THE ECONOMY OF MODERN SINDH

Opportunities Lost and Lessons for the Future

This book is dedicated to
the poor households of Sindh who deserve a better future.

THE ECONOMY OF MODERN SINDH

Opportunities Lost and Lessons for the Future

Ishrat Husain | Aijaz A. Qureshi | Nadeem Hussain

OXFORD
UNIVERSITY PRESS

OXFORD
UNIVERSITY PRESS

Oxford University Press is a department of the University of Oxford.
It furthers the University's objective of excellence in research, scholarship,
and education by publishing worldwide. Oxford is a registered trade mark of
Oxford University Press in the UK and in certain other countries

Published in Pakistan by
Oxford University Press
No. 38, Sector 15, Korangi Industrial Area,
PO Box 8214, Karachi-74900, Pakistan

ISBN 978-0-19-070047-8

Typeset in Adobe Garamond Pro
Printed on 52gsm Book Paper

Printed by The Times Press Pvt. Ltd., Karachi

Acknowledgements

Author photographs courtesy of Arif Mehmood

Cover images:

'Blue Hour in Karachi City' © Israr/Shutterstock.com
'Two women are working in field' © SM Rafiq Photography/Getty Images

Contents

Acknowledgements   vii
Acronyms and Abbreviations   ix
List of Tables   xv
List of Figures   xxii
Preface   xxv
Introduction   xxvii

1. Land and People   1
2. Administrative and Economic History   13
3. Population   41
4. Education   55
5. Health   90
6. Labour and Employment   107
7. Poverty and Inequality   131
8. Agriculture   163
9. Irrigation   189
10. Infrastructure   210
11. Sindh's Industrial Structure: Past and Present   226
12. Energy and Mineral Resources   257
13. Public Finance: Taxation and Resource Mobilisation   294

Conclusion   328
Annexures   333
List of Annexure Tables   335
List of Annexure Figures   339
Annexure Tables   340
Annexure Figures   412
Notes   419
Bibliography   440
Index   457

Acknowledgements

IT gives us immense pleasure to thank our friends who encouraged us to study Sindh's economy. A lot of very kind people have helped us write this book. We are grateful to Fazalullah Qureshi who gave his time and shared with us his immense knowledge of Sindh. We thank him for painstakingly questioning and challenging the data with his deep understanding and rich experience of dealing with official statistics. Dr Fateh Marri, former acting chief economist to the Government of Sindh, discussed and laid out the turf for writing. He has been very keenly interested in studying Sindh's true economic potential, and warmly supported the project from the very start. We would like to thank Arif Hasan for sharing his thoughts on Sindh's urban slums, and his Urban Resource Centre for their in-depth studies. We are deeply grateful to Dr Farrukh Iqbal, Executive Director of the Institute of Business Administration (IBA), Karachi, and Dr Qazi Masood, Director of the IBA Center for Business and Economic Research (CBER) for opening up the facilities of the Center during the conduct of this study.

We are indebted to Abdul Lateef, a young civil servant and scholar, who thoroughly reviewed the manuscript. His suggestions helped us improve the cross-referencing of data tables and figures. He edited our redrawn tables and advised on the infographic representation of hard facts. Without him, the readers might have had to plough through a lot more numbers.

We thank Rahema Obaid, our research associate, for her infectious enthusiasm and faith in making a difference through the writing of this book. She worked diligently in reviewing the literature on Sindh's economic history and labour. Hazkeel Rizvi's consistent hard work needs to be mentioned; his passion in aligning different data sources and making them coherent was unprecedented. Shaheer Ahmed used his sharp eyes to ensure the authenticity of references and helped us prepare the bibliography. Agha Abdul Wahab supported us by using online academic databases and other governments publications

Many people were generous to share their experiences. We thank Nawaz Leghari for tirelessly helping with an in-depth inquiry on Sindh's public finances. Idrees Rajput,Professor Noor Muhammad Memon, and Muhammad Umer Karim provided the latest information on Sindh's irrigation.

We are grateful for the cooperation extended by the libraries of the State Bank of Pakistan (SBP), Applied Economics Research Centre (AERC), and Pakistan Bureau of Statistics (PBS) Karachi Office. We thank Muhammad Anwar, Chief Librarian at the IBA Karachi, and his staff, especially Sadiqa Parveen for making Pakistan's economic surveys, annual budget statements, and Sindh development statistics, from 1970 onwards, available at the Archives section of the IBA libraries. We also would like to thank Bashir Ahmed Zia, Chief Librarian, State Bank of Pakistan, and Naeem Daudpota, Librarian, Sindh Archives, for their assistance.

We are grateful to Imtiaz Ali and Amar Latif Qazi who went through the *Dawn* newspapers of around five decades to sift through and select some of the most significant economic developments in the province. Both of them also conducted a thorough review of tens of English, Urdu, and Sindhi newspapers and periodicals to help us understand the nature and trends of popular development discourse in Sindh.

Our friend Qazi Zulqurnain ul Haq remained invaluable throughout the research process. We highly appreciate Nadia Naviwala, Farid Alvi, Sumaiya Virjee, and Anam Rizvi for sharing their comments on the draft chapters; Zia Muneer and Ijaz Bajwa for helping with statistical software; Zuhaib Shaikh for locating inter-library resources, Hiba Batool for doing the literature review on Sindh's industries, and Ilsa Razzaq for initial proofing.

We owe a great deal of debt to the young IBA undergraduate students who worked with us as research assistants. Without their support the vast amount of official data on various aspects of Sindh's economy would not have been possible to collate. They include Bakhtawar Niaz, Talheen Naqvi, Mustaf Gul, Ahsan Hamid, Seher Khan, Abdullah Hassan Yahya, Syeda Jaisha Ahmed, Fatima Aizaz, Amenah Sajid, Shumaila Abbasi, Zaineb Makati, Aatyka Fatima, Ramsha Sajid, and Imran Nasir. They proved to be critical pillars of support.

We are deeply grateful to the Sindh Bureau of Statistics for generously supporting the study, especially the chairman Planning and Development (P&D) Board, Waseem Ahmed, whose personal interest and drive proved crucial in bringing this book project to fruition.

At the Oxford University Press (OUP) Pakistan, we thank Arshad Saeed Husain, Raheela Baqai, and Ghousia Ali and her team.

Acronyms and Abbreviations

ADP	Annual Development Programme
AERC	Applied Economics Research Centre
AIDS	Acquired Immune Deficiency Syndrome
AJK	Azad Jammu and Kashmir
AKHSP	Aga Khan Health Service Pakistan
AKU	Aga Khan University
ALP	Alternative Learning Pathways
APPM	Accounting Policy and Procedural Methods
AWBs	Area Water Boards
BC	Before Christ
BHP	Broken Hill Proprietary Company
BHUs	Basic Health Units
BOC	Burma Oil Company
BoR	Board of Revenue
BPD	Barrels per Day
BPS	Basic Pay Scale
BTU	British Thermal Unit
CAGR	Compound Annual Growth Rate
CATI	Civil Aviation Training Institute
CBN	Cost of Basic Needs
CBT	Competency Based Trainings
CCI	Council of Common Interest
CETP	Combined Effluent Treatment Plant
CMEC	China Machinery & Engineering Corporation
CMI	Census of Manufacturing Industries
CPEC	China-Pakistan Economic Corridor
CPPA	Central Power Purchasing Agency
CPPs	Captive Power Producers
DBGs	Drainage Beneficiary Groups
DWT	Deadweight Tonne
DAILY	Disease-Adjusted Life Year
DHQs	District Headquarter
DISCOs	Distribution Companies
DPOD	Dhoro-Puran Outfall Drain

ECCE	Early Childhood Care & Education
ECNEC	Executive Committee of the National Economic Council
EEI	Esso Eastern Inc.
EFA	Education For All
EIC	East India Company
EMOs	Education Management Organisations
EMP	Environment Management Plan
EOBI	Employees Old-Age Benefits Institution
ET&N	Excise, Taxation and Narcotics
FAO	Food and Agricultural Organisation
FO	Farmer Organisation
FATA	Federally Administered Tribal Areas
FBR	Federal Board of Revenue
FDA	Food and Drug Administration
FEI	Food Energy Intake
FESCO	Faisalabad Electric Supply Company
FFCEL	Fauji Fertilizer Company Energy Limited
FPAP	Fire Protection Association of Pakistan
FOs	Farmer Organisations
GBP	Great Britain Pound
GCP	Ghee Corporation of Pakistan
GDP	Gross Domestic Product
GENCOs	Generation Companies
GEPCO	Gujranwala Electric Supply Company
GoI	Government of India
GoS	Government of Sindh
GPI	Gender Parity Index
GRDs	Government Rural Dispensaries
GRP	Gross Regional Product
GSP	Geological Survey of Pakistan
GSP	Grup Servicii Petroliere
GST	Goods and Services Tax
HAEB	Hyderabad Area Electricity Board
HANDS	Health and Nutritional Development Society
HDI	Human Development Index
HDR	Human Development Report
HEC	Higher Education Commission
HEI	Harbin Electric International
HELP	Health Education Library for People
HESCO	Hyderabad Electric Supply Company
HFO	Heavy Fuel Oil
HIV	Human Immunodeficiency Virus
HOPE	Health Oriented Preventive Education
HYV	High Yielding Varieties
IBRD	International Bank for Reconstruction and Development
ICT	Information and Communications Technology

ICT	Islamabad Capital Territory
IDBP	Industrial Development Bank of Pakistan
IDU	Injectable Drug Users
IESCO	Islamabad Electric Supply Company
IFMIS	Integrated Financial Management Information System
IHMIS	Integrated Health Management Information System
ILO	International Labour Organisation
IMF	International Monetary Fund
INGOs	International Non-Governmental Organisations
IPPs	Independent Power Producers
IRSA	Indus River System Authority
ISPs	Internet Service Providers
IT	Information Technology
KAIRP	Katchi Abadi Improvement and Regularization Programme
KE	K-Electric
KESC	Karachi Electric Supply Corporation
KM	Kilometre
KP	Khyber Pakhtunkhwa
KPOD	Kadhan Pateji Outfall Drain
KV	Kilo Volt
KW	Kilo Watt
KWH	Kilowatt Hour
LARMIS	Land Administration and Revenue Management Information System
LASMO	London and Scottish Marine Oil
LBOD	Left Bank Outfall Drain
LCDC	Lakhra Coal Development Company
LESCO	Lahore Electric Supply Company
LFS	Labour Force Survey
LG	Local Government
LHV	Lady Health Visitor
LHWs	Lady Health Workers
LNG	Liquefied Natural Gas
LoI	Letter of Intent
MAF	Million Acre Foot
MCH	Mother and Child Health
MDGs	Millennium Development Goals
MEPCO	Multan Electric Power Company
MGCL	Mari Gas Company Limited
MMBTU	Million British Thermal Units
MMCFD	Million Cubic Feet per Day
MMCFT	Million Cubic Feet
MNV	Main Nara Valley
MOL	Hungarian Oil and Gas Plc/Magyar Olaj és Gázipari Részvénytársaság
MPAs	Members of Provincial Assemblies
MPI	Multidimensional Poverty index
MW	Mega Watt

N/A	Not Available
NDP	National Drainage Project
NEC	National Economic Council
NEPRA	National Electric Power Regulatory Authority
NFBE	Non-Formal Basic Education
NFC	National Fertilizer Corporation
NFC	National Finance Commission
NGOs	Non-Governmental Organisations
NJV	Narain Jagan Nath Vidya
NLC	National Logistics Cell
NSC	Nutrition Stabilization Centre
NTDC	National Transmission and Dispatch Company
NWFP	North West Frontier Province
OT	Operation Theatre
ODA	[British] Overseas Development Agency
OGDC	Oil and Gas Development Corporation
OGDCL	Oil and Gas Development Company Limited
OMV	Austrian Mineral Oil Administration/Österreichische Mineralölverwaltung
OOSC	Out of School Children
OPD	Out Patient Department
OPEC	Organisation of Petroleum Exporting Countries
OSR	Own Source Revenue
OZT	Octroi and Zila Tax
PAEC	Pakistan Atomic Energy Commission
PAVHNA	Pakistan Voluntary Health and Nutrition Association
PCMU	Project Coordination & Monitoring Unit
PEFA	Public Expenditure and Financial Accountability
PEL	Petroleum Exploration Limited
PEPCO	Pakistan Electric Power Company
PESCO	Peshawar Electric Supply Company
PFC	Provincial Finance Commission
PFM	Public Financial Management
PFMAA	Public Financial Management and Accountability Assessment
PGDP	Provincial Gross Domestic Product
PIA	Pakistan International Airlines
PICIC	Pakistan Industrial Credit and Investment Corporation
PID	Provincial Irrigation Department
PIFRA	Project for Improvement of Financial Reporting and Auditing
PIHS	Pakistan Integrated Household Survey
PILER	Pakistan Institute of Labour Education and Research
PKR	Pakistani Rupee
PMDC	Pakistan Medical and Dental Council
PMDC	Pakistan Mineral Development Corporation
PPHI	Public-Private Health Initiative
PPIB	Private Power and Infrastructure Board
PPL	Pakistan Petroleum Limited

PPP	Public Private Partnership
PSDP	Public Sector Development Program
PSLM	Pakistan Social and Living Standards Measurement
PTA	Purified Terephthalic Acid
PTV	Pakistan Television
QESCO	Quetta Electric Supply Company
RBOD	Right Bank Outfall Drain
RHCs	Rural Healthcare Centres
SACP	Sindh Aids Control Programme
SAP	Social Action Programme
SAT	Standardized Achievement Test
SAZDA	Sindh Arid Zone Development Authority
SBR	Sindh Board of Revenue
SDGs	Sustainable Development Goals
SECMC	Sindh Engro Coal Mining Company
SEF	Sindh Education Foundation
SEGC	Shanghai Electric Group Company
SEL	Siddiqsons Energy Limited
SEMIS	Sindh Education Management Information System
SEPCO	Sukkur Electric Supply Company
SEZ	Special Economic Zones
SFPSP	Second Floor Protection Sector Project
SIDA	Sindh Irrigation and Drainage Authority
SITE	Sindh Industrial Trading Estate
SIUT	Sindh Institute of Urology and Transplantation
SKAA	Sindh Katchi Abadi Authority
SME	Small and Medium Enterprise
SMEDA	Small and Medium Enterprise Development Authority
SMEs	Small and Medium Enterprises
SOC	Sui Oil Company
SoFWP	Sindh on Farm Water Management Project
SPPRA	Sindh Public Procurement and Regulatory Authority
SPPs	Small Power Producers
SRB	Sindh Revenue Board
SSIC	Sindh Small Industries Corporation
STR	Student-Teacher Ratio
SWMO	Sindh Water Management Ordinance
T&D	Transmission and Distribution
TB	Tuberculosis
TCD	Tons Crushed per Day
TESCO	Tribal Electric Supply Company
TEVTA	Technical and Vocational Training Authority
TFR	Total Fertility Rate
THQs	Taluka/Tehsil Headquarter
TIKA	Turkish Cooperation and Coordination Agency
TOE	Tonne of Oil Equivalent

ToR	Terms of Reference
TransCO	National Transmission Corporation
TV	Television
U5MR	Under Five Mortality Rate
UAE	United Arab Emirates
UCG	Underground Coal Gasification
UEP	United Energy Pakistan Limited
UIB	Upper Indus Basin
UN	United Nations
UNDP	United Nations Development Program
UNESCO	United Nations Educational, Scientific and Cultural Organisation
UNICEF	United Nations Children's Education Fund
USAID	United States Agency for International Development
UTP	Union Texas Pakistan
WAPDA	Water and Power Development Authority
WAR	War Against Rape
WCA	Water Course Association
WFP	World Food Programme
WHO	World Health Organisation
WMOs	Women Medical Officers
WSIP	Water Sector Improvement Project
WWF	Workers' Welfare Fund

List of Tables

Introduction
I: Assignments Transferred/Added to the Federal Legislative List after Eighteenth Amendment   xxviii
II: Division of Functions between the Federal and Provincial Governments   xxviii

1. Land and People
1.1: Administrative Units of Sindh—Divisions and their Districts   11

2. Administrative and Economic History
2.1:   Exports from Various Regions of Sindh   14
2.2:   Population Statistics for Sindh (excluding the Khairpur region) (1856–72)   16
2.3:   Composition of Population in 1856   16
2.4:   Population of Major Cities in 1872   17
2.5:   Population of Sindh including Khairpur (in million) (1901–51)   18
2.6:   Age and Gender Composition of the Population of Sindh (%) (1901–51)   18
2.7:   Population of Karachi (1881–1951)   19
2.8:   Types of Jagirs and their Policy Treatment   21
2.9:   Land Granted to Jagirs Before and After British Annexation   22
2.10: Irrigation Works Under the British (Excluding Sukkur Barrage Canals)   31
2.11: Livestock in Sindh—1945   33
2.12: Exports and Imports of Sindh (in GBP) (1843–44 to 1856–57)   35
2.13: Composition of Imports and Exports (GBP)—1855   35
2.14: Major Trading Partners—1886   36

3. Population
3.1:   Population Growth in Sindh (1891–1941)   41
3.2:   Sindh Urban Demographics (in Hundred Thousand) (1941 and 1951)   42
3.3:   Language Groups in Sindh (in Thousand) (1931–98)   43
3.4:   Sindh-Karachi Comparison and Percentage Shares (in Hundred Thousand) (1931–2017)   43
3.5:   Population Growth in Sindh (1951–2017)   44
3.6:   Area, Population, and Population Density of Pakistan and Sindh (1951–2017)   46
3.7:   Population by Gender in Sindh (1951–2017)   47
3.8:   Sindh's Population Growth Rate and National Rank by Size and Division (2017)   47
3.9:   Percentage Distribution of Rural-Urban Population in Sindh, Punjab, and Pakistan (1951–2017)   48

3.10:   Percentage of Migrants from Other Province/Within Province by Rural Urban (1998)   49
3.11:   Migrants from India as of 1951 (in Thousand)   50
3.12:   Population by Age Groups, Gender, and Rural–Urban Areas of Sindh (in Million) (1998)   51
3.13:   Marital Status by Percentage in Sindh (1998)   51
3.14:   Percentage of Population by Economic Categories, Gender, and   52
        Rural–Urban Areas of Sindh (1998)
3.15:   Population Shares of Pakistan and its Provinces Over the Censuses (1951–2017)   54

4. Education
4.1:   Out of School Children in Sindh (in Thousand) (2015–16)   55
4.2:   Enrolment in Sindh (in Thousand) (2015–16)   56
4.3:   Youth and Adult Literacy Rates (2015–16)   57
4.4:   Pakistan's Primary and Secondary Education Status (2015–16)   58
4.5:   Literacy Rates for Pakistan, Sindh, and Punjab (2001–02 to 2014–15)   58
4.6:   Trends in Public Education (1970–71 and 2015–16)   59
4.7:   Distribution of Public Schools by Level in Sindh (2015–16)   60
4.8:   Student Enrolment by Stage in Sindh (2015–16)   62
4.9:   Gross and Net Enrolment Rates of Sindh (2014–15)   62
4.10:   Stage-wise Enrolment in Public Schools of Sindh as a Percentage of Pakistan (2015–16)   63
4.11:   Sindh Education Budgetary Estimates and Actual Spending   66
        (in PKR Million) (1970–71 to 2015–16)
4.12:   Public Spending on Education as a Percentage of GDP (2006–07 to 2013–14)   67
4.13:   Enrolment in Private School System in Pakistan and Sindh (in Thousand) (2015–16)   67
4.14:   The Evolution of ECCE in Pakistan (1947–2009)   73
4.15:   Enrolment in All Primary Schools of Sindh (2015–16)   74
4.16:   Enrolment in Public Primary Schools of Sindh (2001–02 to 2015–16)   75
4.17:   Out of School Children in Sindh (2015–16)   75
4.18:   Provincial Comparison of Public Primary Enrolment between Sindh and Punjab (2015–16)   75
4.19:   Number of Functional Primary Schools with Facilities (2015–16)   76
4.20:   Overview of Historical Developments   77
4.21:   Beneficiaries of Girls' Stipend (2007–08 to 2015–16)   79
4.22:   Post-Primary Enrolment by Gender (2010–11 and 2015–16)   80
4.23:   Post-Primary Enrolment by Gender (Percentage) (2010–11 and 2015–16)   81
4.24:   Grade-wise Enrolment of Female Students in Government Schools of Sindh   81
        (2008–09 to 2014–15)
4.25:   Transition of Female Students from Grade 5 to Grade 6   81
4.26:   Computer Lab and Library Facilities in Public Secondary Schools of Sindh (2015–16)   82
4.27:   Universities and Degree-awarding Institutions in Pakistan (1947–48 to 2015–16)   83
4.28:   Provincial Status of Technical and Vocational Institutes (2015–16)   85

5. Health
5.1:   Health Status of Pakistan (1990–2015)   91
5.2:   Comparison of Health Indicators in Pakistan, Sindh, and Punjab (2015)   91
5.3:   Dispensaries and Hospitals in Sindh (1947)   93
5.4:   Public Sector Hospital Facilities in Sindh (1970–2015)   93
5.5:   Sindh Urban and Rural Health Indicators (2004 and 2014)   93

5.6:   Usage of Health Facilities (1980)   94
5.7:   Nutritional Status of the Children in Sindh (%)—(2014)   95
5.8:   Comparison of Health Indicators of Tharparkar and Sindh (Percentage)—(2014)   97
5.9:   Public Sector Health Facilities in Sindh (1970–2015)   99
5.10:   Relevant Ratios of Availability of Health Services to Patients in Sindh (2011–16)   100
5.11:   Reasons for Not Opting for Public Health Facilities in Punjab and Sindh (%) (2013–14)   100
5.12:   Medical Personnel in Sindh (Public) (1975–2015)   101
5.13:   Sindh Health Budgetary Estimates and Expenditures (in PKR million) (1970–71 to 2015–16)   103
5.14:   MDG Health Goals and Actual Outcomes as of 2014   104

6. Labour and Employment

6.1:   Population and Labour Force of Pakistan and Sindh (in Million) (1951–2014)   107
6.2:   Labour Force Participation Rates for Pakistan by Area (%) (1990–91 to 2014–15)   108
6.3:   Labour Force Participation Rates and Underemployment Rates for Pakistan by Area   108
        and Gender (%) (1990–91 to 2014–15)
6.4:   Labour Force Participation and Unemployment Rates for Sindh by Area   109
        and Gender (%) (1990–91 to 2014–15)
6.5:   Labour Force Participation and Unemployment Rates for Punjab by Area   110
        and Gender (%) (1990–91 to 2014–15)
6.6:   Labour Force Participation Rates and Unemployment Rates for Sindh by   111
        Age Group (%) (2014–15)
6.7:   Underemployment Rates for Pakistan, Sindh, and Punjab by Age Group (%) (2014–15)   114
6.8:   Percentage Distribution of Employment by Occupation in Pakistan (1963–64 and 2014–15)   115
6.9:   Percentage Distribution of Civilian Labour Force by Level of Education for Pakistan, Sindh,   116
        and Punjab (2014–15)
6.10:   Percentage Distribution of Employed Labour Force by Level of Education   117
        (15 Years and Above) (2001–02 to 2014–15)
6.11:   Percentage Distribution of Population by Education for Pakistan, Sindh, and Punjab   118
        (10 Years and Above) (2014–15)
6.12:   Literacy Rates for Pakistan, Punjab, and Sindh by Area (%) (10 years and above)   118
        (1990–91 to 2014–15)
6.13:   Percentage Distribution of Employed Persons by Agriculture and Non-Agriculture Sector   119
        (10 Years and Above) (2001–02 to 2014–15)
6.14:   Percentage Distribution of Employed Persons by Formal and Informal Sector for Pakistan,   120
        Sindh, and Punjab (10 years of age and above) (1997–98 to 2014–15)
6.15:   Percentage Distribution of Inter and Intra Provincial Migration for Pakistan, Sindh,   121
        and Punjab (2014–15)
6.16:   Percentage Distribution of Employment by Industry for Pakistan, Sindh, and Punjab   122
        (10 Years and Above) (1990–91 and 2014–15)
6.17:   Average Wages for Pakistan by Area and Occupational Group (in PKR)   123
        (2010–11 and 2014–15)
6.18:   Average Wages for Punjab by Area and Occupational Group (in PKR)   124
        (2010–11 and 2014–15)
6.19:   Average Wages for Sindh by Area and Occupational Group (in PKR)   125
        (2010–11 and 2014–15)

7. Poverty and Inequality

7.1:   Nutrition Status vis-à-vis MDG Nutrition Target 2015 (1990–91 to 2014–15)   132
7.2:   Proportion of Poor in Pakistan by Area (Headcount Ratio) (%) (1963–64 to 1999–2000)   133
7.3:   Pakistan's Multidimensional Poverty Index (2015–16)   136
7.4:   MPI, Incidence, and Intensity for Pakistan, Punjab, and Sindh (2014–15)   137
7.5:   Human Development Indicators of Pakistan (1980–81 and 2015–16)   138
7.6:   Comparative Development Indicators for Pakistan, Punjab and Sindh (2014–15)   138
7.7:   Incidence of Poverty among the Districts of Sindh (2012)   140
7.8:   Intensity of Poverty in Districts of Sindh (2012)   140
7.9:   Trends in Income Distribution in Pakistan (1963–64 to 2010–11)   145
7.10:   Average Monthly Income Quintiles in Pakistan, Punjab, and Sindh (in PKR) (2010–11)   146
7.11:   Average Monthly Income Quintiles for Urban Pakistan, Punjab, and Sindh (in PKR) (2010–11)   147
7.12:   Average Monthly Income Quintiles for Rural Pakistan, Punjab, and Sindh (in PKR) (2010–11)   147
7.13:   Percentage Distribution of Monthly Household Income in Sindh (Rural/Urban) (2007–08 to 2013–14)   150
7.14:   Trends in Growth, Poverty, and Income Distribution in Pakistan (1950–2013)   150
7.15:   Average Per Capita Income Estimates by Area for Pakistan, Punjab, and Sindh (2010–11)   152
7.16:   Average Household Size by Quintiles in Sindh (2015–16)   153
7.17:   Average Household Size by Quintiles in Rural Sindh (2015–16)   154
7.18:   Average Household Size by Quintiles in Urban Sindh (2015–16)   154
7.19:   Percentage Distribution of Household Housing Units in Pakistan, Punjab, and Sindh by Area (2015–16)   155
7.20:   Percentage Distribution of Household Housing Tenures in Pakistan, Punjab, and Sindh by Area (2015–16)   155
7.21:   Percentage Distribution of Household in Pakistan, Punjab, and Sindh by Source of Drinking Water by Area (2015–16)   156
7.22:   Agro-climatic Zones of Sindh and Punjab   157
7.23:   Head Count Ratio and Poverty Gap amongst the Different Agricultural Groups (1987–88 and 2004–05)   158

8. Agriculture

8.1:   Shares in Agricultural Value Added (%) (1949–50 to 2015–16)   163
8.2:   Land Ownership and Acreage in Sindh Before 1959   164
8.3:   Land Ownership and Acreage in Sindh (1961–62)   166
8.4:   Land Ownership and Acreage in Sindh—1972   166
8.5:   Cross Sectional Analysis of Important Variables (in Thousand) (1980–2010)   167
8.6:   Land Ownership and Acreage in Sindh (2010)   171
8.7:   Index of Agricultural Production in Pakistan and Sindh by Type of Crop (1970–71 = 100.00) (1970–71 to 2010–11)   171
8.8:   Credit Source by Various Institutions (in PKR Million) (1965–2015)   175
8.9:   Production of Major Crops in Sindh (in 000 Tonnes) (1947–48 to 2015–16)   176
8.10:   Percentage Share of Sindh in Major Crops by Area and Production (2005–06 to 2015–16)   176
8.11:   Livestock Population of Sindh Over the Censuses of 1986, 1996, and 2006 (in Million)   182
8.12:   Tubewell Ownership in Sindh by Type (1987–88 to 2014–15)   185

8.13:   Numbers of Tractors Manufactured in Pakistan (1990–91 to 2014–15)   185

9. Irrigation
9.1:   Canals under Sukkur Barrage Project (1953)   190
9.2:   Allocation of Water to the Provinces by Various Committees/Commissions (MAF) (1945–91)   195
9.3:   Distribution of Water as Per the 1991 Water Accord (MAF)   196
9.4:   Area Water Boards, Divisions, and Barrages   203

10. Infrastructure
10.1:   Road Mileage (Principal Highways) and Motor Vehicles in Sindh (2000–01 to 2014–15)   212
10.2:   Pakistan Railway Movement of Passengers, Freight, and Earnings (1980–81 to 2015–16)   214
10.3:   Cargo Handled at Karachi Port (in Thousand Tonnes) (1990–91 to 2015–16)   217
10.4:   Performance of PIA (1990–91 to 2015–16)   218
10.5:   Annual Cellular Subscriptions (2003–04 to 2015–16)   219
10.6:   Teledensity (2002–03 to 2015–16)   219
10.7:   Annual Broadband Subscribers (2005–06 to 2016–17)   219
10.8:   Growth of Television Services and Revenue in Sindh (1980–81 to 2012–13)   220
10.9:   Government of Sindh Budget Allocation for Housing (in PKR Million)   221
        (1975–76 to 2015–16)
10.10: Number of Households in Sindh (1972–2017)   223
10.11: Housing Ownership and Tenancy Pattern in Sindh (1980–81 to 2014–15)   223
10.12: Percentage Distribution of Households by Number of Rooms in Sindh (1980–81 to 2014–15)   224

11. Industrial Structure: Past and Present
11.1:   Manufacturing Value Added in Sindh (Constant Factor Cost 2005–06)   227
        (1999–2000 to 2014–15)
11.2:   Number of Reporting Establishments in Pakistan and Sindh (1970–71 to 2005–06)   228
11.3:   Locational Breakup of Industrial Establishments in Sindh, Karachi, Hyderabad, and Sukkur   229
        (1970–71 to 2005–06)
11.4:   Average Daily Employment in Pakistan and Sindh (in PKR) (1970–71 to 2005–06)   230
11.5:   Locational Breakup of Average Daily Employment (1970–71 to 2005–06)   230
11.6:   Employment Cost in Pakistan and Sindh (in PKR) (1970–71 to 2005–06)   231
11.7:   Value of Production in Pakistan and Sindh (in PKR Million) (1970–2005)   232
11.8:   Sindh's Share of Production of Selected Major Industries from Total Value of Production   232
        (1970–71 to 2005–06)
11.9:   Total Value of Fixed Assets in Sindh's Manufacturing Sector (in PKR) (1970–71 to 2005–06)   233
11.10: Industrial Growth in Large-scale Manufacturing Sector of Sindh (in PKR Million)   235
        (1970–71 to 2005–06)
11.11: Relative Contribution of Punjab and Sindh in Manufacturing (1970–71 to 2005–06)   251
11.12: Contribution to Seasonal GDP by Punjab and Sindh at Producer Prices (in PKR Million)   252
        (1990–91 to 2005–06)
11.13: Census Value Added by Sindh and Punjab (1970–71 to 2005–06)   252

12. Energy and Mineral Resources
12.1:   Oil and Gas Exploration Efforts in Sindh   257
12.2:   Spud and Completion Dates of Major Offshore Exploratory Wells of Pakistan (1963–2010)   261

12.3:   Production of Crude Oil in Pakistan and Sindh Tonne of Oil Equivalent   263
        (TOE) (1980–81 to 2014–15)
12.4:   Petroleum Energy Products Consumption (TOE) (1980–81 to 2014–15)   264
12.5:   Natural Gas Production (in MMCFT) (1980–2015)   266
12.6:   Number of Consumers of Natural Gas in Sindh and Pakistan (1980–2015)   268
12.7:   Exploratory On-shore Licenses in Sindh (2014)   270
12.8:   Sindh Coal Reserves as of June 2015   271
12.9:   Sindh Coal Quality Proximate Analysis, June 2015   271
12.10: Coal Production in Sindh and Pakistan (in Tonnes) (1980–81 to 2014–15)   272
12.11: Thar Coal Reserves (in Million Tonnes)—2014   273
12.12: Daily Insolation Rates for Various Seasons and Regions of Pakistan (in kwh/m2/day) (2010)   276
12.13: List of GENCOS   279
12.14: List of DISCOS   282
12.15: Power Generation in Sindh (Plant-wise) (in Kwh) (2010–11 and 2015–16)   283
12.16: Generation Capacity of K-Electric (1983–2009)   285
12.17: Distribution and Transmission Network of HESCO   286
12.18: Distribution of SEPCO and HESCO   287
12.19: DISCO-wise Units Billed and Received (2005–06 to 2015–16)   287
12.20: Company-wise Billing Demand and Collection (in KW) (2010–14)   288
12.21: List of IPPS in Sindh as of 2015   288
12.22: Mineral Resources in Pakistan and Sindh   292

13. Public Finance: Taxation and Resource Mobilisation

13.1:   Estimated PGDP of Sindh by Sector (in PKR Billions at Constant Prices of 2005–06)   294
        (1999–2000 to 2014–15)
13.2:   Share of Provinces in National Economic Sectors (2012–13)   294
13.3:   Size of Provincial Economies (in PKR Billions at Constant Prices of 2005–06)   295
        (1999–2000 and 2014–15)
13.4:   Sindh Provincial Budgets: Historical Trends (in PKR Million) (1985–86 to 2015–16)   295
13.5:   Tax Collection in Bombay Presidency (1925)   297
13.6:   Share of Different Provinces of West Pakistan in the Divisible Pool (1970–71 and 1971–72)   298
13.7:   1983 Presidential Order Specifying Provincial Shares in 2nd NFC   300
13.8:   Special Grant to Provinces—1990 NFC Award (in PKR Million)   301
13.9:   Proposed Subventions to Provinces (in PKR Billion)   302
13.10: Share in Tax Collection and Divisible Pool (2000–01)   303
13.11: Distribution Order of 2006   304
13.12: Provincial Percentage Share under NFC Awards (1974–2009)   305
13.13: Share of Provinces in Terms of Indicators NFC (2009)   308
13.14: Criteria for Distribution of National Revenue   309
13.15: Provincial Share in NFC Awards   309
13:16: Changes in the Provincial Share (%) (1974–2009)   310
13.17: Provincial Share in the Divisible Pool Before and After 7th NFC Award (Percentage)   310
        (2008–09 to 2015–16)
13.18: Transfers to Provinces and Sindh (in PKR Million) (2008–15)   311
13.19: Tax Collection Agencies of Sindh by Tax Type   312

13.20: Revised Estimates of Sindh's Provincial Tax Revenue Collection (in PKR Million)   313
(1990–91 to 2015–16)

13.21: Own Source Tax Revenue Collection Before and After the Implementation of 7th NFC   314
(2009–10 to 2015–16)

13.22: Provincial Agricultural Tax (in PKR Million) (2000–15)   316

13.23: Land Revenue Rates (First Schedule)   316

13.24: Progressive Tax Rates Levied by Sindh Agriculture Income Tax Act 2000 (Second Schedule)   317

13.25: Summary of Agro-Based Revenues and Agriculture Income Tax (in PKR Million)   317
(2009–10 to 2012–13)

13.26: PEFA Ratings for PFM Assessment   319

13.27: Annual Development Programme (ADP) Allocations and Expenditure   321
(in PKR Million) (1970–71 to 2015–16)

13.28: ADP Allocations to Education (In PKR Million) (1990–91 to 2015–16)   323

13.29: Sectoral Breakdown of Employment (2013–14)   323

13.30: ADP Allocations to Health (in PKR Million) (1990–91 to 2015–16)   324

13.31: ADP Allocations to Water Supply and Drainage (Approved Schemes) (in PKR Million)   325
(1990–91 to 2015–16)

List of Figures

Introduction

Figure I: Share of Sindh in Pakistan's Economy (in PKR Billion at Constant Prices of 2005–06)   xxxiv
              (1999–2000 to 2014–15)
Figure II: Estimated Sindh's Share in Pakistan's Economy (2014–15)   xxxiv
Figure III: Pakistan's Population vis-à-vis Output of Major Crops (1972–2015)   xxxv
Figure IV: Annual Average Growth Rate of Sindh's Major Crops (%) (1995–2005 and 2005–15)   xxxvi
Figure V: Socio-Economic Standing of Sindh Compared to the Rest of Pakistan (2014–15)   xxxvii

1. Land and People

Figure 1.1:   Area Weighted Mean Temperature of Pakistan (1960–2010)   7
Figure 1.2:   Deviation of Maximum (Represents Day Highest) and Minimum   8
              (Represents Night Lowest) Temperature during Last Decade from Normal in
              Summer and Winter Seasons in Pakistan

3. Population

Figure 3.1:   Trend of Sindh's Population—Annual Growth Rate of Population (%)   45
              (1961–72 to 1998–2017)

4. Education

Figure 4.1:   Enrolment by Stage in Sindh (%) (2015–16)   57
Figure 4.2:   Lack of Basic Facilities in Public Schools Across Sindh (2015–16)   61
Figure 4.3A: Percentage Distribution of Children by Schooling Status and Province   69
              (Age Group: 6–10) (2010–11)
Figure 4.3B: Percentage Distribution of Children by Schooling Status and Province   69
              (Age Group: 11–15) (2010–11)
Figure 4.4A: Percentage Distribution of Children by Schooling Status and Socioeconomic   70
              Sub-group (Age Group: 6–10) (2010–11)
Figure 4.4B: Percentage Distribution of Children by Schooling Status and Socioeconomic   71
              Sub-group (Age Group: 11–15) (2010–11)
Figure 4.5:   Transition of Students in Public Schools of Sindh (%) (2015–16)   78
Figure 4.6:   Comparison between Female Students' Enrolment and Girls' Stipend Beneficiaries   80
              (Class 7 to 10) (2009–10 to 2012–13)

7. Poverty and Inequality

Figure 7.1:   Poverty Headcount in Pakistan (%) (1998–99 to 2013–14)   134
Figure 7.2:   Sindh's Head Count Ratio (2004–05 to 2014–15)   135
Figure 7.3:   Multidimensional Poverty Index   136
Figure 7.4:   Poverty Incidence Map of Sindh 2004–05 (Left) and 2014–15 (Right)   138–9
Figure 7.5:   Poverty Incidence Rates for Rural Areas in Pakistan, Punjab, and Sindh (2010–11) 142
Figure 7.6:   Poverty Measures for Rural Areas in Sindh, Punjab, and Pakistan (2010–11)   142
Figure 7.7:   Poverty Incidence Rates for Urban Areas of Pakistan, Punjab, and Sindh (2011–12) 143
Figure 7.8:   Poverty Measures for Urban Areas of Sindh, Punjab, and Pakistan (2011–12)   143
Figure 7.9:   Distribution of Monthly Household Income in Sindh and Punjab (2007–2013)   146
Figure 7.10:   Average Monthly Income (2010–11)   147
Figure 7.11:   Distribution of Monthly Consumption Expenditure in Pakistan (2007–08 to 2013–14) 148
Figure 7.12:   Percentage Distribution of Monthly Income and Monthly Consumption Expenditure   149
                in Pakistan (2010–11)
Figure 7.13:   Inequality in Per Capita Income for Urban Pakistan, Punjab, and Sindh (2014–15)   151
Figure 7.14:   Per Capita Income Inequality for Rural Pakistan, Punjab, and Sindh (2005 to 2011–12) 152
Figure 7.15:   Economic Situation of Households in Pakistan, Punjab, and Sindh (%) (2014–15)   156
Figure 7.16:   Social Expenditure as Percentage of GDP in Federation, Punjab, and Sindh (2014–15) 159
Figure 7.17:   Education Expenditure as a Percentage of GDP in Federation, Punjab, and Sindh   160
                (2014–15)
Figure 7.18:   Health Expenditure as a Percentage of GDP in Federation, Punjab, and Sindh (2014–15) 160
Figure 7.19:   Water Supply and Sanitation Expenditure as a Percentage of GDP Federation,   161
                Punjab, and Sindh (2014–15)

8. Agriculture

Figure 8.1:   Seasonal Cropping in Sindh   168
Figure 8.2:   Cropping Intensities of 1963–64   168–9
Figure 8.3:   District Badin Crops and Cultivation Area (1991–92 to 2009–10)   168–9
Figure 8.4:   District Thatta Crops and Cultivation Area (1991–92 to 2009–10)   168–9
Figure 8.5:   Hay–Grass Farming in Mirpurkhas   169
Figure 8.6:   Annual Precipitation in Sindh (in Millimeter) (1960–2010)   173

10. Infrastructure

Figure 10.1:   Total Number of Railway Tracks in Sindh (in Kilometers) (1976–77 to 2005–06)   215

11. Industrial Structure: Past and Present

Figure 11.1A: Industrial Production Index of Sindh (1969–70 to 1980–81)   234
Figure 11.1B: Industrial Production Index of Sindh (1980–81 to 2015–16)   234
Figure 11.2:   Automobiles (Excluding Cars) Production in Sindh (1975–76 to 2015–16)   236
Figure 11.3:   Vegetable Ghee Production in Sindh (in Million Tonnes) (1970–71 to 2015–16)   237
Figure 11.4:   Sugar Production in Sindh (in Million Tonnes) (1970–71 to 2015–16)   238
Figure 11.5:   Cotton Fabric Production in Sindh (in million sq. meters) (1970–71 to 2015–16)   239
Figure 11.6:   Cotton Yarn Production in Sindh (In Million Tonnes) (1970–71 to 2015–16)   239
Figure 11.7:   Cement Production in Sindh (in Million Tonne) (1970–71 to 2015–16)   240
Figure 11.8:   Fertilizer (Urea) Production in Sindh (in Million Tonnes) (1970–71 to 2015–16)   241
Figure 11.9:   Value of Chemical Production in Sindh (in PKR Million) (1970–71 to 2005–06)   242

Figure 11.10: Value of Pharmaceutical Production in Pakistan (in PKR Million)   243
              (1970–71 to 2005–06)
Figure 11.11: Value of Electronics and Electrical Machinery Production in Sindh   244
              (in PKR Million) (1970–71 to 2005–06)
Figure 11.12: Value of Iron, Steel, and Non-ferrous Metal Production in Pakistan   246
              (in PKR Million) (1970–71 to 2005–06)
Figure 11.13: Value Leather and Leather Products Production in Sindh   247
              (in PKR Million) (1970–71 to 2005–06)

12. Energy and Mineral Resources

Figure 12.1:   Hydrocarbon Basins   259
Figure 12.2:   New Exploration Blocks in Sindh (2014)   260
Figure 12.3:   Licenses for Gas Exploration in the Indus Basin   262
Figure 12.4:   Production of Crude Oil (in Million TOE) (1980–81 to 2014–15)   263
Figure 12.5:   Petroleum Energy Products Consumption by Province (in Million TOE) (1980–2014)   264
Figure 12.6:   Petroleum Energy Products Production and Consumption in Sindh   265
              (in Million TOE) (2009–14)
Figure 12.7:   Crude Oil Production, GDP of Pakistan, and Crude Oil Price (2007–08 to 2014–15)   265
Figure 12.8:   Oil Consumption, GDP of Pakistan, and Crude Oil Price (1980–2014)   266
Figure 12.9:   Natural Gas Production (in MMCFT) by Provinces (1980–81 to 2014–15)   267
Figure 12.10: Comparison of Natural Gas Consumption and Production by Province   268
              (in MMCFT) (2014–15)
Figure 12.11: Natural Gas Consumption by Sector in Punjab, Sindh, and Pakistan (%) (2014–15)   269
Figure 12.12: Coal Production by Province (in Tonnes) (1980–81 to 2014–15)   272
Figure 12.13: Current Power Structure   280
Figure 12.14: Reformed Power Sector Structure   281
Figure 12.15: Sectoral Consumption in Sindh (in MW) (2004–05 to 2007–08)   283
Figure 12.16: Sectoral Consumption in Sindh (in MW) (2010–11 to 2014–15)   284
Figure 12.17: Province-wise Consumption of Electricity (%) (1976–77 to 2014–15)   284
Figure 12.18: Service Area of HESCO   286
Figure 12.19: Electricity Access as a Percentage of Population (1990–2014)   289
Figure 12.20: Per Capita Electricity Consumption (1975–2014)   289
Figure 12.21: Electricity Consumption Growth Rate for Public Utilities (1976–2014)   290
Figure 12.22: Change in Electricity Consumption of Sindh—Private and Public (1992–2006)   290
Figure 12.23: Number of Electricity Consumers in Karachi by Type (in Million)   291
              (1980–81 to 2015–16)

13. Public Finance: Taxation and Resource Mobilisation

Figure 13.1:   Contribution of the Major Taxes in the Province's Own Source Revenue   312–13

Preface

Economic analyses in Pakistan have largely focused on aggregate, national, and macro economy issues. There is dearth of literature on regional and provincial economies which have assumed importance recently for a variety of reasons. First, both Punjab and Sindh have population sizes that can be compared with many nations. Second, the Eighteenth Amendment to the Constitution has devolved a lot of powers from the federal to the provincial governments. Third, the seventh National Finance Commission has awarded almost 60 per cent of the divisible tax pool and other federal resources to the provinces. Fourth, heterogeneity and initial resource endowments differ among the provinces. Sindh and Balochistan, for example, are both coastal provinces but population density and other factors have set them apart in the level of their development outcomes. All the donor agencies such as the World Bank, Asian Development Bank (ADB), the UK Department for International Development (DFID), and the United States Agency for International Development (USAID) are now carrying analysis of the provincial economies and preparing projects at the regional level to assist in specific areas such as education, health, irrigation, water supply, and public transport. For them, analytical work done across the board, as contained in this volume, would be helpful. In an era of information explosion and connectedness and higher share in the distribution of resources, the expectations of the people from their provincial and local governments have been raised. Therefore, the performance of the economy at the regional and local levels has to match these expectations. Benchmark studies such as the present one would be helpful in evaluating the progress.

The present volume, initially conceived as an update of the book *Economy of Modern Sindh* (the Institute of Sindhology, Jamshoro, 1981), has turned out to be a highly comprehensive account of Sindh's economy based on empirical data. It also presents the contours of a future development strategy based on this analysis for provoking debate and discourse. This is a modest attempt to fill in the gap in the literature on the historical evolution, current situation, and the future direction of the economy of Sindh. It is intended to serve as a text book for university and college students as no such book exists at present, as a reference material for researchers and scholars, and as a guide for policy makers. Bringing together these diverse elements in a single volume aimed at a variety of target audiences is by no means an easy task. We are, however, convinced that the synergies in presenting this material in a single volume would overcome the difficulties that may arise due to omissions, excessive attention to some topics, and incomplete treatment of some issues from the viewpoint of some target groups that are inherent in such an exercise. The effort to bring as much coherence, keep as wide coverage, and maintain as meaningful consistency as possible may keep it relevant and responsive. We are not aware of any volume where such rich longitudinal data set on the economy of the province of Sindh is available in one place. Making this data available in the public domain through this volume (tables in the appendix along with 209 text tables and 77 figures derived from known and reliable sources) would make it possible for many research students and scholars to use it as the starting point in their empirical investigations, and improve, update, upgrade the quality, and expand the series and coverage further. Copious notations, references spread over a number of pages, and careful labelling of the data sources will be helpful to both researchers and students.

One of the distinguishing features of this volume is systematic collection, collation, sifting and selection of data on many socio-economic variables of the province. Consistent time series on a large number of such variables is not available in any one place and therefore raw data as well as analytical tables are constructed using many sources—primary as well as secondary. The limitations of such data sets are quite well known. Sample size for a sub set derived from aggregated national surveys may not be representative or statistically significant. Coverage may vary from one period to another. Definitions may change with the passage of time. The screening and selection of data for this volume had to keep these limitations in mind and a lot of numbers were either rejected or eliminated because they did not meet the tests of consistency and representativeness. Various sources were used to validate the results.

This book is neither an economic history nor a description of the current facts of the Sindh economy, but it weaves together the economic history into the current situation, analyses the constraints and issues facing the economy and to some extent the peculiar configuration of societal interests, and finally proposes a future development strategy that can address these issues and relax the constraints identified. We use a two-stage approach. First, we compare Sindh with the national aggregates to discern whether we are gaining or losing our shares in the national economy. Second, we use Punjab as the comparator because it was far behind Sindh in many respects but has overtaken us in the last decade or so. It is our endeavour to comprehend the factors behind this shift and incorporate those in the proposed strategy. Benchmarking Punjab would help researchers and scholars to inform policy makers about the distance traversed to make up or widen the gap between the two provinces against various economic and social indicators.

The book is organised according to a clear division of time periods before and after the independence of Pakistan. 'Chapter 2' provides a bird's eye view of pre-independence administrative and economic history of Sindh and chapters 3 and onwards examine and analyse the historical evolution since 1947 pertaining to each major economic and social dimension and brings it update to the contemporary scene. 'Chapter 2' is needed to provide a backdrop of the pre-independence era in a succinct manner to enable the reader to form a better understanding as to how we reached the present point. Institutional economics tells us that path dependence has greater sway on our understanding of contemporary economic problems. Naturally, some of the sections in 'Chapter 2' will be dealt with in more detail in the standalone chapters on the respective subjects. It should, therefore, not be construed as repetition but a continuum from 'Chapter 2'. The last chapter in this book uses this detailed sectoral analysis to bring together elements of a future development strategy for Sindh.

Introduction

SINDH is one of the four federating units of the Islamic Republic of Pakistan along with Punjab, Khyber Pakhtunkhwa, and Balochistan. After the partition of India and the formation of Pakistan in 1947, Sindh existed as a separate province with its own government and assembly of elected legislators. However, it was decided in 1956 to merge all the provinces of West Pakistan into One Unit and thus Sindh ceased to exist as a separate province and became part of the West Pakistan province. In June 1970, One Unit was dissolved and Sindh was restored as a province. Elections to the provincial assembly were held that year leading to the formation of the Government of Sindh with the Chief Minister as the chief executive of the province and a Governor appointed by the federal government.

After the separation of East Pakistan, a new constitution was enacted and promulgated in 1973. The constitution established three levels of government—federal, provincial, and local. Moreover, it provided for a bicameral legislature comprising the Upper House and a Lower House, which are the terms used for Senate and National Assembly respectively.[1] According to the 1973 Constitution, the members of the National Assembly must be at least 25 years or older and should be directly elected every five years by the people. The Senate consists of 104 members, of whom the members of each provincial assembly should elect 23.[2] This allocation gives equal representation to the provinces in the Senate and facilitates the role of provinces in the central decision-making process. In addition to the National Assembly and Senate, there is a Council of Common Interest (CCI), which has equal representation from the Federal Government and each constituent unit (provinces). CCI has jurisdiction over the matters which are contained in the Federal Legislative List II. Subjects that lie under the jurisdiction of CCI require collective approval of the federal and provincial governments.

The Eighteenth Amendment to the Constitution was passed by the parliament on 20 April 2010. Significant changes were made to the constitutional framework of Pakistan and as a result of the Amendment, 102 out of a total of 280 articles were amended, substituted, added, inserted, or deleted. The new constitutional framework is a milestone in the political history of Pakistan because it devolved the previously heavily centralised government structure into a decentralised federation and completely changed the political paradigm. The Amendment provided greater autonomy to provinces and emphasised creating a multi-level governance system so that the benefits can trickle down and be observed at the grass-root levels.

The Eighteenth Amendment, proved to be significant in redistributing the power amongst the provinces and the federal government. The Concurrent Legislative List, which was formerly followed, was abolished and the Federal Legislative List I and II were introduced instead, which demarcated the jurisdiction amongst federal, inter-provincial, and provincial governments. According to the Federal Legislative Lists, jurisdiction over 53 subjects is solely granted to the federal government, while CCI is given power over the 18 subjects that are included in the Federal Legislative List II. The authority over the remaining subjects is given to provincial governments.

As a result of the Eighteenth Amendment to the constitution, the role of the CCI was strengthened, particularly because of the replacement of the Concurrent Legislative List with the Federal list. Some functions that were under the sole jurisdiction of the federal government before the Amendment were later moved to the Federal Legislative List II, and now fall under the jurisdiction of the CCI. The more active role of the CCI has enabled greater involvement of the provincial governments in the decision-making process. Table I enlists the assignments that were transferred from Concurrent List and Federal Legislative List I to the Federal Legislative List II, under the Eighteenth Amendment. There were some assignments which were previously not part of any legislative list but were included in the Legislative List II after the constitutional amendment, further enhancing the role of CCI, which has equal representation from the federal and provincial governments.

Table I: Assignments Transferred/Added to the Federal Legislative List
after Eighteenth Amendment

Assignments transferred from Concurrent List	Assignments transferred from Federal Legislative List I	Assignments not included in any legislative list
Electricity	Major ports	All regulatory authorities
Legal professions	National planning and national economic co-ordination	Management of Public Debt
Medical professions	State lotteries	-
-	Census 4	-
-	Appointment of police force (of one province in another)	-

Source: National Assembly, *Eighteenth Amendment to the Constitution of Pakistan 1973*, Islamabad, Government of Pakistan, 2010.

Table II describes the assignment of some important functions to different tiers of government.

Table II: Division of Functions between the Federal and Provincial Governments

Subject	Functional Assignment
Currency	Federal
Defense	Federal
Treaty Ratification	Federal
External Trade	Federal
Interstate/Interprovincial Trade	Federal
Major physical infrastructure	Federal
Primary/Secondary education	Provincial
Post-Secondary Education	Provincial
Income Security	Provincial
Pensions	Provincial
Health Care	Provincial
Mineral resources	Joint/CII

Subject	Functional Assignment
Agriculture	Provincial
Environment	Provincial
Municipal	Provincial
Court System	Federal
Criminal Law	Provincial
Police	Provincial
Custom/excise taxes	Federal
Corporate and Federal taxes	Federal

Source: National Assembly, *Eighteenth Amendment to the Constitution of Pakistan 1973*, (Islamabad, Government of Pakistan, 2010)

Forty-eight federal laws were identified under the Eighteenth Amendment, that require changes to reflect the true intent and purpose of the amendment.[3] Even after eight years, there are certain issues that remain unresolved. The following are some of the issues that await policy decision and require political attention.

Conflict over Oil and Natural Gas

According to the Article 161(1) of the Constitution of Pakistan, the net proceeds of the excise duty imposed by the Federal government on Natural Gas will not be a part of Federal Consolidated Fund and the proceeds will go to the province in which the resource extraction is taking place. Moreover, the same principle applies to oil extraction processes.

There is an ongoing conflict of views regarding the above clause between the federal and provincial governments. For instance, Sindh claims that the province has exclusive right to extend the exploration license of the oil and gas companies operating in the province while the Federal Ministry of Petroleum and Natural Resource (MPNR) is opposed to this idea.

Provincial Borrowings

Provinces are empowered to have access to foreign loans under the Eighteenth Amendment, but the Executive Committee of the National Economic Council (ECNEC) has failed to formulate the policies and rules regarding different aspects of borrowing.

Higher Education Commission (HEC) Conflict

Under the Eighteenth Amendment, the authority over higher education was devolved. Following suit, Punjab and Sindh established their own higher education department/commission but these commissions have been termed as 'unconstitutional' by the Central HEC. The conflict over Higher Education commissions still needs to be resolved.

It is obvious that effective implementation of provincial autonomy will take some time to find a stable equilibrium. More importantly, the third tier of the government—local governments—has been weakened under the new laws passed by Punjab, Sindh, and Balochistan.

An Overview of Sindh's Economy

The province of Sindh, in its present form, came into existence in 1970 when West Pakistan was dissolved after the abolition of the One Unit programme. In the period 1947–55, the province of Sindh had the same territory but excluded the state of Khairpur. Karachi, the capital of Sindh, became the capital of Pakistan in 1947 and remained so until a new capital city—Islamabad—was established in the northern part of the country in 1962.

Forty-eight per cent of Sindh's citizens live in rural areas and around 38 per cent of them derive their livelihood from agriculture, livestock, forestry, and fishing.[4] The organised manufacturing and services sectors have little presence in rural areas, and much of what exists primarily caters to the need of the rural population.[5]

Fifty-two per cent of the province's population resides in the urban areas of Sindh.[6] Within these areas, Karachi Division houses 50 per cent of Sindh's population and is almost exclusively employed in the manufacturing and services sectors.[7] In Pakistan, the agriculture, industry, and services sectors account for nearly 42, 23, and 35 per cent of the urban labour force respectively.[8] From the period of the last two labour censuses, between 1998 and 2014, the average annual addition to Sindh's labour force was estimated at 400,000 compared to that of Pakistan's 1.86 million.[9] While the labour force in the province grew by over 6.5 million over the period of 17 years, the population grew by around 18 million in the same period.

Almost three in every ten people of working age in Sindh are engaged in formal employment.[10] Of Sindh's population, 39 per cent is employed in agriculture whereas almost 34 per cent is in the informal sector.[11] Sindh has a crude labour force participation rate of 43 per cent, which means that more than half of the population is not participating in the labour force, perhaps due to low female participation of only around 28 per cent.[12] This means there are on average at least two people dependent on each employed person, which is muting any potential demographic dividend effect.[13]

The unemployment rate, especially among the youth, is quite high nationally, at 5.9 per cent although it appears to be 4.7 per cent in the province.[14] Mismatch between education and skills required by the economy and those present in the market is the main reason for rising youth unemployment rates. To absorb this additional labour force, Sindh has to deliver growth rates in excess of 7 per cent annually in the next decade.

Mean consumption is much higher in the urban areas as compared to rural Sindh, which relies upon agriculture as the main source of sustenance. Therefore, the labour absorption strategy has to have a differentiated rather than a uniform approach so that the existing income and urban–rural disparities do not get further magnified, thus impairing the already fragile social and political relations between the two major communities living in the province. Choices of occupation—public sector mainly by the rural residents and private commerce and industry by the urban—also affect employment and consumption patterns and a greater inter-sectoral factor mobility would help in arresting the current dichotomy.

Sindh is one of the richest provinces in the Federation and its share in the national GDP is estimated to be at around 30 per cent, while its population share is currently at 23 per cent.[15] On the other hand, Punjab is the most populous province with 53 per cent of the population contributes between 54 per cent to the national economy.[16] These two large provinces account for more than four-fifth of the national income. If the share in GDP is seen relative to population, Sindh has been losing its lead with the passage of time, with Punjab catching up.

According to an unpublished draft report on the Sindh Growth Strategy (SGS) 2015 by the World Bank, Sindh's per capita income at the time of Independence was believed to be nearly 55 per cent higher than that of the rest of the country; by the early 1990s, it was 36 per cent higher and by 2014–15 the difference was further reduced to 17 per cent. The high per capita income of Sindh conceals the low per capita income in the rural areas, which are one-half of that of the urban population. Sindh's per capita income growth has stagnated during the last two decades and was less than one per cent annually, compared to the national average of 2.5 per cent. In the most recent period, i.e. between FY 2011–15, the per capita real GDP grew at only 1.2 per cent on average, compared with Punjab's 2.6 per cent and Khyber Pakhtunkhwa's 3.3 per cent. A further disaggregation reveals that rural Sindh experienced negative growth while urban Sindh enjoyed positive growth. The poorest in rural areas experienced the worst growth rate of any category in that period, losing almost one per cent of income.

Sindh appears to have lost more at every downturn than it gained in the upturn, resulting in a broad-based decline in its share in the national GDP. By the early 2000s, Sindh's share in the national GDP fell in every sub-sector except mining and quarrying, and some of the largest declines were registered in sub-sectors where Sindh is believed to have a competitive advantage, namely large-scale manufacturing; finance and insurance; and transport, storage, and communication. Consequently, industry and services sectors have increased at a rate below the national average during 1998–2014. During this period, the overall value of Sindh (Provincial Gross Domestic Product, or PGDP) increased by almost 90 per cent and stood at PKR 3,193 billion in 2014, while the value of the national GDP rose by 170 per cent. The reason for this relative lag lies in the sharp division between the two major communities inhabiting the province.[17]

Sindh's population grew relatively faster than that of rest of the country because of higher net migration from other provinces. A new method, which estimates multidimensional poverty, puts the poverty head count ratio for Pakistan at 38.8 and for Sindh at 43.1 for the year 2014.[18] This means that the poverty intensity in Pakistan and Sindh is at 50.9 and 53.5 per cent respectively. The trend line shows a decline in poverty headcount when measured against all different poverty lines. According to the old poverty line, the corresponding number at the national level was 6.1 in 2013.[19] This means that the poor made gains as poverty declined in Sindh between 2001–14, as well as in the rest of the country. However, this decline was uneven. Between FY2004–08, the poor had stronger gains relative to the mean growth rate, but far fewer gains between FY2010–14 in comparison to the average person in Sindh. The poverty statistics in rural Sindh are far higher than those in urban Sindh and in the rest of Pakistan.

The main reason for weak economic growth despite an urbanised, educated population has been declining productivity. This is despite the fact that the contribution of manufacturing and services to GDP recorded an increase during this period while agricultural employment in Sindh remained stagnant and agriculture's contribution to the GDP dropped.[20] Labour productivity in agriculture has remained low and steady in Sindh over the last decade. Productivity in industry and services has also started to decline in the last three years after rising for most of the last decade, implying that the reallocation of labour is not transpiring according to the classical economic growth theory.

Further analysis is required to determine the factors responsible for this negative shift in productivity. It is possible that the expansion in the industry and services sectors occurred in low productivity firms or services such as wholesale and retail trade, thereby lowering the average productivity of the sector. Poor outcomes in education and health may have also affected the quality of human capital, which in turn contributed to lower productivity. Underemployment and lower than minimum wage rate in informal economic activities could be other possible factors.

Sindh has historically been one of the most unequal and sharply divergent provinces in Pakistan. Karachi has the highest per capita income with the highest ranking across various social indicators while some of the districts in rural Sindh are among the poorest in the country, with bottom rankings in access to basic social services. The social gap between the urban males and rural females is wide and inter-personal income, gender, and rural–urban inequalities have worsened over time.

The main explanatory factor for this sharp divergence is the congruence of rural–urban divide with the ethnic and linguistic divide. With 99 per cent gross primary enrolment, a 72 per cent literacy rate, and 87 per cent of babies fully immunised, the social indicators of urban Sindh—especially Karachi—equal or surpass the level of development in other developing countries with a comparable per capita income. On the other hand, with 58 per cent gross enrolment at the primary level, a 38 per cent literacy rate, and 62 per cent of babies fully immunised, the level of human development in rural Sindh is worse than many countries in sub-Saharan Africa.

Historically, it has been observed that whenever the two larger communities—Sindhis and Urdu-speaking—worked together in harmony and peace, the province prospered and when they got engaged in mutual recrimination and violence, the province suffered. Over time, the growth and development process of the province has taken a backseat as mistrust, and social and ethnic cleavages have deepened and tainted all economic decisions. Consequently, Sindh has performed worse than the rest of the country on both economic and social fronts.

This underperformance, if not reversed, would pose many challenges for Sindh because of the current demographics, and education and migration dynamics. The province's unemployment situation is likely to deteriorate in the future in the absence of rapid growth. As pointed out earlier, youth unemployment is on the rise and with changes in the demographic pattern, the youth bulge can pose serious economic and social distress in the future. If the progress in social development had been commensurate with its economic advancement and the social divide across gender and geographical dimension was less severe, the youth unemployment problem would have been amenable to certain policy, institutional, and investment interventions. But these additional complicating factors that are peculiar to Sindh make the resolution of the youth unemployment problem more onerous.

The agriculture sector, which is the main driver of its rural economy, has been stagnant because of inequitable land distribution and poor resource management—particularly that of water—coupled with absence of new varieties.[21] Both inequality in access to land and water use have exacerbated the situation. Sindh has the highest incidence of absolute landlessness, highest share of tenancy, and the lowest share of land ownership in the country, according to the latest agricultural census of 2010. The wealthy landlords in Sindh, with holdings in excess of 100 acres, account for 0.45 per cent of all farmers in the province, but own seven per cent of the total farmed land. Their farmed holdings are equivalent to around 75 per cent that of small farmers with landholding less than five acres.[22]

The productivity differentials between the large farmers and small farmers have widened because of lack of access to basic inputs for the latter. Being a lower riparian province, Sindh's water problem appears acute and the shortages hit the small farmers most severely as they are deprived of timely and adequate availability of water for their crops. Tampering of water modules and direct pumping from the canals by the influential and politically well-connected landlords, in collusion with the officials of the irrigation department, have become a common feature of the water conveyance and distribution system of Sindh.

Until recent years, Sindh had been the nation's most efficient cereal producer, with crop yields that exceeded those of every other province in the country. The droughts, floods, and the accompanying decline in canal water release, however, have changed that scenario considerably. During FY1980–90, the output of wheat and sugarcane grew by 17 and 136 per cent respectively while both rice and cotton fell by 7 and 20 per cent respectively. Crop production has increased from FY2010–15 for cotton, rice, and sugarcane but has declined for wheat.[23] The fallout from climate change—floods, droughts, reduced moisture content, and the erratic rainfall pattern—is likely to intensify these trends of low productivity.

Sindh has become a water deficient province and the distribution of the Indus water among the upper and lower riparian provinces has been one of the major sources of long standing tension and discord between Punjab and Sindh. Rapid population growth, industrialisation, and the growing needs of agriculture will aggravate the demand for water in the future. Storages such as Tarbela and Mangla are likely to silt up in the next decades, further exacerbating the problem, while new reservoirs would not come on stream until the late 2020s. In addition, widespread contamination, sea water intrusion below Kotri barrage, increasing quantities of pesticides and fertilisers used in agriculture, industrial run-offs from rapidly growing cities and industries, and inadequate sewage treatment have degraded the quality of water. Previous attempts to train and confine the course of river flow by embankments have raised the river bed higher and higher and, in many lower parts of Sindh, the river bed is higher than the land. As a result, the likelihood of embankment breaches has increased, as have problems of drainage from floodlands. If and when this coincides with unfavourable tidal conditions, the consequence can be disastrous. Careful and judicious water resource management is thus the key for Sindh's agricultural economy.

Sindh's social indicators have either stagnated or have not improved in tandem with the other provinces of Pakistan. In 1998–99, Sindh's literacy rate was six percentage points higher than that of Pakistan; by 2004–05, it was only three percentage points higher. Sindh's net primary enrolment rate in 1998–99 was one per cent higher than the national average; by 2004–05, it was four points lower and by 2011, it was lower by nine per cent. The percentage of households with access to roads in Sindh exceeded the national average by two percentage points in 1998–99; today, it is seven per cent lower.[24] Perhaps the biggest change is with respect to the poverty rate: Sindh's poverty headcount ratio was 10 per cent lower than the national economy in 1995–96; it was three per cent higher in 2001–02.[25] The poor social indicators not only stunt the lives of those who remain afflicted by illiteracy and ill-health, but they also limit the possibilities of economic growth since no country or province can hope to make much progress in a globalised world without an educated and healthy workforce.

Federal revenue transfers to Sindh have more than tripled over the last seven years. The Sindh Government has directed most of this towards development spending. Health and education expenditure has increased in real terms by at least 40 per cent a year between FY2005–15.[26] Outcomes, however, have shown no improvement. There is clear evidence that the efficiency of public expenditure on key services has not improved or may have in fact declined.

The intra-provincial inequity in the social indicators is unacceptably high in Sindh. The inequity runs across two dimensions: gender (male vs female) and geography (urban vs rural). The extent of disparity across these two dimensions is best understood by comparing the development indicators for the two groups in the extremes, that is, urban males and rural females. The disparity in the social outcomes between these two groups starts at birth and perpetuates throughout their lifetimes.

The gender ratio of Sindh is currently 108.58, compared to that of the country at 105.07.[27] For every 100 boys being immunised in urban Sindh, only 70 girls get immunised in rural areas.[28] For every 100 boys enrolling in primary school in Sindh, only 86 girls do so in the province.[29] The disparity widens as one moves to higher education and finally to participation in the job market. Evidence demonstrates that it is 'governance deficit', which has translated into a 'service delivery deficit' in the province. Most surveys, public opinion polls, and media reports point to widespread corruption, and leakage and misuse of public funds, and indifferent attitude of the service providers as the main reason for poor delivery of public services. Private mafias openly operate for supplying water, plots of land, cheating at examinations etc. while private security companies, private educational institutions, and health facilities have proliferated throughout the province. These non-state providers of services motivated by profits are the prime movers behind the social gap in Sindh.

To sum up, the principal challenges faced by the economy of Sindh are:

- How to absorb 300,000–400,000 new entrants every year to the employed labour force and equip them with appropriate education, training, and skills
- How to raise the productivity of agriculture in the face of water shortages, food insecurity, and rising demand for meat, dairy, and fruits by the urban middle class
- How to use the relative strengths of the urban and rural economies to build more synergies between the two and overcome the existing divide
- How to improve governance and make state institutions effective and capable for delivery of public goods and service
- How to bridge the social gap between the underdeveloped districts and the rural female population and the developed districts and urban male population

The strategy proposed in the concluding chapter of this volume has been designed to address these challenges.

Figure I: Share of Sindh in Pakistan's Economy (in PKR Billion at Constant Prices of 2005–06) (1999–2000 to 2014–15)

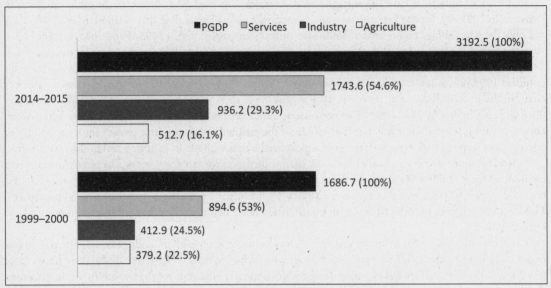

Source: Hafiz Pasha, *Growth of the Provincial Economies,* Lahore, Institute for Policy Reforms, 2015.

Figure II: Estimated Sindh's Share in Pakistan's Economy (2014–15)

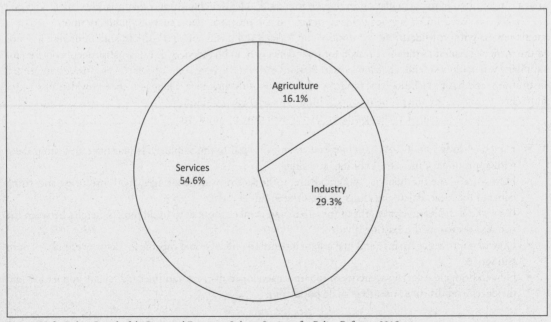

Source: Hafiz Pasha, *Growth of the Provincial Economies,* Lahore, Institute for Policy Reforms, 2015.

Figure III: Pakistan's Population vis-à-vis Output of Major Crops (1972–2015)

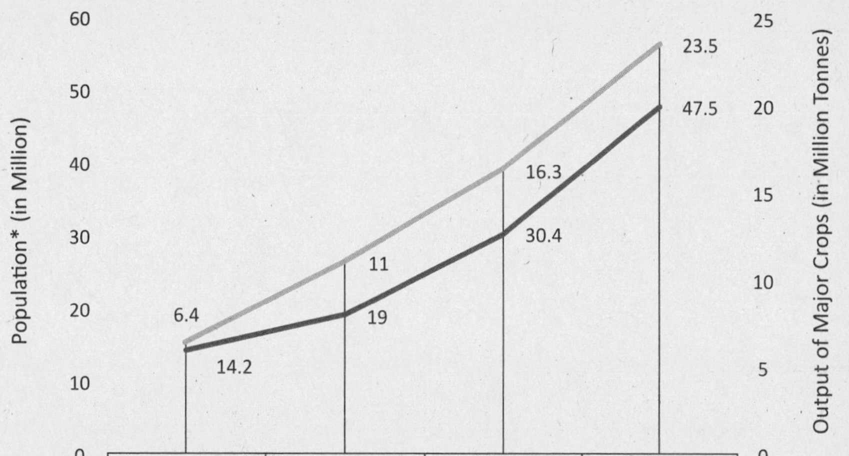

	1972	1981	1998	2015
Output of Major Crops** (in Million Tonnes)	6.4	11	16.3	23.5
Population* (in Million)	14.2	19	30.4	47.5

Source: Population Census Organisation, 1998 Census Report of Sindh Islamabad, Statistics Division, Government of Pakistan, 2000: Pakistan Bureau of Statistics, Provisional Summary Results of Sixth Population and Housing Census, Islamabad, Statistics Division, 2017; Economic Adviser's Wing, *Pakistan Economic Survey* Islamabad, Finance Division, Government of Pakistan, various years; Government of Sindh, n.d. 'Development Statistics of Sindh (1990 to 2010)', Bureau of Statistics, Planning and Development Department; Government of Pakistan, 2007, *50 Years of Agricultural Statistics in Pakistan (1947–2000)*, Islamabad, Ministry of Food, Agriculture and Livestock (Economic Wing), May; 2012, *Agricultural Statistics of Pakistan (2011–2012)*, Islamabad, Statistics Division, Pakistan Bureau of Statistics, February.

Population data incorporated is obtained from the last five censuses held, i.e. 1972, 1981, 1998, and 2017. Source: Population Census Organisation, 1998 Census Report of Sindh, Islamabad, Statistics Division, Government of Pakistan, 2000; Pakistan Bureau of Statistics, Provisional Summary Results of Sixth Population and Housing Census, Islamabad, Statistics Division, 2017; The output of major crops obtained is for the years 1975, 1985, 2000, and 2015. The crops included are cotton, rice, sugarcane, and wheat.

* Provincial figures have been taken from Ministry of National Food Security and Research, Agricultural Statistics 2014–15, Islamabad, Government of Pakistan, n.d.
** National figures were taken from Finance Division, *Pakistan Economic Survey 2016–17*, Islamabad, Ministry of Finance, Government of Pakistan, 2017.

Source: Bureau of Statistics, Development Statistics of Sindh, Karachi, Planning and Development Department, Government of Sindh, various years; Ministry of Food, Agriculture and Livestock, *50 Years of Agricultural Statistics in Pakistan (1947–2000)*, Islamabad, Government of Pakistan, 2007; Pakistan Bureau of Statistics, *Agricultural Statistics of Pakistan (2011–2012)*, Islamabad, Statistics of Division, Government of Sindh, 2013.

Figure IV: Annual Average Growth Rate of Sindh's Major Crops (%)
(1995–2005 and 2005–15)

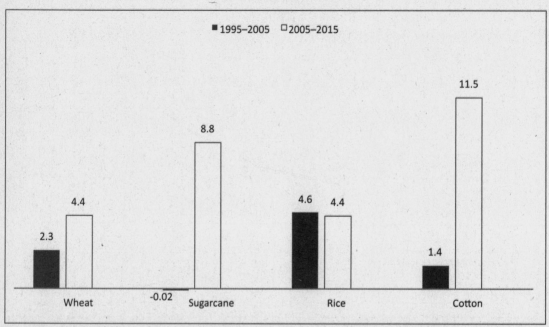

Source: Economic Adviser's Wing, *Pakistan Economic Survey,* Islamabad, Finance Division, Government of Pakistan, various years: Government of Sindh, n.d. 'Development Statistics of Sindh (1990 to 2010)', Bureau of Statistics, Planning and Development Department; Government of Pakistan, 2007, *50 Years of Agricultural Statistics in Pakistan (1947–2000),* Islamabad, Ministry of Food, Agriculture and Livestock (Economic Wing), May; 2012, *Agricultural Statistics of Pakistan (2011–2012),* Islamabad, Statistics Division, Pakistan Bureau of Statistics, February.

Figure V: Socio-Economic Standing of Sindh Compared to the
Rest of Pakistan (2014–15)

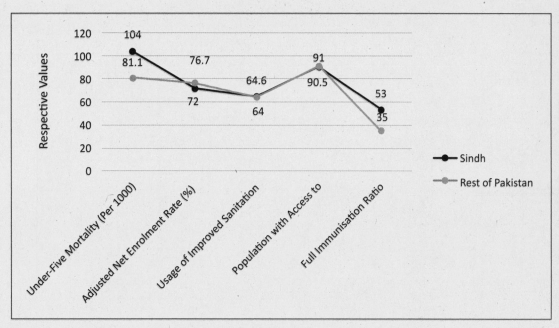

Source: Government of Sindh and United Nations Development Programme, *Sindh Multiple Indicator Cluster Survey 2014,* Karachi, 2015, Ministry of Food, Agriculture and Livestock (Economic Wing), May; Government of Pakistan, 2007, *50 Years of Agricultural Statistics in Pakistan (1947–2000),* Islamabad, Planning and Development Department; 2012, *Agricultural Statistics of Pakistan (2011–2012),* Islamabad, Statistics Division, Pakistan Bureau of Statistics, February; Government of Sindh, n.d., 'Development Statistics of Sindh (1990 to 2010)', Bureau of Statistics.

1

Land and People

Location

SINDH is the southern-most province of Pakistan. It is bordered by the province of Punjab in the north, the Arabian Sea and the Rann of Kutch in the South, Balochistan in the west, and India towards the east. Sindh ranks third in size among Pakistan's four provinces with an area of 54,407.2 square miles (140,914 sq. km). Punjab is the biggest province in terms of population; however, it has an area of 79,542 sq. miles. In contrast, Balochistan is sparsely populated but is the largest area wise; sprawling across 133,107 sq. miles (344,746 sq. km). Khyber Pakhtunkhwa (KP), formerly known as the North West Frontier Province (NWFP), is the smallest with an area of 39,283 sq. miles (101,743 sq. km). The province of Sindh is part of the lower Indus basin and lies between 23–40° and 28–30° north latitude and 66–40° and 71–05° east longitude. It is about 540 km in length from north to south and nearly 250 km in its extreme breadth (281 km average).

Historical Origin of the Province's Name

The Western world knows the river as Indus. The Greeks who travelled along with Alexander the great called it Indus as well as Sindhos. Indus was that great body of the water coming from the Himalayas through the Mansarovar Lake. Sindh in its early history was a part of the subcontinent extending from Kashmir to Arabian Sea and from Sessitan to Thar Desert.[1]

In the local dialect, the Indus River is known as 'Sindhu Nadi' or 'Sindhu Darya'. Sindh's name has been derived from the local name for the river that sustains it. The river bisects the province and cultivates large tracts of land[2] on either side. Moreover, its history is intricately connected to the Sindhi spatial identity.

Major General Henry George Raverty in his book *The Mihran of Sind and Its Tributaries* (Sang-e-Meel Publications, 1979) reiterates the same, 'The name Indus was and is unknown to oriental geographers and historians. It was Europeanised by the Greeks out of Sindhu, as they may have called the Indus, as being the river separating Hind from Iran-i-Zamin, and not intending it to be understood that Indus was the proper name of the river.' Pliny says that the Indus was called Sindhus by the inhabitants. Sindhi locals today call the Indus the Sindhu Nadi. The words Sind, Hind, and Ind are perhaps then the same, Hind and Sind are often interchanged in the Indo-European languages. Hence, Sind, the name of the country, Indus, the name of the river, and Hindustan, the former name of the Indo-Pakistan subcontinentt, are all philologically the same word. No one knows whether the river takes its name from the land, or whether the land takes its name from the river.[3]

Topography

MOUNTAINS

In the extreme west, Sindh is a dominantly flat region. The mountainous region consists of the Kohistan section of the barren Kirthar Mountains. To the east, the sand belt stretches from the borders of the Bahawalpur to the Rann of Kutch, the Kutch State of India. Between these tracts lies the Indus Valley, terminating in the deltaic area in the South West. The Northern portion of this Valley is called the 'Siro' (Upper), the Southern the 'Lar' (Lower), and between them is the 'Vicholo' Middle). These areas have rich alluvial soil and the central portion has a perennial water supply from the Sukkur Barrage which provides the province with enormous agricultural and kindred potentialities.

Except for a small hilly tract in the South East corner of the Tharparkar District (Nagar Parkar), western Sindh is the only region which is mountainous. This region is known as Kohistan. H.T. Sorley explains: 'The mountains here are, however, not high enough to attract rain clouds during the monsoon season with the result that the rainfall in Sind is generally precarious'.[4] Bhago Thoro Mountains are also connected to Kirthar ranges from Sehwan and onwards. The Kirthar region has little soil and is mostly dry and barren. Additionally, there are small hills in Hyderabad such as Ganjo Takar, Makli hills in Thatta, small hills in Tharparkar like Karoonjhar Hills, and other smaller hills in Karachi.

COAST

The coastal region of Sindh is spread over the southern and eastern part of the country between the Indian border along Sir Creek on the east, and the Hub River along the Balochistan coast on the west. This coastal line, which is approximately 350 km long and can be separated into the Indus Delta/Creek and Karachi coast in the south, is located along the Arabian Sea.[5]

Mangrove forests are the main vegetation found in the coastal areas. They not only provide food and a breeding ground for fish, shrimps, crabs, and other marine life but also help sustain all kinds of fisheries. Thousands of people live around the coastal region and earn their livelihood through fisheries and related activities, contributing towards the betterment of the local and national economy.

The coastlands, wetlands, and lakes attract a variety of migratory birds including water fowl. In the coastal area around Karachi, different kinds of turtles are found. Coastal biodiversity is threatened by pollution caused due to industrial effluents and run off from agricultural production. The more insidious form of pollution emanates from effluents containing the heavy metals mercury and lead. Tanneries situated along the coast are also very harmful to the marine life. According to Indus for Ecoregion Programme by the World Wild Life Fund—in association with the Government of Sindh and Embassy of the Netherlands—states: 'It is estimated that annually about 37,000 tons of industrial waste is being dumped in the coastal environment of Karachi, whereas 20,000 tons of oil finds its way to beaches and harbours and the fishing grounds of Karachi annually.'[6]

DESERT

A significant portion of Sindh's land is desert. The eastern border of the province is known as Tharparkar and is characterised by large sand dunes. The desert is also called Rajistan and has an area of 13,100 sq. miles (33929 sq. km). All these tracts are devoid of irrigation facilities. Furthermore, the Kohistan region of Sindh contains large tracts of Dadu, Thano Bola Khan, parts of Larkana and Shikarpur, and Jacobabad near the Bolan Pass. Parts of Thatta and Sehwan, very small regions of desert, and Kohistan are also irrigated by some canals of Guddu Barrage. These regions are irrigated through wells and nars, and dug tube-wells also provide irrigation to the desert.

MINERALS

Sindh is a depository of coal, iron, and large quantities of limestone and salt. A large quantity of coal has been found in Tharparkar and Lakhra. In Thar, it is being excavated by the government for generating electricity. Iron ore is also extracted from multiple regions. Gypsum is another kind of mineral found in large quantities near Maripur, where it is being mined. It is also found on the banks of Nain Gaj in Kohistan near Bhago Thoro Mountain. Petroleum, oil, and gas have been found in copious amounts and are being utilised as resources for the entire country. In the Thar Desert, there is found fine sand, *china* clay, and granite stone.

VEGETATION AND FORESTS

Previously, a large number of forests existed in Sindh and were classified as irrigated and gallery forests. The gallery forests are also called riverine forests. In 1955, the Government of West Pakistan had directed that at least some water was to be reserved for the forests from various barrages in Sindh. However, the preservation of forests through this allotted conservation of water was a futile effort. This is because forests produce firewood and many have been hunting grounds for rulers in the region. The areas of Sindh along the Indus River where vegetation once existed, included the regions ranging from the City of Sann up to District Jamshoro and up to city of Moro district Naushahro Feroz (formerly Nawabshah). There existed thick forests through the area, spread over hundreds of kilometers. In his book, *A Geography of Sind Province, Pakistan*, Mushtaqur Rehman states:

> In the western hills a few patches of trees [are] found along the seasonal rills or small valleys loosely called forests or woodlands. Following Munshey, the main species of these forests are Babul (Acacia Arabica), Kandi (Prosipis spicigera), Khumbat (Acacia senegals), Khaonr (Acacia fernasiana), Dhaonr (Acacia modesta), Rohero (Tecoma undulate), and a few species of Ber (Zizyphus spp). In addition to these trees, medicinal scrubs and herbs grow in the area. Some of these herbs are used either as antidote for a snake bite, or for washing the clothes, or as a cure from skin diseases. It is said that the Baluchi tribes inhabiting this region find most of their needs from the locally growing scrubs and herbs. Kandero (Alghai comclorum), Reho (Bergia aestivosa), Dramah (Fagonia cretica), and Gangethi (Grewia peplifolia) are some of the important herbs found in the western hills.[7]

Unfortunately, in the time period ranging from 1980 onwards, Ziaul Haq's government ordered the destruction of the largest forests including the thick ones ranging from Sann to Moro to eliminate sanctuaries of dacoits. Since then, no systematic effort has been made in revitalising the forest or the vegetation cover in Sindh. Whatever vegetation that occurs is due to the rainfall.

A number of forests also are grown through canal-irrigated plantations in Sindh. Having begun in the 1930s, these plantations are currently irrigated through Sukkur, Kotri, and Guddu barrage irrigation systems. In the coastal region, forests are located in the region of Indus Delta in Karachi and Thatta; mangroves around here offer great ecological value in terms of sanctuaries for fisheries. The practice of selling large parcels of forest land on nominal prices for cultivation purpose without any effort to replace them or bring in new areas under plantation is the major cause of rapid deforestation.

FLORA

Sindh is a tropical area of the country. Under its ancient sun, countless crops have been sown. Two types of annual crops are grown in the province; one is the rabi crop, which is sown in autumn, while the other is the kharif crop and is sown in summer months. The rabi crop consists of wheat, barley, oilseeds, mustard, saffron, garlic, onion, radish, carrots, turnips, indigo, hemp, okra, and senna. The kharif crop consists of cotton, *bajri, jowar,* rice, sunflower, mung, and others. There are plenty of fruits grown including mangoes, bananas, oranges, coconut, dates, grapes, citrus fruits, melons (watermelon and honeydew melon), peaches, and others. Sugarcane is also grown on a large scale.

FAUNA

Fauna found in Sindh consist of animals like tigers, hyenas, wolves, jackals, *gurkhars*, folks, wild hogs, antelopes, hares, pigs, and porcupines. All the animals mentioned above are wild animals found in the fields. Domesticated animals include camels, cows, buffalos, goats, sheep, horses, mules, asses, cats, and dogs. The birds which are found here include vultures, pelicans, falcons, crows, flaming, stork, cranes, *tilur*, *quil*, partridges, water fowl, wild geese, ducks, teals, curlew, snipe, and hens. A wide variety of snakes are also found in Sindh.

Types of Water Bodies

RIVERS IN SINDH

River Indus

As mentioned earlier, Sindh has an important river known as the Indus. This irrigates most of the agricultural land through canals linked with the three barrages constructed on it. For a significant portion of its history, Sindh was known as the inundation country, until the Indus was tamed. The length of the river from Kailash Range to the Sea is between 2,986 to 3,218 km. The Indus is considered to be a lifeline for the people of Sindh. In the past, the fertility of Sindh has always been dependent on floods and the melting of glaciers which the Indus water system has provided. The Indus enters into Sindh near Kashmor (200 feet above sea level), 96 km downstream (south) of Mithankot.

Hub River

The Hub River, a perennial stream, has its headwaters in the Pab Range. Its main stream forms a rough continuation of the axis of the Kirthar range and the western boundary of Sindh. For most of the year, it forms a series of shallow pools. A dam that has been constructed over it at Hub is the main source of water for the residents of Karachi.

The Baran rises near Tako Baran in the Khirthar Range, where it receives the water of the *nais* (hill torrents), and later cutting through it runs eastwards right through Kohistan into the Indus River, a few kilometers from Bholari railway station.[8]

Malir River

Malir is a small, seasonal stream, remaining dry for most of the year. Once there is heavy rainfall in the city, it flows into Gizri Creek, Karachi. Malir River provides water to the various localities. Some notable characteristics of the river include the perennial flow of water, as well as the aquifers that exist underneath the sandy bed of the river. At a later stage in the water cycle, it joins Kadeji.

Lyari Stream

Lyari is another minor stream of the same nature. It flows into Keamari harbour. Most of its smaller waterfalls, like Mohan, rise from east of the Lakhi Range, including Nienaegh. All of them either flow into the Indus or Arabian Sea if they have not been lost in the sandy tracts along their course.[9]

There are many other *nais* and hill torrents which, although not perennial, supply water to some of the localities in good quantity. The other *nais* are known as Gaj, Mazar, Khenji, Delan, Nari, and others.

Alluvial Plains

A significant amount of Sindh's terrain is considered to be alluvial as the floods of Indus bring copious amounts of alluvium material. Some of the hill ranges have sandstone and limestone formations. A major portion of the area that acts as the extension of the alluvial plains is productive. This is found near Shikarpur, Larkana, and Dadu and extends towards Narrow Island from north to south lying between hills, desert, and the Indus delta.

LAKES IN SINDH

Manchar Lake

Lake Manchar is the biggest freshwater lake of Pakistan and Asia. It is situated in the district of Jamshoro (previously district Dadu) in the west of Indus River. The area of the lake fluctuates with the seasons from 400 sq. km to 600 sq. km.

There are numerous small streams and hill torrents in the mountains of Khirthar which fall in Manchar and River Indus during the inundation period and the rainy seasons. This was a small scale natural lake in its earliest history and its size increased in the 1930s when the Sukkur Barrage was built. There are two large canals known as Aral and Danister which feed Manchar from Indus and once it is overflowing, these two canals take the water back to the River Indus from Lake Manchar to save the nearby areas from heavy floods. There are thousands of fishermen (fisher folk) and their families who live on the banks and the nearby cities of Manchar where they also earn their livelihood. The famous small towns on the banks of Manchar include Kot Lashari, Bubak city, Bubak railway station, and some other smaller villages.

During the winter, there are Siberian birds which come to the lake and the fishermen hunt them for commercial gain. Of late, the lake has been spoiled and degraded through pollution, and saline water from upper Sindh. The water comes from various crops, including rice. The saline water is deposited in the Manchar through Main Nara Valley Drain (MNV). In fact, MNV has to transport the saline water to the Indus as a part of the Right Bank Outfall Drain (RBOD), but RBOD work is at present suspended. RBOD-II provides for a disposal of all effluents from Pat feeder to Manchar. RBOD-III takes the saline water to the sea near Gharo. The area of Manchar Lake will continue to suffer unless this link is completed.

The lake irrigates about 0.25 million acres of Sehwan Taluka. Due to pollution, a large chunk of local fisherman known as Mohanas also work as share-croppers with local *zamindar*s.

Keenjhar Lake

Keenjhar Lake (formerly known as Kalri Lake) in district Thatta, southern Sindh, is 122 kilometers from Karachi and some 18 kilometers from Thatta city. Keenjhar is the second largest lake of fresh water in the country. It provides drinking water to Karachi city as well as Thatta district. It is known as a Ramsar Site and is a sanctuary for wildlife.

This lake is also a favourable habitat and breeding ground for the migratory birds in winter such as ducks, geese, flamingos, cormorants, waders, herons, egrets, ibises, terns, coots, and gulls. Lately, Keenjhar has become one of the largest resorts for tourists. A large number of people visit the lake daily from Karachi, Hyderabad, and other parts of Sindh. A folktale about the Sindhi king Jam Tamachi attracts the tourists to the location. The legend says that King Jam Tamachi of Samma tribe married Noori, a daughter of a poor fisherman, after he fell in love with her while visiting Keenjhar. Noori's grave is believed to be located in the middle of the lake. Hundreds of devotees visit the shrine every day.

Haleji Lake

District Thatta is very rich in lakes. Haleji Lake is in Thatta District. Haleji Lake was originally a salt water lake formed by seasonal water collecting in depressions. During World War II, the British administration in Sindh took a decision to increase the capacity of the lake by bringing one big feeder canal from the river to meet the water requirements for Karachi and the British troops. Lately, fresh water was added in Haleji through a canal and salty water was drained out. Presently, Haleji is one of the major resources of water supply to the increasing population of Karachi. Along with Siberian migratory birds from November to February, some crocodiles and fishing cats are also found here.

Hadero Lake

Hadero Lake is also located in the District of Thatta. It is a brackish water wetland. A variety of waterfowl make their home in this lake. It attracts swans, storks, cranes, and feeding flocks of pelicans. It is considered a significant research site for ornithologists. It is about 85 km to the east of Karachi. Hudero was declared a wildlife sanctuary with an aim to conserve and protect the natural environment in and around the lake for different migratory and resident birds. The lake was originally declared a Game Sanctuary under Section 15 of the West Pakistan Wildlife Protection Ordinance 1959 in 1971. In 1977, it was declared a wildlife sanctuary under a notification by the Government of Sindh. There is stony desert around Hudero. Many fishermen depend on this lake for their livelihood.

Drigh Lake

Drigh Lake is situated in Qambar Shahdadkot district, formerly parts of Larkana. It is 29 km from Larkana city and 7 km (4 miles) from Qambar town. It has a surface area of 450 acres.

The lake attracts night heron, grey heron, purple heron, great white egret, little egret, painted anipe, mallard, gadwal, pintail, shoveller, common teal, tufted duck, wigeon, osprey, marsh harrier, white breasted kingfisher, pied kingfisher, small blue kingfisher, purple galinule, white-breasted water hen, moorhen, cormorant, common pilchard, pied harrier, crow pheasant, darter, garage, ferruginous duck, greater spotted eagle, moorhen, marbled teal, and coot. This lake was declared a wildlife sanctuary in 1972 and Ramseur site in 1976.

Hamal Lake

Like Thatta, Larkana and Dadu are also very rich in the water reservoirs namely the Dhands (the lakes in Sindh are called Dhands). Hamal Lake is also situated in Qambar Shahdadkot district, 58 km from Larkana city. The length of the lake is 25 km and the width is 10 km with a surface area of 2,965 acres. It is a freshwater lake and the main sources of water are the streams that come through from Kirthar Mountains.

Like all other lakes, Hamal Lake is also a habitat for Siberian migratory birds like ducks, geese, coots, shorebirds, cormorants, flamingos, herons, ibises, gulls, terns, and egret. It is a nursery for fresh water fish as well. Lately, the environment and the wildlife of the lake have been very dangerously affected by the poisonous and saline water of Hairdin drain coming from Balochistan.

Makhi Lake (Makhi Dhandh)/Chotiari Reservoir

Makhi Lake is in district Sanghar. This was formerly a haunt of Hur fighters in Sanghar (the freedom fighters of Pir Pagaro). Hurs waged war with the British rulers in Sindh. The British tried to quell their opposition through force. However, the Hurs took refuge in the region of the lake and fought back. The British government abolished all the rights of Hurs on Makhi Dhand. In present-day Sanghar, Makhi Dhand no longer exists. The whole area of Makhi has now been changed into Chotiari reservoir which irrigates some parts of Sanghar and the area of Thar adjacent to Sanghar. Many local people including Hurs and their families have settled around Chotiari reservoir.

Climate

The temperature varies daily throughout the province during the daytime. The maximum temperature occurs in the afternoon during summers and is low in the evening especially between sunset and sunrise. Some parts of the region remain extremely hot. Summers that occur for long months bring sweltering heat. Winters are, by contrast, quite moderate. Figure 1.1 shows a sharp rise in temperature during the first decade of the twenty-first century, except for the year 2005. Figure 1.2 depicts the deviation of maximum and minimum temperatures recorded in the last decades.

Pakistan is a vulnerable region as far as climate change is concerned. Global warming is bringing a lot of interactive changes to the physical processes responsible for climate system dynamics. Climate change is likely to affect water resources and agriculture, energy, economic, health, industrial, and other sectors in ways that are not yet clearly known. 'The north of Pakistan hosts more than 5,000 glaciers while the south is composed of hyper deserts despite the closet [*sic*] vicinity of the Arabian Sea'[10]

Sindh in Pakistan is most exposed to climate change as it lies in a zone where temperature increases more than the global ranges. Most of its land area is arid and semi-arid and being predominantly an agricultural economy, it is sensitive to the risks of monsoon rains, large floods, cyclones, and droughts. These in turn, would affect

Figure 1.1: Area Weighted Mean Temperature of Pakistan (1960–2010)

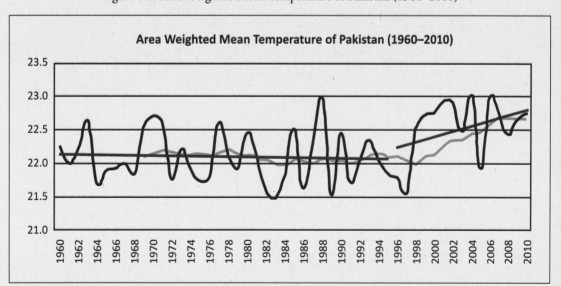

Source: Ghulam Rasul, *Impacts of Climate Change,* Islamabad, Pakistan Metrological Dept, Research and Development Division, n.d., p. 11.

Figure 1.2: Deviation of Maximum (Represents Day Highest) and Minimum
(Represents Night Lowest) Temperature during Last Decade from Normal
in Summer and Winter Seasons in Pakistan

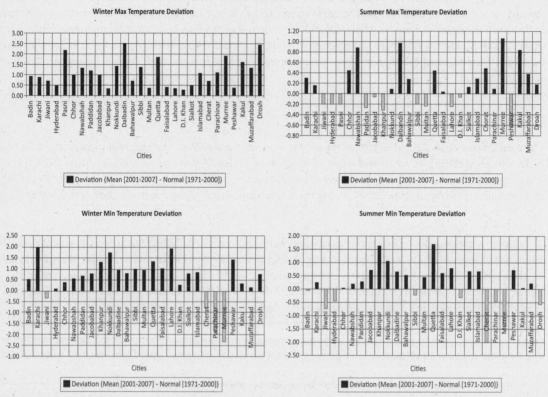

Source: Ghulam Rasul, *Impacts of Climate Change,* Islamabad, Pakistan Metrological Dept, Research and Development Division, n.d., p. 11.

water, food, and energy sectors adversely unless mitigation measures are put in place. Cyclonic activity in the Arabian Sea, rise in sea levels, erosion of the coast, and sea water intrusion are all potential threats to the region.

Although there are many challenges to the livelihood of Indus Delta dwellers due to climate change, there may also be some opportunities. There is a large potential for wind power generation due to the sea being nearby which can attract investment. Potential investments include building climate resilient infrastructure and generating employment for the local population, hence ensuring sustainable livelihood.

RAINFALL

The rainfall in Sindh is scant. It is said that the surrounding hill ranges on the sides of Sindh, especially on the western side, do produce an orographic effect that makes it dry with low or very low rain.

Sindh receives 4 to 5 inches of rain in the monsoon season. The rainfall during the winter seasons consists of a mere 2 inches. Over the last few years, Sindh has witnessed heavy rains resulting in floods. The 2010 floods caused serious displacement of population, losses in incomes and livelihood, and required huge expenditures on relief and rehabilitation of flood affectees. In other cases, Sindh has been facing droughts as mentioned earlier elsewhere in the chapter.

Culture of Sindh

LANGUAGE

The major language spoken in Sindh is Sindhi. This is the most valuable cultural heritage that this land possesses. Sindhi language is fully developed and is being used technically with complete grammatical accuracy. This language has been the primary mode of communication in Sindh throughout the centuries. It has been incorporated into digital dictionaries with new developments like Unicode and transliteration. Its sister languages and dialects include Aer, Bagri, Bhaya, Dhatki, Goaria, Gujarati, Jadgali, Jandavra, Jogi, Kohli, Parkari, Dhatkhi, Kutchi, Loarki, Marwari, Memoni, Mewari, Od, and Rajasthani. With the immigration of the Balochis from Balochistan, a significant number of the people settled in the districts nearing Balochistan speak Balochi as well. It is pertinent to mention here that the British rulers tried their best to standardise the Sindhi alphabet and wrote out the grammar of the language.

The other main language that is spoken in Sindh is Urdu. Majority of the Urdu speaking population who migrated to Sindh from India speak Urdu, other languages spoken are Punjabi and Pushto. Urdu is understood across Sindh and has some sociological influence, affecting Sindhi. It is a highly developed language. There is sparse literature in languages other than Sindhi and Urdu that have been mentioned above. According to some surveys, two books per day are published in Sindhi language on average. This is due to the literary institutions established by the Government.

The dialects and pronunciation of the Sindhi language changes as communities live in different areas, and the habits, and social and cultural behaviour also varies along the towns and cities situated on the banks of the River Indus.

In Sindh there are five to six Sindhi news and entertainment television networks and 25 to 30 daily newspapers besides weekly, monthly, quarterly, literary, and social magazines including research journals by different universities.

Sindhi Literature (Prose and Poetry)

As noted earlier, the Sindhi language has a very rich literature. There are many books written and published in this language. Dr U.M. Daudpota in his survey of Sindhi literature says that like 'all other world of literature, Sindhi literature as well begins with poetry. The people of Sindh were not barbarians when Sindhi poetry came first to be sung and written.'[11]

Prominent names in the early history of Sindhi literature are that of Shah Kareem of Bulri, Shah Abdul Latif Bhittai, and Sachal Sarmast. Another prominent Sindhi author, Mirza Qalich Beg, in his book *Qadeem Sindh, Una Ja Mashhoor Shahar Aeen Manhoon* (Ancient Sindh, Its Famous Cities and People) has given many names of the learned men of Thatta during the period of its greatest splendor.[12]

Likewise, throughout various periods of rulers in the history of Sindh, Sindhi language and literature was given patronage and recognised for its rich cultural value.

TRAITS AND OTHER ELEMENTS

The people of Sindh have strong ethnic loyalty with their language and culture. They have love for their land which they express through regular cultural events for different occasions. They are hospitable. They also believe in *Kachahry* (get together) culture. Their traditional dresses are very different which they wear on celebrations, cultural days, and religious occasions like Eid. These include the *ajrak* (blockprinted shawls), the Sindhi *topi* or cap, *soosis* (a very famous cloth of Sindh for women dresses made at various places of Sindh especially at

Hala and Nasarpur), *loongees* (a type of wraparound), embroidered cloths and Sindhi *jutis* (shoes). The local Sindhi sports are played with lot of enthusiasm like *Malakhro, Kodi Kodi, Wanjhe Wati,* and *Bilharo* (various local traditional games).

Religion

Ninety-five per cent of Sindh's population is Muslim. The remaining five per cent of the population practices Hinduism, Christianity, and Zoroastrianism. Ninety per cent of the total Hindu population of Pakistan lives in Sindh.

Music

Besides prose and poetry, Sindhi music is one of the greatest cultural achievements of the province. Various schools of Sindhi music, especially Sindhi Bhervi, Sindhi Rano, and many other Surs which have been given by the great poets, have been sung throughout the centuries. Shah Abdul Latif Bhittai, the great poet of Sindh himself sung with the Sitar and his *Sangeet* is known as 'Shah jo Raag'. Sindhi music is still very popular in the whole subcontinent. Dr N.A. Baloch, another prominent scholar of Sindhi, has written much on the various instruments of Sindhi music through which various singers have been fulfilling various ragas and Sindhi melodies. The instruments like Sitar, Bhorindo, and Chang have been dealt with in detail.

Arts and Crafts

If we look at recent history, Sindh has been famous for the variety and skills of its cottage industries which contribute towards the economy. The cottage industry comes under the sphere of small industries.

Sindh has historically been famous for the muslin cloth and other textile products which were being woven here and sold across the sea to the various parts of the world, especially Russia, Hong Kong, Hawaii, and Portugal. Thatta, Shikarpur, Sehwan, Naserpur, Boobak, and Rohri have been the main centres of the export of leather goods, also a popular export. Loongees, soosees, and rich scarves earned fame and have greatly contributed towards the flourishing of the small-scale economy. The embroidery and silk work carried on in Sindh uses the gold and silver thread and was always in great demand for the decoration of shawls, coats, caps, ladies shirts, children trousers, and Sindhi topis.[13]

The coloured and glazed tiles of Sindh have been always of great interest to the people of the world. Sukkur, Hala, Nasarpur, Goomi, and Thatta are the main districts for the tiles as well as wood carving work. The Khes and fine loongies and beautiful dresses for the local people are admired widely. The ralli is another beautiful work of Sindh. It is used as a bedsheet or as a quilt in the beginning of the winter season. It is also used as decorative linen for beds and as cutwork for dresses.

Administrative Setup

The province is governed by an elected chief minister who is the leader of the house in the provincial assembly consisting of 168 MPAs (Members of the Provincial Assembly). At the same time, the said person is also chief executive of the province. The governor is a titular head of the province appointed by the federal government as the representative of the federation. The division is headed by the commissioner, the district by the deputy commissioner, the sub-division by the sub-divisional officer or assistant commissioner, and the taluka/tehsil by the mukhtiakar. A local government system exists as well. The metropolitan corporations, municipal corporations, district councils, union councils, and town committees are run by the elected representatives such as the mayors and the chairman.

At present there are six administrative divisions, 29 districts, 125 talukas/tehsils and 1175 union councils in Sindh. Some of the details are provided in Annexure 1A and Table 1.1:

Table 1.1: Administrative Units of Sindh—Divisions and their Districts

Divisions	Districts
Karachi	Karachi West, Karachi East, Karachi South, Karachi Central, Korangi, Malir
Hyderabad	Badin, Dadu, Hyderabad, Jamshoro, Thatta, Sujawal, Matiari, Tando Allah Yar, Tando Muhammad Khan
Larkana	Larkana, Jacobabad, Shikarpur, Kashmor, Kambar ShahdadKot
Mirpurkhas	Mirpurkhas, Tharparkar, Umer Kot
Shaheed Benazirabad	Sanghar, Naushahro Feroze, Shaheed Benazirabad
Sukkur	Ghotki, Khairpur, Sukkur

Source: Local Government Commission, Government of Sindh, Karachi.

Sindh in Different Eras

MOHEN-JO-DARO

Sindh, which was known as the Indus Civilisation, has a rich archeological heritage. The ancient history of Sindh begins in 3,000 BCE. This civilisation is known to have consisted of two large cities, Mohen-jo-Daro and Harappa. It evolved from the villages of neighbours or predecessors using the Mesopotamian model of irrigated agriculture. The city of Mohen-jo-Daro is considered to have been the greatest civilised city in the world 4,500 years ago. Mohen-jo-Daro was an impressively well-planned city of the Indus Civilisation. The city of Mohen-jo-Daro had the oldest drainage system, highly appreciated by scholars and writers today. The people had an impressive social order and were well organised. Economic conditions were also very promising. In Mohen-jo-Daro and Harappa, a number of small seals distinctive in kind and unique in quality have been found. These depict animals such as elephants and tigers as well as human beings. Farming and commerce was the business of the day. Wheat and barley were grown, as were dates, mustard, peas, sesame, and cotton. Domesticated animals like cattle, foul, camels, buffalo, dogs, and cats were also found. The people living there were highly civilised. Those of a higher social class lived in large houses, and the poorer classes lived in small huts. However, the huts were beautifully made with complete drainage systems, a common bath, and stupa.

Multiple archeological sites have been excavated in Sindh which provide evidence of cilvilizations here with rich backgrounds. Among these are Kahoo-a-jo-Daro (Mirpurkhas), Lakhian-Jo-Daro (Khairpur Mirs), Kot Digi (Khairpur Mir's), and Amri-Jo-Daro (District Dadu now Jamshoro). Besides these archaeological sites, some rulers constructed beautiful forts which were used as protection for those kings and were of aesthetic value for visitors. These include Rani Kot (District Dadu, now Jamshoro) and Kot Digi Fort (Khairpur). Other sites are Gorakh Hill, Kute gi Qabar, and Bado Jabal.

Excavations of the Mohen-jo-Daro and Harappa sites provided unquestionable evidence of agriculture, urban life, and a decently advanced civilisation.[14]

MEDIEVAL ERA

Muhammad bin Qasim invaded Sindh in the year CE 712. This area of the Indus Valley was thus introduced to Islam. Prior to this, Hinduism and Buddhism were practised in Sindh. After the Arab conquest of Sindh, Muslim rulers ruled Sindh. These included local rulers and tribes like the Samas, Soomras, Kalhoras, and Talpurs, and non-local rulers like the Arhoons, Turkhans, and Mughals. In 1843, the British took over Sindh from the Talpurs who were the local rulers at the time.

After taking over Sindh, the British made Sindh a part of the Bombay Presidency and ruled it for close to a century. Sindh was governed through a commissionerate till 1936 when it was separated as a province with the Governor as head of the province. The British carried on development such as making of railway tracks, roads, irrigation projects, navigation and the like. The next chapter discusses the colonial era in much detail.

POST-INDEPENDENCE PERIOD

In 1947, the British left India and Pakistan and a sovereign nation-state came into being. As a result of Partition, refugees—especially Urdu-speaking migrants—came from India and settled in Sindh, especially in Karachi, in very large numbers. In 1948, Karachi was separated from Sindh and was made the capital of Pakistan and a federal territory. This continued up until the late 1950s to 1960 when Ayub Khan shifted the capital to Islamabad. Sindh, along with Karachi, reappeared on the map of Pakistan in 1970.

It is pertinent to mention here that in 1955, the One Unit policy was enforced where all the four provinces of West Pakistan were amalgamated and were re-constituted as a single province, West Pakistan. Hence, Pakistan at this point in its history had two provinces: East Pakistan and West Pakistan. In 1971, there were political differences between East and West Pakistan and a military intervention in East Pakistan. This led to the country partitioning into two separate sovereign nations, wherein East Pakistan became Bangladesh. West Pakistan continued to be a new Pakistan of which Sindh is now the southern-most province.

2

Administrative and Economic History

SINDH's economic history has to be chronicled so that it may serve as a background against which to analyse the region's current economic standing. The focus of this chapter will be the period 1800–1947 because Pakistan to a great extent is still not completely detached from the vestiges of the colonial system which, having roots in the Mughal era, was later modified by the British. The evolution of Pakistan's (and hence Sindh's) present economic landscape can be traced back to the time of the British Raj (1858–1947). While many changes have taken place over the years (for example Pakistan can no longer be described as a feudal economy[1] in the true sense of the word), certain remnants of the past remain, one of the most evident manifestations being 'neo-feudalism'.

Although Sindh was not annexed by the British until 1843, it is important to understand what motivated them to intervene and eventually annex the region once deemed not worthwhile.[2] The political history of Sindh up to the start of British intervention serves as a useful backdrop.

Before the British Annexation

The earliest account of Sindh's history dates back to the Indus Valley Civilisation. However, the earliest available recorded history of Sindh begins from the Arab conquest of CE 711.[3] Although history predating the Arab conquest exists, a coherent chronology can only be traced after this event.

The Gazetteer prepared by Sorley divides the history of Sindh in the following order:[4]

1. The period of Arab rule.
2. The middle ages from Mahmud of Ghazni till the establishment of the Mughal Empire over Sindh.
3. The Mughal period.
4. The Kalhora period.
5. The Talpur period.
6. The British period.
7. The post-British period from the partition of India till the present day.

The Arab conquest in Sindh was led by Muhammad bin Qasim—the Umayyad general. The Arab hold of the region gradually passed onto the indigenous Sindhi empires of Sumra (r. CE 1032–1351) and Samma (r. CE 1351–1521), which were later replaced by the Central Asian tribes of Arghuns and Turkhans.[5]

Sindh enjoyed a somewhat semi-autonomous status, until Akbar's forces defeated the last Turkhan, Mirza Jani Beg, the ruler of Thatta. After that, Sindh became a part of the 'Subha of Multan' of the Mughal Empire[6] and was divided into the Upper and Lower region under the 'sarkars' of Bakhar and Thatta respectively.[7] In fact, the *Gazetteer* describes Thatta as '… by far the wealthiest town in Sind in those [Mughal] days and the country round it was the centre of a thriving agriculture.'[8] The city had 5,000 looms and 400 colleges and, apart from other areas in the subcontinent, was engaged in trade with Persia, Afghanistan, Iraq, Central Asia, and Europe.[9]

The locals of Sindh once again assumed ascendancy when the Kalhora clan, a Sindhi dynasty, steadily spread its influence by amassing political power. In 1701, the Mughals loosened their political grip on Sindh by extending governorship to the Kalhoras. In the next three decades, the Kalhoras became the de facto sovereigns of the region.[10] Throughout the rest of the century, the power of the Kalhora dynasty weakened as they had to accept suzerainty first at the hands of the Persians in 1739 and then the Afghans in 1747, and they had to pay 'tributes' to these powers.[11]

The clash between the Kalhoras and the Balochi tribe of the Talpurs in the latter half of the 1770s saw the Talpurs gain control of the reins of Sindh, followed by their recognition from the Afghan king in 1783.[12] The Talpur system of government was a 'confederacy of chiefs' which divided Sindh into different spheres of influence, with Mir Fateh Ali, along with his three brothers (together called the Char Yars) controlling Hyderabad and Mir Sohrab, and Tharo Khan controlling Khairpur and Mirpur.[13] The Talpurs eventually suffered a severe blow at the hands of the British in 1843.

The British Arrival in Sindh

The first time the British showed an interest in Sindh was during the Mughal rule in the seventeenth century. Thatta was an important commercial town and the port of Lahribandar served as the main port through which the exports were sent to the Persian Gulf in the west and to Gujarat and Goa in the east.[14]

At the time, the Portuguese held considerable power in the region's naval trade since they had been the first to arrive there,[15] thereby controlling Sindhi exports. These exports included 'cotton taffetas of yarn and silk, ornamental desks, writing cases, indigo, and saltpetre.'[16] The British were interested in gaining power over Sindh but were stalled by the fear of Portuguese retaliation, given that the latter had 'threatened to destroy the port of Lahribandar if the English were allowed to come to Sind'.[17]

The British enjoyed backing from the Mughal Emperor Jahangir and even bought some local samples of Sindhi produce;[18] this did not amount to much in the presence of the Portuguese. Eventually, the Portuguese signed a treaty with the British in 1635 and in the same year, the first English factory was founded at Thatta.

According to Sorley, the British set up a factory in Sindh for the following reasons:[19]

1.   To keep the supply of cotton cloths for the London markets;
2.   to obtain indigo;
3.   and to carry trade to the Persian Gulf and the western coasts of India.

The exports of the East India Company (EIC) comprised of cotton goods, indigo, saltpetre, fish, and leather and leather goods.[20] Table 2.1 shows the regions which supplied the exports for the British.[21]

Table 2.1: Exports from Various Regions of Sindh

Exports	Regions
Cotton goods	Bhakkar, Rohri, Darbelo, Gambat, Kandiaro, Sehwan, Sann, Dadu, Nasarpur, and Thatta
Indigo	Sehwan, Bubak, and Sann
Saltpetre	Nasarpur and Thatta

Source: Mubarak Ali, *The English Factory in Sindh*, Lahore, Fiction House, 2005.

According to Ali, 'the arrival of the English promoted trade, commerce, and the manufacturing industry of Sind' as the local Sindhi traders, by way of sending their merchandise through English ships, could now participate in international trade without any fear of attack from other European powers.[22]

Nevertheless, the feudal structure of Sindhi society did not help improve the economic conditions of the region. There was no structural change in the economy and hence the opportunity to permeate the European markets was lost.[23] In addition to this, any economic gains that the local craftsmen may have enjoyed due to increased economic activity with the arrival of the British were reversed due to heavy local taxes.[24]

The taxes also became a hurdle for the British who then had to flex their bureaucratic muscles to bypass taxes by obtaining 'royal farmans'.[25] Moreover, the succession dispute in anticipation of the end of Aurangzeb's reign gave rise to chaos in Sindh.[26] Taken together, these unfavourable conditions made the continued operation of business difficult for the British, resulting in the eventual closure of the factory in 1662, after 27 years of operation.

More than a century would pass before the British would turn their attention to Sindh once again. This happened during the time of the Kalhoras in 1758, when Ghulam Shah Kalhora invited them to establish a second factory. The factory, however, was shut down in 1775 owing to 'internal unrest and the decline of textile manufactures formerly characterised as "the flower of the whole parcel and preferred before all others in their making".'[27]

While the British designs in Sindh had an obvious commercial angle, this was to be no longer the case. In the nineteenth century, the nature of the relations between the British and Amirs changed course due to exogenous factors. These included the advances of external powers (the French, Persians, Afghans) and the internal powers (Ranjit Singh and the Marathas) that threatened to disturb the status quo for both the British and the Amirs. The dynamics that played out throughout the first half of the nineteenth century till the annexation of Sindh was not much different from the cold war that played out between the US and the Soviet Union in the latter half of the twentieth century. The external powers had deep suspicion and misgivings about each other while at the same time trying to win over the local Amirs into their sphere of influence.

The threat from Napoleon Bonaparte's army's advance in Asia in 1799, possibly with help from Zaman Shah, so alarmed the British that the Governor of Bombay, Jonathan Duncan, was instructed by the Governor-General, the Marquis of Wellesley, to send an emissary to Mir Fateh Ali Khan to resume friendly ties with the Talpurs and to allow establishing a factory.[28] Subsequently Nathan Crowe, a British representative, was sent on a 'mission' to Sindh.

Huttenback writes that the Governor-General informed Duncan that 'the factory was to be established, "not so much with a view to commercial as to political advantages".'[29] However, the opposition of the other Char Yars among the Talpur dynasty and a threat of annexation from Zaman Shah did not allow the establishment of the factory.

In the face of the renewed Frano-Russian threat in 1807, Hankey-Smith was sent to Sindh and a treaty was signed which called for a native representative of the British to be stationed in Sindh. The influence of the British was further extended through another treaty in 1820 that called for the exclusion of other Europeans as well as Americans from Sindh.[30]

The treaty, concluded in 1832, was the first fissure in the authority of the Amirs as it opened the Indus to trade for the British. The power of the Amirs further eroded when the events in Afghanistan in 1838 required British troops to pass through the Indus—a provision not allowed for in the previous treaty and hence a violation. Resistance at first by the Amirs resulted in the loss of Karachi to the British in 1839. Later, the hostility from their Baloch armies in 1843 served as the final blow to the Amirs with the fall of Hyderabad. Sindh by now had been annexed by the British and General Sir Charles Napier assumed control of the region as its first governor. (General Sir Charles James Napier was the Commander-in-Chief of the British Army in India who led the conquest of Sindh. Upon his successful campaign, Napier became the first Governor of Sindh from 1843–47 and added the region to the Bombay Presidency.)

The British who ruled India and Sindh for a century introduced a modern, elaborate administrative system, run by a few hundred officers of British origin, assisted by the hundreds of thousands of Indian officials and clerks. They invested in physical infrastructure such as railways, roads, and highways, connecting the region from Calcutta in the east all the way to Peshawar in the north-west. They established civil and criminal courts for dispensing justice, resolving disputes, and enforcing contracts. Their efforts in Sindh towards land holdings, revenue administration, the irrigation system, agriculture, communication, and trade are analysed in the sections below; suffice to say that the civil services, court system, and other institutional structures introduced by the British have withstood the test of time. However, the requirements of an independent sovereign country differ greatly from those of the colonial master. The lack of adjustment to new realties and new demands have created some distortions and left some unpleasant legacies. The strong culture of patronages, where the British officers acted as patriarchs and their native subjects petitioned them for relief and redressal, has still survived seventy years after the British quit the subcontinent. The elitist mindset of those 'rulers' created strong fissures in the society. While an objective assessment of the British rule over the Indian subcontinent would reveal some positive gains, there are some equally pernicious influences that they left behind.

Demographics

According to the *Gazetteer* (1876), the record of population statistics for the period preceding the British annexation does not exist. What little—and possibly questionable—information the British gathered was a result of their missions in Sindh. Dr James Burnes deemed the population of Sindh to be 'not more than 1 million'.[31] In contrast, Thornton considered Burnes conclusion to be an overestimate, given the vast desert region and unsatisfactory farming practices.

The first census by the British appears to have been conducted in 1856 and the statistics mentioned therein and in the subsequent census are as follows:

Table 2.2: Population Statistics for Sindh (excluding the Khairpur region) (1856–72)

Year	Population	Annual Percentage Change (%)
1856	1,772,367	-
1859	1,795,594	1.31
1872	2,203,177	22.7

Source: A. W. Hughes, *Gazetteer of the Province of Sind*, London, George Bell and Sons, 1876.

Table 2.3: Composition of Population in 1856

Religious Group	Population	Percentage of Population (%)
Muslims	1,355,891	76.5
Hindus	363,295	20.5
Other	53,181	3.0
Total	1,772,367	100.0

Source: A. W. Hughes, *Gazetteer of the Province of Sind*, London, George Bell and Sons, 1876.

Table 2.2 shows that from 1856 to 1859, the annual percentage change in the population was 1.31 per cent. This is considered to be an overestimate given the famine in the Thar and Parkar district.[32] This rate of change increased to an annual percentage change of 22.7 between the 13 years from 1859 to 1872. Table 2.3 shows that Muslims formed 76.5 per cent of the population in Sindh in 1856, followed by the Hindus who made up one-fifth of the total. The rest, three per cent, belonged to other religions.

The *Gazetteer* (1876) gives a figure of 130,350 for the population of Khairpur state for the year 1872, thereby giving an aggregate figure for the whole Sindh region as 2,333,527.[33]

Table 2.4 presents the population figures for the main cities of Sindh for 1872.

Table 2.4: Population of Major Cities in 1872

City	Population
Shikarpur	38,170
Hyderabad	35,272
Karachi	56,753
Khairpur	-
Thatta	7,951
Mirpurkhas	1,280
Hala	4,096
Larkana	-

Source: A. W. Hughes, *Gazetteer of the Province of Sind*, London, George Bell and Sons, 1876.

Karachi, Hyderabad, and Shikarpur were the main centres of the Talpur confederacy. Of these, Shikarpur wielded the most importance by virtue of its wealthy and well-connected Hindu bankers.[34] Nevertheless, this source of the region's prosperity was inherently precarious, for:

Shikarpur, no doubt, attained its high rank under the Durani monarchy of Afghanistan, and much of the prosperity of its bankers was due to the vicious operation of that institution, and to the errors of the Durani character. Many enriched themselves by loans to the ministers of state, generally careless finances, and by acting as treasurers to nobles, who deposited with them the spoils of their provinces and governments, and who, subsequently, died without revealing the secret to their heirs.[35]

Not surprisingly, the economic edifice of Shikarpur, so dependent on the Durani monarchy, suffered following the collapse of the Afghan empire. The subsequent rise of Punjab as a commercial hub further diminished the region's significance as the budding cities of Multan and Amritsar attracted the migration of the Shikarpur bankers.[36] Thatta's importance diminished as it experienced famine.

Table 2.5: Population of Sindh including Khairpur (in million) (1901–51)

Year	Population including Khairpur	Khairpur
1901	2.73	1.51
1911	3.21	1.70
1921	3.51	1.93
1931	3.27	2.27
1941	4.41	3.06
1951	6.05	3.19

Source: H.T. Sorley, *The Gazetteer of West Pakistan the Former Province of Sind Including Khairpur State*, Lahore, Gazetteer Cell, Board of Revenue, 1968.

Table 2.5 gives the decennial percentage change in population from 1901 to 1951. The data is disaggregated for Sindh and Khairpur. In 1901, the population of Sindh was approximately 2.73 million which increased to 4.41 million by 1941 and 6.05 million by 1951.[37] The table shows a near-consistent increase in the population growth rate from 1901–21, except for the period 1921–31. This negative growth rate, which appears to be in stark contrast to the rest of the table, reflects the influenza epidemic of 1918–19 which resulted in mass fatality.[38] The Gazetteer attributes the increase in the rate in 1931–41 to the increased migration into Sindh following the construction of Lloyd (Sukkur) Barrage. The persistent increase of 34.9 per cent and 37.2 per cent for the next two decades respectively is credited to the irrigation works that were undertaken.

With regard to the gender distribution of the population, the Gazetteer gives a consistent average male-to-female ratio as 55:45 throughout the 1901–51 period. No clear reason for this discrepancy has been mentioned, although it is surmised that this may be due to higher male births—a phenomenon reflected in the then birth registration figures but which cannot be taken at face value due to underreported female births.[39]

Table 2.6: Age and Gender Composition of the Population of Sindh (%) (1901–51)

Age Groups		Gender	Census Years					
1901–41	1951		1901	1911	1921	1931	1941	1951
0–10	0–9	Male	28.8	27.6	27.0	27.0	32.7	27.0
		Female	31.0	30.1	29.9	30.0	35.4	30.8
10–40	10–39	Male	51.6	52.8	54.4	55.6	51.2	50.7
		Female	48.4	50.3	50.3	53.5	49.4	49.5
40–60	40–59	Male	15.5	15.6	15.4	14.4	13.6	16.3
		Female	15.7	15.0	14.9	13.2	12.3	14.2
61 and over	60 and over	Male	4.2	4.0	4.3	3.1	2.5	5.9
		Female	4.9	4.6	4.8	3.3	2.9	5.6

Source: H. T. Sorley, *The Gazetteer of West Pakistan the Former Province of Sind Including Khairpur State*, Lahore, Gazetteer Cell, Board of Revenue, 1968, p. 224.

Table 2.6 shows a 70:30 ratio of the working age to the dependents' population. According to the *Gazetteer* (1968), the figures for the year 1941 were based on a two per cent population sample which is why the figures seem to be a few percentage points off-trend as compared to the corresponding figures of previous decades.

Table 2.7: Population of Karachi (1881–1951)

Census Year	Total	Population	
		Absolute Increase	Percentage Change (%)
1881	68,332	-	-
1891	98,195	29,863	43.7
1901	108,644	10,449	10.6
1911	140,511	31,867	29.3
1921	201,691	61,180	43.5
1931	247,791	46,100	22.9
1941	359,492	111,701	45.1
1951	905,781	546,289	152.0

Source: H.T. Sorley, *The Gazetteer of West Pakistan the Former Province of Sind Including Khairpur State*, Lahore, Gazetteer Cell, Board of Revenue, 1968, p. 225.

Table 2.7 shows a tremendous thirteen-times increase in the population of Karachi between 1881 and 1951. While the figures for 1951 can be attributed to the Partition-related migration (from 1947) and hence are not surprising, the figures for preceding decade show the gradual economic importance of Karachi during the time of the British Raj, not least owing to its function as the port of Sindh.

Agriculture and Land

LANDHOLDING SYSTEM IN SINDH

Sindh, at least till the time of Partition, can be described largely as an agriculture-based economy. However, this dependence on agriculture was not without tribulations. Far from being rain-fed, agriculture in Sindh was dependent on 'the vagaries of the River Indus'.[40] This distinct feature, peculiar to Sindh in the entire Indian subcontinent, gave way to an agricultural system which necessitated an important role for the government.[41]

During the time of the Kalhoras and the Talpurs, the administrative structure in Sindh established by the Mughals remained intact, albeit with great modifications.[42]

The mansabdari system was a pre-Mughal invention but was further solidified by the Mughal Emperor Akbar. As the emperor was the sole owner of all the land, it was by way of the mansabdari system that land was granted to an officer as a reward for military services. At the time of the British annexation, the administrative and revenue units in place in Sindh were of the Mughal era.[43] These units were called parganas which were further divided into *tapas*. The head serving as the chief revenue officer and chief law enforcer of a pargana was called *sazawalkar/mukhtiarkar* and the revenue officers for *tapas* were called *kardars*. The agricultural system followed was *batai* (sharecropping) whereas the landholding system was that of jagirdari—assignment of tracts of land as a reward for services rendered to the state.

This jagirdari system as is understood today evolved during the reign of Amirs. Previously, the Talpur chiefs enjoyed a certain share in the agricultural produce (called *seri*) in the regions of which they were made in-charge in return for various services rendered.[44] These *seri* grants were then transformed into jagir lands after the death of Mir Fateh Ali Khan in 1802, a process during which extra tracts of lands were added liberally. This payment in kind further evolved into cash payments via the exchange rate of one *kora* per *biga* of land.

The holders of these jagirs, the jagirdars, were de facto rulers of their regions besides being responsible for the collection of revenue. This jagirdari system hence enmeshed Sindh in a feudalistic structure. The jagirs, however, were not assigned on a permanent basis and were repossessed by the government upon the death of the jagirdar. The terms jagirdar and zamindar are often used interchangeably in our daily language, although they bear an important difference; while the jagirdars were government officials, the zamindars held sway in their respective regions and '… had the characteristics of a feudal lord … [he was] "the linchpin of the system".'[45] The zamindars were basically the class of men who had either brought land under cultivation themselves or were the descendants of those who had. As such, they also charged fees called *malikano* or *lapo* from the peasants working for them.

Napier came to Sindh with an outlook that focused on the law and order situation of the region. On assuming control, Napier restructured the provincial division and introduced three revenue units, called collectorates—one each at Karachi, Hyderabad, and Shikarpur; under each collector were deputy collectors. While the office of *kardar* was retained, the office of *sazawalkar* was removed, and the former made responsible to collect all the information that may be required by the new, alien government, apart from collecting revenue.

Khuhro notes that the jagirdars did not enjoy any 'special judicial or civil rights in their jagirs' which too were subject to the Amir's authority.[46] Nevertheless, during the British period, Napier was clear in his agenda to prop up the jagirdars as the 'true aristocracy' at the cost of the zamindars, whom he considered the 'middlemen'.[47] In fact, one of the first things that Napier did upon assuming control was to confirm jagirs of the Baloch overlords through issuing *sanads* to clinch the political support of the latter.[48] His policy can be discerned through his words '… It may be said that I thus in reality, make zamindars of jagirdars … If we put them [the jagirdars] down, we shall put ourselves down, in times to come, for injustice will have a reaction sooner or later.'[49] At the same time, Napier wanted to promote the ryotwari system—a system of direct collection of revenue from small landholders, called ryots. This, he believed, would enlarge the revenue base for the government. Khuhro claims that 'the fact that Sind remained so quiet during the "Mutiny" could be considered a tribute to this policy of political reconciliation',[50] a policy she states was applauded by Frere[51] who credited it to Napier.

Nevertheless, Napier's policies with regard to landholding can only be described as incongruous at best. The injudicious policy of confirming jagirs alienated much of the state land, depriving the government of the potential revenue. More than 19 lac *bigas* of land was conferred as jagirs by Napier, which amounts to nearly 7 per cent of the cultivable land.[52] This too is a very conservative estimate given the topographical issues of water logging and salinity and given the termination of the servicemen role of the jagirdars.

The second part of Napier's term then, unsurprisingly, focused on resuming what had been imprudently given away. Sir George Clerk (Governor of Bombay) commenting on this rightly stated, 'There are grounds for believing that in the first, claims were recognised with to great profusion but subsequently the conditions of tenure have been made too stringent … it is plain that the hopes raised by the first measures must have subsequently merged in the feelings of disappointment [for the jagirdars]'.[53]

Lost revenues were redeemed by repossessing wastelands through grants and putting them on rent. The issue of grants raised questions on whether or not to maintain them on a hereditary basis and also required a decision regarding methods of taxation (i.e., taxing on a fixed rate or proportional rate). Eventually, in 1847, a tax of two *annas* per *biga* was imposed following the death of a jagirdar, whereas the wasteland was to be recouped.[54] Another method adopted was to fix a ceiling on the future land grants at 5,000 *bigas* and the transfer of jagirs could take place only via direct male heritage. Napier also advised the consolidation of the otherwise dispersed jagirs into one tract (*yaktarfi*)—an item introduced after the jagir settlement of 1861–62.[55]

After Napier's resignation in 1847, the land settlement process was streamlined by subsequent commissioners, Pringle and Frere.[56] Table 2.8 shows the jagirs classified before Frere's term along with their respective policies. It was eventually decided to regrant all the land under cultivation, subject to conditions mentioned in the table. The jagirdars were also made responsible for payments of the the water rate, *hakabo*, and for the water drawn from the government canals. A 5 per cent liability rate was also placed for roads and education (unless otherwise stated in the table).[57]

Table 2.8: Types of Jagirs and their Policy Treatment

Class	Description	Policy
I	All Jagirs preceding Talpur dynasty (1783).	These were the permanent jagirs, without subject to assessment and reduction, re-granted through direct male heritage.
II	Jagirs given by the Talpurs from coming to power till the death of Mir Ghulam Ali in 1810.	These were of two types: The first of these were given to the Talpur families of Shahdadani, Shahwani, Khanani, and Manikani to whom Napier had promised jagirs. These grants were conditioned on one-third resumption of wasteland upon regrants. They were also liable to pay taxes related to education and roads but were exempt from other dues.* These included jagirs granted to the 'Sardars of Sind'—powerful chiefs carefully selected who were dealt with on an individual basis.
III	Jagirs given during the period 1810–33.	These were granted for one generation, subject to one-fourth government share and resumption of wasteland upon regrant.
IV	Jagirs given between 1833–43.	These were granted for life but to be forfeited upon death.

Source: H. T. Sorley, *The Gazetteer of West Pakistan the Former Province of Sind Including Khairpur State*, Lahore, Gazetteer Cell, Board of Revenue, 1968, p. 380; Hamida Khuhro, *The Making of Modern Sindh: British Policy and Social Change in the Nineteenth Century*, Oxford, Oxford University Press, 1999, pp. 84–5.

* Khuhro, *The Making of Modern Sindh*, p. 94.

There were other types of grants which were dealt with separately. These were the *pattadari* grants, *khairat* grants and garden grants. The first of these, the *pattadari*s, were grants in possession of Pathans since the time of Afghan rule in the region. These were peculiar to the 'Moguly' district of Sindh, straddling the areas of Sukkur, Bukkur, Shikarpur and its adjunct regions.[58] These were the tracts of land, called *patta*s, purchased either from the locals of Sindh or brought to cultivation by the Pathans on which they enjoyed reduced assessment from the then Afghan government.[59] These, and some of the *khairat* grants were a minor part of the first-class jagirs.

The khairat grants were the 'charitable' grants, extended to esteemed religious personalities and men of scholarship, usually the Sayads within Muslims, but also incorporated Hindus. While the Sayads of Rohri and Sukkur occupied land grants, the Sayads of Thatta had cash grants—some of which had their origins in excess of 300 years.[60] These were treated as differently classed jagirs conditioned on their ancientness.[61]

The garden grants were for the lands cultivated as gardens; these were either subject to quarterly assessment or were assessment-free. Other grants included tree grants, called *huri*, to encourage the growth of trees, as well as some *seri* grants.[62]

Table 2.9 shows the acres of land alienated as a result of jagir settlements.

Table 2.9: Land Granted to Jagirs Before and After Britsh Annexation

Class	No. of Grants	Granted Acreage
Pre-British Period		
a) First Class Jagirdars	11	293,000
b) Four Great Talpur Families	17	479,000
c) Sardar Grants	55	56,000
d) Muafi Nashistgah	15	26,000
e) Khairat Grants	8	220,000
f) Garden Grants	266	2,500
Total	372	1,076,500
British Period		
a) Hindu Grants	1	5,800
b) Sodha Rajput Grants	11	17,200
c) Baloch Tribal Grants	23	31,500
Total	35	54,500
Grand Total	407	1,131,000

Source: H.T. Sorley, *The Gazetteer of West Pakistan the Former Province of Sind Including Khairpur State*, Lahore, Gazetteer Cell, Board of Revenue, 1968, p. 383.

Table 2.9 shows that the majority of jagirs were granted in the pre-British period and the contribution of the British government was limited to only 35 grants, covering an area of 55,000 acres.

Land Revenue in Sindh

According to the 1876 *Gazetteer* The system of land tenure was neatly divided into two distinct categories:[63]

(a) Land under State assessment or Alienated included:
1. 'Large proprietors, a comparatively small but important class.
2. Holders of estates of a few hundred acres, the middle class gentry.
3. A large body of peasant proprietors, all paying revenue direct to the Government, or to the Alienee to whom the Government rights in the land have been transferred.'

(b) The other category included:
1. 'Tenants possessing a right of occupancy.
2. Tenants-at-will.'

The first group has already been covered in the previous section. This section will shed light on the second category, the relationship between the two categories, and the various revenue systems which were implemented. The tenants who enjoyed a right of occupancy were called the *marusi haris*—translated as 'hereditary cultivator'.[64] This arrangement, which was common in and peculiar to Upper Sindh, allowed not only for a hereditary but a transferable right to these *haris*.

The concept of zamindari, however, was an elusive one for the British as no clear-cut definition or the role of zamindars existed. As stated before, these were the landholders who enjoyed certain rights on land, often hereditary, by virtue of reclaiming wastelands. But the Amirs of Sindh conferred no exclusive rights to these zamindars and the Amirs were quite free to transfer the land rights of zamindars if they were found to be transgressing their duties.[65] Citing Lieutenant Colonel Dr Haig, the *Gazetteer* of 1968 defines zamindars as:

> On the accession of British rule, it was found that at all events as a fiscal arrangement village communities were commonly divided into principal zamindar, minor zamindars, petty occupants (also calling themselves zamindars), and the *haris* or cultivators of the larger holdings.
>
> Where this organisation prevailed, the principal zamindar transacted all business with Government on behalf of the community and from him or under his supervision, the Government share of the produce of the village lands was collected.[66]

Hence, a zamindar's responsibility consisted of charging a fee called *malikano*—collected from his own tenants—and as zamindari, which he collected from the rest of the occupiers of the village for which he was responsible. *Lapo* was another due charged on the produce of the tenants which a zamindar held claim to. Zamindars' right to collect these dues was recognised by the British insofar that they enjoyed judicial support to extract *lapo* from the tenants in the event that the latter declined to pay.[67]

An important feature that underpinned the relationship between cultivators and the landlords was the *batai* system. According to this practice, the produce which was cultivated by the *haris* was to be divided equally between them and their masters. The *haris* however bore a disproportionate burden of this unfair bargain as they had to supply their labour, plough bullocks, and seeds. Landholders would in fact only contribute towards half of the expenditure of harvesting, threshing, and winnowing.[68] As a result, *haris* would be forced to borrow money and in some cases their masters would rob them of their fair *batai* share, ensnaring them in a debt cycle.

It is perhaps owing to these powers vested in the zamindars that Napier wanted to eliminate or at least limit these powers and wished to supplant this class with the entrepreneurial class of ryots. To this end, he also offered small *takavi* loans to the ryots to free them from their dependence on zamindar masters to some extent.

Nevertheless, the policy of bolstering the ryotwari system was far from being a success. Firstly, the *takavi* loans in themselves were not sufficient and requests for remissions by ryots during bad seasons were perceived as indolence by Napier who believed that no help beyond the loans should be offered. But he did not appreciate the fact that a peasant was highly vulnerable to the vagaries of the weather that determined the amount of produce.

Secondly, although Napier did try to clip the zamindars' wings, he essentially wanted to replace this class with a new class of jagirs whom he considered the 'real aristocracy' in order to extract loyalty from them. In this scheme of things, the position of a ryot hardly underwent any improvement. Thirdly, there was no policy to outlaw the zamindari and jagirdari system altogether as the abolition of the former may not have suited their political interests. The relationship between the zamindar/jagirdar and the ryot was skewed in favour of the former.

Nonetheless, there existed another class of men—banias (money lenders)—who created trouble not just for the cultivators but for the landlords as well. These banias were mostly Hindu and as such were traditionally not entitled to land ownership.[69] The advent of the British Civil Courts (1866) not only declared land to be treated as private property, allowing banias to hold lands, but also for land to be used as a collateral.[70] Consequently, the hitherto landless banias became 'land grabbers', with both the zamindars and them vying for the best quality land.[71] The process continued unbridled till the time of Partition. Quoting A. R. Arain, the *Gazetteer* reports that in 1936, scarcely 13 per cent families in Sindh were unbounded by debt.[72]

REVENUE SETTLEMENTS

The land revenue system in Sindh evolved through experimentation. The first series of these regulations was introduced during Napier's time. Remissions were replaced by the *takavi* loans, and cash assessment was introduced in the form of 7–14–21 year leases of land.[73] These cash rents were fixed separately for Upper and Lower Sindh, irrespective of soil quality and other features.[74] All the existing dues, *abwabs*, were done away with and replaced by a standard tax of four *kassa* on a *kharar*—which were equivalent to one-fifteenth of the produce if rent was taken in kind and 6 per cent of the revenue if rent was taken in cash.[75] To compensate for the loss of remissions to cultivators, the cash assessments introduced were light and certainly 'not more than half and in many cases less than a fourth of the cash rents under Amirs'[76] and one-third of the annual produce was set as the upper limit of the rent to be taken.[77] An extra rate of one-twentieth of the produce was charged for the use of water through government canals.[78]

Although the above regulations appeared quite well-thought out at first glance, its implementation phase proved otherwise. The substitution of remissions by loans proved more taxing for the cultivators. The cultivators were willing to part with a large proportion in *batai* to the government in return for the reassurance of help in times of misfortune owing to the erratic nature of production in Sindh.[79] To Napier, these remissions were no more than a means of making cultivators lethargic and dependent on government support. Moreover, the cash rents deemed fair in times of high grain prices turned out to be an unbearable burden once the prices plummeted due to the opening up of Punjab trade (following its annexation), removal of import duties, and subsiding of demand-side pressures.[80] Not surprisingly, there were demands to restore the *batai* and the system Napier introduced came to a halt in 1853–54.[81]

Sir George Clerk, who took over as the new Governor of Bombay, was of the view that government had involved itself too much in the minute affairs of the province which could be easily dispensed by zamindars and jagirdars, freeing the government functionaries to pay due attention to the important matters of the state.[82] It was decided that information on population distribution, land tenure, and revenue collection should be collected to restructure the existing system.

Consequently, a full-scale topographical survey called *Rough Survey and Settlement* was initiated and completed by the early 1860s.[83] In 1862, a plan to classify land in four categories according to soil characteristics was introduced. Additionally, the type of water available for irrigation was also classified as a) flow (*mok*), b) lift (*charkhi*), and c) flood (*sailabi*) and was used along with other characteristics to determine the water-rate.[84]

The First Settlement (1865) came to be known as the 'diffused-rate' system—so called as it extended the rent applied to cultivated area as well as fallow land. According to Cheesman (1997), landholders found ownership of large landholdings a matter of pride, even if that involved holding parcels that remained uncultivated. As such, the government introduced a policy regarding fallow land; for retaining such lands, landlords were required to either pay rent or forfeit the property. This complicated model is explained by Cheesman in the following words:

> This model … required land to be divided into large Survey Numbers of twenty to thirty acres each. It was assumed that the zamindar cultivated only one-third every year, leaving the rest fallow. If one imagines a thirty-acre field assessed at three rupees per acre then, with ten acres cultivated every year, its annual assessment could be fixed at thirty rupees, giving it a 'diffused rate' of one rupee per acre per year. After three years, each acre could have paid the 'full rate' of three rupees[.][85]

Nevertheless, some cultivators took advantage of the loophole—they would cultivate an entire tract, 'paying only a third of the revenue' and forfeit the entire tract later as a waste. The loss in average revenue during this period as compared to the period before was estimated to be 16 per cent.[86] The First Settlement also gave rise to an increase in the small holdings; there was a 40 per cent increase in holdings of maximum five acres—which saw small landholders in the clutches of debt.[87] In regard to the wasteland policy and its effect, the Governor of Bombay remarked, 'The zamindars naturally clung to their land, though they could not cultivate it. They had to borrow money to pay the assessment and were destroyed.'[88]

Needless to say, a Revised Settlement (1875) had to be introduced to rectify the flaws of the previous system. According to this system only the cultivated land was to be assessed, which was divided into smaller survey numbers, and it allowed for land to lie fallow subject to a certain scale, retaining the cultivators' lien on it.[89] This system, however, took time to be implemented across Sindh as the survey was still underway and hence a transitory system, called the Irrigation Settlement, was introduced in 1881.[90] The system turned out to be so efficient, at least relative to previous attempts, that it was taken up permanently in 1887 throughout Sindh, except for water-scarce areas such as Tharparkar and Kohistan.

Under the new system, the villages in the talukas were categorised according to their access to water as well as the resources available to distribute the crop in the market.[91] The assessment rates then depended on the worth of land, the movement of prices, the condition of the canals and the financial profile of the cultivators. The main characteristics of the 1887 settlement that rectified the flaws of the previous regulations were:[92]

1. Only cultivated land was to be assessed.
2. Assessments would depend on the type of irrigation used.
3. Allowance for remissions in the event of destruction of crops.
4. Allowance for land to lie fallow for four years.

The assessment included both the water rate as well as the land revenue, with a breakup of 90 per cent and 10 per cent respectively.[93] An additional tax of six paisas was charged as the government collection fee.[94] To account for the price oscillation in the agricultural market, a sliding scale assessment was proposed in 1943–44 for cotton, rice, and wheat crops, which fixed assessment according to the value of the crop in a particular season.[95]

Irrigation System

The entire history of irrigation in Sindh during various periods of rule, such as the Mohen-jo-Daro period, Arab Period, Mughal Period, Soomra and Samma period, Kalhora period, Talpur period, and British period has been attempted. The data for periods other than the British period is scanty.

It is said about the River Indus that 'for some it was [a] goddess to be worship[p]ed, for some it was an awe to be seen and a grandeur to be watched. It is [a] lifeline for Sindh.'[96]

Historically, most of the irrigation has been through *moki, chahi, charkhi, moki-madad-charkhi* and *barani*.[97] *Moki* involves withdrawal of water from the river through perennial and inundation canals.

Chahi and *charkhi* refer to two systems of well irrigation. *Chahi* is *boka*-well irrigation and *charkhi* is a *nar*-well irrigation. In *chahi*, irrigation water is lifted using leather bags pulled by ropes with the help of bullocks. The early history of this type of irrigation is not known but it is speculated that it was perhaps available during the time of Mohen-jo-Daro. *Charkhi* irrigation is carried through the *nar*-wells. The word 'nar' is derived from the Arabic word 'noria', a device for raising water from a stream or river, consisting of a chain of pots or buckets revolving round a wheel driven by the water current. The *nar*s were possibly invented by the Arabs and brought by them to Sindh around CE 712. The bullock or camel, blind-folded, operates the nar which is composed of a small cogged horizontal wheel inter-locked with a 'vertical wheel, water is lifted by buckets …while a man or a boy stands by to keep it moving.'[98]

Both these practices of well irrigation cultivate from 2 to 6 acres of land. The practice of well irrigation has now declined because of better irrigation facilities and the assured supply of perennial waters.

Barani irrigation refers to the lands irrigated by the waters of the rains. While this is an old practice in Sindh and acres of land were irrigated using this method, it is still used in most parts of Tharparkar and mountainous areas are cultivated when it rains. It appears that Sindh was a fertile and prosperous country on the eve of the Arab conquest. The lands of Sindh were watered by the great river Sindhu and Hakro. Hakro irrigated the eastern part of the country.[99]

Land tax in the earlier period was derived on the basis of the source of irrigation. The kharaj or the tributum soli was the land tax collected from the non-Muslims at the rate of two-fifths of the produce if the land was watered by the public canals. In case of lifts or other artificial means, three-fifths was recovered and if unirrigated, one-fourth of the probable produce was collected. If any arable land was left fallow, a fine equivalent to one-fourth of the probable produce was imposed to discouraging them from sitting idle. Garden produce and the fruits were charged at one-third and the same was the rate for wines, fish, and pearls etc.[100]

The Arab land holders had to pay the land tax at the concessionary rate of one-tenth of the produce and it was known as 'ushr'. It was levied on all those lands which had irrigation facilities but in case of land watered by lift, a nominal tax at the rate of one-twentieth was recovered.

Foreign invaders would attack Sindh because it was very rich. The Moghuls who were the rulers of India were satisfied with the tributes paid to them through their nominated agents, turkhans and the arghuns. They were never interested in the development of Sindh. On the contrary, they robbed and looted the local people openly. The irrigation system which existed during the Samma period was taken over by the Arghuns and Turkhans. The produce of the local cultivators was taken away by the ruling chiefs of Sindh and poor people remained in perpetual debt; even their crops were burnt and destroyed many times for the same reason.

Yusif Merrak, the author of *Tarikh-i Mazhar-i Shahjahani*, writes in his book that during the Samma rule, Sehwan was highly developed in agriculture and was very prosperous.

> Makhdoom Jafar Bubakai told Mirza Essa Khan Turkhan that when first time in 1515 CE during the period of Jam Nindo, Shahbeg Arghun came to attack this province, he found one thousand camels operating 'Nars' & 'Hurlas' during the night, and all those one thousand camels were forcibly taken away by Shah Beg Arghun and his people. This figure extends only to one district Baghban, of Sehwan province.[101]

The Kalhoras succeeded the Arghuns and Turkhans and focused on the development of Sindh. They contributed significantly towards promoting irrigation in the region. Most historians agree that the Kalhora rulers put their best efforts to develop the canal system and water channels during their reign. Not only did they improve the existing natural canals but dug many new artificial ones as well. The natural branches of the Indus during the Kalhora period, according to Del Hoste, were 'Puran, Nara, Aral, Fuleli, Cuin, Piriyari, Gagro, Lakh Sitta, Baghar … there were also several important water courses and extensive marshes of the former, Nara, Dadaji, Nurwely of the latter the Marui Manchar, Mirpur and Kinjher Lakes.' The Kalhoras dug and constructed by the Kalhoras: 'Charwah' 'Nurwah' 'Shah Jikur' 'Dite ji kur' 'Nusarat Wah' and 'Sarfraz Wah'.[102]

'Mian Nur Muhammad, the grandfather of Mian Sarfraz Khan, was responsible for some of the finest canals in upper Sindh on both the banks of the river'.[103] The Kalhora rulers ought to be praised for their extensive and intensive work in establishing a well-conceived irrigation system in Sindh. They not only constructed the canals but were able to manage and operate them well. These canals were cleaned of silt annually so that the water could easily flow and lands could easily be watered. Dr Sorley is all praise for the irrigation in Sindh in general and about the Kalhoras in particular.

The Talpurs, the Baloch tribe, were the next rulers of Sindh. The evidence suggests that the Talpurs did not pay as much attention to the irrigation system of Sindh as the Kalhoras did. Disunity among and lethargy of the Talpur ruling class contributed towards their poor performance. Dr Chablani is of the opinion that the

'Talpurs did not care to pay attention to even the annual clearance of the inundation canals and the result was the low cultivation'.

Sir Charles Napier, immediately after conquering Sindh in 1843, organised a canal department under Lt Col. Walter Scott but his subordinates were not engineers and the department had to be abolished in 1849. It was not until 1855 that General Fife put forward various suggestions before the government for the improvement of the canals and submitted a report on the remodeling of the whole canal system of the province.

Fife was of the opinion that Sindh lost 'thirty-one lacs' (rupees) of land revenue annually because of the defective irrigation system and that before embarking on future development, it was essential to undertake the following tasks:

1. Clean and deepen the existing canals.
2. The canal head must coincide with permanent banks of the river.
3. The velocity of the canal flow should be such as to carry away the silt.
4. The slope of the canal must be such that not only the silt is carried away but an area for at least thirty miles is also irrigated.

The major proposals of the report were, however, not accepted by the Government of India. Several other views in addition to that of Fife were put forward regarding the prospects of perennial canals in Sindh.

By the end of the nineteenth century, there were two schools of thought grappling with the irrigation problems of Sindh. One favoured that Sindh should be regarded as inundation country and the inundation canals be improved. The other school was of the view that, perennial canals be developed so that there is a stable supply of water to an area of about two million acres. The wasteful, uncertain, and poorly distributed supply from the inundation canals could not meet the objective of increased area under irrigated cultivation. But the recommendations were neither given serious consideration nor properly examined until the late 1920, although several surveys of Sindh were undertaken between 1890 and 1900.

In 1892, the Bombay government appointed a committee which favoured improvement of inundation canals and abandoning the proposal of perennial canals because of financial and engineering considerations. The Bombay government did not agree with these proposals and strongly advocated for perennial irrigation. However, the Indian Irrigation Commission of 1901–03 contested the Bombay government's proposals and recommended a project that consists of the construction of a barrage along with construction of two canals, one on the right bank and the other on the left bank. The Commission regarded such a project feasible but pointed out certain practical difficulties which may have reduced its scope.

In 1910, Mr Summers presented the Rohri Canal project for immediate execution. The triple project recommended by the Indian Irrigation Commission in 1901 thus fell victim to Summer's advocacy of the Rohri Canal Project. But Summer was probably the first to have pointed out the effect on Sindh of the withdrawals of water in Punjab. However, this criticism came too late; by this time, numerous irrigation projects in the Punjab and the United Provinces had already been undertaken. The people of Sindh were not oblivious to the provinces deprivation and the neglect of its legitimate claims. The Bombay government was heavily criticised for having failed to protect the interests of the region. It is no wonder that the demand for the separation of Sindh from Bombay coincided with the prevalent irrigation controversy.

Sindh made little progress in its irrigation projects as compared to other areas in India. Yet it must be said that it did make a strong case for canal development. In Punjab, perennial canal irrigation was becoming the order of the day, whereas in Sindh, non-perennial irrigation from Mahi Wah, Nasrat, and partially from Jamrao canals had begun in 1899, 1902, and 1904 respectively. Even this late development added very little to the total area under irrigation. Even Bombay fared better than Sindh; in 40 years, the irrigated area in the Bombay Presidency had risen nearly six times while Sindh's had little more than doubled.

The Government of India finally came to Sindh's rescue and impressed upon the Government of Bombay that the increasing cold water withdrawals in Punjab would very likely diminish supplies entering the inundation canals in Sindh. Because of the backward nature of Sindh irrigation, the Government of India was determined to make up Sindh's leeway. The Indian government's suggestion and the people's discontent forced the Bombay government to recommend the construction of the barrage and the Rohri Canal in 1910. These had an estimated cost of Rs 215 lac and Rs. 4.38 lac respectively. Even after these recommendations, the project was not undertaken immediately.

In 1913, A. A. Musto[104] was appointed as an executive engineer on special duty under the Chief Engineer to revise the Sukkur project. Musto examined the situation and came to the conclusion that the Barrage be constructed along with seven canals on both sides of the Indus. (North Western Canal, Rice Canal, Dadu Canal, Khairpur feeder West, Rohri Canal, Khairpur feeder East and Nara Canal.) The scheme was put forward for the Secretary of State's approval. It was after eight years of Musto's recommendations that orders were finally issued for construction work to start from 1 July 1923, but even those orders were not implemented immediately; two years passed before the work actually started in July 1925. The construction work was finally completed in 1932. It took more than six decades for the original proposals of Fife and about three decades for the proposals of the Indian Irrigation Commission to be put into effect.

Briefly, the scheme comprised of the construction of the barrage across the Indus at Sukkur, and the excavation of seven main canals with their branches and distributaries, minors, and water courses. The total discharge of the canals was 46,583 cusecs in Kharif and 25,648 cusecs in Rabi and the area commanded was 6.75 million acres.

During the construction period, Sindh had to put up with the ever increasing demand of Punjab to retain more water. At the same time, when the Sukkur project was approved, Punjab wanted its own project—the Sutlej Valley Project—to be sanctioned. The Indian government finally recommended both the projects to the Secretary of State for his approval.

> Upon learning [of] the Secretary of State's sanction of the Sukkur Project in April 1923, the Government of Punjab apparently concluded that Sindh had won the first round. At any rate, it wanted to stake its claim in no uncertain manner and, therefore, entered a protest to the restriction of further withdrawals from both the Indus and the up-stream distributaries.[105]

The Government of Bombay strongly objected to this view of the Punjab government. They stressed upon the statement of Thomas Ward, the Inspector General of Irrigation, who had said that all future schemes of Punjab would have to be carefully examined in relation to possible effects on Sukkur.[106]

> From 1923 on, the Punjab government was in effect attacking Sind on three fronts, Bhakra, Thal and Trimmu, whichever seemed the most promising at the moment, while Sind was purely on the defensive with nothing further to propose until the Sukkur Scheme was completed.[107]

The Sindhi zamindars and local cultivators also hindered its progress. So far, they had enjoyed free access to water. Once the project began, they feared that their supply of water would have to be regulated and controlled. The influential zamindars looked for support and won many adherents among the members of the Bombay Legislative Council who were keen to oblige the landed aristocracy because of their electoral support. The legislators, instead of regarding the project a blessing, criticised it on the grounds that the Bombay government was not in a position to pay for such an expensive undertaking. Therefore, they concluded that Sind would be riddled with loans which it would find difficult to pay back and, consequently, the project would result in the imposition of new taxes on the public. According to the critics, the repayment of loans was to continue until 1986. Criticism for the project came on technical grounds as well. It is interesting to note that the objections raised against the project proved unfounded once the scheme came into being and the loans were paid back by the Sind government within ten years.

As mentioned before, Sindh does not enjoy much rainfall and the cultivation in the region has historically depended on the River Indus. However, the inherent vicissitudes of the Indus required a regulatory system that ensured consistent supply of water to the farmers. The *Gazetteer* of 1962 mentions the following three key features of the Indus:[108]

1. It has a regular inundation which brings with it immense quantities of silt that in the course of centuries have produced the alluvial area of the Sind Valley and are still adding to the land area at its mouth;
2. The river is gradually raising its bed level above that of the surrounding alluvial deposits; it is thus ideal for the development of irrigation …
3. It pursues a westering course and … has shown this tendency to eat into and erode the land on the right bank and leaving the land on the left bank dry, except for occasional breakthroughs.

To derive maximum benefit from the Indus, canals had to be dug and lands divided according to the type of irrigation for the purpose of assessment.[109] During the Mughal rule, the local rulers were responsible for the upkeep of canals and wells, among other facilities. Since an unabated supply of water was necessary to collect revenues at an adequate level, the system was well maintained.[110] However, during the Talpur regime, the upkeep of the canals fell prey to the Amirs' negligence about which Lt Postans in 1841 stated, 'In repeated instances, large tracts of fertile lands have become perfect wastes entirely owing to the neglected state of the canals.'[111] This is in complete contrast to the Kalhoras who have been described as the 'great canal builders'.[112] The two main canals built during their reign were Nurwah and Dite ji Kur; the latter canal was termed 'the finest artificial canal in Upper Sindh'[113] by the Deputy Collector of Chanduka, Hugh James.

At the time of the British annexation, three groups of canals were in existence.[114] The first of these were the ones with natural pathways from the Indus and included the Eastern Nara, the Western Nara, the Ghar, the Dhoro Puran, and the Naurang in Upper Sindh, and the deltaic canals in Lower Sindh. The second of these were the natural and man-made canals and included the Sindwah, the Maharo, the Mirwah, and the Dahar canals in Upper Sindh as well as a few others in Lower Sindh. The third of these were the artificial canals which included the Begari, the Nurwah, the Shah ji Kur, the Dite ji Kur, and the Naulakhi on the right bank, and the Nasratwah, the Ferozwah, the Bagwah, and the Muradwah on the left.

Silting of the Indus posed a great problem as it affected the flow of the water. To tackle this, four mechanisms were put in place:[115]

1. The clearance of the large canals (called 'wah') was done by the government alone in some cases;
2. in other cases, the clearance was done by the government but the cost was partially recouped from the cultivators, called 'sherakati' (or sharing system);
3. in the case of other canals, the smaller ones, the government made an allowance of a certain number of 'khasas' in the 'kharar' of produce as the government share of clearance—mukhadimi;
4. in all other cases, the cultivators cleared each water course and smaller channels, called 'kario' or 'kasi', entirely at their own expense.

While the zamindars oversaw the canals and their tributaries on which their cultivation/revenue depended, the large canals were the government's responsibility for which they charged a water rate called *hakaba*.[116] These water-rates, as mentioned above, were charged depending on the type of irrigation used. *Charkhi* was used to irrigate dry crops such as *bajiri, jowar*, cotton, sugar cane, and vegetables whereas barley and wheat were mostly cultivated using *sailabi* method, and rice on *mok*.[117] Of these, the *mok* (irrigation by flow) was the most costly at Rs. 2 per *biga*—double the amount charged as land tax.[118]

Cognizant of the condition of canals in Sindh at the time of annexation, Napier was very ambitious in his plans for remedying the situation. He, along with Governor-General Ellenborough, wanted to provide dry land of Cutch with access to water.[119] To this end, he established a canal department. However, without proper resources and planning, all these plans amounted to nothing. The supervisor, Captain Baker, who surveyed Sindh to investigate the state of irrigation, had to resign and his successor (Captain Walter Scott), although an engineer himself, did not have a qualified staff.[120]

One of Napier's other plans was to connect Shikarpur with Sukkur to bring economic prosperity to the former which required a building of *bund*. This was a poorly-planned adventure which did not materialise and about which Jacob reprimanded, 'This *bund* was the most absurd affair ever projected by man. Had the work succeeded, it would have reduced a large portion of the country to a desert.'[121] With the conditions in Sindh still politically unstable in the first few years of annexation, it was no surprise that Napier's plan did not succeed. In fact, in the light of Clerk's criticisms of Napier's policies in Sindh, especially the lack of delegation of tasks to *kardar*s, the canal department was dissolved in 1848–49 and the work on the canals fell into disarray.[122]

One positive anomaly in this fiasco was the work of Brigadier-General John Jacob, the founder of Jacobabad. He received a grant of Rs. 130,000 to rejuvenate an area of 181,747 *biga*s of land by March 1854 with Frere's help.[123] Augmentation of the Eastern Nara canal was another scheme that was successfully completed, the advantages of which were enhanced with the completion of the Mithrao Canal in 1879.[124]

Captain Fife is also a key figure who can be credited with improving the state of the canals. Fife was a Canals Superintendent under Major Blois Turner, who was put in-charge of canal supervision during Frere's Commissionership. To tame the caprices of the Indus, Fife conducted a thorough investigation of the features of the river and revealed his findings in a report in 1855.[125] He found that the artificial canals dug in Sindh were very ill-planned, exacerbating the problem of siltation of the Indus, so much so that he gave an estimated revenue loss of Rs. 31 lac in 1853 alone.[126] He proposed a comprehensive, albeit very aspiring, plan to organise the canal system in Sindh—the realization of which was an intermittent process which took decades to complete, reaching culmination with the building of Lloyd Barrage in 1932.[127]

During these decades, much progress was stalled due to political disagreements between two diametrically opposed factions, one favouring the reliance on inundation canals and the other supporting a long-run viable solution of perennial canals.[128] The finance required to initiate and complete the projects was often not released, and the interest of the government to embark on ambitious works greatly subsided after the 'Mutiny' of 1857.[129]

Nonetheless, the *Gazetteer* (1968) declares the improvement in irrigation on scientific grounds to be the second major contribution of the British in Sindh after the stabilisation of government and ascribes it to Lt Col. Walter Scott, Gen. John Jacob, Bartle Frere, and Lt Fife, R.E.[130] Indeed, the state of irrigation before and after the British intervention is described in the following words:

> Until the nineteen twenties[,] Sind lay at the mercy of the Indus, which played 'hide and seek' with it, changing its five-hundred-mile course at will, unleashing calamitous floods, ravaging the fields every now and then and leaving a trail of misery, pain and squalor behind the rivers' wrath. But with the coming of the Lloyd Barrage[,] the river was made to surrender its power before the largest ever irrigation system of the world covering 1,028 miles of main canals[,] 1,071 miles of canal distributaries[,] and 5,196 miles of water courses. Old and new watercourses run for over 50,000 miles, enough to circle the globe twice … 5.25 million acres cultivable as against 2 million acres in the pre-Barrage period.[131]

However, the coverage of the Lloyd Barrage was only limited to central Sindh. In contrast, the northern and southern regions still relied on inundation canals, and the full benefits of the barrage were not to be derived till the construction of Guddu and Kotri barrages after Partition, serving northern and southern Sindh respectively.[132] The following table lists the canals constructed during the British period, along with the cost and the date of completion and operation.

Table 2.10: Irrigation Works under the British (Excluding Sukkur Barrage Canals)

Number of Work	Name of Irrigated Work	Estimated Cost (in Rs.) of Construction, Direct and Indirect	Date of Completion	Date of Commencement of Operations[*]
1	Eastern Nara	8,616,551	1897–98	1854–55
2	Begari Canal	2,477,798	1890–91	1855–56
3	Ghar Canal	678,303	1887–89	1856–57
4	Fuleli Canal	3,201,582	1892–93	1861–62
5	Sukkur Canal	1,485,574	1885–88	1870–71
6	Desert Canal	2,749,968	1891–92	1872–73
7	Alibhar Canal	107,169	1875–76	1873–74
8	Marak Canal	458,028	1881–82	1873–74
9	Sarfarazwah	121,680	1875–76	1873–74
10	Unharwah	795,700	1890–91	1885–86
11	Jamrao Canal	9,954,821	1901–02	1900–01
12	Hasanahwah	304,579	1906–07	1903–04
13	Navlaki	135,678	Not completed	1928
14	Kalri	96,333	1921–22	1922–23
15	Pinigari Canal	1,178,885	1921–22	1922–23
16	Indus Right Bank Canal	88,760	1921–22	1922–23
17	Indus Left Bank Canal	258,938	1921–22	1922–23
18	Sind Canal and Branches	834,656	1921–22	1923–24
19	Ranjiho Chith and Garang	286,928	1921–22	1923–24
20	Canabin Rohri	197,088	1921–22	1923–24
21	Western Nara and Pritchard	2,082,928	1921–22	1923–24
22	Phitta	26,136	1921–22	1923–24
23	Marviwah	9,737	1921–22	1923–24
24	Gharo Mahomudo	109,785	1921–22	1923–24
25	Nasirwah	47,157	1921–22	1923–24
26	Indus Canals (other canals, Fuleli Division)	115,783	1921–22	1923–24
27	Kari Shumali	15,793	1921–22	1923–24
28	Dambhro	51,818	1921–22	1923–24

Source: R. D. Choksey, *The Story of Sind: An Economic and Social Survey (1843–1933)*, Karachi, Indus Publications, 2003, p. 59.

[*] While some of these projects were grandeur[does not make sense here] and completed over several years, some parts of the canals became operational before the completion of the entire project.

Most of the canals were constructed towards the beginning of the twentieth century as water withdrawals in Punjab impressed upon the British government the need for a barrage supported by a system of perennial canals.[133]

Agricultural Production

As stated earlier, Sindh was predominantly an agricultural economy, with 68 per cent of workers directly involved in cultivation according to the 1951 census.[134] The two main cultivating seasons are Rabi and Kharif; the former spans the months from October to March while the latter from June to October. *Adhawa* is a third season mainly peculiar to Hyderabad and a few regions in Upper Sindh, which spans from April to June.[135] However, it comprises a small region due to water requirements of the time.

Kharif crops include rice, bajri, juwar, maize, cotton, saon, chaunra, sesame, sugarcane, indigo, hemp, and tobacco whereas the Rabi crops include wheat, rape and jambho, gram, and chickling vetch.[136] The Kharif crops, accounted for 72 per cent of the total cultivation as compared to the Rabi crops which had a share of 28 per cent.[137]

Of these, rice was the major crop of Sindh. Its total cultivated area is reported to have been one one-fourth million acres. Owing to limited rainfall, it was irrigated mostly through inundation canals.[138] The major rice growing areas are Larkana, Hyderabad, Dadu, Thatta, Khairpur, Sukkur, and Sindh Frontier while the lowest area under rice cultivation was in Nawabshah.

Next in importance was bajri which, along with juwar, was a staple food in Sindh among the working class.[139] Bajri, being a resilient crop, was mostly cultivated in Thar and Parkar and in Nawabshah. Gram was another important crop, commonly consumed as *dal*, grown mostly in the Sindh Frontier as well as in Larkana and Sukkur.

The significance of cotton, of course, cannot be underestimated. It was a major fibre crop occupying a mammoth share of 99.9 per cent among other fibre crops.[140] Not a very popular crop before the British era, cotton cultivation received a major boost owing to increased trade and improved irrigation during the British period. Thar, Parkar, and Nawabshah comprised the major cotton producing regions. Various foreign cotton seed varieties were also introduced but to no avail.[141]

As far as sugarcane was concerned, even after improved irrigation, the cultivation was never more than 4,000 acres.[142] Karachi, Hyderabad, and Thar and Parkar comprised 85 per cent of the total sugarcane producing regions. The annual acreage of indigo was 1,000 acres with Nawabshah being the main producing region.[143] Tobacco, grown in Hyderabad, Sukkur, Nawabshah, and Larkana, made up 7,000 acres.

Despite promising climatic and soil conditions, not much attention was paid to growing fruits.[144] There was some cultivation of fruits.[145] Root vegetables are cultivated during the winters. In contrast, green vegetables are planted in November and December except for Okra (*bhindi*), brinjals, purslain, and amaranth which are planted during the beginning of the Kharif season.[146] In terms of gourds too except for melons, musk melons, and water melons which are planted in the Rabi season, all others are cultivated during the Kharif season. Tomatoes, lettuce, beetroot, cauliflowers, peas and other European vegetables are also cultivated during the winters in various gardens.

As far as spices are concerned, the main varieties included red chillies, coriander, fennel, and mustard. While all vegetables are cultivated in the winters, chillies are the only ones cultivated during both Kharif and Rabi seasons.

Livestock and Animal Husbandry

At the time of British arrival, Sindh was a great pastoral region and continued to be during their rule albeit not as significantly.[147] In fact, 'the cattle of Sind were among the best in India.'[148] Most common were the sheep and goats, after which came the milch and plough cattle, with camels being the least.[149] The highest number of milch cattle—230 per thousand of the human population—were found in Hyderabad. Sukkur, Larkana, and Karachi had 228, 227, and 196 milche cattle per thousand of the human population respectively.[150] This large number is owing to milk exports to Ceylon (present day Sri Lanka) and Zanzibar, and cattle in Karachi (mostly in the hilly areas) were considered to be the best.[151]

In terms of plough cattle, Sukkur, Larkana, and Hyderabad had 56, 54, and 53 cattle per square mile respectively.[152] In Upper Sindh, though, the number was only 30, despite it being a region with greater cultivated area.[153] Hyderabad also had the highest number of goats, 38 per square mile, followed by 15 and 12 in Upper Sindh and Larkana respectively. Camels were more common in Thar and Parkar and Hyderabad and also in a lesser extent in Larkana and Thatta and were once used as a chief mode of transport.[154] They were also exported to as far as Australia.[155]

According to the 1945 livestock census, the following population of livestock was reported:

Table 2.11: Livestock in Sindh—1945

Livestock	Population
Cattle	1,958,764
Buffaloes	702,397
Horses	105,789
Poultry	803,740
Sheep	638,101
Goats	1,414,167
Camels	105,469
Donkeys	125,698

Source: H.T. Sorley, *The Gazetteer of West Pakistan the Former Province of Sind Including Khairpur State*, Lahore, Gazetteer Cell, Board of Revenue, 1968, 430.

Communications

The importance of the Indus for trade purposes was realised by the British from the outset. In fact, it was the significance of the Indus which led to the eventual annexation of the country. Commenting on its commercial importance, Napier remarked:

> If any civilized man were asked … were you ruler of Sindh, what would you do? His answer would be, I would abolish the tolls on the rivers, make Kurrachee a free port, protect Shikarpoor from robbers, make Sukkur a mart for trade and commerce on the Indus. I would make a track-way along its banks. I would get steam boats[156]

Hence, on 13 March 1843, believing taxes to be the reason for restricted trade activities via the Indus, Governor General Lord Ellenborough eliminated transit duties.[157] However, this did not translate into increased trade, more so owing to the inherent features of the Indus: 'in the summer [it] was flooded, and in the winter it was liable to go down so rapidly the steamers were likely to be grounded'. Additionally, the full benefits of the Indus with regard to trade could not have been achieved until Punjab too was annexed.[158] Even the capture of Punjab by the British in 1849, though, did not produce the desired result.

About this, Governor General Dalhousie wrote:

When the conquest of Punjab gave the upper stream of the River Indus into our possession, the government was in hopes that private enterprise would place river streamers upon its stream even more abundantly than upon the Ganges. That hope was disappointed. The Government therefore endeavoured by its own flotilla to establish regular communication by steam between the sea and the rivers of the Punjab[159]

Reports in 1850 of the popularity of Russian chintz threatening the English trade perturbed the British.[160] Upon inquiry, it was found that the English goods had not lost their markets and that the cloth presumed to be of Russian origin was actually an import from Bombay. However, the quality of Russian cloth available in the markets of Kabul and Kandahar was superior to that of the English cloth. Although there was no decrease in English imports, it was thought that bringing together Afghan and Bombay traders would cushion against the Russian commercial influence.[161]

To this end, Frere set out to establish a fair in Karachi to provide Afghan and Bombay traders a meeting ground. However, the success of such a venture depended upon other factors, not least the security issues posed by the Balochi tribes.[162] These tribes under the Khan of Kalat would charge hefty fees and also blackmail the en route caravans. This impediment too was removed as a result of British intervention, guaranteeing a toll of Rs. 5 per camel load, and an annual remuneration of Rs. 50,000 to the Khan in return for providing safe passage to the caravans.[163] The fair was eventually organised in 1852.[164]

This was just the beginning of a series of efforts initiated by the Sindh government to upgrade infrastructure in the region. Frere put in many requests for funds towards roads, bridges, and inns, to revamp the Karachi harbour as well as to introduce steamers for the Indus. Despite support from both Governor General Dalhousie and the Governor of Bombay, Falkland, the efforts were stifled by the bureaucracy.[165]

The government authorised a fund of Rs. 9,500 towards the cleaning of road from Karachi and 126 miles of road had been built in 1851 which cost Rs. 18,525. The next year, another 207 miles of road were built costing Rs. 28,298.[166] Jacob himself took upon the challenge of improving communication in Sindh. During 1847–60, he was able to get 2,589 miles of road constructed and 786 masonry bridges built. This was an improvement because in 1851, Frere had objected that 'there was not a mile of bridged or metalled road, not a masonry bridge of any kind.'[167]

Next in line was the harbour work about which Dalhousie himself stated: 'Without a good harbour at Kurrachee I think you would never have really good trade by the way of Scinde. But with a good harbour there, I know not why it should be very far behind Bombay.'[168] Previously, the orders for the establishment of a harbour mole had been given by Napier and endorsed by the then Governor General Ellenborough, connecting Karachi and Kemari, with funds of Rs. 51, 849.27.[169] This was another instance of poor planning on the part of Napier's administration. The allocated amount was quite meagre; by 1849, just three years since the construction began, Rs. 144,539 had been spent. To complete the project, additional funds of Rs. 130,711 were needed and the project was eventually completed in 1864.

Even with Dalhousie's support, not much was achieved and the harbour could not accommodate the [added?] heavy traffic in 1857.[170] The upgradation and renovation of the harbour was eventually completed in 1883 and a Karachi–Kotri railway line had been established by 1861.[171]

Table 2.12 gives the value of exports and imports for the ten years following the annexation of Sindh.

Table 2.12: Exports and Imports of Sindh (in GBP) (1843–44 to 1856–57)

Year	Imports £	Exports £	Total £	Annual Percentage Change (%)
1843–44	121,150	1,010	122,160	-
1844–45	217,700	9,300	227,000	85.822
1845–46	312,900	40,500	353,400	55.683
1846–47	293,400	49,300	342,700	-3.028
1847–48	287,872	154,730	442,602	29.151
1848–49	344,715	107,133	451,848	2.089
1849–50	419,352	114,378	533,730	18.122
1850–51	425,831	196,461	622,292	16.593
1851–52	489,220	244,122	733,342	17.845
1852–53	535,690	376,337	912,027	24.366
1853–54	508,793	376,310	885,103	-2.952
1854–55	575,196	346,893	922,089	4.179
1855–56	629,813	604,440	1,234,253	33.854
1856–57	685,665	734,522	1,420,187	15.064

Source: W. P. Andrew, *The Indus and Its Provinces: Their Political and Commercial Importance Considered in Connexion with Improved Means of Communication,* Karachi, Indus Publications, 1986, p. 47.

Table 2.12 shows that the annual trade increased almost twelve-fold between 1843–57. Overall, during this period, exports got a big boost and saw an increase of approximately 727 times while the value of imports increased by around six times.

Table 2.13: Composition of Imports and Exports (GBP)—1855

Items	Imports £	Exports £
Cotton	294,000	-
Grain	32,000	66,000
Raw silk	28,000	-
Sugar	28,000	-
Horses and drugs	-	14,000
Indigo	-	42,400
Saltpetre	-	21,000
Oil seeds	-	137,000
Sheep's wool	-	221,000

Source: W. P. Andrew, *The Indus and Its Provinces: Their Political and Commercial Importance Considered in Connexion with Improved Means of Communication,* Karachi, Indus Publications, 1986, pp. 57–58.

The composition of imports and exports for a single year, 1855, is depicted in Table 2.13. The main imports were cotton, grain, raw silk, and sugar while the main exports were wool, oil seeds, grain, and indigo. Grains included wheat and other staples were used mainly by the army deployed in Karachi. Cotton was imported from Manchester whereas raw silk came from Persia and Bukhara. Most of these export items saw a considerable increase relative to previous years. It is important to note also that until the war, all increases in trade transactions occurred without any direct help from the government and was 'natural ... without the aid of British capital'.[172]

Table 2.14: Major Trading Partners—1886

Bombay
Calcutta
Kutch and Kattiawar
England
France
Goa and Demaun
Guzerat and Concan
Malabar
Mauritius
Mekran and Persian Gulf

Source: W. P. Andrew, *The Indus and Its Provinces: Their Political and Commercial Importance Considered in Connexion with Improved Means of Communication*, Karachi, Indus Publications, 1986, p. 62.

Table 2.14 illustrates how most of the trade conducted was intra-regional and international trade and with the colonisers themselves and their allies, highlighting the imperialist nature of mercantilism. The absence of cotton as a major export item puzzled the British too for Sindh was thought to possess favourable conditions for the cultivation of the crop. It was speculated that the reason was either the poverty of the cultivators or the lack of interest from zamindars.[173]

In 1852–53 without apparently the existence of any unusual demand for any particular produce in the home market, the exports of Scinde rose from Rs. 24,41,228 in 1851–52 to Rs. 37, 63,376, or 54 per cent in 1852–53.

This increase was attributed to the fairs being organised in Karachi.[174] Here it is also mentioned that the fair that year was not as successful with the Afghan traders as had been expected because of the absence of British goods, which meant that the traders had to travel extra miles to Bombay which negated the very purpose of the fair.

Whilst the trade of Scinde, despite the difficulties which encompass it, had advanced since the conquest 575 per cent., the trade of Bombay, notwithstanding the many improvements that have taken place in the interior of the country, and other advantages has not increased within the same period more than 33 per cent., including her trade with Scinde.[175]

However, such a comparison does not highlight the difference in the total value of trade between the two vastly different regions in terms of economic importance. Sindh was a new colony and Bombay had been under British possession for nearly two centuries. The difference in the figures might as well be a reflection of the mature status of Bombay's economy relative to that of Sindh's which was still nascent in terms of trade.

Despite the rosy picture depicted by the tables above, it was pointed out that a majority of the trade was handled at Bombay and that propping Karachi as another important port would prove to be more profitable owing to reduced distance.[176] In fact, W. P. Andrews, the Chairman of the Sindh and Punjab Railways and Indus Steam Flotilla, commented:

> Kurrachee is not only the port of the Indus and Central Asia, but, from its geographical position and other advantages, appears destined to become, if not the future metropolis of India, most certainly the second city and the European port of that empire.[177]

Following the launch of several infrastructural schemes mentioned above, substantial increase in trade was also observed during 1855–60: the imports increased by a whopping 2,619 per cent from £629,813 to £1,712,7151 while the exports saw an increase of approximately 57 per cent.[178] However, not all of this can be attributed to the improvements in harbour; it was also a result of other reasons at play, the most important of which was the annexation of Punjab.[179] Sindh now 'assumed a far greater importance as the natural outlet for the Punjab and the entire north west of India',[180] especially for trade with England. At the same time, its importance with respect to trade with Central Asia diminished with the inclusion of the North West Frontier and, hence, the Khyber Pass into British dominion in the subcontinent. Moreover, with the advent of the Russian trade influence in Central Asia during the 1860s, Sindh was now being 'seen in relation to the Punjab' about which Frere commented: 'We must remember that Scinde forms, as it were, but the spout of a funnel, of which the vast province of the Punjab forms the larger portion.'[181]

Stating how the progress in exports during the 1850s resulted without any effort of the government, a newspaper article mentioned:

> When the communication between this province [Sindh] and the Punjab [sic] shall have been completed, by means of railroads and steamers, and the internal communication of the two provinces attended to, by the construction of roads from village to village, connected with the grand trunk road, the trade of Kurrachee will then exceed the present value [of 1857] by as much as the present exceeds the trade of 1847.[182]

Needless to say, the next big project to capture Frere's imagination was a railway network connecting Sindh and Punjab since the route through the Indus was not a reliable one and much of the trade was being carried out via camels.[183] In fact, 'the river above Multan was shallow and tortuous and almost impossible to navigate'.[184] But like other major works requiring substantial investment, the establishment of a railway network too was not an easy task, given the bureaucratic inertia of the government. Besides, an alternative project—that of a development of a canal linking the Indus at Kotri with the harbour—was sought by Jacob who wholeheartedly, albeit senselessly, supported the scheme.[185]

Eventually, the Frere-backed initiative, supported by Hardy Wells who surveyed the country for the railway plan, was adopted.[186] As a result, a company called the 'Scinde Railway Company' was established in 1855 with W. P. Andrews as its chairman. This was in essence a culmination of the project to interlink the two regions of Sindh and Punjab. The new company's aims went beyond just Sindh. In fact, it was:

> … also responsible for the construction of [a] Punjab line from Multan to Lahore and Amritsar, and was also in charge of a flotilla of steam boats on the river between Kotri and Multan to complete the system of communication between the Punjab and Karachi.[187]

The Scinde Railway Company was one part of the grand scheme combining the project with Punjab Railway and Indus Steam Flotilla—each with its own financial accounts but all under the administration of one board of directors.[188] However, the distance between Kotri and Multan via water was a hundred miles longer compared to land and the trade activity was restricted by the limited number of ships.[189] Hence, the need arose for a railway line connecting the two nodes and, eventually, a railway line was constructed connecting Karachi with Multan and Lahore in 1878.[190]

Khuhro, chronicling Sindh's importance in the eyes of the British, shares how initially the Indus was deemed as 'the highway of commerce to the countries of Central Asia' and that the emphasis was on freeing the markets.[191] This approach, however, soon proved inadequate. With the annexation of Punjab, the dynamics of the region changed, calling for direct government provision of infrastructural facilities. This need for effective communication channels in Sindh, Khuhro emphasised, preceded the 'Mutiny'.[192]

The value of trade within just a decade during the 1860s increased significantly by approximately 733 per cent; this was mainly a result of the American Civil War, which increased the value of cotton exports internationally.[193]

The land revenue system, construction of Sukkur Barrage and the associated network of irrigation canals, development of Karachi harbour, the railway line and the highway connecting Sindh with Punjab and the North Western Frontier helped the province in its modernisation and economic integration nationally and internationally.

Public Finance and Local Government

Although infrastructual development was modernised to a certain extent, Sindh remained backward in the areas of revenue generation and local governance. Until the mid-nineteenth century, Sindh remained without any finances for spending on local public utility.[194] It was in 1863 that local funds were introduced across the Bombay Presidency to lend taxpayers a say in the expenditure of their taxes.[195] The plan comprised of a fixed tax of '… 1 *anna* per rupee of assessment of the land revenue, toll and ferry receipts, the surplus income from cattle ponds and other items.'[196] Of the total revenue collected, a third was allocated to education while the rest was spent on the building and maintenance of public infrastructure such as roads and wells.

However, the scheme failed to bear fruit as it was discovered that the sole authority of the management of public funds fell in the hands of the collectors and their deputies.[197] To rectify this, the scheme was later enacted into a law in the form of the Bombay Act I (1884) which brought not only the domain of local funds but also that of local self-government more firmly within the ambit of the general public.[198] Instead of one person, the authority for the management of local funds and matters now belonged to a district local board as well as to a taluka board. The inclusion of the general public becomes apparent from the fact that of the 20–30 members who comprised the Board, half were to be elected (except the president). This arrangement, which was applied to the rest of the Bombay, did not extend to the Upper Sind Frontier and Thar Parkar districts. According to Sorley:

> The elected members represented the Taluka Local Boards, Municipalities and *inamdars* who were holders of entire villages. The nominated members included Collectors, Assistant and Deputy Collectors, Executive Engineers of districts, the Educational Inspector, the Deputy Sanitary Commissioner and the Civil Surgeon, who was the Health Officer, and had the right of attending the meetings and joining in the deliberation of the Board without voting. The Taluka Local Boards consisted of about fifteen members, of whom half were nominated and half elected. The Assistant or the Deputy Collector in charge of the taluka was invariably appointed a member and president of the taluka board … The electorate comprised two classes of persons, the first deriving its privilege from real property situated in the taluka and bearing an assessment on assessable value of 48 rupees per annum, or a value of 5,000 rupees, and the second including residents in the taluka whose annual income was not less than 500 rupees, or whose monthly pension was not less than 50 rupees.[199]

The power enjoyed by the taluka boards, however, was flimsy as budgets prepared at the taluka level required approval from the district board—an exercise which proved futile, resulting in the eventual elimination of the taluka boards in 1936.[200]

The Act was also extended to the village level (in the form of village sanitary boards), municipalities, and cantonments.[201] In terms of the villages, the Act was only introduced upon the presence of local demand, and hence there was no one standard which applied to such committees. Half of the revenue for funds were drawn from the villages themselves, whereas a third and a sixth were derived from the local funds and from the government respectively. As the name suggests, the funds were used towards introducing and maintaining the cleanliness of the villages.

In terms of the evolution towards municipalities in Sindh, Sorley traces the following developments:

> District Municipal Government in Sind falls into three divisions; the first from 1852/1878, during which Act XXVI of 1850 was in force; the second embracing the years between 1878 and 1901, the period covered by Bombay Act VI of 1873 … and third the beginning with the introduction of the District Municipal Act III of 1901 … [and] a fourth stage, 1933–1947, namely the creation of Karachi as a Municipal Corporation in 1933 bringing it into line with the major municipalities of India like Bombay and Calcutta. The period lasted till 1947 when Karachi was assumed by the Federal Government of Pakistan.[202]

During the first period, boards of conservancy set up by Napier only applied to Karachi and Hyderabad, whereas throughout other areas of Sindh the matters of cleanliness rested with local officials and citizens. This was followed by the Act XXVI (1850), at first introduced in Karachi, followed by Hyderabad, Sukkur, Shikarpur and wherever existed the demand for its application, extending municipalities the authority for the outlay of the tax revenue. In the face of opposition to house tax, revenue was mainly drawn from octroi and wool tax.[203]

The Act of VI and its subsequent amendment (in 1875) provided more powers to the municipalities in the form of extending them the charge of some public property, thereby expanding the source of revenue.[204] Municipalities, now divided into city and town municipalities, became elected bodies, were exempt from police related costs, and were made responsible to provide for middle-class and primary schools. This was followed by the Municipal Act III (1901) which provided

> … for municipal councillors vacating their seats on failure, without leave from the municipality, to attend at least one meeting for a period of four months, the appointment of ex-officio counsillors and presidents, the election of counsillors by sections of the inhabitants, public bodies and associations the management of trusts and the enforcing of information as to dangerous diseases and liability to municipal taxation.[205]

Another major development was the application of a Punjab Act, which called for the establishment of 'Notified Areas' in units which were too small to be elevated to the status of a municipality.

The culmination of this gradual evolution of local government came in 1933 in the form of the Karachi Municipal Corporation (KMC).[206]

Lastly, military cantonments were the fourth kind of local self-government entities. Besides Karachi, one was set up at Jacobabad in 1847 and another at Manora in 1903.[207] The control of the cantonments fell with committees established as a result of the Cantonment Code of 1899 and the revenue, which came from the taxes enforced by the Cantonments Act XIII (1889), was spent on 'conservancy, maintenance of roads and other necessary purposes.' [208]

Conclusion

A cursory glance at the administrative and economic history of Sindh very clearly depicts the transformational role played by the British from 1857 to 1947. There is no disagreement that they were mainly motivated by their self-interests to extract as much benefits from their colonies as possible and at the same time to maintain firm administrative control over a diverse, segmented population and the far-flung territory. In this process, the collateral benefits did accrue to the indigenous population of the subcontinentt, including Sindh. This laying down of an elaborate communication network of roads, highways, and railways laid the groundwork for a large national economy for market transactions. The building of Sukkur Barrage despite a long period of trials and tributaries converted Sindh's agriculture into a reliable, high income-earning occupation. Although much can be said about their promotions of jagirdars and zamindars in the body politic of the province, the average incomes of Sindh's inhabitants did increase since this important barrage was commissioned.

3

Population

Background

T HE first census of India, including Sindh (as part of the Bombay Presidency), was conducted in the late nineteenth century. The table below presents the population growth in the province from 1891 to 1941. The British annexed Sindh in 1843 and in 1845, it was merged with the Bombay Presidency as a commissionerate. Its provincial status was reduced; however, the census continued to be conducted every ten years. Sindh was separated from the Presidency in 1936 following the Government of India Act of 1935.

Table 3.1: Population Growth in Sindh (1891–1941)

Census years	Population (in million)	Inter-census rate of increase (%)	Average annual growth rate (%)
1891	2.9	-	-
1901	3.2	10.3	1.17
1911	3.5	9.4	0.94
1921	3.3	- 5.7	0.67
1931	3.9	18.2	1.85
1941	4.5	15.4	1.67

Note: Up to 1941, Khairpur was considered as a separate state. In 1951, it was made as a district of the province.
* Compound per annum.
The figures for the years 1951–98 have been taken from the *1998 Census Report of Sindh*.

Sources: Government of India, *Census of India 1941,* vol. 12, Sindh, n.d., Population Census Organisation, *1998 Census Report of Sindh*, Karachi/Islamabad, Statistics Division, Government of Pakistan, 2000, p. 73.
Pakistan Bureau of Statistics, *Provisional Summary Results of 6th Population and Housing Censu*s, Islamabad, Statistics Division, 2017.

The census for the year 1941 depicted different trends. The Pakistan Resolution was passed in 1940. The migration of Muslims from India and Punjab had already started due to better economic conditions in Sindh and the construction of Sukkur Barrage. The demographics of Sindh were such that different religious communities such as Bahais, Christians, Jews, Hindus, Muslims and, Zoroastrians (or Parsis) had been living in peace and harmony.

The intake of Muslims slowly started to increase in 1941 and from 1947, the migration of Muslims started in huge numbers as the Hindu population, alongwith Jews, Christians, Hindus, and, Parsis, started to migrate to India and other parts of the world.

According to the first census conducted during the British rule in 1891, the population of Sindh (excluding Khairpur state) was less than 2.9 million. From 1891–1921, the populations was growing on an average of 10 per cent in between censuses; however, from 1931 onwards, this doubled to 20 per cent. This means that the population of Sindh was supposed to have doubled every 50 years (between the span of five censuses starting from 1931) and urban planning would have been conducted keeping this pattern in mind.

From 1891 to 1941, the population of Sindh increased from 2.9 million to 4.5 million—an increase of more than 55 per cent as estimated earlier. Table 3.2 shows that the first post-Partition census saw a jump of almost 33 per cent in a decade, reflecting the effect of migration into and from Sindh after the partition of British India.

In terms of demographics, prior to Partition, the urban share of Sindh's population was dominated by Hindus, at 59 per cent during the census year of 1941 (see Table 3.2). The largest urban area of Sindh, Karachi, was home to about 0.4 million people only.

Table 3.2: Sindh Urban Demographics (in Hundred Thousand) (1941 and 1951)

Urban Districts	1941				1951
	Hindu	Muslim	Others*	Total	
Karachi	1.97	1.67	0.31	3.95	10.7
Hyderabad	1.13	0.53	0.03	1.69	2.9
Sukkur	1.07	0.49	0.02	1.58	1.5
Sub Total	4.17	2.69	0.36	7.22	15.1
Rest of Sindh (Excluding Khairpur)	1.13	0.54	0.03	1.70	2.4
Sub Total Sindh (Excluding Khairpur)	5.30	3.23	0.39	8.92	17.5
Khairpur	0.10	0.11	0.01	0.22	0.2
Total Urban Sindh (Including Khairpur)	5.40	3.34	0.40	9.14	17.7
Percentage Share (%)	59	37	4	100	-

* Christians, Jains, and Sikhs and others.

Source: Government of India, *Census of India 1941*, vol. 12, Sindh, n.d; Population Census Organisation, *Census of Pakistan, 1951*, Karachi, Government of Pakistan, n.d.

Partition was poised to change the demographics of the province and caused planners to amend their policies according to the increased migration.

The demographics of the province prior to Partition showed that the dominant language group—Sindhi—stood at 70 per cent during the two censuses of 1931 and 1941. The 1951 census shows that this dominance decreased to 58 per cent as a result of the influx of over 1.5 million Urdu-speaking migrants who formed about 21 per cent of the population after Partition.

The added influx completely changed the demographics of the province and made it even more multi-cultural than before. Sindhi hospitality is a testament to the migrant influx as majority of the province's migrants were resettled in Karachi because of which the population rose to over 1.1 million in 1951 compared to 0.4 million in 1941 (see Table 3.4). This means that the city of Karachi, which was also the capital at the time, was home to 20 per cent of the population compared to 9 per cent in the decade prior to Partition.

Table 3.3: Language Groups in Sindh (in Thousand) (1931–98)

Year	Sindhi	Urdu	Seraiki	Pushto	Punjabi	Others (d)	Total
1931	2,874	73	631	17	72	447	4,114
Percentage	70	2	15	0.4	1.6	11	100
1941	3,175	234**(b)	7,32*(a)	17	87	277 (c)	4,522
Percentage	70	5	16	0.4	2	6.6	100
1951							
1961*	4,850	17,55	7,50	172	361	491	8,370
Percentage	58	21	9	2	4	6	100
1981**	1,422	614	213	83	209	163	2,714
Household Percentage	52	23	8	3	8	6	100
1998	18,181	6,409	944	1,276	2,128	1,501	30,439
Percentage	60	21	3	4	7	5	100
1931–1998 (67 Years Growth)	6 times	88 times	1.5 times	75 times	29 times	3 times	7 times

Source: Government of India, Census of India 1931, Vol. 8, Bombay, n.d. Government of India, Census of India 1941, vol. 12, Sindh, n.d., Population Census Organisation, Population Census Report, Karachi/Islamabad, Government of Pakistan, various years.

*Computed from Census of 1961.
**Population in 000s at the rate of 7.0 persons per household.

a) Including Thari/Dhatki and Jatki and Balochi/Brahwi.
b) Including Hindustanis, Western Hindi, and Rajasthani.
c) Including European and other languages.
d) Christians, Jains, and Sikhs and others,

Table 3.4: Sindh-Karachi Comparison and Percentage Shares (in Hundred Thousand) (1931–2017)

Year	Sindh	Karachi	Rest of the Sindh	Percentage Share (%)	
				Karachi	Rest of Sindh
1931*	41.4	2.62	38.42	6.4	93.6
1941**	45.4	4.4	41.0	9.7	90.3
1951	60.5	11.3	49.2	18.7	81.3
1961	83.7	20.4	63.3	24.3	75.7
1972	141.6	36.1	105.5	25.5	74.5

table continued

| Year | Sindh | Karachi | Rest of the Sindh | Percentage Share (%) | |
				Karachi	Rest of Sindh
1983	190.0	54.4	135.6	28.6	71.4
1998	304.4	98.6	205.8	32.4	67.6
2017	478.8	149.1	329.7	31.1	68.9

* Government of India, *Census of India 1931*, vol. 8, Bombay, n.d.
**Government of India, *Census of India 1941*, vol. 12, Sindh, n.d.

Source: Population Census Organisation, *Population Census Report*, Karachi/Islamabad, Government of Pakistan, various years; Pakistan Bureau of Statistics, *Population Census 2017*, Islamabad, Statistics Division, Government of Pakistan, p. 20.

Introduction

Since the inception of Pakistan, six censuses have been conducted (see Table 3.5). The first in 1951, the second in 1961, the third in 1972, the fourth in 1981, and the fifth census, which was scheduled to be conducted in 1991, was conducted in March 1998. The last census—conducted in the year 2017 after a gap of nineteen years—showed Pakistan with a population of just over 200 million, ranking it as the fifth most populated country in the world as of 2017.[1] Of these 200 million people, almost 47 million people reside in Sindh.[2] The population growth rate is 2.4 per cent, which is higher compared to Pakistan's neighbouring countries.[3]

Table 3.5: Population Growth in Sindh (1951–2017)

Census years	Population (in Thousand)	Inter-census rate of increase (%)	Average Annual Growth Rate (%)
1951	6,048	-	-
1961*	8,367	38.3	3.3
1972*	14,156	69.2	4.9
1981*	19,029	34.4	3.3
1998*	30,440	60	2.8
2017	47,886	57.3	2.4

Note: Up to 1941 Khairpur was considered as separate state. In 1951, it was made a district of the province.
** Compound per annum.

Source: Government of India, *Census of India 1941*, vol. 12, Sindh, n.d.; The figures for the years 1951–98 have been taken from Population Census Organisation, *1998 Census Report of Sindh*, Karachi/Islamabad, Statistics Division, Government of Pakistan, 2000, 73; Pakistan Bureau of Statistics, *Provisional Summary Results of 6th Population and Housing Census*, Islamabad, Statistics Division, 2017.

Between 1891 and 1941, the population of Sindh rose from 2,875,000 to 4,535,000—there was an increase of almost 55 per cent. However, the first post-Partition census shows a big jump to 6,048,000, almost 33 per cent in a decade, reflecting the effect of net migration into and from Sindh after 1947.

Since then, there has been an almost eight-fold increase in the population as observed in the latest census of 2017.[4] While the population has been on the rise, the rate of increase in population shows a mixed pattern.

There was a spike in the rate of increase in the population, almost 70 per cent, during the period of 1961–72. This period was followed by a 34 per cent increase in the next decade. The period of 1981–1998 once again recorded a 60 per cent increase in the population, which rose to about 30 million, largely because of inter-provincial and rural–urban migration.

However, the average annual growth rate of the population declined to 2.80 per cent from 3.3 per cent between 1981 and 1998 and to 2. 4 per cent between 1998 and 2017. The highest growth rate of 4.9 per cent was recorded during 1961–72. If the population of the province continues to grow at the rate of 2.4 per cent, it is likely to double in about 30 years, reaching nearly 100 million by 2047.[5] Therefore, there is an urgent need to contain the population within manageable limits. India and Bangladesh have brought down their growth rate to 1.5 per cent. Sindh is the third largest (by area) and second most populous province of Pakistan accounting for approximately one fourth of the country's total population, rising from 18 per cent in 1951 to 23 per cent in 2017 (see Table 3.6).

Population has been considered a double-edged sword for economic and social development. Large increases in unskilled and untrained population create a heavy demand on public services, while an educated and skilled labour force provides a safety net by finding employment in other parts of the world faced with labour scarcity. The youth forms a large percentage of Sindh's population. Given a carefully planned strategy of education and skill formation, this segment of the population can be turned into an asset.

Figure 3.1: Trend of Sindh's Population—Annual Growth Rate of Population (%)
(1961–72 to 1998–2017)

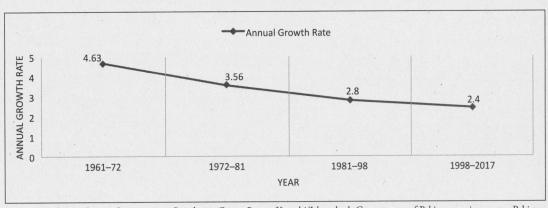

Source: Population Census Organisation, *Population Census Report,* Karachi/Islamabad, Government of Pakistan, various years; Pakistan Bureau of Statistics, *Provisional Summary Results of 6th Population and Housing Census,* Islamabad, Statistics Division, 2017.

Density

As per the 2017 census, the population density, i.e. persons per square kilometres, was 339 for Sindh as a whole (Table 3.6). This has increased from 135/sq km in 1981. Population density varies from one district in the province to another. For example, Karachi, with all its districts, has the highest density. As already stated, due to the lack of availability of complete 2017 census results, the population density in 1998 of Karachi Central District was 76 per kilometre while in contrast, Tharparkar district had the lowest density of 46.6, followed by that of Thatta with 64.1. Other less dense districts, with the population density of less than 100 persons per kilometre, were Dadu and Khairpur.

Table 3.6: Area, Population, and Population Density of Pakistan and Sindh (1951–2017)

Region	Area (sq. km)	Population (in Thousands)						Population Density (Persons per sq. km)					
		1951	1961	1972	1981	1998	2017	1951	1961	1972	1981	1998	2017
Pakistan	796,096	33,740	42,880	65,309	84,254	132,352	207,763	42	54	82	106	166	261
Sindh	140,914 (17.70)	6,048 (17.93)	8,367 (19.51)	14,156 (21.68)	19,029 (22.59)	30,440 (23.00)	47,833 (23.02)	43	59	100	135	216	339

Source: Population Census Organisation, *Population Census Report*, Karachi/Islamabad, Government of Pakistan, various years; Pakistan Bureau of Statistics, *Provisional Summary Results of 6th Population and Housing Census*, Islamabad, Statistics Division, 2017.

Table 3.7: Population by Gender in Sindh (1951–2017)

Years	Male (in Million)	Female (in Million)	Female-Male Ratio
1951	2.7	2.2	0.81
1961	-	-	-
1972	7.6	6.6	0.87
1981	10	9	0.90
1998	16.1	14.3	0.89
2017	24.9	23	0.92

Source: Population Census Organisation, *Population Census Report*, Karachi/Islamabad, Government of Pakistan, various years; Pakistan Bureau of Statistics, *Provisional Summary Results of 6th Population and Housing Census*, Islamabad, Statistics Division, 2017.

Table 3.7 presents changes in the female–male ratio. Although, there is some improvement as compared to 1951, the situation is still unacceptable. The preference for a boy child over a girl is driven by socio-cultural norms which have given rise to a biased female–male ratio, resulting in a shortage of females in the population with large inter-district variations.

As per the 1998 census results, in the more urban areas such as Karachi, Hyderabad, and Sukkur, the size of the household was higher, i.e. between 6.0 and 6.8. The district of Khairpur touched the provincial average while Shikarpur, Larkana, Naushahro Feroz, and Sanghar hovered close to the average. Thatta had on average the lowest number of persons in the household. The other phenomenon that is observable is the rate of urbanisation in cities of Sindh other than Karachi. The fast-growing cities are Mirpurkhas and Sukkur divisions (Table 3.8), with above average growth rates compared to the other cities of Sindh.

Table 3.8: Sindh's Population Growth Rate and National Rank
by Size and Division (2017)

Division	Population 2017 (in Million)	Annual Average Population Growth Rate 1998–2017 (%)	National Rank by Size and Division
Karachi	16.1	2.6	3
Hyderabad	10.6	2.3	8
Sukkur	5.5	2.5	13
Larkana	6.2	2.1	12
Mirpurkhas	4.2	2.6	15
Shaheed Benazirabad	5.3	2.2	14

Source: Population Census Organisation, *1998 Census Report of Sindh*, Karachi/Islamabad, Statistics Division, Government of Pakistan, 2000; Pakistan Bureau of Statistics, *Provisional Summary Results of 6th Population and Housing Census*, Islamabad, Statistics Division, Government of Pakistan, 2017.

Rural Urban Distribution/Urbanisation

The census of 2017 showed an almost even distribution between the urban and rural population in Sindh, the most urbanised province in the country. As of 2017, 52 per cent of Sindh's population lives in urban areas, while the remaining 48 per cent reside in rural area. (Table 3.9). The respective proportions for Pakistan were 36.4 and 63.6, while those for Punjab were 36.8 and 63.2. According to the World Bank Urban Sector Assessment 2014, in Pakistan, out of every three migrants who go to urban centres, one goes to Sindh's towns. Cities in Sindh receive 60 per cent inter-provincial migrants—25 per cent from Punjab and 15 per cent from KP.

Table 3.9: Percentage Distribution of Rural–Urban Population in Sindh, Punjab, and Pakistan (1951–2017)

	Punjab		Sindh		Pakistan	
	Urban	Rural	Urban	Rural	Urban	Rural
1951	17.4	82.6	29.2	70.8	17.7	82.3
1961*	21.5	78.5	37.9	62.1	22.5	77.5
1972	24.4	75.6	40.4	59.6	25.4	74.6
1981	27.6	72.4	43.3	56.7	28.3	71.7
1998	31.3	68.7	48.8	51.2	32.5	67.5
2017	36.8	63.2	52	48	36.4	63.6

Source: Population Census Organisation, *Population Census Reports*, Karachi/Islamabad, Statistics Division, Government of Pakistan, various years.

* Pakistan Bureau of Statistics, *Population By Province/ Region Since 1951*, Islamabad, Government of Pakistan, n.d.

The trend of rapid urbanisation, in recent years, has led to the emergence of many secondary peri-urban and satellite districts, such as N. Feroze, Ghotki, Mirpurkhas, Umerkot, Jamshoro, Qambar Shahdadkot, Tando Muhammad Khan and Tando Allahyar. The planned growth of these districts with opportunities for livelihoods, employment, and basic public services such as education, healthcare, potable water supply and sanitation can ease the pressure on Karachi. Negative push factors for migration would be mitigated if better economic opportunities and social infrastructure are developed in these districts.

The Karachi–Hyderabad Corridor, encompassing districts of Thatta, Jamshoro, Tando Mohammad Khan, and Tando Allahyar, is becoming an attractive centre for manufacturing and employment. The last decade however, was marked by lower GDP growth for Sindh's urban centres. Karachi had the lowest GDP growth rate. The deteriorating security situation in Karachi led to the relocation of many units to Punjab. With the improvement in security and stable electric supply, this trend is reversing.

The unplanned expansion of urban cities and absence of public services and amenities has led to diseconomies of agglomeration.[6] Although relative per capita GDP is higher than other Pakistani cities, their growth has been stunted by slow rate of employment generation and low labour productivity. Haphazard planning, ill-conceived projects, inadequate allocations, and weak institutional capacity have worked in concert to negate most of the economic and social benefits associated with urbanisation. Fragmentation of administrative responsibilities among uncoordinated multiple agencies has compounded the problem. District local governments in the 2001 Ordinance were an improvement but lacked jurisdiction and enforcement powers over land under the control of the Government of Sindh, Defence Authority, cantonment boards, the Civil Aviation Authority, port authorities, etc., which carried out their own mandates independent of the district governments. The Karachi Metropolitan

Corporation/District Government owned only 31 per cent of total land area in Karachi. Ultimately, the citizens suffered the most because of multiple turf-wars, blame-game and inaction.

Migration

Migration is the movement of population from one area to another—one district to another district in the same province, from one province to another province, or people living abroad migrating to any province. Sindh is the province which has received the largest number of migrants in Pakistan.

The lure of economic opportunities has led to massive rural–urban migration in Sindh. Karachi, the financial hub of the country, has been at the receiving end of migration not only from rural Sindh, but also from urban centres in Balochistan, Punjab, FATA, and Khyber Pakhtunkhwa contributing heavily to the urban sprawl in the city. Every year, millions of people add to the workforce of the province in the urban areas. However, this has come at the cost of reduced economic opportunities for locals in the city. Karachi alone, with 16.05 million people in 2017, accounted for 64 per cent of the province's urban population, with the other major urban centres being Sukkur, Hyderabad, and Larkana. Almost three-fourths of urbanites live in these three cities.

According to the census figures of 1998, the number of in-migrants in the province of Sindh was 2,832,937, which made up 9.31 per cent of the total population.[7] Out of these migrants, 21.8 per cent moved from one district to another within the province and 78.3 per cent came from outside the province (40.3 per cent from other provinces, 1.6 per cent from AJK/NA, 0.1 per cent from Islamabad, 0.7 per cent from FATA, and 24.2 per cent from other countries), while 11.3 per cent came from places not reported by the respondents. Table 3.10 provides the origin of the migrants.

Table 3.10: Percentages of Migrants from Other Provinces/Within Province by Rural Urban (1998)

Place of Previous Residence	All Areas (%)	Rural (%)	Urban (%)
Sindh (Within Province)	21.8	55.8	18.0
NWFP	15.2	3.6	16.5
Punjab	22.4	12.5	23.5
Balochistan	2.7	7.7	2.1
Islamabad	0.1	0.1	0.1
FATA	0.7	0.2	0.8
AJK/NA	1.6	0.5	1.8
Other Countries	24.2	8.2	25.9
Not Reported	11.3	11.4	11.3

Source: Population Census Organisation, *1998 Population Census Report of Sindh*, Islamabad, Statistics Division, Government of Pakistan, 2000.

It is interesting to examine the results of the 1951 census, which incorporated the great influx of the migrants in the aftermath of the partition of India in 1947 (see Table 3.11). In all, those who took refuge from India were over 7.2 million people, of which Sindh and Khairpur state received 550,000 of them or 7.6 per cent of the total entrants while Karachi—the capital of Pakistan at the time—received 617,000 or 8.5 per cent of all muhajirs. Those who did opt to settle in Sindh originated from the north and north-west regions.

Table 3.11: Migrants from India as of 1951 (in Thousand)

Province Where Enumerated	Total Muhajirs	Chief Zone of Previous Residence in India				
		North West	Central	North	West	East
Baluchistan & States Union	28	16.5	3	6.3	1.5	0.3
East Bengal	699.1	2	2.7	20.8	1.9	670.7
Karachi	616.9	217.6	49.6	197.6	119.2	19.9
N.W.F.P & Frontier Regions	51.1	31.4	1.7	17.1	0.4	0.5
Punjab & Bahawalpur State	5,281.2	5,146.7	17.2	105.5	5.4	5.6
Sind & Khairpur State	550.3	370.9	21	116.9	32.1	4.3
Total (Pakistan)	7,226.6	5,785.1	95.2	464.2	160.4	701.3

Source: Population Census Organisation, *Census of Pakistan, 1951*, Karachi, Government of Pakistan, n.d.

Sex Ratio

The sex ratio (number of males per hundred females) is another variable of demography. 'It is primarily affected by ratio at birth and later by sex differentials in mortality and migration besides erroneous enumeration.'[8] This ratio denotes mortality rate, fertility, labour force composition, and migration. The sex ratio of Sindh was 108.58 in 2017, compared to 112.2 (see Annex Table R) in 1998 and 110.74 in 1981.[9] It is different in urban and rural areas. In rural areas, it is 107.8 whereas in urban areas it is 109.31. Different age groups have different sex ratios.

Age Structure

As the detailed results of the 2017 census are not available, this section is based on findings from the 1998 census. The latest census of 1998 (Table 3.12) depicts a high dependent population of about 38.3 per cent (considering the number of people aged less than 15 years and those aged 65 and above). The working population comprises 61.7 per cent of the total population. Taking the two together, we get a very high age dependency ratio of 83.6. This ratio is significantly higher in rural areas (96) as compared to the urban areas (72). However, this high figure includes the youth who will become part of the working population in a few years. While this is better than the diametrically opposite scenario—aging population outstripping youth population—as the former cannot contribute to economic potential, this should by no means be a state of comfort for the government. The large youth demographic should spur the government to invest in their education, and vocational and employment programmes so that they are better able to integrate into the active labour force in the future.

Marital Status/Females Reproductive Ages by Marital Status

Almost all the individuals aged 15 years and above counted in the census of 1998 were asked about their marital status (married, unmarried, never married, widowed, divorced). About 64.1 per cent were currently married, 30.6 per cent had never married, 5.0 per cent were widowed and a very small percentage were divorced. Of those classified as 'never married' there was a higher proportion of males (62.6 per cent) as compared to the females (37.4 6 per cent). Roughly equal proportion was shared by both genders for the 'currently married' category. In terms of the categories of 'widowed' and 'divorced', however, there was a significantly greater proportion of females than males.

Table 3.12: Population by Age Groups, Gender, and Rural–Urban Areas of Sindh
(in Million) (1998)

Age Groups	All Areas			Rural			Urban		
	Total	Male	Female	Total	Male	Female	Total	Male	Female
Less than 1 year	0.64	0.33	0.31	0.33	0.17	0.16	0.31	0.16	0.15
Less than 5 years	4.56	2.33	2.23	2.64	1.35	1.29	1.92	0.98	0.94
Less than 10 years	9.29	4.83	4.46	5.34	2.80	2.54	3.95	2.03	1.92
Less than 15 years	13.02	6.86	6.16	7.19	3.85	3.34	5.82	3.01	2.81
18 years and above	15.89	8.41	7.48	7.79	3.99	3.80	8.10	4.42	3.68
21 years and above	13.26	7.13	6.13	6.36	3.33	3.03	6.89	3.80	3.09
15 to 64	16.58	8.79	7.79	7.95	4.10	3.85	8.63	4.68	3.95
65 years and above	0.84	0.45	0.39	0.45	0.24	0.21	0.39	0.21	0.18

Source: Population Census Organisation, *1998 Population Census Report of Sindh*, Islamabad, Statistics Division, Government of Pakistan, 2000.

Table 3.13: Marital Status by Percentage in Sindh (1998)

Marital Status	All Areas			Rural			Urban		
	Total	Male	Female	Total	Male	Female	Total	Male	Female
Never Married	30.6	62.6	37.4	23.5	63.7	36.3	37.3	61.9	38.1
Currently Married	64.1	50.5	49.5	71.3	49.4	50.6	57.4	51.9	48.1
Widowed	5.0	27.2	72.8	5.1	28.7	71.3	5.0	25.8	74.2
Divorced	0.2	32.9	67.1	0.1	32.0	68.0	0.3	33.3	66.7
Total	100			100			100		

Source: Population Census Organisation, *1998 Population Census Report of Sindh*, Islamabad, Statistics Division, Government of Pakistan, 2000.

According to the census of 1998, the total percentage of the female population aged between 15 and 49 was 47.8; an increase of 4.75 percentage points was marked when compared to the 1981 census. In the census of 1981, the percentage was 43.0. The percentage of such cases was higher in urban areas than the rural areas. For the percentage of reproductive ages by marital status and urban rural areas, see Annex Table S.

Economic Characteristics

The active population of either sex involved in various productive activities is considered to be of value to the economy. The scope of the manpower data in the 1998 census is defined as the economically active population which comprises persons of either sex who are engaged in some work for pay or profit, including unpaid family helpers. People not working but looking for work are also considered to be part of the economic population.[10] The population groups not included in the labour force comprise children below 10 years of age, housewives, students, and others.

Table 3.14: Percentage of Population by Economic Categories, Gender, and Rural–Urban Areas of Sindh (1998)

Economic Category	All Areas			Rural			Urban		
	Both Sexes	Male	Female	Both Sexes	Male	Female	Both Sexes	Male	Female
Labour Force	22.8	41.2	2.0	21.4	39.3	1.7	24.1	43.2	2.5
Not in Labour Force	77.3	58.8	98.0	78.6	60.7	98.3	75.9	56.8	97.6
Children Below 10 Years	30.5	30.0	31.1	34.2	34.1	34.3	26.6	25.7	27.7
Domestic Workers	31.9	2.6	64.7	31.9	3.4	63.3	31.8	1.6	66.3
Students	8.1	13.8	1.6	5.2	9.5	0.4	11.1	18.4	2.9
All Others	6.8	12.4	0.5	7.3	13.7	0.3	6.3	11.1	0.7
Labour Force Participation Rate (Refined)	32.7	58.8	3.0	32.6	59.7	2.5	32.9	58.1	3.4
Unemployment Rate	14.4	14.9	4.7	12.0	12.3	3.7	16.8	17.3	5.4

Source: Population Census Organisation, *1998 Population Census Report of Sindh*, Islamabad, Statistics Division, Government of Pakistan, 2000.

There is significant variation between male and female participation rates. As per the 1998 census, it is 58.8 per cent of males compared to only 3 per cent of females. This shows a very low participation rate compared to other countries. The labour force participation rate is affected by the level of industrialisation, agriculture development, education, and socio-economic norms but in the case of Sindh, the participation rate is primarily offset by low levels of female participation. Rural–urban refined activity rates do not differ much; they are 32.6 per cent in rural and 32.9 per cent in urban areas.[11]

Reasons and Consequences of High Growth Rate of Population

The major reasons for the high growth rate in Sindh, especially in the city of Karachi, are its two seaports and the economic markets. People from all over Pakistan come to the province of Sindh in search of economic opportunities. At the same time, the push factors that induce mass migrations from the different parts of the country are the other determinants for high population growth. During the years 1978–83, it was expected that the agricultural sector would yield jobs but this did not happen. Within the next few years, real wage rates fell because of the cheap supply of labour from rural areas. Between 1983 and 1988, net migration was expected to be 5.5 million for five years.[12] Another reason for the increase in population are improved health facilities, which led to a reduction in the mortality rate and limited supply of contraceptives to meet the demand of the families who wish to space out in the births of their children.

The high fertility rates and early marriages also contribute to an increase in population. Parents and relatives belonging to destitute families sell their young girls for a few thousand rupees.[13] Although the custom is not widely practised in rural societies today, it has not been completely eliminated. Another factor is illiteracy among females, especially in rural areas. Even though an increase in literacy rate and participation in the workforce has meant that women on average in urban centres marry later, generally, there is a lack of awareness among females, especially in rural centres, about family planning and use of contraceptives, which has also contributed to the population boom in the province. Moreover, the government has largely failed to draft an effective national policy on population control, which has resulted in low outreach by family planning organisations. Low allocation of funds and low spending have actually reduced the efficacy of the programme. Many programmes were suspended mid-course. This low spending can be judged by the fact that less than one per cent of GDP was spent although there were foreign donations available for this purpose. The low level of spending can be attributed to the political leadership's ambivalence about family planning, partly due to fear of backlash from some of the clergy if an aggressive campaign is launched. The experience of Bangladesh shows that the religious imams played a positive role in promoting family planning practices.[14] In addition, most of the family planning workers hired in Pakistan were from urban areas and were unable to win the trust of the rural population. Better results could be achieved if people from the same community were hired as family planning workers. In order to ensure that there is maximum community involvement in such programmes, it is imperative to take local, influential ulemas into confidence.

In developing countries, it is observed that a high population growth rate has disadvantages as it puts a burden on scarce public resources and infrastructure. In these countries, resources generally grow at an arithmetic rate while population grows at a geometric rate.[15] Resources that would be more relevant to population growth are food, shelter, clothing, etc. Despite the fact that Pakistan is an agro-based country, its agricultural productivity has remained stagnant. The decline in output, if not addressed, may lead to food shortages and an increase in food prices. The high demand of food products would lead to increased imports of food items, placing pressure on foreign exchange reserves. Rapid population growth has also put strain on the feeble infrastructure of the province. Power and gas shortages observed in the latest decade are an example of the demand outstripping the supply.

Provincial and Country-wise Comparison

Sindh performs poorly as compared to the other provinces of Pakistan in terms of population growth rate and labour participation but better in terms of urbanisation. The average population growth rate of Sindh from 1981 to 1998 was around 2.8 per cent while that of the country was 2.7 per cent.[16] By 2017, however, both the national and provincial rates had converged to 2.4 per cent. Punjab's growth rate declined more sharply from 2.7 to 2.1 per cent.[17] Sindh's share in the national population has risen from 17.9 to 23 per cent in the last six decades, while that of Punjab has fallen from 60.9 to 53 per cent (Table 3.15). This is one of the reasons why Sindh out-performs Punjab; this differential of growth rate over the decades is now translating into difference in terms of per-capita income growth in the two provinces.

As discussed in the previous sections, a decline in mortality rates and increase in birth rates have raised the natural growth rate of the population. Reproduction rates are higher in low-income families who view their children as a source of augmenting family income.

Table 3.15: Population Shares of Pakistan and its Provinces Over the Censuses
(1951–2017)

	1951	1961	1972	1981	1998	2017
Pakistan	100.0	100.0	100.0	100.0	100.0	100.0
Sindh	17.9	19.5	21.7	22.6	23.0	23.1
Punjab	60.9	59.3	57.6	56.1	55.6	53.0
Khyber Pakhtunkhwa	13.5	13.4	12.8	13.1	13.4	14.7
Baluchistan	3.5	3.2	3.7	5.2	5.0	5.9
Fed. Area (FATA and Islamabad)	4.2	4.6	4.2	3.0	3.0	3.3

Summing Up

There is negligence in governance and bureaucracy, especially when it comes to controlling the ever-increasing population—witnessed through the past censuses—and planning to accommodate the generations to come.

The lack of planning with respect to the increasing population and urbanisation can be witnessed in the sprawling and congested cities of Sindh. The pressure on infrastructure is evident through the overflowing sewerage lines as a result of which roads constantly break down in the urban areas of Sindh.

Population planning was one of the major priorities of the government in the 1960s and many developing countries had taken Pakistan as the benchmark for their own efforts. Since then, it has fallen from the radar of policy makers. Even the population censuses, quite crucial for elections, finance awards, and national planning were postponed and conducted after a considerable lapse of time. The 2017 census, after several postponements, took place after nineteen years.

Sindh has gained a share in the national population since 1951 although the latest census shows a flat line between 1998 and 2017. As the economic hub of country, Sindh is the most urbanised province, with 52 per cent of the population living in cities compared to 36 per cent for the entire country. Karachi, the largest city of Pakistan, is the magnet for migration from the rest of the country. Its ethnic composition reflects the microcosm of Pakistan. However, haphazard urbanisation has created negative externalities with congestion, pollution, environmental degradation, and crime. Investment in housing for the poor, drinking water, sanitation, solid waste disposal and transport has not kept pace with the rate of urbanisation. Although per capita income in the country and the province is rising, income inequalities are also simultaneously becoming starker. Gender discrimination and male dominance also engender reluctance in controlling the population in the rural areas of the province. The 2017 census results are believed to have understated the population growth rate in Sindh.

If the state is to clamp down on out of control migration and sprawl of cities then it is imperative to incentivise investment in rural areas and create ample economic opportunities to ease the pressure on infrastructure.

4

Education

Introduction

THEORETICAL and empirical evidence across countries linking education and economic development is quite strong. But a well-functioning system of inclusive and relevant, quality education remains one of the major challenges facing Pakistan even after seven decades. The uneven and faltering economic development is a result of the low priority accorded to education, training and skill development. Education not only expands economic opportunities but also helps build a socially cohesive and responsible society embedded with democratic values. A well-educated society also exhibits more tolerance and respect for other nations, societies, and groups.

The significance attached to education has to be matched by consistent policies, robust institutions and well-targeted investment. The record in this respect has been lacklustre and Pakistan lags behind other countries in the region in educational indicators. Efforts were initiated right after Independence by convening an Educational Conference in November 1947 for formulating a structure for the promulgation of quality education in the country. In pursuance of this, the then education minister of Sindh, Pir Illahi Bukhsh, piloted the Sindh Primary Education Act, 1947, to introduce a scheme of free and compulsory elementary education in six talukas of Sindh every year till it was extended to the whole province.[1] However, the Act was later repealed in 1962.

The practice of introducing schemes and policies and later rescinding them, without any proper evaluation, has become a recurring feature in Pakistan and Sindh's history. A major setback to the development of the education sector was the nationalisation of all private institutions in the early 1970s. The subsequent regimes only paid lip service to the education and social sectors. Financial allocations remained inadequate, supply of schools and teachers lagged behind the growing demand, and the quality of instruction remained sub-par. As a consequence, the present state of education in the country and in Sindh particularly does not appear very promising. High unemployment and poverty in the province can be traced back to the weak education system.

Article 25A of the Constitution of Pakistan has declared that the state shall provide free and compulsory education to all children aged 5 to 16. However, after the Eighteenth Amendment to the Constitution in 2010, this responsibility was delegated to the provinces who were then to decide their respective educational trajectories. Sindh is the first province to enact the Free and Compulsory Education Act (January 2013). This declaration by the government built dual expectations: one that the state shall provide opportunities to all to acquire education, second, that there will be no compromise on quality. This promise of equitable access is not limited to constitutional provision only; in fact, there are several conventions and accords that also bind the state. The Universal Declaration of Human Rights by the United Nations in 1948, the Millennium Development Goals (MDGs) till 2015, and Sustainable Development Goals to be achieved by 2030 are some of them. However, the province has failed to achieve targets for universal education by 2015 as over 6.6 million children are still out of school.[2] Moreover, access to educational facilities is still a major problem for the poor and less privileged segments of the population.

Table 4.1: Out of School Chidren in Sindh (in Thousand) (2015–16)

	Male	Female	Total
Primary	770	1,097	1,867
Middle	997	986	1,983
High	677	674	1,351
Higher Secondary	727	740	1,467
Total	3,171	3,497	6,668

Source: Ministry of Federal Education and Professional Training, *Pakistan Education Statistics 2015–16*, Islamabad, Government of Pakistan, 2017.

Table 4.2: Enrolment in Sindh (in Thousand) (2015–16)

Stage	Urban			Rural			Total		
	Boys	Girls	Total	Boys	Girls	Total	Boys	Girls	Total
Pre-Primary	560	491	1,052	365	244	610	926	736	1,662
Primary	1,013	878	1,891	1,271	735	2,005	2,284	1,612	3,896
Middle	359	333	692	265	125	390	623	458	1,081
High	217	202	418	154	59	214	371	261	632
Higher Secondary	108	97	205	141	62	203	249	158	408
Degree	-	-	-	-	-	-	48	41	89
Total	2,257	2,001	4,258	2,196	1,225	3,422	4,501	3,266	7,768
Total (Excluding Pre-Primary)	1,697	1,510	3,206	1,831	981	2,812	3,575	2,530	6,106

Source: Ministry of Federal Education and Professional Training, *Pakistan Education Statistics 2015–16*, Islamabad, Government of Pakistan, 2017.

At the provincial level in Sindh, out of 12.7 million children, almost 6.0 million (47 per cent) are enrolled in schools from primary to higher secondary while as many as 6.7 million (53 per cent) are out of school (see Table 4.2). The comparable figure at the national level is 55 per cent in schools and 45 per cent out of schools. The main reason for this lag is the low enrolment rates in Sindh's rural areas.

Sindh's adult literacy rate is higher than that of Punjab and the national average (Table 4.3) but it lags behind in the youth literacy rate. The main factor behind this indicator is the relatively low literacy among females. This finding is contrary to conventional wisdom that Sindh is urbanised province—with the highest per capita income it should have been at top.

Considering the trend over the years (Table 4.2), there has been a greater percentage increase in enrolment in different levels of institutions as compared to the percentage increase in the number of institutions. The increase in teachers does not translate well across all levels of institutes in relation to the corresponding increase in enrolment and is concentrated mostly at primary and secondary levels.

Before examining the status of education at the provincial level in some detail, it is advisable to look at the national picture to place Sindh in a comparative context.

Figure 4.1: Enrolment by Stage in Sindh (%) (2015–16)

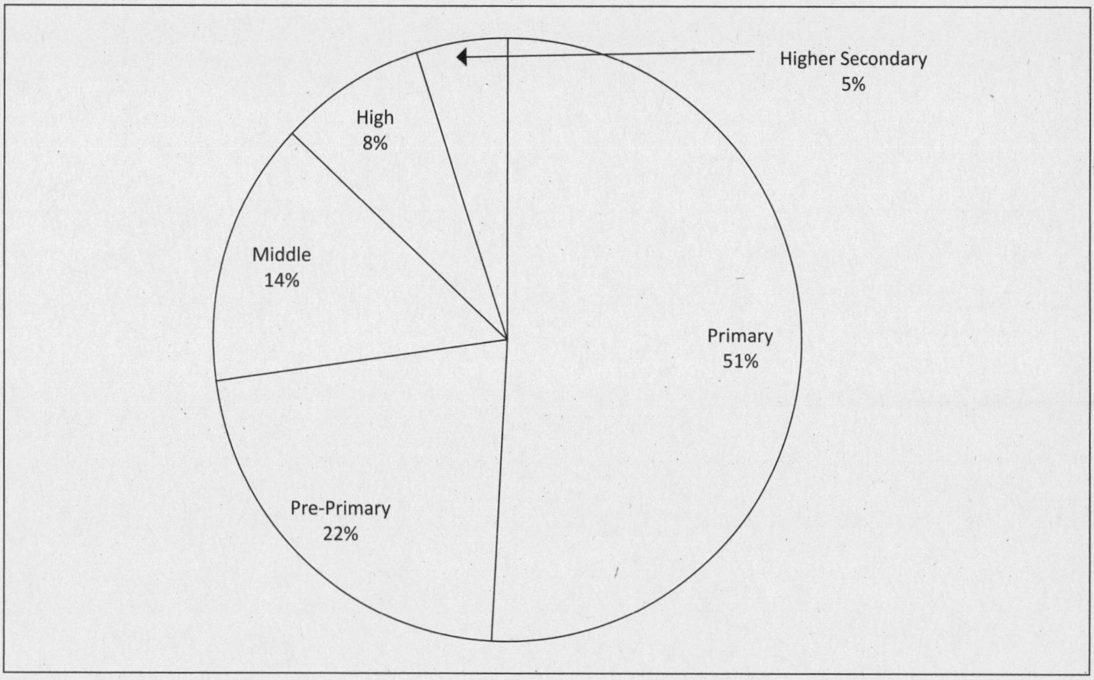

Source: Sindh Education Management Information System (SEMIS), *Sindh Education Profile 2015–16*, Karachi, Government of Sindh, n.d.

Table 4.3: Youth and Adult Literacy Rates (2015–16)

	Youth Literacy Rate (%)			Adult Literacy Rate (%)		
	Male	Female	Total	Male	Female	Total
Pakistan	80.6	64.1	72.4	69.1	45.2	57.2
Punjab	80.7	69.7	75.1	68.1	49.8	58.8
Sindh	77.8	61.2	70.2	72	46.2	59.8

Source: Ministry of Federal Education and Professional Training, *Pakistan Education Statistics 2015–16*, Islamabad, Government of Pakistan, 2017.

Table 4.4 shows that the net enrolment ratio of 56 per cent is much below that of the other countries in the region, falling short of the Article 25(1) requirement, and is a serious impediment for the absorption of the bulging youth population in the productive and employable labour force.

Before examining the status of education at the provincial level in some detail, it is advisable to look at the national picture to place Sindh in a comparative context.

Table 4.4: Pakistan's Primary and Secondary Education Status (2015–16)

	Gender	Population (in Million)	Gross Enrolment (in Million)	Net Enrolment (in Million)	Adjusted Net Enrolment Rate (%)	Out-of-School Children (in Million)
Primary Classes 1–5 (Age Group 5–9)	Male	11.49	12.02	9.51	83%	1.98
	Female	10.64	9.53	7.60	71%	3.05
	Total	22.13	21.55	17.10	77%	5.03
Middle Class 6–8	Male	6.53	3.90	3.46	53%	3.06
	Female	6.02	3.03	2.68	45%	3.33
	Total	120.55	6.92	6.15	49%	6.40
Secondary	Male	8.55	3.30	3.06	35%	5.49
	Female	7.95	2.37	2.22	27%	5.73
	Total	16.50	5.67	5.28	32%	11.21
Primary to Secondary Classes 1–12 (Age Group 5–16)	Male	26.56	19.21	16.03	60%	10.53
	Female	24.61	14.93	12.50	51%	12.11
	Total	51.17	34.14	28.53	56%	22.64

Source: Ministry of Federal Education and Professional Training, *Pakistan Education Statistics 2015–16*, Islamabad, Government of Pakistan, 2017.

Table 4.5: Literacy Rates for Pakistan, Sindh, and Punjab (2001–02 to 2014–15)

	2001–02	2004–05	2005–06	2006–07	2007–08	2008–09	2011–12	2012–13	2013–14	2014–15
Pakistan (%)	45	53	54	55	56	57	58	60	58	74
Punjab (%)	47	55	56	58	59	59	60	62	61	75
Sindh (%)	46	56	55	55	56	59	59	60	56	75

Source: *Pakistan Social and Living Measurement Survey 2014–2015*, Pakistan Bureau of Statistics, <http://www.pbs.gov.pk/sites/default/files//pslm/publications/PSLM_2014–15_National-Provincial-District_report.pdf>.

According to Table 4.4, literacy rates have increased over the years for Punjab, Sindh, and Pakistan. However, Pakistan and its provinces still lag behind neighbouring countries and strategies should be formulated so that out-of-school children can acquire literacy and numeracy, and contribute to society.

Public Education in Sindh

Public sector is the main provider of education in Sindh and therefore an analysis of the achievements and shortfalls of this sector is critical to complete understand the picture. From a quantitative perspective, the achievements with respect to increasing the number of schools, hiring more teachers, and raising enrolment falls short of the goals. Quality has also been declining. All these factors contribute to sub-standard education and may jeopardise the future of the children.

Table 4.6: Trends in Public Education (1970–71 and 2015–16)

Primary		1970–71	2015–16	Percentage Change (%)
Institutes		10,033	41,131	310
Enrolment	Total	830,754	2,429,921	192
	Male	661,894	1,485,534	124
	Female	168,860	944,387	459
Teachers		25,575	92,942	263
Middle				
Institutes		546	2,329	327
Enrolment		33,736	602,430	1,686
Teachers		2,957	13,610	360
Secondary				
Institutes		557	1,696	205
Enrolment		221,724	367,701	66
Teachers		9243	38,811	320
Colleges				
Institutes		112	235	109
Enrolment		71,994	438,064	509
Teachers		2,640	6,758	156
Technical and Vocational				
Institutes		39	603*	1,446
Enrolment		5036	79,801*	1,484
Teachers		343	2,970*	768
Universities				
Institutes		2	17	750
Enrolment		4,999	217,311	4,247

*Includes figures for public, private and other public. Source: Pakistan Bureau of Statistics, *25 Years of Statistics*, Islamabad, Government of Pakistan, n.d.; Ministry of Federal Education and Professional Training, *Pakistan Education Statistics 2015–16*, Islamabad, Government of Pakistan, 2017.

With a total of 45,447 schools across the province,[3] Sindh appears to have a dense network of schools. While this may seem like education is becoming accessible, it is not so. Out of 45,447 schools, 40,063 (88 per cent) are functional, i.e. having enrolment and teachers, whereas 4,123 are temporarily closed and the remaining 1,261 are non-viable, i.e. cannot be made functional.[4] The problem is further aggravated by inadequate transition to higher levels, depicting a deficit of planning and effective resource allocation.

Only 60 per cent of these completing primary education get to the middle school. While there are 41,131 primary schools, the number of middle schools in the province is a paltry 2,329. Most out-of-school children can therefore be found at this and a higher level of schooling.

Almost 90 per cent of total schools terminate at the primary level, creating a serious bottleneck right away for those completing primary education and aspiring to pursue further education. This lopsided approach has not been corrected as the entire emphasis seems to be on setting up primary schools throughout the province. While this emphasis is right, attention should be equally given to build up a pipeline transition by expanding the number of middle and secondary schools.

For every twenty-one primary schools, there is only one secondary school which shows that school rationalisation has been severely neglected. As per the Sindh Education Profile 2015–16, 58 per cent of the total students in Sindh are enrolled in primary classes.[6] The number of secondary schools is insufficient to accommodate these students upon their transition.

Table 4A (see Annexure) shows the imbalance between primary and post-primary schools which also varies across the province. Almost 50 per cent of the 29 districts have less than 10 per cent post-primary schools. This imbalance is one of the reasons why most out-of-the school children are in the age groups of middle and secondary schools.

This ratio is comparatively better only for Karachi where the percentage of post-primary schools ranges from 20 to 40 per cent.

As Karachi has a higher proportion of post-primary schools, it enjoys a comparative advantage in higher, professional, vocational, and technical education. The employment opportunities for these students are thereafter plentiful as compared to districts where post-primary institutions hardly exist.

Table 4.7: Distribution of Public Schools by Level in Sindh (2015–16)

School Level	Number	Percentage Share (%)
Primary	41,131	90.5
Middle	2,329	5.12
Secondary	1,696	3.73
Higher Secondary	291	0.64
Total Schools	45,447	100

Source: Sindh Education Management Information System (SEMIS), *Sindh Education Profile 2015–16*, Karachi Government of Sindh, n.d.

Although Sindh has a considerably large number of functional schools; their suitability for effective quality learning is open to question—9,499 schools in Sindh are one-room schools and 18,293 schools have only one teacher. With only one room in the school, students of multiple grades sit in the same classroom with a single teacher teaching multiple grades and multiple subjects. These teachers have no formal training to teach a variety of subjects of different levels of difficulty in such a setting. The distinction between grade levels and adherence to multiple curricula at the same time gets blurred in this process. The practice of a single teacher teaching multiple subjects to kids of different age groups should be a part of non-formal education for which teachers are particularly trained. However, owing to mismanagement, the distinction between formal and informal schooling seems to be eroding day by day.

The other area of concern is the dismal physical condition of the schools. There is a considerable consensus around basic dimensions of quality of education today. One such dimension includes the following definition:

'Environments that are healthy, safe, protective and gender-sensitive, and provide adequate resources and facilities.'[5]

In the light of this definition, a significant number of schools in Sindh do not have basic facilities which results in an environment non-conducive to learning.

There are altogether 7,120 schools in Sindh which do not have formal school premises.[6] Students either take their classes in open spaces or under the trees. Even if the school buildings exist, they are either dilapidated or do not have the requisite paraphernalia for a proper learning environment. Figure 4.2 shows that 50 per cent of the schools in Sindh do not have safe drinking water; 46 per cent are without toilets; 63 per cent without electricity; and 41 per cent without boundary walls.[7] There are only 10,155 schools in Sindh that have all the four basic facilities available within school premises. There have been unfortunate incidents of roofs falling down on students, costing their lives.

Figure 4.2: Lack of Basic Facilities in Public Schools Across Sindh (2015–16)

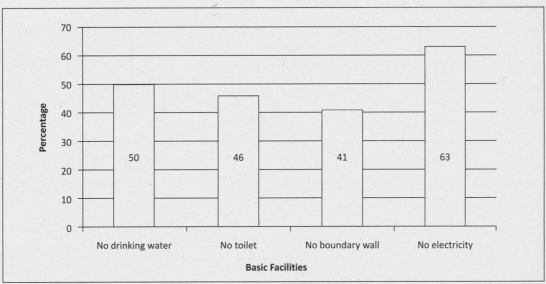

Source: Sindh Education Management Information System (SEMIS), *Sindh Education Profile 2015-16*, Karachi, Government of Sindh, n.d., pp. 30–3.

Having too many schools without required facilities exhibit poor planning and inert management. The non-availability of these basic amenities acts as a deterrent for parents to send their children to schools. Parents are particularly reluctant to send their daughters to schools without boundary walls and toilets as they add to their insecurity. Combining the percentages of girls' schools and mixed schools, there are altogether 77 per cent schools where girls are enrolled.[8] There is a high probability that the enrolment of girls in these schools might rise further if the essential facilities are provided, thus reducing gender disparity. Furthermore, non-availability of these amenities is also a strain on students' learning time, e.g. having to go out of school to fetch water and use the toilet. Some might not even return once they leave the school for these chores.

The government carries out school construction and their major repair and maintenance through the Education Works Department. Their teams visit schools to observe the situation and to confirm the need for construction and promise to revert later to commence the work. However, the school management awaits their return in despair knowing that the work will not begin anytime soon. Due to poor inter-department coordination and no regular follow-up to track progress, actions are put in abeyance with impunity. Even where schools are constructed or repaired, low-quality material is used, which defeats the very purpose of repair/construction in the first place.

ACCESS

Almost 70 per cent of the enrolment in Sindh falls in the combined pre-primary and primary enrolment category (Table 4.8). Having a share of 31 per cent of the total primary schools in Pakistan, the primary enrolment of 22 per cent (Table 4.10) against the national figure reflects underutilisation of resources, indicating a significant number of out of school children.[9]

Table 4.8: Student Enrolment by Stage in Sindh (2015–16)

School Stage	Enrolment	Percentage Share (%)
Pre-Primary	641,038	15
Primary	2,429,921	55
Middle	602,430	14
Secondary	367,701	8
Higher Secondary	353,289	8
Grand Total	4,394,379	100

Source: Sindh Education Management Information System (SEMIS), *Sindh Education Profile 2015–16*, Karachi, Government of Sindh, n.d., p. 13.

Table 4.9: Gross and Net Enrolment Rates of Sindh (2014–15)

School Level	Overall (Government, Not-for-Profit and Private Schools)		Government Schools Only*	
	GER (%)	NER (%)	GER (%)	NER (%)
Primary	79	61	34	27
Middle	55	34	16	13
Secondary	51	25	20	16
Higher Secondary	-	-	5	5

Source: Pakistan Bureau of Statistics, *Pakistan Social and Living Standards Measurement Survey 2014–15*, Islamabad, Statistics Division, Government of Pakistan, 2016.

* Sindh Education Management Information System (SEMIS), *Sindh Education Profile 2014–15*, Karachi, Government of Sindh, n.d.

Considering the gross and net enrolment ratios, enrolment falls significantly as students move up the academic level. With 11.6 per cent average drop-out rate at the primary level, which adds up to almost 58 per cent over five years of primary education, the remaining students who eventually transition to the secondary level do not have a sufficient number of secondary or higher secondary public schools to opt for. It is alarming to note that the difference between gross and net enrolment rates is wider when the level of schooling increases, resulting in 18 per cent, 21 per cent, and 26 per cent difference at primary, secondary, and middle levels respectively. Table 4.9 shows the rates for the government schools alone as well, where the same trend of lower gross enrolments could be observed from primary to secondary. However, it is interesting to note that enrolment rates depict a slight increment of 4 per cent from middle to secondary level, reflecting that students from low-cost private schools get themselves enrolled in government schools to complete their matric (grade 10). Keeping aside the very slight increase in the public schooling enrolment at the secondary school level, it does not refute the argument that enrolment rates decrease as the students move up in the hierarchy of school levels.

This, however, puts a burden on the economy since the pathway to adding to human capital is disrupted, leading to economic loss for the province and the state at large. Similarly, without proper education, these children get stuck in an unending cycle of poverty, which traps future generations as well.

Table 4.10: Stage-wise Enrolment in Public Schools of Sindh as a Percentage of Pakistan (2015–16)

School Stages	Sindh	Pakistan	Sindh's Percentage (%)
Pre-Primary	641,038	4,412,936	15
Primary	2,429,921	11,088,762	22
Middle	602,430	3,907,828	15
Secondary	367,701	2,155,758	17
Higher Secondary	353,289	1,302,834	27

Source: Ministry of Federal Education and Professional Training, *Pakistan Education Statistics 2015–16*, Islamabad, Government of Pakistan, 2017, p. 63.

Table 4.10 shows Sindh's contribution to national enrolment. Sindh has a small share of 15 per cent in pre-primary enrolment which could be due to absence of Early Childhood Care Education (ECCE) classes. However, the percentage increases for primary with even higher percentage of 27 per cent for higher secondary.

When it comes to ensuring access to education for all, it is the state's responsibility to ensure it, while the providers could be diverse. The record of public sector schools is far from being satisfactory. Sindh's public school system is extensive but it is marred by serious issues. Besides improper schools, teacher rationalisation, and poor infrastructure, the students who do manage to attend schools have very low learning levels. The Government of Sindh has been conducting the Standardised Achievement Test (SAT) for the past four years (since 2012–13) to gauge the students' competence in language (English, Sindhi and Urdu), science, and maths. However, the overall results are stagnant at around 22 per cent for the past four years, which, by any standards are extremely low.[10] As per its reform plans, SAT is conducted for grade 5 and grade 8 students, but a low score on this test is not a failure of grades 5 or 8 alone; in fact, it shows sub-standard learning in all previous grades as well. It also reflects a lack of intervention to alter the results in these four years or blatant failure in case there has been any intervention per se.

STUDENT–TEACHER RATIO (STR)

The public school system in Sindh has a total enrolment of more than 4 million students across the province with almost 0.15 million teachers.[11] The overall Student–Teacher Ratio (STR) as per the Sindh Education

Management Information System (SEMIS) 2015–16 is 30:1 for Sindh. Seventy-four per cent of the total students in government schools are enrolled in rural areas, whereas 26 per cent of students are in urban areas. Sixty-five per cent of the total teachers are posted in rural areas, whereas the remaining 35 per cent are in urban area (see Table 4P, Annexure).

This gives an interesting contrast between STR of schools in rural and urban areas of Sindh. There is one teacher for every thirty students in rural areas as opposed to one teacher for every twenty students in urban areas. However, these are averages which mask large variations across districts. Karachi Central and Hyderabad districts have ratios as low as 14:1 and 17:1 respectively. Ghotki has 37 students per teacher and Tando Allahyar 36—almost thrice as many students as in Karachi Central or Hyderabad schools.

The student–teacher ratio is an indicator of resource allocation, i.e. teachers by the government, but the process seems to have become highly politicised. Besides the reckless construction of schools for political gains, teacher deployment is yet another impediment to quality education. Teachers use their political affiliations to stay or get transferred to schools of their preference or convenience even if there is no need in that school for another teacher. This results in a serious imbalance as some schools have more students without a sufficient number of teachers while in others there is an excess of teachers because there is not enough enrolment. This misallocation of teacher resources particularly in subjects such as Science and Mathematics perpetuates backwardness in less developed districts. As these teachers are in greater demand they choose to opt for large urban centres with all amenities for themselves and their families.

Another serious problem until recently was teacher absenteeism. As the teachers were largely appointed to their jobs by their political patrons, they did not bother to turn up to their duties. The schools were open but there were no teachers available to teach. The change in the recruitment system to evolve selection on merit rather than connections is beginning to make some difference.

In 2015, the government introduced a biometric system whereby every employee in the education department (teaching and non-teaching) was biometrically entered in the system for official record.[12] It was the first time that the department tried compiling data of all of its employees. Teachers in government schools had to get themselves registered and many had to return to their schools of original posting in case they were working somewhere else. Due to this exercise, a number of ghost teachers were identified who were previously drawing salaries but never physically went to school. This was a significant step by the government which received severe backlash from the teaching staff/teachers' unions who blamed the government for unnecessary, stringent, and unfair intervention. Since teachers were made to go back to their original schools due to the biometric system, the schools of their current posting ended up having no teachers and consequently many schools had to be temporarily closed. While introducing interventions, the government should think holistically and devise remedial actions for all possible outcomes.

This biometric system was the first step of the major reform of Monitoring and Evaluation. The Education Department set up its own monitoring and evaluation directorate and established district offices to keep monitoring assistants for random school visits to monitor teachers' attendance, verify students' enrolment, and capture information on the state of schools' infrastructure. This monitoring system has also helped in containing teachers absenteeism. Teachers would previously only draw salaries and either not work at all or work somewhere else for additional earning while retaining their jobs in schools. As teachers' attendance is taken through biometric device, hence implanting a temporary replacement to complete the number of teacher count in the school was curtailed. Initially teachers' salaries were being stopped for being absent from school, giving a huge jolt to teachers who had taken their jobs for granted. This indeed is a commendable step but those with connections can still find a way out. Some of the incidents have been reported where monitoring assistants have submitted complaints against certain teachers and their complaints were removed from the digital record. This adds an element of partiality in education governance which has to be rectified for the system to remain effective.

GOVERNANCE

To rationalise physical and human resources and to improve the overall management of schools, the School Education and Literacy Department of the Government of Sindh introduced the School Consolidation Policy in 2012. Through this initiative, distinct government schools operating in the same campus, or catering to the same child population in the local community are converted into a single functional school. As a result of this policy, 4,095 schools have been merged into 1,350 campus schools so far.[13]

This policy is a step towards improved governance. After the implementation of the School Consolidation Policy, several primary schools have been merged into secondary schools, which has increased the probability of the students transitioning to further grades instead of dropping out. Prior to this policy, teachers in nearby school units would strictly teach in their respective units and would not try compensating for teacher absenteeism or shortage in other (nearby) schools. The policy, after merging the nearby school units into a single campus school, has tried breaking this barrier to improve teacher rationalisation. Furthermore, before consolidation, the resources which were commonly used by all schools would not be taken care of as no one would hold the responsibility of doing so. For instance, if multiple schools had a common playground, then none of them would clean it, stating that it was not being used solely by them. Hence, after consolidation, all resources come under one management which improved resource allocation and utilisation.

However, in reality, this has not been as successful as it was thought to be. Upon merging multiple schools into a single campus school, the headmasters (or headmistresses) of the previous school units now become section in-charges and report to the campus head, which they find demeaning. Further, it is deemed unacceptable if the section in-charges have a higher basic pay scale (BPS) grade than that of the campus heads. Similarly, teachers do not always agree to teach a different grade or a different subject which obstructs cooperation and understanding that this policy significantly rests on. The school consolidation policy has a strong human element which needs proper handling for a successful change of school management and the attainment of intended objectives. These have not so far been attained. Policies tend to fail when they are imposed on schools without taking the stakeholders into confidence and building their support for the policy since they are the actual implementers. Furthermore, a proper mechanism of continuous support needs to be devised by the government so that the schools are not left on their own.

EDUCATION BUDGET

It is generally believed that the government does not have the required financial resources to revamp the public education system. In reality, the major problem with Sindh's education is underspending and not a lack of funds.

Table 4.11 shows that the total budget allocation for education in Sindh jumped from PKR 5.1 billion to PKR157.5 billion over the last decade—a spectacular increase of over thirty times. The corresponding change in enrolment, student–teacher ratio, learning outcomes, and, facilities improvement shows no perceptible impact of higher allocations. The utilisation rate varied between 84–87 per cent in this period but access, quality, or governance indicators hardly depict any advance or upward movement.

Although this exceptional escalation in allocations and utilisation is recent, the education budget has been continuously increasing since 1970. On average, there has been an increase of more than 250 per cent in the education budget every five years from 1970–71 to 2015–16. However, almost 88 per cent of the total education budget on average had been recurrent expenditures, leaving too little for development expenditures. Of course, education is a highly labour-intensive activity but the salaries of the teachers have risen at an accelerated pace regardless of their competence and contribution. The education budget for FY 2015–16 was 157.7 billion with 92 per cent (144.7 billion) in recurrent budget, whereas the remaining 8 per cent (12.8 billion) was for development.

Table 4.11: Sindh Education Budgetary Estimates and Actual Spending (in PKR Million)
(1970–71 to 2015–16)

	1970–71	1975–76	1980–81	1985–86	1990–91	1995–96	2000–01	2005–06	2010–11	2015–16
Total Education	162	463	865	2,266	4,562	11,463	15,087	5,099	25,618	157,517
Recurrent	107	401	740	1,802	3,893	10,202	14,210	4,099	18,678	144,678
Development	56	62	125	464	669	1261	877	1000	6,866	12,839
Percentage share of Budgeted Recurrent and Development Expenditure (%)										
Particulars	1970–71	1975–76	1980–81	1985–86	1990–91	1995–96	2000–01	2005–06	2010–11	2015–16
Total	100	100	100	100	100	100	100	100	100	100
Recurrent	66	87	86	80	85	89	94	80	73	92
Development	34	13	14	20	15	11	6	20	27	8

	Actual Spending									
Particulars	1970–71	1975–76	1980–81	1985–86	1990–91	1995–96	2000–01	2005–06	2010–11	2015–16
Actual Total Spending	122	412	N/A	1,731	3,643	8,497	11,869	27,448	19,462	131,938
Recurrent	N/A	N/A	N/A	1,555	3,540	8,417	11,856	25,010	14,246	123,608
Development	N/A	N/A	N/A	176	102	80	13	2437	5,216	8,330
Actual Spending as a Percentage of Budgeted Figures (%)										
Particulars	1970–71	1975–76	1980–81	1985–86	1990–91	1995–96	2000–01	2005–06	2010–11	2015–16
Percentage of Actual Total Spending	N/A	N/A	N/A	76	80	74	79	538	87	84
Percentage of Actual Recurrent Spending	N/A	N/A	N/A	86	91	83	86	610	76	85
Percentage of Actual Development Spending	N/A	N/A	N/A	38	15	6	1	244	75	65

Source: Finance department, *Annual Budget Statement*, Karachi, Government of Sindh, various years.

The distinction between recurrent and development budgets in sectors such as education and health should be replaced with an integrated programme budget. The planned outcomes should be costed out and allocations should then be made for each component and input needed to achieve those outcomes. The drivers of the budget should be desired indicators of access, quality, and relevance.

Table 4.12 indicates that the public spending on education as a percentage of GDP has been increasing on both the federal and provincial levels over the years. For Sindh, there has been a 90 per cent increase in education spending as a percentage of GDP from 0.22 in 2006–07 to 0.42 in 2013–14.

Table 4.12: Public Spending on Education as a Percentage of GDP (2006–07 to 2013–14)

	Federal (%)	Provincial (%)	National (%)	Sindh (%)
2006–07	0.39	1.16	1.55	0.22
2007–08	0.40	1.39	1.79	0.36
2008–09	0.34	1.50	1.84	0.37
2009–10	0.32	1.45	1.77	0.36
2010–11	0.33	1.45	1.78	0.40
2011–12	0.28	1.63	1.91	0.33
2012–13	0.31	1.78	2.09	0.43
2013–14	0.34	1.77	2.11	0.42

Source: Muhammad Sabir, *Agenda for the 8th NFC: Lessons from the 7th NFC Award, Post-7th NFC Developments and Emerging Issues*, Karachi, Social Policy and Development Centre, 2014.

The Private School System

The constitutional pledge emphatically underscores that the state will provide free and compulsory education to all children beyond societal barriers. The rationale behind this promise is to promote social equality by enabling equal access to educational opportunities. However, there is a misperception that the constitutional obligation implies that the government would be the exclusive provider of schooling. The government has to ensure that the goal of universal access to primary education is met but it can rely upon an array of delivery channels and service providers such as private, non-governmental, non-profit community, charitable, and philanthropic organisations. It would be incumbent upon the government to ascertain that the poor students are not deprived of education because they cannot afford the direct and indirect expenses of schooling. A voucher scheme has been introduced whereby the government finances education of the children of poor families who choose to study at private schools. A rising middle class aspiring to provide better education to their children in this competitive environment is also pushing the demand for private schooling.

Table 4.13: Enrolment in Private School System for Pakistan and Sindh (in Thousand) (2015–16)

Stage	Urban			Rural			Total		
	Boys	Girls	Total	Boys	Girls	Total	Boys	Girls	Total
Pakistan									
Pre-Primary	1,294.3	1,099.6	2,303.9	1,053	765.7	1,818.6	2.347.3	1.865.3	4,212.6
Primary	2,153.5	1,790	3,943.5	1,974.7	1,372.7	3,347.5	4,128.2	3,162.7	7,290.9
Middle	755.0	629.7	1,384.7	597.5	423.7	1,021.2	1,352.5	1,053.4	2,405.9
High	440.8	359.1	799.9	229.5	180.5	410	670.4	539.6	1,209.9
Higher Secondary	152.6	108.4	261	54.7	56.4	111.1	207.3	164.7	372.0

table continued

Stage	Urban			Rural			Total		
	Boys	Girls	Total	Boys	Girls	Total	Boys	Girls	Total
Degree	72.6	54.8	127.4	0.3	1.3	1.6	72.8	56.2	129
Total			8,826.4			6,710.0			15,620.3
Total (excluding Pre-Primary)			6,522.5			4891.4			11,407.7

Sindh									
Stage	Urban			Rural			Total		
	Boys	Girls	Total	Boys	Girls	Total	Boys	Girls	Total
Pre-Primary	505.0	430.0	935.0	40	28.0	68.5	545.4	458.3	1,003.8
Primary	688.0	574.0	1,263.0	63.8	41.9	105.6	751.8	616.4	1,368.2
Middle	235.0	193.0	428.0	15.6	7.2	22.8	250.7	200.6	451.3
High	132.0	112.0	245.0	4.4	2.1	6.6	136.9	114.6	251.4
Higher Secondary	27.0	22.0	49.0	2.0	0.188	2.2	29.0	21.9	50.9
Degree	1.7	2.6	4.2	-	-	-	1,668	2,565	4.2
Total	1588.7	1333.6	2924.2	125.8	267.2	205.7	3381.8	1,414.2	3,129.9
Total (excluding Pre-Primary)			1,989.2			137.2			2,126.1

Source: Ministry of Federal Education and Professional Training, *Pakistan Education Statistics 2015–16*, Islamabad, Government of Pakistan, 2017.

A comparison with Table 4.2, which covers the total public and private school enrolment in Sindh, shows that the share of private schools in all stages of schooling has reached almost 40 per cent of the total in 2015–16.

There has been an explosion of private schooling mostly at the primary but at higher levels as well and, somewhat surprisingly, private schooling cannot be considered an urban elite phenomenon alone.[14] One out of three school-going children in Pakistan is enrolled in a private school.[15] Private schools range from high-cost elite schools (charging very high fees, around PKR 20,000 per month) to low-cost schools (charging around PKR 100 per month). Hence, private schooling has become accessible to varying socio-economic strata of the society. It is interesting to see that the growth of private schools is not limited to urban Sindh alone—it engulfs rural Sindh as well.

Figures 4.3A and 4.3B give a quick glimpse of the percentage of children enrolled in public and private schools across different provinces. For both the age groups (6 to 10 and 11 to 15), the participation rate in private schools in Sindh was around 19 per cent in 2010–11 which was lower than that of Punjab's. But it must have risen by now. However, the participation rate in public schools across various provinces has a slight variation. In provincial comparison, it is also evident that a fall in participation rate in private schools is offset by a rise in the percentage of out-of-school children.

Figures 4.3A and 4.3B also show a correlation between the choice of schooling system and socio-economic standing. Those with sound economic backgrounds lean towards private schools, whereas the drift towards public education is greater among households with poor economic status.

Figure 4.3A: Percentage Distribution of Children by Schooling Status and Province
(Age Group: 6–10) (2010–11)

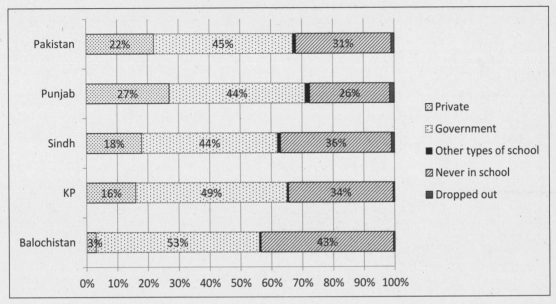

Source: Quynh T. Nguyen and Dhushyanth Raju, 'Private School Participation in Pakistan', *Lahore Journal of Economics*, 20/1, pp. 1–46.

Figure 4.3B: Percentage Distribution of Children by Schooling Status and Province
(Age Group: 11–15) (2010–11)

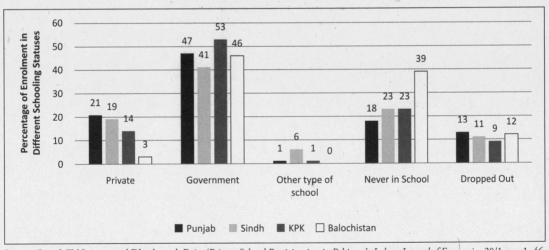

Source: Quynh T. Nguyen, and Dhushyanth Raju, 'Private School Participation in Pakistan', *Lahore Journal of Economics*, 20/1, pp. 1–46.

However, the growing numbers of low-cost private schools in the province are attracting children from low-income and disadvantaged households also. Parents prefer low cost private schools over public schools because the learning outcomes are perceived to be better in the former.

The characteristics that contribute towards the growth of low-cost private schools in rural Sindh are moderately educated teachers who by and large live in the same village, relatively low teachers' salaries compared to public schools which minimises the fee structures, co-educational structure, and geographical accessibility.

As opposed to the lower class, children of belonging to the upper-middle class residing in urban localities mostly attend high-cost private schools offering foreign curricula and international examination systems (O and A levels). These schools are staffed with more qualified and trained teachers, well-equipped classrooms with all essential facilities of good quality, and imported teaching–learning materials.

This concept of private elite school system was initially introduced by the British colonisers with the sole purpose of educating the ruling class. Adam Curle emphasises, 'in fact, as in England, so in [the] Indian subcontinent the education of the ruling elite was carried out in a virtually separate parallel school system from which the children of the lower order were excluded by both social and economic sanctions.'[16] During Zulfikar Ali Bhutto's regime, a massive campaign was launched to nationalise educational institutes as a result of which 175 private colleges and 3,334 private schools were nationalised by 1 September 1972.[17] This step was well-received by teachers, media and the general public as it promised a framework of social mobility for the underprivileged with greater participation in education with better access, but the results proved to be a setback of educational quality and access. Teachers became unionised, using political affiliation and collective bargaining to obtain higher pay and greater benefits, which preoccupied them at the expense of their professional duties. Seniority and length of service became the sole criteria for promotion and performance whereas dedication suffered.

Figure 4.4A: Percentage Distribution of Children by Schooling Status and Socioeconomic Sub-Group (Age Group: 6–10) (2010–11)

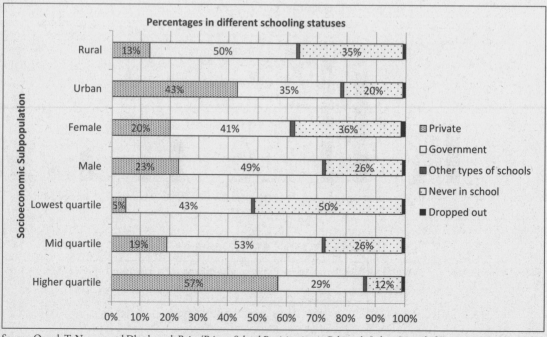

Source: Quynh T. Nguyen and Dhushyanth Raju, 'Private School Participation in Pakistan', *Lahore Journal of Economics*, 20/1, pp. 1–46.

Figure 4.4B: Percentage Distribution of Children by Schooling Status and Socioeconomic Sub-Group Age Group: 11–15 (2010–11)

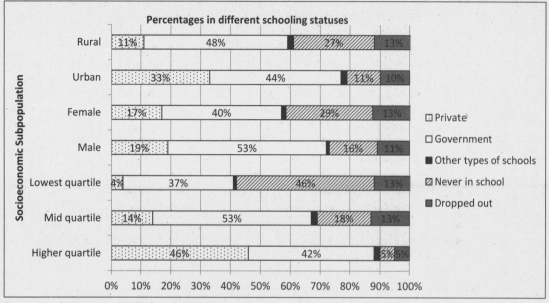

Source: Quynh T. Nguyen and Dhushyanth Raju, 'Private School Participation in Pakistan', *Lahore Journal of Economics*, 20/1, pp. 1–46.

However, elite schools were exempted from nationalisation on the condition that they would admit students on merit, disregarding their financial background. About 221 high-fee schools were exempted as they agreed to admit lower-class children.[18] This concession did not prove to be much beneficial as children from low-income households could not clear the admission tests.

The distribution of children of age group 11–15 shows that one-fourth of the students in the rural areas are out of school compared to only 11 per cent of their urban counterparts. The lowest and mid quartiles send their children to government schools while the higher quartiles preferred to send their children to private schools.

Figures 4.4A and 4.4B illustrate the participation rate in public and private schools across different socio-economic sub-groups. For both the age groups (6–10 and 11–15), it can be seen that the enrolment in private schools is greater in urban areas than in rural areas whereas it is opposite for public schools which have larger share in the total enrolment in rural areas. This disparity is also evident across genders. It is interesting to note that the gender disparity is comparatively lower in private schools than in public schools. For instance, for the age group 6–10, the difference between male and female percentage of enrolment is 3 percentage points, whereas it is 8 percentage points for public schools. Similarly, for the lower quartile, i.e. low income households, the participation rate in private schools is lower, which increases for the middle quartile and reaches the highest rate for those in the higher quartile.

In the 1980s, Public-Private Partnership (PPP) was invoked to provide education to the masses and the private sector was invited to share the responsibility.[19] Following this announcement, non-elite private schools began emerging. They used the English language as a catchy educational product which was not being offered by public schools.

The Sindh Public-Private Partnership Act was passed in 2010, under which the government and its agencies could enter into agreements with private parties to jointly design, finance, operate and maintain projects. Sindh was a late comer in adopting this mode of delivery. On 3 December 2013, the first Public Private Partnership (PPP) node was set up in the Education Department with the mandate of engaging with the private sector and signing and administering contracts. The PPP node currently has ten partners with over $15 million provided by the government for on-going and new innovative schemes.

Under the PPP, the government of Sindh began contracting out management of public sector schools to credible education management organisations (EMOs) from the private sector. These organisations were to improve the functioning of public sector schools by introducing innovations, modernising the education system, addressing management gaps, maintaining and upgrading the school facilities (where required), and working cooperatively with teachers, schools staff, school management committees, surrounding communities, and local tiers of the Education Department. Initially, the roll-out of EMOs was carried out in schools under the USAID-Sindh Basic Education Programme and is now being extended to other public schools. Similarly, the government is trying to improve schools through bilaterals, NGOs, INGOs, and foundations. For instance, World Vision is helping the government rehabilitate schools in flood-devastated areas. The government is also providing endowment funds to private organisations for revitalisation of public schools. Recently, the Sindh government entrusted Akhuwat Foundation with the management of Narain Jagan Nath Vidya (NJV) School—the first and oldest public educational institute established in 1855 in the province—with the same mandate.

The idea behind private sector participation was to lend a helping hand in this endeavour of educational provision by the government. However, looking at the scale of the public school network, the reach of public–private partnership still remains insignificant. For instance, selecting two schools in Thatta and Shaheed Benazirabad districts for state-of-the-art construction through the Turkish Cooperation and Coordination Agency (TIKA) may not create much of a difference as the majority of the school buildings in these two districts are in dilapidated conditions.[20] The long-term sustainability of such high-cost projects financed by external donors would remain open to question. Even if the web of PPP is further woven, it would still leave a significant burden on the government to improve and upgrade the already existing public school system to an acceptable level.

The Government of Sindh also established the Sindh Education Foundation (SEF) in 1992 as an initiative to promote quality education and empower the youth of this country, primarily focusing on those living in the remote and disadvantaged areas. Initially the Foundation started by giving grants and loans to educational institutes but today, with support from the School Education & Literacy Department of the Government of Sindh, they have a network of over 2,000 schools and educational centres and over 350,000 beneficiaries.

SEF is promoting education through projects such as the Adopt-A-School-Programme, Early Learning Programme, Existing School Support Programme and the Adolescent and Adult Learning and Training Programme. The Sindh Education Foundation is one of the largest educational foundations in Pakistan and has drawn support from private non-government organisations and individuals who want to contribute to education. Combining financial resources and outreach from the government and management capacity from the private sector, SEF is trying to overcome the problems faced by the public sector schools. If scaled up and successfully executed, this can become an impressive model solution to improve access to the children of poor households to quality education.

Low-cost private schools attracted students on the premise that the learning outcomes would be better than those in the public sector schools. Preliminary evidence suggests that the quality of education and learning outcomes are no different in private schools. The private school advantage over public school is only marginal.[21] In this case, a significant percentage of students enrolled in low-cost private schools and public schools are at stake because their compromised learning will hardly enable them to transcend beyond their current social strata, hindering their social mobility. The government has to introduce an effective monitoring mechanism for gauging learning outcomes so that they adhere to minimum acceptable standards. This mechanism should be applicable to both private and public schools.

Early Education Childhood Care and Education (ECCE)

It has been globally recognised that early childhood education is a significant investment to help children engage in early child survival, protection, learning, and development with far greater chances of transition to primary and later, secondary education. Research shows that children exposed to stimulating environments at an early age have enhanced cognitive, verbal, and social development skills which are maintained into the first few years of school.[22] These kids are also more likely to have higher IQ and tend to demonstrate higher levels of school achievement and better social adjustment.[23]

Early Childhood Care and Education in Pakistan was first touched upon in the first National Education Conference in November 1947. It was then decided that the primary education committee would provide guidelines to include pre-primary education in the mainstream education system. Early Childhood Care and Education has been the focal point in educational policies thereafter.

Table 4.14: The Evolution of ECCE in Pakistan (1947–2009)

Timelines	Policy Developments on ECCE
1947	Viewing Nursery as an integral part of mainstream education at the Education Conference in 1947
1950s–1980s	Kachi classes as a means of familiarising children with the school setting; No education policy during the four decades made any reference to ECCE
1992	Education policy proposed to mainstream Kachi classes
1998	National Education Policy charts out the need for ECCE
2001–15	National Plan of Action for EFA (2001–15) charts out a complete plan for mainstreaming ECCE in the formal education system, through sensitisation of stakeholders, allocation of funds, engaging with the private sector, etc.
2002	National ECCE Curriculum developed Sindhi version of the revised National ECCE Curriculum made available
2001–04	In the Education Sector Reform Action Plan, ECCE is introduced as an Innovative Programme implemented across Pakistan with federal funds.
2009	National Education Policy proposes that ECCE is made part of mainstream education, integrated in all primary schools, and suggests action plans.

Source: School Education and Literacy Department, *Sindh Education Sector Plan 2014–18*, Karachi, Government of Sindh, n.d.

Public schools offer one year of Kachi as opposed to three years of pre-primary education in private schools. A major milestone was achieved in 2002 when the ECCE curriculum was devised. However, it is rather disappointing to see that something which was highlighted in 1947 could not materialise until 2002—more than fifty years later. In fact, when the ECCE need was again reiterated in the 1998 National Education Policy, a new chapter was opened and the previous policies which could serve as a baseline were discontinued.

The Government of Pakistan is a signatory of Education for All (EFA) declaration which was signed in 2000 at the Dakar Conference. Therefore, Pakistan abides by the agreement to allocate necessary resources to achieve the objectives of EFA, one of which is to improve and expand early childhood education and care. The Sindh Education Sector Plan (2014–18) also recognises the importance of Early Childhood Education and Early Childhood Development in helping the transition from pre-primary to primary and post-primary education levels. However, it seems verbal emphasis is yet to be translated into organised and effective action.

According to the Sindh Education Sector Review 2015–16, the task of prescribing minimum standards for ECCE is still in process. The School Education and Literacy Department is still aiming to begin implementation on ECCE policy with 1,100 teachers yet to be recruited. Similarly, the curriculum to be followed also needs to be reviewed and revised. So far, only two ECCE centres have been set up and more ECCE classes in campus schools are being planned. At present, the teachers teaching in Kachi/ECCE classes do not hold relevant qualification which negates the very purpose of the initiative. Untrained teachers actually do more harm. Planned, systematic and consistent efforts need to be made for effective Early Childhood Care and Education for better child learning and development. This is essential as these ECCE classes later serve as feeder classes for primary and later post-primary education.

Primary Education

Primary education has been a focal point of policies since Independence. National Education Commission of 1947 stressed on achieving universal primary education in twenty years. Furthermore, the subsequent five-year plans realised the need for promoting primary education. Therefore, new primary schools were constructed and teacher training centres were established to ensure adequate transmission of knowledge. In 1970, it was claimed that Pakistan was likely to attain 100 per cent literacy by 2010; however, we are still lagging behind, giving ourselves more time to attain goals for which deadlines have long been missed.

Sindh has a total of 41,131 public-primary schools, which account for almost 91 per cent of the total number of government schools in the province. Seventy-nine per cent of these schools are functional with an enrolment of around 2.5 million students.[24] Over the years, there has been a steady rise in the number of primary schools in Sindh; from 2000 to 2015, the number of primary schools increased by almost 52 per cent. The rise in the number of primary schools can be attributed to educational policies which have focused on building primary schools across the nation. For example, the fifth 5-Year Plan (1978–83) proposed to spend 33 per cent of development expenditure on primary education. However, in recent years the number of primary schools has fallen due to the government's School Consolidation Policy due to which a number of schools have been merged with other nearby schools to constitute a single school unit for better management.

Table 4.15: Enrolment in All Primary Schools of Sindh (2015–16)

Population of School Going Children (in Million)	Enrolment			Participation Rate (%)
	Public	Private	Other Public Sector	
7.3*	2.4	1.4	0.1	53.4

* Projected Population from the *Sindh Education Profile 2015–16*.

Source: Ministry of Federal Education and Professional Training, Academy of Educational Planning and Management, Islamabad, Government of Pakistan, 2017.

Table 4.15 shows that the enrolment in public primary schools was 62 per cent that of the total enrolment. The Global Education Monitoring Report 2016 estimates the total number of out-of-school children in Pakistan at all three levels at 21.5 million. Most of these children are from the middle, secondary, and higher secondary stages in Sindh. At the primary stage, the proportion is much lower compared to the higher stages (Table 4.17).

Table 4.16: Enrolment in Public Primary Schools of Sindh (2001–02 to 2015–16)

Year	Population (Age Group 5–9)			Enrolment			Participation Rate (%)		
	Boys	Girls	Total	Boys	Girls	Total	Boys	Girls	Total
2001–02	3,274,910	2,951,165	6,226,075	1,517,606	831,078	2,348,684	46	28	38
2005–06	2,973,691	2,657,645	5,631,336	1,708,472	1,098,001	2,806,473	57	41	50
2010–11	3,382,723	3,026,474	6,409,197	1,582,415	1,071,387	2,653,802	47	35	41
2015–16	3,853,975*	3,451,906*	7,305,881*	1,485,534	944,387	2,429,921	39	27	33

* Projected values.

Source: Sindh Education Management Information System (SEMIS), *Sindh Education Profile* (various years), Karachi, Government of Sindh (various years).

Table 4.17: Out of School Children in Sindh (2015–16)

Levels	Ages	No. of Children enrolled*	Number of Out of School Children (OOSC)
Pre-Primary	1 to 4	1,662,033	-
Primary	5 to 9	3,896,177	1,866,464
Middle	10 to 12	1,081,480	1,982,472
Secondary	13 to 16	631,959	1,350,659
Higher Secondary	16 to 18	407,743	1,467,673

*Enrolment includes public, other public and private sector schools however, the enrolment in unregistered madrassas is not included.
Source: Ministry of Federal Education and Professional Training, *Pakistan Education Statistics 2015–16*, Islamabad, Government of Pakistan, 2017.

Table 4.18: Provincial Comparison of Public Primary Enrolment between Sindh and Punjab (2015–16)

	Primary Enrolment		Percentage of Total Enrolment (%)	
	Sindh	Punjab	Sindh	Punjab
Male	1,485,534	2,664,165	61	52
Female	944,387	2,493,806	39	48
Total	2,429,921	5,157,971	100	100

Source: Ministry of Federal Education and Professional Training, *Pakistan Education Statistics 2015–16*, Islamabad, Government of Pakistan, 2017.

Table 4.18 shows that Sindh has a greater gender difference in its primary enrolment as compared to Punjab's. Punjab has almost reached a parity point between male and female enrolment but Sindh is still beset with greater gender disparity and that is because of the low ratio of female enrolment in the rural areas. One of the strong influences on female enrolment rates is security and inadequate toilet facilities for the girls. Table 4.19 shows that only half of the schools have toilet facilities and boundary walls.

Table 4.19: Number of Functional Primary Schools with Facilities (2015–16)

Facilities	Number of Schools	Percentage (%)
Electricity	13,487	33
Toilets	20,068	49
Drinking Water	18,679	45
Boundary Wall	21,576	52
Library	88 (132*)	0.3
Playgrounds	5,317 (6043*)	15
No. of Schools with all the amenities stated above	34 (430*)	0.08

* Schools of all levels Source: Sindh Education Management Information System (SEMIS), *Sindh Education Profile 2015–16*, Karachi, Government of Sindh, n.d.

It is alarming to see that there are only thirty-four schools in Sindh that have all the facilities listed above. The lack of facilities discourages parents from sending their children to schools. In addition to lack of basic physical facilities, parents have serious reservation regarding learning outcomes. According to SAT (2015–16), learning outcomes for grade 5 students are around 23 to 24 per cent on an average which also raises questions about teacher competence.

The enrolment in schools gradually drops as students move up. However, the reasons are not too difficult to comprehend. There is a serious shortage of middle schools even in areas where there is a large cluster of primary schools that can act as the feeder for them. Ninety-three per cent of the primary schools have less than five classrooms.[25] This means primary schools have a significant barrier as they have to turn down students who are underage for grade 1 and in the absence of Kachi, they might never be academically eligible. Similarly, an ideal primary school should have at least five classrooms, assuming that there is only one section for each grade. With less than five classrooms, students of multiple grades have to be adjusted in one, which hinders students' learning. Therefore, the students either move to other schools with proper classrooms or simply drop out. As per the SEMIS 2015–16, the transition rate from primary to middle education was 61 per cent for Sindh.[26] With an average drop-out rate of 11.6 per cent for primary (grades 1–5),[27] almost 40 per cent of the students discontinue their education post-primary.[28]

The construction of one or two classroom schools or schools without a minimum required number of classrooms cannot be backed by any rational educational policy. They simply reflect an ad hoc approach to providing employment to teachers who then serve as election officials. This mutual promotion of self-interest is damaging the progress of the education sector.

Post-Primary Education

Secondary education in Sindh refers to grades 9 and 10, also known as Matriculation, while Higher Secondary education refers to 11 and 12, also known as Intermediate education. Middle, secondary, and higher secondary government schools share the same burden of problems as borne by primary schools. However, in our current education system, students in secondary schools have to make an early career choice; hence their subject-choice in secondary education defines their later academic study for their intended career. Students in secondary schools can choose between Science and Arts, whereas students in higher secondary schools can choose between Science, Commerce, Arts and Home Economics (only for females).

Table 4.20 shows the various attempts made by successive governments to improve secondary education in Pakistan. Despite these oft-repeated pronouncements, the shortfall in the numbers of those graduating from primary to middle and secondary stages has become quite acute.

Table 4.20: Overview of Historical Developments

National Education Policies	Focus on Secondary/Higher Secondary Education
1947 First Educational Conference	The 'Committee of Primary and Secondary Education' of the Conference proposed that 'the intermediate stage should be abolished and these Grades (i.e. 11 and 12) should be added to the secondary level'.
1951 Second Educational Conference	The policy was concerned about untrained teacher and emphasised teachers' training at secondary levels.
1957 National Education Commission	Based on thorough analysis, emphasised that secondary education should be recognised as a complete stage in itself. At secondary level of education, the curriculum should offer a common core of subjects compulsory for all students and a variety of elective courses designed to prepare students for careers.
1969–70 The New Education Policy	Building on 1959 policy, it proposed the creation of a District School Authority in each district. The Authority was to be autonomous with specific functions, to streamline the primary and secondary school system.
1972–80 The Education Policy	Noticed the malpractices in the system of terminal examinations by the boards of Intermediate and Secondary Education and put emphasis on making every effort to eliminate these malpractices—a goal yet to be achieved.
1979 National Education Policy	Proposed replacement of the existing four-tier system; namely, primary, secondary, college, university to three tiers, namely, elementary, secondary and university. All schools need to be upgraded as higher secondary schools
1992 National Education Policy	The policy proposed shifting of classes XI and XI1 from the colleges to the general schools and vocational schools.
1998–2010 National Education Policy	Proposed a conceptual framework to reform secondary education. The features were: enhancing access to secondary, integration with technical and vocational education based on our experiences and adequate development of a student to enter into world of work or further studies.

Source: School Education and Literacy Department, *Sindh Education Sector Plan 2014–18*, Karachi, Government of Sindh, n.d.

The National Education Policy of 2009 points out that the narrow base of the secondary education system excludes a large number of students. This issue of access is then exacerbated by low quality of skills added to these students during their secondary education.

Figure 4.5 shows that students from 90 per cent of the schools in Sindh have only 10 per cent of schools to transition into. There has been a 58 per cent increase in the number of primary schools from the year 2001–2 to 2015–16. However, there was only an 11 per cent collective increase in middle/elementary, secondary, and higher secondary schools during the same time period.[29] This results in low enrolment in post-primary institutes, where it dips to nearly half while transitioning from primary education. There exists no defined policy to maintain a reasonable balance between primary and post-primary educational institutes, which could reflect the government's march towards pre-set educational vision.

SEMIS 2015–16 reports the total number of students in post-primary schools at 1,456,818 across Sindh.[30]

Figure 4.5: Transition of Students in Public Schools of Sindh (%) (2015–16)

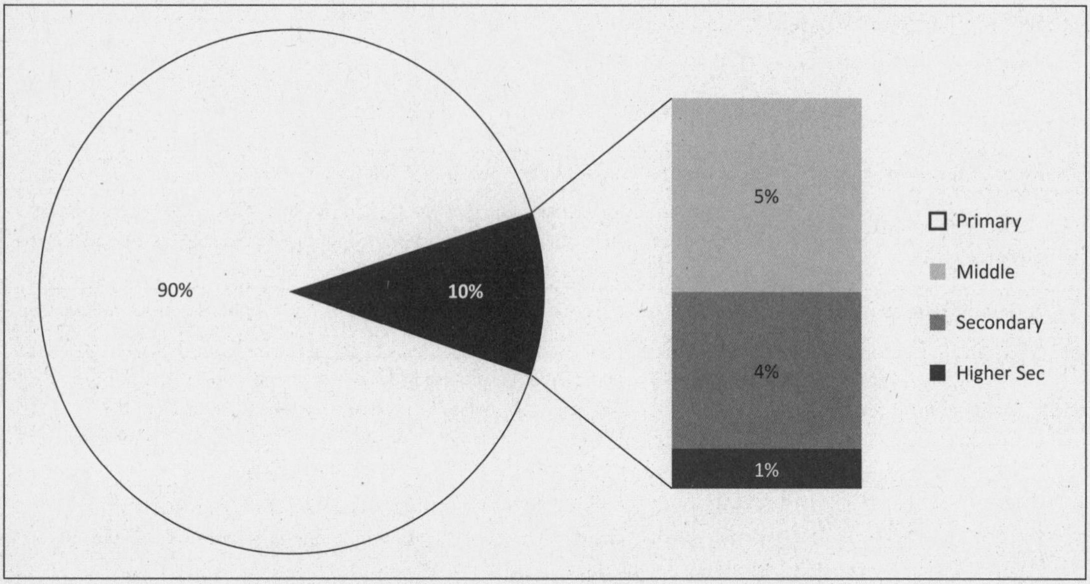

Source: Sindh Education Management Information System (SEMIS), *Sindh Education Profile 2015–16*, Karachi, Government of Sindh, n.d.

Sixty per cent of these students are male whereas the remaining 40 per cent are female. This shows the continuation of gender disparity that seeps in during primary education. However, the government introduced a girls' stipend programme in 2006 whereby every female student from grade 6 to 10 receives PKR 2,500 at the end of the academic year. There are 45 talukas subjected to the 'Differential Stipend Policy' where female students receive PKR 3,500 instead due to extremely low transition rates there. This financial support was provided to encourage academic transition among female students beyond primary education. However, considering the transition rate from grades 5 to grade 6 among female students, it can be seen that there is a persistent drop among female students which questions the effectiveness of the entire initiative. This monetary incentive is aimed at increasing girls' transition post primary education. As compared to 2010–11, female enrolment in 2015–16 in post-primary education has increased by almost 26 per cent compared to 35 per cent for boys, thus widening the gender gap. It is not clear as to whether female enrolment would have been lower than this in absence of the stipend policy. In other words, is the stipend policy keeping these girls in the post-primary institutions who would have otherwise dropped out?

Table 4.21 presents a very bleak picture of stipend distribution to female students. There is a sharp decline in the proportion of female students receiving stipends. For example, 85 per cent of those enrolled in grade 6 used to receive the stipend in 2008–09 but by 2014–15, this number was down to 78 per cent. A similar trend is observed in the case of grade 10, where the ratio has fallen from 95 to 75 per cent.

According to Figure 4.6, there were a total of 83,732 female students in grade 7 in 2009–10, and 98 per cent of these girls received the due amount and almost 99 per cent of these students moved on to the next grade. Similarly, almost 99 per cent of the same batch in 2010–11 received the stipend amount and 84 per cent of these students thereafter transitioned to the next grade. It can be seen that the girls' stipend initiative had been effective in ensuring student transition since only 15 per cent of the female students dropped out over two years (from 2009–11). This to an extent indicates that the female students' retention is comparatively easier once the

Table 4.21: Beneficiaries of Girls' Stipend (2007–08 to 2015–16)

	Class 6			Class 7			Class 8			Class 9			Class 10		
	Total female students	Stipend recipients	Percentage received	Total female students	Stipend recipients	Percentage received	Total female students	Stipend recipients	Percentage received	Total female students	Stipend recipients	Percentage received	Total female students	Stipend recipients	% received
2007–08	82,562	69,912	84.68	74,771	67,617	90.43	70,834	61,760	87.19	59,420	55,080	92.70	52,496	-	-
2008–09	82,001	73,133	89.19	78,270	71,987	91.97	72,228	68,247	94.49	62,983	62,436	99.13	56,771	54,138	95.36
2009–10	98,560	94,250	95.63	83,732	81,561	97.41	78,240	75,660	96.70	67,343	67,232	99.84	61,029	60,557	99.23
2010–11	103,084	97,158	94.25	94463	93,959	99.47	81,740	81,346	99.52	69,030	68,193	98.79	61,166	60,281	98.55
2011–12	102,114	100,453	98.37	96,766	96,525	99.75	88,658	88,533	99.86	68,278	67,968	99.55	60,520	60,134	99.36
2012–13	99,621	Not distributed	-	99,002	Not distributed	-	93871	Not distributed	-	77,166	Not distributed	-	64,018	Not distributed	-
2013–14	83,496	63,807	76.42	93,932	72,708	77.40	94,282	71,594	75.94	78,498	72,381	92.21	68,991	64,077	92.88
2014–15	79,658	62,133	78.00	81,318	56,188	69.10	86,992	64,100	73.68	73,371	61,115	83.30	67,042	49,961	74.52
2015–16	82,364	38,007	46.15	80,736	62,403	77.29	77,788	62,498	80.34	70,907	57,134	80.58	68,557	53,047	77.38

Source: Reform Support Unit, Education and Literacy Department, Karachi, Government of Sindh.

students have transitioned to post-primary education. However, it is more challenging to ensure female student transition from primary to secondary education in the first place.

Figure 4.6: Comparison between Female Students' Enrolment and Girls' Stipend Beneficiaries (Class 7 to 10) (2009–10 to 2012–13)

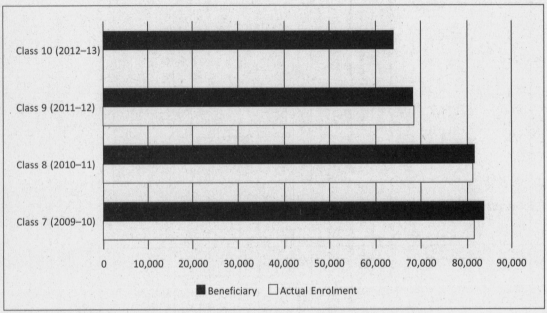

Source: Reform Support Unit, Education and Literacy Department, Karachi, Government of Sindh.

Table 4.22: Post-Primary Enrolment by Gender (2010–11 and 2015–16)

	2010–11			2015–16		
	Boys	**Girls**	**Total**	**Boys**	**Girls**	**Total**
Middle/Elementary	119,227	117,776	237,003	147,898	117,948	265,846
Secondary	366,074	254,877	620,951	490,291	346,103	836,394
Higher Secondary	161,371	91,694	253,065	232,384	122,194	354,578
Total	646,672	464,347	1,111,019	870,573	586,245	1,456,818

Source: Sindh Education Management Information System (SEMIS), *Sindh Education Profile*, Karachi, Government of Sindh, various years.

As Tables 4.22 to 4.23 show, there has been an overall increase in female enrolment across all levels of schools. However, gender disparity between boys' and girls' enrolment widened at the middle/elementary stage as the ratio of girls enrolled dropped from 50 to 44 per cent between 2010–11 and 2015–16. There was a slight fall at the higher secondary and no change at the secondary stages during this period.

Table 4.23: Post-Primary Enrolment by Gender (Percentage)* (2010–11 and 2015–16)

	2010–11			2015–16		
	Boys	**Girls**	**Total**	**Boys**	**Girls**	**Total**
Middle/Elementary	50	50	100	56	44	100
Secondary	59	41	100	59	41	100
Higher Secondary	64	36	100	66	34	100

*Calculated from post-primary enrolments figures in Table 4.22.

The problem of large proportion of out-of-school children in Sindh is largely due to a low effective transition rate from the primary to lower secondary level. As compared to the national average of 82 per cent, Sindh fares poorly with 69 per cent transition rate, which is lower than that of Balochistan.

Table 4.24: Grade-wise Enrolment of Female Students in Government Schools of Sindh
(2008–09 to 2014–15)

Year/Grade	Grade 5	Grade 6	Grade 7	Grade 8	Grade 9	Grade 10
2008–09	149,642	82,001	78,270	72,228	62,983	56,771
2009–10	159,118	98,560	83,732	78,240	67,343	61,029
2010–11	157,578	103,084	94,463	81,740	69,030	61,166
2011–12	153,647	102,114	96,766	88,658	68,278	60,520
2012–13	147438	99,621	99,002	93871	77,166	64,018
2013–14	142,444	83,496	93,932	94,282	78,498	68,991
2014–15	139,251	79,658	81,318	86,992	73,371	67,042

Source: Reform Support Unit, Education and Literacy Department, Karachi, Government of Sindh.

Table 4.25: Transition of Female Students from Grade 5 to Grade 6

Year	Grade 5	Grade 6	Drop-Out Rate (%)
2008–09	149,642	-	-
2009–10	159,118	98,560	38
2010–11	157,578	103,804	34
2011–12	153,647	102,114	33
2012–13	147,438	99,621	32
2013–14	142,444	83,496	41
2014–15	139,251	79,658	43
Average Drop-out Rate	37		

Source: Reform Support Unit, Education and Literacy Department, Karachi, Government of Sindh.

The rate of transition from grade 5 to grade 10 for female students in 2008–09 was 38 per cent and has gradually improved to reach 48 per cent by 2014–15 in the government schools. What seems surprising is the reversal in the trend of overall female enrolment since 2011–12. Whether the private schools are now absorbing most of the incremental enrolment is a question that needs to be explored.

Another way of looking at this problem is to measure the dropout rate from grade 5 to grade 6, i.e. the terminal point for the primary and the initial point of entry to the middle school. On average, a 37 per cent drop-out rate is observed among female students upon transitioning from primary to secondary education. The underlying factors contributing towards the drop out could range from cultural limitations to low expectations from public education.

The quality of secondary education is unsatisfactory because of inadequate resources for instructional support.

Table 4.26: Computer Lab and Library Facilities in Public Secondary Schools of Sindh (2015–16)

Number of Schools Having Computer Lab Facilities				
Location	Primary	Middle/Elementary	Secondary	Higher Secondary
Urban	32	20	245	66
Rural	40	30	160	102
Total	72	50	405	168
		695		
Number of Schools Having Library Facilities				
Location	Primary	Middle/Elementary	Secondary	Higher Secondary
Urban	46	14	255	55
Rural	86	24	216	115
Total	132	38	471	170
		811		

Source: Sindh Education Management Information System (SEMIS), Education and Literacy Deparment, Government of Sindh.

Table 4.26 presents an overview of computer labs and library facilities in different schools. It is a sad commentary on educational priorities that only one-fourth of secondary schools have computer labs while library facilities exist in 28 per cent of schools. There is some improvement in higher secondary schools where these facilities exist in 60 per cent of the schools. The adverse effect on the students from the schools where these facilities do not exist is likely to have a bearing on their future capabilities. The presence of facilities per se is not a very helpful indicator. What really counts is whether there are enough qualified teachers engaging with students in computer labs.

The Education Department had made allocations of PKR 4.685 billion in 2015–16 for non-salary expenditures including library and laboratory facilities. Only 5 per cent of this allocation was utilised. One of the reasons for non-utilisation is the timing and complex procedures involved in the release of these allocations. The need for reform in the procurement, disbursement, and drawing of funds is compelling. In the absence of such procedural reforms, schools would continue to suffer and budgetary allocations would lapse.

Table 4.27: Universities and Degree-awarding Institutions in Pakistan (1947–48 to 2015–16)

Year	Public				Private				Total			
	Pakistan		Sindh		Pakistan		Sindh		Pakistan		Sindh	
	No. of insti-tutes	Enrol-ment	Institutes	Enrol-ment	Institutes	Enrol-ment	Institutes	Enrol-ment	Institutes	Enrol-ment	Institutes	Enrol-ment
1947–48	2	644	N/A	N/A	N/A	N/A	N/A	N/A	2	644	N/A	N/A
1959–60	5	4,092	N/A	N/A	N/A	N/A	N/A	N/A	6	4,092	N/A	N/A
1970–71	10	17,690	2	4,999	N/A	N/A	N/A	N/A	10	17,690	2	4,999
1980–81	21	42,688	5	18,992	N/A	N/A	N/A	N/A	21	42,688	5	18,992
1990–91	23	61,857	6	25,236	N/A	N/A	N/A	N/A	25	61,857	6	25,236
2000–01	38	142,652	8	40,173	22	43,873	N/A	N/A	60	186,525	8	40,173
2005–06	62	242,879	12	43,311	54	78,934	N/A	N/A	116	321,813	12	43,311
2015–16	91	669,709	17	217,311	72	274,734	30	67,632	163	944,443	47	284,943

Note: The figures for 2000–01 and 2005–06 were obtained from HEC.

Source: Federal Bureau of Statistics, 50 years of Statistics, Karachi, Statistics Division, Government of Pakistan, 1998; Bureau of Statistics, *25 Years of Statistics in Sindh*, Karachi, Planning and Development Department, Government of Sindh, n.d.; Ministry of Federal Education and Professional Training, *Pakistan Education Statistics 2015–16*, Islamabad, Government of Pakistan, 2017.

Non-Formal Education

Non-formal education is an additional commitment by the government to attain education for all through special educational provisions for out-of-the-school children and adults who could not get formal education. With 55 per cent literacy rate[31] and persistent and pronounced regional and gender disparities, Sindh needs concerted efforts along with planned action to address its literacy problem. Non-formal basic education in Sindh aims to provide access to children aged 6 to 14 who are out of the formal schooling system and prepare them through an accelerated programme for eventual reabsorption in the mainstream education system.

The Directorate of Literacy and Non-Formal Basic Education (NFBE) was setup in 2002 with the responsibility to carry out programmes on literacy and non-formal education in Sindh. It was also responsible for initiating Alternative Learning Pathways (ALP) to increase literacy and life skills to enable economic survival of individuals. NFBE programmes include Non-Formal Basic Education, an accelerated programme for 6 to 14 years, and the Adult Literacy Programme for 10+ years.

The National Education Policy 2009, prior to the Eighteenth Amendment, emphasised on improving the quality of NFBE programmes. The low quality of NFBE programmes was attributed to poor teaching due to low capacity. Teachers in these centres were under-qualified and would not undergo professional development. Though the directorate was setup in 2002, it still lacked adequate resources—financial, technical and administrative. However, considering the magnitude of the problem, the outreach of NFBE and the Adult Literacy Programme is very limited, and without proper curriculum to increase literacy and life skills of students enrolled in NFBE schools the desired outcome cannot be attained.

The Sindh Education Sector Plan 2014–18 has detailed objectives for NFBE starting with a comprehensive policy for NFBE and ALP along with innovative approaches to increase their reach. It also aims to increase the quality of programmes through curriculum development and teachers' capacity building. It underscores the strengthening of the Literacy and NFBE directorate for better monitoring and implementation of set standards, coupled with proper accreditation mechanisms to re-route children to mainstream education. However, an appropriate policy for NFBE and ALP and a new curriculum still do not exist. It has already been two years since the plan was launched. To achieve the set target, the pace needs to be accelerated, resources provided, and progress monitored regularly.

Vocational and Technical Training

There are a total of 3,746 technical and vocational institutions in Pakistan.[32] Of these, 1,123 (30 per cent) are in the public sector, whereas 2,630 (70 per cent) are in the private sector. It has been seen that 30 per cent of the public technical and vocational institutions have a share of 44 per cent of the total technical and vocational enrolment, while 70 per cent of private institutes are catering to the remaining 56 per cent. Sixteen per cent of the total technical and vocational centres are in Sindh. Having technical and vocational centres is essential as all students enrolled in formal education do not complete secondary education or make it to higher education.

Sindh contributes 25.1 per cent to the total enrolment of technical and vocational centres.[33] Considering that the percentage of total enrolment in public schools nationally falls to 30 per cent by the time students reach grade 10,[34] the burden of responsibility on technical and vocational institutes is far greater. However, several technical certifications or programmes have a minimum qualification requirement of matriculation, which makes a huge chunk of students ineligible since they drop out before completing grade 10. This chunk can opt for vocational trainings such as CBT (competency-based trainings) which can later help them earn a living. However, it is to be ensured that the skills taught at these centres are in line with market demands.

Table 4.28: Provincial Status of Technical and Vocational Institutes (2015–16)

Province	Level	Total Institutes		Total Enrolment		Total Teachers	
		Number	Percentage	Number	Percentage	Number	Percentage
Punjab	Technical	664	20.4	53,049	18.4	6,303	41.9
	Vocational	1,153	35.4	117,701	40.8	2,756	18.3
	Total	1,817	55.8	170,750	59.2	9,059	60.2
Sindh	Technical	192	5.9	57,573	19.9	2,136	14.2
	Vocational	411	12.6	21,508	7.5	834	5.5
	Total	603	18.5	79,081	27.4	2,970	19.7
KP	Technical	34	1	4,989	1.7	2,037	13.5
	Vocational	670	20.5	30,233	10.5	595	4
	Total	704	21.5	35,222	12.2	2,632	17.5
Balochistan	Technical	11	0.3	1,788	0.6	203	1.3
	Vocational	124	3.8	1,971	0.7	180	1.2
	Total	135	4.1	3,759	1.3	383	2.5
Grand Total		3,259		288,632		15,044	

Source: Ministry of Federal Education and Professional Training, *Pakistan Education Statistics 2015–16*, Islamabad, Government of Pakistan, 2017.

Deeni Madrassas

Madrassas mainly impart Islamic education but they also fill the vacuum created by public schools. With private schools charging money and public schools offering substandard education gratuitous, madrassas provide another option to those families with limited financial means who wish their children to get an education along with boarding and lodging.

Despite having produced renowned scholars in the past such as Hassan Ali Effendi and Maulana Ubaidullah Sindhi, madrassas today are associated with obscurantism and conservative attitudes in thought and practice. A number of madrassas are alleged to be breeding grounds for fanatics and extremists who then indulge in violence.

During the Soviet–Afghan war, many madrassas received funding from conservative Islamic Middle Eastern countries to recruit men for jihad. As a result, thousands of youth were brainwashed, trained, and planted in the war theatre of Afghanistan. After the disintegration of the Soviet Union, the Western powers and their Islamic allies abandoned the support of jihadis. This eventually led to the return of the jihadis into their native countries, where they formed small militant groups and turned weapons against their own states.

Madrassas in Pakistan mainly support two schools of thought—Sunni and Shia. Within the Sunni school of thought, Deobandi, Barelvi, and Ahl-e-Hadith are the most prominent sub-sects. Each of these schools of thought has a different ideology and curriculum, which is not in line with the curriculum taught by private and public schools. This in turn leads to lack of coherence and coordination. This simultaneity of different curricula and ideologically-charged pedagogical techniques has, according to National Education Policy of 2009, led to learning gaps and social rifts.

Despite all the problems associated with madrassas, since Independence, a rapid growth in the number of madrassas has been observed. From 189 at Independence, the number of madrassas has increased to 13,000 in 2002, and 40,000 in 2008. However, according to the 2016 statistics, the enrolment in madrassas is 2.26 million, which is almost 5 per cent of the total student enrolment in the country.[35] The National Action Plan requires all madrassas to be registered with the government to enable regulation; however, a large number of them still remain unregistered. The absorption of 300,000 to 400,000 graduates from these madrassas in the job market is a big challenge that has not been properly addressed by the sponsors of the madrassas or the government. Infusion of skills in the curriculum could be one possible option to mitigate this problem. The fact remains that madrassas are regarded as the best choice for the children from the poorest segment of the society, since they provide free lodging, boarding, clothing, and education.

Educational Policies

Soon after independence in 1947, the Pakistan Educational Conference was convened to establish the significance of education for the country's prosperity. This was essential to address the grave issue of illiteracy as 85 per cent of the population was illiterate. The situation was even worse for people from under-served areas. Hence, the conference was arranged where universalisation of primary education in the next twenty years was unanimously agreed upon. Though there has never been an absence of educational policies in Pakistan, the track record in poor implementation of these policies is evident in the form of poor literacy rate and low ranking in various educational indicators.

Education policies have not followed a consistent path in Pakistan. They have ranged from nationalisation during Bhutto's regime to Islamisation during Ziaul Haq's era and to modernisation and decentralisation during Musharraf's rule. Immediately post-Partition, Pakistan ran into unravelling its ideological dilemma, attempting to define the role of Islam in its curriculum. As Pakistan was founded to provide a separate homeland for Muslims, there had always been strong sentiments towards Islam and its position in education. The prominent suffusion of Islam in education was evident during Ziaul Haq's regime in the 1980s when he ordered the of review all textbooks to delete anything repugnant to Islam and to the ideology of Pakistan. Islamiat and Pakistan Studies were made compulsory and were introduced in all sorts of educational institutions and Arabic was introduced as a compulsory subject from grade 6 to grade 8.

Along with other issues, the medium of education is another matter which has long been under debate. There has been a persistent contest between Urdu, English, and the regional languages as the dominant medium of instruction. This debate remains fierce but inconclusive and unsettled. The simultaneity of multiple hegemonies and identity politics have been entangled with the question of the dominant language. Should it be Urdu, to ensure unity and solidarity among people or English—the lingua franca—to face the daunting global competition and to avail further prospects of employment? Or should it be the mother tongue/regional language to promote the value of heritage among children? A satisfactory response to this heated debate is still awaited.

In 2010, the devolution of power from the federal to the provincial level through the Eighteenth Amendment was a significant step to empower provinces to hold the reins of previously federal subjects. One such subject is education. After this amendment, the scope of the federal ministry has been redefined with greater provincial autonomy. The provinces will now have to manage their own educational affairs but it has given rise to a new set of problems of coordination. The Council of Common Interest (CCI) would have to play a more proactive role in coming up with solutions to these problems.

Policy-making in Pakistan has been more of an exercise to produce documents with elaborate targets with barely any mechanisms set out. These ambitious targets do not take into account the impediments. Effective and good public policy is aimed at solving problems which affect the masses. They are, therefore, devised based on proper ground research followed by realistic targets. Pakistan has so far made six education policies. Their evaluation reflects that the subject of education has been handled on a trial and error basis. There is a frequent jump from one idea to another without testing it for implementation and learning. The knee-jerk reaction is to keep extending the deadlines to achieve set targets without questioning the realism of targets themselves in light of the experience gained.

The target of attaining universal primary education has continuously shifted from one year to another, indicating lack of consideration for on-ground challenges. If there was adherence to policies, Pakistan would have attained universal primary education by 1980 as per the 1970 policy. The same target was later pushed to 1984 in the next policy of 1972 and yet again to 1992 in the 1979 policy. It was then shifted to 2010 and finally as per the 2009 policy, it should have been attained by 2015. However, the target has still not been achieved by 2019. It is quite evident that targets in these policies had been set without much contemplation and without considering their attainability.

Our policies also reflect a confused approach and inability of the policy makers to prioritise available options. The government seems to aim for and promise everything and then fails on all counts. For instance, the idea of utilising the latest practices to impart education effectively was rightfully considered in the 1970 education policy. The policy action of supplying radios and TV sets to schools (covered by telecasting facility) was novel as TV was then recently introduced in Pakistan. However, it was mere rhetoric—nothing of the sort materialised. In fact, the commitment announced in the 1979 policy to provide one teaching kit to every school, which was certainly far more important than the stated gadgets or educational toys, remained unfulfilled as only 30 per cent of the schools were provided these kits by 1998. In Pakistan, public administration ends at the stage of policy formulation because the next stage of implementation is rarely reached in the right manner.

There have been policy actions that would have proved valuable if they were implemented. For instance, the suggestion for a uniform curriculum in both private and public schools would have been a step in the right direction if it had only been taken. If implemented this would curb the prevalent disparity in the education system which has bifurcated the societal fabric into privileged and under-privileged. However, for policies to be effective and successfully implemented, commitment and willingness by the government is required which has been found to be lacking.

One of the major loopholes in education policies has been the absence of evaluation and regular monitoring. The focus mainly on inputs and outputs completely disregards the outcomes. It is the outcomes that add the element of sustainability to the policy itself, making implementation inevitable.

Since education serves as the grounds for preparing the population for economic progress, it should be flexible and broad enough to cater to diverse interests of the students and changing needs of the economy and society. Our current education system, at a very early stage, gives students rigid academic plans from which they can choose. They have to decide between strands of science and humanities in grade 9 which limits their possible academic choices and restricts their chance of exploration. This was observed in the 1979 policy where it was suggested that strict division of medical and non-medical groups should be removed to broaden course choices for students. However, this division still exists. As opposed to the intermediate system, O and A levels are far more flexible with a wide range of subjects for students to choose from. This enables students to acquaint themselves with a wide range of subjects and even wider available career options.

Besides wider options, education should be imparted in a way that it equips students with all the elements that make them responsible citizens, making valuable contribution to the state's economy. Therefore, a focus on imparting scientific and technical skills at the secondary level is important as it is at this stage that students acquire skills essential for contribution towards the economy. For this very reason, units for science and technical skills for matric and intermediate were proposed in the 1979 policy. Almost the same significance was granted to these aspects in other education policies as well. However, how much of it was practically implemented is not obvious. As per SEMIS 2015–16, there are only 2.5 per cent[36] schools in Sindh alone that have science facilities, which present a striking contrast between the intended and the actual. It was suggested in 2009 that school rankings should be introduced to inject a level of competition. However, any such ranking would be useless.

Where 70 per cent of the student population eventually ends up out of schools, there should be structures in place to ensure that scarce human resource is not wasted.

As per the education policy of 2009, the total participation rate in universities across Pakistan was 4.8 per cent in 2008 and it was aimed to increase this to 15 per cent by 2020. Since then, the number of universities in Pakistan has risen to 163 with 47 universities in Sindh (17 in public sector and 30 in private sector) and the rate has risen to 10 per cent.[37] The surge in private sector universities is a good sign as more students can get access. However, most students from lower-income backgrounds cannot afford to go to these universities. A proper geographical spread of these universities is also important as everyone might not be too open to travel for studies.

Tertiary Education

Table 4.27 shows that most of the increase in enrolment and in the number of students has taken place in the post-2000 period. The number of universities almost tripled, whereas tertiary enrolment expanded by 550 per cent. The formation of a Higher Education Commission as an independent, autonomous body, liberal budgetary allocations to HEC for recurrent and development expenditure, overseas training of faculty members in large numbers, and improvement in governance structure all contributed to this phenomenal growth. However, the policies regarding higher education have been inconsistent. The government that came to power in 2008 reversed the growth momentum by curtailing budgetary allocations and taking away the autonomy of the HEC management. The Eighteenth Amendment also created confusion regarding the responsibilities for tertiary education. Punjab and Sindh claimed that tertiary education had also devolved and formed their own provincial commissions. The huge quantitative expansion led some observers to question the dilution of quality and research. Monetary incentives and promotion imperatives have pushed many teachers to indulge in malpractices such as plagiarism but the number of research publications in referred journals has indeed increased significantly. The proponents of such expansion argue that access takes precedence as poor areas of the country do not benefit if these high degree awarding institutes are largely located in the better-off urban areas. Once the situation stabilises and the system reaches a steady state, competitive forces would induce improvement in quality. Meanwhile, employability of graduates and post-graduates being produced by the universities remains a matter of concern.

Another bone of contention in the provinces is about the internal control of the universities. According to the University Act, the governor as the chancellor exercises most of the powers of appointments, removal, supervision etc. The elected chief ministers feel that this an infringement upon their mandate as the public at large would hold them accountable for the performance of the universities or the lack of it. This has further clouded the governance of universities.

University teachers have protested against the intrusion of the chief ministers in the affairs as they suspect this would lead to politicisation. Appointments would not be made on merit but on connections to the political parties in power. Retribution would take place against those who do not fall in line. According to this group, academic freedom, which forms the cornerstone of the universities, would be jeopardised.

This ongoing tussle between governors and the provincial chief executives has to be settled once and for all. The jurisdictions of the HEC and the provincial HECs should delineate the governance structure of universities, including setting and compliance of standards, a mechanism of strengthened accountability and sustained level of funding. Unless these steps are taken, the progress made so far may be reversed.

Summing Up

Despite the constitutional amendment under Article 25(A), universal primary education has remained an elusive goal and the target dates for achieving this goal have been extended several times. Spending on education has increased since the last NFC award and the Eighteenth Amendment but net enrolment rates remain sub-par. Recent reforms in teacher recruitment and biometric attendance have reduced teacher absenteeism to some extent but the quality of teaching still remains in doubt. A more decentralised system of management and governance of school education from primary to high school may bring about better results. The burning issue of out-of-school children requires focus on the missing link in the education value chain, i.e. nonexistence of middle and secondary schools.

A mere glimpse of our education system indicates that the value chain with a desirable pyramid structure has not yet taken roots. Ninety per cent of schools are at primary level and 10 per cent for the remaining levels. The education value chain starts with recruiting of teachers, their continuous training, curriculum shows, classroom instructional methods, quality assurance, and examination and assessment systems that enable students to enter subsequent levels—middle, secondary, higher secondary etc. The chain has been broken in many places. Teachers until a few years ago were not recruited on the basis of subject matter knowledge but on the basis of their connections with politically influential persons. Training was unsystematic and not linked to acquiring professional competence and was more ritualistic rather than substantive. Curriculum and instructional methods encouraged rote learning, discouraged questioning, and promoted conformity. These tendencies were reinforced by an outdated examination and assessment system. Those who passed primary school did not have much options to pursue further education or any skills training. This was particularly true in the case of girls from rural areas. These weaknesses have led to poorly trained individuals and wide urban–rural disparity. The transitions from primary to higher education are too many and too disruptive.

Every primary school does not have an ECCE class, which is the first stage to turn the child away. After primary, a school has to be changed to cater to attend middle level. Post-middle level, there is another transition to attend grades 9 and 10 which is then followed by yet another transition to another institute for grades 11 and 12. These frequent transitions shed the number of students on the way. After intermediate, some opt for a two-year degree programme which does not have the same worth and recognition that a four-year undergraduate degree holds. Similarly, those who opt for vocational training might never get an opportunity to transition into tertiary education; diploma courses also do not have any link to tertiary education. This is further divided by a parallel madrassa educational system. This gets worse when quality is compromised from curriculum to examination. Students resort to rote learning and then resort to plagiarism and cheating which destroy the entire purpose of education. Furthermore, people in the education department fail to utilise the education budget since they fear being questioned later for transparency. Every year a significant percentage of the education budget lapses which is why the state of schools in the public sector is as it is. The government has an understanding of existing problems. However, the commitment to ensure the implementation of reforms is still awaited.

5

Health

Introduction

Health forms an integral part of human development and well-being. It has widespread benefits that extend to nutrition, population, planning, labour, productivity, environment, and many others. The World Health Organisation (WHO) defines health as 'a state of complete physical, social, and mental well-being, and not merely the absence of disease or infirmity'.[1]

Food and nutrition are some of the essential components of health. The availability of adequate food helps sustain the nutritional level of a person. When the required nutritional intake is secured, a person is capable of fighting off diseases and deficiencies. Hence, if a society wants growth and minimal inequality, access to nutrition and health care needs to be prioritised.

Low nutritional levels inevitably lead to several health issues such as stunting and wasting. These preventable diseases have a negative impact on the economy. The economic consequence of such diseases has already been felt on Pakistan's economy; various types of malnutrition are responsible for a 3 to 4 per cent loss to the country's GDP.[2]

According to the Global Nutrition Report, malnutrition and diet are by far the biggest risk factors for the global burden of disease. The economic consequences are measurable in losses of 11 per cent of the GDP every year in Africa and Asia. Relatively low-cost maternal and early-life health and nutrition programmes offer very high returns on investment. India had a higher rate of child stunting than Pakistan but it has almost doubled the rate of stunting reduction in the past ten years compared with the previous decade.

Changes in the indicators of the health status of Pakistan over the last twenty-five years are presented in Table 5.1. Life expectancy has risen, infant and maternal mortality rates have declined, and access to sanitation has improved, while access to drinking water has remained unchanged. The most worrisome aspect is an almost four times increase in child malnutrition—the stunting rate has gone up from 12 to 45 in this period.

An Overview

Table 5.2 presents a comparative analysis of the most recent health indicators of Pakistan and Sindh along with those of Punjab. This analysis shows that the province performs poorly as compared to Punjab and the national average. Poor health indicators come as a surprise where the province leads in per capita income, urbanisation, and adult literacy. A closer look at the factors responsible for the relative success of Punjab shows that better management, improved governance, and higher public expenditures have collectively reinforced this outcome.

In 2015–16, Punjab allocated 11.5 per cent of its budget to health compared to 7.7 per cent by Sindh.[3] Punjab's graph on public health spending is on the rise. Autonomous boards have been formed at the district level to supervise and operate various health facilities. The data shows that Punjab has done particularly well in reducing child mortality, maternal mortality, and contraceptive prevalence rates. The Sustainable Development

Table 5.1: Health Status of Pakistan (1990 and 2015)

Health Indicator	1990	2015
Life Expectancy	60.1	66.4
Child Mortality (Under the age of 5)	138.6	81.1
Maternal Mortality (Deaths per 100,000 live births)	431	178
Improved water source (% of population with access)	86	91
Improved sanitation facilities (% of population with access)	24	64
Total Expenditure on Health (% of GDP)	2.5	2.61
Child Malnutrition (Stunting in Children Aged Under-5)	12*	45
Physicians per 1,000 population	0.5	0.8
Contraceptive prevalence (any method) (% of women aged 15–49)	14.5	35.4**

* Value obtained pertains to 1995 because the relevant data for 1990 is not available.
** Value obtained pertains to 2013 because the relevant data for 2015 is not available.

Source: United Nations Development Programme, *Human Development Report,* New York, various years; World Bank Open Data <https://data.worldbank.org/>.

Table 5.2: Comparison of Health Indicators in Pakistan, Sindh, and Punjab (2015)

Indicators	Pakistan	Sindh	Punjab
Infant Mortality (Per 1,000 Live Births)	65.8	82	75
Maternal Mortality (Per 1,000 Live Births)	178	214*	189*
Under-five Mortality (Per 1,000 Live Births)	89*	105*	93*
Malaria Treatment Using ACT* (Malarial Drug) for children under age 5	-	15.9	9.4
Hospital Beds per 1,000	0.6	-	-
Nurses and midwives per 1,000	0.61	2.8	
Hospitals per 1,000	-	1.7	-
Life Expectancy	66.4	-	64**
Physicians per 1,000 population	0.8	0.59	0.63
Full Immunisation Coverage	53.0	35	56
Contraceptive Prevalence Rate (any method) (% of women ages 15–49)	35.4	29	38.7

* Artemisinin-based Combination Therapy (ACT).
**Pakistan Demographic and Health Survey (2012–13).
*** Health Department, 'Punjab Health profile', 2017, <http://health.punjab.gov.pk/Punjab_Health_Profile>.

Source: National figures are taken from World Bank Open Data <https://data.worldbank.org/> and Global Health Observatory (GHO) data <http://www.who.int/gho/en/>; Government of Sindh and United Nations Development Programme, *Sindh Multiple Indicator Cluster Survey 2014,* Karachi, 2015; Government of Punjab and United Nations Development Programme, *Punjab Multiple Indicator Cluster Survey 2014,* Lahore, 2015, Pakistan Medical and Dental Council.

Goals (SDG) report of the UNDP pushes developing economies towards attaining the goal of a maternal mortality of 70 per 100,000 births—the rate in Sindh is 214 for the same.[4] Additionally, the Under Five Mortality Rate (U5MR) is 104 per 1,000 live births in Sindh compared to that of the SDG goal of 25 per 1,000 births.[5] In addition, Sindh's performance in respect to child mortality rate is also poor.

Another alarming aspect of Sindh's healthcare system is the disparity, which exists between the rural and urban areas. The maternal mortality rate of rural areas is twice that of urban areas.[6] Disparity in income levels, access to quality education, infrastructure, and healthcare facilities, are the variables that help to explain this phenomenon.

The province can proudly claim to have developed several first-rate health facilities, such as Aga Khan University Hospital (AKUH), Jinnah Postgraduate Medical Centre (JPMC), National Institute of Cardiovascular Disease (NICVD), Sindh Institute of Urology and Transplantation (SIUT), and Indus Hospital, but preventive services such as immunisation vaccination, and prenatal and antenatal care particularly in the rural areas lag behind and require serious attention. It is the government that is the sole provider of preventive services.

In Sindh, both the public and private sectors help provide curative healthcare services. It is the government that is supposed to provide curative services in the rural areas but the unqualified private practitioners dominate the scene. Some of them are frauds and others are faith healers. Healthcare facilities in the public sector are divided into three categories: primary, secondary, and tertiary. The primary sector comprises basic health units (BHUs), rural healthcare centres (RHCs), government rural dispensaries (GRDs), maternal and child health (MCHs) and tuberculosis centres. These centres of basic health provide services ranging from preventive to curative measures. Secondary healthcare is provided by the taluka/tehsil headquarter hospitals (THQs) and district headquarter hospitals (DHQs). The tertiary care is provided mainly by teaching, private, charitable, specialised, and military hospitals.

In an attempt to promote services at the grassroot level, lady health workers (LHWs) were introduced in 1994. LHWs are trained to provide advice and health care to people living in rural areas. They are responsible for reproductive health, vaccinations, control of diarrhoea, and promotion of access to clean water. According to the Planning and Development Department of Sindh, there are 14,243 general medical officers/ lady health supervisors and 1,347 LHWs in Sindh.[7] The Sindh Health Profile 2016 states that there are 790 BHUs and 124 RHUs. There are 3,075 people per doctor, 12,308 persons per nurse, and 1,527 persons per bed.[8]

Evolution of the Healthcare Delivery System

At the time of Independence, Sindh's health sector faced a lack of resources in terms of infrastructure as well as healthcare staff. Table 5.3 shows the highly underdeveloped health system in Sindh in 1947. There was not a single tertiary level facility worth its name in the whole province. Mostly it was dispensaries of various kinds that provided most of the curative services and that too of a rudimentary nature. The situation worsened following the influx of migrants into the province, which further stretched already limited resources. Government civil hospitals were located at district headquarters, while there were few dispensaries in rural areas.

Since 1970, there has been some expansion in the health infrastructure, but it remains inadequate in relation to the needs of the population. The ratio of hospital beds to population is still quite low and therefore access is highly limited. Even if access became easier, the quality of care is poor. Medical staff absenteeism in the rural centres is quite rampant. Some of the health centres are not even equipped with diagnostic tools and just one or two maternity and child centres exist. Whenever epidemics hit the rural areas, the situation could not be controlled because of a lack of staff employed in the public health service.[9] Clearly, there is still a wide gap between the demand and supply of health services.

Health indicators for Sindh are relatively worse among the rural population of the province (Table 5.5). Maternal and child health indicators are precarious, and immunisation and vaccination coverage rates are

Table 5.3: Dispensaries and Hospitals in Sindh (1947)

Type of Dispensary or Hospital	Sindh
Purely Municipal Dispensaries	21
Purely DLB Dispensaries	18
Municipal Hospital	3
Grant-In-Aid Dispensaries	67
Government Dispensaries	15
Government Hospitals	10
Grant-In-Aid Hospitals	2
Women Grant-In-Aid Hospitals	4
Women Private Hospitals	4

Source: Government of Sindh, *Post War Development Schemes (1947–1952)*, Karachi, n.d., pp. 13–14.

Table 5.4: Public Sector Hospital Facilities in Sindh (1970–2015)

	Hospitals		Hospital Beds	
	Teaching	Civil, Specialised, Taluka, and Others	Teaching	Civil, Specialised, Taluka, and Others
1970	2	21	1775	2084
1975	6	30	2892	2464
1980	6	51	4195	5615
1985	6	65	3402	4079
1990	6	74	4384	4833
1995	7	78	5116	5059
2000	5	81	5330	5414
2005	5	83	5474	6040
2010	6	82	5799	5878
2015	7	99	6017	6499

Source: Figures for 1970–2005 were taken from Bureau of Statistics, *Sindh Development Statistics*, Karachi, Planning and Development department, Government of Sindh, various years; Bureau of Statistics, *Health Profile*, Karachi, Planning and Development Department, Government of Sindh, various years.

Table 5.5: Sindh Urban and Rural Health Indicators (2004 and 2014)

Indicators	2004		2014	
	Urban	Rural	Urban	Rural
Maternal mortality	240	410	-	-
Infant mortality	50	80	57	106
Child mortality (Under 5)	68	117	69	139

Source: Government of Sindh and United Nations International Children's Emergency Fund, *Multiple Cluster Indicator Survey 2014*, Karachi, 2015.

unsatisfactory. The contraceptive prevalence rate is low and unmet demand is rising with the passage of time. Only 29 per cent of the couples of childbearing ages in Sindh at present use contraception.

Table 5.6: Usage of Health Facilities (1980)

	Private	Government
Rural Sindh	53.9	38.8
Urban Sindh	51.6	43.5

Source: M. B. Abbasi, *Socio Economic Characteristics of Women in Sind Issues Affecting Women's Status*, Karachi, Economic Studies Centre, Sind Regional Plan Organisation, 1980.

Table 5.6 shows that as far as back 1980, private clinics in both urban and rural areas filled the void that had been created by poor health facilities provided by the government. The trend has picked up in the last few decades because of deterioration in government health and service delivery. People previously unable to afford fees charged by private providers, particularly in rural areas, can now go to charitable dispensaries, clinics, and hospitals.

Free eye clinics by Layton Rahmatullah Blindness Trust (LRBT) and free dialysis and transplantation by SIUT are some of the shining examples of excellent charitable health service providers.

Several attempts to reform the health sector have been made, some with the assistance of donors such as the World Bank. For example, during 1993–94, the government of Pakistan launched a social action programme (SAP) with the funding from the World Bank, the objective of which was to improve delivery of social services to citizens and provide easy access to facilities. In the health sector, efforts were focused towards the provision of proper nutrition, better maternal and child care, effective family-planning programmes, and proper control of communicable and non-communicable diseases.

However, a flawed system of governance inhibited an effective execution of the projects that SAP had ambitiously set. Staff absenteeism was widespread because there was no proper mechanism for monitoring the goals set by the social action programmed and no action was taken against them. The reporting was inaccurate and timely remedial action to solve the problems was not taken. The critical part of female paramedical staff was not filled. The initiatives such as health committees, cost recovery, and health programmes were actually not implemented. Releases of funds were sporadic and much below what was required to meet the programmatic goals. Consequently, due to poor governance and management, the goals set by the social action programme could not be attained.

One of the positive aspects of SAP was that it introduced and promoted the concept of public-private partnership in healthcare delivery. Other components where progress was made were family planning services provision through health outlets and training of women medical officers (WMOs) and paramedics. Overall, Sindh's performance under SAP was far below the satisfactory level.

Punjab, on the other hand, was applauded for its will and determination to excel in the field of health. A tight monitoring system and merit-based recruitment made Punjab's performance under the programme impressive.

Women, Children and Nutrition

The role of women in health care, spacing of children, nutrition, and cleanliness is critical. Education and empowerment provide women with the confidence and knowledge to better take care of their children, such as in diagnosing a child's disease at an early stage and monitoring the nutritional intake of their families.

A lack of awareness among women aggravates the health situation in Sindh. According to a survey, few women receive prenatal and antenatal care.[10] However, prenatal and antenatal care are crucial during pregnancy, which help improve the health of both the mother and her child. Research suggests that the tetanus toxoid vaccination had slightly increased amongst married women in both rural and urban areas in recent years.[11] This finding is important as the lack of tetanus toxoid is understood to contribute to the maternal mortality rate.[12]

The delivery of preventive healthcare, particularly immunisation and vaccination of children to protect them from diseases and malnutrition, is not up to mark. Prenatal and antenatal care should be a priority along with the provision of maternity healthcare centres in rural areas. In Sindh, 50 per cent of the total health budget is allocated to Karachi while the remaining districts share the remaining 50 per cent.[13] Tertiary health and medical institutions receive a disproportionate share of the budget allocation.

Child Malnutrition

Child malnutrition, which contributes towards stunted mental as well as physical growth, is one of the most serious issues in Pakistan.

According to the National Economic Council (NEC), one in three Pakistanis is deprived of nutritious food.[14] Adequate provision of nutrition requires food security and equitable distribution and access. In recent years, the decline in the agricultural sector, has resulted in food shortages in some areas.[15] Climate change has also increased fluctuations in the seasonal cycle, affecting food production, and has also increased the spread of diseases. In 2010, flooding in Sindh caused huge devastation and dislocation, resulting in accelerated migration from flood affected areas to urban centres. Around 2.6 million acres of crop were damaged.[16] The people who migrated had to switch from producing crops to seeking jobs or self-employment opportunities, exacerbating the low food production problem.

Table 5.7: Nutritional Status of the Children in Sindh (%)—2014

Indicator	Percentage
Stunting (Moderate and Severe)	48
Underweight (Severe)	17
Wasting (Moderate)	15
Overweight	1

Source: Government of Sindh and United Nations International Children's Emergency Fund, *Multiple Cluster Indicator Survey 2014*, Karachi, 2015.

Sindh's nutritional crisis has hampered the growth of children. As shown in Table 5.7 almost quarter of the children (48 per cent) are too short for their age, i.e. severely stunted. Stunting occurs as a result of malnourishment or contact with infections at birth. Poor environmental conditions also hinder a child's ability to grow. Other problems such as wasting (15 per cent) and being underweight (17 per cent) have also surfaced due to nutritional imbalance. Wasting, when the child is underweight for their height, reduces their immunity, putting them at the risk of death. Underweight is defined as being of a lower weight compared to an average child of the same age. This increases the risk of mortality amongst children.[17]

The poorest households are hit the hardest—64 per cent of children belonging to the lowest income quintiles are stunted as compared to 24 per cent for the highest quintile.

Karachi division, with the highest literacy rate and plentiful economic opportunities, has the lowest prevalence of stunted children (31.2), while on the other extreme, Kashmore has the highest rate (66.2).[18] There are more stunted children in rural areas than in urban areas. The prevalence of stunted children is lower in rich households (22.6) as well as in households where the mother is educated (15.7).[19]

School feeding programmes have been found to enhance nutritional levels and school attendance but attempts in the past such as the Tawana Pakistan Programme have failed to yield positive results. An integrated approach towards nutrition and food along with proper monitoring and supervision should be able to overcome difficulties faced in the provision of nutritious food to school-going children.

Maternal Health and Family Planning

One of the main indicators of the poor health status of women in Sindh province is the high maternal mortality rate, which is 214 per 100,000 births compared to the national average of 178 (Table 5.2). This vividly demonstrates the poor socio-economic conditions which women are accustomed to in the province. In rural areas, Girls are married off quite young in the country at large and especially in rural areas, which leads to longer reproductive cycles in some cases and high maternal deaths in others.

Longer reproductive cycles have led to a total fertility rate (TFR) of 4 in Sindh.[20] This is propelled by a low contraceptive prevalence rate of 29. Family planning programmes have faced major backlash due to the conservative mindsets of the people. Women do not use contraceptives either by their own choice or by that of their husbands. Less than one-third of currently married women actually use modern methods of contraception. Utilisation of protection strongly correlates with the number of living children, woman's educational level, and wealth status. Contraceptive prevalence was the highest in the divisions of Karachi and Hyderabad, and lowest in the divisions of Larkana, Sukkur, and Mirpurkhas.

The key to family planning lies in empowering women through education and an improvement in their economic status. An increase in knowledge allows them to better understand the social and economic problems they face. They can be more confident in communicating with health professionals and will be willing to take decisions related to their personal health. This will eventually lead to an increase in the utilisation of reproductive health services.

To achieve the SDG of a maternal mortality ratio of 70 per 100,000 live births, the provision of antenatal care is essential. Antenatal care entails informing women about the risks associated with pregnancy, particulars of labour and delivery, and the importance of breast-feeding. Furthermore, guidance on birth spacing can increase the chances of an infant's survival. It is an instrumental step in improving maternal health since it boosts the nutritional intake of mothers, such as that of tetanus toxoid, which helps in controlling maternal deaths.

As many as three-fourths of women in Sindh received antenatal care in 2014, mostly provided by a medical doctor in the ratio of 40:60 in public and private centres.[21] Two-thirds of deliveries are undertaken by a skilled attendant, i.e., a medical doctor, nurse, midwife, or a lady health visitor. Less than a third of deliveries take place at home, with an enhanced risk of fatality for both.

Disease Prevention

Among common diseases, malaria has been a source of much distress recently due to outbreaks of dengue fever. The detection of tuberculosis (TB) cases amount to 57 per cent on an average.[22] However, Sindh has an above national average figure of 87 per cent for treatment success rate.[23] Hepatitis B and C incidences in the general population of Sindh was reported to be 2.5 per cent and 5 per cent respectively in the recent Multiple Indicator Cluster Survey.[24]

According to the Sindh Aids Control Programme (SACP) of 2014, there were 994 new cases of HIV/Aids in Sindh with 91 per cent of the patients being men.[25] Children had been infected either because of mother-to-child transmission or because of thalassemia.[26] More than one half of the reported HIV cases in Pakistan were from Sindh of which 81 per cent were from Karachi. Injectable drug users (IDU), and male and female sex workers are most vulnerable to HIV. Jail inmates and street children are also at a high risk of contracting this disease.[27] Mental health issues have also been growing in Sindh. They account for 12 per cent of the total foregone Disability-Adjusted Life Year (DALY), a majority of which is due to clinical depression. The actual rates are much higher, due to increasing inflation and violence over the years. This area of health has not been explored in depth.[28]

Intra-Regional Disparity

Stark disparity in health exists even between districts for a variety of reasons such as differences in government attention, geographical location, budget allocation, role of the private sector, and development schemes. It may be useful to examine the condition of the most backward district of the province, Tharparkar, which is also the most health-stressed district. A number of factors such as unreliable livelihood, backwardness, geographical location in arid zones, and inadequate health coverage have placed Pakistan at the list of medium development countries—with the likes of Botswana, El Salvador, Iraq, Kiribati Nicaragua, and Zambia—in the 2016 Human Development Index (HDI). Over the past few years, children of Thar have been dying at an alarming rate. Challenging living conditions comprising poor sanitation, inadequate supply of food, sparse health service, lack of awareness of diseases, and an unhealthy lifestyle have contributed to the grim situation of Thar.

Table 5.8: Comparison of Health Indicators in Tharparkar and Sindh (Percentage)—2014

Indicators	Tharparkar	Sindh
Low-birth weight infants	10.3	7.8
Underweight (Severe)	68.8	17
Stunted (Severe)	63	24
Wasted (Moderate)	32.9	15
Children who have ever been breastfed	93.9	95.6
Children who received minimum dietary diversity	1.2	10.8
Neonatal Tetanus Protection (Percentage of women who received at least 2 doses during last pregnancy)	34.2	47.4
Use of Improved drinking water	53.7	90.5
Use of Improved sanitation	18.9	64.6
Total Fertility	5.7	4.0
Antenatal care from any skilled provider at least once	30.6	79.7
Delivered in Health Facility	20.7	65.3

Source: Government of Sindh and United Nations Development Programme, *Sindh Multiple Indicator Cluster Survey 2014*, Karachi, 2015.

A comparative analysis of health indicators of Tharparkar with that of Sindh raises severe concerns. Food insecurity is of major concern and has resulted in malnutrition among children and put most of them at the verge of death. Thar's statistics for stunting, wasting, and being underweight are higher than Sindh's average. Minimum dietary diversity is also the lowest in Thar. High maternal and infant deaths can also be attributed to a lack of neonatal tetanus protection, at an appalling rate of 34.2, combined with low rates of antenatal care from a skilled provider (30.6) and less deliveries taking place at a health centre (18.9). Since more children are dying, this has led women to choose to have more children, which is evident from a high fertility rate of 5.7.

Most of the health problems of Tharparkar can be attributed to its climactic condition of frequent droughts, absence of alternative livelihood earning arrangements, lack of access to drinking water, etc. The climatic situation of Thar remains unchanged over the years and it has taken a heavy toll on the lives of the people. The climatic conditions have amplified the vulnerability of the poor and the weak. After the drought, women have been reported to have stopped or reduced breastfeeding, which is a circumstance that is strongly correlated with malnutrition.[29] Drought-struck areas have severe health problems like diarrhoea (87), fever and malaria (82), cough and respiratory tract infections (79), and, skin diseases (41).[30]

Although 113 health facilities are available for the people of Thar, the services and facilities are inadequate as only one district headquarter hospital has a capacity of fifty beds and three tehsil/taluka headquarter hospitals have a capacity of 80 beds.[31] This leads to overcrowding and long waiting times even in emergency cases. Sixty-six per cent of the locals reported that the nearest facility, BHU, or dispensary, is at a distance of more than 5 km. Only 32 per cent of the villagers agreed that the nearest facility was not functional.[32]

The cost of reaching the nearest health facility has a price range of PKR 1,000 to PKR 4,000 attached to it, making access to healthcare virtually unaffordable. The average travel time to the closest health facility is of about 2 to 4 hours. Brackish water from the wells is the main source of water and sanitary toilets are almost non-existent.[33]

Nevertheless, there have been initiatives attempting to address the crisis of Tharparkar. After the alarming rates of malnutrition in Thar, the WHO, WFP, and UNICEF took immediate steps. Eighty children were admitted at the nutrition stabilisation centre at DHQ Mithi. As many as seventy-one children were cured.[34]

However, the government needs to initiate development schemes to elevate the conditions of Thar. The worst-stricken areas need to be provided with food supplements to mitigate malnutrition amongst children. In order to maintain a hygienic standard of living, drinking water and sanitation need to be improved. The government also needs to undertake water conservation projects and reinstall water facilities. Mobile health teams should visit inaccessible areas. Lastly, awareness programmes on health and hygiene should be conducted so that people can respond almost immediately to the symptoms of prevalent diseases.

Healthcare Providers

PUBLIC SECTOR

The usage of the public-sector health facilities in Sindh is only 22 per cent, compared to 29 per cent at the national level. In rural and urban areas, private services are sought after for treatments and check-ups. Although some healthcare centres in the rural areas are designed properly, they are under-utilised due to poor maintenance, staff shortage, and mediocre management of equipment and facilities. Since the primary healthcare system is not properly functional, tertiary and teaching hospitals are utilised beyond their maximum capacity. The LHW programme is a commendable initiative on the preventive side but its coverage extends to 20–43 per cent. This programme needs to be expanded and reformed with better supervision, training, and resources to increase accessibility.

The number of teaching hospitals in the province has risen from two to seven (Table 5.9) with almost three times the increase in hospital beds. However, meeting the demand still remains a major challenge. As low-income families invariably use these hospitals, the rationing takes place through administrative discretion or rent seeking. Instances of poor patients denied immediate help at these hospitals have become commonplace due to this demand–supply gap. Poor governance and weak management have been major stumbling blocks. Several experiments, such as the introduction of autonomous boards of governors, were done but with little success. Political interference in the human resource management of these hospitals has been a bane as most specialists serving therein are politically well-connected. They do not wish to abandon their lucrative private practices in large urban centres and move to places such as Larkana, Khairpur, and Nawabshah, where there is a dearth of qualified specialists. The imbalance in the quality of medical personnel acts a 'pull' factor for people from the interior districts of Sindh rushing to Karachi's Civil or Jinnah hospitals.[35]

The number of non-teaching hospitals such as those at the district headquarter or taluka combined have multiplied almost five-fold, and their capacity is almost equal to that of the teaching hospitals. Upgradation of facilities at these hospitals with diagnostic equipment, appropriate medical and paramedical staff, and incentives could relieve much pressure on the teaching hospitals. Hospital beds have expanded more than two times since 1970; however, the population has grown more than three times. A backlog is accumulating as the capacity in these hospitals has failed to keep pace with population growth. The shortages therefore crowd out the poorest among the poor who deserve public sector facilities the most. This inequitable access to basic service such as health is one of the main contributory factors to the rural–urban disparities. An increasing number of philanthropic organisations and individuals, who are donating funds, equipment, and volunteers to upgrade public sector hospitals wards and theatres selectively, is making some difference, but this momentum has to be sustained over time. Civil Hospital, Karachi, has two-thirds of its funds emanating from philanthropic and charity organisations and individuals and only one-third from the provincial budget.

Some teaching hospitals do not have proper equipment or machinery for the patients. This leads to less patients and has an adverse impact on medical education.[36]

Table 5.9: Public Sector Health Facilities in Sindh (1970–2015)

	Dispensaries		Rural Health Centres		Tuber-culosis Clinics	Basic Health Units		Maternal and Child Health Centres	Teaching Hospitals	
	Number	Beds	Number	Beds	Number	Number	Beds	Number	Number	Beds
1970	44	49	19	82	9	-	-	-	2	1,775
1975	47	60	27	108	13	-	-	-	2	2,205
1980	85	60	52	640	14	-	-	-	6	4,195
1985	100	14	60	700	13	33	-	-	6	3,402
1990	94	12	67	814	126	372	804	-	6	4,384
1995	111	12	83	1,252	158	615	1,286	-	6	4,658
2000	221	4	92	1,364	169	701	1,450	36	5	5,330
2005	340	6	99	1,464	174	753	1,550	40	5	5,474
2010	420	6	106	1,582	186	772	1,586	40	6	5,799
2015	865	6	129	1,629	187	798	1,598	94	7	6,017

Sources: The figures from 1970–2005 have been taken from Bureau of Statistics, *Development Statistics of Sindh*, Karachi, Planning and Development Department, various years; Bureau of Statistics, *Health Profile*, Karachi, Planning and Development Department, Government of Sindh, various years.

An analysis of the current public health centres such as dispensaries, RHCs, and BHUs has been presented in Table 5.9. From a glance at the data, it would appear that there has been a phenomenal increase in the number of facilities over the last thirty-five years. From only nineteen rural health centres with eighty-two beds in 1970, there has been a tremendous rise to 129 RHCs with 1,629 beds supplemented by 798 BHUs with 1,598 beds.

Table 5.10: Relevant Ratios of Availability of Health Services to Patients in Sindh (2011–16)

Year	Population per Doctor	Population per Nurse	Population per Bed
2011	3,017	11,413	1,406
2012	2,986	11,584	1,436
2013	2,997	11,739	1,476
2014	3,014	11,966	1,488
2015	3,075	12,308	1,527
2016	3,159	12,441	1,455

Source: Bureau of Statistics, *Health Profile of Sindh*, Karachi, Planning and Development Department, various years.

Table 5.10 shows that the ratio of availability of health services to population have remained stagnant without any substantial improvement despite expansion in health facilities in the province.

However, this quantitative expansion does not depict an accurate picture as far as access, responsiveness, and quality of care is concerned. Unfilled vacancies of medical doctors, absenteeism of medical staff, poor patient care, management, shortage of drugs, and sparse diagnostic equipment make it difficult for the sick to seek relief at these centres.

A survey carried out in the context of PSLM (Table 5.11) indicates that the four main reasons for not opting for public sector health facilities are inaccessibility to a government facility, absence of government facilities, insufficient medicines, and inhospitable behaviour of the staff.

Table 5.11: Reasons for Not Opting for Public Health Facilities in Punjab and Sindh (%) (2013–14)

Reasons	Punjab	Sindh
Too far away	30	25
No Government Facility	18	9
Not enough medicines	15	12
Staff not courteous	8	14

Source: Pakistan Bureau of Statistics, *Pakistan Social and Living Standards Measurement Survey (PSLM) 2013–14*, Islamabad, Statistics Division, Government of Pakistan, p. 93.

The recent initiative of the Sindh government to outsource these facilities to private or non-governmental organisations under Public-Private Partnership is a step in the right direction. According to the health facilities Sindh provincial report, only 55 per cent of infrastructure components were available and functional at BHUs.[37] Labour rooms and LHV residences were available in 37 per cent and 59 per cent of BHUs respectively.

There has been a proliferation of private medical colleges in Sindh in the recent years. Serious questions have been raised about the quality and accreditation of some of the medical colleges. Standards are lax, violation and infringements of standards are rampant, and enforcement is weak. The Pakistan Medical and Dental Council (PMDC) was revamped recently but it is too early to assess the results.

The new medical colleges established in Mirpurkhas and Sukkur, for example, do not have the minimum number of qualified teachers, or the laboratories or equipment needed for a standard medical college. There is already an excess of doctors being produced every year by the existing universities and colleges, but their effective participation in the delivery of healthcare is contained by two main factors. Primarily, the majority of the graduates are females, which is highly commendable, but only a small fraction of them enter the profession. Thus, the huge public subsidy incurred in their education has a negative social return.

Secondly, those admitted in medical institutions on rural domicile wish to stay in big urban centres and use connections to avoiding postings in the rural districts. Thus, the two sources of disparity—gender and a rural–urban—divide remain unaddressed despite substantial investment.

Table 5.12: Medical Personnel in Sindh (Public) (1975–2015)

Year	Doctors	Nurses	LHV technicians	Radiographer	Health technicians
1975	926	415	107	14	95
1980	969	436	135	15	105
1985	1,758	607	158	13	82
1990	7,213	837	220	13	295
1995	7,702	1,343	218	11	1,027
2000	7,953	1,639	306	11	1,369
2005	6,626	1,581	406	11	-
2010	7,145	1,565	464	-	-
2015	7,990	1,630	786	-	-

Source: The figures for 1975–95 have been taken from Bureau of Statistics, *Development Statistics of Sindh*, Karachi, Planning and Development Department, Government of Sindh, various years; Bureau of Statistics, *Health Profile*, Karachi, Planning and Development Department, Government of Sindh, various years.

Table 5.12 shows a continuous increase in the number of doctors, nurses, and LHV technicians. The population to doctor ratio has improved significantly but nurses are still in short supply. Technicians are now getting places in the system. Two distinct trends are visible from this data. The number of doctors has appreciably gone up almost eight times in the last thirty years, but there was a downward movement from 1995 to 2005. This has reversed because of the growth of private colleges. This may be increasing the number of doctors, but professional competence and adequate training according to acceptable standards remain open to serious questions. Most of these colleges are driven mainly by profit with little attention to the quality of instructions.

The number of LHV assistants, operation theatre (OT) technicians, *dais*, and lab assistants continuously increased, which is a positive sign as they serve as the backbone of an efficient and responsive healthcare delivery system.

PRIVATE SECTOR

The private sector has assumed the role of a leading provider of primary, secondary, diagnostic, pharmacy, and ambulance services. Fifty-nine per cent of private hospitals of the country, which run for profit, are located in Sindh. The private healthcare provision now encompasses a full range of medical and dental services. Private clinics are expensive since they operate at market prices, yet they are preferred because the alternative, i.e. public sector, suffers from a number of weaknesses. In rural areas, unqualified practitioners, quacks, compounds, faith healers, and *hakeems* dominate the scene as the poor cannot afford to pay for the services of qualified, private-practising doctors. The introduction of the public-private initiative over the last several years is beginning to divert patients towards government clinics, dispensaries, health units, and health centres.

The private health sector is divided into profit and non-profit ventures. The province also constitutes the largest network of not-for-profit health services. Private healthcare has a strong footing in urban areas. Attempts to set up clinics in rural areas have met with limited success but as rural incomes rise, there would be an increased demand for private clinics and dispensaries.

NON-GOVERNMENTAL ORGANISATIONS (NGOs)

NGOs have contributed immensely to increasing access of the poor to healthcare. Edhi Foundation, which has the largest ambulance service in Pakistan, has contributed immensely and is complemented with an efficient communication system. The Indus Hospital and the SIUT provide free services to those who cannot afford medical care.[38] Edhi Foundation runs the world's largest ambulance service and so do many others including Aman Foundation, Chhipa etc.

The NGOs are building and ramping up specialised wards or units in public-sector hospitals. This is a positive move as a majority of the poor turn up at these hospitals rather than visiting the charitable or philanthropic facilities.

Other active organisations in this field include the Marie Stopes Society, Pakistan Voluntary Health and Nutrition Association (PAVHNA), Fire Protection Association of Pakistan (FPAP), Health and Nutritional Development Society (HANDS), Thardeep, Health Oriented Preventive Education (HOPE), and Health Education Library for People (HELP). Similarly, AKHSP is operating in secondary maternal care and primary health care.

Some of the NGOs are engaged in raising awareness for social issues. Aahung is an organisation that focuses on improving reproductive health. War against Rape (WAR) is productive in raising awareness regarding sexual violence. Aurat Foundation concentrates on the role of women in political and governance spheres.

Health Expenditures

Under the Eighteenth Amendment, the responsibility of health was delegated to the provinces. This has resulted in a gradual increase in budget allocation for this sector. The total spending on health jumped from PKR 8.2 billion in 2005–06 to PKR 48.4 billion in 2015–16—a six-fold increase over ten years. Most of the budget was incurred on recurring expenditure. The provincial development spending for the health sector jumped from PKR 2,335 million in 2005–06 to PKR 8,368 million in 2015–16.[39] Increased expenditure in the absence of adequate governance and management may not improve healthcare delivery services particularly to poor segments of the population. Therefore, the Government of Sindh's initiative of public-private partnership deserves close scrutiny. Benchmark indicators should be established against which progress in achieving performance indicators is regularly measured, monitored, and course correction made where necessary. Preventive healthcare facilities including potable drinking water and sanitation facilities should be allocated adequate resources and given equal

Table 5.13: Sindh Health Budgetary Estimates and Expenditures (in PKR Million)
(1970–71 to 2015–16)

	1970–71	1975–76	1980–81	1985–86	1990–91	1995–96	2000–01	2005–06	2010–11	2015–16
Total Health	53.425	132.727	77.445	811.66	1,469.02	2,971.78	4,128.31	4,965.36	14,265.81	66,503.90
Recurrent	26.561	65.227	7.025	347.66	1,098.02	2,214.30	3,734.98	4,170.36	10,786.57	54,090.96
Development	26.864	67.5	70.42	464	371	757.48	393.33	795.00	3,479.24	12,412.95
Percentage share of Budgeted Recurrent and Development Expenditure (%)										
	1970–71	1975–76	1980–80	1985–86	1990–91	1995–96	2000–01	2005–06	2010–11	2015–16
Total	100	100	100	100	100	100	100	100	100	100
Recurrent	50	49	9	43	75	75	90	84	76	81
Development	50	51	91	57	25	25	10	16	24	19
Actual Spending										
	1970–71	1975–76	1980–81	1985–86	1990–91	1995–96	2000–01	2005–06	2010–11	2015–16
Actual Total Spending	61.14292	7.25	N/A	391.96	1,198.13	2,293.24	3,327.99	8,244.68	13,321.64	48,473.27
Recurrent	N/A	N/A	N/A	346.58	1070.12	2118.17	3211.03	5,909.81	9,458.95	40,105.73
Development	N/A	N/A	N/A	45.37	128.01	175.07	116.96	2334.865	3,862.69	8,367.54
Actual Spending as a Percentage of Budgeted Figures (%)										
	1970–71	1975–76	1980–81	1985–86	1990–91	1995–96	2000–01	2005–06	2010–11	2015–16
Percentage of Actual Total Spending	N/A	N/A	N/A	48	82	77	81	166	93	73
Percentage of Actual Recurrent Spending	N/A	N/A	N/A	100	97	96	86	142	88	74
Percentage of Actual Development Spending	N/A	N/A	N/A	10	35	23	30	294	111	67

Source: Finance Department, Finance Budget Book, Government of Sindh, various years.

attention. The crowding out of health managers' time and financial resources in the form of curative health facilities is one of the main reasons for the relative neglect of tackling the challenges of malnutrition, child and maternity health, family planning etc.

The following has been achieved in the period 2008–09 to 2011–12:

- The Hepatitis Control and Prevention Programme was initiated, which included vaccinations, treatment of afflicted patients, additional laboratories, awareness on a large scale, and training of staff. As many as 4.572 million people were vaccinated, of whom 0.75 million were children. Around 93,664 patients were treated for Hepatitis B, C, and D.
- In different secondary and tertiary care hospitals, 43 specialised units were built and 2,800 of the health staff was trained to improve service delivery in Sindh.
- The Public-Private Health Initiative (PPHI) was established in 2007. It operates in 21 districts, and manages 1,135 health facilities comprising 651 BHUs, 34 MCHs, 429 dispensaries, 9 RHCs, and 12 other facilities. Its performance over the years has made some difference owing to cost-saving techniques, efficient management, and strict monitoring. PPHI has a long list of satisfied patients who are highly impressed by and indebted to its proficient services. PPHI ensures that it is well-stocked with equipment such as X-ray machines, which allows for speedy diagnosis and treatment. The rates of antenatal and prenatal care, OPD attendance, and delivery coverage are a testament to PPHI's performance in improving the health of rural Sindh. It has confronted urban bias and removed the need for the locals to visit big cities for medical check-ups. It is a successful example of a public-private partnership.
- Expanded Programme of Immunisation, Tuberculosis Control Programme, Malaria Control Programme, and HIV/AIDS Control Programme took place.

Table 5.14: MDG Health Goals and Actual Outcomes as of 2014

Indicator	Sindh (2014)	MDG Target
Infant mortality rate (deaths per 1,000 live births)	82	52
Child mortality rate (under 5–mortality)	104	40
Proportion of fully immunised children aged 12–23 months	35	>90
Lady health workers coverage (as a percentage of the target population)	52.3*	100
Proportion of children 12–23 months immunised against measles	52.7	>90
Children Under 5 who suffered from diarrhoea in the last 30 days	28.4**	<10
Maternal mortality ratio (per 100,000 live births)	214***	140
Proportion of births attended by skilled birth attendants	65.3	>90
Contraceptive prevalence rate	29	55
Total fertility rate	4	2.1
Antenatal care coverage (at least once)	79.7	100

* Percentage of women aged 15–49 years who were visited by lady health workers during the past three months.
** Percentage of children with diarrhoea, under age five in the last 2 weeks.
*** Refer to table 5.2.

Source: Government of Sindh and United Nations Development Programme, *Sindh Multiple Indicator Cluster Survey 2014,* Karachi, 2015; Government of Sindh and United Nations Development Programme, *Report on the status of the Millennium Development Goals Sindh,* Karachi, 2012.

The report on MDGs-Sindh, published in March 2011, for almost all the indicators observed that some of the districts performed far better than the others, and yet the crux of the problem was due to an urban bias. This was persistent even in districts which produced good results.

A trend analysis showed fluctuation in the immunisation rates, where 'between 1991 and 1999 immunisation coverage increased, declined, and then picked up again'.[40] However, the report concluded that the pace was not sufficient for the MDG targets to be met. Furthermore, a majority of the districts showed disturbing cases of diarrhoea along with underweight children.

Disparity between rural and urban areas was also highlighted in this report. The performance in big cities such as Karachi and Hyderabad, and to some extent Nawabshah and Sukkur, has been relatively better due to the availability of quality health services and generous funds.

It was also pointed out that social factors influence child health and the provision of child care. Literacy levels, gender disparity, access to safe drinking water and sanitation, and food supply reflect the challenges faced by the society. Moreover, the health sector suffers from weaknesses of its own which prevent execution of its services with excellence. These include poor management and governance systems, chronic staff, absence of complementary supervision techniques, unfair financial disbursement between urban and rural areas, and weak decision-making and planning.

Pakistan has now adopted the SDGs which aim to end hunger and poverty by 2030. This is an opportunity for the government to execute plans that could work towards the attainment of the following goals:

- Maternal mortality to be reduced to less than 70 per 100 000 live births
- Neonatal mortality to be as low as 12 per 1000 live births
- End to AIDS, tuberculosis, malaria, and waterborne diseases
- Universal access to reproductive healthcare facilities

Summing Up

The poor health status of Sindh's population, particularly in rural areas, requires an integrated multi-sectoral strategy. An integrated health sector approach includes family planning services, immunisations, emphasis on nutrition, water supply, and sanitation. LHWs should be continuously trained better by focusing on their skills, especially communication ones, to help in reaching out to poor families. Messages should be effectively targeted in regional languages and must have the feedback mechanisms to respond to the concerns and questions of the families/contacted. Parallel organisations, although some may claim that these are efficient, work in isolation and are compartmentalised, making them neither cost effective nor efficient.

The devolution of primary, and secondary healthcare facilities to the local governments with adequate financial and human resources would bring relief to the population as well as the overcrowded tertiary and teaching hospitals. The PPHI should be carefully monitored, and its impact and outreach evaluated, and the initiative expanded to cover other districts. The provincial health department should concentrate on policy making, and regulation along with developing options for health financing. The procurement of spurious drugs is supported by public hospitals for supplying to the patients while genuine drugs procured for the public sector are sold to private pharmacies, contributing to the loss of trust in the public health system. Therefore, high out-of-pocket expenditures are incurred on drugs by the patients and their families.

Staffing of nurses and lady health workers in rural health facilities should be increased and incentivised to help attract qualified personal to those areas. Uniform national pay scales have done a great disservice in the way of promoting the rural population's access to health services. These scales have to be replaced by labour market differentiated compensation packages, where scarcity premia are paid to those services in the rural areas.

The integrated health management information system (IHMS) should be updated, verified, and validated to assist in planning and introducing missing services as well as setting up new health facilities in various parts of the provinces.

Plans to educate and train nurses, technicians, radiographers, and pharmacists ought to be drawn in order to fill in the current and future vacancies in the health system. Private medical colleges should be screened and those below par should be closed down.

The budget allocations have to be revisited in terms of salary and non-salary components. The present ratio of 65:35 does not leave much scope for enhancing the quality of services rendered. A large portion of the salary component is pre-empted by the general and support staff, some of which is not required but employed only on political considerations or humanitarian grounds. The salary saved from the attrition and non-replacement of this type of staff can be diverted to finance non-salary expenditures.

6

Labour and Employment

Introduction

IN economics, labour constitutes one of the four main factors of production, with the other three being land, capital, and entrepreneurship. In developing countries such as Pakistan, capital and entrepreneurship are scarce while land is a fixed resource. The only mobile and plentiful factor of production is labour. Recent work on developing economies shows that human capital embodied in labour can become a potent force in boosting growth and reducing poverty.

Pakistan depends on land and labour as the main ingredients of its economic growth. With land yield in Sindh being volatile due to the vagaries of the River Indus, labour assumes greater importance.

Unfortunately, as important as labour is to the economy, the paucity of data and literature exploring labour issues and the government policies that relegate labour to oblivion have made it difficult to develop its full potential. This chapter draws heavily on the Labour Force Survey (LFS) of the Federal Bureau of Statistics as the provincial labour department and the Sindh Bureau of Statistics do not have much to add to our understanding of the issues related to this sector.

An Overview

Table 6.1: Population and Labour Force of Pakistan and Sindh (in Million)
(1951–2014)

Year	Pakistan		Sindh	
	Population	Labour Force	Population	Labour Force
1951	33.7	9.5	6.0	1.64
1961	42.9	12.8	8.4	0.8
1972	65.3	19.0	14.2	-
1981	84.3	22.6	19.0	5.1
1998	132.4	29.4	30.4	7.8
2014	188.0	61.0	45.0	14.3

Source: The population figures in 1951–98 have been taken from the Population Census Organisation, *Population Census Report*, Karachi/Islamabad, Government of Pakistan, various years; The population figures in 2014 have been taken from Ministry of Finance, Population, Labour Force and Employment', in *Pakistan Economic Survey 2015–16*, Islamabad, Government of Pakistan, 2016. Labour force figures have been obtained from Pakistan Bureau of Statistics, *Labour Force Survey*, Karachi/Islamabad, Government of Pakistan, various years.

Table 6.2: Labour Force Participation Rates for Pakistan by Area (%)
(1990–91 to 2014–15)

Years	Pakistan		
	Total	Urban	Rural
1990–1991	43.2	37.6	44.2
1997–1998	43.3	36.3	45.4
2005–2006	46.0	39.6	48.6
2010–2011	45.7	38.5	48.8
2014–2015	45.2	37.9	48.9

Source: Pakistan Bureau of Statistics, *Labour Force Survey*, Islamabad, Statistics Division, Government of Pakistan, various years.

According to the Labour Force Survey, Sindh's labour force of 14.3 million accounted for almost one-third of the province's population in 2014. Similarly, the labour force to population ratio of Pakistan in the same year was 32 per cent (Table 6.1). However, the latest data from the Human Development Report (HDR) shows that the employment to population ratio (15+ years of age) in Pakistan is 51.6 per cent. The labour force participation rate or the refined activity rate (as termed in the LFS) is defined as 'the currently active population expressed as a percentage of the population 10 years and above.'[1]

Since the 1990s, the Labour Force Participation rate for Pakistan has increased gradually from 43.2 in 1990–91 to 45.2 in 2014–15. The average rate during this period has been 45 per cent (Table 6.2).

Table 6.3: Labour Force Participation Rates and Underemployment Rates for Pakistan by Area and Gender (%) (1990–91 to 2014–15)

Years	Labour Force Participation Rates					Unemployment Rates				
	Total	Male		Female		Total	Male		Female	
		Rural	Urban	Rural	Urban		Rural	Urban	Rural	Urban
1990–91	43.2	73.6	66.6	14.8	8.6	6.3	3.9	5.9	13.3	27.8
1997–98	43.3	73.4	65.2	17.4	7.4	5.9	3.5	5.8	11.9	28.6
2005–06	46.0	73.8	68.7	23.4	10.6	6.2	4.6	6.9	7.7	15.8
2010–11	45.7	70.0	66.4	27.6	10.7	6.0	4.0	7.1	6.4	20.7
2014–15	45.2	69.0	65.7	28.8	10.0	5.9	4.3	6.2	6.7	20.4

Source: Pakistan Bureau of Statistics, *Labour Force Survey*, Islamabad, Statistics Division, Government of Pakistan, various years.

If we use the HDR definition of the working population of 15 years and above, the rate goes up to 54.4 per cent. This implies that almost one half of the country's potential labour force is not engaged in monetised economic activities. They may be children in the school system, or elders who have retired, or those who are physical disabilities or handicaps. There may be others who may have voluntarily withdrawn from active search in the market. Pakistan fares poorly in labour force participation rates compared to other developing countries having the same income levels. The main reason for this low rate is the absence of females from the active labour market. Even in rural areas, females are engaged mostly as unpaid family help. A further breakdown by urban–rural and male–female (Table 6.3) shows that in urban areas, only 10 per cent of the females are doing a gainfully employed job. This non-utilisation or underutilisation of almost half of the potential labour force is a matter of serious concern.

Table 6.4: Labour Force Participation and Unemployment Rates for Sindh by Area and Gender (%)
(1990–91 to 2014–15)

| Years | Labour Force Participation Rates | | | | | Unemployment Rates | | | | |
| | Total | Male | | Female | | Total | Male | | Female | |
		Rural	Urban	Rural	Urban		Rural	Urban	Rural	Urban
1990–91	41.6	76.6	65.7	9.5	5.9	3.5	1.3	4.0	10.7	16.7
1997–98	39.8	76.5	62.3	8.2	4.6	3.0	1.3	2.6	13.4	20.0
2005–06	42.9	77.2	68.5	12.4	6.2	4.4	2.6	5.4	5.4	13.1
2010–11	45.0	75.2	65.5	25.2	7.2	5.1	1.8	8.0	2.3	21.7
2014–15	43.0	72.5	66.1	21.7	6.2	4.7	1.7	5.5	5.3	28.7

Source: Pakistan Bureau of Statistics, *Labour Force Survey*, Islamabad, Statistics Division, Government of Pakistan, various years.

The low recorded unemployment rates do not tally with common observation and casual empiricism, raising scepticism about the validity of the data. In fact, unemployment and underemployment need to be clubbed together as Pakistan has a large underemployed population. The reported open unemployment is low because of the family support system. A shopkeeper or a farmer may employ a relative at a very minimal cash wage or in-kind compensation even when there is no obvious need for an additional hand. In the surveys, this individual ceases to fall in the category of 'unemployed'.

In case of Sindh, the labour force participation rate has averaged around 42 per cent during the 1990–2015 period except that it declined from 41 per cent to 39.76 in 1997–98 (Table 6.4). The rate increased subsequently, peaking at 45 during 2010–11. An objective analysis of this erratic behaviour has not been undertaken but it can be deduced that political economy factors and the unstable law and order situation may have contributed to the dips. Alternatively, migration from rural areas and other parts of the country to the Middle East may have diverted the potential supply. But these factors fall in the realm of speculation rather than informed analysis. It may also be possible that the 1997–98 data may simply be a statistical quirk. The stability in labour force participation can be gauged from the fact that as early as 1974–75, the rate was 43.1—not much different from recent years.

It is worth noting that although Sindh is relatively more urbanised, the female urban participation rate in the survey is about 6 per cent which is below the national average and almost one-half of that in Punjab. This finding is contrary to the observed trend of females increasingly taking part in education, health, and financial services sectors in Karachi, Hyderabad, and Sukkur.

Punjab has performed relatively well with its average labour force participation of 47 per cent during the 1990–2015 period, outstripping not just Sindh's but also the national average (Table 6.5). The rate increased by four percentage points during this period as compared to only one and two percentage points for Sindh and Pakistan as a whole, respectively.

A stark difference can be observed not only between male and female labour force participation rates but also between rural and urban areas. While the (national) female labour force participation rate in rural areas has increased over the years by 14 percentage points (Table 6.3), on average, the differential in the rate for male (rural) is still approximately three times that of females. This rises to five and three for Sindh and Punjab respectively, highlighting a higher gap in labour participation between males and females in Sindh as compared to Punjab.

Table 6.5: Labour Force Participation and Unemployment Rates for Punjab by Area and Gender (%) (1990–91 to 2014–15)

Years	Labour Force Participation Rates (%)					Unemployment Rates (%)				
	Total	Male		Female		Total	Male		Female	
		Rural	Urban	Rural	Urban		Rural	Urban	Rural	Urban
1990–91	44.3	73.6	67.3	17.6	10.8	7.5	4.6	7.3	14.6	31.9
1997–98	46.3	75.2	67.7	22.4	9.6	6.5	3.8	7.7	9.1	29.9
2005–06	48.9	74.2	69.5	30.3	14.0	6.0	4.7	7.8	5.1	14.9
2010–11	48.3	70.6	68.0	33.2	13.4	6.1	4.6	6.6	6.2	19.2
2014–15	48.5	70.9	66.7	35.5	12.8	6.3	5.2	6.7	6.1	17.0

Source: Pakistan Bureau of Statistics, *Labour Force Survey*, Islamabad, Statistics Division, Government of Pakistan, various years.

Looking at the urban population (national), however, this gap is even higher with the male labour force participation rate seven times that of females. This number for Sindh is 11 while that for Punjab is 6, again reinforcing the fact that when it comes to women's participation in the labour force, Punjab is performing better.

Moreover, on average, labour force participation is higher in rural areas as compared to urban areas. This may not be of much surprise in the case of females as a majority in rural areas are employed in the agricultural sector. In the case of males, the rate is higher for those in rural areas as compared to those in urban areas.

Interestingly, while the female labour force participation rate has increased by 14 percentage points in rural areas in Pakistan and by two percentage points in urban areas, it has declined for males for both urban and rural areas. Similar is the case for Sindh and Punjab.

An analysis of age-specific rates (Table 6.6) shows that the labour force participation rate jumps after the 15–19 age bracket from 32 to 51 for ages 20–24, thereafter increasing to reach the peak of 65 for the age groups 45–49 and then tapers off gradually to 29 for 65 and above. The 10–14 age bracket signifies that 9 per cent of children in the school-going age in Pakistan work as child labourers (Annex Table 6A). Commenting on the economically active population as defined in the LFS, Hisam argues:

This definition is contradictory to the definitions given in the Constitution of Pakistan (Article 25-A) and the national law on child labour, which sets the limit of 14 years for the person to enter labour market. Also, the ILO core labour convention (No.138) on the minimum age stipulates that the person entering the labour force should not 'be less than the age of completion of compulsory schooling and, in any case, shall not be less than 15 years'.[2]

To that effect, the HDR uses the working population entry age as 15, which makes sense. However, the presence of employed boys and girls in the age bracket 10 to 14 revealed in the survey should raise alarms and policy and institutional measures ought to be taken to eliminate child labour from the province. A significant proportion of these children are out of school while they work as labourers. They must be enabled to attend school as is their constitutional right.

Table 6.6: Labour Force Participation Rates and Unemployment Rates for Sindh by Age Group (%)
(2014–15)

| Age Groups | Labour Force Participation Rates | | | | | Unemployment Rates | | | | |
| | Total | Male | | Female | | Total | Male | | Female | |
		Rural	Urban	Rural	Urban		Rural	Urban	Rural	Urban
Total (All Ages)	30.58	48.79	50.52	14.28	4.66	-	-	-	-	-
Total (10 Years and Over)	42.96	72.45	66.1	21.67	6.18	4.66	1.74	5.48	5.27	28.69
10–14	8.54	19.11	3.7	8.15	0.71	2.38	1.7	-	2.35	38.46
15–19	32.27	66.12	34.95	16.19	4.79	5.48	2.66	7.98	7.28	22.69
20–24	51.41	88.83	75.77	26.96	11.02	8.66	3.91	9.06	9.54	38.66
25–29	56.16	97.95	96.73	27.76	11.01	5.41	1.34	4.62	5.36	43.02
30–34	54.82	98.67	99.22	26.93	7.49	2.39	1.2	0.92	5.92	19.73
35–39	60.01	99.29	99.67	28.28	8.12	1.49	0.49	1.01	3.3	14.2
40–44	60.59	99.32	99.01	30	7.08	1.08	0.29	0.66	1.93	14.65
45–49	65.09	99.24	98.79	33.43	5.74	1.59	0.54	1.76	2.33	14.4
50–54	60.8	97.65	97.95	31.15	5.2	2.25	0.61	3.19	2.03	12.33
55–59	64	97.03	95.94	22.2	5.26	3.99	2.32	3.83	10.26	23.76
60–64	50.35	83.84	69.36	17	5.08	14.77	3.96	24.58	17.8	44.66
65 Years and Over	29.1	49.3	51.32	6.71	3.18	38.63	3.36	64.8	4.95	100

Source: Pakistan Bureau of Statistics, *Labour Force Survey 2014–15*, Islamabad, Statistics Division, Government of Pakistan, 2015.

Annex Table 6A also shows that the labour force participation for the 10–14 age bracket is more pronounced in rural areas. As compared to urban areas, the labour participation rate is two times higher for males and eight times higher for females in rural areas. Another glaring difference is in the rates of child labour force, where child labour appears to be slightly more prevalent in Punjab (11.5) than in Sindh (8.5). In terms of rural–urban breakup, the prevalence of child labour is primarily a rural phenomenon (refer to Annex Tables 6A and 6B).

While Punjab and Khyber Pakhtunkhwa had already amended The Employment of Children Act 1991, Sindh has just recently followed suit.[3] This, while a step in the right direction, is by no means an end to tackling the child labour issue as there has historically been a huge gap in the ratification and implementation of bills.

The variance in labour force participation rates in both Sindh and Punjab for different age brackets seems to follow a similar pattern as that of the national level.

Unemployment

Unemployment is the other important indicator, along with labour force participation rates and employed-to-population ratio, to discern the real contribution of labour to the economy.[4] The LFS defines unemployment as:

Unemployment in Pakistan comprises all persons ten years of age and above who during the reference period were:

(i)   'Without work', i.e. were not in paid-employment or self-employment; and

(ii)   'Currently available for work', i.e. were available for paid employment or self-employment; or

(iii)   Not currently available for the following reasons: illness, will take a job within a month, is temporarily laid off, is an apprentice and is not willing to work; or

(iv)   Seeking work during last week.[5]

In terms of unemployment, the national rate averaged at 6 per cent during the 1990–2015 period (Table 6.3) and did not fluctuate much. This invariant behaviour of the unemployment rate in the face of high and low economic growth rates raises a lot of scepticism about its definition and coverage. A hopeful finding from the data is that female unemployment is gradually decreasing over time, albeit the labour force participation is still dismally low compared to Bangladesh or Sri Lanka. This may point to changing societal attitudes towards female employment and may also be a result of the burgeoning informal sector which readily absorbs semi-skilled and unskilled labour.

The average unemployment rate for Sindh stood at 4 per cent during 1990–2015 while that of Punjab was relatively higher at 6 per cent (Tables 6.4 and 6.5). Unemployment rate has been lowest for rural males throughout the years for both the provinces. In Sindh, while male unemployment has increased during 1990–2015, that of females has decreased, irrespective of the area. In Punjab, however, it is surprising to find that female unemployment rate for urban areas has increased by five percentage points although female education status has improved. In contrast, the unemployment rate of females in rural areas has decreased by eight percentage points. This may be owing to increased urbanisation of rural areas that opens up more job opportunities for women, for example, in low-cost private and NGO schools and health work. These young women may prefer to get jobs in their immediate vicinity so they do not have to relocate and leave their families. This makes sense as a research study in Karachi shows that young, educated women living in the outskirts are hesitant to join the labour force in the main centres in absence of safe and reliable transport arrangements.

The highest unemployment rate is recorded for the 15–24 year age bracket (10.6 per cent). This constitutes youth unemployment and may be a source of concern.[6] The rate is higher in urban areas and is as high as 12 per cent for males and 27 per cent for females, as compared to 8 per cent and 10 per cent for their rural counterparts. One of the possible reasons is that the enrolment at tertiary level of education has risen quite rapidly in the last decade and as many as 1.8 million students in this age group are receiving education. While this is a healthy trend for the future employability of those students, it is reflected in current labour statistics as increased youth unemployment because those enrolled may be doing part time jobs. Open University, Virtual University, and evening class students may fall in this category, reconciling the high youth unemployment rate with increased tertiary enrolment. Another factor may be that this cohort does not possess much work experience and therefore the search period for finding jobs may be relatively longer for them.

Comparing Sindh and Punjab (Annex Tables 6B and 6C), youth unemployment is higher in Punjab with an average rate of 11.7 per cent as compared to that of Sindh of 7 per cent. In urban Sindh, this rate is 2.6 and 3.6 times higher than rural Sindh for males and females respectively. In Punjab, this ratio falls to is 1.5 and 3.1 for males and females respectively.

In investigating the reasons for 'not being currently available [for work]', the LFS reports on the following main factors influencing a worker to remain out of work:

1. Illness
2. Will take a job within a month
3. Temporarily laid off
4. Apprentice and not willing to work

Analysing the national data for 1997–2015 (Annex Table 6C), illness remains the biggest reason for unemployment, even though this has gradually declined from 71 per cent in 1997 to 44 per cent in 2014. This may partly be a reflection of relatively better health enjoyed by the working age population today compared to twenty years ago. Apprenticeship is the second most important reason which, on average, accounts for 31 per cent of the reasons for unemployment. The increase on this account from 21 per cent in 1997 to 46 per cent in 2014 is a favourable trend because the young men and women are equipping themselves with marketable skills that would reduce their chances for remaining unemployed. The other two reasons, 'will take a job within a month' and 'temporarily laid off', can be classified as frictional and cyclical unemployment respectively and this on average accounted for 4 per cent and 5 per cent of the total reasons between 1997 and 2014.

However, it is surprising that illness factors appear more pronounced in Punjab as compared to Sindh. While only 14 per cent term illness as a reason for unemployment in Sindh, there is a marked jump to 74 per cent for Punjab. One spurious point that emerges from this finding could be the poor healthcare system in Punjab, but this is not based on facts. The reasons behind this discrepancy needs further explanation.

The authenticity of this data is also open to question as the responses about apprenticeship in the two provinces at times appear quite implausible and difficult to understand. Therefore, it is advisable to take this information with a lot of scepticism and avoid formulating any policies based on this data.

Underemployment

According to the ILO:

> Underemployment reflects underutilisation of the productive capacity of the labour force … The indicator is important for improving the description of employment-related problems, as well as for assessing the extent to which available human resources are being used in the production process of the country concerned.[7]

The 2014–15 LFS defines underemployment as:

> Underemployment (time-related) comprises all employed persons who during the reference period satisfied the following two criteria simultaneously:
>
> (i)   Worked less than 35 hours per week,
> (ii) Sought or were available for alternative or additional work.
>
> Underemployment (time-related) Rate is the time-related underemployed population expressed as a percentage of the currently active population.[8]

According to the LFS data, the underemployment rate increases with age at first, after which it decreases. Table 6.7 shows age-specific underemployment for Pakistan, Sindh, and Punjab.

As stated earlier, underemployment in Pakistan is a more representative manifestation of labour market conditions and the data corroborates this finding. Three-fourths of the total underemployed population for Pakistan as well as Sindh and Punjab is accounted for by the age group 15–44. This finding, unlike unemployment rate, is identical for the country, Punjab, and Sindh. The highest rate of underemployment is observed in the age group 20–24, i.e. the youth, and the reasons for this are manifold. As these new entrants to the labour force do not have any work experience or are fresh out of colleges and universities, it is difficult for them to find full-time jobs. Therefore, they have to get part-time jobs to acquire experience or while waiting for the right job, engage in some odd jobs below their capabilities or join some family relative in a temporary arrangement. Underemployment is more apparent in agriculture and informal urban sectors where labour productivity is quite low. Increased mechanisation in agriculture does not fully displace labour but reduces work hours. Self-employment that is highly rampant in big urban centres in the form of *thelas*, kiosks, footpath vendors, and daily wage earners in construction does not keep them fully employed for thirty-five hours a week. Skill mismatch between what is being produced by the educational and vocational institutions and the demand of the market is one of the main contributing factors to this observed phenomenon of underemployment. In pure economic terms, this is tantamount to underutilisation of one of the key factors of production resulting in low productivity and low incomes, thus pulling down the national average income. The policy implication is to align the educational curriculum and assessment methods with the needs of the employers.

Table 6.7: Underemployment Rates for Pakistan, Sindh, and Punjab by Age Group (%)
(2014–15)

Age Total (All Ages)		Pakistan	Sindh	Punjab
Young Dependents	10–14	6.0	8.2	6.3
	Average	6.0	8.2	6.3
Working Population	15–19	18.2	22.2	18.5
	20–24	20.6	22.9	20.3
	25–29	11.9	11.1	12.0
	30–34	10.9	9.5	10.8
	35–39	9.0	8.9	7.5
	40–44	7.1	8.0	7.2
	45–49	5.7	3.3	5.5
	50–54	3.7	1.5	4.1
	55–59	3.2	2.7	3.6
	60–64	1.2	1.2	1.4
	Average	9.15	9.13	9.09
Elderly Dependents	65 and over	2.5	0.5	2.9
	Average	2.50	0.50	2.9

Source: Pakistan Bureau of Statistics, Labour Force Survey 2014–15, Islamabad, Statistics Division, Government of Pakistan, 2015.

The various responses from the LFS for the reasons for underemployment have been combined in the following categories (Annex Tables 6D to 6F):

1. Normally works the same number of hours
2. Illness or injury
3. Strike or lockout or layoff
4. Holiday, Ramzan, vacation or leave of absence
5. Educational and training leave
6. Involuntary reasons
7. Supply-side issues
8. Economic issues (external)
9. Voluntary reasons

As expected, working below capacity as 'normally works the same number of hours' accounted for 81 per cent of the total reasons for underemployment on average for 1948–2014. Moreover, there appears to be relatively more underemployment in rural areas as compared to urban areas. The next category that is of involuntary reasons, comprising 7 per cent of the total share. All the remaining categories are insignificant.

Occupation Groups

There has been a noticeable change in the occupational mix of labour force. Professionals, managers, technicians, and associate professionals who did not count much in the earlier period of Pakistan's history now form about 10 per cent of the total employment compared to 6.5 per cent fifty years ago. This is not a big jump but is a positive development in the spread of professional and managerial skills. It shows that the skill mix of our workers is beginning to match the country's market demands but the gap between supply of trained, technical, and skilled workers and the demand for these vocations is still large. This is reflected in the average years of schooling that, according to the Human Development Report, has risen to 5.1 years in 2015 from 1.8 years in

Table 6.8: Percentage Distribution of Employment by Occupation in Pakistan
(1963–64 and 2014–15)

Occupational Groups	1963–1964			Occupational Groups	2014–2015		
	Total	Urban	Rural		Total	Urban	Rural
Managers	-	-	-	Managers	2.19	1.62	0.57
Professional and Technical Related Workers	3.05	1.69	1.36	Professionals	4.73	2.60	2.14
Administrative, Executive and Managerial Workers	0.80	0.59	0.21	Technicians and Associate Professionals	3.13	1.75	1.38
Clerical Workers	2.68	1.96	0.72	Clerical support workers	1.51	1.02	0.49
Sales Workers	7.35	4.32	3.03	Service and Shop and Market Sales Workers	15.7	8.42	7.27
Farmers, Fisherman, Hunters, Loggers and Related Workers	59.34	1.78	57.6	Skilled agricultural, Forestry and Fishery workers	37.13	1.43	35.70
Mines, Quarrymen and Related Workers	0.06	0.01	0.05	Craft and Related Trade Workers	13.54	6.83	6.72
Workers in Transport, Storage and Communication	2.11	1.27	0.84	Plant and Machine Operators and Assemblers	6.24	2.80	3.44
Craftsmen, Production Process Workers and Labourers, n.e.c.	17.83	5.97	11.86	Elementary Occupations	15.83	4.13	11.69
Service, Sports and Recreation Workers	6.02	2.54	3.48				
Workers not Classified by Occupation	0.76	0.41	0.35				

Source: Pakistan Bureau of Statistics, Labour Force Survey, Islamabad, Statistics Division, Government of Pakistan, various years.

Table 6.9: Percentage Distribution of Civilian Labour Force by Level of Education for Pakistan, Sindh, and Punjab (2014–15)

| | | Total (Illiterate + Literate) | Illiterate | Literate | Literate Categories | | | | |
					No Formal Education	Pre-Matric	Matric	Inter	Degree, Post Graduate & PHDs
Pakistan	Population	100	39.3	60.7	0.7	61.8	19	9.4	9.1
	Civilian Labour Force	45.2	42.9	57.1	0.7	52.2	22.0	10.3	14.9
	Employed	42.5	44.2	55.8	0.7	53.6	22.4	9.9	13.4
	Unemployed	2.7	32.8	67.2	0.5	33.5	18.4	14.5	33
	Not in Civilian Labour Force	54.8	37.2	62.8	0.7	69.1	16.9	8.6	4.8
Punjab	Population	100	38.1	61.9	0.3	38.7	12.2	5.2	5.5
	Civilian Labour Force	48.5	44.7	55.3	0.7	55.9	21.8	8.2	13.4
	Employed	45.4	46	54	0.7	57.5	22.3	7.9	11.5
	Unemployed	3.1	25.9	74.1	0.4	38.9	16.4	10.2	34.1
	Not in Civilian Labour Force	51.4	31.8	68.2	0.4	67.5	18	8.7	5.4
Sindh	Population	100	37	63	0.3	36.5	12	7.6	6.6
	Civilian Labour Force	42.96	38.4	61.6	0.5	45.4	21.6	14.4	18.2
	Employed	40.96	39.4	60.6	0.5	46.1	21.7	14	17.6
	Unemployed	2.7	19.5	80.5	0.0	33.5	19.3	20.5	27.3
	Not in Civilian Labour Force	57.04	36	64	0.4	67.1	17.2	10.4	5

Source: Pakistan Bureau of Statistics, *Labour Force Survey 2014–15*, Islamabad, Statistics Division, Government of Pakistan, 2015.

1980. The expected years of schooling in that period has moved up from 3.7 years to 8.1 during the said period. As Pakistan's population is mostly comprises the youth, investment in education and skills training would bear fruits not only in the domestic labour market but in the global market as well.

An examination of labour force distribution by educational level is required. Looking at level of education with respect to its effect on employment and unemployment, one would expect a literate workforce to comprise a majority of the employed workforce. Literacy rate in the 2014–15 Labour Force Survey has been defined as 'all those persons ten years of age and above who could read and write in any language with understanding, as percentage of the population ten years and above.'

The data presented in Table 6.9 shows that 39 per cent of the population as a whole above the age of 10 is still illiterate in Pakistan and the deviation from this average is negligible for the two provinces either in population or the civilian labour force of Punjab and Sindh.

Table 6.10: Percentage Distribution of Employed Labour Force by Level of Education (15 years and above) (2001–02 to 2014–15)

		Pakistan		Sindh		Punjab	
		2001–02	**2014–15**	**2001–02**	**2014–15**	**2001–02**	**2014–15**
Illiterate	Both	49	44.2	42.1	39.4	49.7	46
	Male	78.3	61.2	91.7	72.3	70.7	55.9
	Female	21.7	38.8	8.3	27.7	29.3	44.1
Literate	Both	51	55.8	57.9	60.6	50.3	54
	Male	92.1	88.8	95.8	95.1	89.7	85
	Female	7.9	11.2	4.2	4.9	10.3	15
Literate Categories							
No Formal Education	Both	1.4	0.7	1.7	0.5	1.3	0.7
	Male	89.3	76.5	89.2	83.33	85.2	70.6
	Female	10.7	23.5	10.8	16.67	14.8	29.4
Pre-matric	Both	57.8	53.6	50.5	46.1	61.5	57.5
	Male	93.4	88.6	98	95.3	90.9	85
	Female	6.6	11.4	2	4.7	9.1	15
Matric	Both	22.6	22.4	19.2	21.7	23.2	22.33
	Male	92.8	92.3	96.7	96.5	90.9	89.6
	Female	7.2	7.7	3.3	3.5	9.1	10.4
Inter	Both	8.4	9.9	11.1	14	7.3	7.9
	Male	87.6	91.1	93.5	95.4	83.2	87.2
	Female	12.4	8.9	6.5	4.6	16.8	12.8
Post-graduate	Both	9.9	13.4	17.5	17.6	6.7	11.5
	Male	87	83	90.8	92.9	82.5	75.9
	Female	13	17	9.2	7.1	17.5	24.1

Source: Pakistan Bureau of Statistics, *Labour Force Survey*, Islamabad, Statistics Division, Government of Pakistan, various years.

Table 6.11: Percentage Distribution of Population by Education for Pakistan, Sindh, and Punjab (10 years and above) (2014–15)

Region	Nature of activity	Total (Literate + Illiterate)	Literate			Illiterate		
			Total	Male	Female	Total	Male	Female
Pakistan	Population	100	60.7	59.8	40.2	39.3	36.6	63.4
	Civilian Labour Force	45.2	57.1	86.9	13.1	42.9	61.5	38.5
	Employed	42.5	55.8	88.9	11.1	44.2	61.4	38.5
	Unemployed	2.7	76.9	64.1	36.4	23.1	62.9	37.1
Sindh	Population	100.0	63.0	62.1	37.9	37.0	37.3	62.7
	Civilian Labour Force	43.0	61.6	93.4	6.6	38.4	72.1	27.9
	Employed	41.0	60.6	95.1	4.9	39.4	72.3	27.7
	Unemployed	2.0	80.5	67.1	33.5	19.5	59.0	41.0
Punjab	Population	100.0	61.9	56.5	43.5	38.1	38.7	61.3
	Civilian Labour Force	48.5	55.3	83.3	16.7	44.7	56.2	43.8
	Employed	45.4	54.0	85.0	15.0	46.0	55.9	44.1
	Unemployed	3.1	74.1	64.2	35.8	25.9	64.6	35.4

Source: Pakistan Bureau of Statistics, *Labour Force Survey 2014–15*, Islamabad, Statistics Division, Government of Pakistan, 2015.

Sixty per cent of Pakistan's population and 57 per cent of the civilian labour force is literate. The corresponding proportions for Sindh are 63 per cent and 62 per cent and for Punjab, 62 per cent and 55 per cent. Table 6.11 shows that among the literate in the labour force, 87 per cent are male and 13 per cent are female. In Sindh, the male-female ratio among the literate labour force is 93:7 and in Punjab, 83:17. As most of the females are employed in rural areas and are unpaid family workers, their literacy rates are relatively low.

Table 6.12: Literacy Rates for Pakistan, Punjab, and Sindh by Area (%) (10 years and above) (1990–91 to 2014–15)

Region		1990–91	2000–01	2014–15
Pakistan	Rural	30.5	40.5	51.9
	Urban	58.9	67.8	76.0
Punjab	Rural	32.7	44.3	54.6
	Urban	56.9	67.4	75.6
Sindh	Rural	29.0	36.0	45.0
	Urban	64.5	71.0	79.6

Source: Pakistan Bureau of Statistics, *Labour Force Survey*, Islamabad, Statistics Division, Government of Pakistan, various years.

Of the 60.7 per cent literate population (national), 60 per cent are male and 40 per cent are female.[9] Of the literate civilian force (males) in rural areas, the highest proportion is that of males with pre-matric level of education. This is true for both the employed and unemployed population and the urban areas also show a similar rates.

The case is similar for (rural) females but for the unemployed, a higher proportion is that of the population with post-graduate education. In urban areas, the highest proportion of unemployed females are those with post-graduate education, which indirectly highlights gender discrimination.

Table 6.12 presents the data on the evolution of the literacy rate since 1990–91. Literacy rates have improved during the last twenty-five years both for rural and urban areas in the country as well as the provinces. But the rate of improvement has been quite slow not only compared to the national planned targets but also in relation to other neighbouring countries in the region.

Employment by Sectors

In terms of sectors, instead of reporting for all three—agriculture, manufacturing, and tertiary—the LFS reports the data for the two categories—agriculture and non-agriculture. Within the latter, a further breakdown of formal and informal sector is also reported. According to the ILO, 'Sectoral employment flows are an important factor in the analysis of productivity trends, because within-sector productivity growth needs to be distinguished from growth resulting from shifts from lower to higher productivity sectors.'[10]

There has not been any major structural shift in the last fifteen years and employment patterns have remained stable at both the national as well as the two provincial levels. As non-agricultural activities are expanding and taking up a large share of GDP, the same is happening in the allocation and utilisation of labour. However, on a single sector basis, employment-wise, agriculture is still a dominant sector (Table 6.13) although its share in national employment has declined over the years from 60 per cent in 1963–64 to 42 per cent in 2014–15.

Table 6.13: Percentage Distribution of Employed Persons by Agriculture and Non-Agriculture Sector (10 years above) (2001–02 to 2014–15)

Region	Major Sector of Employment	2001–02	2005–06	2010–11	2014–15
Pakistan	Agriculture	42.1	43.4	44.9	42.3
	Non-agriculture	57.9	56.6	55.1	57.7
Sindh	Agriculture	37.6	37.3	45.3	39.3
	Non-agriculture	62.4	62.7	54.7	60.7
Punjab	Agriculture	42.8	44.3	45.3	44.7
	Non-agriculture	57.2	55.6	54.7	55.3

Source: Pakistan Bureau of Statistics, *Labour Force Survey*, Islamabad, Statistics Division, Government of Pakistan, various years.

Data for the provinces for the earlier years is not available; however, it can be surmised that a similar pattern would be discernible for Punjab and Sindh too. The distinguishing feature for Sindh is that non-agricultural sector has a slight edge over the national average and Punjab. In terms of changes between 2001–02 and 2014–15, both the direction and the magnitude are almost identical. As the share of agriculture in the national economy recedes and mechanisation spreads, it is but natural that employment in agriculture would also take a downward path.

Table 6.14: Percentage Distribution of Employed Persons by Formal and Informal Sector for Pakistan, Sindh, and Punjab (10 years of age and above) (1997–98 to 2014–15)

Region	Major Sector of Employment*	1997–98	2005–06	2010–11	2014–15
Pakistan	Formal	32.2	27.1	26.2	27.4
	Informal	67.8	72.8	73.8	72.6
Sindh	Formal	44.8	33.3	36.1	33.6
	Informal	55.2	66.7	63.9	66.4
Punjab	Formal	27.2	23.2	22.0	25.6
	Informal	72.8	76.8	78.0	74.4

* The values are percentages of the non-agriculture sector.

Source: Pakistan Bureau of Statistics, *Labour Force Survey*, Islamabad, Statistics Division, Government of Pakistan, various years.

The share of the non-agricultural sector in Sindh decreased from 62.7 per cent in 2005–06 to 54.7 per cent in 2010–11 but again picked up to reach 60.7 per cent in 2014–15. For Punjab, this share has hovered around 55 per cent for the same period without major deviations. This points to the growing importance of the service sector in the economy which is labour intensive and has higher elasticity of employment with respect to growth.

Another important variable to explore, especially for developing economies such as Pakistan, is the informal sector. The ILO elucidates the importance of the sector in the following words:

> The informal economy plays a major role in employment creation, income generation and production in many countries. In countries with high rates of population growth or urbanisation, the informal economy tends to absorb most of the growth in the labour force. Work in the informal economy is generally recognised as entailing absence of legal identity, poor working conditions, lack of membership in social protection systems, higher incidence of work-related accidents and ailments, and limited freedom of association. Knowing how many people are in the informal economy is a starting point for considering the extent and content of policy responses required.[11]

Table 6.14 shows that the informal sector continues to be the major provider of jobs in Pakistan. What is more worrisome is that unlike other developing countries at similar income levels, informal sector employment is expanding at the expense of the formal sector. It now accounts for almost three-fourths of total employment in the country. The informal sector consists of low productivity economic activities. Economic theory and cross-country evidence suggests that it is because of the shift of labour from low productivity to high productivity sectors that growth takes place. Surplus labour released by agriculture is absorbed in urban industrial and services sectors, raising the overall rate of productivity growth in the economy. This shift is certainly taking place in Pakistan in the form of rural–urban migration, but unplanned urban sprawl has resulted in diseconomies of agglomeration. Migrants to urban areas remain trapped in informal, low productivity activities such as hawking, vending, domestic servitude etc. The more enterprising among them migrate to the Middle East, thus further depleting the pool of productive workers. The tax collection efforts of the federal and provincial governments are also thwarted by the rising informalisation of the economy.

In the case of Sindh, employment in the informal sector has expanded from 55.2 per cent in 1997–98 to 66.4 per cent in 2014–15. This share is comparatively lower than that of Punjab where almost two-thirds subsist on informal employment. One of the recent measures has attracted some attention and the Pakistan Institute of Labour Education and Research (PILER) comments:

A positive state intervention to address 'informality' of economy was the imposition, in June, of a 0.6 per cent tax on all kinds of banking instruments of over Rs. 50,000 of non-filers of income tax. Faced with stiff resistance from the business circles, the government relented and reduced the tax to 0.3 per cent in September. This intervention could impact governance issues in the informal economy and '…may be a method of engaging firms with the state, and thus promoting legitimacy, good governance, and political accountability'. But there was no debate or analysis by labour economists that the measure deserved praise.[12]

Within the informal sector, the categories of self-employed and employees dominate both the urban and rural economies.[13]

Migration

Rural–urban migration and international migration are the main determinants of labour market conditions, employment opportunities, and living standards, and these considerations act as important push factors from rural to urban areas, and then onwards overseas. Almost seven million Pakistanis are currently working overseas, thus easing pressures on the domestic labour market. The remittances they send to their families sustain our balance of payments. However, this section focuses mainly on domestic rural–urban migration as detailed data is available for it.

Table 6.15: Percentage Distribution of Inter and Intra Provincial Migration for Pakistan, Sindh, and Punjab (2014–15)

| Region | Migration | | | | | | | | |
| | Total | | | Inter-Provincial | | | Intra-Provincial | | |
	Total	Male	Female	Total	Male	Female	Total	Male	Female
Pakistan	100	100	100	100	100	100	100	100	100
Sindh	20.6	22.7	19.2	34.8	31.8	38.6	16.7	20.2	16.9
Punjab	68.2	61.8	72.5	45.4	42.1	49.3	74.6	70.3	76.9

Source: Pakistan Bureau of Statistics, *Labour Force Survey 2014–15*, Islamabad, Statistics Division, Government of Pakistan, 2015.

In terms of migration, Punjab accounts for the highest proportion amongst all the provinces, followed by Sindh. The better linkage of urban and rural areas in Punjab owing to widespread urbanisation as compared to Sindh becomes apparent from Table 6.15. Of the total migration, Punjab experiences more intra-provincial migration whereas in Sindh, there is more inter-provincial migration. In Sindh, Karachi can support the rural migrants from within the province as well as other provinces and acts as a magnet economically. Punjab, which is quite vast, fast urbanising, and has a rapidly growing economically, provides ample opportunities to absorb those originating from backward districts of the province. Lahore acts in similar way for migrants from other parts of Punjab as Karachi does for other provinces. Substantial investments in infrastructure, education and health in Lahore have made the city an attractive place and it is expanding in all directions, engulfing some of the rural areas in the vicinity. In 2017 census, Lahore district emerged as a completely urban centre. Secondary towns are also emerging and absorbing rural migrants.

Comparing the years 2010 and 2014 (Annex Table 6K), the main motivation that appears to encourage migration is family-related, which accounts for around 80 per cent of total migration. Next come job-related factors that account for around 12 per cent of total migration while the other 8 per cent belong to non-job/family related factors.

The results remain relatively unchanged for 2014 and LFS reports similar results for Punjab. However, in Sindh, the job-related reasons accounted for approximately 15 per cent of total migration in 2010–11 which increased to 17 per cent in 2014–15. Although not clearly apparent, the economic neglect of the province in recent decade may have influenced this result.

As the detailed information about international migration by province of origin is not available, it may be fair to surmise that a majority of the migrants belong to Khyber Pakhtunkhwa and arid districts of Punjab. As they have already experienced inter-provincial migration mainly to Karachi and have relatives and friends in the Gulf states, it becomes much easier for them to relocate overseas. There has been some migration from Sindh to Saudi Arabia but the numbers are not impressive.

Distribution by Industry

Pakistan was an agro-based economy to begin with but as economic theory and historical evidence suggests, structural changes take place when economic development occurs. Agriculture loses its share in the national income and employment and industry and services sectors gain. As pointed out earlier, the latter exhibit relatively higher productivity—the shift of resources from a low productivity sector to a high productivity sector improves the efficiency of resource use and stimulates economic growth. Pakistan's agriculture has also followed this line over decades, both in terms of contribution to GDP and total employment.

Table 6.16: Percentage Distribution of Employment by Industry for Pakistan, Sindh, and Punjab
(10 years of age and above) (1990–91 and 2014–15)

Major Industry Division	1990–91			2014–15		
	Pakistan	Sindh	Punjab	Pakistan	Sindh	Punjab
Agriculture, forestry, hunting and fishing	47.5	40.2	48.9	43.5	39.3	45.4
Mining and quarrying	0.2	0.2	0.1	0.2	0.1	0.1
Manufacturing	12.2	14.4	13.0	14.6	15.2	15.8
Electricity, gas, and water	0.8	1.1	0.7	0.5	1.4	0.4
Construction	6.6	5.9	6.7	7.3	7.0	6.5
Wholesale and retail trade and restaurants and hotels	13.2	15.8	12.4	14.6	15.8	13.8
Transport, storage and communication	5.3	6.1	4.8	5.0	8.4	4.3
Financing, insurance, real estate and business services	0.9	1.6	0.7	0.5	1.8	0.4
Community, social, and personal services	13.3	14.7	12.7	11.1	11.0	11.1
Activities extraterritorial organisations and bodies	0.1	0.1	0.1	0.01	0.0	0.02

Source: Pakistan Bureau of Statistics, *Labour Force Survey*, Islamabad, Statistics Division, Government of Pakistan, various years.

The employment shares of the agriculture, forestry, hunting, and fishing industry declined from 53 per cent in 1982–1983 to 47 per cent in 1990–1991, recording a change of six percentage points in eight years. Since then, the rate of decline has slowed down and in the last fifteen years, only five percentage points were lost in agricultural employment (Annex Tables 6L and 6M). As against 11 percentage points for Pakistan, the corresponding decline in Sindh was 13 percentage points and in Punjab by just eight percentage points, highlighting Punjab's continued dependence on the sector. The share of manufacturing and construction in national employment increased roughly from 18 to 22 per cent over the said period, and Sindh and Punjab also follow a similar pattern.

The tertiary sector consists of wholesale and retail trade and restaurants and hotels; transport, storage and communication; financing, insurance, real estate and business services; community, social, and personal services; and activities of extraterritorial organisations and bodies. The tertiary sector's contribution to national employment expanded from 33 per cent in 1982–83 to 34 per cent in 2014–15, in Sindh from 38 to 37 per cent, and in Punjab from 31 to 32 per cent. In Sindh, only 11 per cent employment was generated in rural areas and 26 per cent in the urban areas whereas in Punjab, the rural and urban areas generated equally, i.e. 15 per cent in rural areas and 16 per cent in urban areas.

In the long run, it is advisable to develop medium-sized, secondary cities or industrial towns as is happening in Punjab, to support the migrant rural population, rather than relying on one big metropolis alone. The diseconomies of scale would at some time or other offset the agglomeration effects of urbanisation. Already the urban sprawl has put a great deal of stress on Karachi's infrastructure and living conditions.

Wages and Pensions

Table 6.17: Average Wages for Pakistan by Area and Occupational Group (in PKR)
(2010–11 and 2014–15)

Major Occupational Groups	2010–11			2014–15		
	All Areas	Rural	Urban	All Areas	Rural	Urban
	Total	Total	Total	Total	Total	Total
Managers	25,835	17,644	27,739	51,573	42,948	53,361
Professionals	21,117	14,075	25,377	26,876	23,067	30,029
Technicians and Associate Professionals	13,164	12,993	13,329	23,107	19,966	25,200
Clerical Support Workers	14,006	13,426	14,309	21,766	21,943	21,682
Service and Sales Workers	8,546	8,852	8,320	12,866	13,027	12,746
Skilled Agricultural, Forestry and Fishery Workers	7,804	7,233	10,760	11,554	10,950	12,667
Craft and Related Trade Workers	8,222	8,020	8,416	13,342	12,496	14,046
Plant and Machine Operators and Assemblers	9,049	8,855	9,304	13,088	12,656	13,619
Elementary Occupations	6,658	6483	7,096	9,474	9,075	10,655

Source: Pakistan Bureau of Statistics, *Labour Force Survey*, Islamabad, Statistics Division, Government of Pakistan, various years.

One of the main correlates of poverty reduction in developing economies is the rate at which real wages rise. In case this rate is higher than that of the national income, there is a relative gain in the share of employed labour, gradually lifting people above the poverty line. A consistent time series data which is reliable, comparable, and representative does not exist and therefore drawing any meaningful inferences becomes quite difficult.

Tables 6.17 to 6.19 depict the changes that have taken place in nominal wages in the last four years among different categories of workers for Pakistan, Punjab, and Sindh. The data shows that the highest increases have been recorded by managers, technicians, and associate professional workers while those least benefitted were surprisingly professionals.

As most of the professionals—doctors, lawyers, accountants, architects, IT experts—are self-employed they may be understating their incomes for tax purposes. What is even more puzzling is how professionals earn only PKR 26,876 per month—an amount which appears highly unrealistic.

Table 6.18: Average Wages for Punjab by Area and Occupational Group (in PKR) (2010–11 and 2014–15)

Major Occupational Groups	2010–11			2014–15		
	All Areas	Rural	Urban	All Areas	Rural	Urban
	Total	Total	Total	Total	Total	Total
Managers	24,101	16,399	27,249	52,687	43,620	55,594
Professionals	18,236	12,665	22,619	22,935	19,310	25,822
Technicians and Associate Professionals	12,411	12,082	12,722	22,168	19,290	24,361
Clerical Support Workers	13,416	12,800	13,960	20,567	19,944	20,917
Service and Sales Workers	7,977	8,031	7,933	12,012	11,979	12,035
Skilled Agricultural, Forestry and Fishery Workers	7,362	6,940	9,927	11,369	11,270	11,718
Craft and Related Trade Workers	7,903	7,673	8,168	11,946	12,011	11,877
Plant and Machine Operators and Assemblers	8,646	8,534	8,823	12,768	12,412	13,260
Elementary Occupations	6,302	6,130	6,827	9,043	8,707	10,233

Source: Pakistan Bureau of Statistics, *Labour Force Survey*, Islamabad, Statistics Division, Government of Pakistan, various years.

Government mandated minimum wages also do influence the average wage levels. The minimum wage was raised from PKR 12,000 to PKR 13,000 in 2015 by the federal government. The provincial governments of Punjab, Sindh, and Balochistan raised the minimum wage to PKR 13,000 in their budgets for 2015–16.[14] However, due to weak regulatory mechanisms and non-compliance of labour laws, a large number of workers remained deprived of their minimum wage in the year 2015. According to the recent Pakistan Labour Force Survey, the national average monthly wages stood at PKR 13,154. The survey noted that 17 per cent of workers were getting PKR 5,000 and 41 per cent between PKR 5,000 to PKR 10,000 per month as salary.

Pakistan still appears to be struggling to transition to the post-Eighteenth Amendment decentralisation era. One aspect where this becomes apparent is wage-setting. Although the minimum wage determination authority now rests within the purview of the provincial governments, the federal and the provincial governments continue to rely on the outdated 1961 Minimum Wage Ordinance for West Pakistan.[15] Sindh has only recently passed the Minimum Wages Bill, in early 2016, and its effectiveness is yet to be determined.[16] Moreover, despite the existence of minimum wage boards in the provinces, the process of wage-setting is far from satisfactory. This tripartite body comprising of an independent chairperson and representatives from workers and employers organisations can only suggest wage-rates whereas the final authority rests with the provincial governments who 'look to the annual federal budget for an indication of the minimum wage rate set by the federal government for ICT [Islamabad Capital Territory], and then follow suit.'[17]

Table 6.19: Average Wages for Sindh by Area and Occupational Group (in PKR)
(2010–11 and 2014–15)

Major Occupational Groups	2010–11			2014–15		
	All Areas	Rural	Urban	All Areas	Rural	Urban
	Total	Total	Total	Total	Total	Total
Managers	28,003	21,891	28,385	51,308	32,439	51,866
Professionals	27,396	19,528	28,700	34,039	29,746	35,917
Technicians and Associate Professionals	14,029	14,322	13,863	24,148	18,475	25,763
Clerical Support Workers	14,324	14,612	14,259	22,190	25,218	21,631
Service and Sales Workers	9,063	10,001	8,725	12,954	12,741	13,062
Skilled Agricultural, Forestry and Fishery Workers	8,207	7,542	11,685	11,040	10,594	11,363
Craft and Related Trade Workers	8,659	7,864	8,842	16,091	11,497	17,095
Plant and Machine Operators and Assemblers	8,958	7,776	9,470	12,691	11,092	13,457
Elementary Occupations	6,723	6,167	7,268	9,165	8,207	10,536

Source: Pakistan Bureau of Statistics, *Labour Force Survey*, Islamabad, Statistics Division, Government of Pakistan, various years.

Furthermore, 'There is nothing in the law that either requires the government to follow the recommendations of the Minimum Wage Board nor anything that requires it to give reasons for departing from the Minimum Wage Board's recommendations.'[18] Once the provincial government announces the wage-rate to be set, the Board is notified and after some discussions, the recommendations are relayed to the provincial government before it finally sends the official notification.[19] 'The gap between announcement and notification impacts the workers who are often deprived of their dues in minimum wages raise. Even in those units where employers agree to pay minimum wages, payment of arrears remains in doubt.'[20] Moreover, while the Board is asked to consider 'changes in economic conditions, costs of living, and other relevant factors', none of these have been statistically defined.

Another contention in the post-Eighteenth Amendment era is the status of Employees Old-Age Benefits Institution (EOBI) and the Workers' Welfare Fund (WWF). The devolution of these two institutions has been described as 'controversial' since 'the devolution of the EOBI would benefit Punjab and Sindh as the two provinces are the major contributors to the EOBI fund whereas the militancy-hit KP province and under-developed Balochistan would be affected adversely.'[21] Regarding the allocation of assets, Sindh government maintains that the assets be distributed in accordance with the 'source of collection of fund' whereas the Punjab government supports the NFC-based distribution which takes into account 'the number of registered industrial units and workers.'[22] KP and Balochistan, on the other hand, are satisfied with the status-quo formula.

Although, the Sindh government passed the EOBI Act in 2014, as of 2015, the government was still wrestling with its proper implementation.[23]

Gender Disparity

As pointed out earlier, female participation in the labour force is quite low compared to other developing countries. There are several factors contributing towards this phenomenon such as education, discrimination, and socio-cultural norms. The rate of employment of women is extremely low in formal markets—around 30 per cent. Most of the work done by women is concentrated in the agricultural sector or menial jobs having low job security. This is the core reason why women constitute only 2 per cent of memberships of trade unions in Pakistan. Being unaware of their basic working rights, women are faced with situations against which they cannot raise a voice due to absence of adequate representation. The Pakistan Workers' Federation struggled for a year to finally grant women the basic right of privacy and separate access to washrooms at IESCO.[24]

According to a 2008 study by the Ministry of Labour and Manpower and the ILO, there was a 33 per cent difference in the wage gap between men and women. The lack of awareness regarding this phenomenon even among literate women has led to the gender gap widening even further. Minimum wage according to Nadia Tahir is 'a means available for reducing wage gap for the poor and redistribute resources in a welfare enhancing way.'[25] Despite the promulgations of minimum wages, weak regulatory mechanisms and discriminatory treatment (women workers are generally perceived to be more docile and less vocal compared to male workers) deprives many female workers of their fair dues. The workers at the textile industry face even worse conditions; they are paid per the piece rate rather than the hours contributed towards the produce.

The dual role of a woman which comprises catering to both the home and workplace discourages many from entering the job market and maintaining work–family balance remains a tough challenge. However, with the growing emphasis being put on women education and a decline in taboos attached to working women due to a changing society, white-collar jobs have substantially risen over the past few years for women. The Federal Bureau of Statistics (FBS) concluded that the total fertility rate has declined to 3.8 children per women.[26] Various programmes and organisations have been established to increase technical skills and provide training which are required in the commercial and industrial sectors such as the National Vocational and Technical Education Commission.[27]

A new crop of women entrepreneurs is taking shape, particularly in the metropolitan areas and large cities. Beauty parlours and salons, clothing outlets, and boutiques are proliferating the city. Women are also entering other professions and occupations which were traditionally out of bounds for them. Access to microfinance, which has expanded to almost 4 million borrowers, is helping small-scale women traders and businesses. The Benazir Income Support Programme provides cash transfers to women in poor households. Stipends for female students are also encouraging the retention and completion of school education. It has been observed that education and economic independence empower women to tackle domestic violence issues and contributes toward breaking vicious cycle of malnutrition, illiteracy, fertility, and health, all of which hinder the sustainable development of the country.

Agricultural Labour

The land ownership pattern in Sindh is skewed compared to other provinces and, therefore, highly influential landlords who combine political, economic, social, and administrative powers have created an asymmetric relationship between owners and tenants. It would not be wrong to claim that the feudalistic structure that the British left behind after Partition more or less continued to operate in the province with tenants divested of their rights until the land reforms of the early 1970s[28] which introduced a ceiling on land that an individual could hold. This ceiling was further reduced in 1977.[29] As mentioned earlier, the first major breakthrough to improve the conditions of peasants came in 1950 in the form of the Sindh Tenancy Act which focused on dynamics involved in tenant–landowner relationships, but the act fell short of implementation.[30]

In contrast, in Punjab, ambitious steps were taken to address the issue which included:

a. repeal of *jagir*s,
b. extension of ownership to 'occupancy tenants',
c. provision of security of tenure to 'tenants-at-will', and
d. abolishment of 'non-statutory cesses and levies'.[31]

Moreover, to protect against the eviction of tenants, the Punjab Protection and Restoration of Tenancy Rights Act of 1950 was approved.[32]

Nevertheless, in Punjab too the intent of all the legislations passed have not translated well into practice. Remnants of bonded labour were found in Punjab, but such instances were localised in some areas of Hafizabad and Attock districts, in central and northern Punjab, although the study focused mainly on southern Punjab where dependence on agriculture, and hence prevalence of bondage was believed to be the highest.[33] Also, the study claims that bondage, rather than being a consequence of debt is more a result of unavailability of other employment opportunities for agricultural workers.

With regard to tenants, the mistreatment was a direct effect of contravention of government legislations.[34] A feature of abuse found common in both Sindh and Southern Punjab (regions of cotton and sugarcane cultivation) was the 'bad maintenance of account or their delayed clearance' from which it is understandably impossible for the illiterate tenants to escape.[35] The contracts between the *haris* and their landlords are of verbal nature which means that even a sufficiently literate worker would have to find himself at the mercy of his master.[36] Arif (2004) reports the following instance which summarises the predicament of the tenants:

> In Rahim Yar Khan district, it was found that landlords do not maintain accounts fairly, and payments to tenants are delayed. All tenants agreed that account registers are kept but did not consider the entries to be correct. Some pointed out that due to illiteracy they could not challenge the accounts and, in any case, they had no proof that would stand in a court of law. We also found some extreme cases where the landlord had not settled accounts with tenants for 20 years. Tenants consider it as an exploitative and coercive way to keep them tied to the landlord.[37]

Bonded Labour

One manifestation of extreme violation of decent work conditions in Pakistan, particularly in Sindh, is the presence of bonded labour. Forced labour, of which bonded labour is a subgroup, is described by the ILO as: '…all work or service which is exacted from any person under the menace of any penalty and for which the said person has not offered himself voluntarily.'[38]

Debt bondage has been referred by the *UN Supplementary Convention on Abolition of Slavery, the Slave Trade and Institutions and Practices Similar to Slavery (1956)* as a phenomenon whereby:

> … a debtor pledges his personal services or those of a person under his control as security for a debt, if the reasonable value of those services is not applied towards the payment of the debt or if the length and nature of these services are not limited or defined.[39]

Bonded labour, then, is a practice of extorting forced labour from individuals as a retribution for the non-payment of debt. While this arrangement sounds fair on the surface for the stakeholders involved, the conditions surrounding this unwritten informal contract heavily favour the creditor at the expense of the debtor.

Pakistan currently ranks sixth in the Global Slavery Index (2016) out of 167 countries, with a population of approximately 2.1 million persons living under conditions of modern slavery.[40] Although the 1973 Constitution of Pakistan proclaims slavery 'non-existent' in the country, it gets obscured under the guise of modern slavery.[41] To address this issue, the Bonded Labour System (Abolition) Act was ratified in 1992.[42]

Nevertheless, not many concrete steps have been taken by the government to ensure that modern slavery is no longer practised.[43] The act passed itself lacks implementation power since 'the definition of "bonded labour system" given under Section 2(e) of the act is vague and imprecise and it does not take into account an array of customary and non-customary practices which amount to bonded labour.'[44] In fact, the Global Slavery Index puts the 'Government Response Rating' as CCC for Pakistan, where the category corresponds to 7/10 rank, with 10 being the lowest.[45]

The condition is worst in Sindh compared to the rest of the provinces of Pakistan due to widespread prevalence of bonded labour by powerful feudal landlords. The peculiar tenant–landowner relationship creates apt conditions for the exploitation of the former.[46] This skewed and one-sided relationship is exacerbated by the practice of extending *peshgi* (advance payment) to the tenants.[47] As the amounts are not fully recovered and rolled over, the hold of the landlord who also now assumes the role of the lender perpetuates the bondage of the tenants who become borrowers also.[48] On the other hand commercialisation of agriculture in Punjab and Khyber Pakhtunkhwa has helped to dilute this extreme form of exploitation.[49] However, there too the influence of the powerful class has not been uprooted completely, with the nature of bondage merely shifting from traditional to contract-based which Breman (2007) has described as 'neo-bondage'.[50]

It is important to note that *peshgi*, although associated with bondage, is not a necessary precursor. The glass bangle-making and football-stitching industries in Hyderabad and Sialkot have been cited as evidences where *peshgi* does not lead to debt-bondage.[51] The intervening factors identified between *peshgi* and bondage in Hyderabad and Sialkot have been 'patrilineage (*biradari*) ties' and 'shared geographical and "class" origins' respectively.[52] These factors have helped to keep at bay extreme forms of bondage such as threat and use of violence, but these factors imperceptibly serve to maintain some form of domination of employers over their employees.[53]

The issue of deferred payment, low wages and 'fiddling of accounts' have also been cited in the mining sector, particularly in Sindh and Balochistan.[54] Another issue in the legal ambit that forces workers into bondage is the non-registration of national identity cards.[55] Non-possession of identity cards excludes them from safety net schemes, financial support which could have otherwise prevented them from seeking *peshgi*s or other loans from their superiors, eventually ensnaring them into bondage.

According to a survey conducted by the Asian Development Bank, the districts with high incidence of debt-bondage, namely Badin, Dadu, Mirpurkhas, Thatta, and Umerkot in Sindh had 60 per cent of the families working as *hari*s or sharecroppers.[56] This coexistence of high intensity and high incidence of debt-bondage conditions underlines the inherent and widespread bondage-driven labour environment in the abovementioned districts. Within the sharecroppers too, a distinction has been drawn between the settled *hari*s and the non-settled *hari*s. While the former enjoy hereditary tenancy and are cognizant of their rights, the former belong to non-Muslim minority nomadic tribes which makes them most susceptible to debt-bondage.[57] In fact, it has been reported that, 'According to one source, an estimated 10,000 households from Thar are caught in a bonded labour type situation. It is generally contended that a migrant from Thar will always return to the desert, and if he has not done so, it is only because he is constrained by bondage.'[58]

The type of labour contracts governing the relationship between agricultural workers and their masters differs for the different types of workers: skilled/ unskilled and permanent/ seasonal.[59] Unskilled labour is hired frequently whereas the skilled labourers on the other hand comprise the usual middlemen called the *kamdar*s who supervise the land and the *hari*s, as well as tractor operators.[60]

The workers from nomadic tribes and others without employment opportunities contribute to the seasonal labour, especially those from Thar who in times of drought find no recourse but to work as casual labourers elsewhere.[61] Those who enjoy hereditary tenancy are usually permanent workers settled on a farm land and contrary to their casual counterparts, work for the same landowner.[62] The plight and state of helplessness of the agricultural workers becomes obvious from the statement that 'Haris who are indebted to the zamindar are also often sold on to other zamindars, with or without their consent, if the landowner needs money or wants to get rid of his haris for some reason.'[63]

As stated earlier, those most vulnerable to bondage are the nomadic haris but it was found that:

> … almost all hari families interviewed during the field survey in the camps in Hyderabad who had fled bondage indicated that they owed money to the zamindar, debts carried over for many years. Although hari families work on a half-share tenancy basis, they rarely receive half-shares from the production due to the deduction of input costs and debts … A crucial aspect of the bonded labour story is that it highlights the use of apparently legitimate and voluntary economic transactions as the means of extracting forced labour … These haris receive further loans of grain to sustain themselves, compounding the debt as part of the cycle of debt bondage.[64]

The permanent haris, however, are in a relatively better position for they cannot be evicted from their lands. According to the Sindh Tenancy Act of 1950, this permanency status is conferred on 'those who farmed on at least four acres of land under the same landlord for a continuous period of three years.'[65] Their tenancy cannot be revoked if they pay their rent regularly and hence 'it is common to rotate temporary haris from one farm to another in different seasons to prevent them from making any claims to the land they cultivate.'[66]

Interestingly, despite the above-mentioned findings, the landlords when interviewed were resolute in their denial of the adverse labour conditions. Hussain et al. note that:

> Zamindars from Sindh … felt that the relationship between the hari and zamindar is a contractual one, entailing no exploitation. In fact, many of the landlords felt that the tenants know their rights and can effectively negotiate their due share from the landlord. In fact, they felt that they had to be watchful to protect themselves from routine pilfering by hari households. Many zamindars see themselves as benefactors and are surprised by the suggestion of exploitation. A few did, however, admit that coercion and maltreatment could exist in some cases.[67]

The condition for women in particular, however, is worse. Ahmed argues that since women in the patriarchal culture of Pakistan are treated as an emblem of a family, in particular a man's honour, they are easy targets for threat to coerce households into bondage.[68] Expounding on women's role in upholding a family's honour, Ahmed claims that:

> It is in this context, one in which women's bodies and their protection are inscribed by very specific gendered meanings, that I suggest that violence or the threat of violence against women in bonded labour has the potential of being differentially effective in maintaining the status-quo.[69]

Women are more vulnerable in agricultural and brick-making sectors which employ households and hence female labour.[70] The use of threats against women and publicised punishments then serves to 'make an example out of them [for disregarding authority] … [which becomes] one of the reasons why the abuse often takes place in front of other family members or community members.'[71]

In fact, use of threat against women seems more prevalent in Sindh as:

> … haris in rural Sindh are relatively less stigmatised when [their women are raped] may also be connected to the frequency with which kamdars use rape as a tool for control, and/or a strong feeling of helplessness over the course of events in their life.[72]

This feeling of extreme helplessness not only forces workers into submission but also prevents them from taking any action against their inhumane treatment.[73] Citing a finding from a joint survey of the ILO and Human Rights Commission of Pakistan, Ahmed (2016) states that 79 out of 100 liberated tenants never ventured to file a complaint against their superiors, despite threats of and use of violence, because they believed doing so would serve no purpose owing to their landlords' clout.[74] Ahmed cites a case of a tenant 'who once called the police in an attempt to stop their landlord from harassing his wife but he ended up spending years in jail because of false allegations made against him by that landlord … [and that the landlord] "would tease any woman in the village".'[75]

As far as governmental action to prevent bondage in Sindh is concerned, the Provincial Assembly of Sindh passed the Sindh Bonded Labour (Abolition) Act in 2015, which came into force in June 2016 following the Governor's approval.[76] Punjab, has already passed the Bonded Labour System Abolition Act.[77] The text of the act declares:

> …the bonded labour system shall stand abolished and every bonded labourer shall stand freed and discharged from any obligation to render any bonded labour… [and outlaws *peshgi* stating] no person shall make any advance under, or in pursuance of, the bonded labour system or compel any person to render any bonded labour or other form of forced, labour.[78]

Not only does the act nullifies all past and future contracts leading to bondage, it also proclaims all liabilities to 'stand extinguished'. Moreover, the act also calls for the restoration of property to their rightful owners which may have been surrendered in order to pay towards *peshgi*.

However, while the act prescribes punishments and sufficiently addresses how it is to be implemented, there still appear loopholes for the perpetrators to circumvent penalties. As stated above, those forced into bondage are usually illiterate without any recourse to legal help. Since the contracts are entered into verbally, the workers may not possess any written document to prove bondage and may also face difficulty reclaiming ownership to property forfeited as a consequence of bondage. Since it has been less than a year since the enforcement of the act, its legal strength is yet to be ascertained.

Summing up

The labour force in Sindh broadly follows the pattern of employment at the national level. Participation rate hovers around 45 per cent with males dominating the scene. Unemployment rate is below the national average while highest underemployment is observed among the age group 20–24. The occupational mix has undergone a change and about 13 per cent of the employees fall in the high and mid skilled categories.

Sixty-two per cent of the civilian labour force in Sindh is literate. There has not been any major structural shift in sectoral allocation of employment. Non-agriculture sector employs about 58 per cent and agriculture 42 per cent of the labour force. The discomforting finding is that the population of those in the formal sector is shrinking while informalisation is spreading. Sindh has not benefitted from international migration as much as Punjab and KP but it is the popular destination for migrants from these provinces.

The data for wages is not robust but from whatever information is available it appears that the average wage level has been rising in the recent years. Perhaps the government mandated in minimum wages may be influencing this outcome. Female workers receive lower wages as they are usually docile and not vocal and are perceived as such. Only 2 per cent unionised labour is female.

The dominance of powerful feudal landlords has given rise to some exploitation of agricultural labour, particularly casual workers. The tenant–landlord relationship being one sided in favour of the landlord has given rise to the practice of bonded labour that prevails in Sindh.

7

Poverty and Inequality

Overview

Official data and studies have revealed that 4 out of 10 people live in multidimensional poverty in Sindh, home to six of the ten worst performing districts in terms of human development in Pakistan which also have the highest proportion of the poor. Within the province, poverty also varies across sub-groups of the population, as households headed by illiterate persons working as unskilled or semi-skilled workers are poorer than those that are headed by literate persons engaged in well-paid jobs. Chronic poverty is often concentrated in the most rural parts of the province, which can further hamper progress in these areas.

To analyse the state of poverty in the province, this chapter looks at the metrics of the incidence and intensity of poverty, along with multidimensional indicators of poverty and the state of human development in the province. It also looks at the patterns of inequality in Sindh, along with public expenditure on social services and poverty. It finally ends with some policy recommendations, calling for an emphasis on long term development plans for the most poverty-stricken areas of the province.

Defining Poverty

Poverty is a complex and multifaceted human development issue, the definition of which cannot be adequately encapsulated within a single sentence. However, there have been various attempts to capture the essence of poverty. The UN has defined poverty as:

> Fundamentally, poverty is a denial of choices and opportunities, a violation of human dignity. It means lack of basic capacity to participate effectively in society. It means not having enough to feed and clothe a family, not having a school or clinic to go to, not having the land on which to grow one's food or a job to earn one's living, not having access to credit. It means insecurity, powerlessness and exclusion of individuals, households and communities. It means susceptibility to violence, and it often implies living on marginal or fragile environments, without access to clean water or sanitation.[1]

The phenomenon can only be understood in relative terms which is why the poverty line has been revised various times in the past. Poverty, on the other hand, has also been defined in absolute terms to have a time invariant and universal understanding. Absolute poverty was defined as 'a condition characterised by severe deprivation of basic human needs, including food, safe drinking water, sanitation facilities, health, shelter, education and information. It depends not only on income but also on access to social services' at the World Summit on Social Development in Copenhagen in 1995.[2] To arrive at a measure of absolute poverty, the number of people who are deprived of the above-mentioned basic needs are counted as 'the total number living below a specified minimum level of real income—an international poverty line.'[3] This line is currently set at USD 1.90 a day by the World Bank.[4]

The importance of addressing this condition is clear from the fact that the eradication of absolute poverty comprised the first of the eight Millennium Development Goals (MDGs), which provide concrete, numerical benchmarks for tackling various dimensions of extreme poverty. When it comes to Pakistan, the country, unsurprisingly, failed to achieve most of the set targets except for the elimination of poverty.[5] Initial reports by the UN, tracking Sindh's progress against the MDGs, presented quite a bleak picture of the rate of progress.

Table 7.1: Nutrition Status vis-à-vis MDG Nutrition Target 2015
(1990–91 to 2014–15)

Indicators	1990–91	2005–06	MDG Target 2015	2014 (Latest National Statistics)	Current Status
Proportion of population below the caloric based food plus non-food poverty line	26.1	23.3	13	12.4	On-Track
Prevalence of underweight children under 5 years of age	40	38	<20	31.5	Off-Track
Proportion of population below minimum level of dietary energy consumption	25	N/A	13	30	Off-Track

Source: Pakistan Institute for Parliamentary Services (PIPS), *National MDGs Orientation for Parliamentary Task*, Islamabad, National Assembly of Pakistan, 2014.

Table 7.1 presents the outcomes of Pakistan's performance with respect to the MDGs. Pakistan's conventional measure of poverty, based on minimum calories, has lost its efficacy and the Planning Commission along with the UNDP and World Bank has constructed a new poverty line based on basic needs. Both the series differ in measurement of poverty but consistently show a declining trend since 2001–02.

Moreover, poverty, while prevalent throughout Pakistan, differs in its intensity subject to agro-climatic differences and socio-economic variations across different provinces as well as districts and this is what we intend to cover in the following passages.

Historical and New Poverty Lines for Pakistan

The historical data on estimation of poverty in Pakistan suffers from major methodological and conceptual weaknesses, including choices of poverty lines, conversion from calories into values, changing definitions, varying coverage in the surveys, and differing assumptions. Therefore, a clear picture is hard to discern from simply examining the historical data. Table 7.2 provides the historical series published by the government of Pakistan, but this is not a definitive picture.

According to Table 7.2, 40 per cent of the country's population was living below the assumed poverty line in 1963–64. This ratio had declined substantially to 17 per cent by 1987–88 but then gradually witnessed an upward swing ending up to around 32 per cent by the end of 1990s. The fall in urban poverty was much steeper compared to the rural poor as it was almost halved from 45 to 26 per cent in this thirty-five-year span.

It was interesting that at the beginning of the 1960s rural poverty incidence was lower than that of urban but by the end of the 1990s, the decline in rural poverty was marginal and was almost ten percentage points higher than urban poverty.

Table 7.2: Proportion of Poor in Pakistan by Area (Headcount Ratio) (%)
(1963–64 to 1999–2000)

Years	Total	Rural	Urban
1963–64	40.2	38.9	44.5
1966–67	44.5	45.6	41.0
1969–70	46.5	49.1	38.8
1979–80	30.7	32.5	29.4
1984–85	24.6	25.9	21.2
1987–88	17.3	18.3	15.0
1990–91	22.1	23.6	18.6
1992–93	22.4	23.4	15.6
1996–97	31.0	32.0	27.0
1998–99	32.6	34.8	25.9
1999–2000	33.5	-	-

Source: Ministry of Finance, *Pakistan Economic* Survey, Islamabad, Government of Pakistan, various years.

The reliability of long term trends beginning from the 1960s is always open to question for a variety of reasons—definition of poverty line, estimation procedures, sample size and coverage, methodological approach, non-response ratios, and underlying assumptions with regards to interpolation in the intervening years between the surveys. Accepting these reservations, it appears that the most rapid decline in the incidence of poverty took place during the 1980s—a period of high economic growth.

It appears from the data presented in the table that the proportion of poor fell sharply from 46.5 per cent in 1969–70 to 17.3 per cent by 1987–88. The trend reversed in the 1990s and the poverty incidence almost doubled to 34 per cent by 1998–99, i.e. in about a decade. This increase is understandable because the economic growth rate itself had taken a dip from average 6 per cent in the 1980s to 4 per cent in the 1990s. There has been a secular decline since 2000–01 when the growth rate picked up once again (Figure 7.1). However, the momentum was not broken ever after 2008–09 when the economy was once again under severe stress. The only deviation from the accepted norm that high economic growth is associated with reduction in poverty incidence was observed for the decade of the 1960s—the fastest growth rate in Pakistan's history.

There has been a lot of controversy about poverty estimates in the last decade as income poverty based on Food Energy Intake (FEI) showed a precipitous fall from 35 per cent in 2001–02 to about 9.3 per cent in 2013–14.

The Planning Commission along with the UNDP and World Bank has constructed a new poverty line that is based on the Cost of Basic Needs (CBN) approach. The CBN poverty line is constructed by taking both the minimum caloric threshold and necessary non-food expenditures such as clothing, shelter and education. Both the FEI and CBN poverty lines are then updated for inflation using the Consumer Price Index (Figure 7.1).

Figure 7.1: Poverty Headcount (%) in Pakistan (1998–99 to 2013–14)

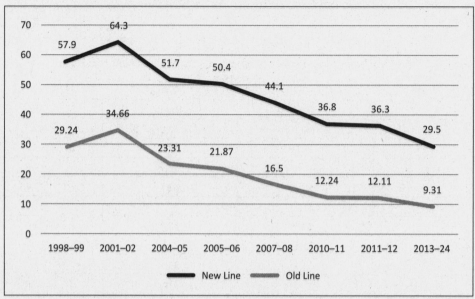

Source: HIES and World Bank calculations.

Under the new poverty line, there was a similar trend using this (CBN) method but the headcount was 64 per cent in 2001–02 and less than one half (29 per cent) in 2013–14. There is a smooth downward sloping curve witnessed in both these cases. It is more realistic to count the poor meeting their basic needs rather than simply their caloric intake. The absolute numbers, despite such a sharp fall, are still staggering. Almost 60 million people in Pakistan are still living below the poverty line and this poses a big challenge for policy makers. It is gratifying that the Benazir Income Support Programme has been retained by successive governments and its scope and coverage are being extended. Five million poor households living in extreme poverty are receiving cash grants to sustain their families.

Poverty Indicators of Sindh

The poverty rates in some areas of Sindh, particularly rural Sindh, are alarming, where weather changes, such as floods and droughts, often push people back in poverty given the vulnerable conditions of these areas, which often do not have the infrastructural capacity to deal with natural disasters.

The extent and intensity of the issue of poverty in Sindh can be gauged from the data presented in Figure 7.2. As per latest estimates, 43 per cent of the population in Sindh still lives below the poverty line. The national head count ratio is 39 per cent and therefore a greater proportion of Sindh's population is poor, as compared to the national average. Sindh is marked with stark urban–rural differences, one which is pervasive and rife in nature.[6]

As of 2016, almost 75 per cent of the rural population in Sindh is reported to be afflicted with extreme poverty.[7] As the rural population continues to depend heavily on natural endowments like water, forest, and arable land, environmental degradation and poor natural resource management are likely to have a greater effect on them as compared to those in the urban areas.

Figure 7.2: Sindh's Head Count Ratio (2004–05 to 2014–15)

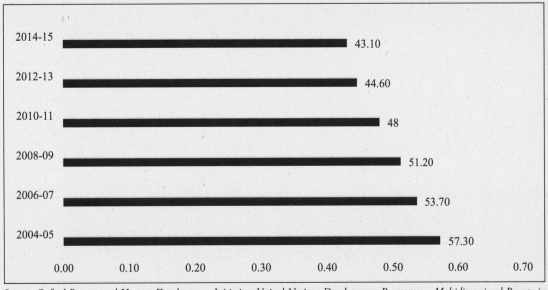

Source: Oxford Poverty and Human Development Initiative, United Nations Development Programme, *Multidimensional Poverty in Pakistan*, Islamabad, Planning Commission of Pakistan, Ministry of Planning, Development and Reform, 2015.

A visible declining trend is observed in the poverty rates for Sindh in the last decade (Figure 7.2). Although these figures show a massive decrease in the head count ratio during the years of rapid economic growth, the rates have slowed down in subsequent years.

Multidimensionality of Poverty and Human Development

In recent years, to capture the multidimensionality of poverty usually ignored by monetary measures, a more comprehensive measure of poverty, the Multidimensional Poverty Index (MPI) has been developed and used by the UNDP in its Human Development Report.

As Pakistan's Vision 2025 has pledged to create more inclusive economic growth, one that promises sustainability in the years to come, it is appropriate to use the MPI. The merit of this measure is that it not only looks at monetary deprivation but takes health, education and living standards into account. It can be deconstructed on a number of dimensions, such as provinces, districts and other groupings, which makes it a valuable tool for policymaking, as it can be used for specific targeting of the most vulnerable groups.

The index is based on the Alkire and Santos' (2010, 2014) methodology for international MPI but it has been modified for Pakistan.[8] Figure 7.3 outlines the Alkire-Foster methodology used to calculate Pakistan's MPI.

The MPI for Pakistan covers the same three dimensions of education, health, and standard of living as are covered in the global MPI, where each of these three dimensions equally weigh one-thirds in MPI calculation.[9] The specific indicators within these dimensions, however, are weighted according to their relative importance but together add up to one-thirds. 'The choice of indicators, however, reflects the country's particular context and political priorities, as well as the data available in the PSLM surveys.'[10] Hence, the Pakistan MPI is based on 15 indicators, where 7 of these are those derived from the global MPI.[11]

Figure 7.3: Multidimensional Poverty Index

Sabina Alkire and James Foster created a new method for measuring multidimensional poverty (MPI). It identifies who is poor by considering the intensity of the deprivations they suffer and includes an aggregation method.

Mathematically, the MPI combines two aspects of poverty:

MPI = H x A

1) Incidence (H) of poverty i.e. the percentage of people who are multidimensionally poor, or simply the headcount of poverty.

2) Intensity (A) of Poverty i.e. the average percentage of dimensions in which poor people are deprived.

Source: Oxford Poverty and Human Development Initiative and United Nations Development Programme, *Multidimensional Poverty in Pakistan*, Islamabad, Planning Commission of Pakistan, Ministry of Planning, Development and Reform, 2015.

It is to be noted that the indicators that have been selected for Pakistan reflect gendered understandings of poverty.[12] For instance, the gendered component incorporated in the 'Years of Schooling' indicator 'requires that at least one man and one woman in the household above the age of 10 has completed a minimum of 5 years of schooling', thus underlining gender equity in the household. [13] The highest weight has been given to years of schooling and access to health facilities, reflecting the significance of lack of basic rights to education and healthcare, enmeshing individuals into poverty traps (Table 7.3).

Table 7.3: Pakistan's Multidimensional Poverty Index
(2015–16)

Dimension	Indicator	Weights (%)
Education	Years of Schooling	16.67
	Child School Attendance	12.50
	School Quality	4.17
Health	Access to health facilities/clinics/ Basic Health Units (BHU)	16.67
	Immunisation	5.56
	Ante-natal care	5.56
	Assisted Delivery	5.56
Standard of Living	Water	4.76
	Sanitation	4.76
	Walls	2.38
	Overcrowding	2.38
	Electricity	4.76
	Cooking Fuel	4.76
	Assets	4.76
	Land and Livestock (Only for the rural areas)	4.76

Source: Oxford Poverty and Human Development Initiative, United Nations Development Programme, *Multidimensional Poverty in Pakistan*, Islamabad, Planning Commission of Pakistan, Ministry of Planning, Development and Reform, 2015.

While the inclusion of a gendered component enhances the MPI's efficacy, it can be argued that poverty needs to be captured more broadly by allowing MPI to capture other important socio-political aspects such as justice, rights, and participation.

Table 7.4: MPI, Incidence, and Intensity for Pakistan, Punjab, and Sindh
(2014–15)

	Index	Value
Pakistan	MPI	0.197
	Incidence (%)	38.8
	Intensity (%)	50.9
Punjab	MPI	0.152
	Incidence (%)	31.4
	Intensity (%)	48.4
Sindh	MPI	0.231
	Incidence (%)	43.1
	Intensity (%)	53.5

Source: Oxford Poverty and Human Development Initiative and United Nations Development Programme, *Multidimensional Poverty in Pakistan,* Islamabad, Planning Commission of Pakistan, Ministry of Planning, Development and Reform, 2015. MPI was calculated from PSLM.

Table 7.4 provides evidence for Sindh's poor performance relative to the national average and Punjab. For the year 2014–15, Pakistan had an MPI of 0.197 which means that the poor people of Pakistan 'experience 19.7 per cent of the deprivations that would be experienced if all people were deprived in all indicators'.[14] While Punjab shows an MPI of 0.152, Sindh on the other hand gives a much higher figure of 0.231, depicting a greater degree of deprivation.

It is also useful to present an overview of human development indicators of Pakistan that have a bearing on the incidence, depth, and intensity of poverty. These consist mainly of income, education, health etc. Table 7.5 presents trends in human development for Pakistan between 1980 and 2015 for which the data is available.

Pakistan has improved in almost all indicators in the said thirty-five years but other developing countries have done much better (Table 7.5). Pakistan is, therefore, ranked consistently low and in 2015 it was at 147 out of 188 countries. In 1994, Pakistan, ranked at 132, was ahead of India (135) and Bangladesh (146). By 2015, India had moved up to 131 and Bangladesh to 139, leaving Pakistan behind. In the Gender Inequality Index, it is almost at the lowest rung.

Sindh faces one of the largest disparities in terms of district HDIs amongst the provinces, according to a UN assessment. With an HDI of 0.640, Sindh has been categorised as having medium human development, compared to 0.732 for Punjab.[15] The overall provincial HDI figure for Sindh might be misleading since around 40 per cent of the population in Sindh lives in Karachi and Hyderabad, the two most developed districts of the province which coincide with the main hubs of economic activity. This is reflected in the fact that most of the districts in Sindh fall in the low to low-medium levels of development.

In terms of basic human development indicators and Sindh's performance relative to Punjab, Table 7.6 shows that Sindh falls behind the national average in four indicators—primary gross and net enrolment ratios, pre-natal consultation, and under five mortality rate. It equals the national average in two indicators (literacy rate and immunisation) while excels in two indicators (adult literacy, and postnatal consultation). Punjab as a province has done comparatively well, except in the case of under five mortality rates and postnatal consultation.[16]

Table 7.5: Human Development Indicators of Pakistan
(1980-81 and 2015–16)

	1980	2015	Percentage Change (%)
HDI Value	0.353	0.55	56
Life Expectancy (Years)*	57.0	66.4	16
Expected Years of Schooling	3.7	8.1	119
Mean Years of Schooling	1.8	5.1	183
Gross National Income per capita 2011 (PPP in USD)	2,437	5,031	106
Adult Literacy Rate (%)	26.2	58.7	124

*Values obtained from the Worldbank.org portal.

Source: United Nations Development Programme, *Human Development Report*, New York, United Nations (UN), 2016.

Table 7.6: Comparative Development Indicators for Pakistan, Punjab and Sindh
(2014–15)

Basic Indicators	Pakistan	Punjab	Sindh
Primary Gross Enrolment Rate	91	98	79
Primary Net Enrolment Rate	67	70	61
Literacy Rates (10 Years and Older)	60	63	60
Adult Literacy Rates (15 Years and older)	57	60	58
Under 5 Mortality Rates	89	105	93
At least 1 Immunisation	99	99	99
Pre-Natal Consultation	73	78	72
Post-Natal Consultation	29	29	33

*Values pertain to the year (2012–13) and are taken from Pakistan Demographic and Health Survey (2012–2013).

Source: Pakistan Bureau of Statistics, *Pakistan Social and Living Standards Measurement Survey 2014–15,* (slamabad, Statistics Division, Government of Pakistan, 2016.

Another report highlighted that during the period 2001–14, Sindh had the slowest growth rate in HDI due to poor law and order, weak governance, and skewed priorities.[17]

Figure 7.4: Poverty Incidence Map of Sindh 2004–05 (left) & 2014–15 (right)

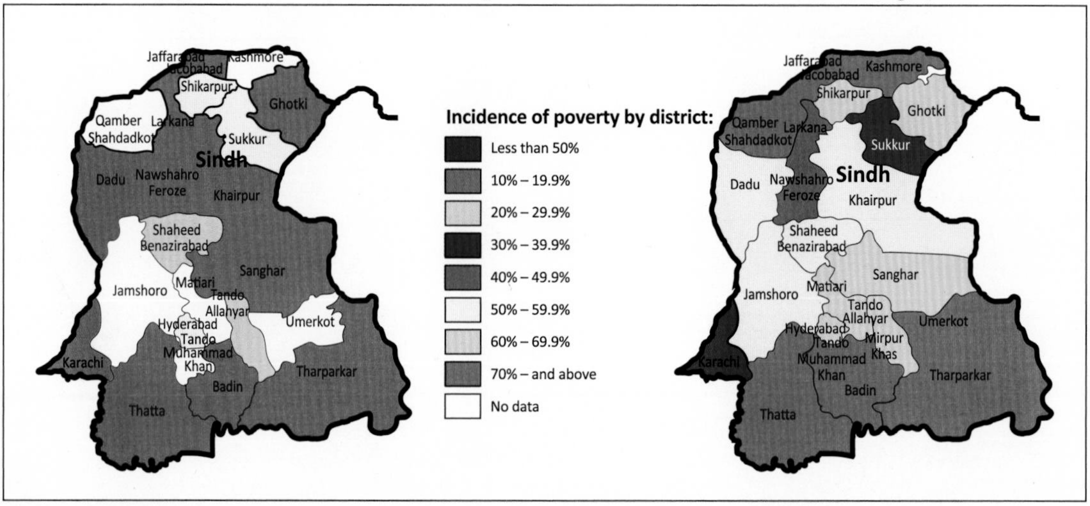

Source: Oxford Poverty and Human Development Initiative and United Nations Development Program, Multidimensional Poverty in Pakistan. Islamabad: Planning Commission of Pakistan, Ministry of Planning, Development and Reform, 2015.

Variation in Poverty in Sindh

INTER-DISTRICT VARIATION

Karachi is the only district classified as the 'least poor' in the province, while many districts come to be classified as very poor. The southeast part of Sindh is the poorest region in the province, with Central Sindh being relatively less poor, and the southwest part of the province being the least poor region

Citizens' access to and utilisation of public services can, to a large extent, have a bearing on monetary and non-monetary measures of poverty. Particularly, access to education and healthcare facilities and municipality services can significantly determine the human development progress of a region. It follows that the areas with high levels of poverty in Sindh are characterised with poor service delivery.

According to the indicators of poverty, southern districts of Sindh, excluding Karachi and Hyderabad— districts such as Tharparkar, Umerkot, and Sujawal—have the highest concentration of the poor, with Tharparkar experiencing severe deprivation. The state of governance, limited or no access to public services aggravated by local power structures, and the quality of public services are characteristic of some of the poorest districts. Poor governance results in inefficient delivery of critical social services, such as health and education, which have severe implications for human development in Sindh.

The districts in Sindh that face a lower incidence of poverty also happen to have a concentration of industry and required infrastructure. In contrast, the poorest districts in Sindh lack the industries and infrastructure required to integrate them into the national economy. Some districts in Sindh might also face the resource curse, as the benefits of endowment and subsequent exploitation of natural resources often does not reach the local communities.

Figure 7.4 illustrates a district-level analysis of the incidence of poverty in Sindh. The districts which have shown improvement in terms of the poverty incidence rate include Gothki, Shaheed Benazirabad, and Dadu. Sukkur, Naushahro Feroz, Larkana, and Hyderabad have done outstandingly well by having jumped to more than one category upwards. The worse-off districts in the province are Tharparkar, Mirpurkhas, Badin, and Tando Mohammad Khan. Shikarpur has worsened over the years and moved lower. Since no data was available in 2004–2005 for the districts Tando Muhammad Khan, Tando Allahyar, Umerkot, Qamber Shahdadkot, Matiari, and Kashmore, the extent to which poverty has changed in these districts cannot be deduced. However, the later years do suggest that more than half of the population is below the poverty line. Unsurprisingly, Karachi is the only district that seems to have a low proportion of the poor.

It is to be noted that the northern districts of Sindh have generally worsened over time while the southeastern ones have not changed much in terms of the incidence rate.[18] This district-wise analysis clearly highlights that even within rural Sindh, there is heterogeneity, and government policies and public spending does not seem to work effectively in the relatively more deprived districts of Tharparkar, Umerkot, Badin, Thatta, Mirpurkhas, and Tando Muhammad Khan.

Table 7.7 provides a list of the extreme and the least poor districts in Sindh and corroborates the findings that the southeastern part of Sindh is relatively poorer as compared to its central counterpart. As per the Clustered Deprivation Report from SDPI, the desert areas of District Tharparkar, Mirpurkhas, and Umerkot are among the poorest. With Karachi and Naushahro Feroze being the least poor districts, the regional dimension of poverty becomes clear.[19]

While incidence is a simple measure of the fraction of the population that lies below the poverty line and should not be considered on its own, intensity, on the other hand, reflects the extent to which income of the poor lies below the stated line. Intra-provincial intensity of poverty in Sindh is exhibited in Table 7.8, which shows that Naushahro Feroze has the lowest intensity of poverty, closely followed by the districts lying in the northern part of Sindh. Interestingly, Karachi appears under the extreme poor districts, highlighting inequality arising from migration from interior districts of Sindh, and the pressures and cost of increasing urbanisation

Table 7.7: Incidence of Poverty among the Districts of Sindh (2012)

Extremely Poor Districts			Least Poor Districts		
Rank	Districts	Headcount Ratio (H)	Rank	Districts	Headcount Ratio (H)
1	Tharparkar	47	1	Karachi	20
2	Mirpurkhas	44	2	Naushahro Feroze	20
3	Badin	42	3	Hyderabad	25
4	Tando Muhammad Khan	41	4	Sukkur	25
5	Thatta	40	5	Khairpur	27
6	Shaheed Benazirabad (Nawabshah)	39	6	Shikarpur	28
7	Jamshoro	39	7	Sanghar	28
8	Larkana	38	8	Dadu	29
9	Shahdadkot	38	9	Matiari	29
10	Jacobabad	36	10	Tando Allah Yar	32

Source: Naveed, Arif and Nazim Ali, *Clustered Deprivation: District Profile of Poverty in Pakistan*, Islamabad, Sustainable Policy Development Institute, 2012.

Table 7.8: Intensity of Poverty in Districts of Sindh (2012)

Extreme Poor Districts			Least Poor Districts		
Rank	Districts	Average Intensity of Deprivation (A)	Rank	Districts	Average Intensity of Deprivation (A)
1	Mirpurkhas	0.59	1	Naushahro Feroze	0.48
2	Jamshoro	0.54	2	Shikarpur	0.49
3	Karachi	0.53	3	Kashmore	0.49
4	Shaheed Benazirabad (Nawabshah)	0.53	4	Larkana	0.49
5	Hyderabad	0.53	5	Badin	0.5
6	Tharparkar	0.52	6	Jacobabad	0.5
7	Thatta	0.52	7	Sukkur	0.5
8	Sanghar	0.52	8	Shahdadkot	0.51
9	Tando Allah Yar	0.51	9	Ghotki	0.51
10	Matiari	0.51	10	Dadu	0.51

Source: Naveed, Arif and Nazim Ali, *Clustered Deprivation: District Profile of Poverty in Pakistan*, Islamabad, Sustainable Policy Development Institute, 2012.

including the absence of family support systems. In rural areas, those without jobs can always look to their extended families for support, but once they migrate to urban areas, they have nobody to fall upon and have to fend for themselves

URBAN–RURAL VARIATION

It is argued that poverty in rural areas needs to be treated differently than that in the urban districts of the economy. For an equal comparison, it has been suggested that if the urban poverty line lies at 2,350 minimum calories per adult for each day, then it should be 2,550 in the case of rural areas.[20]

Besides, the official data and poverty lines, there have been some other studies by researchers on this subject that are worth mentioning here. These studies have their own estimates, but they supplement the headcount ratio with other measures such as poverty gap and severity of poverty. While the incidence of poverty gives only a share of the population whose income or consumption is below the poverty line, the poverty gap index provides the depth or the magnitude of how far off the households are from the poverty line. Another appropriate measure of poverty is the squared poverty gap which simultaneously accounts for the poverty gap (distance) and inequality amongst the poor.

Amongst all of the provinces, Sindh seems to have the highest urban–rural disparity in poverty; the province is home to the city with the highest per capita income in the country and has rural districts with some of the poorest inhabitants.

Figures 7.5 to 7.8 attempt to provide an in-depth analysis for the period 2010–12 on the intensity of poverty for both the urban and the rural areas of Pakistan, Sindh, and Punjab. For the year 2010–11, 39 per cent of the rural population of Pakistan falls below the poverty line where Sindh has a percentage as high as 43 per cent. Moreover, the severity is much more prominent in Sindh as compared to Punjab.[21]

Some structural issues can help explain the pervasive poverty levels (the poor who have not experienced any change in their standard of living), such as the land ownership patterns in rural Sindh which can help in explaining the vulnerability of the poor. Areas that have greater feudalism tend to have high levels of rural poverty, since sharecropping arrangements are structured to favour the landowner, which is evident in most of rural Sindh, which happens to have the lowest proportion of owner-operated farms.

Ownership of even small landholdings can help households absorb economic shocks, ensuring food security. However, in Sindh, the rural poor are majorly engaged as *haris* (landless peasants) with no ownership of the land they work on—a pattern that carries across generations. In cases where they may own the land, they do not have accurate, accessible land title records, which makes them unable to protect their assets. There is also the problem of clustering of most basic infrastructure and social services in rural Sindh, raising the cost of living and limiting the access that the poor have to these services since they also happen to be situated in far-flung areas.

Sindh houses 36 per cent of the urban population that lies below the poverty line. It is indeed surprising to note that the severity index of urban Sindh is much higher (2.24) than that of rural Sindh (2.01) which points to higher inequality in urban areas as compared to the rural. Hence, it can be argued that while poverty has always been high for those living in rural areas, urban areas are becoming increasingly riddled with poverty-related issues owing to rising urbanisation and rural–urban migration. The depravity that rural migrants and urban poor have to contend with, in the form of unemployment, living in slum areas, and adapting to a sub-standard lifestyle, may in fact be higher than that faced by their rural counterparts.

Contrary to popular perception, Punjab, according to this study, does not compare much different from Sindh in the incidence of consumption poverty, poverty gap or severity of poverty. The closeness of these estimates do raise questions about their veracity and accuracy.

Figure 7.5: Poverty Incidence Rates for Rural Areas in Pakistan, Punjab, and Sindh
(2010–11)

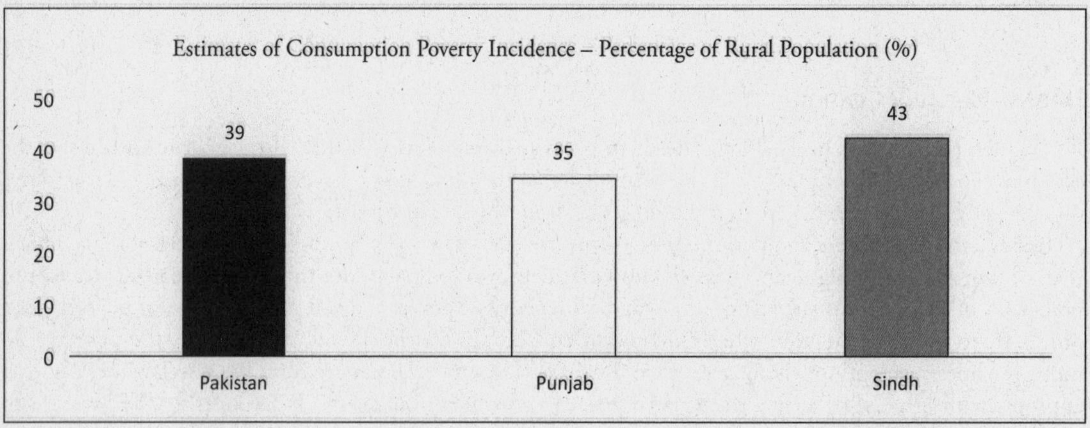

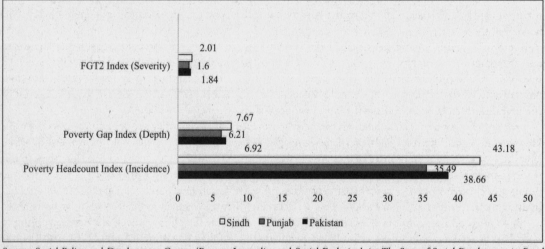

Source: Social Policy and Development Centre, 'Poverty, Inequality and Social Exclusion', in *The State of Social Development in Rural Pakistan*, Karachi, 2014, pp. 85–115.

Figure 7.6: Poverty Measures for Rural Areas in Sindh, Punjab, and Pakistan (2010–11)

Source: Social Policy and Development Centre, 'Poverty, Inequality and Social Exclusion', in *The State of Social Development in Rural Pakistan*, Karachi, 2014, pp. 85–115.

Addressing Inequality

Closely related to poverty is the problem of inequality. Inequality, in the simplest terms is disparity or unevenness. When referred to in economic terms, inequality is usually combined with income and wealth which connotes the disparity in the income of different groups in a particular area. Thus, when we talk about income inequality in Sindh, we intend to refer to the disparities in income earned by different groups. Stephen Jenkins explains

Figure 7.7: Poverty Incidence Rates for Urban Areas of Pakistan, Punjab, and Sindh (2011–12)

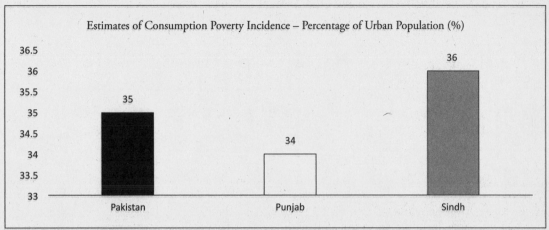

Source: Social Policy and Development Centre, 'In the State of Social Development in Urban Pakistan', in *Counting the Poor in the Urban Context*, Karachi, 2016, 137–57.

Figure 7.8: Poverty Measures for Urban Areas of Sindh, Punjab, and Pakistan (2011–12)

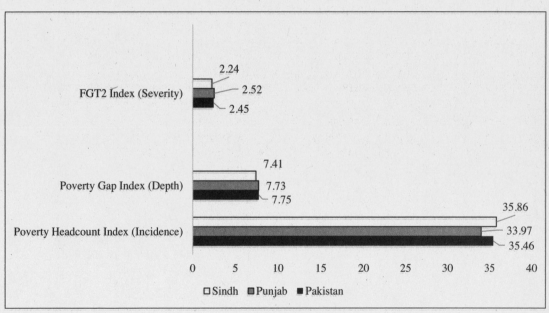

Source: Social Policy and Development Centre, 'In the State of Social Development in Urban Pakistan', *Counting the Poor in the Urban Context*, Karachi, Social Policy and Development Centre, 2016, pp. 137–57.

the study of economic inequality as 'the analysis of differences across the population in access to, and control over, economic resources.'[22] This entails that economic inequality, quite commonsensically, is directly related to 'economic resources'. Thus, the most common indicator and determinant of inequality in economics is income, which we will be focusing upon in the chapter. This brings us to the oft-repeated term 'income inequality'. This term has become a common part of our daily discourse and therefore needs to be understood properly. Considering Jenkins's definition of economic inequality, we can conclude that it is the difference in the income earned across the population. Thus, an income inequality analysis will ideally include a representative sample of all households in the country to critically examine statistics on distribution of income and consumption by various households.

Inequality is not only an economic concern but also carries political ramifications. Amartya Sen notes in his book, *On Economic Inequality*, that there is a close relation between economic inequality and rebellion.[23] This is not a surprising fact since many countries have experienced massive revolutions just because of the pervasive inequality. A case in point is the USSR.[24] One of the major reasons attributed towards its collapse is the increased amount of inequality in the Soviet Union. A more recent example is of the Arab Spring. While the achievement of democracy was a motive of the people, it was fuelled by the huge income disparity in these countries particularly in Egypt and Tunisia. Nevertheless, it can safely be established that income inequality is closely related to economic and political stability. Increasing inequality will result in frustration among the masses who tend to become disillusioned with the ruling elite. This might result in rebellions and attempts to overthrow the ruling government.

Karl Marx, an eminent thinker of the nineteenth century whose theories have significantly impacted the course of politics in the twentieth century, also argues that growing inequality will result in a disillusionment of the working class which will ultimately rise against the ruling capitalist class and bring about a revolution following which an equal society will be established. Although Marx's prediction is quite idealistic, it should motivate governments to work towards eliminating inequality and poverty and consequently achieving a more egalitarian society in which the benefits of economic growth are shared widely.

Moreover, there have also been attempts to establish a link between crime and income inequality. The greater the inequality, the greater chances there are of increased rates of crime and violence. All in all, inequality has detrimental effects on society. Although a perfectly equal society is possible only in theory, this should not stop governments from working to minimise stark inequality, be it income, regional, or gender.

This brings us to the state of inequality in Pakistan. Pakistan suffers from a high rate of income inequality which is evident from the fact that in 2013, the top 20 per cent of Pakistan's population shared 40.3 per cent of the total income of the country, while the lowest 20 per cent only 9.2 per cent of the country's total income.[25] Such statistics reflect wide disparity in income generation. If the lower stratum also records a low rate of growth in real income, then over time, the gap between top and bottom quintiles will keep on widening, threatening social cohesion.

Not surprisingly, Sindh is no different than the rest of the country in this respect. The situation is even worse because of the sharp differentials in rural and urban incomes. Urban Sindh is much better off than rural Sindh in terms of income per capita. A pertinent example is that of Thar, where people are forced to survive in abysmal conditions. It is one of the poorest regions of the country which is frequently devastated by droughts and famine. The people of Thar are forced to live in conditions of abject poverty and malnourishment, with a dearth of even the most basic necessities such as food and water. At the same time, some residents of Karachi enjoy living standards that are comparable to those in Southern Europe.

The historical trends of income distribution presented in Table 7.9 shows that the average Gini Coefficient has ranged within 0.33 to 0.41, while the ratio of the incomes received by the top 20 per cent of those of the bottom 20 per cent has been around 5.2 to 8.6. (The Gini coefficient is 'an aggregate numerical measure of income inequality ranging from 0 [perfect equality] to 1 [perfect inequality]'.)[26] The highest Gini Coefficient was recorded in 1992–93 and the relative income ratio in 1990–91. If a long-term view is taken there is no discernible change in these two indicators in 1963–64 and 1998–99. The Gini Coefficient was 0.39 in 1963–64 and 0.40 in 1998–99. Relative income ratio was 7.0 in 1963–64 and 8 in 1998–99. There have been wide fluctuations in the intervening years. For example, both the Gini Coefficient and the relative income ratio (top 20 per cent to bottom 20 per cent) recorded to its lowest value in 1969–70. This finding is indeed puzzling as the 1960s was the fastest growth period in Pakistan's history and Ayub Khan was taken to task for promoting concentration of income in the hands of twenty-two rich families of the country. Both popular media and academic literature attacked the Decade of Development Model for creating sharp income inequalities. The reason for this finding may be that there may be growing income disparities between the two regions— East Pakistan and West Pakistan—while the intra household income distribution within West Pakistan was improving. The other problem may be the quality of data upon which inferences are drawn.

Table 7.9: Trends in Income Distribution in Pakistan
(1963–64 to 2010–11)

Year	Percentage share of income (%)			Household Gini Coefficient	Number of Poor as a Percentage of Population			Ratio of Highest 20% to Lowest 20%
	Lowest 20%	Middle 60%	Highest 20%		Urban	Rural	Total	
1963–64	6.4	48.3	45.3	0.386	44.5	38.9	40.2	7.1
1966–67	7.6	49	43.4	0.355	41	45.6	44.5	5.7
1969–70	8	50.2	41.8	0.336	38.8	49.1	46.5	5.2
1979–80	7.4	47.6	45	0.373	25.9	32.5	30.7	6.1
1984–85	7.3	47.7	45	0.369	21.2	25.9	24.5	6.2
1987–88	8	45.3	46.7	0.348	15	18.3	17.3	5.5
1990–91	5.7	45	49.3	0.407	18.6	23.6	22.1	8.6
1992–93	6.2	45.6	48.2	0.41	15.5	23.4	22.4	7.8
1996–97	7	43.6	49.4	0.4	27	32	31	7.0
1998–99	6.2	44.1	49.7	0.4	20.9	34.7	30.6	8.0
2004–05	7.2*	44*	48.8*	0.41*	27.7**	30.85**	29.85**	6.8*
2010–11	7.0*	44.3*	48.7*	0.41*	34.09**	39.37**	37.62**	6.9*

Source: Finance Division, *Pakistan Economic Survey*, Islamabad, Ministry of Finance Government of Pakistan, various years.

* Haroon Jamal, *Growth and Income Inequality Effects on Poverty: The Case of Pakistan (1988–2011)*, Karachi, Social Policy and Development Centre, 2014.

** Haroon Jamal, *Pakistan Poverty Statistics: Estimates for 2011*, Karachi, Social Policy and Development Centre, 2013.

Different surveys and different researchers have not used consistent methodological approaches or coverage may have varied.

According to conventional wisdom, rapid growth does reduce the incidence of poverty but its impact on income distribution remains ambiguous. In this case, the poverty incidence was at its peak in 1969–70 while income distribution was better. This paradox defies logic and betrays broad empirical patterns of relationship between income growth and poverty incidence, and income growth and changes in income distribution. Therefore, the results contained in Table 7.9 should be interpreted keeping these caveats in mind.

In terms of inequality, Figure 7.9 clearly shows the disparities in incomes of different income groups in Sindh and Punjab. It reflects a general decrease in inequality over the period studied. Inequality in Punjab is considerably higher than in Sindh. For each year studied, the proportion of income earned by the lowest 20 per cent of the population was lower in Punjab than in Sindh. Similarly, for every year studied, the proportion of income earned by the highest 20 per cent of the population was considerably higher in Punjab than in Sindh except for the year 2011–12.

Figure 7.9: Distribution of Monthly Household Income in Sindh and Punjab (2007–2013)

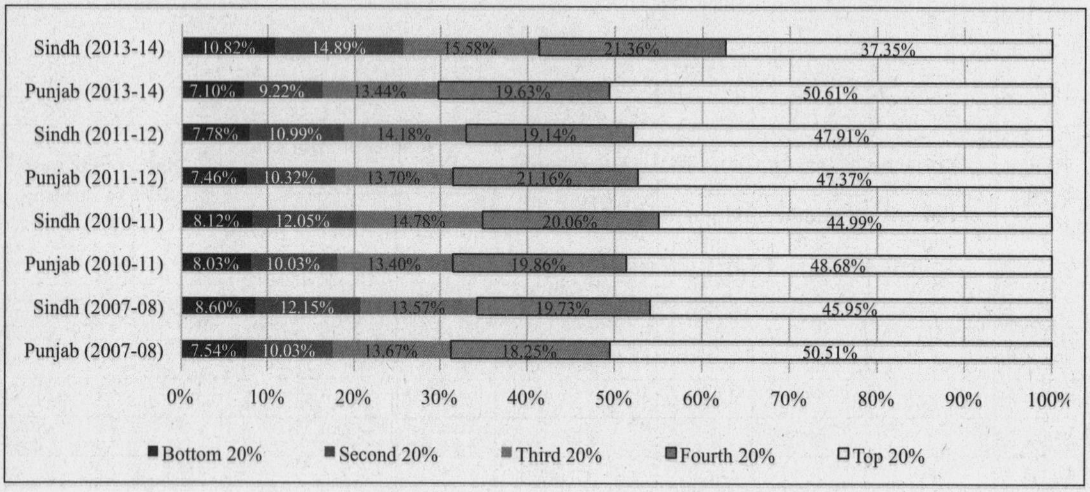

Source: Pakistan Bureau of Statistics, *Household Integrated Economic Survey*, Islamabad, Statistics Division, Government of Pakistan, various years.

Tables 7.10 to 7.12 and Figure 7.10 for 2010–11 corroborate the data shown in Figure 7.9.

Table 7.10: Average Monthly Income Quintiles in Pakistan, Punjab, and Sindh (in PKR) (2010–11)

	Total	1st	2nd	3rd	4th	5th	Ratio of Top 20% to Lowest 20%
Pakistan	21,785	11,385	14,274	16,841	20,784	37,727	3.31
Punjab	22,859	11,144	13,936	16,829	20,904	40,968	3.67
Sindh	20,606	11,047	14,441	15,964	20,249	32,914	2.98

Source: Pakistan Bureau of Statistics, *Household Integrated Economic Survey 2010-11*, Islamabad, Government of Pakistan, 2011.

Table 7.11: Average Monthly Income Quintiles for Urban Pakistan, Punjab, and Sindh (in PKR) (2010–11)

	Total	1st	2nd	3rd	4th	5th	Ratio of Top 20% to Lowest 20%
Pakistan	27,663	11,970	16,481	17,382	22,295	40,876	3.41
Punjab	29,491	11,584	15,898	17,605	22,891	44,996	3.88
Sindh	25,253	12,196	17,352	16,572	20,982	34,378	2.82

Source: Pakistan Bureau of Statistics, *Household Integrated Economic Survey 2010-11*, Islamabad, Government of Pakistan, 2011.

Table 7.12: Average Monthly Income Quintiles for Rural Pakistan, Punjab, and Sindh (in PKR) (2010–11)

	Total	1st	2nd	3rd	4th	5th	Ratio of Top 20% to Lowest 20%
Pakistan	18,712	11,265	13,613	16,617	19,921	33,932	3.01
Punjab	19,778	11,062	13,354	16,521	19,971	37,142	3.36
Sindh	15,499	10,713	13,043	15,533	19,115	26,320	2.46

Source: Pakistan Bureau of Statistics, *Household Integrated Economic Survey 2010-11*, Islamabad, Government of Pakistan, 2011.

Figure 7.10: Average Monthly Income (2010–11)

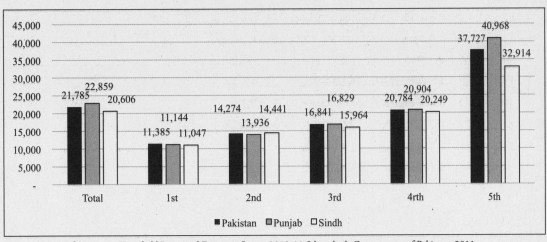

Source: Bureau of Statistics, *Household Integrated Economic Survey 2010-11*, Islamabad, Government of Pakistan, 2011.

Consumption Inequality

Low income and income disparities are closely linked with consumption inequality as well. A low income will inevitably result in suppressed consumption while differences in income will also be reflected in consumption patterns of different groups in the country. Although consumption patterns remained quite steady during the time period studied, a wide gap in the consumption of the richest and the poorest is also visible in Figure 7.11. The year 2011–12 was the most unequal in terms of consumption expenditure. The poorest stratum of the province had a 9 per cent share of the consumption in the province while the richest 20 per cent had a mammoth 43.7 per cent share of consumption. An important thing to note here is the fact that monthly consumption exceeded the poor household's income. The monthly household income in the year 2011–12 was PKR 12,551.72 while the monthly consumption expenditure of the poor for the same year was PKR 13,354.57. The poor spend significantly more than the rich on consumption of inferior goods such as food. Across years, almost 60 per cent of the poor's income was being consumed in food and housing.[27] The remaining part of the income is spent on utilities, leaving very little for their children's education, creating an inescapable cycle of poverty. The inevitable consequence is persistence of the gap between the rich and the poor beyond the present generation.

If we consider the distribution of monthly consumption expenditure in the provinces of Sindh and Punjab, it is worth noticing that Punjab is considerably 'more unequal' in terms of consumption expenditure. The gap between the richest and the poorest in quintiles in Sindh was lower than that in Punjab. While there is a general decline in the consumption expenditure of the richest in Sindh, the data contains the phenomenon of an expanding middle class in the country.

Figure 7.11: Distribution of Monthly Consumption Expenditure in Pakistan
(2007–08 to 2013–14)

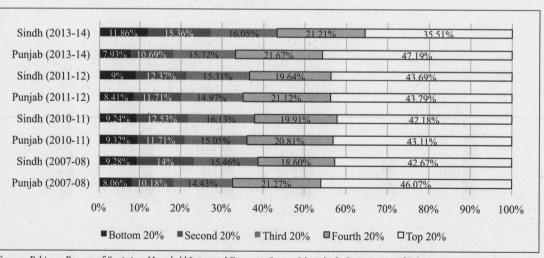

Source: Pakistan Bureau of Statistics, *Household Integrated Economic Survey*, Islamabad, Government of Pakistan, various years.

Comparing monthly income and expenditure across the various quintiles, it becomes apparent that savings are done by the top quintiles only while dissaving by 60 per cent of the population (Figure 7.12.)

Figure 7.12: Percentage Distribution of Monthly Income and Monthly Consumption Expenditure in Pakistan (2010–11)

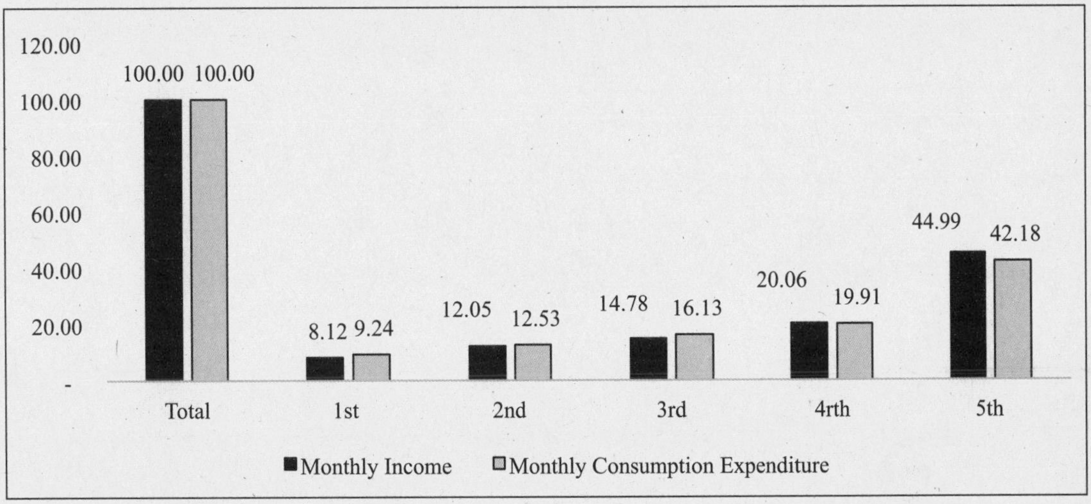

Source: Bureau of Statistics, *Household Integrated Economic Survey 2010-11*, Islamabad, Government of Pakistan, 2011.

Excess of expenditure over income indicates inadequacy of assets they hold and the returns they receive on their assets. In the rural areas, these quintiles represent landless peasants, share croppers, and causal labourers. In urban areas, they are mostly working in the low skill-using informal sector. The difference between income and expenditure results in their state of indebtedness. The fourth quintile barely makes it even and it is only the top quintile that can save some proportion of their incomes—about 6 to 7 per cent monthly. The low domestic savings rate in Pakistan reflects this propensity to save being limited to a very small fraction of the population.

Urban–Rural Nexus

Besides the well-known problem of disparity between the urban and rural areas, inequality within urban areas is sharper. More than 60 per cent of the income in urban areas accrued to the richest 20 per cent of the population while a meagre 2 to 3 per cent was earned by the poorest 20 per cent. In the rural areas on the other hand, incomes of the poor expanded to 12.8 per cent in 2013–14[28] from 10.57 per cent in 2007–08,[29] while those on the top quantile decreased simultaneously, thus narrowing the income gap between the two classes. This can partly be attributed to an increasing rural–urban migration over the past decade or so which has resulted in an ever-expanding lower class in cities that can hardly survive in the midst of the relatively higher cost of living in cities. The urban poor also do not enjoy support from the family—something quite common in rural areas.

The above trend can be discerned in the province of Sindh (Table 7.13) also; income disparity between the top and the bottom quintiles was considerably higher in urban areas than in rural areas in 2007–08. While the top quintile in the urban areas received 67.4 per cent of the province's income, the poorest quintile had only 1.2 per cent. However, by 2013–14, there was some improvement in urban areas. The top 20 per cent's share had declined to 51.5 per cent of the total income while the bottom 20 per cent increased theirs to 3.6 per cent. The relative income ratio between the two groups, bottom and top 20 per cent, was 14.3 compared to 57.2 six years ago. In rural areas, the share of the poorest expanded over the years to reach 23.4 per cent in 2013–14 from 19.2 per cent in 2007–08.

Table 7.13: Percentage Distribution of Monthly Household Income in Sindh (Rural /Urban)
(2007–08 to 2013–14)

		Bottom 20%	Second 20%	Third 20%	Fourth 20%	Top 20%
Rural	2007–08	19.22	23.15	21.74	20.71	15.18
	2010–11	17.03	20.53	23.47	20.74	18.24
	2011–12	18.91	22.36	20.89	19.22	18.62
	2013–14	23.37	26.03	20.66	16.97	13
Urban	2007–08	1.18	4.46	7.87	19.05	67.44
	2010–11	3.15	7.32	9.93	19.68	59.92
	2011–12	2.08	5.16	10.74	19.11	62.91
	2013–14	3.56	8.44	12.63	23.91	51.46

Source: Pakistan Bureau of Statistics, *Household Integrated Economic Survey*, Islamabad, Statistics Division, Government of Pakistan, various years.

Ascension of Poverty and Income Distribution

A high rate of economic growth has been found to be a strong correlate of poverty reduction. According to Todaro and Smith 'it is not just the rate but also the character of economic growth (how it is achieved, who participates, which sectors are given priority, what institutional arrangements are designed and emphasised, etc.) that determines the degree to which that growth is or is not reflected in improved living standards for the poor.'[30]

Table 7.14: Trends in Growth, Poverty, and Income Distribution in Pakistan
(1950–2013)

Decade	Growth	Poverty	Income Distribution
1950–60	Stagnated	Persisted	Unknown
1960–70	Rapid Increase	Increased	Improved
1970–80	Lower	Declined	Worsened
1980–90	Rapid Increase	Declined	Rapid deterioration, followed by rapid improvements
1990–00	Lower	Increased considerably	Worsened
2000–07	Rapid Increase	Declined	Probably worsened
2008–13	Lower	Declined	Unknown

Source: Akbar Zaidi, *Issues in Pakistan's Economy: A Political Economy Perspective*, Karachi, Oxford University Press, 2015.

In Pakistan, the evidence does point in the same direction except that the data for the 1960s—a period of high growth—points in a different direction. The 1980s and the period 2000–07 certainly show a close correlation between higher rates of economic growth and poverty reduction. In the 1990s, declining growth reversed the trend, making it consistent with the above hypothesis. The paradox appears for 1970s and 2008–13 where slowdown in growth was not accompanied by increase in poverty. As a matter of fact, poverty did decline despite lower growth rates. Presumably, the pattern of growth in this period was pro-poor.

At this point it must be noted that 'growth is indeed a necessary but not a sufficient condition for ensuring poverty reduction',[31] which means that there is a need for growth to be complemented by strong policy measures. The picture pertaining to income distribution remains hazy for a variety of reasons. In most of the last five decades, both international and national efforts were concentrated on poverty reduction. Surveys, statistical methods, refinements, and policy analyses made it possible to track the changes and trends in poverty. Millennium Development Goals (MDGs) made this the most important goal for all developing countries. World Bank's analytical work in international income comparison and a uniform poverty line ($1.25/day per person) made it easier for policy makers to have a clearer picture and take remedial measures.

However, while the international community was engaged in self-congratulatory celebrations on achieving the MDG target of reducing global poverty by one half between 1990 and 2015 and bringing almost one billion people out of the poverty net, inequality in income surfaced. Several seminal studies have demonstrated that income inequality is not only a phenomenon confined to the developing countries but developed countries are also faced with this malaise. Attention is now beginning to shift to accurately measure and track income inequality along with gender (male–female), region (urban–rural) and other dimensions.

The data available on income inequality in Pakistan is quite limited and therefore a lot of time these numbers are extrapolated or intrapolated. A popular measure is the Gini coefficient.

Figures 7.13 and 7.14 indicate the Gini coefficients for urban and rural areas for Pakistan as a whole as well as for Sindh and Punjab. Inequality seems to be marginally higher in urban Sindh as compared to not only urban Punjab but urban Pakistan as well, perhaps owing to increased burden of rural–urban migration, lack of urban planning, and overdependence on a few urban centres in Sindh. When looking towards the rural Gini coefficients, it is quite evident that the Gini coefficient for Sindh has risen over the years as compared to the fall in that for Punjab. Access to ground water, increased owner-operated farms, division of land holdings because of inheritance laws and diffusion of new technologies may have contributed to this outcome.

Figure 7.13: Inequality in Per Capita Income for Urban Pakistan, Punjab, and Sindh (2014–15)

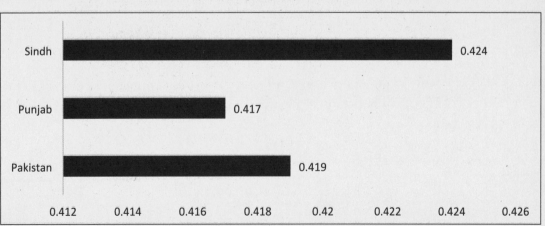

Source: Social Policy and Development Centre, 'Geographical Unevenness in Urban Human Development', in *The State of Social Development in Urban Pakistan*, Karachi, 2016, pp. 129–35.

Figure 7.14: Per Capita Income Inequality for Rural Pakistan, Punjab, and Sindh
(2005 to 2011–12)

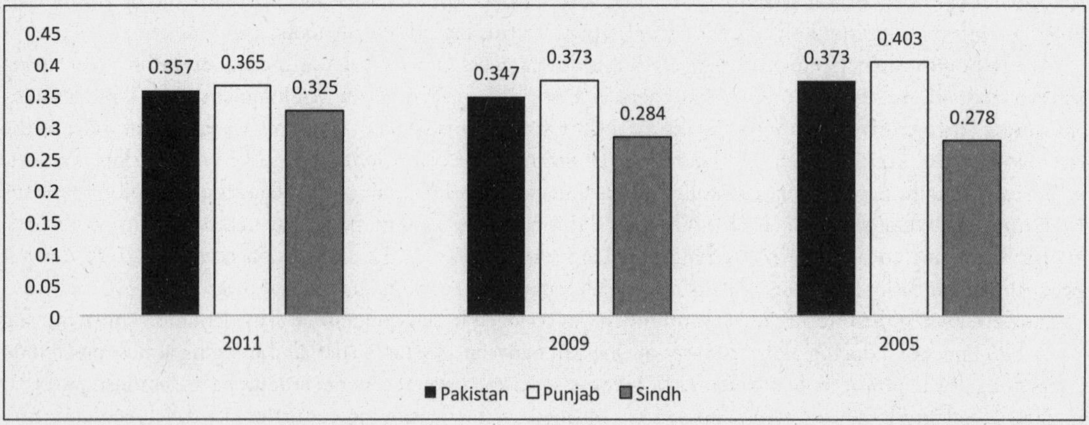

Source: Social Policy and Development Centre, 'Poverty, Inequality and Social Inclusion', in *The State of Social Development in Rural Pakistan*, Karachi, 2014, pp. 85–115.

Table 7.15: Average Per Capita Income Estimates by Area for Pakistan, Punjab, and Sindh
(2010–11)

		Population (in Million)	Gross Regional Product (in PKR Billion)	Per capita Income (in PKR Thousand)	Ratio of Urban to Rural Incomes
Pakistan	Total	177.1	17,107	96,595	
	Rural	117.1	8,703	73,942	1.9
	Urban	59.4	8,704	141,481	
Punjab	Total	96.6	9,375	97,100	
	Rural	65.3	5,054	77,434	1.8
	Urban	31.3	4,321	138,139	
Sindh	Total	42.2	5,050	119,724	
	Rural	22.1	1,813	82,151	2
	Urban	20.1	3,237	160,956	

Source: Social Policy and Development Centre, 'Poverty, Inequality and Social Inclusion', in *The State of Social Development in Rural Pakistan*, Karachi, 2014, pp. 85–115.

Poverty and inequality analysis is marred by inconsistent results derived from different data sets (Table 7.15). The SPDC uses the national income data to construct provincial Gross Regional Product (GRP) and then estimates per capita incomes for the provinces further divided into rural and urban per capita incomes. Based on the national income accounts data and assumed distribution, the ratio of urban to rural per capita income for Pakistan comes up to 1.9; for Punjab, 1.8, and for Sindh, 2.0. If we compare these ratios with those presented in Table 7B of the Annexure derived from Household Income and Expenditure Surveys of 2010–11, the same ratios turned out to be 1.6 for Sindh, 1.5 for Punjab, and 1.5 for Pakistan. The relative order ranking remains the same, confirming high disparity in urban–rural incomes in Sindh but the absolute numbers are quite different. This may be ascribed to the under reporting of incomes and expenditures when people are asked questions in the surveys compared to national income accounts data that is built upon hard output and value added numbers.

Although the Gini coefficient is a good representation of income inequality, it must be noted that it too has certain limitations because of its major sensitivity to the middle part of income distribution. For a more thorough representation of the extreme parts of income distribution, it is necessary to review income distribution data quintile-wise.

This ratio of incomes received by the top 20 per cent to bottom 20 per cent shows that, in contrast to the picture emerging from the examination of Gini coefficients, income distribution in Sindh, as a whole, is much better as compared to Punjab and the overall national average. While the Gini coefficient for Punjab is lower, both the ratio of incomes received by top 20 per cent income to bottom 20 per cent, and the average income in the urban areas, is quite high, as compared to the national average and Sindh.

The popular notion about large urban–rural income disparities in Sindh is corroborated by the data on the differentials in average incomes for the urban and rural areas. For Pakistan, the average urban income is only 48 per cent higher than that in the rural incomes. In Punjab, it is almost the same but in Sindh the differential widens to as high as 63 per cent. In other words, an urban citizen in Sindh earns almost two-thirds more than his counterparts in the rural area.

Economic Situation of the Poor Households in Sindh

While the previous section covered how average monthly income varies amongst different quintiles, this section delves into the characteristics of households, housing tenure, and access to services. It further presents a breakdown of poverty across agro-climatic zones.

Household size and dependency ratios have a direct relation with poverty incidence, while education level and employment status of the household head have an inverse relation. It follows that small families, headed by an educated, employed male with more working individuals, have a better chance of escaping poverty. Households headed by women are generally poorer as compared to those dependent on men, since their earning potential might be hampered due to less access to education and health facilities.

Table 7.16: Average Household Size by Quintiles in Sindh
(2015–16)

		Total	1st	2nd	3rd	4th	5th
Average Number of	Members per Household	6.22	8.23	7.33	6.44	5.55	4.51
	Employed person per Household	2.15	2.71	2.62	2.39	1.90	1.48

Source: Pakistan Bureau of Statistics, *Household Integrated Economic Survey 2015–16*, Islamabad, Statistics Division, Government of Pakistan, 2016.

Tables 7.16 to 7.18 bring out the characteristics of households that can explain some of the correlates of the incidence of poverty. It can be observed that the household size of the lowest income quintile is eight—almost twice that of the highest quintile. While the members of the family to support are too many, the income earners are only two, i.e. four persons are dependent on the earning of one individual. In case of the better off households, the number dwindles to three persons. Thus, lowering income earned combined with higher number of people to support is one of the reasons for the incidence of poverty. Either the numbers must be curtailed by better planning of children reproduced or household incomes should be supplemented by non-earning adults joining the labour force.

Table 7.17: Average Household Size by Quintiles in Rural Sindh
(2015–16)

		Total	1st	2nd	3rd	4th	5th
Average Number of	Members per Household	6.62	8.11	7.15	6.00	4.83	3.71
	Employed person per Household	2.59	2.81	2.82	2.74	1.98	1.66

Source: Pakistan Bureau of Statistics, *Household Integrated Economic Survey 2015–16*, Islamabad, Statistics Division, Government of Pakistan, 2016.

Table 7.18: Average Household Size by Quintiles in Urban Sindh
(2015–16)

		Total	1st	2nd	3rd	4th	5th
Average Number of	Members per Household	5.87	8.77	7.70	6.93	5.95	4.63
	Employed person per Household	1.76	2.24	2.18	2.01	1.85	1.45

Source: Pakistan Bureau of Statistics, *Household Integrated Economic Survey 2015–16*, Islamabad, Statistics Division, Government of Pakistan, 2016.

Focusing on the rural–urban analysis, the average number of members and employed members in a household are naturally higher for the rural districts where entire households are involved in economic activities, compared to urban districts. Analysing the economic situation of the households also requires an understanding of the housing facilities enjoyed by the households, which determines the extent to which the members are living a comfortable and liberating lifestyle.

According to Table 7.19, more than half of the population in both Sindh and Punjab, lives in a house with approximately two to four rooms in it.

Similar is the case for Pakistan. However, the urban–rural differential in Sindh is noticable. While 25 per cent of urban households have one room, it is almost 50 per cent for rural households.

Table 7.20 presents the recent information on housing tenure. Although Punjab has a higher percentage of owned households (approximately 85 per cent) as compared to that of Sindh, when broken up by rural–urban, there is not much difference in rural ownership but in Punjab a slightly higher proportion of urban housing is owned. This finding is consistent with the higher average per capita income of urban Punjab. Moreover, Sindh (rural) has almost an insignificant proportion of those who live on rent. Nevertheless, even if what has been discussed above is a true representation for the provinces, the quality of housing is not known.

Table 7.19: Percentage Distribution of Household Housing Units in Pakistan, Punjab, and Sindh by Area (2015–16)

Province	District	Housing Units		
		One Room (%)	2–4 Rooms (%)	5 & More Rooms (%)
Pakistan	Total	27.51	66.69	5.8
	Urban	23.71	69.67	6.62
	Rural	29.74	64.93	5.32
Punjab	Total	27	66.72	6.28
	Urban	24.08	68.42	7.5
	Rural	28.46	65.87	5.67
Sindh	Total	35.27	62.25	2.49
	Urban	25.07	71.04	3.89
	Rural	47.43	51.76	0.81

Source: Pakistan Bureau of Statistics, *Household Integrated Economic Survey 2015–16*, Islamabad, Statistics Division, Government of Pakistan, 2016.

Table 7.20: Percentage Distribution of Household Housing Tenures in Pakistan, Punjab, and Sindh by Area (2015–16)

Province	Housing Tenure			
	Own (%)	Rent (%)	Free (%)	Subsidised Rent (%)
Pakistan	84.1	8.2	6.3	1.4
Urban	73.7	17.9	5.1	3.3
Rural	90.2	2.4	7.0	0.4
Punjab	84.7	7.4	7.0	0.9
Urban	74.6	16.7	6.3	2.4
Rural	89.8	2.8	7.3	0.1
Sindh	81.0	10.6	6.0	2.4
Urban	72.6	19.0	4.3	4.2
Rural	91.0	0.6	8	0.4

Source: Pakistan Bureau of Statistics, *Household Integrated Economic Survey 2015–16*, Islamabad, Statistics Division, Government of Pakistan, 2016.

Table 7.21: Percentage Distribution of Households in Pakistan, Punjab, and Sindh by Source of Drinking Water by Area (2015–16)

Province	Water Delivery System				
	Tap Water (%)	Hand Pump (%)	Motor Pump (%)	Dug Well (%)	Others (%)
Pakistan	27	26	33	3	11
Urban	51	7	27	1	14
Rural	13	38	36	5	9
Punjab	18	28	45	1	9
Urban	35	7	40	1	18
Rural	9	38	47	1	4
Sindh	41	33	11	4	10
Urban	69	8	11	1	11
Rural	7	63	12	8	9

Source: Pakistan Bureau of Statistics, *Household Integrated Economic Survey 2015–16*, Islamabad, Statistics Division, Government of Pakistan, 2016.

Safe drinking water and sanitation are critical factors for maintaining good health of the population as most of the disease in Pakistan are waterborne. The latest survey shows that tap water is available to only one quarter of the total population with half of the urban areas population having access. The surge in consumption of bottled water in the recent years does raise serious doubts about the quality of tap water even in the urban areas. Rural population is still heavily dependent upon hand pumps and motor pumps.

Figure 7.15: Economic Situation of Households in Pakistan, Punjab, and Sindh (%) (2014–15)

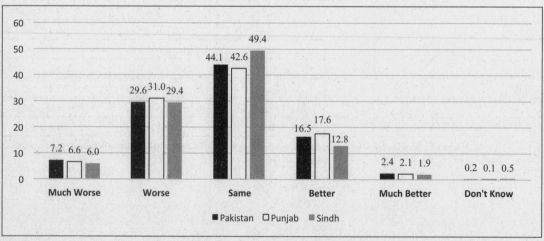

Source: Pakistan Bureau of Statistics, *Household Integrated Economic Survey 2015-16*, Islamabad, Statistics Division, Government of Pakistan, 2016.

In urban Sindh, as many as 69 per cent of the urban households can rely upon tap water as their main source while 63 per cent of rural households draw their water from hand pumps.

The HIES Survey 2015–16 inquired from the respondents about their economic situation. In Sindh, almost 50 per cent felt that there was no improvement while only 12–15 per cent believed it to be better or much better than during the period of previous survey.

Geography of Poverty and Poverty in the Agro-Climatic Zones

While it is important to understand poverty in terms of income distribution and disparities between rural and urban areas, it is also important to map out its geography to understand the inherent inequality that may be driving it. It has been highly debated as to why the economic fortunes have been clustered in some areas and not the rest. Focusing on about reasons such as lack of education in the labour market, or not having sufficient access to technology and productive systems can be the 'proximate' causes of poverty, but do not provide any insight as to why this has occurred in some areas and not in others. The two most popular perspectives pertaining to the differences in prosperity are 'geography and institutions'.[32]

Pakistan has been bestowed with a versatile geography which leads to a diversified cropping pattern, soil, and availability of water.[33] As discussed above, such variations in natural resource endowments play an important role in influencing poverty.

Table 7.22: Agro-Climatic Zones of Sindh and Punjab

Punjab	Rice/Wheat	Sialkot, Gujrat, Gujranwala, Sheikhupura, Lahore, Kasur, Narowal, Mandi Bahauddin, Hafizabad
	Mixed	Sargodha, Khushab, Jhang, Faisalabad, Toba Tek Singh, Okara
	Cotton/Wheat	Sahiwal, Bahawalnagar, Bahawalpur, Rahimyar Khan, Multan
	Low Intensity	Dera Ghazi Khan, Rajanpur, Muzaffargarh, Layyah, Mianwali, Bhakkar and Dera Ismail Khan
	Barani	Attock, Jhelum, Rawalpindi, Islamabad, Chakwal
Sindh	Cotton/Wheat	Sukkur, Khairpur, Nawabshah, Hyderabad, Tharparkar, Nowshero Feroz, Ghotki, Umerkot, Mirpurkhas, Sanghar
	Rice/Other	Jacobabad, Larkana, Dadu, Thatta, Badin, Shikarpur, Karachi

Source: Social Policy and Development Centre, 'Poverty, Inequality and Social Exclusion', in *The State of Social Development in Rural Pakistan*, Karachi, 2014, pp. 85–115.

Punjab and Sindh are divided into seven agro-climatic zones. Some parts of Punjab are considered non-irrigated, with the mountainous areas of Balochistan and Khyber Pakhtunkhwa, where the major crop production is that of wheat and maize. Northern Punjab falls in the category of irrigated areas, where mostly rice, and in some cases wheat, is grown. Southern Punjab and some adjoining areas of Sindh are characterised as areas where cotton and wheat rotation is practised. Moreover, the southern part of Sindh is known for growing Irri rice and sugar in those areas where water availability is sufficient for sugar production.[34]

The above disaggregated analysis sheds further light on the factors contributing to the incidence of poverty. Barani or non-irrigated and low intensity districts of Punjab are hit hardest because of low agricultural productivity translating into lower incomes. The better-off districts are those which grow rice/wheat and mixed crops in Punjab. The cotton/wheat ecological zone in Sindh is better off compared to the rice/other crops zone. The incidence of poverty in the former is lower than the provincial average.

What needs to be noted here is that the Barani and northern Punjab have a comparatively more established culture of peasant proprietorship in their agricultural sector contrary to the feudal culture more prominently entrenched in southern Punjab and Sindh.

Interestingly, Irfan (2007) states that the urban–rural poverty incidence is closely linked to zonal classifications in the case of Punjab. However, in Sindh, the rural areas of the same zone are astonishingly far worse off than the urban districts.

Land Tenure and Poverty

Many analysts and observers have attributed the political and economic domination in southern Punjab and Sindh to the feudal land ownership pattern. Land reforms attempted by Ayub Khan and Z. A. Bhutto did not make much of a dent in the ownership pattern. What has made a difference is the application of the inheritance law. Many large holdings of the 1950s and 1960s have been split up among the descendants of the jagirdars and large zamindars. These parcels of land are further divided among the second generation inheriting from their fathers. As can be seen from the agriculture census results, the average size holding has been on a declining trajectory and the share of total farm area among these owning 150 acres or more is also falling. Owner-operated farming has caught on but it has repercussions for rural employment, wages, and poverty.

Table 7.23: Head Count Ratio and Poverty Gap amongst Different Agricultural Groups
(1987–88 and 2004–05)

	Head Count Ratio	Poverty Gap	Poverty Gap Squared
1987–88			
Landless	0.624	0.422	0.327
Tenant	0.8	0.402	0.243
Owner Tenant	0.47	0.219	0.132
Land Owner	0.37	0.145	0.075
2004–05			
Landless	0.742	0.408	0.301
Tenant	0.918	0.59	0.479
Owner Tenant	0.623	0.398	0.283
Land Owner	0.626	0.339	0.231
Percentage Change (%)			
Landless	11.84	-1.46	-2.597
Tenant	11.82	18.75	23.593
Owner Tenant	15.3	17.907	15.147
Land Owner	25.62	19.334	15.587

Source: Hari Ram Lohana, *Poverty Dynamics in Rural Sindh, Pakistan*, Bath, Chronic Poverty Research Centre, 2009.

Table 7.23 attempts to shed light on the extent to which the head count ratio and poverty gap have changed from 1987–88 to 2004–05 for different agricultural groups in rural Sindh. It is explicitly shown that poverty levels have increased for all agricultural groups for the stated time period. If comparisons are made among the agricultural groups, it is observed from the Poverty Gap Squared Index that tenant groups have experienced the worst change in terms of severity of poverty.

Public Expenditures on Social Sectors and Poverty

Having understood the role of agro-climatic zones in Punjab and Sindh as well as the impact of landlessness on rural poverty, the data above allows one to understand the variation that exists in the sources of income for these households. While wage income is the major contributor in urban areas, livestock and crop form the primary source in rural areas.

Having analysed agro-climatic zones it is the turn to analyse another critical determinant and consequence of poverty, i.e. access to basic social services such as education and health. In a resource-contained economy, particularly in the domain of public finances, access of the poor to social services is limited due to inadequate supply. Shortages arise due to poor allocation of public expenditures, poor governance, and mismanagement of expenditures. Pakistan has historically been spending very little on education and health and whatever is being spent does not have the desirable impact either in terms of access or quality. Underinvestment and misallocation therefore hurt the poor families most as they are the ones that are excluded. They do not have asset such as land and are denied accumulating another asset, i.e. human capital. The consequence is perpetuation of poverty and widening of income inequalities.

Figure 7.16: Social Expenditure as Percentage of GDP in Federation, Punjab, and Sindh
(2014–15)

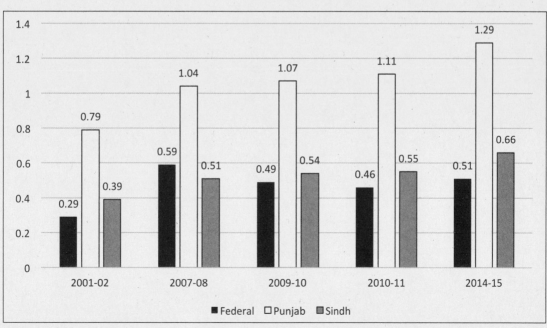

Source: Social Policy and Development Centre, 'Financing of Urban Social Service Delivery', in *The State of Social Development in Urban Pakistan*, Karachi, 2016, pp. 57–81.

Figure 7.17: Education Expenditure as a Percentage of GDP in Federation,
Punjab, and Sindh (2014–15)

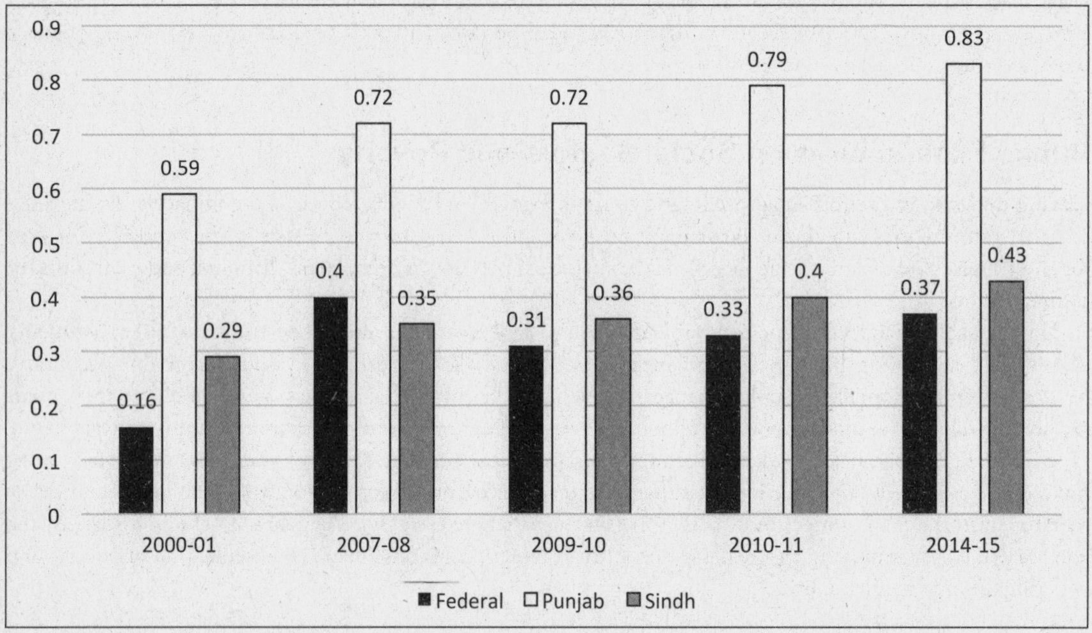

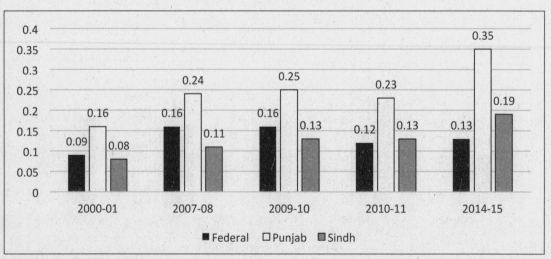

Source: Social Policy and Development Centre, 'Financing of Urban Social Service Delivery', in *The State of Social Development in Urban Pakistan*, Karachi, 2016, pp. 57–81.

Figure 7.18: Health Expenditure as a Percentage of GDP in Federation,
Punjab, and Sindh (2014–15)

Source: Social Policy and Development Centre, 'Financing of Urban Social Service Delivery', in *The State of Social Development in Urban Pakistan,* Karachi, 2016, pp. 57-81.

Figure 7.19: Water Supply and Sanitation Expenditure as a Percentage of GDP in Federation, Punjab, and Sindh (2014–15)

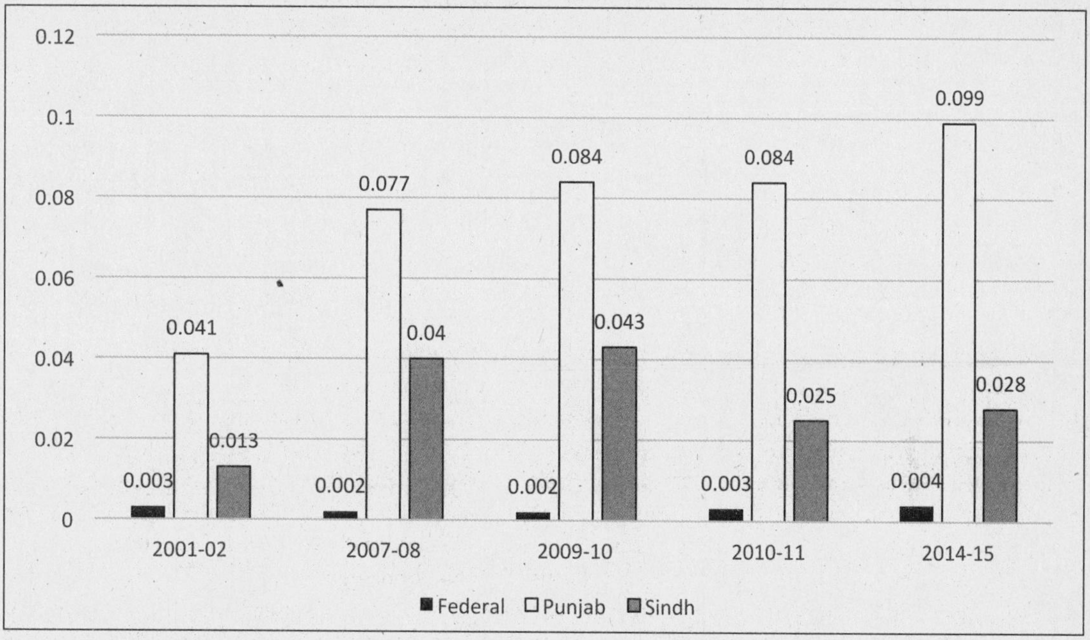

Source: Social Policy and Development Centre, 'Financing of Urban Social Service Delivery', *The State of Social Development in Urban Pakistan*, Karachi, 2016, pp. 57–81.

Figures 7.16 to 7.19 show that public expenditures in social sectors have been consistently below or around 2 per cent of the GDP. It is only in recent years, after the Eighteenth Amendment, that the allocations for social sectors have been rising. For 2016–17, it is estimated that allocations for education and health together by the federal and provincial governments now account for 3.7 per cent of GDP—higher than defence expenditures for the first time. The problem in these sectors is the efficiency in the use of these resources. Education is the major beneficiary, claiming almost two-thirds of the total social sector expenditure. Health receives only 27 per cent of the total while the residual amount goes to water supply and sanitation. Although the government has committed itself to expenditure on education rising to 4 per cent of GDP and to compulsory universal primary education, both these goals have proved elusive so far.

Summing Up

Poverty in Sindh is characteristic of a large household size, illiterate, with one or two income earners leading to a high dependency ratio, in households situated in non-irrigated, arid agro-climate, rural district, with little access to public services such as education, health, drinking water, and sanitation. Furthermore, landless peasants have the highest probability of being below the poverty line.

There has been significant progress in the reduction of poverty incidence particularly since 2001–02 against different measures of national and international poverty lines. The most recent best practice is to use the Multipurpose Poverty Index (MPI) that not only takes income into account but also access to education, health, and living standards. Sindh, according to this measure, has 43.1 per cent of its population below MPI, as compared to the national average of 39 per cent. Inter-district variation in poverty is quite large, with Karachi having 1.9 per cent of its population below MPI, while 48 per cent of people in Tharparkar are poor according to MPI. Pakistan shows some slight improvement in its human development indicators, but still did not fare so well when compared to other countries. Urban–rural income and gender disparities are much higher in Sindh compared to the rest of the country. The three lowest income quintiles spend more than their monthly incomes while the top quintile is saving a small fraction of their income. Sindh's Gini coefficient, measuring income inequality, is higher than that of Punjab and the national average.

Public expenditures on social sectors have started rising in recent years after a long period of stagnation. However, the efficiency of resource use poses a serious problem in achieving the desired results.

Districts with the highest poverty headcount ratios need to be prioritised not only for poverty reduction strategies but also for overall economic development plans in Sindh. Such form of specific targeting can help reduce severe horizontal inequalities and bring down the overall poverty headcount ratio. The poorest districts also need greater investment and implementation of education and healthcare service delivery plans.

The poorest of the districts in Sindh either suffer from weak public service delivery or from low population density scattered in far flung areas. Policymakers must make use of non-monetary indicators of poverty such as the MPI and HDI to identify and target low development pockets in the province, and to focus funding and resources on the specific aspects of human development in which the areas are lagging. Interventions, thus, need to be targeted district or region wise, with special emphasis on those areas that fare low on multidimensional indicators of poverty, focusing on improving governance, enhancing the outreach and efficiency of public service, and on finding innovative ways to reach the poor. Public service delivery needs to be accessible to all and not just concentrated on the needs of the high density urban population.

For districts vulnerable to recurring natural disasters, there needs to be long-term policy planning for developing infrastructure that can improve the resilience of these areas towards surviving disasters instead of resorting to short-term emergency relief measures.

8

Agriculture

Introduction

Pᴀᴋɪsᴛᴀɴ's economy has undergone a structural transformation from the period 1949–50, in which the share of agriculture in the GDP dominated the economy (53 per cent) to the current situation, where it is less than 20 per cent today. Within the agriculture sector, crops are no longer the major contributors—the livestock, dairy, and the poultry sub-sectors have assumed prime position. Sindh, a relatively high urbanised province, has followed the same pattern as agriculture's contribution to gross provincial product has come down to 17 per cent. Table 8.1 depicts this transformation over the years.

Table 8.1: Shares in Agricultural Value Added (%)
(1949–50 to 2015–16)

	1949–50	1980–81	2002–03	2015–16
Major Crop	52.0	51.9	40.6	26.2
Minor Crop	12.4	17.8	15.9	11.1
Livestock	34.4	26.7	38.9	58.3
Forestry and Fisheries	1.2	3.6	4.6	4.4

Source: Unofficial estimates.

It is estimated that 40 per cent of this province has arable land, the total cultivated area is 7.64 million acres, and the net area sown is 7.51 million acres.[1] The total area cropped is 12.4 million acres.[2] The two major varieties of crops grown in Sindh are food crops and cash crops.[3] As pointed out in Chapter 7, two-fifths of Sindh is poor according to multidimensional indicators.[4] Since almost half the population suffers from socioeconomic deprivation, social cohesion and stability appear to remain unattainable goals till now.

The development of the agriculture sector in Sindh should be considered in its historical context. Previous rulers such as the Mughals, Kalhoros, Soomras, Samas, Talpurs (the Mirs), and the British had left an entrenched system of feudalism wherein landlords exercised enormous economic, political, and social control over the *haris*, who cultivated their jagirs. Most of the jagirs (as mentioned in 'Chapter 1') were given as rewards to the rulers of the day for their loyal services. This indirect method of subjugation of the population served the ruling and colonial interests well. However, the consequential legacy of a rich and powerful class of landlords enjoying large concentration of wealth and income, and a poor, deprived peasant population subservient and dependent on this class, has created difficulties in terms of economic efficiency, equity, democratic governance, and capture of state institutions. Although the situation in Sindh has been further exacerbated by the migration of numerous refugees from India in the post-Partition period and subsequent migration from other provinces of the country, the vested interests of the powerful landholding class and their agriculture-based incomes have been the main driving force behind a lack of broad-based economic and social progress in the province.

Agricultural produce in Sindh is heavily dependent on two factors: irrigation and climate. Although, Pakistan's climate is generally hot and arid, the United Nations Educational, Scientific, and Cultural Organisation (UNESCO) has divided the province of Sindh into three main climatic regions: coastal or southern (southward from Thatta), central (Hyderabad to Nawabshah), and northern (from Nawabshah northward to Jacobabad).[5] Each district has different characteristics that encourage the cultivation of various crops. Northern or upper Sindh is suitable for growing rice, wheat, cotton, mustard, and sunflower; central Sindh is a dry tract and suitable for producing cotton and mustard; and southern Sindh is most suitable for producing sugarcane, banana, cotton, wheat, *mash*, and *masoor*. During winters, when the temperatures fall to 25°C and the soil loses its acidity, wheat, i.e. the major rabi[6] crop, is suitably planted. Kharif[7] crops such as rice, cotton, onions, tomatoes, and mung are far more tolerant of higher temperatures and acidity, requiring more water to be sown than wheat. When temperatures rise to 35°C, kharif crops can easily be planted.[8] Interestingly, sugarcane is both a rabi and a kharif crop.

Post-Partition Era

LANDOWNERSHIP AND TENANCY

Unfortunately, climate and irrigation are not the only factors that dictate crop production. Factors such as landlord–tenancy relations, state policies, state–society interactions, and market models have complicated the performance of the agricultural sector in Sindh. Immediately after 1947, Sindh saw a massive inflow of culturally diverse people, but they were not agriculturalists nor did they have the means to buy land from the Hindus migrating to India. The departing Hindu landlords abandoned their holdings, which were taken over by the existing powerful landowners, thus further concentrating land ownership. Table 8.2 shows the landownership pattern before 1959. Around 27,000 large landowners with holdings above 100 acres of land or more owned over 54 per cent of the land area, whereas less than 256,000 small *khatedar*s or around 22 per cent of the total farms.

Table 8.2: Land Ownership and Acreage in Sindh Before 1959

Acreage	Owners		Land	
	Numbers	Percentage	Acres	Percentage
Up to 5 Acres	100,601	29.8	365,817	3.6
5–25 Acres	155,163	46.0	1,937,073	18.8
25–100 Acres	54,792	16.2	2,390,358	23.3
100–500 Acres	24,064	7.1	2,600,123	25.3
500–above Acres	3,045	0.9	2,991,650	29.1
Total	337,665	100.0	10,285,021	100.0

Hunting Technical Services Limited and Sir MacDonald and Partners, *Lowers Indus Project Report*, Hyderabad, West Pakistan Water and Power Development Authority, 1966, vols. 1–16.

It is estimated that immediately post Partition, Hindu landowners abandoned approximately 1.3 million acres of land, which were occupied or taken over by powerful landowners.[9] Some of the evacuee property lands left by the Hindu owners were allotted to non-agriculturalists—some being migrants from India. This situation created initial dislocation and uncertainties. Concentration of landownership in the hands of absentee landlords, non-utilisation of land by non-agriculturalists, and lack of security of tenure for the tenant-at-will (or sharecropper) resulted in a very stagnant phase in Sindh's agriculture. Thus, a Hari Enquiry Committee was formed by the government to examine land tenure and related questions.[10] Yet, it failed to put forth one of the most vital recommendations i.e. security for tenants; it only put forward regulations governing tenancy agreements.

In the past, the pattern of land ownership in the province has been feudalistic as there were no restrictions on landholdings. Hence, land continued to be disposed-off without any limit to the intending purchasers. This strengthened feudal landlords, who reaped the benefits without corresponding gains to the *haris* who continued to toil under them. *Hari* committees were therefore set up by the government to suggest methods for improving the living standard and social status of *haris*.[11]

In 1950, the Sindh Tenancy Act was passed to supervise the traditional sharecropping land revenue system.[12] It marked the difference between four different sharecroppers: permanent *hari* (one who cultivates at least four acres of land for the same landlord for at least three years), temporary *hari* (one who is rotated between landlords on a seasonal basis), seasonal *hari* (one who works on a farm for only one season), and share labourer[13] (one who is employed in a rush, or as a backup).[14] It accorded permanent *hari*s with a lifelong right to cultivation on the condition that the *hari* had to be cultivating the same piece of land (of at least 4 acres) for the same landlord for three continuous years prior to the enactment of the act. The *hari* could not be expelled from the land unless he had failed to meet his landlord's obligations, or if the landlord wished to self-cultivate his land by mechanisation. In such a situation, the landlord had the responsibility of providing the *hari* with some other similar tract of land for cultivation or compensate him in some other way.[15] However, feudal lords employed a clever technique of not keeping a *hari* on their farm for more than three years to prevent them from becoming permanent *hari* and enjoying their rights.

The Sindh Agriculture Commission, which was set up in 1953 to investigate the prevailing conditions of Sindh, found that 2,588,000 landless peasants formed nearly 79 per cent of the total population of Sindh. This further substantiated the core finding of the 1951 population census that 73.8 per cent of agricultural workers owned a part of, or no land while 954,000 acres of land were owned by jagirdars.[16] The introduction of the Sindh Tenancy Act was followed by the inauguration of the Kotri Barrage in lower Sindh in 1955. The construction and opening of this barrage proved to be extremely beneficial as it provided perennial irrigation to some of the seasonally irrigated lands and helped increase the crop yield. This barrage enabled new lands to be brought under cultivation, aiding in the rise of commodity production. Table 8.3 represents the landownership pattern in Sindh during the fiscal year 1961–62.

Some landowners, who earlier had lands even beyond 500 acres, had to relinquish some of their inferior land in exchange for government bonds.[17] As a result of the Land Reform Regulation, 401 landowners gave up 967,000 acres of their land.[18] Furthermore, the surrendered land was given to 32,900 landless peasants—reducing their numbers to 4 per cent.[19] Table 8.3 reveals that 0.9 of Sindh's elite and powerful population still owned more than one-fifth of the land area, and 3.2 per cent, belonging to 125–250 acres' category, held 16 per cent of the land. Together, this 4.1 per cent of the population had recourse to 37.5 per cent of the total land in Sindh. In contrast, the majority of small landholders constituting 88.5 per cent of the population could subsist on only 43 per cent of the land area—an average of 15 acres per owner—in the category who owned less than 64 acres. Table 8.4 represents the landownership pattern in Sindh in 1972.

Table 8.3: Land Ownership and Acreage in Sindh
(1961–62)

Acreage	Owners		Land		Average Farm Size (Acres)
	Number	Percentage	Acres	Percentage	
Less than 16 Acres	245,034	61.1	2,156,463	17.3	8.8
16–64 acres	110,021	27.4	3,191,350	25.7	29.0
64–125 acres	29,489	7.4	2,427,691	19.5	82.3
125–250 acres	12,986	3.2	2,022,267	16.3	155.7
More than 250 Acres	3,750	0.9	2,641,260	21.2	704.3
Total	401,280	100	12,439,031	100	31.0

Source: Hunting Technical Services Limited and Sir MacDonald and Partners, *Lowers Indus Project Report*, Hyderabad, West Pakistan Water and Power Development Authority, 1966, Vols. 1–16.

Table 8.4: Land Ownership and Acreage in Sindh—1972

Size (Acres)	Owners		Land	
	Numbers	%	Numbers	%
Under 5	138,000	18.4	424,000	4.0
5–12.5	387,000	52.0	3,261,000	34.0
12.5–25	165,000	22.0	2,766,000	29.0
25–50	39,000	5.0	1,247,000	13.0
50–150	13,000	2.2	1,013,000	11.0
150 and above	3,000	0.4	748,000	8.0
Total	745,000	100.0	9,460,000	100.0

Source: Ishrat Husain, *Economy of Modern Sindh*, Jamshoro, Institute of Sindhology, University of Sindh, 1981.

As a result of the Ayub and Bhutto land reforms, there was a substantial shift in the pattern of land ownership. The top 8 per cent of the owners had a share of 32 per cent in 1972, down from 54 per cent in 1959. This pattern does not depict the actual picture as the land area was sub divided into smaller parcels among the individual family members but the control of the entire landholding still rested with the patriarch of that family. In some instances, land was given to *benamidar*s, i.e. the servants of the family, but the landlord still derived all the benefits.

There seems to be a huge upsurge in the number of owners with holdings between 5–25 acres in 1972 compared to 1959. This group formed 77 per cent of the total farm owners compared to 46 per cent in 1959. The major decline took place in those below 5 acres as their proportion went down from 30 per cent to 18.4 per cent in the same period. This trend in ownership is however, not consistent with the results of the subsequent agriculture censuses.

Table 8.5, shows the cross-sectional analysis of important variables in agriculture and the increase in the number of farms in various years. The cross-section further shows the owners, tenant, and owner-cum-tenant relationship with farm areas and cultivated areas.

Table 8.5: Cross-Sectional Analysis of Important Variables (in Thousand)
(1980–2010)

Variables All Farms	1980	1990	2000	2010	Percentage change (1980–2010)
All Farms	793	803	1070	1115	40.25
Owner	323	406	704	784	142.72
Tenant	385	336	323	286	-25.71
Owner Cum Tenant	85	61	43	45	-47.06
Farm Area (Hectares)	3730	3493	4327	3993	7.05
Cultivated Area (Hectares)	3166	2873	3256	3093	-2.31

Source: Bureau of Statistics, *Development Statistics of Sindh*, Karachi, Planning and Development Department, Government of Sindh, various years.

The changes in the ownership pattern between 1980 and 2010 are also recorded in this table. There has been an almost doubling of owners and a decline in the number of tenants and owner-cum-tenants. Mechanisation and subdivision of land resulting from inheritance were the main factors behind this shift.

Cropping Pattern and Water Shortage

Cropping patterns in Sindh were documented in the completion reports of Sukkur Barrage (1932) as rice, rabi crops, and kharif crops. The renowned agriculturist M. H. Panhwar further elaborated summer crops, e.g. Millet, sorghum, and rice, and winter crops as wheat, oats, oil seeds, vegetables, and Dubari.[20]

During the development of the Lower Indus Plan (LIP) 1966 study, the consultant, Messer's Hunting Technical Services Limited and Co., in association with Mott MacDonald and Partners, identified existing cropping patterns and intensities. The findings of the LIP report on seasonal cropping is presented in Figure 8.1.

The cropping patterns were catering to the population at the time and under designed water availability, i.e. around 47.61 million acre feet.[21] The cropping intensities of that time are presented in Figure 8.2. The increase in population and liberalisation of water distribution controls has led to a complete shift in cropping patterns and its intensities in Sindh. The dilemma of cash crops is that while they help generate significant revenue, they hamper the equitable distribution system and cause serious degradation to soil.

The irrigation system was designed on the principles of equity and limitation of soil to sustain cultivation intensities. The cropping intensities were fixed between 35 to 45 per cent of total command area of different canals in Sindh.[22] On the other hand, overall supply of irrigation water from the Indus Basin has historically been inconsistent.

Figure 8.1: Seasonal Cropping in Sindh

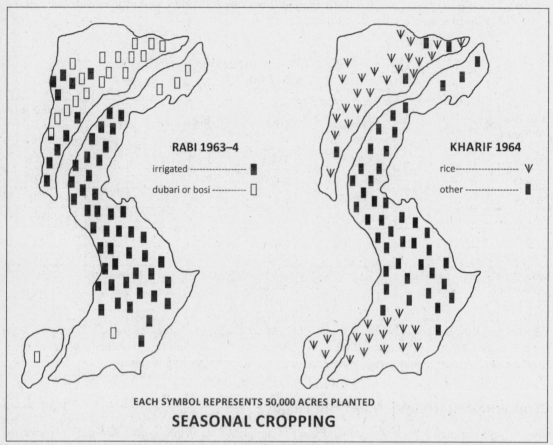

SEASONAL CROPPING

EACH SYMBOL REPRESENTS 50,000 ACRES PLANTED

Source: Wapda, 'Water Availability and Future Projections', *Lower Indus Development Study*, Hyderabad, Wapda, 1966.

The analysis of Sindh canal abstractions from 1977 to 2014 show several years with lowest supplies of 41 million acre foot (MAF) whereas our requirements are almost 48 MAF.[23] The average consumption during the said years was 43.69 MAF. The injudicious distribution of water, coupled with water shortages at the national level, has serious impact on the tail-enders of the water conveyance system. Ultimately, the farmers in Sindh face the wrath.

The irrigation system is divided into three parts: Head, Middle, and Tail. The head areas get the maximum water supply and their cropping intensity touches the 150 per cent mark, while the middle areas do also get the substantial supplies of water range between 80–100 per cent intensities.[24] The tail end areas are below 30 per cent crop/landholding percentage. Due to such continuous uncertainties in water supplies, the tail-end growers are left with indecisiveness over sowing crops. The farmers who pro-actively prepare fields and sow seeds are left disheartened.

Resource scarcity has forced the farmers to change their cropping patterns. The Master Plan of 2013 by WSIP-SIDA for the Left Bank of River Indus, Delta, and Coastal Zone shows significant change in crops in the tail-end delta districts of Sindh. The spread of drought and salt-resistant crops, e.g. Sunflower, indicate resource scarcity in these areas, referred to in Figures 8.3 and 8.4.[25]

Figure 8.2: Cropping Intensities of 1963–64

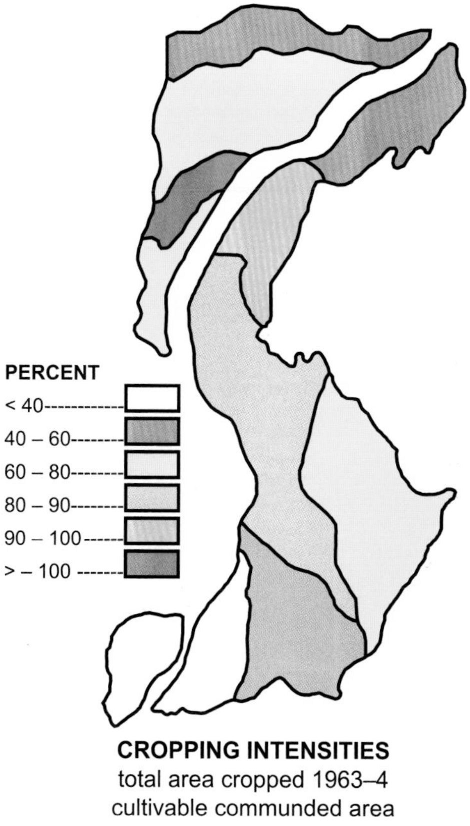

PERCENT

< 40------------
40 – 60--------
60 – 80--------
80 – 90--------
90 – 100------
> – 100 -------

CROPPING INTENSITIES
total area cropped 1963–4
cultivable commumded area

Source: Wapda, 'Water Availability and Future Projections', *Lower Indus Development Study*,
Hyderabad, Wapda, 1966.

Figure 8.3: District Badin Crops and Cultivation Area (1991–92 to 2009–10)

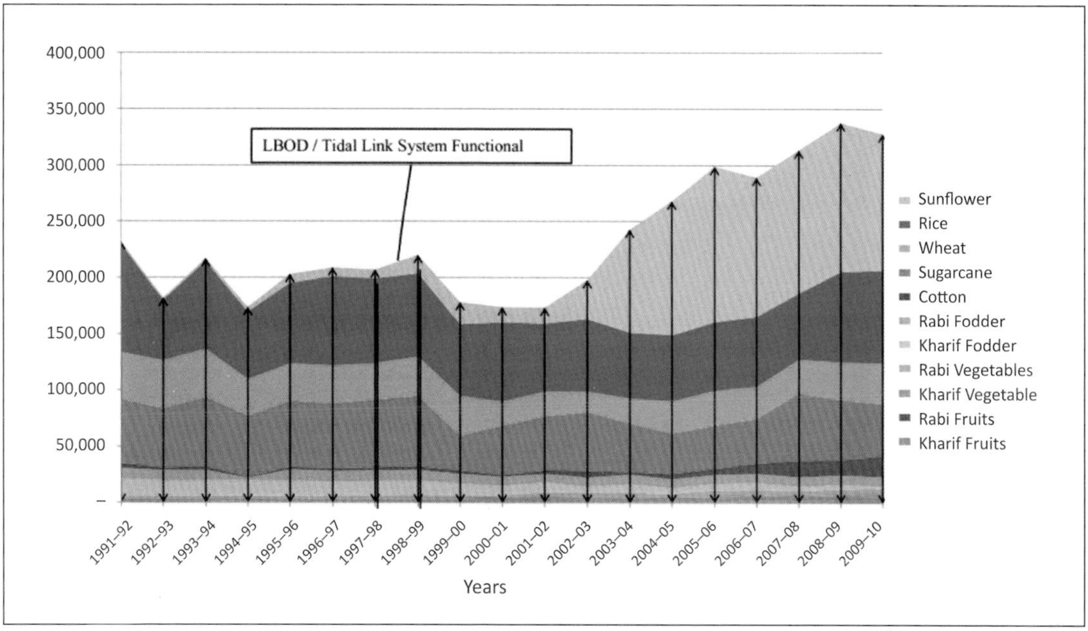

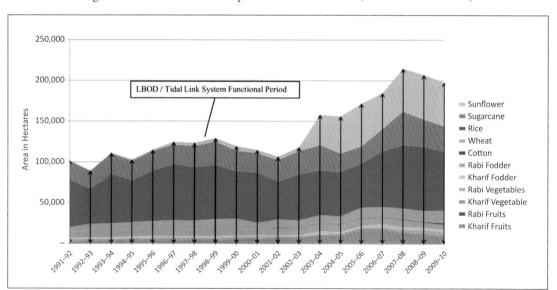

Source: Sindh Irrigation and Drainage Authority, *Master Plan for Left Bank of River Indus, Delta & Coastal Zone*, Karachi, Water Sector Improvement Project (WSIP), 2013.

Figure 8.4: District Thatta Crops and Cultivation Area (1991–92 to 2009–10)

Source: Sindh Irrigation and Drainage Authority, *Master Plan for Left Bank of River Indus, Delta & Coastal Zone*, Karachi, Water Sector Improvement Project (WSIP), 2013.

Similar conditions are observed in several areas, including Mirpurkhas and Badin, where farmers have opted for hay-grass cultivation, a currently flourishing industry. This type of grass is basically a bio-saline crop with a high nutritional value for livestock. It is directly exported to the vet farms of the Middle East where a good foreign exchange is earned on the crop (Figure 8.5).

Figure 8.5: Hay–Grass Farming in Mirpurkhas

Source: Sindh Irrigation and Drainage Authority, *Master Plan for Left Bank of River Indus, Delta & Coastal Zone*, Karachi, Water Sector Improvement Project (WSIP), 2013.

Ayub Reforms

In 1945, a tenancy laws committee in Sindh recommended that occupancy rights be given to the *hari*s who cultivate four to five acres of land with the same zamindar for eight years. 1n 1947, the Hari Committee of Sindh was formed. This Hari committee, however, defended the interests of the landlords. Two members of the committee, G. M. Syed and Masood Khadarposh had to record their notes of dissent which favoured *hari*s more than the landlords. In 1950, the Sindh Tenancy Act, which recommended permanent rights of tenancy to long-term tenants and eviction rights to landlords under certain conditions, was passed.[26] Likewise, the Punjab Tenancy Act was passed in 1950. In 1952, the Punjab Tenancy (Amendment Act) was passed which recommended abolition of occupancy tenancy, transfer of ownership, rights to occupancy tenants, and a reduction in the share of landlords from 50 to 40 per cent.[27] In 1955, an executive order was passed by the Government of Pakistan for the abolition of jagirs and other revenue-free grants, as well as calling on the jagirdars to pay land revenue like other zamindars. In the same year, this executive order was challenged but was upheld by the Sindh High Court.[28]

In 1959, the Land Reform Commission formed by Ayub Khan submitted a report which prompted the government to announce new reforms: no one could own more than 500 acres of irrigated land, 1,000 acres of unirrigated land, and 150 acres of orchard; landowners were to be compensated for any lands surrendered, and jagirs were abolished altogether. The reforms were so imprecise that anyone who had an expected heir, direct heir, or family for that matter could easily evade surrendering property. In fact, out of the 401 people who surrendered their lands, only 967,000 acres were free of any encumbrances. 2,025,000 acres were allowed to be retained, and 32,900 acres were transferred to landless peasants. By 1959, around half of the allotted land surrounding the barrage had been claimed to have been given to the *hari*s. However, the *hari*s complained of never receiving the acclaimed lands as they were in possession of the wealthy landlords, even though the land was in their (*hari*s') name.[29] Similarly, a major proportion of the other half of the allotted land fell into the hands of the army personnel and farmers who belonged mostly to Punjab and Khyber Pakhtunkhwa.

From 1958–69, Ayub Khan encouraged the introduction of high-yielding varieties of wheat and maize that started what is today hailed as the Green Revolution.[30] But the benefits to Sindh were not as widespread as expected due to the accumulation of vast land in the hands of what is termed 'traditional elites'. The *hari*s had hoped to obtain tracts of lands left behind by the Hindu landlords during Partition or through the land reforms of 1959. However, in a society marked deeply by unequal distribution of resources, social hierarchy further solidified and left the peasantry even more dependent on their feudal benefactors as Ayub's government distributed the lands to the Urdu-speaking refugees from India and created a class of 'urban absentee landlords'.[31] By 1965, land allotted to *hari*s had increased from 115,454 acres to 165,000 acres only. However, the number of landowners owning more than 500 acres increased from 3,045 before 1959 to 3,750 in 1962–63.[32]

BHUTTO REFORMS

In addition to the land reforms that took place under Ayub Khan's government, further reforms were introduced in 1972 which became effective in 1973. The West Pakistan Land Reforms Commission was designed to reduce social disparity, owing to unequal land distribution. In 1972, Zulfikar Ali Bhutto's government reduced and fixed the ceiling for individual holdings, provided protection to sharecropping tenants, and reserved state land for landless tenants. Individual land ownership was brought down to 150 acres for irrigated and 300 acres for non-irrigated land, with no exemptions for gardens and trees.[33] These limitations on landownership were made a little flexible in the case of poor quality land. Also, no concessions were to be made to any class of people in the name of presents, trusts, etc. and all the land retained because it was held illegal under these reforms was to be distributed amongst the landless farmers, and that too free of cost (Table 8.4).

Such land reforms could have proven (and did so in the initial years) to be a turning point in the history of Sindh for it would have taken excess land from the wealthy landowners and would have granted it to the poor *hari*s. However, due to lack of a proper follow-up by government officials, these land reforms remained mainly ineffective and many landlords took to saving their lands through *benami*[34] transfers, and where they were unable to do so, they gave up only those pieces of lands that were barren and not fit for cultivation.[35] Apart from *benami* transfers of land, many landlords even transferred their lands to their *hari*s, but it was only the name of the *hari* that was used; in reality, the land continued to remain the property of the actual landowner.[36]

It is quite evident that despite the land reforms under Ayub and Bhutto, landownership remained skewed. Approximately 20 per cent of the farm area was owned by just 2 per cent of the wealthy landowners and around 68 per cent of farm area was held by a total of 93 per cent land owners.[37] This skewed distribution of land also tilted the balance of political power in the hands of a few large landowners.

In 1977, another land reform act by the Bhutto government was passed whereas the ceiling of 100 acres of irrigated land and 200 acres of unirrigated lands were fixed. This act was cancelled by the martial law government under General Ziaul Haq, who took over the reins of the country in 1977.

The Agriculture Census of 2010 shows that 5,575 landlords in Sindh (less than one per cent of the total owners) with holdings of 100 acres and above own 10 per cent of total farm area, while 56 per cent with holdings less than 5 acres own 17 per cent of the farm area. Those in the middle (25–100 acres) represent 8 per cent of the total owners but own 32 per cent of the area. In contrast, those holding 100 acres and above in 1959 constituted 8 per cent of ownership, possessing 54.4 per cent of farm area. Thus, there has been de-concentration and dispersal of farm ownership during the last five decades.

Table 8.6: Land Ownership and Acreage in Sindh (2010)

Acreage	Owners		Land	
	Number	Percentage	Acres	Percentage
Less than 5 acres	624,544	56.3	1,776,382	17.0
5–25 acres	390,340	35.2	4,342,268	42.0
25–100 acres	89,221	8.0	3,335,538	32.0
100–150 acres	3182	0.3	350,581	3.0
More than 150 acres	2393	0.2	615,016	6.0
Total	1,109,680	100.0	10,419,785	100.0

Source: Pakistan Bureau of Statistics, *Agricultural Statistics of Pakistan (2011–2012)*, Islamabad, Statistics Division, Government of Pakistan, 2013.

The share of the middle-class farmers has expanded in this period from 23 to 32 per cent of the total farm area and that of small *khatedars* (with less than 5 acres) has risen significantly from 3.6 to 17 per cent—the highest rate of increase.

It may be questioned whether this fragmentation of farm area may be adversely affecting productivity because of the diseconomies of scale and sub-optimal utilisation of land. On the other hand, it is eroding the political stranglehold and economic exploitation practised by the big landlords. The evidence on the latter point does not show any significant change.

Agricultural Production

Table 8.7: Index of Agricultural Production in Pakistan and Sindh by Type of Crop (1970–71 = 100.00)
(1970–71 to 2010–11)

Year	All Crops		Cash Crops		Non-food Crops		Food Crops	
	Pakistan	Sindh	Pakistan	Sindh	Pakistan	Sindh	Pakistan	Sindh
1970–71	100	100	100	100	100	100	100	100
1980–81	139.9	147.8	139.1	151.8	154.7	159.3	154.1	140.9
1990–91	287.3	387.1	399.3	616.1	244.6	174.4	195.5	150.4
2000–01	329.1	405.6	466.1	620.0	325.4	281.2	233.9	157.2
2010–11	366.3	443.8	485.9	644.7	409.9	387.0	317.1	215.8

Source: Ministry of Food, Agriculture and Livestock, *50 Years of Agricultural Statistics in Pakistan (1947–2000)*, Islamabad, Government of Pakistan, 2007; Pakistan Bureau of Statistics, *Agricultural Statistics of Pakistan (2011–2012)*, Islamabad, Statistics Division, Government of Pakistan, 2013.

The Index of Agriculture Production with 1970–71 as the base year shows that the progress in Sindh, relative to Pakistan, has been impressive. While nationwide, the multiple between 1970–71 and 2010–11 was 3.6 for all crops, it was 4.4 for Sindh. This better performance can be attributed to the spectacular increase in cash crop production that multiplied by a factor of 6.4, far exceeding the national average of 4.8. However, in case of food crops, Sindh lagged much behind and was hardly able to double food production over a forty-year period compared to more than a three times increase at the national level. The progress was quite spectacular in the decade 1970–80 when production rose by as much as 41 per cent. This was the decade when new varieties introduced under the Green Revolution got widely diffused. However, the pace slowed down in the 1980s and 1990s. It was only in the decade of 2000–10 that food crop output once again recorded a 37 per cent increase.

Green Revolution

Green revolution refers to the adoption of new, high-yielding varieties (HYV) in agriculture, especially wheat, rice, and other food grains. This was adopted in the mid-1960s by importing new varieties of wheat developed at CIMMYT in Mexico and of rice developed by IRRI in the Philippines. Norman Borlaug, the inventor of Mexi-Pak seed, won a Nobel Prize for his research that made India and Pakistan's food production more secure. This revolution and the new technologies accompanying this enabled a three times increase in the output of food grains between the mid-1960s to end-1980s. During this time period, agricultural and economic growth accelerated. The requirement of the new technology was timely application of HYV seeds, chemical fertilisers, and irrigation water.[38]

The Green Revolution (through higher yields per acre) gave support to the rich farmers as they had the financial resources to manage the adoption of new technologies and purchase fertiliser as well as the appetite to take risks with these new varieties. The poor farmer did not benefit much from this revolution for quite some time, leading to unequal income distribution and social inequity. Due to increased incomes, the social and political clout of the landlords was further strengthened. The government, in the pursuit to demonstrate success, gave all the facilities to the richer landlords, whereas the poor farmers were not able to access the required inputs, credit, and even water. It was only when a subsidy was given for the use of fertilisers that some of the medium-sized landowners began adopting these new varieties. The demonstration effect spilled over to the small farmers after a considerable time lag. Almost 60 per cent of tenants who worked on a sharecropping[39] basis did not benefit proportionally.[40] By 1989–90, the demonstration effect was widespread and a 75 per cent increase was recorded in the cropping of these varieties in Sindh. At present, almost 96 per cent of the farmers have adopted these varieties.

The cumulative effect of the increased area under cultivation due to Kotri Barrage and Guddu Barrage, introduction of high yielding varieties of wheat and rice, incentivised production of/ cotton and sugarcane, and subsidised distribution of fertilisers, tractors, and irrigation pumps led to an increase in acreage, production, and yields of major crops.

Apart from increasing interpersonal income inequality, the Green Revolution in Pakistan also accentuated regional economic disparities. This is because the yield increase associated with the adoption of HYV seeds required irrigation. Since Punjab and Sindh had a relatively larger proportion of their area under irrigation, they experienced much faster growth in their incomes compared to Balochistan and the NWFP (now KP). For the same reason, the intra provincial regional income disparities between the irrigated and non-irrigated districts also increased.[41]

Annual Precipitation in Sindh

Since water availability is an essential element in agricultural production, it is important to understand the pattern of rainfall in the province (Figure 8.6). Long-term average precipitation in Sindh is 160 millimetres, taking into account the data of fifty years. Figure 8.6 depicts Sindh as a drought-prone area with occasional surplus extremes leading to flooding conditions in the province's districts. The province's long history of droughts that persisted over a stretch of at least a couple of years is also quite evident from the graph. For instance, periods of 1968–69, 1971–74, 1985–87, and 1999–2002 are known for their damages to crops, livestock, soil, and the natural ecosystem. This can account for the dips in the production of rice (and of other crops too) especially during these years. The problem of floods in Sindh has been persisting because of the flow of water from upstream through the mighty River Indus than because of local rain storms, which are relatively rare in nature. Hence, attention should be focused simultaneously on both local conditions as well as the changing behaviour of precipitation in the Upper Indus Basin (UIB). These flooding phenomena have occurred in the province during 2010 when heavy rainfall in Khyber Pakhtunkhwa inundated the Indus Delta, followed by another in 2011. Similarly, adverse effects of drought conditions resulting from a lack of rainfall in the Indus Delta can be mitigated if required water supply is maintained through canal irrigation from upstream water reservoirs.[42]

Figure 8.6: Annual Precipitation in Sindh (in Millimeter) (1960–2010)

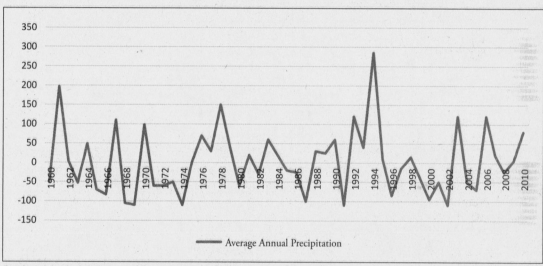

Source: Salma, S., S. Rehman and M.A. Shah, 'Rainfall Trends in Different Climate Zones of Pakistan', *Pakistan Journal of Meteorology*, 9/17, 2012, pp. 37–47.

Impact of Migration

In 1947 when Pakistan came into being, massive inward and outward migration took place. Millions of people from both sides were displaced; from Sindh, those displaced were the Sindhi Hindus who were mainly urban residents but a large chunk of them were also agriculturalists having large lands. They were a hard-working section of the population and looked after agriculture in a much better way than the existing zamindars. The Hindu zamindars left Sindh, went to India without any proper or prior planning, and left their agriculture lands behind. The urban and rural property left by Hindus was declared evacuee property. As per the Evacuee Property Act and the decision of the federal government, the urban property and the agriculture lands were distributed to the immigrants who were Muslims from India; some of the agriculture land was also distributed amongst the local Sindhi zamindars. Nevertheless, since most of the migrants were not agriculturalists, they did not give their full attention to agricultural production in terms of employing new technologies as the Hindu zamindars were doing. Many of the Muslim immigrants, however, came to urban areas and settled there and became absentee landlords. Their contribution to overall agricultural production was not adequate to make up for the output loss caused by the migration of Hindu agriculturalists.

The Sindhi Muslim landowners who were big zamindars did not apply new technologies on their lands and agricultural production remained stagnant. This combination of absentee landlordism and the indifferent role of large landowners did not produce satisfactory outcomes. With the passage of time, the absentee landlords sold their lands to the newly emerging and educated class of rural Sindh. As the locals was more informed than the absentee landlords, they were able to give a new life to farming as a profession. In the meantime, arrival of new technologies and assured water supply, and availability of pesticides and fertilisers under the green revolution did change the scenario dramatically. These young, educated zamindars played a pioneering role in the adoption and diffusion of these new technologies.

The high yields of wheat and rice produced on the field of these pioneers encouraged other large landowners to follow their lead. The tried and tested techniques of their neighbours, i.e. the early adopters, reduced the fear of failure and mitigated the risks of applying new varieties of seed and fertiliser on their own fields.

Agricultural Credit

Credit is considered to be one of the major inputs as far as agriculture production is concerned. In the early years after the establishment of the country, there was no organised credit facility/ institution. The local landlords or zamindars used to provide financial support to small farmers or the *hari*/tenant who cultivated their land and used that amount for personal expenses. This is informal credit. Institutions such as banks, which include Zarai-Taraqiati Bank Limited (ZTBL), micro-finance banks, co-operatives, and other such institutions i.e. institutions of formal credit, were not established then. The Agricultural Development Bank of Pakistan (ADBP)—the first financial institution dedicated to providing credit to farmers—was set up in the year 1961. They started disbursing loans for inputs but these were limited to large zamindars. In the initial years, the government extended Taccavi loans directly to agriculturalists. But these loans were never recovered and therefore had to be phased out.

Although the State Bank of Pakistan had directed commercial banks to disburse loans for agriculture and assigned them yearly targets, the volume of loans disbursed remained paltry. Loans granted at lower than market interest rates for agriculture created distortions. The loan recipients availed of the subsidised loan schemes of ZTBL but used the proceeds for non-agricultural activities. Loan recovery was poor and the ZTBL had to suffer losses and capital erosion. In 2000–01, the entire credit disbursed by all financial institutions was only PKR 45 billion (Table 8.8). Most of it was disbursed by ZTBL. The commercial banks paid penalties for not meeting the targets, but did not take any serious interest in lending to the farmers with middle and small holdings.

It was only in the early 2000s when the SBP abolished the mandatory directed credit schemes and allowed the financial institutions to charge market-based mark-up rates that the pace picked up. The volume of credit disbursed doubled in four years from PKR 52 Billion in 2001–02 to PKR 169 billion by 2004–05. The share of commercial banks in the total amount disbursed jumped from 26 per cent in 2000–01 to 60 per cent by 2004–05. Not only did this raise the loan amounts, but credit also reached a much larger proportion of the target population of farmers. Simplification of the procedures, whereby loans could be granted on the basis of pass books issued by the Board of Revenue showing the landholding of the applicant, also contributed to the spread of credit to the segment of agriculturalists who did not have access previously. By 2015–16, the amount of agricultural credit had reached almost PKR 600 billion—a six-fold increase in a decade.[43] Private and public commercial banks were the main suppliers of credit—almost three fourths of the total disbursements, while the share of ZTBL has dwindled to only 15 per cent. Another new player in the agriculture credit field are microfinance institutions and microfinance banks whose clients were small farmers requiring small loans. Despite the fact that they are still in a nascent stage, they have contributed 10 per cent of the total amount disbursed.

The SBP has recently introduced new types of schemes such as the agricultural value chain financing (AVCF), especially for livestock/dairy and poultry sub-sectors, warehouse receipt financing scheme (WHRF), credit guarantee scheme for small and marginalised farmers, and crop loan insurance scheme. The thrust of all these schemes is to promote agricultural financing particularly to small and medium-sized farmers. As a result of these initiatives, the subsistence farmers now receive almost half of the farm credit.

Farmers in Sindh have lagged behind their counterparts in Punjab as their participation in total credit disbursement is not commensurate with the value of production in the province or the number of farm holdings. The main reason has been the delayed issuing of pass books by the Sindh Board of Revenue.

A study on access to finance carried out in May 2009 shows that despite this large expansion in formal credit through multiple channels, only 14 per cent of all Pakistanis, rural and urban, use a financial product or service of a formal financial institution. However, 50 per cent of all Pakistanis have access to some sort of financial service, whether from the nonbanking, informal unorganised or informal organised sectors. The comparative figures for formal credit for Bangladesh are 32 per cent and 48 per cent for India. This shows that there is a lot of scope for access to formal financial institutions particularly for the rural population in Pakistan. The picture for Sindh does not appear any better.

Majority of the farmers in Sindh continue to rely upon informal sources of credit—from their zamindars, money lenders, input suppliers, *arthis* (middle men), and shop keepers etc. Their rates are exorbitantly high and therefore microfinance institutions, which charge interest rates of 25 to 30 per cent annually are able to attract customers. The latest numbers of microfinance borrowers have reached almost 5 million or 25 per cent of the target population. Table 8.8 provides data regarding institutional and non-institutional credit.

Table 8.8: Credit Source by Various Institutions (in PKR Million)
(1965–2015)

Year	ZTBL	Co-operatives	Commercial banks	Total
1965–66	222.0	194.3	-	416.3
1970-71	127.5	54.0	-	181.5
1975–76	532	102.05	-	808.1*
1980-81	1,066.6	1,128.25	1,816.13	4,010.98
1985–86	5,307.87	2,048.58	5,324.00	12,680.45
1990-91	8,323.95	3,017.45	3,517.79	14,859.19
1995–96	7,551.32	2,510.13	4,144.91	14,206.36
2000-01	27,610	5,124.2	12,055	44,789.2
2005–06	47,594.14	5,889.4	67,967.40	137,474.32*
2010-11	65,400	7,200	140,300	263,000*
2015–16	102,000	12,500	305,700	600,000*

*The total figure is not the sum of the figures for ZTBL, co-operatives, and commercial banks.

Source: Finance Division, *Pakistan Economic Survey*, Islamabad, Ministry of Finance, Government of Pakistan, various years.

Major Crops

Table 8.9 presents the data on output of four major crops grown in Sindh for the last seven decades. Annexure Tables 8A, 8B, and 8C represent the area, yield, and production of the major crops of Sindh from 1947–48 up until 2015–16. Wheat output has expanded 11 times, sugarcane 86 times, rice only 6 times, and cotton almost 10 times in this period of seven decades. Population growth during the same period has increased about 8 times per capita availability of wheat, sugarcane, and cotton, which shows an upward moving trend, while rice per capita availability shows decline.

Table 8.9: Production of Major Crops in Sindh (in 000 Tonnes) (1947–48 to 2015–16)

	Wheat	Sugarcane	Rice	Cotton
1947–48	381	192	412	63
1957–58	422	985	524	98
1970–71	1,120	3,239	1,121	156
1980–81	1,945	5,007	1,549	239
1990–91	2,274	11,815	1,433	191
2000–01	2,226	12,650	1,682	364
2010–11	4,288	13,766	1,230	602
2015–16*	3,672	16,614	2,653	607

*Data obtained is for 2014–15 from *Agricultural Statistics 2014–15*.

Source: Bureau of Statistics, *Development Statistics of Sindh*, Karachi, Planning & Development Department, Government of Sindh, various years; Ministry of Food, Agriculture and Livestock, *50 Years of Agricultural Statistics in Pakistan (1947–2000)*, Islamabad, Government of Pakistan, 2007; Pakistan Bureau of Statistics, *Agricultural Statistics of Pakistan (2011–2012)*, Islamabad, Statistics of Division, Government of Sindh, 2013; Ministry of National Food Security and Research, *Agricultural Statistics 2014–15*, Islamabad, Government of Pakistan, n.d.

Table 8.10 Percentage Share of Sindh in Major Crops by Area and Production
(2005–06 to 2015–16)

	2005–06		2010–11		2015–16	
	Production	Area	Production	Area	Production	Area
Wheat	12.9	11	17	12.9	14.3	12
Sugarcane	25.2	20.2	25	22.9	25.4	28
Rice	31	22.6	25.5	15.3	39	28.5
Cotton	20.3	20.5	30.9	17	36	20.5

Source: Bureau of Statistics, *Development Statistics of Sindh*, Karachi, Planning and Development Department, Government of Sindh, various years. Pakistan Bureau of Statistics, *Agricultural Statistics of Pakistan (2011–2012)*, Islamabad, Statistics of Division, Government of Sindh, 2013; Ministry of National Food Security and Research, *Agricultural Statistics 2014–15*, Islamabad, Government of Pakistan, n.d.; Finance Division, *Pakistan Economic Survey 2016–17*, Islamabad, Ministry of Finance, Government of Pakistan, 2017.

The share of Sindh in the total wheat production of the country had risen to 17 per cent in 2010–11, but it has not kept pace with other provinces. However, rice is an export commodity, i.e. surplus to domestic consumption. There has been a significant increase in the production of cotton and the province accounts for more than one-third of the national output. A brief analysis of the four major crops is given below.

WHEAT

Wheat is a staple food, not only in Sindh or Pakistan, but also in many parts of the world. Sindh's climate can support the intensive cultivation and production of wheat—a winter crop that requires 25°C, loamy soils high in organic matter, and a neutral to slightly alkaline pH level. Wheat is sown across Sindh from early November to mid-December. While it is harvested in southern Sindh in March, farmers in northern Sindh harvest it in May.[44] Undue rain, floods, or dry spells during the germination stage can damage wheat yields.[45]

The area under wheat cultivation in Sindh remained stagnant till 1958; the dislocation caused by Partition, the influx of refugees from India, the migration of professional Hindus from Sindh, and absence of perennial canals all contributed to this phenomenon. However, there was a spectacular rise in the area under wheat cultivation which expanded by almost 108 per cent in the next thirty-five years.

As pointed out earlier, this was triggered by the high yield Mexi Pak Seed, uptake of fertiliser, new barrages, perennial canals, and increase in water availabilities. The yield per hectare also went up from 811 kg per hectare to 2,119 kg per hectare between 1957–58 and 1995–96—an exceptional increase of 261 per cent. There was again a hiatus between 1995–96 and 2010–11 as there was no perceptible expansion in the area under cultivation (Annexure Table 8A). The factors at play were water shortage, quantity and timing of rainfall, inadequate supply of inputs (especially phosphate fertilisers), and rise in input prices. Although wheat production has exceeded the population growth rate so far, the worrisome aspect is the tendency observed for the last two decades where the yields and production level are not rising as they did in the past. Agricultural research and development of new varieties have not had any breakthrough so far and the proliferation of seed producers in the private sector with questionable quality has also done a lot of harm to these efforts.

COTTON

Pakistan is the fourth largest producer and the third largest consumer of cotton in the world.[46] Like wheat, the major cotton growing areas lie in Punjab (which accounts for 80 per cent area and 77 per cent production) and Sindh (which accounts for 19 per cent area and 36 per cent production), mainly in Sanghar, Dadu, Khairpur, Sukkur, Ghotki and Nawabshah lying in Sindh. Cotton is planted in the months of June and July, while the time period from September to December tends to be the crop's harvesting period.[47]

Pakistan has witnessed a gradual decline in its cotton production in the last decade, while India through the adoption and diffusion of bt cotton has doubled its production during the same period. As a result, Pakistan has to import cotton from India to meet its consumption needs. Sindh's share of cotton production declined from approximately 33 per cent in 1947 to 20 per cent in 2005–06 (Annexure Table 8C). The number of farms and the area devoted to the cultivation of cotton have been receding since 1990s. There was some pick up in the mid-2000s but it could not be sustained.[48] According to the Sindh Cotton Commissioner, the fall in the area sown and the volume produced is due to the shortage of water at the time of sowing and growers' preference to cultivate more profitable crops like wheat and sugarcane in areas around Ghotki, a traditionally cotton-growing district. In addition, rice has made inroads in the cotton-growing belt, and even a district like Sanghar, which otherwise tops in cotton production, is fast witnessing a shift to rice cultivation. This crop switching is unfortunate as both rice and sugarcane are highly water-intensive crops while cotton is not.

However, it is interesting to note that the per hectare yield for cotton in Sindh has continued to increase in the last decade due to the introduction of new technology, but it is still lower in relation to the best practice yields across the border. Pakistan can catch up only if bt cotton is introduced. Additionally, since cotton cropping and picking are incredibly labour-intensive endeavours, it is necessary that farmers' baseline be kept in mind before legislating policies.[49]

RICE

Rice is an important food crop as it is a domestic staple and an export item. In Pakistan, it is the second most popular staple after wheat, and it is the second largest earner of foreign exchange after cotton.[50] It accounts for 3.0 per cent of the value added in agriculture and 0.6 per cent of GDP of Pakistan.[51] The cultivation of rice is only suited to regions with low labour costs and high rainfall since it is very labour-intensive and requires plenty of water for irrigation.[52] It is often grown in paddies, water from which is drained once the crop has established dominance of the field and preparations for the harvest need to be done. In Sindh, the major rice-growing areas include Larkana, Dadu, Shikarpur, Qambar-Shahdadkot, Jacobabad, and Kashmore districts in upper Sindh while Thatta, Badin, and Tando Muhammad Khan are major areas in lower Sindh.[53] Sindh only cultivates the Irri varieties in Kacha areas of Indus River.[54]

Area utilised for growing rice and its production has been increasing throughout the years with dips observed in the years 2010 and 2012. As explained earlier, the rising trend in all the three variables for rice—area, production, and per acre yield—can be attributed to the incentives enjoyed by the farmers in the form of relatively higher profitability by growing rice and sugarcane. For instance, in 2013–14, Ghotki district—located on the left bank of the Indus and fed by the Ghotki Feeder of Guddu Barrage—had 54,800 hectares under rice compared to 8,500 hectares in 2007–08. Large commercial rice farmers are in a position to get excess supply of irrigation water, much above their entitlement, and pay almost insignificant water use charges; resultantly, they waste a lot of scarce resource at the expense of the tail-enders whose productivity remains low. This leaves these subsistence farmers with little choice to grow other crops with little to no water.[55]

SUGARCANE

Sugarcane is both an important cash crop as well as a vital food crop of Pakistan. It is an important source of income and employment for the farming community of the country. As is evident from Annexure Table 8C the sugarcane production has been escalating since the time of partition particularly with the disbanding of the zoning. It is grown in the lower regions of Sindh in the areas south of Hyderabad. Since it is a high delta crop, it requires 64–66 inches of water in Sindh. Also, the crop needs nitrogen, phosphorus, and potash.[56]

Since 1947, the area under-sugarcane has been increasing till early 2000, after which an uneven trend can be witnessed, and only stabilises after 2011. The oscillation in area can be attributed to the availability of water, particularly rainfall. In the years there was little or no rain, farmers had to shift to the cultivation of other dry crops.[57] In terms of the production, in 1993, the government introduced agriculture assistance policies, including increased support prices for many agricultural commodities and expanded availability of agricultural credit. Henceforth, we see a continuous rise in the production of sugarcane. The yield per hectare of sugarcane (Annexure Table 8B) depicts an upward moving trend with an almost doubling of the yield between 1947 and 2015. The public policy tilt towards sugarcane is likely to have adverse consequences in the future as irrigation water availability becomes stressed due to climate change. The political economy of sugarcane, with above world market procurement prices resulting in production of sugar surplus to domestic demand that is once again exported with government financial assistance, is creating distortions in the efficient allocation of water and financial resources.

Fruits

Pakistan's fruits are in great demand not only locally but internationally as well. It is Punjab and Sindh which produce and export most of the fruits from Pakistan, a new source of earning foreign exchange. The three major fruit crops of Sindh are mango, dates, banana, and to a lesser extent guava.

Pakistan produces approximately 1.7 million tons of mangoes annually, of which almost 40 per cent comes from Sindh. Grown mainly in Hyderabad, Sanghar, Shaheed Benazirabad (Nawabshah), and Mirpurkhas districts, this highly-admired fruit is not only one of Sindh's but Pakistan's leading exports. The famous *Sindhri* mangoes are of high quality and are dried and used for purposes other than fresh juices and eating. However, insufficient knowledge of appropriate amounts of nitrogen-based fertilisers, and pest control methods leads to farmers cutting trees off to contain damage, resulting in slumped yields. Furthermore, lack of post-harvest facilities leads to an increasing loss of fruit. The only mango drying facility available to export dried mangoes for powders, extraction purposes, synthetic juices and jams, etc. is at Tando Allahyar.[58] One hundred and twenty-five different kinds of mangoes are found in Sindh.[59]

While pulping units are scarce in Pakistan, the demand for mango pulp around the world is increasing by the day. Since Pakistan, and Sindh in particular, is the main producer of the fruit, pulping facilities provide a good investment opportunity for those interested in agriculture. Inappropriate care facilities and poor management post-harvest result in mangoes over-ripening due to latex, or get damaged due to bad packaging. Recent reports suggest that production of mangoes is going down because of vagaries of weather.[60] Mango trees need low temperatures to enter their dormancy stage whereby the budding process begins. However, heat waves all across Sindh, even during winter months, result in temperatures rising to almost 30°C. Immense heat during the dormancy stage speeds up the growth rate of the mangoes and results in a higher yield but lower quality.

Around 50 per cent of the date production in Pakistan takes place in the province of Sindh.[61] Khairpur and Sukkur are the main districts which have the most suitable climatic and soil conditions resulting in almost 80 to 85 per cent of date production in the province.[62] The area under dates in Sindh has been increasing consistently throughout the years (Annexure Table 8E). The rise can be attributed to the emergence of Pakistan as an exporter of dates. A viral disease in 2011–12, however, destroyed the date palm in Ahmedpur, Pir Jo Goth, and Babarloi areas.[63]

Most of the banana crop of the country is cultivated in Sindh. The production level, which was hardly 1,000 tons in 1958–59, reached almost 134,000 tons by 2005–06. Since then, there has been a gradual decline in area cultivated and, consequently, production levels. Banana is suitable for tropical and semi-tropical climatic conditions of the Indus Delta zone of Sindh but is prone to diseases. As it is easily perishable, other commercial uses of the fruits need to be explored for adding value as well as augmenting the incomes of the farmers solely producing bananas as the cash crop.

Of the 490,000 tons of Guava produced nationally, Sindh's share is only 14 per cent, fluctuating between annual outputs of 60,000–70,000 tons. Larkana is the largest producer of guavas, contributing to 45 per cent of the total produce, followed by Hyderabad, Shaheed Benazirabad (Nawabshah), Mirpurkhas, and Naushahro Feroze.

Almost all the citrus fruits are cultivated and produced in Punjab, which account for almost 99 per cent of the national production, and this is the trend that has persisted ever since 1990.

However, it should also be noted that Khyber Pakhtunkhwa and Balochistan produce peaches, apricots, apples, and cherries, which are largely consumed domestically.

Vegetables

The cultivation and production of vegetables in Sindh has progressed well in the past few years owing to climate and better farming techniques. The total area under vegetable cultivation has increased since the 1950s to 51,769 hectares in 2014–15.[64] Correspondingly, total production has increased to 356,879 tonnes. The production upsurge has been possible due to the introduction of subsidised fertilisers, harvesting methods, and improved seed varieties.[65] Reports show that whenever climatic conditions get adverse for the production of commercial cash crops such as cotton, farmers switch over to vegetables as a coping strategy. Due to dry and hot spells in Sindh, tomatoes, chilies and onions are abundantly grown in the province (Annexure Tables 8F and 8G). In periods of plentiful rain, gourds and cucumbers are grown. During winter months, cultivators turn to peas, cauliflower, cabbage and spinach. Additionally, farmers in Sindh grow garlic and potatoes in the region (Annexure Tables 8H and 8I). However, potato production here has remained extremely low historically. Punjab is the largest producer of potatoes in the country.

One major reason behind the lower production of vegetables in Sindh as compared to Punjab is the problem of salinity. Around 0.94 million hectares of saline patch exists in Sindh with only 0.45 million hectares and 0.5 million hectares in Punjab and Khyber Pakhtunkhwa, respectively.[66] This affects the growth of vegetables negatively mainly because the salt tolerance of vegetables is low.

Onion is sown mainly in the districts of Hyderabad, Sanghar, Mirpurkhas, Shaheed Benazirabad, and Sukkur, during July–August and October, whereas harvesting takes place in September and January. Although, the production of onion shows a decent trend in Sindh, it is necessary that the government must initially subsidise and make available higher-yielding varieties of onion seeds, popularise weeding strategies, and teach farmers methods to make onions last longer. Onions are perishable and catch maggots if not sold when fresh. Hence, a lot of the surplus is lost due to the heat and ill-storage capacities in Sindh. While Punjab is the major tomato-producing province of Pakistan, Sindh is not too far behind. Tomato production in Sindh has faced problems such as lack of suitable pesticides for white fly and other insects, as well as inadequate refrigeration facilities. These have resulted in grave losses despite crops being harvested all year round.

Sindh is the major chili-producing province of Pakistan and contributes to approximately 90 per cent of the national produce as seen in Annexure Table 8G. Chilli is used in chilli powder, ketchup, and *masalas*. Despite an increase in the area allotted to chilli cultivation, production of chillies has seen a drastic decline since the year 2000.[67] The biggest cause of damage that has struck cultivators from Hyderabad, Badin, and Mirpurkhas are various fungi, insects, and viruses. What is required is immediate research to counter the various pests and insects in order to increase yield, and bring Sindh back to its high chili-yielding province status.

The Food and Agriculture Organisation of the UN ranked Pakistan the nineteenth largest producer of garlic worldwide.[68] In Pakistan, garlic is sown around October and reaped in April. Among many other uses, it is particularly sought after for its savoury qualities, making it most suitable for seasoning.

Pulses

All varieties of pulses are produced mostly in Sindh and Punjab. However, the production as well as area figures have been consistently falling in Sindh in the recent years and Punjab's share has continued to dominate lentil production (Annexure Tables 8J and 8K). Due to inappropriate weather conditions in the region, the production of pulses has remained significantly low. In addition to and because of this, farmers in the region have shifted to utilising their lands for the purpose of growing other cash crops, such as sugarcane, which are tolerant of unpredictable weather patterns. Low yields per hectare of pulses have forced the country to spend huge foreign exchange for importing pulses.

Forestry

The British occupation in Sindh saw the clearing of several otherwise rich forests for the purposes of construction, particularly the Indus Flotilla Company and State Railways. When the realisation about the ill effects of such deforestation occurred in 1875, Sindh Forests Management was finally launched. Ever since Partition, governments have invested resources into putting forests to best use by planting different varieties in order to yield diversely useful products. These forests provide various qualities of raw material for chipboard, plywood, paper and pulp, rayon, and many more. Additionally, since these forests are the natural habitat of a whole range of animal species, it is necessary that they be protected and sustained. Hence in 1972, the Government of Sindh created a separate department for forest and wildlife.

Riverine forests of Sindh constantly face multiple threats. They were destroyed in the 1980s and 1990s as they had become safe havens for dacoits. Influential zamindars are using the fertile riverine land for cultivation purposes. The policies introduced for forest protection in 2004 have not produced satisfactory results and proved inefficient.[69] Several media reports have cited that forests are fast disappearing because of lack of proper water flow, illegal cutting of trees, and encroachment of land and cutting for security issues.[70] These issues went unaddressed for almost four decades,[71] such that local appeals to the government have not been taken seriously.[72] Due to reduction in several creeks, in the Indus delta, many mangrove forests have vanished. The forest department of the Government of Sindh has to take care of the mangrove forests which were in abundance and are now shrinking.

Poultry

Modern poultry farming, which started in 1963, was not well documented until the 1980s. After the formation of the Poultry Research Institution, some data such as names and numbers of poultry farm owners, types of livestock owned, scale of farming, and many others was finally recorded.[73] Poultry forms an integral part of the daily diet in Sindh. As incomes rise, demand for poultry rises and investment in rearing and commercial production becomes relatively profitable. The poultry industry began with rearing chicken in backyards and rose to constructing proper infrastructure to house increasing number of broiler and chick production for commercial purposes. Although government subsidies, tax exemptions and easy loan facilities made growth industry easier, the poultry industry is still swamped with innumerable problems.[74]

Poultry farms are normally located around large urban cities like Karachi so that the increasing fodder demands of the broilers can be met on a regular basis. However, there are government plans to expand poultry farming to rural areas to meet the rising demand for chicken. To increase overall production in the rural areas, modernisation efforts need to be implemented.[75] Lack of adequate supervision and surveillance of hygienic conditions and low quality poultry lead to a spread of diseases such as white diarrhoea, bronchitis, chicken pox and bird flu, leading to a further drop in sales and consumption.[76] Poultry farming employs approximately 1.5 million people in Pakistan but the existence of a gap between demand and supply necessitates the investment of resources into infrastructure construction and management (such as shed and hatchery ventilation, spacing, and other factors), manufacturing of poultry healthcare products, poultry fodder manufacturing, meat processing and packaging factories, and packaged and alive poultry transportation.[77]

Fisheries

Sindh's myriad of lakes, ponds, and rivers, notably the Indus River, have been breeding various kinds of fish for centuries. The Arabian Sea is another major source for the fisheries. The fish produced from the sea is called marine fish and the fish produced through Indus, its tributaries, lakes, and other water ponds is known as inland fish. The types of marine fish are known as sole (flat fish, Singhara fish, khagga), catfish, hira, dother, sua mushka, dhand, gisser, bhambor, bako, kund, pomfret (white), pomfret (black), sangro, rawas, aal, mullets boi, kakkar/bangra, tarli, surmai, asp mahi, mangra, pitton, kikat lobsters, zahric and others.

The inland fisheries produce palla, kuriro, theri and many other kinds. Millions of tons are produced every day and sold not only in Pakistan but all over the world and foreign exchanges earned out of it. Having a long coastal line, fisheries ports, and infrastructure, the potential for exploitation of the marine products for exports (estimated at one million tons per year) has not been fully realised. Poor environmental, processing, and hygienic conditions have led to suspension of imports of fish and allied products by the European Union several times. Unprofessional handling of the sub-sector by well-connected and influential persons has been a major stumbling block. Private sea lords operating their own jetties did not allow the PKR one billion modern Korangi Fish Harbour to operate for the benefit of the small and medium scale fishery business.

Livestock

Sindh is very rich in livestock production such as cattle like buffaloes, cows, sheep, goats, camels, horses, asses (donkeys), and mules. It is a culture of the rural population to have livestock in their homes at their villages. The rural population uses livestock as their bank and use the livestock in difficult times by selling them in the market. As per the Sindh Development Statistics of 2016, the total (latest) figure of livestock as of 2006 is 31.88 million.[78] Livestock production over three decades (1986–2006) increased by 84.5 per cent, which has been bolstered by doubling of cattle, buffaloes, and goat. There has been a decrease in the number of horses, most probably due to the high costs associated with raising them.

Almost 60 per cent of agriculture value added in Sindh originates from the livestock, poultry, and dairy sectors. The demand for these products is likely to rise and investment in processing, hygiene, and environmental safeguards would be greatly required. Quality research and veterinary services are also lacking and need to be boosted. Halal meat exports offer a very lucrative business due to proximity with the Middle East. This avenue can be explored if quality standards are maintained.

Table 8.11: Livestock Population of Sindh Over the Censuses of 1986, 1996, and 2006
(in Million)

Species	1986	1996	2006	Average Growth Rate (%)
Cattle	3.87	5.46	6.93	3.95
Buffaloes	3.22	5.62	7.34	6.40
Sheep	2.62	3.71	3.96	2.56
Goat	6.76	9.73	12.57	4.30
Camels	0.22	0.22	0.28	1.36

Source: Government of Pakistan, *Livestock Census 1996*, Agricultural Census Organisation, Statistics Division, Islamabad, 1986, 1998, and 2006.

The estimated consumption of meat and dairy products in Sindh, every day, is at thousands of tons, which adds to a healthy diet of the population. Unfortunately, the government has almost failed to assure the quality or strictly control prices over the years. Given how nutritious livestock products are, if concentrated upon, the food security situation of the province will immensely improve. Continued practice over a long period of time might even lead to lower costs attributed to health (in form of expenses on hospitals and check-ups) and promote a healthy province. For any province to succeed, the labour force is the backbone of economy and a well-fed work force can surely add to the productivity and make Sindh even more prosperous.

There are almost no government-owned farms, milk chillers, and modern meat and milk testing laboratories. The lack of government attention is evident from the fact that the last scheme to incentivise and increase milk and meat production was completed in 2006–07.[79] The Asian Development Bank and the World Bank have supported a good number of projects but those could not be sustained for a long time.[80]

Unfortunately, there have been inconsistencies in the data collected and published over the last three livestock censuses. This means that any analysis on the subject is quite limited.

Agricultural Inputs

FERTILISERS AND MECHANISATION

Fertiliser use for major crops has surged in Sindh over the last seventy years from almost a non-existent use. Empirical evidence clearly shows a positive cost benefit ratio for fertiliser consumption. During the 1960s, Ayub Khan was the first to emphasise the need to invest in mechanisation and in the fertiliser industry in order to boost the agricultural economy of Pakistan. The first private sector fertiliser plant, ENGRO, was founded in Dharki in 1958 to increase production of fertilisers and reduce reliance on imported foods and fertilisers. Fauji Fertilisers was established in 1977, paving the way for more plants across the country. By the early 1980s, manure was gradually replaced with locally produced, inorganic chemicals.[81] In 1986, subsidies on nitrogenous fertilisers were abolished, and phosphate-based fertilisers provided more nutrients, and increased soil fertility; therefore, crop yield also increased.[82] In 1989, Benazir Bhutto's government introduced a policy whereby the supply of gas to fertiliser plants was guaranteed, no tax was to be charged on the sale of fertilisers, and manufacturers were allowed to expand their plants and branches across the country.[83] Food crop production in the country increased from 10 million tonnes in 1970 to 25 million tonnes in 2002–03, nationally[84] and one of the several contributing factors was the rising fertiliser usage. Phosphate fertilisers were subsidised in 1993 and after the introduction of the 1994 Sindh Fertiliser Control Act,[85] potassium was also subsidised for growers in 1997.[86] The act proved beneficial according to government and international reports.

Crop response to fertilisers and use of tractors is affected by seasonal, climatic, soil, and irrigation factors such as soil acidity or alkalinity, deficiency of nutrients, sowing dates, precipitation, and crop rotations. In the late 1990s and early 2000s, for example, droughts, dehydration, and a lack of precipitation posed a problem. In 2001, prices for fertilisers increased because the government imposed 15 per cent sales tax.[87] Hence in 2002, growers started buying more affordable, second-rate fertilisers.[88] In 2003, the Sindh Agricultural Board petitioned for the federal government to increase Sindh's share from 23 to 25 per cent in order to prevent growers from resorting to sub-standard fertilisers as a result of high prices and extreme shortage.[89]

But the shortage continued in 2004 and it took two years for the Sindh High Court to issue notices to suppliers, inspectors, and manufacturers of sub-standard fertilisers.[90] Eventually, orders were released to seize the production of fertilisers by unregistered companies.[91]

Compared to the average for Pakistan, and Punjab in particular, there is still room for greater usage of fertiliser. In 2010, 30 per cent of private farms across Pakistan made use of fertilisers and manure. Similarly, 30 per cent of private farms in Punjab reported the use of fertilisers and manure, while in Sindh, only 17 per cent of the total private farms used fertilisers and manure.[92] The consumption of fertilisers in Sindh increased twenty-seven times in the last forty-seven years compared to twenty-two times for the whole country. This is reflected in the higher per acre yield of major crops in Sindh relative to the national average.

The use of fertilisers varies each year, depending on the availability of water, prices, supply of feed stock needed to make fertilisers, and the import policy. One of the recently commissioned urea plants was shut down for an extended period due to non-availability of natural gas. This created shortages and rise in prices. In 2015–16, there was an 11 per cent decline in the off take of fertilisers. It is unclear whether it was a fall in the area under production that triggered the decline or high prices of fertilisers acting as a disincentive leading to reduced area. Another subsidy scheme amounting to PKR 20 billion was announced for the year 2016–17.

Fertiliser supply constraints and inequitable distribution of irrigation water, subsidised tractors, and machinery have in recent years been holding Sindh's agrarian economy back from reaching its full potential as the difference in productivity between the progressive farmers and the average farmer is still wide. Most of the subsidised inputs and equipment are pre-empted by large farmers and feudal politicians.

In recent years, several measures were taken by the governments of Pakistan and Sindh to improve the supply of inputs,[93] but weaknesses in their implementation have not been able to bear desired results. In 2006, the Government of Pakistan issued a subsidy of PKR 12 billion for agricultural mechanisation. Money was handed directly to the producers. Farmers protested that those government schemes never benefitted or even reached them.[94] In 2010, PKR 1.6 billion were issued to start a subsidised tractor scheme for growers who owned between 25 and 50 acres of land.[95] Fertilisers and seeds[96] were to be distributed across Sindh, and cheap tractors were to be supplied on installments but increased taxes on the production of farming machinery in 2011 decreased sales considerably.[97]

Since the measures were implemented only on a first-come-first-serve basis, rightful farmers from Sindh Abadgar Tahreek threatened to protest across Sindh because their problems instead of reaching resolution, worsened.[98] Feudals and politicians had started hoarding fertilisers and seeds that were meant originally to be distributed, in their homes. Action was not taken, and fertiliser prices increased while crop prices were lowered once again, adversely affecting the small farmers. Fertiliser deficits continually have to be met through imports. The same holds true for agricultural machinery, such as sprayers for chemicals, for which Pakistan spends approximately USD 100 million annually.[99]

Mechanisation has been slow to penetrate in Sindh because of issues in the acquisition, utilisation, and maintenance of farming machinery and equipment. Small-scale subsistence farmers and small landowners cannot normally afford big machinery, and even if they could, a cost-benefit analysis would deem it unprofitable; rising fuel prices, small plots or land, limited cultivation, and other factors do not favour ownership of expensive farming tools. Table 8.12 shows that the ownership of tubewells has generally increased, especially between 2007–08 and 2014–15 when the numbers of tubewells installed multiplied almost 2.4 times.

While domestic ownership of tubewells shows an upward moving curve, the same is not the case with tractor ownership. Table 8.13 presents domestic manufacturing of tractors. From a modest scale of about 10,000 in 1990–91, production reached its peak in 2010–11 but has fallen to the level below 2005–06. The inconsistent government policies explain most of the fluctuations in the domestic industry response.

Media reports have repeatedly highlighted that the unorganised sector in Pakistan manufactures a lot of other equipment and machinery for the agriculture sector but there is no data available to provide a clear picture. Hence, mechanisation in Pakistan is officially limited to tractors and tubewells. In 2014, there was a rise in local demand for tractors, thrashers, loaders, and the use of solar-powered tubewells and drying units. However, implementation delays did not allow the benefits to be passed on to the users.

SEED

Seed is another major input along with fertiliser and water. It is also a major component in the chain of agriculture production systems. Up to 1970, there were no institutions which catered to seed production. For many years the farmers had been breeding and storing their own seeds. It was only after the Sindh Seed Corporation was established that quality seeds for major crops became available. In the 1990s and thereafter, many private firms also entered the field of production and distribution of improved seed varieties.

Table 8.12: Tubewell Ownership in Sindh by Type*
(1987–88 to 2014–15)

Year	Number		
1987–88	**Public**	**Private**	**Total**
Electric	3,857	11,648	15,505
Diesel	1	4,463	4,464
Total	**3,858**	**16,111**	**19,969**
1997–98			
Electric	4,300	13,705	18,005
Diesel	128	5,455	5,583
Total	**4,428**	**19,160**	**23,588**
2007–08			
Electric	13,099	18,623	31,722
Diesel	1,116	62,377	63,493
Total	**14,215**	**81,000**	**95,215**
2014–15			
Electric	1,153	82,261	83,414
Diesel	1,142	145,834	146,976
Total	**2,295**	**228,095**	**230,390**

*Cumulative owners.

Source: Ministry of Food, Agriculture and Livestock, *50 Years of Agricultural Statistics in Pakistan (1947–2000)*, Islamabad, Government of Pakistan, 2007; Pakistan Bureau of Statistics, *Agricultural Statistics of Pakistan (2011–2012)*, Islamabad, Statistics Division, Pakistan Bureau of Statistics, 2013.

Table 8.13: Number of Tractors Manufactured in Pakistan (1990–91 to 2014–15)

Years	Tractors
1990–91	13,841
1995–96	16,218
2000–01	32,553
2005–06	49,642
2010–11	71,550
2014–15	45,860

Source: Ministry of Food, Agriculture and Livestock, *50 Years of Agricultural Statistics in Pakistan (1947–2000)*, Islamabad, Government of Pakistan, 2007; Pakistan Bureau of Statistics, *Agricultural Statistics of Pakistan (2011–2012)*, Islamabad, Statistics Division, Pakistan Bureau of Statistics, 2013; Ministry of National Food Security and Research, *Agricultural Statistics 2014–15*, Islamabad, Government of Pakistan, 2017, p. 177.

Meanwhile, the Seed Act XXIX of 1976 passed by the National Assembly envisaged the setting up of an institutional framework for regulating the quality of seeds. Soon after the promulgation of this Act, institutes like the National Seed Council, Provincial Seed Council, Seed Certification Agency, and National Seed Registration Agency were established.

The Federal Seed Certification Department was established as an attached department of the Ministry of Food and Agriculture on 1 June 1976, and since then has been responsible for exercising quality control of various crop seeds.

The Atomic Energy Commission of Pakistan (Sindh Chapter) at Tando Jam and the Sindh Agriculture University have also been working on the research and development of different varieties of seeds suited for the ecological conditions of Sindh.

PESTICIDES

Pest attacks are common wherever agriculture is practised. Pests are insects which destroy the crops in part or in entirety. In the modern usage of the term, pests include fungi, bacteria, and various types of viruses. These are major constraints for agricultural production. Control of such damage requires pesticides or insecticides which are now widely used in agricultural crops throughout the world. The diseases that attack cotton include bollworms, cutworms, whiteflies, jassids, mites, and leaf rollers. For rice, these diseases include rice-hoppers, cutworms, bugs, paddy borers and rice maggots and for fruits these are fruit flies, fruit moths, leaf rollers, bugs, and aphids amongst others. For vegetables, these are cabbage worms, thrips, aphids, and mites. To control these diseases, air spray is used, the use of which has been increasing.

With the introduction of new technologies in 1960s, pest attacks had actually risen and pesticides also caught speed with an increased production and consumption of fertilisers (Annexure Tables 8L and 8M). This trend persistently continued throughout the 1970s and 1980s and millions of tonnes of pesticides and insecticides were used in Sindh. This was true for Punjab and other provinces of Pakistan as well. The recent data of pesticides and herbicides can be referred to in Annexure Tables 8N, 8O, and 8P. During the same period, sub-standard and adulterated pesticides were sold by many dealers to the growers.

In August 1999, the Plant Protection Department, Government of Sindh, collected as many as 1,668 samples of pesticides from the various parts of Sindh for testing at the Pesticide Quality Control Laboratory. Out of the total collected samples, forty-seven were found adulterated and substandard. The substandard and adulterated pesticides are partly imported under various brand names and partly manufactured by local manufacturers.[100]

The Pesticides Act was passed by the government of Pakistan in 1971 to govern the pesticide industry. Due to lack of implementation of rules and regulations, Sindh has been facing adulteration to a large extent. It has also been found that some of the government agencies like the Agriculture Extension Department has not been taking serious action against the use of such outdated and fake pesticides. No proper action has been taken against the companies and the dealers who are involved in such practice. There has been a sale of banned pesticides as well in the past. In Sindh, pesticide is being used indiscriminately and at a high level which is also harmful for the crops as well as for the people. There is no monitoring for the application of these pesticides and requisite safety measures are also not taken.

Since the rural population of Sindh is not literate, farmers do not know the ways and the techniques for spraying pesticides, which has also resulted in many casualties.

Summing Up

Concentration of land ownership in Sindh is getting diluted with the passage of time because of inheritance laws but large landowners in the rural areas of Sindh still continue to exercise disproportionate influence both on politics as well as the agrarian economy. They own not only the lands, but also the people who work on them. Land reforms in the 1960s and 1970s did not make much of a dent on the landholding pattern and effective control by large families. The legacy of feudal dominance by large landowners is, however, not weakening at the same pace as dilution of land ownership because of the nexus between the state and big landlords. Political parties seek the help of these landlords at the time of elections and as a quid pro quo they oblige these landlords once they assume power. The patronage–client relationship reinforces political power with access to economic resources and institutions.

Productivity gaps between large and small farmers remain wide because the latter have little access to the resources, inputs and institutions. Whenever there is scarcity of subsidised fertilisers or seeds the large farmers are the ones who, because of their influence and connections, pre-empt these inputs for their own lands. Water does not reach the tail-enders because the same elites breach the modules and divert water towards their lands or have implicit state sanction to pump water directly out of the canals.

Land revenue and *abiana* charges that are required for maintenance and operations have fallen into disuse because large and medium landowners collude with officials and evade these charges. Public procurement of wheat and sugar at above the international prices is also confined to the marketable surpluses of the same elite group. Agriculture credit is not available on time and small farmers have to repay their loans soon after harvest, when output prices are low, pushing them to make distress market sales. The *arhthis* who lend them seasonal credit at exorbitant rates take advantage of the situation and purchase the output from these distressed sellers at prices much below the prevailing market price.

The landless labour or *haris* working on share cropping and *batai* system have to forfeit their shares to the landowners who had advanced them money during the post-harvest period for consumption purposes. The combination of a flawed land tenure system, a tilted agriculture marketing arrangement, absence of a robust credit system, and lack of access to institutions supplying critical inputs has resulted in inefficient allocation of resources and inequitable distribution of the benefits from agricultural growth. The control of the landlords on law and order agencies leads to kidnapping, beating, rape and even murders of those who dare show defiance of these outlandish practices.

However, it is not only fear that binds the *haris* to *waderas*. As big landowners are also either powerful politicians, or have strong affiliations with political parties, they can promise a poor farmer's son a government job in the city thereby leaving *haris* and their forthcoming generations feeling indebted to the merciful feudal for the rest of their lives. Since their survival depends on pleasing the feudal landlords, farmers stay loyal to them and to their political parties. Consequently, a political party creates a strong regional hold, solidifies the feudal control and the landlords purposefully keep their *haris* and servants poor and uneducated. Hence, successive governments in Sindh have never implemented any significant reforms that open up land markets and protect the rights of the tenants.[101]

Pakistan was able to make significant progress by transitioning from being an importer of food crops to become an exporter of food crops. Pakistan's agriculture performance was quite up to the mark until 1990 but has not kept pace since then. The duality in Sindh is not along urban–rural dimensions but also irrigated and non-irrigated areas in the rural landscape, manifested by the high incidence of poverty levels and deprivation in Tharparkar, Umerkot, Thatta, and Badin.

An alternative measure to advance Sindh's agrarian economy is to allocate state land and particularly that in the riverine area presently occupied by influential big landlords to the landless and peasants. They should also be given the required inputs and credit to bring the land under cultivation. If this land is put to intensive use, there would be increased productivity and rising incomes for the poor segments of the population.

There must also be a penalty on absentee landowners who have large tracts of land in their possession but are not bringing them under cultivation. Either they should be asked to pay heavy non-utilisation fees or surrender their surplus parcels to the state. This pool can be consolidated for redistribution.

A renowned Karachi-based architect, urban planner, and researcher maintains that English-language newspapers have reported more than seventy-two protests since 2010, in Sindh.[102] In fact, both anecdotal evidence and archival research have revealed that Sindh has numerous peasant protests against feudal–police links, police looting, and burning peasants' homes and crops, kidnapping of children, raping of girls, water shortages, price hikes, and food shortages to name a few issues. Police storming these protests and rallies on the feudal lords' command spark more protests from peasants, sometimes leading to death or injuries to the protestors. The media reports that when *haris* are engaged in protests against landowners, their crops get destroyed. However, so far *haris* have only protested disjointedly hence, as an interest group they are not organised enough to make any gains for their rights.[103]

Urbanisation and mechanisation, are beginning to change class dynamics, and may work against traditional feudalism. Villages are no longer self-contained, self-sustaining entities. Urbanisation has provided alternative outlets, making the rural population dependent on towns and cities. Telecommunications and particularly mobile phones are opening up new channels of information and awareness. Where farmers and artisans were once able to sell their skills for an exchange of commodity, today few *kumbhars*, *lohars*, *trakhnars*, and other such skilled labourers exist. The rural population relies on urban industries to provide fine fabrics, services, entertainment, modern marketing, warehousing, and agro-processing etc. Industries can strengthen the linkage between the two. Agriculture credit flows and microfinance are also helping ease the constraints in access to finance.

Markets for leasing and renting agriculture equipment and machinery, tractors, maintaining and repairing them, and even offering services to operate need to be developed to widely share the benefits of mechanisation and modernisation. Small farmers would then be able to increase productivity and cross the threshold of subsistence farming which is keeping them under the tutelage of large farmers.[104] As per the last agricultural census of 2010, of the 1. 115 million total farms in Sindh, 56 per cent are under 5 acres, 35 per cent are between 5 and 25 acres, and only 8 per cent are between 25 and 100 acres.[105] The chances for the remaining one per cent landowners, owning 10 per cent of the agricultural land, making hefty profits through leasing and renting, appear promising.

The growing urban population, the slowdown in the rate of increase of major crops in the last two decades, shrinking irrigation water supply per capita along with its inefficient utilisation and distribution, and absence of any breakthrough in new varietal development have created a worrisome situation for Pakistan's agriculture. The province of Sindh, the highest urbanised area of the country and being lower riparian, faces heightened risks. Public policy changes, investment, and institutional renewal are needed to avert this slowdown. Food security, adequate nutrition of children, rural incomes formation, and employment are likely to be adversely affected unless reforms in agriculture policy and institutions are made and investment in agriculture research and water infrastructure are undertaken.

9

Irrigation

Introduction

WITH rich alluvial soils and sufficient supply of water from the Indus River, Sindh is rightly known as the 'Gift of the Indus'. Sindh has always been an area with a surplus of food. Irrigation from the Indus has depended on inundation as well as perennial canals. Inundation canals take their supplies through cuts in river banks and are dependent on the water level in the river. Since the construction of barrages in Sindh, the irrigation is done through the weir-controlled waters of perennial canals. The perennial canals take their water supply through constructed head works and water level is controlled through the weirs constructed on the barrages across the river. Perennial canals provide a reliable supply throughout the year.

There are certain lands which depend on rain fall and are known as 'Barani' lands. Since rainfall is very low and scanty in Sindh, the traditional means of irrigation are wells, canals, tanks, tubewells, nars etc. With three barrages in operation, covering 13.5 million acres, Sindh now has an impressive modern irrigation system. Sukkur Barrage was the first to be built in 1932. It is the largest barrage system in Pakistan with more than 7.5 million acres as its command area. This is the largest single irrigation system in the world. Kotri Barrage, completed in 1955, commands more than 3 million acres of land. The greater part of the command is non-perennial, with rice and sugarcane as main crops. Guddu Barrage was completed in 1962 and it commands more than 3 million acres. Rice has been the main crop. Sukkur Barrage is fully perennial; the other two barrages are mostly summer barrages. During winter, the water level in the river is very low and this hampers agriculture production.

The irrigation system works through big or main canals or feeder canals. These offtake from the river directly. There are branch canals which offtake from the main or feeder canals, and distributaries offtake from these. There are minor canals and water courses as well. The water courses are privately owned and distribute water to the fields.

Modern Irrigation System

SUKKUR BARRAGE, 1932

The entire project, called the Sukkur Barrage Canals Project, was finally approved after much delay in 1920–21. The seven canals constructed were the northwestern canal, the rice canal, the Dadu canal, the Khairpur feeder west, the Rohri canal, the Khairpur feeder east, and the Nara canal.[1] Of these, only the rice canal is a seasonal canal, the rest being perennial.[2]

Before the construction of Lloyd Barrage, inundation canals were the main sources of water supply for cultivation. During the period from 1870 to 1932, there was almost 115 per cent increase in the area of cultivated land under inundation canals (from 14.19 lac acres in 1873–4 to 30.6 lakhs of acres in 1931–32).[3]

189

The importance of Lloyd barrage can be gauged from the fact that within the first twelve years of its completion, nearly 52 per cent of cultivated land was receiving water through the barrage, compared to 28.6 per cent through inundation canals, and 14 per cent relying on rainfall. For alienated lands, the barrage and inundation canals were the main sources of water supply.[4]

Table 9.1: Canals under Sukkur Barrage Project (1953)

Canal	Cultivable Areas (in Hundred Thousand Acre)	Discharge	
		Kharif	Rabi
Northwestern Canal	9.33	5,042	3,639
Rice Canal	4.81	10,215	-
Dadu Canal	4.99	2,837	2,525
Khairpur Feeder West	3.89	4,000	2,625
Rohri Canal	25.35	10,887	9,900
Khairpur Feeder East	3.36	4,000	2,625
Nara Canal	18.33	13,602	6,959

Source: Sorley, *The Gazetteer of West Pakistan the Former Province of Sind including Khairpur State*, Lahore, Gazetteer Cell, Board of Revenue, 1968, p. 459.

The difference in the magnitude of the coverage of the two types of canals can be deduced from the area brought under cultivation. While the coverage of inundation grew two-fold to cover 30 lac acres in the six decades from 1870 to 1932, the construction of the perennial canals brought about extra 65 lac acres under cultivation within two decades.

The opening of the Sukkur Barrage brought about a sort of revolution for the agricultural development of Sindh, although it does not cover the whole of Sindh. The gross area commanded under the canals is 8.28 million acres and cultivable area commanded is 7.63 million acres. An additional area of 6.5 million acres was brought under cultivation after the barrage and its canals became operational. The area under actual cultivation is about 8 million acres. The Rohri Canal which passes through Khairpur, Shah, and Hyderabad districts, is designed to supply water to 2.7 million acres. This is the largest single canal of the Sukkur system which stretches to 200 miles.

The barrage is a huge river regulator consisting of 66 spans, each 60 feet wide. The regulation of these openings is carried out by means of steel gates, each weighing about 50 tons, operated by electric power. These can also be operated by hand if electric power fails. There are two bridges over this regulator. The lower bridge is called Road Bridge, which is used for traffic and connects the main road on the right bank of the river with that on the left bank. The length of the barrage is one mile. Total length of water courses is 47,800 miles and the total length of the canals regulated by the barrage is 6,473 miles. The monthly withdrawals vary from a minimum of 23,482 cusecs in November to 47,763 cusecs in July through September. The immediate effect of the Sukkur Barrage was a substantial increase in Rabi cropping.

Nearly 32,000 men worked all the year round during the construction phase. In addition, 3,800, 2,100, and 1,100 men were employed daily to operate the large-, medium- and, small-sized machines respectively. In some parts the excavation was carried out by keens, the primitive way of scraping up and depositing the earth outside the canal bed, by means of pairs of bullocks drawing a metal edge board scoop. The Sukkur Barrage scheme cost PKR 20 crore (or 200 million). The funds for the construction of the project were mainly supplied by the Government of India in the form of loans. These loans were repaid by the Bombay government. The funds, required for building roads, strengthening agriculture staff etc. amounting to PKR 10 lac, were provided from the famine funds and supplemented by a grant of PKR 6 lac from the general revenues up to the end of 1934–35. Thereafter, these expenses were met from the revenues collected from the lands brought under cultivation as result of the project. The sale of land in the area was another main source of income. Zamindars and jagirdars, in expectation of irrigation facilities, purchased large tracts of land. A part of the available land was allocated as peasant grants on nominal charges. The opening of the barrage had created new opportunities for land speculators. There was large influx of population from the Punjab eager to make purchases of lands. The result was that the Sindh government—the successor to the Bombay government—was able to repay all the loans within ten years of construction of the barrage.

Crop production received a new impetus with manifold expansion in total area cultivated. Special research was undertaken to improve wheat crop, and high-yielding seeds were introduced with excellent results. Experiments on wheat cultivation showed that under post-barrage conditions of irrigation, early irrigation water could be utilised for wheat fields in October and early November provided suitable tillage methods, designed to preserve the moisture, were adopted. The area under cotton cultivation also expanded significantly. Cotton was an important cash crop even before the barrage construction. New high-yielding varieties of cotton were introduced by the Agricultural Research Department after experimentation. The earlier varieties were Punjab American Cotton and Sindh Desi Cotton which were followed by imported American Cottons and Egyptian Cottons.

Besides cotton and wheat, rice cultivation got a boost in Larkana, Dadu in upper and middle Sindh, and in Badin and Thatta in lower Sindh. The rice canal, which feeds Larkana and other parts of upper Sindh, is helpful for the rice crop. Other crops like jowar, bajra, and a variety of fruits were also brought under cultivation after the construction of the Rohri, Nara, and Dadu canals. Besides the above mentioned crops, oil seeds, pulses, soya beans, berseem, onions, potatoes, and different types of fruits are also grown on a modest scale.

Kotri Barrage, 1955

Some time after the construction of the Sukkur Barrage, it was felt that another barrage should be constructed on the lower Indus. Jamshoro was the chosen site for this barrage and work began in the early 1950s. The barrage was completed in 1955.

The barrage itself is 3,000 ft. long and is designed to pass a maximum flood of 875,000 cusecs. It consists of 44 bays of 60 ft. spans. Each span is provided with gates 21 ft. deep which hold up water 20 ft. above the crest of the barrage. The maximum designed head between the upstream and downstream sides in the cold weather is about 31 ft.

The barrage is provided with a lock channel to facilitate river traffic. That portion of the road bridge over the lock channel is designed to lift to allow boats to pass. A lock is also provided into the Fuleli Canal which will be navigable in part of its length.

There are two dividing walls, one on each side, to enclose the pockets containing the head regulators of the canals. These form de-silting devices, enabling the canals to draw water free from heavier grades of silt, which deposit in the pockets. When sufficient silt is thus deposited, the pocket gates are lifted and the silt scoured out into the river downstream of the barrage. Two piers wider than normal have been built to permit the passage of a very high tension electrical transmission line across the Indus, if required later.

The important city of Hyderabad, which used to get inadequate and unsatisfactory supply of drinking water through pumping from the Indus downstream of the barrage, now receives augmented and improved supply from above the barrage by flow for part of the year and by pumping during the winter.

The barrage is provided with a road bridge of 20 ft. wide with footpaths 4 ft. wide on each side. This additional means of communication proved exceedingly valuable at normal times and particularly so whenever it was necessary to repair the existing Kotri road bridge, which is integrated with the railway bridge. The barrage road bridge is carried on pre-stressed, pre-cast beams.

An over-bridge carried on steel trestles has been provided for operation of gates. The barrage is made of concrete, and the piers and abutments are faced with stone.

The barrage project, as originally designed in the year 1949, was estimated to cost PKR 701 lacs. Due to increase in the cost of labour materials by 60 per cent, the revised cost on the basis of the old design would have been PKR 11 crores. However, the design was modified by Sir Thomas Foy and the main structure was completed at a cost of PKR 6.95 crores.

Under the Kalri Baghar feeder, the canal system on the right bank of the Indus River, below Kotri, commands a cultivable area of about 600,000 acres. The fringe of practically the whole of this alluvial tract lies about 56 miles away from the Kotri Barrage and extends up to the Arabian Sea. This has necessitated construction of the feeder for assured water supply to the network of the existing and the proposed irrigation channels of the lower alluvial tract.

This feeder was named Kalri Baghar feeder because it was to supply water to the two main existing inundation canals, i.e. Kalri and Baghar canals. The Kalri Baghar feeder falls into a lake which has been formed out of natural depressions provided at the end of the hills. This huge reservoir when filled to its designed level of R.L. 54 would spread over an area of about 50 square miles with a length of about 17 miles. The maximum depth of water in the lake is expected to be in the vicinity of 37 feet. At its final level, the live storage of the lake would be about 175,000 acre feet which in a flat country is no mean asset to meet irrigation needs.

The Lower Pinyari feeder is a non-perennial canal with a designed discharge of 13,800 cusecs at head. Up to the twenty-third mile, Old Fuleli serves as feeder, and below that, i.e. Hyderabad Tando Muhammad Khan railway bridge which is called 'C' point, the Lower Pinyari feeder starts. At this point, it has a designed discharge of 13,204 cusecs. It tails at Daro Branch where it bifurcates into two main canal systems, Daro Branch and Pinyari Branch.

This feeder supplies assured supply to Taluka Guni of Hyderabad District and Mirpur Bathoro, Sujawal, Jati, and Shah Bunder of Thatta district. Previously this area, which is quite fertile, suffered due to deficiency of water from inundation canals drawing from the Indus River. Now, after the construction of the Kotri Barrage this area gets assured supply and the Nakkabuli land, which was lying fallow, has been brought under plough. This will yield revenue to the state through sale of land and revised assessment. In addition, it will increase food production for the country.

Fuleli New is a non-perennial canal with a designed discharge of 14,350 cusecs at the head. There is no offtaking channel up to the thirtieth mile cross regulator. At this point, a new canal, Guni Branch, with a discharge of 5,097 cusecs takes off. Below this point, this canal follows the alignment of the existing inundation Fuleli up to the sixty-second mile cross-regulator, and almost all the existing channel are retained with the addition of a few distributaries and minors.

The command of this feeder has also undergone many changes from that of the original project design. Under the project design a perennial area of 281,519 acres, a garden area of 2,868 acres, forest area of 222 acres, and dry Kharif area of 4,593 acres, totalling to an area of 289,202 acres was provided. This perennial area was located on the tail of Fuleli with various distributaries mixed with non-perennial land and their distributaries as well. A separate perennial canal namely Lined Canal with a cultivable area of 187,347 acres was introduced. Likewise, the Guni Branch which was to take off from Pinyari was fixed on this feeder. The Guni Branch is the biggest offtake on this feeder with a discharge of nearly 5,997 cusecs while the remaining offtakes would need to be remodelled for higher discharges. The feeder now provides assured irrigation water to Guni Matli, Tando Bago, and Badin talukas instead of inundation canals with inadequate and erratic supply resulting in low produce. With this assured supply, not only have production levels in the existing land increased but additional area has come under plough as well, thus increasing food production in Sindh.

Lined Channel

The Lined Channel is a perennial canal with a designed discharge of 4,100 cusecs at the head. It runs idle up to RD 110 except withdrawals by pumps near Hyderabad for growing vegetables. It runs idle up to RD 322 from where offtaking channels start getting water. As the name denotes, this canal is lined from head to R 191.8 and below this point it is an earth canal. The Lined Channel commands a gross area of 539,276 acres out of which an area of 487,347 acres is cultivable.

The Gaja Branch is the biggest canal which takes off from the Lined Channel at RD 110. The Gaja Branch, with all its distributaries and minors, commands a cultivable area of 115,274 acres. Its designed capacity is 830 cusecs at the head. The remaining offtaking channels are the existing channels of the Fuleli Feeder which require remodelling for revised discharges.

The main canal is designed on the basis of 8 cusecs per thousand acres of CCA. The Kharif discharge at 45 per cent intensity of various crops is 6.0 cusecs per thousand acres. The canal has thus a provision of 2 cusecs for future utilisation. Moreover, provision has also been made for lengthy water courses at 2 per cent of the discharge and 5 cusecs for 100 sq. miles for road plantation.

Of the total cultivable command area of 487,347 acres, more than half, i.e. 270,324 acres, is Na-Kabuli land and is owned by the government. Only a small proportion of 47,214 acres has been released so far for cultivation. When the remaining area of 198,031 acres is released, as work proceeds, there would be a further boost in crop production.

Guddu Barrage, 1962

The Guddu Barrage on the Indus River is located in the Kashmore district in the north of Sindh. It is the last of three barrages on the Indus River to be constructed for meeting the growing irrigation water requirements of Sindh and parts of Balochistan. Construction of Guddu Barrage began in 1959 and it was completed in 1962. The barrage structure is 4,445 ft. (1,355m) long and consists of 65 spans of 60 ft. each and is a gate-controlled weir type with one navigation lock of 50 ft. span. It has a system of four main canals; two on the left side (Beghari Sindh Feeder/Desert Par Feeder) and two on the right side (Ghotki Feeder and Rainee Canal). Rainee Canal happens to be a flood canal, which is supposed to be operated on receipt of 250,000 cfs discharge at Guddu.

Guddu barrage is used to control water flow in the Indus River both for irrigation and flood control purposes. The canals provide water for irrigation of over 2.6 million acres of agriculture land of Jacobabad, Larkana, Shikarpur, Kashmore, and Sukkur districts of Sindh, and Naseerabad and Jacobabad districts of Balochistan. The Guddu Thermal Power Station, located immediately downstream of the barrage, on the right bank, draws cooling water from the Beghari Sindh Feeder.

With a discharge capacity of 1.2 million cubic feet per second (34,000 m3/s), the maximum flood level height of Guddu barrage is 26 ft. (8m). The 7 meters-wide road bridge over the barrage has reduced the road distance between Lahore and Quetta. The distance between Rahimyar Khan and Kashmore has almost been halved.[5]

The area which receives water from the Guddu Barrage comprises the following districts and talukas:

Right Bank Area:
(i)   Balochistan: Tehsil Nasirabad (Part)
(ii)   Upper Sindh Frontier district (Sindh)
       Taluka Jacobabad Takula Kashmore
       Taluka Kandhkot Taluka Thul
       Taluka Ghari Khairo (Part)
(iii) Larkana district (Taluka Shahdadkot [Part])
(iv)   Sukkur district (Taluka Sukkur [Part])
       Taluka Shikarpur Taluka Ghari Yasin (Part)
Left Bank Area:
(v)   Sukkur district (Sindh) Taluka Ubauro
       Taluka Mirpur Mathelo (Taluka Ghokti)
       Taluka Panoakil, Takula Rohri (Part)

The total gross area under Guddu Barrage is 4,161 square miles, including 311 square miles of Balochistan. The area lying on the right bank of the Indus River is bounded by hills on the north-western side and by the Indus River on the south-east. The ground sloping from the hills in the north towards the south has a very steep slope up to the desert canals, after which it flattens and forms a valley line which the other ridge is the Indus River itself.

The total length of the feeder, Begari–Sindh, is 83.9 miles with the full supply (FS) discharge of the feeder at the head of 15,494 cusecs. The feeder has been remodelled to suit the revised discharges. Seventy-four miles of new channels have been laid out for irrigation to katcha (riverine) area. The total length of old canals remodelled is 391 miles, and the length of new channels constructed is, 89 miles feeder and 232 miles for other channels.

Ghotki feeder

The feeder is 83.6 miles long, inclusive of the length of the left marginal (LM) bund excavated in 1940 and 1947. The FS discharge of the feeder at head is 8,490 cusecs.

The total length of old channels remodelled is 380 miles, and the length of new channels constructed is 54 miles for feeder and 296 miles for and other channels. The length of new channels include the intermediate links proposed to remove bad bends, tortuous courses of channels, and extension of old channels.

The total gross area (including forests) under the command of the Guddu Barrage is 2,663,184 acres and the cultivable command area (excluding forests) is 2,144,590 acres. Of the total CCA, 193,459 acres fall within Balochistan and the remaining within Sindh. The entire forest area of 150,320 acres lies in Sindh only. The command area covers 311 square miles of both provinces.

Under this project, water is made available for growing dry kharif crops at 60 per cent intensity with full supply flow (FSF) of 90 to the entire command on the left bank side. The established rice areas are exceptions. The rice area has been taken as the highest yearly rice cultivation in each Deh and provided with water supply at 100 per cent intensity and 45 FSF. Forest areas are provided at 100 per cent intensity and 66 FSF as on the right bank side. Due to rice cultivation season, the water table also rises and is approximately 15 to 30 ft.

Water Disputes

As stated earlier, the dispute over water sharing between the lower and upper riparian provinces began well before Pakistan came into being. The main dispute has been between Punjab and Sindh. Various committees and commissions were formed from time to time to resolve this issue. All the provinces pleaded their cases before the committees and commissions, but a final settlement could not be reached. Prior to this, in 1945, a Punjab–Sindh agreement was signed but could not get the approval of the governor general. In 1960, the Indus Water Treaty under the auspices of the World Bank was signed between India and Pakistan in which the case of the provinces was also discussed. According to the agreement, three eastern rivers—Bias, Sutlej, and Ravi—were given to India and three western rivers Chenab, Jhelum, and Indus to Pakistan. India however paid compensation for the use of eastern rivers. During the negotiations of the treaty, no representative from Sindh was made a member of negotiating team or the advisory committee.

Sindh has been blaming Punjab for diverting its waters including violation of the 1945 Punjab–Sindh agreement and this is one of the major reasons for the shortage of water in Sindh. Table 9.2 presents a summary of the allocation of water recommended by the various committees and commissions. Sindh province has adhered to the latest 1991 water accord.

Table 9.2: Allocation of Water to the Provinces by Various Committees/Commissions (in MAF) (1945–91)

Region	Sindh Punjab Agreement 1945	Fazal-e-Akbar 1970 Post Indus Water Treaty	Haleem Commission 1976	Ad-hoc Sharing Post Replacement Works 1966–1990	1991 Water Accord
Sindh	48.74	43.79	43.52	50% of Indus Water in early Kharif 67% of Indus water in Rabi	48.76
Punjab	48.33	52.43	54.79	Full Mangla, Jhelum, Chenab rivers. 50% of Indus waters in early Kharif. 33% of Indus water in Rabi	55.94
KP	5.0	5.32	N/A	Full requirement	8.78
Balochistan	1.22	2.7	N/A	Full requirement	3.87
Total	103.29	104.24	-	-	117

Source: Documents of various commissions and committees pertaining to allocation of water to the provinces.

INDUS WATER ACCORD, 1991

The deliberations of committees/commissions such as the Akhtar Hussain Committee, Justice Fazl-e-Akbar Committee, Justice Anwar-ul-Haq Commission, Justice Haleem Committee remained inconclusive as no agreement could be reached and the issue remained unresolved. Only ad-hoc arrangements were made from time to time which created serious bitterness among the provinces. However, in 1991, Nawaz Sharif's first government brought all the provinces together and a water accord was signed on 16 March 1991. The accord was then approved on 21 March 1991, by the Council of Common Interests (CCI). This was considered a sort of achievement for water distribution among the provinces. A formula for the water accord on the basis of water calculation was devolved. Table 9.3 shows the distribution among the provinces for Kharif season, Rabi season, and total allocation.

Table 9.3: Distribution of Water as Per the 1991 Water Accord (in Million Acre Foot)

Province	Kharif	Rabi	Total
Punjab	37.07	18.87	55.94
Sindh*	33.94	14.82	48.76
KP (a)	3.48	2.3	5.78
(b) Civil Canals**	1.80	1.20	3.00
Balochistan	2.85	1.02	3.87
Total	77.34 +1.8	37.01 +1.20	114.35 +3.00

*Including already sanctioned urban and industrial uses for metropolitan Karachi.
**Ungauged civil canals above the rim stations.

Source: Ministry of Water and Power, *The Water Accord 1991*, Islamabad, Government of Pakistan, 1991.

As per the accord, the balance of river supplies (including flood supplies and future storages) were agreed to be in the following ratios: Punjab 37 per cent, Sindh 37 per cent, Balochistan 12 per cent, and Khyber Pakhtunkhwa 14 per cent.

Studies for Downstream Kotri Needs

Clause 7 of the water accord reads as under:

> The need for certain minimum escapage to sea, below Kotri to check sea intrusion was recognised. Sindh held the view, that the optimum level was 10 MAF, which was discussed at length, while other studies indicated lower/higher figures. It was, therefore, decided that further studies would be undertaken to establish the minimal escapage needs downstream Kotri.[6]

Since 1991, studies could not be initiated due to differences of opinion on Terms of Reference (TOR). Upper riparian insisted on the conduct of a study on a single point term of reference of 'sea intrusion'. Lower riparian emphasised study on all needs as per decision incorporated in clause 7 of the accord.[7] However, during 2005, two studies were started through international consultants under supervision of international panel of experts and they have given their reports.

A panel of experts which monitored the two studies, has given the following recommendations for downstream Kotri needs:

(i) Flow of 5,000 cusecs throughout the year.
(ii) A quantum of 25 MAF in five years.

It is pointed out that there is no mention of 'sea intrusion' in the TOR of two studies although there is mention of 'sea water intrusion'. The two terms have different significance. In sea water intrusion, salinity effect by sea water entering into river is found, which has been taken into account under these studies. For checking this coastal erosion, a flow in the river is required to counter-balance it. No study for water requirement to counteract sea intrusion has been done. Thus, the downstream Kotri requirements worked out by two studies are lower than the actual requirements.

The 1991 Accord also established an authority, namely the Indus River System Authority (IRSA), to manage water distribution among the provinces. The headquarters of IRSA are located in Lahore, with the representatives of four provinces as members and one member from the federal government.[8]

The basic purpose of the authority is to allocate water in an equitable manner to the satisfaction of all the federating units.

It is unfortunate to note that there are serious conflicts among the members from time to time and the provinces are claiming that fair distribution of water is not taking place. Sindh claims that it has been the worst sufferer and has always been adversely affected whenever there is overall shortage of water, whereas Punjab does not suffer. However, Punjab does not agree with this view.

Construction of New Dams—Viewpoint of the Provinces

Pakistan needs reservoirs and dams to store excess water during the monsoons and then release it for use in the lean months of winter. Tarbela Dam and Mangla Dam were completed in the 1960s and 1970s and since then there has been no addition to storage. The most contentious project has been the Kalabagh Dam. That project was initiated in the 1980s and feasibility reports were completed in the early 1990s. It had to be abandoned due to protests, particularly by Sindh and the then NWFP (now Khyber Pakhtunkhwa). The construction of the dam would have created discontentment and resentment in Sindh, Balochistan, and Khyber Pakhtunkhwa. The provincial assemblies of all these three provinces have passed resolutions against the construction of the dam. Technical experts of these three provinces have also been providing evidence that Kalabagh was not a feasible project, whereas Punjab has been favouring its construction.

Sindh

Sindh's viewpoint is that Punjab overuses the water and consequently Sindh's share is hugely reduced. This charge is denied by Punjab. Sindh feels that Punjab and KP, being upper riparians, take a major share at the expense of the lower riparian, i.e. Sindh, in accordance with the agreement and accepted practices and policies. Sindh further claims more rights under the Sindh–Punjab agreement of 1945 as three eastern rivers have been transferred to India. Punjab also gets more water through the Chashma–Jhelum Link Canal and Taunsa Punjnad. It is further argued that Punjab has 20–40 inches rainfall per year whereas Sindh has only 4–12 inches. Also, in Punjab the available ground water is 2,500 MAF per year and Sindh has only 3 MAF per year.

During British rule, Sindh had only one barrage that is Sukkur, built in 1932, whereas Punjab had many barrages and other canals on the Indus Basin system. Tarbela and Chashma are also on the Indus River. Twelve link canals were also built to transfer water from western rivers to eastern rivers or the tributaries of the Indus River, all of which benefit the farmers in Punjab.[9]

Issues like loss of coastal land, environmental degradation, adverse effects on biodiversity, health problems, and shortage of drinking water, as well as disappearance of mangrove forests, salinity, problems of pollution, lakes desertification, and deforestation will emerge if Kalabagh is constructed. It is feared that the Indus Delta will disappear and therefore the livelihood of the people drawing sustenance from the delta will vanish. Kalabagh Dam, besides creating acute water shortage and devastating the Indus Delta, would be located in a highly seismic zone.[10]

Punjab

Punjab is reluctant to accept any of the arguments advanced by Sindh against Kalabagh. Punjab's viewpoint is that the water escapage to sea is about 35 MAF which is a big loss.[11] It also argues that 14 MAF water is lost between Sukkur and Kotri barrages.[12] They are of the view that Tarbela and Mangla were built to provide water replacement for three eastern rivers given to India under the treaty. Chashma–Jhelum and Taunsa Punjad were built under the Indus Basin Water Treaty. Punjab says that it needs more water to keep up with the pressure of its growing population; the water is demanded for industrial and agricultural production. Punjab fully supports the Kalabagh Dam.

Committees Formed by General Pervez Musharraf

General Pervez Musharraf, the then chief executive and president of Pakistan, wanted to build Kalabagh Dam. He tried his best and travelled to all the provinces to convince and mobilise the politicians, researchers, intellectuals, civil society and all others to support Kalabagh. His final tour was to Sindh in August 2003, where he announced two committees to examine the Kalabagh Dam issue and give their recommendations for the future reservoirs. One parliamentary committee was formed under the chairmanship of parliamentarian Nisar Ahmed Memon and the other committee was a technical committee on water resources under the chairmanship of A. N. G. Abbasi, a renowned engineer of the country, with members from across Pakistan. The committees were asked to study various projects and give their recommendations. The committee toured across Pakistan and came to the conclusion that Kalabagh Dam was not feasible for the country and some other sites may be selected or studied. The technical committee under the chairmanship of A. N. G. Abbasi was given the following terms of reference:

1. Review issues relating to the distribution of water according to 1991 water apportionment accord and submit recommendations for streamlining water distribution among the provinces.
2. Assess the need for constructing dams/reservoirs for future requirements and make up for shortages of water due to silting of Tarbela and Mangla dams and recommend future storages.
3. Review the progress achieved so far regarding the study on escapages below Kotri and recommend measures to expedite the completion of study.
4. Determine water availability for future reservoirs and irrigation schemes.
5. Ascertain actual quantity of water past downstream Kotri from 1976–2003.
6. Examine operational criteria of link canals and future reservoirs.
7. Examine the filling criteria for Mangla reservoir.
8. Complement the parliamentary committee on water resources.

The technical committee with its eight members held deliberations for two and half years. The data was collected, collated, and computed by various organisations such as WAPDA, Commissioner, Indus River Commission, and members of the technical committee. After the deliberations, the committee was of the view that there would be no surplus water either on the basis of upstream flows or downstream flows except in the flood years which can be stored under a full management. Future reservoirs may be considered and WAPDA has already submitted that three projects were already under construction, namely Greater Thal Canal (Punjab), Rainee Canal (Sindh), and Kachi Canal (Balochistan). The report was submitted to the Government of Pakistan in 2005 but no step has been taken to consider and implement the recommendations of the technical committee.

Left Bank Outfall Drain (LBOD)

To tackle water logging and salinity in the province which was making large tracts of land uncultivable, the Government of Pakistan and Government of Sindh came up with the proposal to construct an outfall drain in which the saline water pumped out could be disposed. As a result, a project was prepared in the late 1970s and presented to the World Bank for financing called Left Bank Outfall Drain (LBOD).

LBOD was constructed to drain water from more than two million hectares of land of Shaheed Benazirabad, Sanghar, Mirpurkhas, and Badin districts into the Arabian Sea. The effluent of LBOD (spinal drain) flows into Dhoro Puran Outfall Drain (DPOD) with a capacity of 2,000 cusecs and Kadhan Pateji Outfall Drain (KPOD) having a capacity of 2,600 cusec. The DPOD empties into Shakoor Lake (a shallow saline of an area about 150 sq. km stretched into Pakistan and India), whereas effluent of KPDO is directly discharged into the sea through the 41 km long Tidal Link Canal.

It is a known reality that after heavy rainfalls, lands in Lower Sindh–Badin used to remain under water for more than six month before LBOD was constructed.[13] The stand-up of rain/flood water for a long period created a serious problem of water logging on the left bank, especially Badin district. Agriculture lands in Badin would turn into marshy sumps after heavy rains.

To address the problems of waterlogging, a large number of saline tubewells were installed in Nawabshah, Mirpurkhas, and Sanghar districts under the LBOD project, which helped a lot in reclaiming the lands in these districts. Now, all these four districts are major produce of cash crops contributing to the agrarian economy of Sindh and Pakistan. These tubewells pumped out the saline water of electrical conductivity (EC Value) ranging from 65,000 million moles to 92000 million moles, as the sea water salinity is about 32,000 million moles.[14]

Draining out such highly saline water into DPOD and ultimately to Shakoor Dhand (estuarine water body/lake in Rann of Kutch distributed by Pakistan–India international border) was objected to by the Indian government and it was also against environmental standards followed by donor agencies. Ultimately the LBOD spinal was connected with the already working KPOD that was designed to convey this highly saline effluent to Shah Samando Creek of the Arabian Sea passing through Kadhan Pateji Dhand Complex. To cure the environmental hazards, two weirs were also designed and constructed. One was constructed at DPOD at the start where its purpose was to stop the saline effluent going into Shakoor Dhand in dry season and allow flood storm water bypassing it (saline water used to flow low in dry times). The second weir was a big one called Cholri Weir, constructed to maintain water level of Kadhan Pateji Dhand Complex through which KPOD was passing. Its purpose was to avoid saline water intrusion in that system and allow storm water to refresh it. (Later in 2001, Cholri Weir also collapsed due to tidal scouring and connected tidal link with Kadhan Pateji Dhand Complex).

Spinal drain with internal drains were proposed to provide access to saline water to the sea so that the sea water in Badin could be pushed back. The spinal drain is fully working now and the water is drained into the sea. Some large tracts of land have been restored to cultivation. During heavy rains, LBOD does not help to drain the water to the sea due to its low capacity. In either of the seasons, rains and intrusion of sea water play havoc in Badin district. The villagers of Badin especially are of the view that the design of LBOD is not according to the required wind direction as the water does not flow properly and does not fulfill the purpose it was built for. As a result of the farmers' pleas, a panel of international experts was appointed by the World Bank. The panel has visited the LBOD area but no positive solution has been found till today.

Due to a lack of maintenance of LBOD, it has wreaked havoc at the tail-end districts, i.e. Mirpurkhas and Badin, due to breaches and overtopping of banks. There have been many issues like weed growth, weak banks, low discharge capacity of LBOD, and silting affecting the area.

The people affected by LBOD see huge risks especially for those living along KPOD, the Tidal Link Canal, and the coastal belt, due to breaches and overtopping of water during monsoon. They believe that Badin being a disaster prone district might face calamity and destruction similar to the floods in 1995, cyclones in 1999, and 2007, and floods again in 2001.

Problems with LBOD

The primary problem with LBOD is lack of clarity about the agency responsible for its operation and maintenance. The system was first handed over to the Irrigation Department but because of negligence and indifference, it was transferred to the SIDA without any significant allocation of incremental funds for O&M expenses.[15]

The operation and maintenance of any system needs continuous supply of funds; in the current system, these funds are generated from revenues of irrigated and cultivated areas.

The secondary problem during the early years of completion was complaints of sea intrusion in tidal link and bed erosion. High tide continues for eight hours, blocks the drainage effluent going into sea, creating back water curve, which results in obstruction of flow with a continuous rise of hydraulic head at the upstream of the obstruction. If not controlled, it further results in damage to structures. During low tide, drainage water speeds upto sixteen hours, causing erosion to the channel bed.

During high tide and storm flood drainage, another problem occurred—the back flow of drainage effluent of the Kotri Barrage surface drain from KPOD into adjacent areas of Badin.

There is also an enforcement, which actually means intervention of local people for short term benefits causing long term losses. Now, when the Sub-Surface System of LBOD (tubewells) is not operational, LBOD is used by people upstream for draining surplus agriculture waste water. Nowadays downstream farmers make cuts to the LBOD spinal drain wherever it is adjacent to Dhoro Puran and use these Dhoras for storage and use that water for agriculture. Then, during heavy rains when the LBOD starts flowing at full supply level, it breaches from the same spot.

Environmental hazards such as drainage from sugar mills and industrial effluents have also exacerbated the situation. Starting right from Sanghar passing through Mirpurkhas and Badin, almost all the sugar mills are producing alcohols and its residue after fermentation of molasses along with used potassium is disposed of in LBOD sub-drains, main drains, and the spinal drain, which causes bad odour, skin diseases, and other health problems for the people living in the area.

During the past sixteen years two major disasters have been reported on the Tidal Link until 2010. The first was a cyclone on 21 May 1999, resulting in the 2001 collapse of Cholri Weir at Dhand complex on KPOD, and the second was in the monsoon rains of 2003, causing overtopping of the spinal drain near Kadhan and Tando Bago. Both the disasters have wreaked havoc on the system and many important lessons were learned including remodelling and redesign of the outfall drain to increase the capacity of the system to carry large volumes of storm efficiently. Besides engineering solutions, a management strategy for O&M was greatly emphasised. For example, in 2003, during heavy monsoon rains irrigation channels like Nara Canal were not closed from the barrage in time. It was only when the conditions got out of control (overtopping/breaches of irrigation canals), that the irrigation channels were given escape into LBOD; it was already flowing at its full design discharge capacity of 4,600 cusecs—resulting in rain flood water of about 12,000 to 14,000 cusecs. When the water was flushed towards the sea, it was faced with a high tide—the timing of which has been ignored while opening canal gates resulting in an overflow of LBOD near Kadhan. This brought a silent death wave and an inundation of adjacent areas up to Tando Bago and Pangrio. Several casualties and loss of agricultural crops and livestock was also reported. The LBOD was the only water way that drained out flood water back into the sea after one week.

Under the national drainage programme, the army engineering corps took some remedial measures. As a result, the size of the LBOD spinal drain and that of the Mirpurkhas main drain was increased.

LBOD is the only way out of drainage and flood effluence because the Indus River flows on a ridge and Shakoor Dhand has a limited capacity.

Suggestions for the Improvement of LBOD

1. The capacity of LBOD should be further expanded so that it can withstand and discharge runoff of torrential monsoon rainfall safely into sea.
2. The banks and bed of LBOD, if possible, should be lined.
3. Like irrigation network, drainage network should also be continuously operated, maintained and repaired.
4. The groundwater quality of the coastal belt should be continuously monitored in order to assess and keep watch on the sea water intrusion.
5. A scientific study should be carried out on the mitigation of impacts of soil salinisation. The land reclamation programme for coastal soils should be initiated.
6. Mangroves should be planted along the coastal belt in order to minimise erosion along tidal creeks, provide feed and natural habitat to fish stocks, and to minimise environmental degradation due to sea water intrusion.
7. A comprehensive strategy should be prepared for protection, promotion, and restoration of livelihood and sources such as agricultural land, livestock, fisheries, grazing areas, and forests for the people of Badin.

Right Bank Outfall Drain (RBOD)

RBOD was also conceived for the districts on the right bank. The work of RBOD was divided into three phases, but has still not been completed. During his tenure, General Musharraf had given a boost to the construction of RBOD but work has slowed down since 2008 and has been suspended subsequently.

RBOD-I

This covers Larkana, Qambar Shahdadkot, Dadu and Jamshoro districts. The scope of the work is to provide outfall facilities to the existing and proposed drainage project and improve environmental conditions in Manchar and Hamal lakes. It also includes rehabilitation of the existing drainage system, Indus link discharge, extension of RBOD up to Miro Khan zero point, remoulding of MNV drain for 3,500 cusecs, Ratodero Surface Drainage Project, Miro Khan Surface Drainage Project, Shahdadkot Surface Drainage Project, and monitoring the quality of effluent of the project area. The executing agency is WAPDA.

RBOD-II

RBOD-II is also a mega drainage project spread over 273 km running along the right bank of the Indus River. The drain will be connected to RBOD-I at Sehwan and will carry the effluent directly to the sea at Gharo. RBOD-II extends from Sehwan to the Arabian Sea. It would cost PKR 14 billion and is expected to be the third largest drain in the world. The covered area under the project is 4.30 million acres. The designed discharge of RBOD is 3,525 cusecs. Initially, the disposal was planned for Manchar Lake, the biggest ever natural lake in the country. However, this would have spoiled the environment of Manchar Lake and would affect the livelihoods of those dependent on the lake. It must be mentioned here that the Main Nara Valley Drain (MNV), bringing effluents from Balochistan, is already emptying into Manchar Lake. The Government of Sindh has expressed strong reservations and there is general public outcry against this disposal directly to Manchar or to Indus at Sehwan. It is said that the completion of the RBOD-II is expected by June 2017. The revised cost now is PKR 64 billion.

RBOD-III

The project is located on the right bank of the Indus River, within the area of districts Nasirabad and Jafarabad of Balochistan and district Jacobabad and Kambar Shahdadkot of Sindh province.

The main objective of RBOD-III is to provide disposal facilities for the existing and proposed drainage projects to reclaim the agricultural land to area (GCA) of 67,930 acres. The components to be covered under RBOD-III are as follows: Hairdin carrier drain extension from Chukhi to MKZP and 6 km north of Chukhi, construction of irrigation channel form re-utilisation of 400 cusecs of Balochistan effluent, RBOD extension from MKZP to Hairdin pump station, re-modelling of Shahdad Kot main drain, surface drainage system of Usta Muhammad unit, Hadero drainage unit and Usta Muhammad drainage unit.

Institutional Reforms

SINDH IRRIGATION AND DRAINAGE AUTHORITY (SIDA)

Recognizing the need for a new strategy of participatory irrigation management, the Government of Pakistan during in 1996 decided to introduce institutional reforms in irrigation and established provincial irrigation and drainage authorities in each province. In 1997, a new programme of a self-sustaining irrigation system was established which involved (a) transforming provincial irrigation departments into provincial irrigation and drainage authorities (PIDAs); (b) creating area water boards (AWBs); (c) organising farmers into farmer organisations (FOs). Under these reforms, all provinces established irrigation and drainage authorities through an Act passed by the assemblies in their respective province. This was in fact the first move for introducing participatory irrigation management (PIM) at a larger scale throughout the country.

The Sindh Assembly passed the Sindh Irrigation and Drainage Authority (SIDA) Act in 1997, and as a result, SIDA was established in 1998 followed by one area water board on Nara Canal in 1999 and two area water boards in 2002 on the Ghotki Feeder Canal and left bank canals.

The SIDA Act 1997 was replaced/repealed by the Sindh Water Management Ordinance (SWMO) 2002. The main functions of SIDA are:

- Operation and maintenance of barrages in the province of Sindh.
- Distribution of irrigation water from the barrages to the AWBs.
- Construction, operation, and maintenance of the outfall drains.
- Receive effluent drainage water from AWBs and convey it to the sea.
- Maintain the flood protection infrastructure along the Indus River.
- Act as the prime agent of change, giving advice to AWBs and FOs.
- Provide advice to the government.

SIDA is being managed by a board in which farmers play an important role. Besides farmers, there are some independent members from fields such as that of agriculture, social development, environment, irrigation, and drainage, etc.

CANAL AREA WATER BOARDS

The second tier of the water management system consists of Area Water Board (AWB). The AWBs will be responsible for:

- Operation and maintenance of the main and branch canals.
- Distribution of irrigation water to the FOs.
- Maintenance of intermediate drainage infrastructure.
- Paying SIDA for the irrigation water received.
- Charging FOs for the irrigation water they distribute to them.

The AWBs also have members who oversee the management. In Sindh, out of fourteen canals, six were notified and passed into five AWBs (Table 9.4). The last two canals have not been handed over to SIDA as yet.

Table 9.4: Area Water Boards, Divisions, and Barrages

Number	Area Water Board	Division	Barrage
1	Nara Canal Year of Establishment: 1999 Total FOs to be formed: 170 FOs formed: 162	Jamrao, Mithrao and Thar Divisions, Sanghar and Mirpurkhas Drainage Divisions Mechanical Division	Sukkur
2	Left Bank Canal Circle Year of Establishment: 2002 Total FOs to be formed: 105 FOs formed: 81	Phuleli Division Akram Wah Division Guni Division Tando Mohammad Khan Drainage	Kotri
3	Ghotki Feeder Canal Year of Establishment: 2002 Total FOs to be formed: 94 FOs formed: 70	Ghotki Irrigation Mirpur Irrigation Ghotki Tubewell	Guddu
4	Western Canal Year of Declaration: 2002 Total FOs to be formed: 127 FOs formed: nil (area not yet handed over)	Rice Canal Division Northern Dadu Bund Division Southern Dadu Division Northern Dadu Canal Division	Sukkur
5	Begari Feeder Canal Year of Declaration: 2002 Total FOs to be formed: 85 FOs formed: nil (area not yet handed over)	Begari Division Begari Sindh Feeder Division Sukkur Begari Bund Division	Guddu

Source: Adapted from documents of Sindh Irrigation and Drainage Authority (SIDA), Government of Sindh, and Water Sector Improvement Project (WISP), Planning and Development Department, Government of Sindh.

FARMER ORGANISATIONS

Farmer organisations (FOs) have been established at the distributary/minor level in order to transfer the management responsibility from public/irrigation department to farmers. The responsibility includes channel operation and maintenance, abiana assessment and collection, equitable water distribution, organisational management, and conflict resolution. The management of the system at the distributaries/minor level has been progressively transferred to the FOs which are owned and controlled by them. The FOs receive water from the AWBs and supply it to the farmers and users at the water course/field levels.

The FOs are formed on the minor/distributary system through elections by farmers. The water course associations are the constituent bodies of the FOs. Formed through the process of social mobilisation, 354 farmer organisations have been formed on all three canal AWBs and the process for the remaining FOs is under way, while 314 FOs have taken over the management of water distribution and collection of abiana and small rehabilitation works.

It seems that the demand for irrigation reforms in Sindh province has achieved a high degree of support from farmers, especially small and tail-end farmers.

PHYSICAL PROGRESS

SIDA has executed many physical projects under the National Drainage Project (NDP), Sindh On-Farm Water Management Project (SOFWP), and Second Flood Protection Sector Project (SFPSP) as follows:

National Drainage Project (NDP)

- Modernisation of forty-six channels in three AWBs under NDP.
- Rehabilitation of Ghorabari surface drainage system and Ghorabari regulator in progress.
- Construction of Phul and Daulatpur surface drainage system in progress.
- Rehabilitation of Thatta II surface drainage system, Part II (five packages) complete.
- Rehabilitation of Nagan Dhoro surface drainage system, Part I and II complete.
- Rehabilitation of Jamsakro I and II surface drainage system.

Sindh On-Farm Water Management Project (SOFWM)

- Rehabilitation/Improvement of Distributaries/Minors (eleven channels completed).
- Rehabilitation/Improvement of Distributaries/Minors (work on more than eighty channels is in progress).
- Rehabilitation/Improvement of Branch Canals (six channels in progress).

Second Flood Protection Sector Project (SFPSP)

- Twenty sub-projects (twenty-three contracts) of flood protection works under SFPSP funded by Asian Development Bank (ADB 75 per cent share and GoP 25 per cent share) have been completed.

WATER SECTOR IMPROVEMENT PROJECT

To enhance long term sustainability of the irrigation system through participatory irrigation management, modernisation of irrigation and drainage system, and flood control issues of the province, a project, namely the Water Sector Improvement Project, was negotiated with the World Bank by the Government of Sindh in 2006. The main aim of the project was to increase agricultural production and employment and incomes of farmers cultivating about 1.8 million hectares of land, i.e. more than 30 per cent of the irrigated area in Sindh. The project Phase I—at a total cost of PKR 30,353 million, with a World Bank share of PKR 28,840 million and PKR 1,513 million as a share of the Government of Sindh—was approved by ECNEC in September 2007. The project has many components as follows:

a.   Community development and capacity building of SIDA, AWBs, and FOs.
b.   Rehabilitation and improvement of irrigation and drainage network.
c.   Assess management and measure irrigation and drainage infrastructure.
d.   Project monitoring and evaluation, and project impact.
e.   Project coordination and management.

The project covers three area water boards, i.e. Nara Canal Area Water Board, Left Bank Canals Area Water Board, and Ghotki Feeder Canal Area Water Board.

One of the major objectives of the project is to enhance long-term sustainability of the irrigation system through participatory irrigation management, to address the modernisation needs of irrigation, and drainage of the system in a systematic way, leading to increased agricultural production and employment.

The project covers the districts of Ghotki, Sukkur, Khairpur, Sanghar, Mirpurkhas, Umer Kot, Tando Muhammad Khan, Hyderabad, and Badin. WSIP has the following components:

1.   Community development and capacity-building of SIDA and AWBs, enabling them to perform their responsibilities according to the Sindh Water Management Ordinance. The project would enhance capacity-building of FOs to carry out operation and maintenance of the irrigation and drainage system effectively.
2.   Rehabilitation and Improvement of Irrigation and Drainage System: Rehabilitation and improvement of the irrigation and drainage network of three AWBs including 7 main canals, 28 branch canals, 130 distributaries/minors, and 200,000 ha. drainage area.
3.   Assets Management of Major Irrigation and Drainage infrastructure: The feasibility study for rehabilitation of Guddu Barrage will have to be prepared and assistance will be provided for preparing studies for rehabilitation of Sukkur and Kotri barrages. A regional master plan would be prepared to deal with floods and drainage issues on the left bank of the Indus River and designing measures for improvement of the Indus delta and the coastal zone.
4.   Monitoring and Evaluation of the Project Impact and Environmental Management Plan: This would be for monitoring and evaluation and supervision of the Environment Management Plan (EMP) and Social Action Plan (SAP).
5.   Project Coordination, Monitoring, Technical Assistance, and Trainings: For proper coordination, monitoring of implementation activities, management and supervision of the procurement by FAO Team, and technical assistance and training.

SIDA is the lead implementing agency with close coordination and support of respective AWBs and FOs. The irrigation department is one of the project partners for implementation of the barrage studies component. The planning and development (P&D) department is responsible for overall project coordination, supervision, and monitoring through the Project Coordination Monitoring Unit (PCMU) established in the P&D department to handle day-to-day coordination activities of the project.

Sediment inflow into the Nara command area has been reduced through the construction of three fall structures on the Upper and Lower Nara Canal as well as remodelling of both. The fall structures act to reduce the velocity of flow, reducing erosion within these canals. This in turn reduces the concentration of sediment carried into the downstream system, where it would otherwise deposit on the bed of secondary and tertiary canals where flow velocities are reduced. The ultimate result is to increase the conveyance efficiency and capacity of canals within the command area to ensure full design discharges can be delivered to farm outlets through the following works:

- Rehabilitation of Makhi Complex (including construction of new Makhi cross-regulator, Mithrao and Khipro Canal head regulators, and Bakar Distributary head regulator).
- Remodelling of Khipro Canal from head to RD 70.5 (14th Mile Cross-Regulator).
- Replacement of 6nr. cross-regulators on Khipro Canal.
- Construction of new Samarjo Branch head regulator.
- Replacement of 14nr. minor and distributary head regulators offtaking from Khipro Canal and all existing direct outlets.
- Construction of SIDA offices in Hyderabad.
- Refurbishment of Nara AWB offices in Mirpurkhas.
- Flow measurement at Jamrao Head and Makhi Complex, with remote sensing using SCADA.

All the above works as a package are completed from every aspect.

The major cost of PKR 77.0 billion is earmarked for civil works for activation of Dhoras, constructions surface drains and rehabilitation and improvement of existing drainage systems within implementation period of seven years.

Some community structures such as hand pumps, village foot and road bridges and washing ghats etc. have been constructed under the project. Installation of hand pump in project area provided safe drinking water to all sections of rural life. Health conditions have improved due to significant reduction in cases related to waterborne diseases like malaria, hepatitis etc. In addition, the construction of washing ghats has positive impact on village women who now get their clothes washed in a safe and convenient manner. Washing ghats have proved a point of assembly for social interaction for women as well.

Assessment of Institutional Reforms

Lately, it has been seen that the institutions responsible for irrigation management are not functioning properly and efficiently, and there is a visible lack of coordination. This is affecting the future management of the Irrigation Department and Sindh Irrigation & Drainage Authority (SIDA). There are not at the collaborative level and there were initially thought to be.

Irrigation Department and the farmer organisations are not able to address the institutional reforms and reap the expected benefits of user participation. It can be said here that the problems as described below should be addressed sooner so that governance in the irrigation and water sector can be improved and starts giving better results.

There is a bigger issue of tail-end farmers who are still not able to get a proper share of the water supply and have been complaining even though the FOs have worked well in water distribution. There is less accountability, 'at this level, where the task is management of main canals, the SIDA model and the 2002 (SWMO) required an organisation of FO and the AWB to manage the canals. This has not worked well, and this is the organisational level that needs review and restructuring.'[16]

As per the Sindh Water Management Act (SWMO) 2002–14, canal AWBs were to be formed but only three have been formed. The irrigation department was approached by SIDA a number of times to establish more AWBs and FOs to strengthen institutional reforms but all in vain. The three AWBs, at work since 2002, have been doing so without elections although as per the Ordinance 2002, elections have to take place every three years. Elections can bring better people as members of the board otherwise the government nominates people of their choice on political basis and this does not work. The lower tier members such as the governing body of the farmer organisations and water users' association (WUA) are elected. These are quite popular with the farmers who then support this system.

Following the SIDA Act 1997 and promulgation of Ordinance 2002, lack of noticeable improvement has been observed in terms of arresting the deterioration of the irrigation system and providing more satisfactory services to water users since institutional reorientation. The irrigation department and SIDA should adhere to SWMO 2002 to reform institutions such as AWBs, FOs, and WUAs and also monitor their performance.

The intended institutional reforms still need to be implemented in the remaining eleven canals which the irrigation department shall transfer to SIDA. This requires a lot of social mobilisation for which new AWBs are required to be established to distribute the water at the lowest level and reduce conveyance losses. The canals under the irrigation department have many direct outlets which are completely illegal and there seems to be no pragmatic mechanism to stop direct outlets. SIDA and the AWBs have put in efforts to improve the delivery system and reduce theft and curb direct outlets which are a menace for the irrigation system in Sindh. Through these illegal direct outlets, thousands of cusecs are being stolen by the big landlords and jagirdars in the entire Sindh.

The original Ordinance of 2002 did not provide for the minister of irrigation as the chairperson of SIDA; the idea was to keep SIDA purely a business concern managing irrigation and drainage. As such, the first chairperson of SIDA was a non-politician. It was only when the elected government was installed in 2008 that the then minister irrigation was inserted in the Ordinance and became its chairperson. Perhaps that is when the inevitable political considerations crept in SIDA's working.

The first managing director SIDA was a graduate of the world-renowned Wharton School of Finance & Business Management and hired by the SIDA Board as per SWMO. Subsequent managing directors have been posted by the irrigation department. The present managing director of SIDA is also a serving superintending engineer of ID, (posted in SIDA) which is not favourable to reforms. Thus, the autonomous corporate character of SIDA is compromised. Likewise, the directors of AWBs are also from ID.

Institutional reforms envisaged under the SWMO 2002 have actually been sabotaged. This can be judged from the fact that the SIDA board, which now consists of government nominees, is not serious about the organisation. The board is supposed to meet bi-monthly but meets only occasionally. The objective of SIDA becoming an autonomous, accountable, and participatory water management authority cannot be achieve under such circumstances. The same conditions prevail at the lower levels.

None of the three AWBs have drafted and approved required regulations for the election and the farmer members of the board have been selected directly by the government according to their political affiliations. Initially, the irrigation department posted their engineers as directors of AWBs till the Sindh High Court ruled that directors shall be appointed by the boards in a transparent manner as laid down in the Ordinance—a triumph for reformers. But this euphoria proved short-lived since very soon the board appointees were booted out and irrigation department engineers were reposted, which shows the disregard for the Ordinance (and by implication the reform).

Farmer participation is the spirit of the system and both the Water Course Associations (WCAs) and CAC were designed in this sense; however, no AWB has established WAC or CAC so far. According to the Ordinance 2002, the FO membership shall be open only to WCAs and Drainage Beneficiary Groups (DBGs) and the FO shall act through its general body comprising representatives of the WCAs and DBGs. Daily management of the FO affairs shall be carried out by the board of management consisting of elected members (chairman, vice-chairman, secretary, treasurer, and two additional members), ex-officio member, advisory member, and co-opted advisory member. According to the Ordinance 2002, FOs are also supposed to establish in their command areas WAC and CAC committees like SIDA and AWBs. The organisational structure designed by the Ordinance for the FOs is too ambitious and complex.

SWMO 2002 assigns enormous responsibility to the FO, almost similar to those of a sub-division of the irrigation department. To be able to discharge all these functions, the FO require extensive support, on-the-job training, guidance, and incubation. This is hard to come by, considering the state of development and commitment of its supposedly mentor organisations, SIDA and AWB.

- So far, only 17 per cent of FOs in the project area have attained enough capacity to handle some of their responsibilities. The development level achieved by the FOs is not enough to shoulder their total responsibilities.
- FOs are keeping alive the reform process, despite limited support which they can get from SIDA and/or AWBs.
- The major difference between 'effective' and 'non-effective' FOs is leadership capacity of the chairman and the dedication of the FO members.
- Construction of the FO office buildings is the most visible sign of the reform initiative and this creates a sense of participation and cooperation.
- Relatively easier and more comfortable contacts of the FO chairman or vice chairman with the AWB management is a very important change introduced by the reform process.

Improvement of managerial skills and technical knowledge of FOs is the most crucial SIDA activity in the period of transition for their participation and system sustainability. The SIDA has held twenty-three training programmes for FOs so far.

Abiana assessment and collection is the most critical issue in terms of the creation of a financially viable system. According to the Ordinance 2002, FOs are supposed to carry out Abiana assessment and collection tasks but, the task is beyond the capacity of many FOs. As a matter of fact, only 37 per cent of FOs have the needed capacity. The Abiana collection target was fixed at PKR 1,034.69 million for the period 2001–02 to 2011–12 and by the end of the first quarter of 2013, a total recovery of PKR 488.41 million (47.20 per cent) was made.

The performance of FOs is monitored and evaluated on a quarterly basis by monitory and evaluation committees. Based on some performance criteria such as organisational development, irrigation service delivery, management of physical conditions of channels, dispute resolution, and Abiana assessment and collection, the performance level of the FOs by end of March 2013 show that 37 per cent FOs scored 'good' in the organisational development category. Regarding irrigation service delivery, no FO reached the 'good 'category, while, thirty-three of sampled FOs scored a 'satisfactory' grade. The performance in management of physical conditions of channels was 'good' for 25 per cent of sample FOs. The data shows that all the sampled FOs are 'good' on dispute resolution. The lowest FO performance was found in Abiana assessment and collection, where none of the sample FO qualify for the 'good' category, while, only 4 per cent of FOs were found 'satisfactory'.

In other words, the irrigation department and their political masters have captured the SIDA and its ancillary organisations by not allowing elections of the SIDA board by the water users in a democratic way and selecting members of their own choice. This fragmented approach should be abandoned.

Summing Up

Ever since being introduced, the irrigation system has sustained Sindh's agricultural economy and is the key to Sindh's future. The irrigation system, which has been stretched over the years, has been able to miraculously cope up with the increased demand and pressure. An important indicator, testament to the monumental sustenance of the irrigation system, are the cropping intensities and these now stand at 150 per cent—way beyond the 90 per cent foreseen at the inception of the system.[17]

The irrigation system is also crucial for the myriad of services that it delivers. The canal system not only provides water to the crops, but it is also the source of drinking water for the population and livestock. It also used to provide a lot of opportunities related to fisheries and navigation. The canal and drainage system infrastructure are important for transport and tree plantation and can play a role in housing and leisure. Being the defining element in the rural landscape of Sindh, the management of the irrigation and drainage systems goes way beyond agriculture, touching upon all economic and social functions.

The problems facing the irrigation institutions are well known: finance, innovation, performance, governance, and, engagement with all stakeholders. The stress placed on the irrigation system also comes at a price—in terms of less rigor, more encroachment, interference in maintenance, and uncertain financing. In order to fulfil its role towards a more prosperous future, the said complexities need to be fixed—if the irrigation sector is to be protected. The challenge of climate change has already added to the woes and the frequent flood events of the last five years are a testament to it.

The irrigation sector still uses 91 per cent of the water in Sindh yet the efficiency is still low.[18] It is estimated that 60 to 65 per cent of delivered irrigation water is lost due to seepage at the main canals, lack of governance, i.e. notorious direct outlets (DOs) at the distributary canals, and poor water management at the on-farm level. While the Government of Sindh is trying improve efficiency in various projects, the effort so far has been piecemeal, mainly due to the lack of collaboration between the irrigation department and the agriculture department. It should be noted that the loss of surface water would not only waste the precious resources, but also harm agricultural production through more salinisation.[19]

As mentioned above, the irrigation system is far more intensely used than it was ever meant to and it has been able to deliver. There are now far higher crop intensities because many canals carry more water than their design capacity and there is an intense use of the irrigation and drainage network for other functions. Moreover, there is an almost complete conversion of the riverine flood plains to farmland.

The only way forward for Sindh's water management is to opt for a balanced supply of surface water, in order to promote the conjunctive use of ground and surface water wherever possible. This is due to the fact that the salinity levels have risen and there is a need to free up water in the process for multifunctional use. This would also entail controlling the incessant pollution, which is caused by the discharge of untreated wastewater and enforcing treatment as well as promoting reuse of wastewater—the latter is profitable in some cases.

The province of Sindh has limited fresh groundwater aquifers, which are also facing over-utilisation. This is an open invitation for saline aquifers to permanently encroach upon this precious resource. Limited areas of Sindh, including the riverine area upstream Dadu, South Rohri Canal Command and Northern Right Bank aligned with the Indus, have fresh groundwater available for use; however, it is not a viable option for the majority of agricultural lands.

It is pertinent to mention here that water is scarce in Sindh and there is a need to change the cropping pattern such as sugarcane, rice, etc.—crops, which consume a lot water. Landlords do not pay heed to the problem and issue of water shortage and continue with their old crops. It is only the small and tail-end farmer, who eventually bears the brunt of the fixed cropping-pattern. The only feasible way forward for Sindh is to reform, rationalise and revitalise the canal irrigation system along with legislation for regulation of groundwater use as well as the cropping pattern as per water availability.

10

Infrastructure

Introduction

INFRASTRUCTURE, particularly electricity and roads, are essential for economic growth. If such facilities become available in backward areas, the incidence of poverty declines. The dualistic economy of Sindh with advanced urban and metropolitan areas coexisting with the rural villages makes it more critical. Farm to market roads connecting to the main arteries can fetch better prices for the farmer's produce, while electricity can enable processing, storage, and preservation of perishable commodities. This leads to increased productivity and economic efficiency.

Another important component of infrastructure is telecommunication. Accessibility of telecommunication, especially in rural areas, has improved the price discovery mechanism and bargaining power of small and medium farmers. Teledensity has made a spectacular jump from 4 to 80 per cent between 2003 and 2013. Broadband growth has boomed after the introduction of the 3G and 4G spectrum. Consequently, the Information and Communications Technology (ICT) industry has shown momentum, providing jobs to young talented professionals.

One of the major constraints facing infrastructure development in Sindh is the weak institutional capacity of departments responsible for provision of infrastructure. Technical expertise is outdated, processes and procedures are antiquated, project management capability is poor and rent-seeking is rampant. Therefore, cost overruns and time delays in completion of the projects are quite common and the gap between planned cost-benefit ratios and the actual becomes wider.

The other area that has been neglected is the maintenance of existing infrastructure. There is glamour, visibility, and recognition associated with the inauguration of new roads, highways, bridges etc. but nothing to brag about keeping an existing highway in good operating condition. Allocations for maintenance are made sparsely and are either consumed in wages and salaries or misappropriated. The benefits to the citizens, farmers, and businesses from a well-maintained road or a railway track far exceed those from scanty allocations made for a large number of new construction projects that remain incomplete for a long period of time.

Roads

The total road network in Pakistan is approximately 259,618 km of which 12,000 km consist of national highways and 2,207 km of motorways under the responsibility of the federal government. There are 180,000 km of high quality roads. Pakistan ranks 79 out of 137 countries on quality of roads.[1] Road density stands at just 33 per cent compared to 113 per cent in India.

At the time of Independence, the share of Sindh in the national road network was limited to approximately 1039 km of blacktopped roads.[2] The National Highway that accounted for 63 per cent of this inheritance (664 km from Karachi to Reti), was the only properly constructed road. To this date Sindh, despite the increase in its total high type road mileage to 19,673 km, lags far behind the standard road length of 1 km per square km of area.[3]

A couple of years into the post-Independence era, the road network in West Pakistan served to lend support to the railway-centric transport system.[4] However, Sindh did not have a road network as well-developed as the rest of West Pakistan, a characteristic it shared with Balochistan and tribal areas. By 1955, the Road Transport Board in Sindh had been restructured to allow for the representation of railways to achieve railroad coordination. Retention and full utilisation of an existing road network was given preference over the construction of another in the First Five-Year Plan. The improvement of the Karachi–Lahore–Peshawar–Landi Kotal road was given priority.[5]

The focus of the Second and Third Plan period remained on road development, expansion, and improvement of existing roads. However, allocations were made to initiate targeted projects such as the mobilisation of rural and newly developing areas through secondary roads and construction of super highways. The construction of Malir Bridge (Karachi), the super highway connecting Karachi to Hyderabad, and the bridge over the Indus River in Thatta–Sujawal section were achieved in the Third Plan period.[6]

The emphasis on the development of roads vis-à-vis railways development in West Pakistan was also part of the Fourth Plan period. Out of the total Fourth Plan allocation of PKR 2,200 million, the allocation for roads was 50 per cent, surpassing that of railways.[7] The share of roads in the public sector, in the Annual Development Programme of Sindh in 1970–71 was 39 per cent. Upgradation of the Peshawar to Karachi road to a two-lane super highway and improvement of the West Circular Route connecting Karachi Port with the terminal of Karachi–Hyderabad highway was completed under the fourth Five-Year Plan.[8]

From 1970 to 1978, road mileage of 2,690 miles in Sindh were either constructed or improved, contributing 31.7 per cent to the total national road network. The shift of development from railways to roads became more pronounced in 1975–80, as posited by the allocation of provincial public sector funds entirely to highways.[9] However, the development of the highway network was undermined due to inadequate primary road network, poor quality of the roads, and deficient capacity within the planning and executing agencies. Construction of Dadu–Moro Bridge over the Indus River was undertaken during the Fifth Plan period.[10] The major highway projects conceived during the Sixth Five-Year Plan period 1983–88 included overlay on the Karachi–Hyderabad Super Highway and 850 km of second carriageway along the Karachi–Peshawar Highway.[11]

By the beginning of the last decade of the twentieth century, Karachi–Hyderabad and Hyderabad–Hala sections had been completed under the fourth IBRD Highway Project, and work had been initiated on the Nuriabad–Sehwan section of the Indus Highway.[12]

The Eighth Five-Year Plan introduced projects to restrict short lead traffic to roads aimed at furthering the shift of freight traffic to railways. Induction of private sector and tolling were planned to complement road infrastructure development. The focus during this period was to fill the gaps in the existing infrastructure to improve the efficiency of roads. Dualisation and rehabilitation of N-5 to a considerable extent had been achieved by 1995–96. Construction of Gharo–Keti Bandar Road and Sukkur Bypass were also the major projects initiated in 1995–96.[13]

Dualisation of N-5 extended till 2000–01 and was expected to continue beyond. The same year saw the completion of Kotri–Manjhand–Sehwan, Khrappa Chowk–Badabher and Ratodero–Ghouspur–Shori Nullah sections of the Indus Highway, Khuzdar–Shahdadkot Road, and ongoing work on the improvement of N-65 and Ratodero–Shahdadkot–Quba Saeed Khan road.[14] In 2005–06 began the upgradation of the Karachi–Hyderabad Super Highway to a motorway.[15]

By 2010, freight traffic carried by roads rose to 95 per cent, marking its clear domination in the transport sector.[16] In the first five years of the 2000s' decade, new roads covering 4,990 km were added and 2,940 km of the existing network was improved. This included the rehabilitation and improvement of certain stretches of N-5 and N-25.[17] Sindh achieved a road length of 0.57 km per square km of land area,[18] which although below the norm, was the highest among all the provinces. The construction of Sehwan–Khairpur–Nathan Shah–Ratodero section of the Indus Highway, bridge over the Indus River at Larkana, road from Gharo to Ketti Bunder, Karachi–Hyderabad Motorway, and Lyari Expressway were expected to be completed till 2015 but some of these projects have run into difficulties.[19]

Under the tenth Five-Year Plan, the road maintenance plans in Sindh were largely curtailed, and only 750 km of road network was envisioned to be improved out of total rehabilitation of 9,610 km of road network across Pakistan.[20] The new projects envisaged were the construction and improvement of Hyderabad–Mirpurkhas–Umerkot–Khokhropar Road (N-130) and construction of bridges over the Indus River at Kandhkot–Ghotki and Jherruck–Mulla Katyar to provide east–west links between N-5 and N-55.[21] Between the years 2007–2012, the mileage of high type roads increased by more than 7,000 km. Khairpur district benefitted the most as more than 1,450 km were added to the existing road network in the district.

Table 10.1: Road Mileage (Principal Highways) and Motor Vehicles in Sindh
(2000–01 to 2014–15)

Year	Total Mileage of Roads (km)	Rate of Change (%)	Total Motor Vehicles on Road	Rate of Change (%)
2000–01	7,098.6	-	973,516	-
2005–06	9,716.0	36.9	1,056,519	8.5
2010–11	16,868.1	73.6	1,905,304	80.3
2014–15	33,427.9	98.2	1,008,255	-47.1

Source: Transport and Mass Transit Department, Government of Sindh, Karachi, n.d.

Table 10.1 presents the progress made in expanding the road network in the province, i.e. more than four-fold since 2000–01. Consequently, the number of motor vehicles on the roads also multiplied, creating traffic congestion and air pollution, and increased accidents. Cities such as Karachi, Hyderabad, Sukkur, and Larkana had to invest in flyovers, underpasses, bridges, and ring roads to ease traffic problems. It is, however, ironical that such improvements do induce greater penetration of the motor vehicles. The absence of a reliable and affordable public transport system has further exacerbated this problem.

Railways

The broad-gauge railway network inherited at the time of Independence, served as the cornerstone of Pakistan's transport system in the early decades. The railway network was the backbone for the movement of goods from the port in Karachi, and a system of main lines made its way into Sindh through the valley parallel to the Indus River. Rehabilitation of railways received a great deal of attention and by 1955, 100 miles of railway lines had been added to the existing network with other ancillary services of quality.

The First Five-Year Plan focused primarily on the rehabilitation of track and rolling stock. Major projects undertaken during this period included the reconstruction of Lansdowne Bridge in Sukkur, remodelling of Landhi Station to share the traffic load of Karachi City Station and improvement of the latter, conversion of Jacobabad–Kashmore line to broad gauge, and completion of Drigh Road–Khadda track for the Karachi Circular Railway project.[22]

By the Third Plan period, the railways continued to play a significant role in Pakistan's transport system as it was still being used for bulk transportation and handling heavy volume of traffic, but it lagged behind in meeting the traffic demand both for passengers as well as freight. In passenger miles, the growth was only 2.8 per cent between 1960 and 1964.[23] By the end of the Third Plan period, the railways began to lose their share in the total traffic volume to roads. Projects completed under the Third Plan were conversion of the meter gauged Hyderabad–Mirpurkhas railway track to broad gauge. Other projects within the plan period were doubling of track on the Hyderabad–Kotri section, and establishment of a metre-gauge carriage and wagon shop in Hyderabad and Karachi Circular Railway.[24]

The Fourth Plan maintained the previously held stance of replacement and modernisation of assets to boost productivity and cut down on costs. Railways bagged almost half of the total investments in the transport sector. However, on account of heavy backlog, new projects had to be restricted. The plan provided for conversion of the Hyderabad–Mirpurkhas railway, mechanised marshalling yards at Pipri and Samasata, and a feasibility study for electrification of the Karachi–Kotri section.[25]

In the Fifth Plan, construction of railways was considerably curtailed. In Sindh, the only projects were sleeper and rail renewal along Karachi–Peshawar and Kotri–Peshawar tracks and the portion pertaining to renewal of the Karachi–Lahore track.[26] Ongoing projects—the doubling of Kotri–Hyderabad track and construction of Pipri Marshalling Yard under Crash Development Programme—were also completed during the Fifth Plan period.[27] During this period, underutilisation and inefficiency of existing railways capacity led to a decline in its freight traffic by 4.5 per cent per annum.[28] Despite, the Sixth Plan's proposal for long-term policies to avert this declining trend (as railways still offered least cost transport solution, the internal capacity of a railway as a commercial organisation became a major hindrance in meeting the envisaged goals. In this plan period, renewal work on 470 km of main line and sleeper renewal of 422 km of main and branch lines were undertaken.[29]

The induction of the National Logistics Cell (NLC)—an army-managed organisation with its new fleet of modern trucks into inter-city road movement—provided the last nail in the coffin of the railways. The biggest drop in freight traffic was seen in 1990–91, when railway freight fell by more than 42 per cent.

Construction of overhead the railway bridge at Nawabshah was one of the highlights of the projects running during the Seventh Plan period.[30] The policies proposed under the Eighth Plan were to allocate long lead traffic to railways and to privatise the sector. These policies, however, never saw the light of the day.

In 2000–01, the government once again turned towards the railway and approved a rehabilitation plan for the next five years which included rehabilitation and replacement of locomotives and modernisation of railways as a whole.[31]

By 2005–06, conversion of the Mirpurkhas–Khokhropar track to broad gauge was completed.[32] Despite sustained efforts to transfer traffic to railways, it was only able to secure limited freight traffic which dropped as low as 5 per cent by 2010.[33] Its inability to offset declining revenues on freight handling with heavy pricing on passenger traffic rendered the sector a financial burden on the national economy. Pakistan Railways continued to suffer huge losses during the last decade and was therefore not in a position to rehabilitate its infrastructure or rolling stock.

The Tenth Plan once again attempted to bolster railways as a primary service, provider for freight transportation through consolidation of available infrastructure and resources. To accomplish this goal, projects such as linking of private freight forwarders, and truckers for door-to-door services in Karachi were initiated. Even though the tracks from Landhi to Khanpur were rehabilitated and provision of rail links from Badin to Thar coalfields were approved, progress remained unsatisfactory.[34]

By the Eleventh Plan period, the railways had shown slight improvement, having secured 6 per cent of the total freight traffic. This did not do much to reduce the imbalance between the roads and railways network.[35] Under the China–Pakistan Economic Corridor (CPEC) upgradation, expansion, reconstruction, and laying of new tracks of the spinal railway line from Karachi to Peshawar are to be undertaken at a total cost of $8 billion. It will be for the first time after seventy years that such a mammoth investment is being made in the railway network. China is ideally suited to spearhead this effort as they have demonstrated their prowess in high speed railway systems.[36] Revival of the Karachi Circular Railway (43 km) is also envisaged under the CPEC.[37]

Table 10.2: Pakistan Railway Movement of Passengers, Freight, and Earnings
(1980–81 to 2015–16)

Year	No. Of Passengers Carried (in thousand)	Rate of Change (%)	Freight Carried by Railways (in thousand Tonnes)	Rate of Change (%)	Gross Earnings Rupees (in million)	Rate of Change (%)
1980–81	122,676	-	11,354	-	2,779	-
1985–86	82,829	-32.5	11,805	4.0	4,376	57.5
1990–91	84,899	2.5	7,715	-34.7	6,760	54.5
1995–96	69,000	-18.7	6,000	-22.2	9,785	44.8
2000–01	69,000	0	6,000	0.00	11,939	22
2005–06	81,000	17.4	6,000	0.00	18,182	52.3
2010–11	65,000	-19.8	3,000	-50	18,612	2.4
2015–16*	52,000	-20	5,000	66.6	36,582	96.5

* The figures for 2015–16 are from Finance Division, *Pakistan Economic Survey 2016–2017*, Islamabad, Ministry of Finance, Government of Pakistan, 2017.

Source: Bureau of Statistics, *Development Statistics of Sindh*, Karachi, Planning and Development Department, Government of Sindh, various years.

Table 10.2 presents a summary of the performance of Pakistan Railways over the last four decades. The addition to tracks throughout this period was insignificant, slow speed and unreliability were the hallmarks, and customer service and convenience were totally neglected. As a result, there was a substantial decline in both passengers as well as freight carried. The Indian Railways is still the main carrier for low and lower middle-income population and their share of freight traffic remains high. In Pakistan, there is a downward moving trend even compared to 2005–06 when passengers had reached 81 million while freight traffic carried had crossed 6 million tons. There has been some perceptible improvement in the performance of railways in the last three to four years. It is too early to judge whether it will be able to sustain itself in the future.

Ports

In 1947, Pakistan started off with little or no shipping resources. Karachi Port was the only port in West Pakistan and had to handle a large influx of international and coastal traffic directed to and from West Pakistan. It was subjected to an upsurge of traffic volume from 2.5 million tons in 1948–49 to 4 million tons in 1952–53. By 1955, seven national shipping companies had been established and twenty merchant ships had been commissioned.

In the First Five-Year Plan, emphasis was laid upon the rehabilitation and improvement of Karachi Port in view of the growing needs of international trade. In line with this plan, thirteen of the oldest berths of East Wharf were reconstructed.[38]

Figure 10.1: Railway Tracks in Sindh (in Kilometers)
(1976–76 to 2005–06)

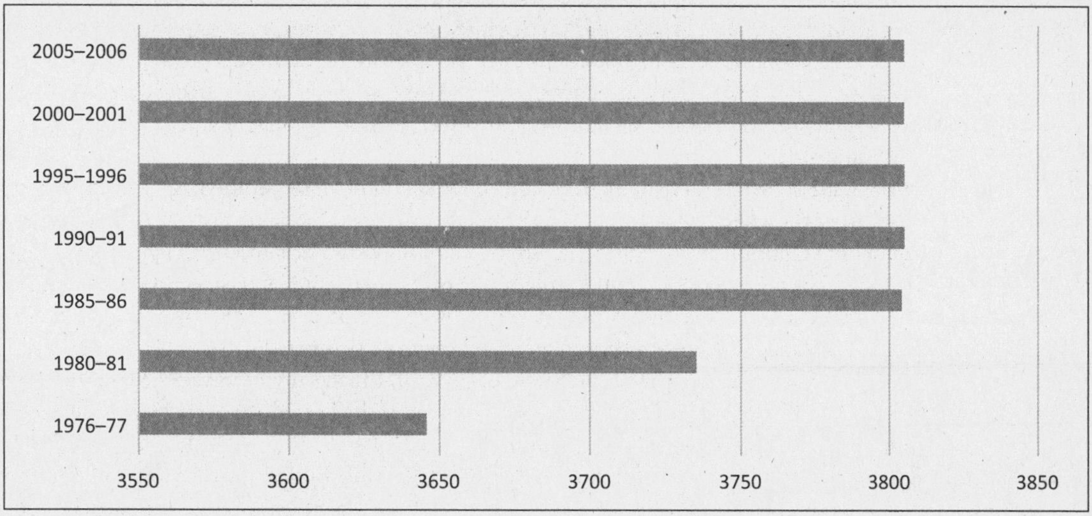

Source: Bureau of Statistics, *Development Statistics of Sindh*, Karachi, Planning and Development Department, Government of Sindh, various years.

Under the Second Plan, reconstruction works on berths numbered 1–4 and 5–17 at East Wharf continued. Reconstruction of the Bulk Oil Pier and rehabilitation of the Manora Breakwater was also completed.[39]

By 1965, the Karachi Port was working beyond its available capacity of 4.5 million tons as traffic volume experienced an increase of 62 per cent during the Second Plan period due to economic growth.[40] Thus, the plan to increase the port capacity by construction of additional berths in the space available at West Wharf was undertaken as a short-term measure. A secondary programme was also designed which included the development of a West Wharf, Oil Berth, construction of two new lighter age berths at Juna Bunder, and rehabilitation of Manora Breakwater.[41] The need for a subsidiary port was realised at the beginning of the Third Plan period and a feasibility study to build another port on Makran Coast was undertaken.

The congestion of Karachi Port persisted in the Third and Fourth Plan period as the rapid growth of traffic volume resulting from high economic growth could not keep pace with the capacity of the port. In order to meet the estimated requirement of fifty general purpose berths to accommodate the projected traffic volume amounting to 10 million tons of dry cargo,[42] schemes for both the expansion of Karachi Port and construction of a new port were made part of the Fourth Plan. It was proposed to bring the number of berths up to thirty-two. New studies on constructing a port at Sonmiani or any other potential location were also taken up, but no considerable progress was made.

In the Fifth Five-Year Plan, the width and depth of the navigable channel was increased, Berths no. 1 to 4 at East Wharves were reconstructed, and additional berths were constructed at West Wharf.[43] The construction of four multi-purpose and dry cargo handling berths at Juna Bunder, construction of the fourth oil pier for 4,500 Deadweight Tonne (DWT) oil tankers, coal/ore terminal at Port Qasim, and procurement of trailing suction Hopper dredger were the major projects that were completed in this period. Napier Mole Bridge also began to be reconstructed as a modern pre-stressed reinforced concrete bridge in view of increased traffic.[44] Studies on construction of new ports were renewed with increased vigour along with the plan for the initiation of construction at Gwadar.

The second port of Pakistan was established at Port Qasim in 1973—28 nautical miles southeast of Karachi. It is located on the trade route of the Arabian Gulf and has eased the congestion at Karachi Port.

The transport demand of dry cargo suffered a major decline during the Fifth and Sixth Plan period. However, liquid cargo held its ground with a slight increase.[45] Therefore, focus shifted to the completion of ongoing schemes and small-scale enabling projects to achieve optimal exploitation of Karachi Port and Port Qasim. The resultant projects were construction of transit silos at Port Qasim, acquisition of a dredger, development of an oil terminal of 3-million tons capacity, and construction of a 1.7-million-ton container terminal and an oil products berth at Karachi Port.[46]

In the Seventh Plan period, further development of and construction of an oil terminal at Port Qasim and Gwadar Fish Harbour were completed.

It was decided under the Eighth Plan to induct the private sector in ports and shipping in light of the cargo traffic demand increasing by an annual compound growth rate of 3.6 per cent.[47] Construction of a deep sea port at Gwadar and container and oil terminal at Port Qasim were proposed to further this objective. The idea of a Central Ports Authority to facilitate coordination between the two major ports and optimal use of equipment and existing infrastructure proposed under the plan did not make any headway.[48] Modernisation of Karachi Port was taken up in 1995–96 under which establishment of the Liquid Products Marine Terminal was established along with the construction of Jinnah Bridge.[49]

Reconstruction of the Oil Pier, Napier Mole Boat Wharf, and Napier Mole Bridge was approved and initiated in the second half of 2001. Sixty per cent of the imports and exports were handled through the Karachi Port, while the remaining 40 per cent of the volume was handled by Port Qasim and Gwadar Port.[50] Port Qasim is operating an iron and coal berth, multi-purpose berths, an oil terminal, a container terminal, and terminals for chemicals, liquid cargo, grain, and fertiliser.[51] The Karachi Port, which has completed 125 years, operates two container terminals, one silos terminal, three multi-purpose oil terminals, thirty dry cargo berths (seventeen at East Wharf and thirteen at West Wharf) for bulk, break bulk, and containers.

Deep-water containers port project with ten berths at 18 metre depth is being completed as public–private partnership at a total cost of $1.6 billion. As economic growth revived in the 2000–07 period, the capacity of the two ports was overstretched to meet the growing traffic demand. It was decided to construct a deepwater container port, reconstruct berths navigation channels, and reconstruct jetties/facilities at Karachi Port. At Port Qasim, projects such as container terminal, grain fertiliser terminal, coal and cement terminal, LNG terminal, and capital dredging to deepen channels to handle large ships were undertaken. Construction of East Bay Expressway and additional container terminals at Gwadar Port were envisaged.[52]

The ongoing projects include the construction of a cargo village in the western backwaters by Karachi Port Trust, as well as the construction of a second LNG terminal, and the construction of coal, clinker, cement, and grain fertiliser terminals. Moreover, the deepening and widening of the navigation channels and capital dredging by Port Qasim Authority are also planned.[53]

Gwadar Port was constructed in the mid-2000s and handled over to the Port Authority of Singapore but it did not make much headway. It has now been taken over as a CPEC Early Harvest project and the Chinese are carrying out several ancillary projects to make it fully operational. With the full operation of Gwadar Port on the Arabian Sea, the congestion on the two Karachi ports would be somewhat eased.

Air Transport

Pakistan ranks 85 out of 142 countries on air transport infrastructure—not at par with international competitors.[54] Air transport was of special significance during the first two decades after Pakistan's independence as it provided the quickest connection between East and West Pakistan. At Independence, Pakistan had inherited one major airport and limited quantity of obsolete equipment in the name of aviation; something as basic as an airline for commercial air transport was non-existent in the country. Initially, Orient Airways relocated and based its operations in Karachi. This provided the structure upon which the future of air transport in Pakistan was built.[55]

Table 10.3: Cargo Handled at Karachi Port (in Thousand Tonnes)
(1990–91 to 2015–16)

Year	Imports	Exports	Total
1990–91	14,714	3,995	18,709
1995–96	18,719	4,862	23,581
2000–01	20,064	5,918	25,982
2005–06	25,573	6,697	32,270
2010–11	28,589	12,843	41,432
2015–16	40,259	9,786	50,045

Source: Finance Division, *Pakistan Economic Survey*, Islamabad, Ministry of Finance, Government of Pakistan, various years.

By 1955, Karachi had become an internationally recognised airport as one of the largest in Asia. Pakistan International Airlines (PIA) was established as a semi-autonomous public corporation in the same year and it absorbed the Orient Airways. PIA entered the international market after the acquisition of three Super-Constellation aircraft.[56] An air training centre to train local and foreign trainees in fields necessary for smooth air transport operations was established in Karachi. Three flying clubs were also established to provide training to pilots.[57] The existing facilities at the airport were upgraded to make them functional for expanded domestic and international services and operations.

During 1960–65, air passenger traffic witnessed an annual mean rate of 50 per cent, surpassing traffic in other transport sectors by a wide margin. The aviation sector, therefore, needed significant investment.[58] Air links were established between Karachi, Tehran, and Ankara. A jet runway was constructed at the Jinnah International Airport and arrangements were made for handling Boeing 720-B in Lahore. Construction of the new airfield in Hyderabad and improvisation of a landing ground at Mohen-jo-Daro made headway during the Third Plan period.[59] To reach out to the farther areas of the country, local area/feeder services were initiated by PIA.

By the Fourth Plan period, air traffic in West Pakistan had the highest growth rate among all modes of transportation. However, its relative share was quite low.[60] Accommodation of large-bodied aircraft by providing necessary airports and ground facilities at Karachi was envisaged.[61] There was an upsurge in passenger miles that grew by of 17 per cent between 1971and 1977.[62]

To accommodate increased usage of airways for passenger movement and freight, new terminal buildings were built at the Jinnah International Airport, Karachi, and other airports were enlarged during the Sixth Plan period. Nawabshah airport was developed as an alternative to the airport in Karachi, and cargo handling facilities were installed at a number of airports.[63] Efficiency gains were realised by PIA as it rationalised the number of workers per aircraft and increased the utilisation of fleet. It was at that time that in pursuit of its policy of liberalisation, the government allowed private airlines to operate domestically to ease pressure on PIA and introduce some semblance of competition.[64]

The new schemes undertaken in Sindh during the Seventh Plan included strengthening of the secondary runway and reconstruction of the main runway at Jinnah International Airport, Karachi, and development of Sukkur airport.[65]

The most significant achievement in the next plan period was completion of ongoing work at the Jinnah Terminal Complex, upgradation of runways at Karachi, and establishment of a new airport at Sehwan Sharif.

By 2000–01, the private sector had acquired a foothold in the aviation sector as four airlines had started their operations. However, PIA still remained a dominant player with a market share of 87 per cent of the passenger and freight traffic. Two of the four private airlines could not keep up the competitive pressure and had to wrap up their businesses. The frequent changes in the top management and the boards of PIA in the 1990s led to heavy financial losses and decline in the market share on international routes. The company which had helped establish Emirates Airline fell victim to its own mismanagement and poor governance. Major projects under the Tenth and Eleventh Plan included construction of a satellite terminal, boarding bridge, and new control tower at Jinnah Terminal Complex at Jinnah International Airport.[66] These also include the establishment of the Civil Aviation Training Institute (CATI) in Hyderabad and cold storage facilities at the Karachi airport.[67]

Currently, PIA is heavily subsidised by the government compared to private airlines but its performance remains lacklustre. Its fleet has not been upgraded, costs are above industry average, and productivity is low. Middle Eastern airlines offer excellent services and have become a hub for easy connections to other continents. PIA's downward slide can only be averted if it is either privatised or other private airlines are provided a level playing field to compete with PIA. For example in India, Air India, i.e. a government owned airline, has only a 25 per cent share in the domestic aviation market while 75 per cent share is held by private airlines which are efficient, cost effective, and customer-oriented. The private companies have placed orders for several hundred new airplanes to cater to the growing demand.

Table 10.4: Performance of PIA (1990–91 to 2015–16)

Year	Revenue Passengers Carried (in thousand)	Revenue Tonne (Million kms)	Operating Expenses (Rs. Million)	Operating Revenue (Rs. Million)
1990–91	5,033	1,228	16,966	16,849
1995–96	5,399	1,402	27,150	27,505
2000*	5,297	1,452	42,033	39,228
2005–06	5,828	1,818	73,074	67,574
2011*	5,935	1,678	132,970	117,536
2015*	4,393	1,191	121,222	91,269

*PIA financial year is based on calendar year, i.e. January to December.

Source: Finance Division, *Pakistan Economic Survey*, Islamabad, Ministry of Finance, Government of Pakistan, various years.

Telecommunication

The one sector which has undergone a major transformation in Pakistan is undoubtedly the telecommunication sector. From the teledensity of 4 in 2002–03, the cellular subscriptions have multiplied by more than twenty-six times by 2015–16 (Table 10.5), raising the teledensity to 71 (Table 10.6). It clearly shows that conducive liberal investment policy, technological assimilation, and competition among private sector players can bring about enormous benefits to the economy as well as the consumers who enjoy low calling rates domestically and internationally. The introduction of 3G/4G technology has raised the number of mobile broadband and Internet users to over 44 million (Table 10.7) up from 26,000 in 2005–06.

Table 10.5: Annual Cellular Subscriptions
(2003–04 to 2015–16)

Year	Cellular Subscribers
2003–04	5,002,908
2005–06	34,506,557
2010–11	108,894,518
2015–16	133,241,465

Source: Pakistan Telecommunication Authority, *Annual Reports*, Islamabad, Government of Pakistan, various years.

Table 10.6: Teledensity (2002–03 to 2015–16)

Year	Total Teledensity (%)
2002–03	4.3
2005–06	26.3
2010–11	68.2
2015–16	70.8

Source: Pakistan Telecommunication Authority, *Annual Reports*, Islamabad, Government of Pakistan, various years.

Internet and Broadband

An optical-fibre system between Karachi and Islamabad laid in the 1990s served as the foundation for digitalisation, cellular phones, and Internet penetration. By August 2000, universal Internet access had been extended to 350 cities, up from 29. The establishment of the Pakistan Internet Exchange at Karachi had also been initiated.

Table 10.7: Annual Broadband Subscribers (2005–06 to 2016–17)

Year	Broadband Subscribers
2005–06	26,611
2010–11	1,491,491
2015–16	32,295,286
2016–17	44,586,733

Source: Pakistan Telecommunication Authority, *Annual Reports*, Islamabad, Government of Pakistan, various years.

According to recent statistics, 138 cities and towns of Sindh have acquired Internet access in the form of dial-up networking because of the propagation of point of presence telecommunications. However, the quality of service remains compromised. Most of the companies that have obtained licenses for the provision of Internet services are based in Sindh.[68]

Broadband access has become increasingly popular in Karachi as private companies are making optic fibre infrastructure available. Karachi is one of the two cities in Pakistan to have Pakistan Internet exchanges which serve as international gateways for Internet service providers (ISPs).[69]

Television

Karachi was one of the three cities where fully operational television (TV) stations were established in 1966. At the time, programmes were only aired for thirty-six hours weekly; 5 KW transmitters, each with a coverage of 40 miles radius, were made available for each station.[70]

The TV industry started from scratch and the training of manpower, and the provision of technical facilities took precedence in allocations under the Fourth Plan. A television institute was established, and film processing workshops were set up.

By the Fifth Plan, television had spread its network to 74 per cent of the population. The Karachi station benefitted as facilities for broadcasting a second channel for educational programmes were developed.

The focus of the Sixth Plan revolved around expanding the outreach of TV services in the far-flung and remote areas of Pakistan. The less developed regions of Sindh were also included in the development programme designed to achieve this objective.

In the next plan period, ongoing projects such as establishment of a broadcasting house, and an installation of a 100 (Kilo Watt Medium Wave) KWMW transmitter in Karachi were completed. Extension of a broadcasting house in Hyderabad, establishment of rebroadcast centres in Shikarpur and Thana Bulla Khan, and a television centre in Karachi were among the new schemes undertaken.[71]

During the Eighth Plan period, the need for rehabilitation, consolidation, and modernisation of the physical infrastructure had risen. The private sector was encouraged to take part in expansion of TV channels. The new schemes, which were more concentrated in far-flung regions included the setting up of a 1,000 KWMW transmitter for the Gulf and Middle East in Karachi.[72]

Table 10.8: Growth of Television Services and Revenues in Sindh
(1980–81 to 2012–13)

Year	Total No. of TV Licenses Issued	Rate of Change (%)	Revenues Paid by TV Set Holders (in Rupees Thousand)	Rate of Change (%)
1980–81	301,764	-	60,553	-
1985–86	471,339	56.2	59,039	-2.5
1990–91	548,766	16.4	47,849	-18.9
1995–96	625,396	14.0	45,110	-5.7
2000–01	978,907	56.5	119,268	164.4
2005–06	1,561,448	59.5	390,540	227.4
2010–11	2,250,401	44.1	660,918	69.2
2012–13	2,561,736	13.8	849,496	28.5

Source: Bureau of Statistics, *Development Statistics of Sindh*, Karachi, Planning and Development Department, Government of Sindh, various years.

During the 2000s, the television industry went through a revolutionary phase with the establishment of a plethora of private television channels. Pakistan Television Network (PTV), which had the monopoly, and still has a heavy penetration in the terrestrial domain, has been sidelined by the enormous growth of private television channels. Talk shows on various subjects such as current affairs, dramas, plays, 24-hour news services, sports, religious channels in Urdu, and regional language channels dominated the airtime. Consequently, the number of television licenses jumped almost four-fold between 1995 and 2010. Revenues collected from television set holders rose to almost fourteen times in the same period.

Housing

At the time of Independence, housing and accommodating millions of refugees migrating to Pakistan posed one of the biggest challenges faced by the newly created state. Although, the availability of evacuee property assuaged the problem to some extent, the required accommodations still fell half a million short of the required number in 1955. As the capital shifted to Karachi, it benefitted from investment in water supply and sewerage that helped establish new colonies and settlements.

The First Five-Year Plan failed to make any considerable contribution in the housing sector except construction of government offices and buildings, public servant housing, and limited housing for homeless families.[73]

The Second Plan made limited progress in basic development programmes since efforts were still directed towards immediate housing for displaced persons. Development of water, sewerage, and drainage systems for Karachi was, however, given priority. The construction of 150,000 housing units during the Second Plan period failed to meet the growing demand of urban population during 1960–70.[74]

By the Third Plan period, the backlog of urban dwellings that had reached almost a million, almost doubled in a decade. Rural areas suffered from a lack of sustainable access to clean drinking water, and proper sanitation and drainage facilities and therefore, migration to urban areas was an attractive alternative.[75] Construction of 160,000 urban dwellings in West Pakistan was intended primarily for the accommodation of the low-income groups and slum dwellers.[76] Comprehensive planning and establishment of water, sewerage, drainage and, garbage disposal for Karachi and Hyderabad among other cities was initiated.

Table 10.9: Government of Sindh Budget Allocation for Housing (in PKR Million)
(1975–76 to 2015–16)

Year	Budget Estimate	Revised Estimate	Rate of Change (%)
1975–76	159.2	148.737	-7
1980–81	273.23	373.121	37
1985–86	400.83	385.259	-4
1990–91	631.034	1,937.782	207
1995–96	1,251.306	1,391.006	11
2000–01	1,082.458	995.912	-8
2005–06	365.959	213.148	-42
2010–11	6,268.818	4,725.19	-25
2015–16	3,330.654	3,433.127	3.1

Sources: Finance Department, *Annual Budget Statement*, Karachi, Government of Sindh, various years.

Table 10.9 provides a summary of the total expenditure incurred by the Sindh government in the area of public housing. These allocations were mainly for the purpose of accommodating government servants of all categories in the main towns of Sindh. Housing provision for the citizens was left mainly to the private sector.

The attempts to develop Korangi and North Karachi housing schemes for low-income groups did not make much headway, despite an allocation of PKR 900 million for low income housing. The absorptive capacity of the public sector department was limited. Although the allocation for physical planning and the housing sector witnessed a dramatic increase of more than 674 per cent from 1970–71 to 1977–78, the physical achievements were far behind the targets. The onslaught of a growing population resulted in overcrowding, informal settlements, and lack of basic sanitary as well as recreational facilities. This created a demand for an additional 1.3 million of additional housing units during 1970–75. The Fourth Plan provided for centres for regional and urban development and building and housing research centres at Karachi.[77] Provision of water, sewerage, drainage and sanitation facilities in large cities and urban centres inclusive of Sindh's were emphasised upon. An experimental housing scheme for industrial workers was initiated at the Sindh Industrial Trading Estate (SITE) in Karachi.[78] A comprehensive water supply and sewerage system for Karachi was also to be completed during the Fourth Plan period.[79]

To strengthen the capacity, a housing and physical planning department was established by the Government of Sindh. A development authority was created in Hyderabad, and the Sindh Development Authority and Regional Planning Organisation for Sindh were created.[80] The rate of house construction rose to 40,000 houses per year in 1977–78 from 10,000 during the Third Plan.[81] The development of 130,000 plots[82] and the Katchi Abadi Improvement and Regularisation Programme (KAIRP) for improvement of slums and katchi abadis covering a population of 0.5 million[83] in Sindh was initiated during the Fifth Plan. KAIRP failed to keep up with its objectives due to multiple structural problems such as dependence on foreign loans and corruption. The Fifth Plan proposed installation of 40,000 hand-pumps per year in Sindh to ensure provision of piped water supply in rural areas.[84] Implementation of the third phase of the Bulk Water Supply Scheme in Karachi was made possible by the utilisation of Karachi's water share from Hub Dam. This scheme increased access to drinking water by one million of the population. But still by the end of the 1970s, only 20 per cent of the population had access to piped water and sewerage facilities. An additional 0.55 million people were to be served through the Lyari Slum Improvement Project.

The phased programme for improvement of katchi abadis in Karachi and Hyderabad[85] was once again resumed in the Sixth Plan period, aiming at the development of 110,000 plots for low income groups during 1975 to 1985.[86] Water supply projects based on the Indus River and Hub Dam as well as two new sewage treatment plans were included in the plan to fill the water supply and sanitation gap in Karachi.[87]

Sindh Katchi Abadi Authority (SKAA) was established in 1987, driven by the realisation that some form of formalisation of katchi abadis should be carried out through regulation, improvement, and integration in the province's urban plan.[88] Different phases of Sind Goth Abad Scheme were also included in the Seventh Plan for Hyderabad, Tharparkar, Badin, Thatta, Nawabshah, Larkana, Jacobabad, Sukkur, Dadu, Sanghar, Khairpur, and Shikarpur.[89] In 1992, SKAA initiated a programme on similar lines as KAIRP but with greater effectiveness.

The Eight Plan provided for provincial governments to undertake construction of houses for the homeless on the plots allotted under the 7-Marla plot schemes in the rural areas.[90] Introduction of housing scheme on ownership basis for federal government employees in Karachi was also planned in this period.

In 1998, housing units showed an increase of 80 per cent, mostly by the private developers, as the total housing units reached over 5 million—of which 43 per cent were in rural areas. This increase brought about some ease on the household size, which went down to 6 in 1998 from 7.1 in 1980. Housing units with one room were replaced with two or more rooms. The percentage of houses constructed with baked bricks also increased to 48 per cent from 40 per cent. A reduction in the level of congestion, which according to the census of 1998 is defined in terms of people per housing unit or household size, was complemented by an increase in the average housing capacity and this marked a considerable improvement in the standard of living.[91]

Progress in middle class and high-income housing in the urban areas also did make much headway in the 2000's, but low cost housing which was not so profitable from the private sector's viewpoint was neglected. The supply of housing stuck at 40,000 houses per annum, falls drastically short of the demand of 120,000.[92]

Table 10.11 indicates that rental to owned housing remained the same although there has been a shift from one room to 2–4 rooms in the households of Sindh (Table 10.12). This bodes well but there has been proliferation of katchi abadis as the newcomers from northern areas to Karachi cannot find any place to live. They therefore fall prey to land mafias who provide them illegally occupied plots of land acquired in connivance with the officials of Land Administration and the police. In 2013, these katchi abadis were home to half of the population of the two major cities of Sindh—Karachi and Hyderabad. There was an addition of 32,000 housing units per year. Karachi also witnessed the demolition of 7,438 units in katchi abadis since 1992 for carrying out projects of urban development, causing displacement and further impoverishment of low-income groups.[93] By 2015, informal settlements, covering 23 per cent of Karachi's residential area, were home to 62 per cent of Karachi's population with lack of basic necessities reflected by the sharing of one toilet by approximately twenty people. In contrast, 77 per cent of the residential area is occupied by formal settlements that houses 36 per cent of varying degrees of privileged masses.[94]

Table 10.10: Number of Households in Sindh (1972–2017)

Year	Total	Rural	Urban
1972	2,287,299	1,350,376	936,923
1981	2,714,420	1,544,773	1,169,647
1998	5,022,392	2,850,989	2,171,403
2017	8,585,610	4,185,828	4,399,782

Source: Population Census Organisation, *Population Census Reports*, Islamabad, Statistics Division, Government of Pakistan, various years.

Table 10.11: Housing Ownership and Tenancy Pattern in Sindh (%)
(1980–81 to 2014–15)

Year	Rental Housing	Owned Housing	Free Housing	Subsidised Rent	Total	Houses with No Latrine
1980–81	10.72	77.04	-	-	-	-
1998–99	12.2	76.9	-	-	-	34.08
2006–07	9.43	83.93	5.27	1.37	100	18
2010–11	9.31	84.14	4.55	2	100	8
2014–15	10.61	80.98	5.97	2.44	100	7

Source: The figures of 1980–81 and 1998–99 were taken from Arif Hasan, *Sindh State of Environment and Development*, Karachi, Sindh Programme, IUCN Pakistan, 2004; The figures of 2006–7, 2010–11, and 2014–15 were taken from Pakistan Bureau of Statistics, *Pakistan Social and Living Standards Measurement Survey (PSLM)*, Islamabad, Statistics Division, Government of Pakistan, various years.

Table 10.12: Percentage Distribution of Households by Number of Rooms in Sindh
(1980–81 to 2014–15)

Year	One room (%)	2–4 Rooms (%)	5 or more rooms (%)	Total (%)
1980–81	61.0	8.6	-	-
1998–99	56.9	10.6	-	-
2006–07	29.0	66.7	4.3	100
2010–11	25.7	70.9	3.4	100
2014–15	35.3	62.3	2.4	100

Source: The figures of 1980–81 and 1998–99 were taken from Arif Hasan, *Sindh State of Environment and Development*, Karachi, Sindh Programme, IUCN Pakistan, 2004; The figures of 2006–7, 2010–11, and 2014–15 were taken from Pakistan Bureau of Statistics, *Pakistan Social and Living Standards Measurement Survey (PSLM)*, Islamabad, Statistics Division, Government of Pakistan, various years.

Karachi's housing infrastructure development has been seriously hampered by the absence of an urban design plan which has led to densification and congestion.[95] The large number of informal housing projects taken up in recent years to fill the gap created by the absence of social housing programmes can lead to a serious problem of integration in future.[96] A large number of patches of land in Karachi are not committed to any formal use and serve as homes to drug addicts, the homeless, and garbage.[97] Elite housing settlements impinge on the outfalls to the sea while informal settlements encroach on sewerage canals.[98] Water and sanitation schemes planned over the years for Karachi failed to meet their objectives and were consequently abandoned, stagnating the housing infrastructure development.[99] So far, SKAA has regularised 354 katchi abadis in Sindh—110 in Karachi, 97 in Hyderabad, 54 in Mirpurkhas, 55 in Sukkur, and 38 in Larkana respectively.

Summing Up

The location of the two sea-ports in the country and a major international airport has placed an enormous pressure on Karachi in terms of infrastructure requirements. Cargo handled at Karachi Port has increased from 18,000 tons to 50,000 tons in the last twenty-five years. Freight movement normally makes extensive use of the affordable railway network connecting the city with the rest of the country. But the performance of the railways has deteriorated over time and therefore alternate modes such as roads and highways have to be used for this purpose.

Investment in highways, superhighways, and motorways therefore accelerated and the metalled road network has expanded almost four times since the formation of the province in 1970. Consequently, the number of motor vehicles on road has also multiplied by a factor of ten, mostly the motorcycles. Within cities, overhead bridges, underpasses, and ring roads had to be constructed to accumulate the exceptional traffic growth. The missing link in the urban transport system was the mass transit system, which could also have moderated environmental pollution and road congestion.

Air transport has also blossomed as Middle Eastern airlines offering excellent services, competitive rates, and convenient locations were allowed freedom to fly from Karachi and other airports and pick up passengers for other connecting flights originating out of their hubs. Although PIA has lost its market share, the passengers have gained by the entry of these airlines in the form of convenience, price, and access. International travel has grown more rapidly than domestic travel. Domestically, private airlines are beginning to nibble into the pie of PIA's monopoly as the latter has lost its edge.

In the area of telecommunications, there has been an unanticipated revolution with teledensity giving up from 4 to 71 in a decade's time and broadband and Internet connections becoming widely available throughout the country.

Housing, particularly for low income groups, has not kept pace with the demand, resulting in congestion and backlog. The private sector and defence authorities are playing an active role in providing housing for upper and upper middle-income groups. However, affordable housing for low income families in the urban areas has been neglected, resulting in the mushrooming and unplanned growth of informal settlements.

11

Sindh's Industrial Structure: Past and Present

THE industrialisation process in Sindh began right after Partition with the establishment of the Sindh Industrial Trading Estate (SITE), meant to serve as the industrial hub of the country.

Pakistan had no industries of any sort, except two sugar mills, one cement factory, a few spinning units, a dozen cotton ginning factories, railway workshops etc. and was dependent on the rest of India for its industrial goods. The new government had to therefore begin its industrialisation process from scratch. The country has seen five waves of significant policy changes, the impact of which trickled down to the provinces.

The first wave came right after Partition, when India imposed restrictions on imports to Pakistan in 1948. Since Pakistan was heavily dependent on India for consumer goods, this ban led to Pakistan adopting the policy of import substitution resulting in high investment in consumption goods and protection of such goods from external competition. The imposition of trade embargo on Pakistan by India and the subsequent strategy of import substitution led to widespread industrialisation in Sindh, spearheaded by the consumer goods industry.

The second wave occurred during the regime of President Ayub Khan and was a part of the second (1960–65) and third (1965–70) five-year development plans. It implemented the industrial licensing policy and in order to fund and facilitate industrialisation, the Industrial Development Bank of Pakistan (IDBP) and Pakistan Industrial Credit and Investment Corporation (PICIC) were set up to provide financing for industrial units. Both these institutions were funded by The World Bank.[1] The Pakistan Industrial Development Corporation (PIDC)—a public sector holding company—set up several manufacturing plants which were subsequently sold to the private sector. This sped up the process of industrialisation in the province and many large, medium, and small scale units, in and around the industrial centres of Karachi were established. One of the positive impacts of this policy, on Sindh's industrial sector, was that the investment and related goods industries grew almost twice as fast as the rest of the manufacturing sector.[2]

The third wave of industrial policy occurred during 1971–73, under the tenure of President Zulfikar Ali Bhutto, and involved the nationalisation of large-scale manufacturing. At that time, it was a popular move in reaction to the concentration of wealth in the hands of twenty-two families but in retrospect this policy was a big setback to the industrial growth of the country. The Board of Industrial Management and Pakistan Industrial Development Corporation together took over thirty-two major manufacturing units[3] from their private owners. Since the units were nationalised and controlled by government-owned organisations, new projects were chosen on political rather than on basis of economic considerations, making the industrial sector inefficient. For example, sugar mills were established in areas where no sugarcane was grown.

When democratically elected governments resumed power in 1989, the country witnessed the fourth wave of industrial policy. This fourth wave consisted of a deletion policy, deregulation, and privatisation. The deletion policy was aimed at achieving import substitution in the engineering sector to promote technology transfers. The privatisation policy was aimed at offsetting the damage done by the nationalisation of the 1970s, which imposed heavy costs on the economy. Along with this, the deregulation policy was pursued to attract private investment and entrepreneurs for active participation in the resurgence of industrial development in the country. This era also marked the establishment of the Small and Medium Enterprise Development Authority (SMEDA).

The fifth wave (1999–2008) moved the private sector to the frontline. The implementation of better fiscal and monetary policies and structural reforms, together with deregulation and adjustments of tariff rates, brought about stabilisation of macroeconomic factors leading to a rise in the GDP growth rate from 5.1 per cent in 2003–04 to 9.1 per cent in 2004–05.[4] Major developments were seen in the automobile and consumer electronics industries. The upward trend in the agriculture and manufacturing sector led to accelerated growth in output and exports.

Sindh has always been viewed as the backbone of Pakistan's economy and rightly so since it has played a major role in promoting industrialisation in the country. Sindh's formal industrial sector mainly comprises agro-industries, textiles, pharmaceuticals, cement, chemicals, and automobile industries. The informal sector is dominated by small-scale manufacturing units, mainly responsible for production of consumer goods.[5]

Table 11.1 Manufacturing Value Added in Sindh (Constant Factor Cost 2005–06)
(1999–2000 to 2014–15)

Year	Value (in PKR Billion)	Percentage share in Provincial GDP
1999–2000	257.7	16.0
2004–05	390.4	18.6
2009–10	455.2	18.1
2014–15	525.5	17.7

Source: Unofficial estimates.

Sindh's value addition—as a percentage of provincial GDP—to the manufacturing sector was 16 per cent (PKR 258 billion) in 1999–2000 and it rose up to 18.6 per cent (PKR 390.4 billion). The value addition has started to increase at a decreasing rate since then from 18.1 per cent (PKR 455.2 billion) in 2009–10 to 17.7 per cent. Overall, Sindh has only improved its value addition by almost 11 per cent in the span of fifteen years.

The industrial sector accounts for 12 per cent of the provincial GDP. Large scale manufacturing accounts for 70 per cent of the manufacturing sector of Sindh and contributes 29 per cent to Pakistan's overall manufacturing GDP.[6,7] The manufacturing sector is unofficially estimated to account for almost 17 to 18 per cent of the provincial GDP. It is estimated that 26 to 30 per cent large-scale units are located in Sindh. Developed industrial zones such as SITE and Korangi, Landhi, Nooriabad, Kotri, Sukkur, Hyderabad, and Port Qasim are home to a large number of manufacturing units. Industrial clusters are spread throughout the province leading to a diverse manufacturing base (Annexure Figure 11B). Textiles dominate the manufacturing sector in terms of size and contribution. It is followed by food manufacturing, which generates the second highest employment.[8] Three of the largest oil refineries of Pakistan are also present in Sindh, with the Pakistan Refinery having a capacity of 2.3 million tons per annum,[9] National Refinery having a capacity of more than 2.7 million tons per annum,[10] and Byco with a capacity of 1.75 million tons per annum.[11] Karachi Steel Mills, with an installed capacity of one million tons, was established in the 1970s. The Karachi Shipyard and Engineering Works is fully equipped to handle the dismantling of old ships and building of new ones and contributes to employment generation.[12]

Industrial Landscape of Sindh

NUMBER OF ESTABLISHMENTS

Table 11.2 shows the share of Sindh in Pakistan's number of establishments for the large scale manufacturing sector. Sindh had 1,534 industries in 1970–71 which accounted for 43 per cent of the country's industries. Since then, there have been variations over time. Due to nationalisation of industries, the number had declined to 1,362 by 1975–76 but bounced back again in 1980–81 to 1,557 and reached 1,751 in 1990–91. In the first year of the next decade, there was only a marginal increase of 1,768. Since then, the number has increased at a relatively slow pace as only 171 units are estimated to have come into existence in the next fifteen years, i.e. approximately twelve a year on average. But most of them were established in 2001–07 when there was economic boom in the country. There was a downturn after that, and the level of new industrial activity also remained subdued.

According to CMI, the share of Sindh had dwindled to 28.4 per cent in 2005–06 from 43.2 per cent in 1970–71. It may be mentioned that the Census of Manufacturing Industries (CMI) on which this data is based has become highly non-responsive and does not represent an accurate and complete picture of the actual state of the manufacturing industry. Sindh did suffer in the past decade because of the poor law and order situation including an increase in the number of kidnappings for ransom and extortion. Some of the industries shifted to Punjab or were freed to shut down. The actual data on this is not readily available and this finding is by and large based on anecdote evidence.

Table 11.2: Number of Reporting Establishments in Pakistan and Sindh
(1970–71 to 2005–06)

Year	Pakistan	Sindh	Share of Sindh (%)
1970–71	3,549	1,534	43.2
1975–76	3,248	1,362	41.9
1980–81	3,815	1,557	40.8
1985–86	4,349	1,609	37
1990–91	4,792	1,751	36.5
1995–96	4,474	1,528	34.1
2000–01	4,528	1,768	39.1
2005–06	6,417	1,825	28.4

Source: Pakistan Bureau of Statistics, *Census of Manufacturing Industries*, Islamabad, Statistics Division, Government of Pakistan, various years.

Industrial units in Sindh are concentrated in highly developed areas of the province while the under-developed areas were largely ignored. There is a huge difference between the number of establishments in Karachi and the rest of Sindh, as shown in Table 11.3. Karachi alone accounted for 75 per cent of Sindh's establishments in 1970–71, compared to Sukkur's 4.2 per cent and Hyderabad's 8.4 per cent, which means only 13 per cent of the industries were present in rest of the province.

In subsequent years, the combined share of Karachi, Hyderabad, and Sukkur has come down from 95 per cent in 1975–76—the peak—to 74 per cent by 2005–06. This can partially be attributed to the shifting of industries or location of new industries out of Karachi in the wake of the deteriorating law and order situation.

Another factor could be the growing urbanisation and emerging demand in other parts of Sindh acting as the magnet for basic consumer goods industries. Another likely reason may again be the absence of data for the recent years and poor quality of coverage and reporting. The major takeaway from the above analysis is that the pace of industrial growth in the province has slowed down in the last seven and eight years.

Table 11.3: Locational Breakup of Industrial Establishments in Sindh, Karachi, Hyderabad, and Sukkur (1970–71 to 2005–06)

Year	Sindh	Karachi	Share of Karachi (%)	Hyderabad	Share of Hyderabad (%)	Sukkur	Share of Sukkur (%)
1970–71	1,534	1,148	75	129	8	64	4
1975–76	1,362	1,208	89	66	5	25	2
1980–81	1,557	1,245	80	94	6	30	2
1985–86	1,609	1,236	77	93	6	48	3
1990–91	1,751	1,273	73	89	5	48	3
1995–96	1,528	1,062	70	69	4	36	2
2000–01	1,768	1,218	69	88	5	31	2
2005–06	1,825	1,198	65	98	5	54	3

Source: Bureau of Statistics, *Census of Manufacturing Industries of Sindh*, Karachi, Planning and Development Department, Government of Sindh, various years.

The total reported employment in manufacturing sector in Pakistan is about one million, which is roughly 2 per cent of total labour force of the country. As pointed out earlier, this is gross underreporting as the actual number of employees in this sector is much higher—perhaps twice or thrice the reported number. The analysis of trends rather than the absolute numbers, is more important. In 2005–06, Sindh's share in the total reported employment in the sector was about 30 per cent which was roughly the same as its share in the number of industrial establishments in the country.

Table 11.4 shows the historical data for five years intervals since 1970–71. The table lends support to the earlier finding that Sindh's share of employment has fallen from almost one half in the peak period of 1975–76 to slightly less than one third in the next four decades.

Employment in the manufacturing sector has lagged behind growth in output for a variety of reasons. Technological advances have substituted capital and skills for unskilled labour. Rigid labour laws and rising minimum wages have shifted the pattern of employment from regular to contractual or daily wage workers. These numbers are not reflected in the CMI data. Informal employment has thus been expanding at the expense of the organised sector. Finally, there is a tendency to outsource work to smaller units that do not pay any taxes and thus the large manufacturers share costs of labour. Therefore, the data presented in this section is not fully representative of the actual development taking place and should be interpreted with the above-mentioned caveats in mind.

Table 11.4 shows the average daily employment across the province. It is apparent from the data in Table 11.5 that employment has always been concentrated in Karachi and the city has been home to three-fourths to two-thirds of the industrial workers of the province over the years.

Table 11.4: Average Daily Employment in Pakistan and Sindh (in PKR)
(1970–71 to 2005–06)

Year	Pakistan	Sindh	Share of Sindh (%)
1970–71	427,411	176,226	41.2
1975–76	506,601	234,498	46.3
1980–81	451,710	191,251	42.3
1985–86	506,593	218,396	43.1
1990–91	622,234	254,647	40.9
1995–96	561,921	202,580	36.1
2000–01	689,692	259,267	37.6
2005–06	941,283	290,376	30.8

Source: Pakistan Bureau of Statistics, *Census of Manufacturing Industries*, Islamabad, Statistics Division, Government of Pakistan, various years.

It can be observed from the data in Table 11.5 that the combined share of Karachi, Hyderabad, and Sukkur in employment has recorded a decline from 92 per cent in 1975–76 to 78 per cent in 2005–06. But the fall in employment is not as steep as that in the reported number of establishments. The underlying reason for this non-congruence in the two series may be a larger drift towards informal labour markets in other parts of Sindh represented by relatively smaller scale and size of their units compared to Karachi, Hyderabad, and Sukkur.

Table 11.5: Locational Breakup of Average Daily Employment
(1970–71 to 2005–06)

Year	Sindh	Karachi		Hyderabad		Sukkur	
	Numbers	Numbers	Share (%)	Numbers	Share (%)	Numbers	Share (%)
1970–71	176,226	132,953	75	23,591	13	2,629	2
1975–76	234,498	181,446	77	31,784	14	2,091	1
1980–81	191,251	142,196	74	17,182	9	2,502	1
1985–86	218,396	160,832	74	17,154	8	2,953	1
1990–91	254,647	182,281	72	2,143	0.8	3,378	1
1995–96	202,580	142,813	71	15,554	8	2,726	1
2000–01	259,267	186,384	72	19,039	7	3,028	1
2005–06	290,376	199,077	69	24,160	8	2,893	1

Source: Bureau of Statistics, *Census of Manufacturing Industries of Sindh*, Karachi, Planning and Development Department, Government of Sindh, various years.

EMPLOYMENT COST

Wage growth in the manufacturing sector is a powerful variable impacting poverty reduction. If the average wage rises to cross the current poverty line ($1.9), the number of people lifted out of poverty would be relatively significant provided the level of employment in the sector is equally significant.

Sindh's employment cost and its share in the national employment cost over the years is given in Table 11.6. In 1970–71, Sindh's employment cost was PKR 570 million and Sindh's share was 50 per cent of all the country's employment cost, rising consistently over the next two decades. By 1990–91 total employment cost had risen almost thirty-six times in nominal terms and the average wage also multiplied by a factor of thirty-two. Although the rise in employment costs were the same, the average wage growth was much higher in Sindh compared to the national average. The pace did become moderate in the next decade as modest increases were achieved in the total employment cost as well as average employee cost, both at the national level and at the Sindh provincial level.

Table 11.6: Employment Cost in Pakistan and Sindh (in PKR)
(1970–71 to 2005–06)

Year	Pakistan			Sindh		
	Average Daily Employment	Employment Cost (in PKR Million)	Average Cost per Employee (in PKR Thousand)	Average Daily Employment	Employment Cost (Rupees million)	Average Cost per Employee (in PKR Thousand)
1970–71	427,411	1,138	2.7	176,226	570	3.2
1975–76	506,601	2,860	5.6	234,498	1,376	5.9
1980–81	451,710	5,624	12.4	191,251	2,768	14.5
1985–86	506,593	12,120	23.9	218,396	6,437	29.5
1990–91	622,234	26,546	42.7	254,647	13,798	54.2
1995–96	561,921	41,603	74.0	202,580	20,499	101.2
2000–01	689,692	65,522	95.0	259,267	32,526	125.4
2005–06	941,283	132,413	140.7	290,376	53,060	182.7

Source: Pakistan Bureau of Statistics, *Census of Manufacturing Industries*, Islamabad, Statistics Division, Government of Pakistan, various years.

Table 11.7 shows how Sindh has done quite well over time in terms of the reported value of production in the last thirty-five years. Sindh produced almost one half of the national manufacturing output in the first fifteen years period until 1990–91. Since then, its share has been declining and is now around 40 per cent. Anecdotal evidence shows that there has been some shifting of industrial units from Karachi to up-country due to deterioration in law and order. More recent data, if available, would show some reverse of this trend, since the law and order situation has improved since 2014.

Table 11.7: Value of Production in Pakistan and Sindh (in PKR Million)
(1970–2005)

Year	Pakistan	Sindh	Share of Sindh (%)
1970–71	13,336.25	6,178.18	46
1975–76	30,674.16	15,060.65	49
1980–81	84,288.33	44,936.66	53
1985–86	171,123.65	85,497.62	50
1990–91	374,858.50	181,493.08	48
1995–96	693,010.48	285,289.79	41
2000–01	1,145,063.40	535,387.20	47
2005–06	2,929,319.77	1,200,402.29	41

Source: Pakistan Bureau of Statistics, *Census of Manufacturing Industries*, Islamabad, Statistics Division, Government of Pakistan, various years.

Composition of Output

This section is about the composition of output and the changes over time. Table 11.8 shows that two industries during 1970–71, Textile, and Food and Beverages, accounted for over two-thirds of manufacturing output in Sindh. Although together they still formed almost two-fifths of the total production in 2005–06, chemicals, rubber and plastics have shown a very impressive turnaround. This industry contributed almost one-thirds to the total output in 2005–06. Other industries that have expanded their output during this thirty-five-year span are metal products, machinery, and equipment. This should be an expected outcome as the skill reservoir and capital base in Karachi is quite developed compared to other parts of the country.

Table 11.8: Sindh's Share of Production of Selected Major Industries from Total Value of Production
(1970–71 to 2005–06)

Category of Industry	1970–71	1975–76	1980–81	1985–86	1990–91	1995–96	2000–01	2005–06
Food, Beverage, and Tobacco	28.0	17.9	20.7	19.7	15.7	15.6	13.7	14.1
Textile	34.4	27.3	24.1	22.6	28.1	27.6	31.0	24.6
Chemicals, Rubber, and Plastics	11.7	12.3	13.3	33.5	29.8	27.6	34.1	33.1
Non-Metallic Mineral Products	3.7	3.6	2.7	3.7	3.3	3.3	1.7	3.2
Basic Metal	3.7	4.8	3.2	6.6	8.5	7.5	5.0	5.2
Metal Products Machinery and Equipment	9.8	17.0	9.9	11.5	11.9	15.2	12.9	18.1
Other Industries	8.6	17.0	26.1	2.2	2.6	3.0	1.5	1.6
Total of Sindh	100	100	100	100	100	100	100	100

Source: Pakistan Bureau of Statistics, *Census of Manufacturing Industries*, Islamabad, Statistics Division, Government of Pakistan, various years.

An examination of the Industrial Production Index—a better indicator than CMI—reveals that in the 1970s' decade, the quantum of increase was limited to 43 per cent. The next decade, the 1980s, however saw a sharp increase of 62 per cent followed by a slowdown in the 1990s. As expected, the pace picked up in the 2000s—a period of high aggregate demand and economic growth—and by 2015–16, the index had registered a more than two-fold increase between 2000–01 and 2015–16.

The pattern of industrial growth was relatively capital-intensive as the employment numbers according to the CMI data are not very spectacular. Table 11.9 presents the value of fixed assets in the manufacturing sector over the same period, i.e. 1970–71 to 2005–06. A cursory examination of the data clearly shows that manufacturing in Sindh has been relatively capital-intensive. From a base of PKR 2.2 billion in 1970–71, the total value of fixed assets has jumped to PKR 351.6 billion—a highly impressive outcome. This finding is corroborated by the shift in the composition of output (Table 11.8) whereby capital-intensive industries such as chemicals, metals, machinery, and equipment have overtaken the relatively labour-intensive industries of textiles, and food and beverages. Employment growth has naturally been lacklustre because of this shift in factor intensity of production.

Table 11.9: Total Value of Fixed Assets in Sindh's Manufacturing Sector (in PKR)
(1970–71 to 2005–06)

Category of Industry	1970–71	1975–76	1980–81	1985–86	1990–91	1995–96	2000–01	2005–06
Food, Beverage, and Tobacco	324,599	532,506	1,661,369	4,255,465	6,875,310	12,522,115	21,357,788	39,506,277
Textile	755,633	1,543,912	2,438,157	5,666,176	12,768,417	20,181,621	43,865,654	106,974,542
Chemicals, Rubber, and Plastics	285,908	608,275	2,762,109	5,838,031	5,854,918	13,404,482	48,046,324	103,095,663
Non-Metallic Mineral Products	280,005	381,094	769,461	2,583,354	4,429,540	5,130,420	4,943,613	33,436,318
Basic Metal	62,758	103,676	141,288	22,347,369	22,545,955	19,304,034	33,431,734	19,194,325
Metal Products Machinery and Equipment	230,384	640,699	1,395,935	2,176,696	3,960,237	8,931,978	15,265,025	39,131,849
Other Industries	266,583	285,577	940,889	702,725	1,429,150	1,559,135	1,906,331	10,298,320
Total of Sindh	2,205,870	4,095,739	10,109,208	43,569,816	57,863,527	81,033,785	168,816,469	351,637,294

Source: Pakistan Bureau of Statistics, *Census of Manufacturing Industries*, Islamabad, Statistics Division, Government of Pakistan, various years.

Figure 11.1A: Industrial Production Index of Sindh
(1969–70 to 1980–81)

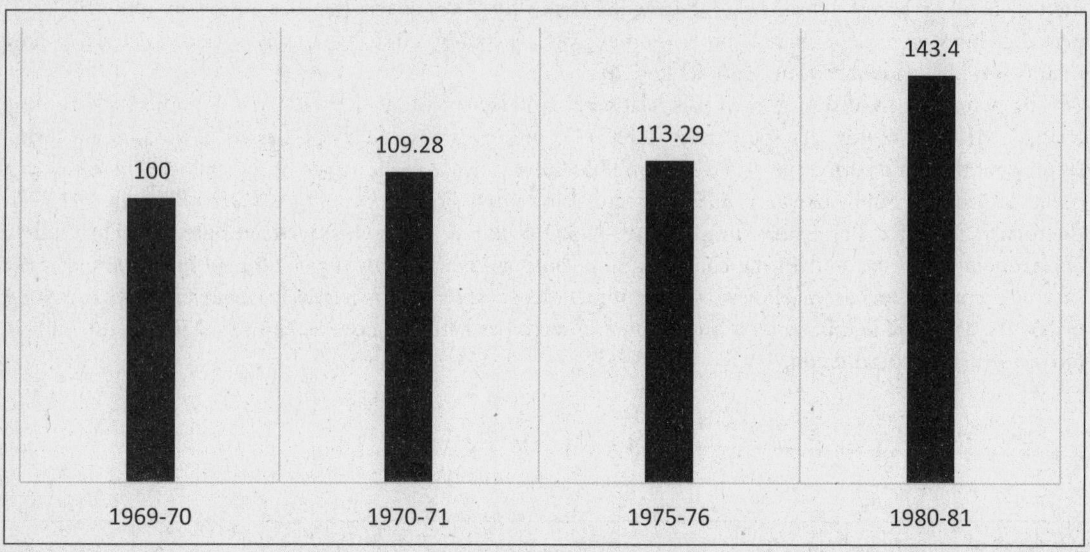

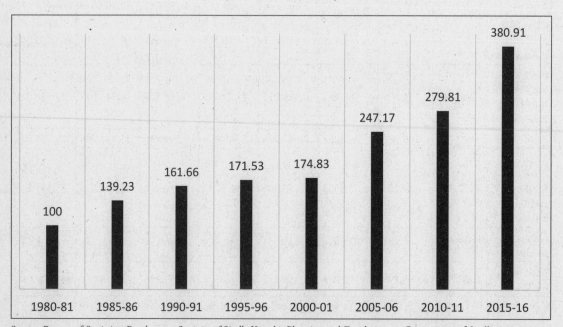

Source: Bureau of Statistics, *Development Statistics of Sindh*, Karachi, Planning and Development Department, Government of Sindh, various years.

Figure 11.1B: Industrial Production Index of Sindh
(1980–81 to 2015–16)

Source: Bureau of Statistics, *Development Statistics of Sindh*, Karachi, Planning and Development, Government of Sindh, various years; Bureau of Statistics, *Monthly Survey of Industrial Production and Employment (2015–16)*, Karachi, Planning and Development, Government of Sindh, 2016.

Table 11.10: Industrial Growth in Large-scale manufacturing Sector of Sindh
(in PKR Million)
(1970–71 to 2005–06)

	No. of Reporting Establishments	Average Daily Employment	Employment Cost	Value of Fixed Assets	Value of Production	Industrial Cost	Value Added During the Year at Factor Cost
1970–71	1,534	176,226	570	2,205.9	6,178.18	3,626	2,552
1975–76	1,362	234,498	1,376	4,095.7	15,060.65	10,161	4,899
1980–81	1,557	191,251	2,768	10,109.2	44,936.66	31,148	13,789
1985–86	1,609	218,396	6,437	43,569.8	85,497.62	57,617	27,880
1990–91	1,751	254,647	13,798	57,853.5	181,493.08	127,992	53,501
1995–96	1,528	202,580	20,499	81,033.8	285,289.79	193,329	91,961
2000–01	1,768	259,267	32,526	168,816.5	535,387.20	356,972	178,415
2005–06	1,825	290,376	53,060	351,637.3	1,200,402.29	751,700	425,627

Source: Pakistan Bureau of Statistics, *Census of Manufacturing Industries*, Islamabad, Statistics Division, Government of Pakistan, various years.

Table 11.10 brings together a summary of the main variables that have affected industrial development in Sindh over the last thirty-five years. The main findings from a perusal of this table are that the policy makers should not expect employment absorption, particularly in large-scale manufacturing industries. Despite the advent of contractual labour, part time labour, outsourcing of work, and underrepresenting of data in the CMI, it is obvious that the pattern is moving towards capital-intensive industries or where labour can be substituted by capital in a cost-effective manner. As the demand for cement, automobiles, consumer electronics, chemicals, and petrochemical products, and oil refining keeps on rising due to an emerging middle class, the capacity to absorb unskilled or semi-skilled labour in the manufacturing sector is likely to recede.

Trends in Production of Major Industries

AUTOMOBILES

In the 1950s, General Motors set up the first automobile plant in Karachi for the assembly of Bedford Trucks. Today, Sindh has five of Pakistan's six auto-assembling plants.[13] Automobile production (Figure 11.2) has recorded a compound average annual growth rate of 7.1 per cent during 1975–76 to 2015–16. Collection of data on production levels of automobiles did not start until 1975–76, hence no data is available for 1970–71.

In 1975–76, the number of automobiles produced was 32,327, which remained unspectacular and reached merely 52,973 by 1985–86. The next fifteen years proved disastrous for the industry due to a highly uncertain import policy on used cars under the Personal Baggage Scheme. Production sank to 51,290 by 2000–01. An improvement in the auto policy and buoyancy in the overall economy resulted in an unprecedented expansion of the industry as it reached a figure of 174,897 in the next four years. The momentum once again slowed down in the period after 2008–09 and the recovery has begun only in the last two years. The taxi scheme introduced by the Government of Punjab gave a major boost to Suzuki cars and the overall industry production jumped up to 504,504 by 2015–16.

Figure 11.2: Automobiles (Excluding Cars) Production in Sindh
(1975–76 to 2015–16)

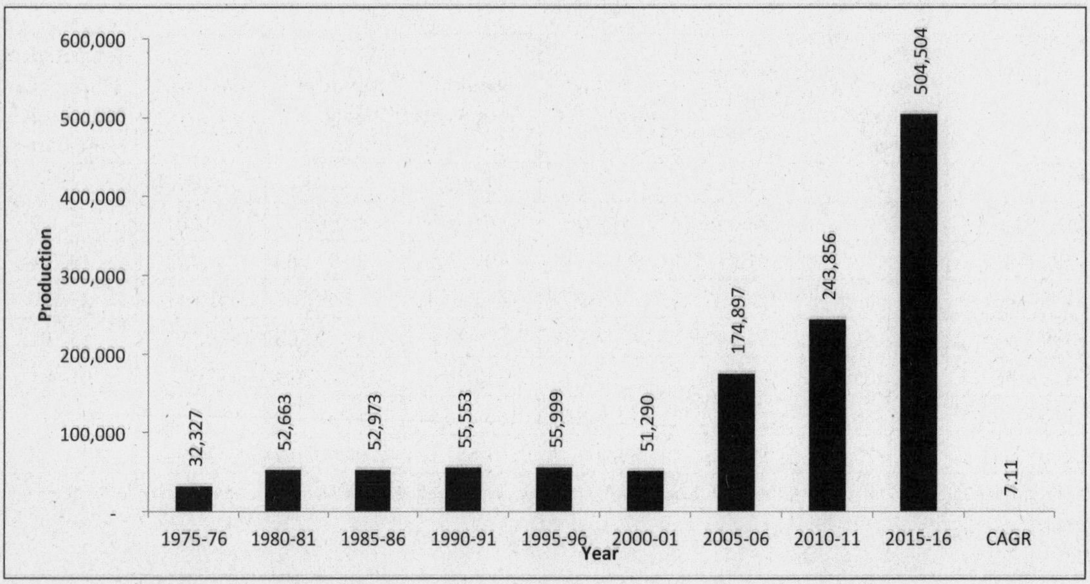

Sources: Bureau of Statistics, *Development Statistics of Sindh*, Karachi, Planning and Development, Government of Sindh, various years; Bureau of Statistics, *Monthly Survey of Industrial Production and Employment (2015–16)*, Karachi, Planning and Development, Government of Sindh, 2016.

CAGR—calculated using data from the mentioned sources.

VEGETABLE GHEE

The vegetable ghee industry was set up as part of the private sector in the beginning but was nationalised in 1973 and put under the Ghee Corporation of Pakistan (GCP). During the period 1974–75 there were eight vegetable ghee units operating in Sindh with a total installed capacity of 3,000 tons on a three-shift basis.[14] Today, 35 per cent of the country's total edible oil processing units are in Sindh.[15] Figure 11.3 shows the production levels of vegetable ghee and the compound annual growth rate (CAGR) over the period 1970–71 to 2015–16. The industry has grown at an average annual rate of 4.7 per cent in the 45-year time period. The production level of vegetable ghee during 1970–71 was 54,189 tons, which has risen to 437,482 tons by 2015–16 or almost eight times the 1970–71 level. This shows the surge in demand due to high income elasticity of vegetable ghee.

Figure 11.3: Vegetable Ghee Production in Sindh (in Million Tonne)
(1970–71 to 2015–16)

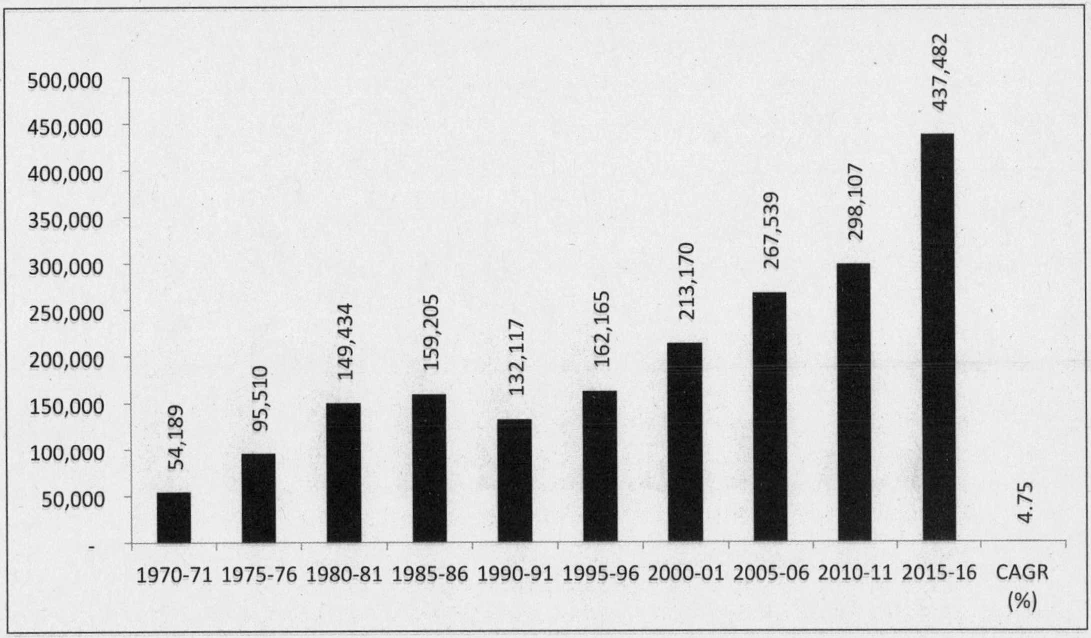

Sources: Bureau of Statistics, *Development Statistics of Sindh*, Karachi, Planning and Development, Government of Sindh, various years; Bureau of Statistics, *Monthly Survey of Industrial Production and Employment (2015–16)*, Karachi, Planning and Development, Government of Sindh, 2016.

CAGR—calculated using data from the mentioned sources.

SUGAR

The sugar industry is an agro-based industry using sugarcane as its basic input. At the time of Independence, Pakistan inherited two sugar mills.[16] Today, there are 78 sugar mills with a total capacity of 365,000 TCD (tons crushed per day) which can produce about 31,025 tons of sugar daily.[17] Thirty-two of the seventy-eight sugar mills, or 41 per cent of the total, are located in Sindh.[18] Sindh has a suitable climate for the growth of sugarcane and it is easier to set up the manufacturing base where the raw material is readily available. About 87 per cent of the sugarcane grown in Sindh is used by the sugar mills. Production levels shown in Figure 11.4, indicate that the industry has had an annual compound growth rate for this period of 5 per cent.

In 1970–71, the production level was 202,808 tons which tripled by 1985–86 and grew fivefold by 2000–01. By 2015–16, Sindh produced 1.84 million tons of cane sugar which represents nine times increase over the base period thus indicating an increase in the per capita consumption of refined sugar in the country, by both the domestic households as well as the commercial and industrial users of sugar.

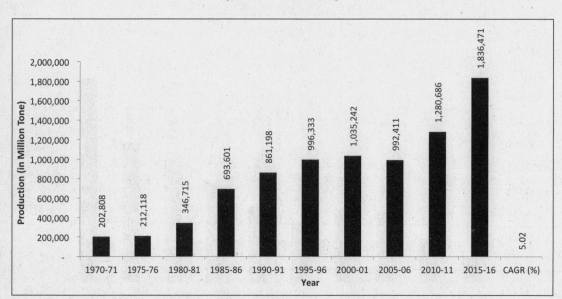

Figure 11.4: Sugar Production in Sindh (in Million Tonne)
(1970–71 to 2015–16)

Sources: Bureau of Statistics, *Development Statistics of Sindh*, Karachi, Planning and Development, Government of Sindh, various years; Bureau of Statistics, *Monthly Survey of Industrial Production and Employment (2015–16)*, Karachi, Planning and Development, Government of Sindh, 2016.

CAGR—calculated using data from the mentioned sources.

COTTON TEXTILE

Pakistan is the fourth largest producer of cotton in the world and ranks third in the world in terms of yarn production. The manufacturing of textile and garments is not an alien concept in the province as well. Sindh has a history in manufacturing of textiles dating back to the Indus Valley Civilisation, around 3,000 BC.

The textile manufacturing sector still holds salience in the industrial sector of the province with cotton textile dominating the sector. This sector has the longest production chain with potential for value addition at each stage from cotton ginning, spinning, fabric, dyeing, finishing, and garments.

One reason for the domination of cotton textiles is that the input, cotton, is easily available in the province with one million acres sown every year mainly in the districts of Naushahro Feroze, Benazirabad, Sanghar, Sukkur, Ghotki, Hyderabad, and Mirpurkhas.

Cotton Fabric

Cotton fabric production reported in the official data is partial and incomplete as it does not capture the production outside the organised sector. The highest production level during the forty-five-year time period was 324 million square metres recorded in the year 1970–71. Since then, there has been a gradual decline and the present production level (2015–16) has come down to 224 million sq. metres. The low value-added cotton yarn and cotton cloth have lost their weightage as the relatively higher value-added garments, knitwear, and apparels have made inroads.

Figure 11.5: Cotton Fabric Production in Sindh (in million sq. meters)
(1970–71 to 2015–16)

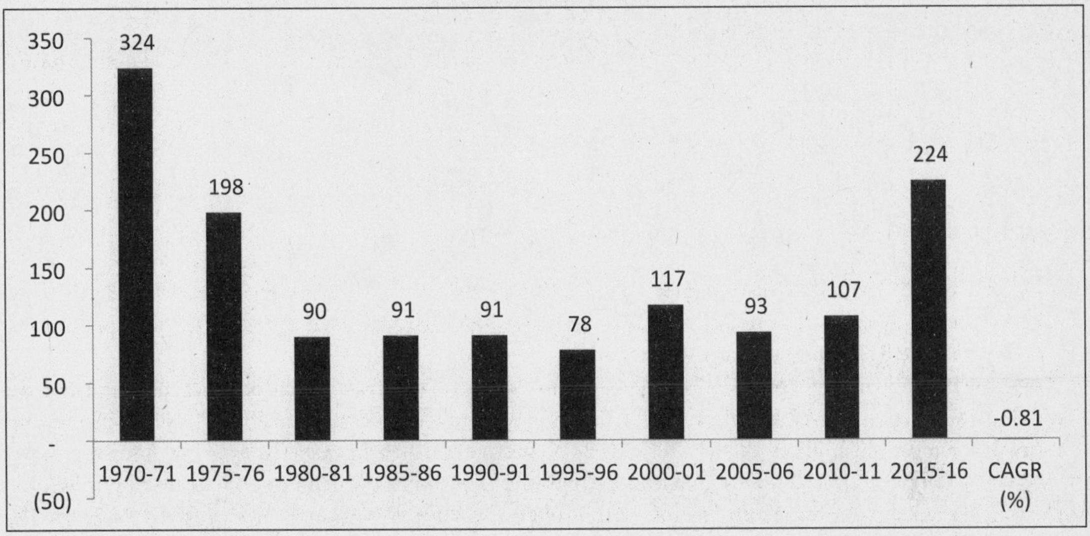

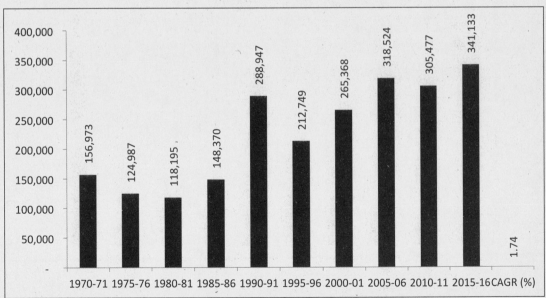

Sources: Bureau of Statistics, *Development Statistics of Sindh*, Karachi, Planning and Development, Government of Sindh, various years; Bureau of Statistics, *Monthly Survey of Industrial Production and Employment (2015–16)*, Karachi, Planning and Development, Government of Sindh, 2016.

CAGR—calculated using data from the mentioned sources.

Figure 11.6: Cotton Yarn Production in Sindh (in Million Tonnes)
(1970–71 to 2015–16)

Sources: Bureau of Statistics, *Development Statistics of Sindh*, Karachi, Planning and Development, Government of Sindh, various years; Bureau of Statistics, *Monthly Survey of Industrial Production and Employment (2015–16)*, Karachi, Planning and Development, Government of Sindh, 2016.

CAGR—calculated using data from the mentioned sources.

Cotton Yarn

As compared to cotton fabric production, cotton yarn has not done so badly. The annual rate of growth over the forty-five-year period was close to 2 per cent.

In 1970–71, the production level was 156,973 tons, which kept declining until 1980–81. The turnaround took place in 1985–86 and despite some temporary shortfalls, it almost doubled by 2000–01. The production accelerated by 11.7 per cent between 2010–11 and 2015–16. The yarn production in 2015–16 was twice more than that of the level in 1970–71.

CEMENT

Cement was one of the few industries that existed in Sindh, although at a modest scale, before 1947. The production grew at an annual rate of 4.66 per cent over the last forty-five years. By 1970–71, Cement production had already reached 1.396 million tons.

The growing demand by construction industry and infrastructure gave a big boost to the industry. By 1985–86, it was producing 2724,654 tons. The industry suffered a big setback in the 1990s and the output was down by almost one million tons by 2000–01 or about one third of the installed capacity. A big uptake in the demand took place after 2000–01 due to fast economic growth rates which not only led to full utilisation of the existing capacity for recovering the lost output but also a huge expansion in new capacity. By 2015–16, the cement factories in Sindh were producing 10 million tons—over six times the output in 2000–01.

Figure 11.7: Cement Production in Sindh (in Million Tonnes)
(1970–71 to 2015–16)

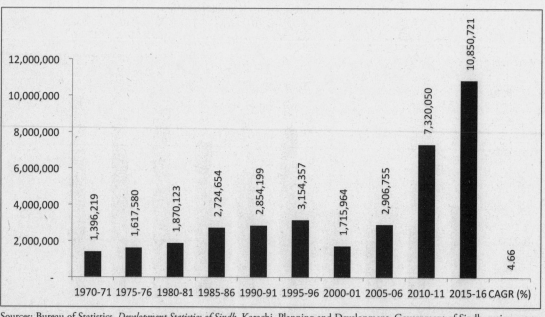

Sources: Bureau of Statistics, *Development Statistics of Sindh*, Karachi, Planning and Development, Government of Sindh, various years; Bureau of Statistics, *Monthly Survey of Industrial Production and Employment (2015–16)*, Karachi, Planning and Development, Government of Sindh, 2016.

CAGR—calculated using data from the mentioned sources.

FERTILISER

The Food and Agricultural Organisation (FAO) made an assessment of Pakistan's agriculture sector that led to an agreement with the Government of Pakistan for setting up the Rapid Soil Fertility Survey and Popularisation of the use of Fertilisers Project in 1958.[19] The project concluded that Pakistan's agriculture output can be enhanced with the use of fertilisers. Hence, improving the fertiliser sector was a major part of Ayub Khan's Green Revolution in the 1960s. The National Fertiliser Corporation (NFC) set up the first fertiliser plant in 1958. Exxon set up the first private sector fertiliser plant in 1965 at Daharki. Fauji Foundation set up another private plant in 1977 and was followed by Dawood Hercules later on.[20]

In 1975, there was only one fertiliser factory operating in Sindh and it was located in Daharki. The capacity of the unit was 175,000 tons but during 1974–75, the actual production was 205,000 tons.[21] However, the demand for fertiliser exceeded the supply and another plant was set up in 1980–81 at Mirpur Mathelo by the National Fertiliser Corporation with a capacity of 570,000 tons,[22] a mega boost to meet the future demand.

Figure 11.8 shows the movement over time in production of fertilisers in Sindh. The annual average compound growth rate between 1970–71 and 2015–16 is 4.25 per cent. In 1970–71, the production level was 175,796 tons, which tripled to 565,123 tons in the next ten years, i.e. a jump of 221.4 per cent. It more

Figure 11.8: Fertiliser (Urea) Production in Sindh (in Million Tonnes)
(1970–71 to 2015–16)

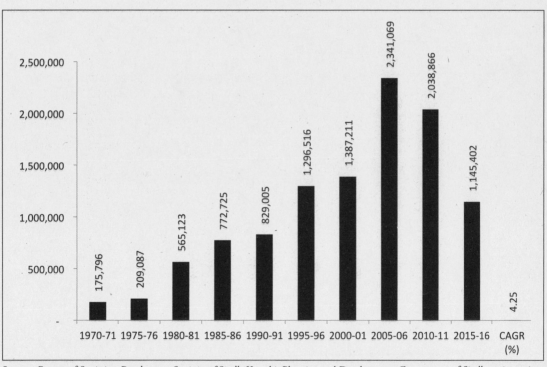

Sources: Bureau of Statistics, *Development Statistics of Sindh*, Karachi, Planning and Development, Government of Sindh, various years; Bureau of Statistics, *Monthly Survey of Industrial Production and Employment (2015–16)*, Karachi, Planning and Development, Government of Sindh, 2016.

CAGR—calculated using data from the mentioned sources.

than doubled again by 2000–01. As a growing number of non-progressive farmers found out the benefits of fertiliser usage, additional demand kept on soaring and the production level reached a peak of 2.34 million tons in 2005–06—an addition of almost one million tons in five years' time. Since then, the imposition of sales tax and shortages of natural gas—the feedstock for the fertiliser industry—have caused a setback and production has fallen to 1.15 million tons by 2015–16. The gains of the early 2000s have been neutralised.

Chemical

Sindh's chemical industry is based on natural gas-based liquid fuels and petrochemicals and has attracted large capital flows.

Figure 11.9 shows that this industry, starting from a small base, has grown the fastest at an average annual rate of 16.9 per cent over the 1970–71 to 2005–06 period.

In 1970–71, the production value was PKR 338 million which multiplied quite rapidly to reach PKR 42.98 billion by 2000–01. The next five years witnessed a doubling of the production value.

The induction of a highly capital-intensive purified terephthalic acid (PTA) plant by a reputable multinational company at Karachi gave a big boost to the industry. It is estimated that the value of production currently would be as high as PKR 384 billion.

Figure 11.9: Value of Chemical Production in Sindh (in PKR Million)
(1970–71 to 2005–06)

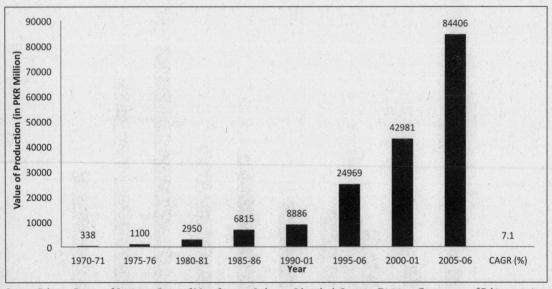

Source: Pakistan Bureau of Statistics, *Census of Manufacturing Industries*, Islamabad, Statistics Division, Government of Pakistan, various years.

CAGR—calculated from the mentioned source.

PHARMACEUTICALS

At the time of Independence, Pakistan had no pharmaceutical manufacturing unit. Today, it has 386 local companies and has attracted 30 multinational companies. Sindh occupies a dominant position in this industry as 92 of 386 local companies and 23 of the 30 multinational companies are operating in Sindh. The top five pharmaceutical companies have a market share of 26 per cent and all five of them are located in Karachi.[23]

The annual average growth rate of drug production and pharmaceuticals over the thirty-five-year time period shown in Figure 11.10 was quite high, i.e. 16.3 per cent.

In 1970–71, the production value was only PKR 309 million which stood at PKR 60.5 billion in 2005–06. The present estimates of the value of national production of drugs and pharmaceuticals is approximately PKR 315 billion and the bulk of the industry is located in Sindh, estimated roughly between PKR 120–130 billion. The scope of exports from this industry is limited ($200 million) because there are no FDA-approved plants in Pakistan. On the other hand, the Indian industry exports products worth $12 billion annually or sixty times as high as ours as it has twenty FDA approved plants in the country.

Figure 11.10: Value of Pharmaceutical Production in Pakistan (in PKR Million)
(1970–71 to 2005–06)

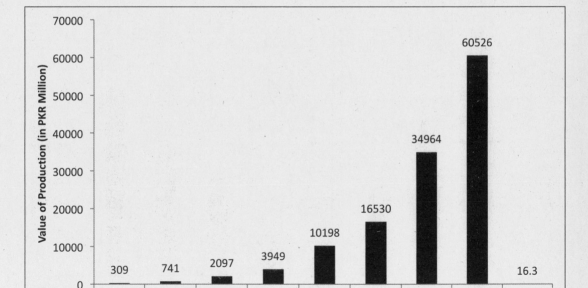

Source: Pakistan Bureau of Statistics, *Census of Manufacturing Industries*, Islamabad, Statistics Division, Government of Pakistan, various years.

CAGR—calculated from the mentioned source.

ELECTRICAL MACHINERY AND ELECTRONICS INDUSTRY

The electronics industry in Sindh, from an international perspective, is still in its early stages. However, Sindh's strategic location makes it an attractive place for foreign investments due to the availability of cheap and efficient labour engaged in quick assembly operations. This industry can help Sindh emerge as a major part of the global value chain as it can help in merging with the final assembly operations of firms in other international locations.[24]

Production of electronics in Figure 11.11 grew at an annual rate of 15.9 per cent over thirty-five years, albeit from a very low base. Investments by several large multinationals such as Siemens, Phillips, LG, and other contributed to this phenomenal growth.

In 1970–71, the production levels were PKR 163 million, which escalated to PKR 1.5 billion by 1980–81—a nine-fold increase in nominal terms in just a decade.

The growth momentum was maintained in subsequent years and by 2005–06, the electronics produced in Sindh amounted to PKR 29.5 billion—almost twenty times the level attained in 1980–81. The latest estimates show that the middle-urban class has been a major driver of the demand for consumer electronics and the domestic industry is gradually substituting imported products in response to this demand.

Figure 11.11: Value of Electronics and Electrical Machinery Production in Sindh
(in PKR Million) (1970–71 to 2005–06)

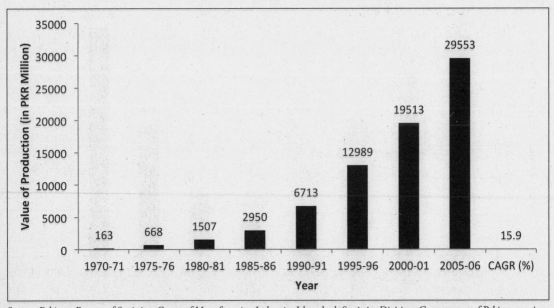

Source: Pakistan Bureau of Statistics, *Census of Manufacturing Industries*, Islamabad, Statistics Division, Government of Pakistan, various years.

CAGR—calculated from the mentioned source

METAL

Sindh's metal industry consists mainly of iron ore, steel, non-ferrous metals, and metal products. However, it lacks in technological sophistication, which requires infusion of capital and know-how by the established players in the global industry.

Steel Mill

In 1953, a senior bureaucrat, Ghulam Faruque, established the Pakistan Industrial Development Corporation (PIDC) with an aim to promote industrialisation in the public and private sectors of Pakistan.[25] PIDC was tasked to arrange finance and technology through potential investors.[26]

Haq Nawaz Akhtar, one of the first chairmen of Pakistan Steel Mills (PSM), states that one of the first projects of PIDC was to make possible a steel mill because it was considered to be a vital component in paving the way for the industrialisation of the country.[27]

By 1956, Pakistan had already received a proposal from the Union of Soviet Socialist Republics (USSR), which offered financial and technical assistance to build the proposed steel mill.[28] In April 1965, President Field Marshal Ayub Khan paid a visit to Moscow, where his government decided to finally build a steel mill.[29]

An agreement with the USSR was signed to provide financial and technical assistance for a coastal-based steel mill near Karachi in 1969. On 30 December 1973, then Prime Minister Zulfikar Ali Bhutto laid the foundation stone of Pakistan Steel Mills as an end-to-end integrated steel mill under the nationalisation programme.[30]

The PSM is based on an area over 18,600 acres, south-east of Karachi, and is linked to the National Highway, railway network, and Port Qasim.[31] Out of the area, over 10,000 acres of land is dedicated to main plants, 8,070 acres is for township, and 200 acres is for the water reservoir.[32] The plants include multiple functionaries: over twenty different plants, including a thermal power station, warehouses, railway tracks, storages for huge fork-lifts, and, stockyards.[33]

Hot and cold rods, and billet (a bar/slab of metal) of various sizes form the portfolio of the Pakistan Steel Mill. The mill has coke ovens, a by-product plant, and blast furnaces. The latter was commissioned on 14 August 1981 and allowed Pakistan to become a proud member of a small group of iron and steel producing nations. Pakistan became a member of the World Steel Association, an elite club, in 2014.[34]

As per the data from World Steel Association's 2010–17 statistical year book, Pakistan is estimated to have produced around 3.6 million metric tons of crude steel in 2016 compared to 2.9 million metric tons of crude steel in 2015.[35] This shows a jump of over 24 per cent in a year, and production has been increasing from 2007.

It is commendable to note that the production of crude steel in the country has increased by almost 2 million metric tons in the past six to seven years while it is equally worrisome to note that the capacity of the PSM alone stands at 1.1 million metric tons per annum, expandable up to 3 million metric tons per annum, although its production levels are negligible.[36] The levels of unemployment and inflation can be controlled, if the PSM is revived and led to function to its operational capacity. This step will provide another added benefit that the losses would be cut, thereby relieving the burden to the exchequer, and the funds could be utilised on infrastructure and welfare elsewhere.

The reason behind the recent dwindling of production is operational losses, political interference—largely in the form of jobs—and unavailable gas, which has worsened the operational and financial situation of the PSM. It is interesting to note that the Steel Mill was already operating at 33 per cent capacity when its gas supply was cut off due to overdue payments.[37]

There is also widespread fear that the machines might no longer function in the future as a result of prolonged stoppages, haphazard and poor maintenances, high-priced imports, low-capacity utilisation, and dwindled funds.

The steel mill was the largest project of its kind at the time and remains the biggest mega corporation of Pakistan. The project, despite being an ambitious and profitable venture by concept, has been marred in controversies surrounding corruption, inefficiency, and political interference. This has led the mega project to become a money drain because of huge losses accumulated over the past decade. The inefficiency and loss to the exchequer has led to calls for the institution to be privatised; however, the attempts to do so are considered to be attempts to sell it off on low prices.

The Pakistan Steel Mill incurred a loss of PKR 16.9 billion in 2008–09, which jumped to PKR 118.7 billion in a matter of five years right about the time when the PML-N government came to power.[38] The accumulated losses of the mill soared to PKR 166 billion while the total liabilities rose to PKR 173bn in 2015–16 from PKR 26.50 billion and PKR 35 billion respectively, in 2008–09.[39]

At present, the total employee strength is 12,800 while their monthly salary bill comes up to about PKR 380 million.[40] The manpower requirements run anywhere between 13,000 and 14,000 personnel—including technical and non-technical employees.[41] Workers have not been paid because of financial problems and the work suffers largely because of lack of gas provision caused by unpaid dues.[42] If the circular deficit problem is not resolved, it will further burden the already under pressure treasury, largely due to a deteriorating rupee and other loss-making industries.

China now accounts for half of the world's steel production. Pakistan, despite its close relations with China, has not derived any benefits by not seeking Chinese collaboration. Recent joint ventures with the Japanese and Korean firms may bring about some technological sophistication. The private sector mills are gearing up by getting themselves listed on the stock market and raising finances for expanding their capacity. The iron and steel industry mainly produces primary iron and steel products including railway track material, wire rod, seamless tubes, and plates. The outputs of non-ferrous metal industries include aluminium, copper, brass, zinc, and tin.[43]

Value of production for the metal industry is (Figure 11.12) given at an annual rate of 17.3 per cent over the 35-year period.

Figure 11.12: Value of Iron, Steel, and Non-ferrous Metal Production in Pakistan
(in PKR Million) (1970–71 to 2005–06)

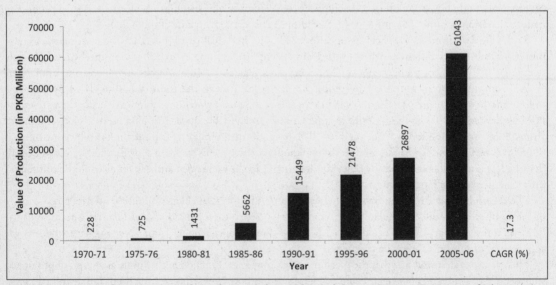

Source: Pakistan Bureau of Statistics, *Census of Manufacturing Industries*, Islamabad, Statistics Division, Government of Pakistan, various years.

CAGR—calculated from the mentioned source.

In 1970–71, the production level was PKR 228 million which rose by over six times in nominal terms to PKR 1.43 billion in 1980–81. A buoyant economy in the 1980s pushed the production levels to PKR 15.4 billion by 1990–91, or ten-fold in a decade.

This pace slowed down in the 1990s and by the end of the decade, the industry had attained a size of PKR 26.9 billion which was only 74 per cent higher than that of the 1990–91 level. If translated in constant prices, the volume of output would either remain unchanged or show a drop. As there is a close correlation between steel consumption and the rate of overall GDP growth, there was a big jump in the five-year period up to 2005–06. The value of production rose to PKR 61 billion by a factor of 2.3 in this short duration. There has been a setback in the last few years as the state-owned Pakistan Steel Mills Corporation has almost shut down its operations due to dire financial difficulties. Dumping of Chinese steel products because of excess capacity has also been a constraining factor in the growth of the industry. Action taken by the National Tariff Commission to offset the material injury to the domestic steel industry has helped the producers.

LEATHER AND LEATHER GOODS

There are currently thirty-three producers of leather and leather goods in the province. The low level of technology is one of the main reasons behind the inefficiency of the industry. If collaboration is established with international partners, many investment opportunities can come to fruition, resulting in efficient production of high quality items for local as well as international consumption.[44]

Figure 11.13: Value of Leather and Leather Product, Production in Sindh (in PKR Million) (1970–71 to 2005–06)

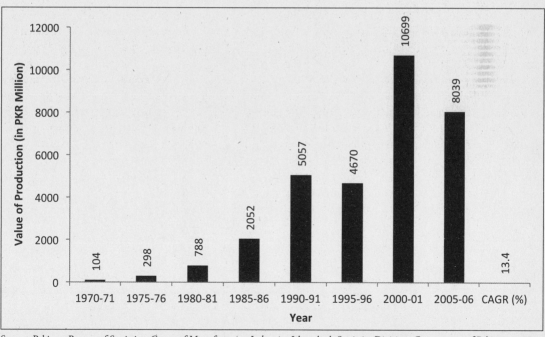

Source: Pakistan Bureau of Statistics, *Census of Manufacturing Industries*, Islamabad, Statistics Division, Government of Pakistan, various years.

CAGR—calculated from the mentioned source.

Production of leather and leather products (Figure 11.13) grew at an annual compound rate of 13.4 per cent over the period. In 1970–71, the production level was PKR 104 million which multiplied almost eight times to reach PKR 788 million in 1980–81. The rate of growth picked up even more in the decade of the 1980s and the value of production touched PKR 5 billion. There was some slippage in the early 1990s but the decade ended up with a doubling in the value. However, the reasons for a decline in the next five years that were the days of the economic boom are not obvious. Exports of leather and leather goods during this period were also quite buoyant.

Small Scale Manufacturing

Small scale manufacturing operates largely in the domain of unorganised or informal economic activities. The surveys carried out are also too infrequent and the national accounts estimates small and medium manufacturing suffer from assumed interpolation during the intervening years between the surveys.

With the lack of data about the composition, value of production, and structure, there is very little information available to carry out any meaningful analysis or discern any trends. Most of it falls in the unorganised or informal sector. Hence, reported data suffers from incompleteness and inaccuracy. Most of the discussion that follows in this section is therefore subject to a certain degree of uncertainty and is mostly speculative, drawing on casual empiricism and scattered observations.

At the time of Partition, very few cottage industries were present in Sindh. According to the Census of 1951, only one out of twenty people was working in the industry.[45] The absence of large scale manufacturing meant that most of the people working in the industrial sector were employed by the small scale sector. The most popular small scale industries were handloom weaving, tanning, shoe manufacturing, pottery, lacquer work, fibre ware, soap manufacturing, and embroidery.[46] However, as industrialisation began and large scale manufacturing came to the province, the small scale manufacturing sector rose in tandem although incentives and privileges were given to large scale manufacturers only. The public policy stance towards SSM was that of indifference.

Today, 25 per cent of small scale manufacturing in Pakistan is located in Sindh.[47] Small and medium enterprises (SMEs) have done quite well as far as employment—both self-employment and number of employees—is concerned. Credit, finance, and labour training facilities[48] have become available over time but their scope is limited. Bank credit to the SME sector accounts for only 6 per cent of total advances as the ratio of non-performing loans is relatively high. Training and vocational institutes under the public sector have failed to perform and Sindh TEVTA has now brought in the private sector to participate in various training schemes. It is also encouraging that philanthropic organisations and foundations have set up modern training facilities in vocations for which there is market demand. As the certification requirements are quite rigorous and learning standards and environment are highly conducive, the output from these few institutes is finding its way readily in the industry, start-ups by enterprising individuals, and to the Gulf countries.

A brief description of the main small-scale industries operating in Sindh is given below.

Lacquer Work

Known commonly as *Jundry Jo Kam*, this sector is responsible for the production of chairs, *masehris*, *jhoolas* (*Peengho/Peenghas*), cot legs, and flower pots. The manufacturing bases for these products are located at Hala and Khanote in Hyderabad district and Khairpur and Kashmore in Jacobabad district. New products have also made way in this industry and include but are not limited to match boxes, cigarette boxes, ashtrays, table lamps, pedestal lamps, walking sticks, toys, and sofa sets.

HANDLOOMS

Spinning wheel and handloom weaving continue to play a major role in rural areas. Clothes are made mainly from silk and cotton. For women, shirts are made from Susi and trousers are made from Mathra, keeping in line with Sindhi colour combination and design. Ajrak is used in making clothes like chaddars etc. and is not gender specific. Niwar and Khes are also important part of silk and cotton handicrafts. The production bases for textiles are located in Nasarpar, Matiari, Hala, and Gambut. Tharkparkar district is famous for the production of Jazim, Mod, and Farasi, and Loi, made from wool, goat hair and camel hair, as the inhabitants possess the inputs required.

EMBROIDERY

Embroidery work or *Bherat Jo Kam* uses cotton, silk, and leather for base inputs. The embroidery industry is no longer limited to producing Guj and Patti but has diversified their outputs which now include bed covers, table covers, screens, and curtains. This sector is popular in both rural and urban areas and has been commercialised due to the popularity of its products. Leather embroidered articles are no longer limited to production of saddles for horses but have expanded to include purses, chappals, shoes, and belts. Hyderabad is a famous production site for leather work.

JEWELLERY

Throughout Sindh, a wide range of traditional jewellery can be found ornamented with enamel in shades of blue, green, red, and yellow. Jewellery is mostly produced by setting uncut stones in gold or silver. Hyderabad is known for its glass bangles.

POTTERY

This sector is famous for production of tiles, made from red clay and lime stone, hinting at a Persian influence. These tiles are commonly known as blue tiles. This sector has become more diverse in terms of products. From producing household utensils such as common plates and bowls, it has started producing quality coffee sets, dinning sets, wall plates, and decoration pieces. The pottery industry also includes building materials such as bricks. Glazed pottery is one of the famous products of this industry and its production sites include Hala, Nasarpur, and Thatta.

MARBLE CRAFT

Onyx, commonly known as green marble, is a major output of this industry. It is used in making lamps, stands for various items, flowerpots, jars, paper weights, bowls, table tops, and ashtrays. Green marble is also used as a material for construction of buildings.

METAL CRAFT

This industry uses brass and copper as main inputs and in addition to shaping them artistically, they employ embossing and cut work. The final output of this industry includes flowerpots, decoration pieces, table tops, and ashtrays. Karachi and Hyderabad are amongst the famous locations for such work, while Khairpur is known for Bidri work.

CARPET KNOTTING

This industry was famous in the province even before Partition. Hand-knotted carpets are among the most important export commodities. This industry has kept up with changing times in terms of design and patterns, and remains valid even today. Hyderabad Central Jail has been very famous for knitting carpets. The prisoners jailed on longer sentences were trained in carpet-making.

AUTO PARTS INDUSTRY

This industry is classified as SME and auto parts made by such SMEs have made a significant contribution to Sindh's economy. There are 850 industrial parts manufacturers in Pakistan and 50 per cent of them are located in Sindh.[49] These SMEs are responsible for the creation of 110,000 jobs in the country out of which 60,000 are Sindh-based.[50] Investment recorded in this industry in the country is PKR 26 billion out of which PKR 12 billion is invested in the auto parts industry in Sindh.[51] The output of this industry includes but is not limited to bumpers, belts, condensers, splash guards, automobile water tanks, and punching pieces.

Small industries are also responsible for the production of Banarsi saris, scarves and suits not only locally but also internationally. Karachi and Khairpur are major production sites for Banarsi textiles. Ivory, wood, and bone carving to make decoration pieces and jewellery are some of other output of small industries.

Institutional Support for SMEs

To facilitate the small industries of Sindh, the Sindh Small Industries Corporation (SSIC) was set up in 1972. It is one of the three institutions supporting industrialisation in the province. SSIC is responsible for providing training to the workers, development of infrastructure to facilitate small industries, development of marketing facilities, and supply of raw materials. It is currently involved in the development of the handicraft industry by building 100 housing units and a workshop by investing PKR 133 million.[52] A handicraft colony has also been established in Mithi that can attract new investments and generate employment.

Despite all the efforts, the small scale industry is not receiving the marketing, advertising, and promotional support it needs and cannot afford on its own. For example, handicraft used to be a major source of livelihood among people in rural Sindh and contributed 50 per cent to their overall incomes.[53] It used to be the most common trade amongst rural people but during the last 15–20 years, the production has fallen and people have shifted to other trades such as agriculture and livestock breeding. There used to be 700 ajrak makers but in 2010 it was recorded that only 10–15 were left in this trade.[54] There used to be 10,000 workshops in Hala Town alone and today, the number has fallen to a few.[55] SSIC has been blamed for being irresponsible and indulging in corrupt practices and the lack of monitoring of its activities seems to be the reason behind the fall of the once booming handicraft industry.

Small scale industries can be developed further with skilled craftsmen, better investments, and facilities. These industries have proved to be an excellent source of foreign exchange earnings, for example in 1973–74, the five handicraft shops established by SSIC sold handicrafts worth PKR 27 lac which included foreign exchange earnings of PKR 6 lac.[56] Accelerating that pace by a 600,000-vigorous institutional support system would have brought the exports of handicraft across the mark of USD 100 million by now.

Boosting this industry will not only have a positive effect on the country's income but also provide employment opportunities to the people.

Comparative Analysis of Sindh, Punjab, and the National Average

In this section, a comparison has been made between Punjab and Sindh in terms of their industrial sectors over a thirty-five-year period from 1970–71 to 2005–06.

The same variables are used for comparison of Sindh with the national level. In doing so, shares of Sindh and Punjab have been calculated for the variables used to determine the health and performance of the industrial sector of the economy in two advanced provinces of the country.

Since the last Census for Manufacturing Industries (CMI) was conducted in 2005–06, the analysis is limited. Just like Sindh, Punjab is industrialised and progressing. Though its industrialisation started later than Sindh's, Punjab has fared well and is ahead of Sindh in almost all the variables used for comparison.

Table 11.11: Relative Contribution of Punjab and Sindh in Manufacturing
(1970–71 and 2005–06)

	Pakistan (%)		Sindh (%)		Punjab (%)	
	1970–71	2005–06	1970–71	2005–06	1970–71	2005–06
No. of Reporting Establishments	100	100	43.2	28.4	53.7	55.9
Average Daily Employment	100	100	41.2	30.8	51.7	59.3
Employment Cost	100	100	50.1	40.1	43.2	51.2
Value of Fixed Assets	100	100	42.6	30.6	46.9	56.5
Value of Production	100	100	46.3	41.0	45.6	48.0
Industrial Cost	100	100	44.9	41.2	47.4	49.3
Value Added During the Year at Factor Cost	100	100	48.5	41.6	42.9	46.3

Sources: Statistics Division, *Census of Manufacturing Industries 1970–71*, Islamabad, Statistics Division, Government of Pakistan, 1977; Pakistan Bureau of Statistics, *Census of Manufacturing Industries 2005–6*, Islamabad, Statistics Division Government of Pakistan, 2009.

Table 11.11 presents a comparative picture of the historical evolution of the manufacturing sector in Pakistan. The two large provinces—Punjab and Sindh—account for 80 per cent of the country's population and almost 86 per cent of the national GDP. The locational advantage of the port city, a relatively large pool of skilled and unskilled labour, and a bourgeoning educated middle class with purchasing power has attracted a number of industrial units. But the deteriorating law and order situation, extortion and kidnapping of businessmen, target killing of professionals, and poor conditions of roads, bridges, water supply, garbage collection, and sanitation in the last decade or so have led to shifting of industries from Karachi or a slowdown in the establishment of new units. Lahore, on the other hand, is a high liveable city enjoying peace, good infrastructure, and responsive administration, a constellation of reputable institutions of higher learning. Therefore, there was a natural tendency to prefer Lahore over Karachi for industrialists and entrepreneurs. As the data ends in 2005–06, the above developments are not reflected.

The data in Table 11.12 reflects very clearly that Sindh had an edge, which it enjoyed in the 1990 but that space has been occupied by Punjab. There is certainly a palpable increase in the relative share of the latter under each variable mirrored by a simultaneous decline in that of Sindh. In other words, the other two provinces—Khyber Pakhtunkhwa and Balochistan—have remained on the periphery and have not benefitted as much from this transfer of industry out of Karachi and the rest of the province.

Table 11.12: Contribution to Seasonal GDP by Punjab and Sindh at Producer Prices
(in PKR Million)
(1990–91 to 2005–06)

Year	Pakistan	Punjab	Share of Punjab (%)	Sindh	Share of Sindh (%)
1990–91	87,852	38,230	43.5	42,323	48.2
1995–96	169,207	67,403	39.8	74,736	44.2
2000–01	279,821	105,093	37.6	147,131	52.6
2005–06	912,147	411,990	45.2	373,429	40.9

Source: Pakistan Bureau of Statistics, *Census of Manufacturing Industries*, Islamabad, Government of Pakistan, various years.

Table 11.13: Census Value Added by Sindh and Punjab (1970–71 to 2005–06)

Year	Sindh	Punjab
1970–71	48.2	42.9
1975–76	44.7	44.2
1980–81	48.1	42.8
1985–86	50.4	38.0
1990–91	48.2	43.2
1995–96	43.3	41.2
2000–01	48.7	41.1
2005–06	41.6	46.3

Source: Pakistan Bureau of Statistics, *Census of Manufacturing Industries*, Islamabad, Statistics Division, Government of Pakistan, various years.

Recent Developments

The restoration of law and order in Karachi, since 2014 has halted the relocation of industries away from the city. Existing capacity is being expanded and new plants are in offing. The main constraint right now is the availability of land in the established industrial zones or clusters.

The government has started rehabilitation of SITE Sukkur, Hyderabad, and Small Industrial Estates in Sukkur and Larkana as possible centres for new industries. PKR 800 million have been allocated for setting up for the rehabilitation of the industrial estates' rehabilitation.[57] The government has also established Small Industrial Estate for Power Looms on 500 acres in Hyderabad.[58] In addition, it invested PKR 1,148 million for establishment of the Khairpur Special Economic Zone for the Agro Industry in Khairpur.[59] Moreover, the water supply pipeline from Keenjhar Lake to SITE Nooriabad has been laid and a water filter plant, which provides 5 million gallons per day, has been constructed at SITE Hyderabad.[60]

One Combined Effluent Treatment Plant (CETP) at Kotri and four CETPs for the industrial areas of Karachi have been established. A number of special economic zones and mega industrial zones are being established all over the province.[61] These zones are said to be the gateway for better investment and employment opportunities in the province since they offer incentives such as duty and tax-free import of equipment, income tax exemption, depreciation allowance, and provision of utilities.[62] Larkana, Nawabshah, Tharparkar, Thatta, Hala, Badin, and Khairpur have been indicated as the main locations for these SEZs.[63]

COMPARATIVE ADVANTAGE

The manufacturing sectors of Sindh exist in large clusters, mostly in or close to urban areas and many clusters are concentrated around Karachi. This eases the flow of technology, knowledge, and know-how among businesses and increase competition by intensifying business rivalries. This also expands the employment opportunities available to skilled workers. As the migration to Karachi from various parts of the country is quite high, labour shortages are seldom a constraint faced by the industry.

The availability of low-cost factors of production such as agricultural inputs and cheap labour in Sindh makes the province an attractive low-cost investment destination. Furthermore, Sindh has access to the rest of the world through the sea and holds an excellent position along the regional trade and energy corridor. The province is home to the country's oldest and most well-developed seaport through which Sindh serves as a trade gateway to Pakistan. Sindh is also home to the country's largest international airport, located in Karachi, which further increases the province's position as the major trade gateway. Sindh's industrial clusters are export-oriented and being a major trade gateway, the costs of transportation are relatively lower than other provinces. In addition to this, the province possesses a strong telecommunication sector. The human resource base of urban Sindh is highly developed. Literacy rates, enrolment rates, retention rates, and completion rates are among the highest in the country. The presence of reputable universities, professional colleges, schools and top-class health facilities have attracted managerial, technical, and professional manpower resources to the cities, particularly Karachi. Nooriabad, Hub, and Kotri have benefitted from their proximity to Karachi and Hyderabad metropolises while Khairpur and Shikarpur have to become integrated with the greater Sukkur metropolitan areas.

The social diversity of the province has played a major role in the development of new businesses, entrepreneurship, and links with other provinces. Hence, in addition to being large and young, the workforce of the province is diverse.

WEAKNESSES

The province has seen arrested development in the last decade as deteriorating security issues restricted flow of investment and talent. The foreigners were reluctant to come to Karachi even for a visit while the established businesses are relocating to other safer and secure places.

There were serious power and electricity shortages, which reduced the operating hours of the mills/industries, causing them to work below their optimal level and reduced their efficiency in terms of quality and quantity of output. Irregular power supply also increases the cost of production and adds to the reasons of lack of investment. In the absence of new hydropower plants, usage of thermal power, based on rise in oil import prices, had led to a pricing disadvantage.

High protection offered to local industries has caused them to become complacent, leading to inefficient and uncompetitive local production and discouraged foreign investment. Though production in the province is moving away from primary products towards high value-added output, this movement has been slow and needs to pick up pace in order to increase diversification and improve quality.

The migration of skilled and trained workers to Gulf countries who could effectively operate large, complicated, modern plants has further added to the problems in the manufacturing sector of the province. Though Sindh is abundant in cheap labour, the supply of adequately trained personnel possessing vocational-technical education and having acquired job-oriented skills is inadequate. Sindh faces a major issue of poor management and misgovernance. Though the province is rich in natural resources, poor management has caused much of it to be misutilised, inefficiently allocated, and wasted. Bureaucratic hassle and intrusion has added to the woes of the manufacturing sector. The communication gap between the different departments of the province has led to a constant state of confusion regarding their roles and responsibilities. This leads to inefficient execution and delivery of development projects.

Sindh has a weak data and research base. The last CMI was done in 2005–06 and even then, the representativeness of sample, the coverage of industrial units particularly newly established, non-response rate, and lack of quality checks on the accuracy of reported data make it extremely difficult to carry out any meaningful analysis. The province has been bearing all the costs of having a large nerve centre of the national economy with a seaport and airport. There is no additional resource transfer to the province to compensate for the costs incurred on behalf of the entire country.

Finally, the stunted growth of small and medium enterprise played a significant part in the inhibited growth of the manufacturing sector of. High cost of doing business, difficulties in finding access to finance, complicated procedure and legal requirements, antiquated production technology, and lack of skilled workers are some of the factors which play a part in stunting the development of small and medium enterprises. This in turn has an adverse effect on the manufacturing sector of the province.

Summing Up

Sindh had developed a reasonably sound industrial base but there has been a slow-down in the pace of industrial growth due to a variety of reasons, the most important being the deteriorating law and order and security challenges in Karachi. The security situation has improved since 2014 but the ease of doing business has not. Looking towards the future, the major challenges faced by Sindh in its industrial sector are rapid urbanisation, rural–urban disparities, job creation for the bulging youth and continuous migration from the rest of the country.

Rapid urbanisation has led to an urban sprawl and the economies of scale and agglomeration have given way to a fragmented, divisive, and inefficient system of urban planning and management. Multiple agencies operating independently in different jurisdictions follow their own rules, norms, and practices. There is an urgent need for establishing dedicated and integrated industrial zones with all the utilities and facilities available within the zone. Coordination among various agencies by an effective district government can bring this about. Master plans for water, sewerage, solid water disposal, electric power, and mass transit should take into account the requirements of these industrial zones. Priority should be accorded to industries in the provision of utilities, facilities, and services. The allottees of the plots who do not utilise them for the purpose within the specified time should be penalised by mandatory cancellation and no bilateral transfers or sub-leasing of plots must be allowed.

Technical and vocational training institutes should be managed and operated throughout the province according to the needs of the particular place. For example, Daharki is now the centre for fertiliser production and the firms operating these plants have set up training institutes which draw young people from the adjoining areas and train them in the skills they would need. Upon successful completion of their training, these youths are employed by these firms. A similar initiative has been taken around Thar coal exploration and development area where the company is recruiting local youth and imparting training for the jobs that would have to be filled at the production and operation stage. AKU and SIUT have training programmes for nurses, laboratory technicians, paramedics, and other vocations who are subsequently absorbed in the same or other institutions. This model has many advantages, e.g., reducing rural–urban disparities, employment of younger population, overcoming critical skill shortages, and improving the productivity of industrial units. The current mismatch between supply of unemployable graduates from colleges and universities and demand by the industries for marketable skills would be minimised to the larger advantage of Sindh and Pakistan's economy.

For accelerating industrial growth:

(a) Infrastructure deficiencies and constraints need to be overcome.
(b) Ease of doing business should be given utmost attention.
(c) Efforts to develop human capital and train labour forces should be increased.
(d) Upgradation of machinery and equipment.

There is a need to eliminate energy shortages and invest in the power and natural gas sector. The Sindh government needs to play a major part in formulation and execution of policies and push the federal government to quickly end the lingering crisis of circular debt in power sector. Furthermore, Sindh needs to build better inter-provincial and intra-provincial transport links. Since most of the trade is done by trucks through the region, a better road network is needed in order to increase the reach of industrialisation. The province also needs to work in the area of telecommunication. In order to secure local and foreign investments, great attention should be paid to improve business environment and maintain law and order. Industrial zones must have their own security forces within their perimeters to protect and preserve property and lives. This will stabilise the social and economic environment and provide security to investors, causing the province to become an attractive investment destination once again.

The province also needs to pay attention to human capital. Though labour is cheap and abundant, most of it is unskilled, which reduces Sindh's industrial productivity. The province needs to upgrade the curriculum in educational institutions, focus more on job-oriented education and training, and develop special training schemes such as the Benazir Bhutto Shaheed Youth Development Programme. This will prepare a skilled and efficient workforce, leading to an increase in the productivity of the province. In addition to this, the health infrastructure needs to be revisited and reformed. A healthy population will lead to lower absence from educational and training programmes which in turn will produce a better, more informed, and trained workforce. Reduced absences from jobs will increase productivity and timely delivery of the work.

A level playing field should be provided to all industries and competition among them should be encouraged. The present patronage-ridden system, where selected few favourites get all the preferences in the allocation of scarce public goods and services, has to be disposed of. Sindh has suffered a lot in the recent years due to this inequitable system which has led to flight of capital and talent. This tendency has to be curbed and if possible, eliminated, to give investors some confidence and assurance of fair play and even-handed treatment.

The Sindh Board of Investment (SBI) has to actively explore opportunities in export-oriented industries in the province to set up joint ventures. China is relocating some of its textile units to Vietnam, Cambodia etc. Pakistan is a low cost producer and Sindh has major ports; the production and transport costs would confer an advantage upon it.

Keti Bandar Industrial Estate under CPEC is an ideal site for the relocation of Chinese industries and other direct investors. The changed security situation needs to be brought to the attention of foreign investors through specially organised visits.

Moreover, Sindh's industrial sector is in dire need of technology upgradation and modernisation. The sector must upgrade its machinery. Upgradation of machinery will reduce cost of production and time consumption. The sector also needs to invest in innovation and value-addition. It needs to move away from the production of primary product for exports and shift towards value-added products. It needs to seek out and collaborate with successful international organisations and firms, and study, learn, and implement their structure and skills. It should invite foreign technocrats and professionals to train its workers. It should work towards transfer of technology and knowledge from such organisations. Implementation of this recommendation will lead to a better-structured and competent industrial sector.

Sindh needs to expand its research and development base. By building a better research base, Sindh can increase its industrial productivity in a short time. More university–industry links need to be established and funds should be created for research grants. Investment in R&D will be beneficial in the long-run and returns on this investment will be visible in the increased productivity in the sector.

Clusters of industries should be carefully planned to cut down costs. Agro-based industries should be near the location of input so that perishable inputs are not wasted during long hours of transportation. Industries should be located keeping in mind factors such as infrastructure, land, public utility, services, education, medical care, and cost of material, labour, fuel and power, duties and taxes, cost involved in procurement of raw materials and distribution of output. Foot-loose industries i.e. those industries that are not tied to any particular source or market, or their access to input is based on their location, should be established in places which are not suitable for supply-oriented industries i.e. those industries for which such factors are decisive in their location.

Diversification, technological upgradation, and competitiveness, push towards high value-added products to meet global competition.

12

Energy and Mineral Resources

Energy Resources of Sindh

Before the late 1950s, Sindh was not known to be rich in hydrocarbons. The Government of India began exploratory activity in Sindh in 1893 by drilling a well in Sukkur, which did not yield anything. The next attempt for the search of oil and gas in Sindh began after an interval of more than three decades by Burmah Oil Company, a Scottish oil business in Khairpur. Like its predecessor, the project did not result in discovery of oil. Until 1947, exploration was underway mainly in Punjab where four oil discoveries were made since the initiation of the process in 1868.

After the creation of Pakistan, the nascent country strove to meet its energy requirements independently. Pakistan Petroleum Limited was founded in 1950. Its first project involved drilling near the town of Sui, Balochistan, leading to the discovery of the largest gas field of the country.

Several players were involved in oil and gas exploration in Punjab, Balochistan, and Sindh. Table 12.1 shows, however, that no gas was discovered in Sindh until 1956 and no oil was found until 1981.

Table 12.1: Oil and Gas Exploration Efforts in Sindh

Well Name	Operator	Spud Date	Status
Sukkur	GOI	1893	Abandoned
Khairpur	BOC	29 Oct 1925	Abandoned
Drigh Road	BOC	05 Jan 1939	Abandoned
Lakhra	BOC	02 May 1948	Abandoned
Karachi	PPL	07 Aug 1956	Abandoned
Khairpur	PPL	14 Sept 1956 Completion date: 06 Apr 1957	Gas
Followed by over 100 exploratory wells, which resulted in 7 discoveries of gas.			
Khaskeli	UTP	14 May 1981 Completion date: 02 Jul-1981	Oil

Source: Hydrocarbon Development Institute of Pakistan, *Pakistan Energy Year Book 2014*, Islamabad, Ministry of Petroleum and Natural Resources, Government of Pakistan, 2015.

OIL AND GAS DISCOVERED IN SINDH

In 1957, Pakistan Petroleum discovered natural gas in Khairpur. In the same year, gas reserves were found both in Mari (of 6.3 trillion cubic feet, the second largest gas reserves in Pakistan) and Talhar by Pak-Stanvoc Petroleum Project (a joint venture by the Government of Pakistan and Esso Eastern Incorporated). The next year, the Burmah Oil Company drilled and discovered some gas in Lakhra, Badro, and Phulji Dadu. And in 1959, Pak-Stanvoc Petroleum Project discovered small gas reserve in Bathoro and some gas and oil in Nabisar. The project also attempted to drill oil in Badin, but did not discover any reserves. In the same year, Pakistan Petroleum Limited discovered a small amount of gas in Kandhkot and Mazarni.

However, during 1960–70, gas exploration shrunk and the focus shifted to oil exploration all over Pakistan. The companies that were involved in exploration during this period were Sun Oil Company (SOC), ESSO Eastern Inc. (ESSO), and OGDC (Oil and Gas Development Corporation established in 1961). Sun Oil Co. focused mainly on coastal areas; it drilled wells in Patiani Creek and Dabbo Creek in 1964, and Korangi Creek in the following year. Oil exploration proved fruitless all over the country; 453 exploratory wells were drilled out of which 60 were located in Sindh, and as a result of these efforts, only one small gas field was discovered at Sari, Sindh, by OGDC in 1966.

In the decade 1970–80, 417 exploratory wells were drilled out of which 127 were in Sindh. Only five significant gas fields were discovered, out of which, two were located in Sindh. The two discovered oil fields were both in Punjab. Companies that were most active during this period in Sindh were Pakistan Petroleum Limited (PPL), ESSO, OGDC, and Union Texas Pakistan (UTP). Offshore drilling was carried out for the first time in Sindh by Wintershall, a German company. The company drilled Indus Marine A-1 and Indus Marine B-1 in 1972, and Indus Marine C-1 in 1975. OGDC drilled and found gas in substantial amounts in Kothar in 1973 and Hundi in 1977. Husky Refining Company, an American company, drilled a well in Karachi South A-1 in 1978 and also located gas. However, no major discovery was registered.

During 1980–1990, widespread exploration for hydrocarbons was carried out in Pakistan; 5,775 wells were drilled, out of which 1,724 were located in Sindh and resulted in the discovery of large oil reserves. The companies leading the drilling expeditions were UTP, ESSO, PPL, and OGDC. The Khaskheli Oil Field was a breakthrough discovery in the coastal district of Badin by UTP in 1981. In 1984, Tando Adam Oil Field was also drilled and completed. This was followed by more significant oil discoveries in Laghari and Mazari.

In the 1990s, a total of thirty-one oil fields were discovered in Pakistan out of which twenty-three were in Sindh (the rest being in Punjab). The contribution of Sindh in gas production exceeded Balochistan's (Figure 12.10). In 1990, the third largest gas field in Pakistan was discovered in Qadirpur by OGDC. In the same year, Kadanwari was discovered by LASMO (now Eni). This discovery was followed by Miano by OMV in 1993, Bhit by LASMO in 1997, Sawan by OMV in 1998, Zamzama by BHP in 1998, and Mari Deep by MGCL in 1997–98. More than a decade later, Sindh continues to be the focus of oil and gas exploration and discovery in Pakistan.

Hydrocarbon Basins

Hydrocarbon basins in Sindh include the following.

LOWER INDUS/MIDDLE INDUS BASIN

The oil discovery in the lower Indus basin made by Union Texas Pakistan in 1981 at Khaskheli was the second major breakthrough in the exploration of hydrocarbons after Sui. It is located to the south of Mari–Kandhkot High and to the east of Kirthar Foldbelt.[1] The exploration in the Middle Indus Basin started in 1989 with

Figure 12.1: Hydrocarbon Basins

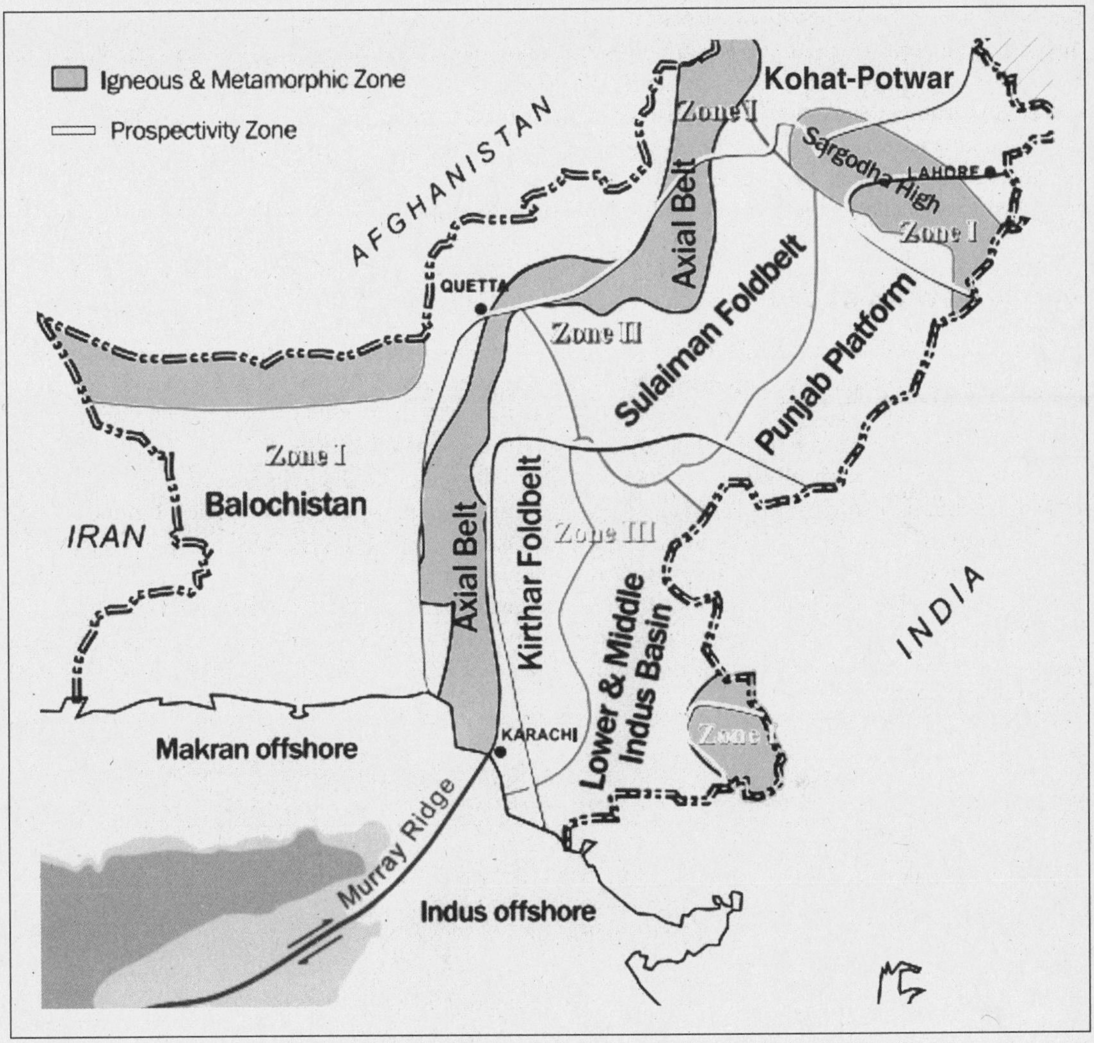

Source: Nasim A. Khan, *Energy Resources and Their Utilization in Pakistan*, Karachi, Hamdard University Press, 2010.

the discovery of Qadirpur by OGDCL followed by various discoveries by OMV and Eni in partnership with OGDCL, PPL, and others.

KIRTHAR FOLDBELT

Kirthar Foldbelt is the north–south trending tectonic feature. It includes Kirthar Foldbelt, Kirthar Foredeep, and the southern Axial Belt. Proven or potentially viable plays range in age from Triassic to the recent age. The first commercial discovery was made in 1998 by Eni followed by another discovery in the same year by BHP.[2]

INDUS OFFSHORE BASIN

Similar to the prolific gas and oil of Mahakam, Nile, and Niger deltas, the Indus offshore basin is the second largest submarine fan system in the world. The Indus Fan is bounded by Murray Ridge on the west. Potentially viable plays range in age from Lower Eocene-Middle Miocene to Oligocene-Neogene.

The first exploration venture in the basin dates back to 1961 when the Sun Oil Company (USA) drilled three exploratory wells followed by three wells drilled by Wintershell (Germany). The basin holds immense potential for hydrocarbons. The Indus Offshore has only undergone limited exploration and provides a lucrative opportunity for big discoveries through drilling and seismic techniques.

Recent Developments

While Pakistan has shown a subpar success rate of oil and gas discovery of 1:3 (compared to the world's 1994 rate of 1:1.3), the country has yielded significant amounts in recent years.[3] In the span of three years since 2013, eighty-three oil and gas discoveries have been made. These have added 631 million cubic feet per day (mmcfd) gas and 27,359 barrels per day (bpd) crude oil to the total reserves of Pakistan.[4]

In 2015, 1,095 bpd crude oil supply was found at Tando Allahyar by OGDC.[5] In June 2016, a total number of six discoveries were made across Pakistan, adding 50.1 mmcfd of gas and 2,359 of crude oil to the existing production levels. Out of these six discoveries, four were made in Sindh. This included one discovery each by PEL and UEP and two by OGDC. These discoveries comprised more than 63 per cent of the gas, but only 14 per cent bpd of crude oil. The other two discoveries were made in KP by MOL Pakistan.[6]

The focus of oil and gas exploration has now shifted from Sindh to the other provinces. Fifty new exploration blocks were created in January 2014, of them only 12 per cent lie in Sindh. The chart below describes their distribution by province.

Figure 12.2: New Exploration Blocks in Pakistan (2014)

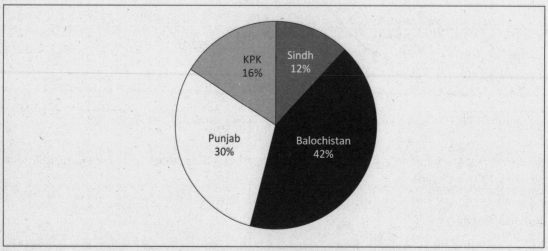

Source: '50 licences awarded for exploration of gas, oil', *Dawn*, Karachi, 24 January 2014.

DISCOVERY (OFF-SHORE)

Offshore Pakistan is divided into two basins: the Indus Basin and the Makran Basin, separated by the Murray Ridge (Figure 12.1). Mainly driven by its similar geology with other deltas rich in hydrocarbons, offshore areas of the Indus delta have indicated tremendous potential of oil and gas in seismic surveys. The interest in the Indus Delta is more recent, only since 1961, but poor success rate offshore in this delta has been a cause of discouragement. Moreover, the cost of such projects is enormously high—a single exploration well can cost in the range of $60 million to $200 million. A list of major exploratory wells that had been drilled offshore in Pakistan until 2010 is shown in Table 12.2. The spud dates and completion dates are also mentioned. None of these resulted in any substantial discovery.[7]

Table 12.2: Spud and Completion Dates of Major Offshore Exploratory Wells of Pakistan (1963–2010)

	Spud (Initial Drilling)	Completion Dates of Major Offshore Exploratory Wells in Pakistan
Dabbo Creek	20 November 1963	8 August 1964
Korangi Creek	25 October 1964	21 February 1965
Indus Marine	12 September 1972	14 December 1972
Indus Marine	15 December 1972	14 March 1973
Indus Marine	4 March 1975	13 May 1975
Jal Pari	30 December 1976	13 February 1977
Karachi South	28 February 1978	9 May 1978
Pakcan	27 September 1985	1 February 1986
Sadaf	22 December 1989	8 March 1990
Pasni	11 October 1999	5 January 2000
Gwadar	31 January 2000	5 January 2000
PakG2	12 May 2004	N/A
Pasni	18 February 2005	N/A
Anne Ax	10 January 2007	N/A
Shark	17 January 2010	19 November 2007

Source: Hydrocarbon Development Institute of Pakistan, *Pakistan Energy Year Book 2014*, Islamabad, Ministry of Petroleum and Natural Resources, 2015.

Note: completion dates of Shark, Pasni Anne Ax and Pak G2 Pasni are not available.

As of 2013, the Ministry of Petroleum and Natural Resources, Government of Pakistan, has given sixteen licenses for gas exploration in the Indus Basin, while no licensees are working in Makran. The areas for which these licenses are applicable are shown in Figure 12.3. While private companies are still interested in exploring, the high risk, cost, and time required relative to onshore exploration repels potential investors. If the government wants to exploit offshore areas, it must encourage public–private partnerships and share the risks.

Figure 12.3: Licenses for Gas Exploration in the Indus Basin

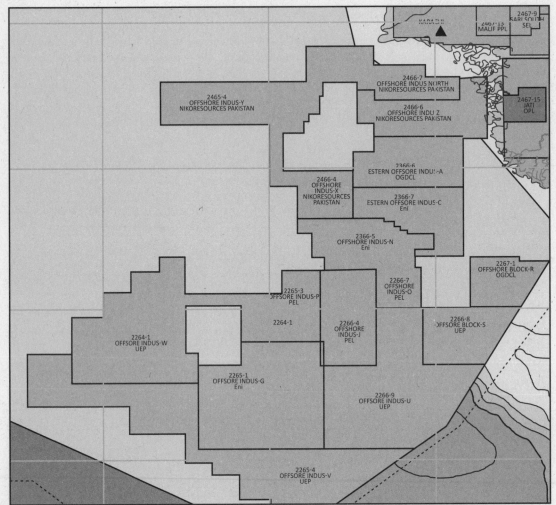

Source: Directorate General of Petroleum Concessions, *Upstream Petroleum Activities 2016*, Islamabad, Pakistan Petroleum Information Service, Government of Pakistan, 2016

Production and Consumption of Oil

From almost no production in 1980, Sindh started providing 47 per cent of the total oil production of the country in 1985–86. This rate went up gradually to reach 65 per cent in 2000. This has been dwindling and reached an all-time low of 38 per cent by 2014. The absolute volume came down to 1.75 million TOE in 2014 from 1.78 million TOE in 2005. The country as a whole has witnessed an increase of 43 per cent in quantitative terms in the same period. Most of the new oil discoveries in recent years have taken place in Khyber Pakhtunkhwa, which has now replaced Sindh as the top domestic producer of oil.

Table 12.3: Production of Crude Oil in Pakistan and Sindh Tonne of Oil Equivalent (TOE)
(1980 to 2014–15)

	1980–81	1985–86	1990–91	1995–96	2000 –01	2005–06	2010–11	2014–15
Sindh	0	902,277	1,688,213	1,673,877	1,836,840	1,784,182	1,477,343	1,745,865
Pakistan	476,811	1,924,872	3,150,986	2,825,731	2,828,498	3,211,113	3,225,270	4,627,054
Share of Sindh (%)	0	47	54	59	65	56	46	38

Source: Hydrocarbon Development Institute of Pakistan, *Pakistan Energy Year Book*, Islamabad, Ministry of Petroleum and Natural Resources, various years.

In Figure 12.4, Khyber Pakhtunkhwa has shown a steady rise in oil production since 2005, while Punjab's yield has declined and has been constant from 2010 to 2014. Punjab's trend in oil production over the years follows a set pattern showing a period of steady rise followed by a gradual decline. The resource-rich province of Balochistan displays a dismal trend; its production has been constant and significantly less than the production of all other provinces.

Figure 12.4: Production of Crude Oil (in Million TOE) (1980–81 to 2015)

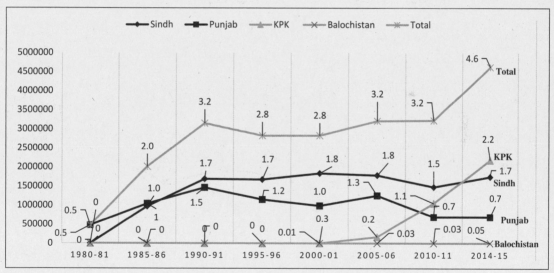

Source: Hydrocarbon Development Institute of Pakistan, *Pakistan Energy Year Book*, Islamabad, Ministry of Petroleum and Natural Resources, Government of Pakistan, various years.

Table 12.4 and Figure 12.5 show consumption of petroleum products at the national and provincial levels. As the industrial and commercial hub of Pakistan, the consumption of petroleum products in Sindh was at its peak during the 1950s. But as economic growth slowed down for a variety of reasons, there has been a gradual decline and the share of petroleum consumption is down to 23 per cent compared to 42 per cent in 1980–81. In absolute terms, oil consumption has risen 2.8 times during this period. For the last two years, the precipitous decline in international oil prices has boosted the domestic demand and furnace oil (FO) once again became an acceptably priced fuel for power generation. Substitution of FO by RLNG for power generation plants under way would, however, reduce the demand for imported FO. Domestic refineries would produce the required quantities.

Table 12.4: Petroleum Energy Products Consumption (TOE)
(1980–81 to 2014–15)

	1980–81	1985–86	1990–91	1995–96	2000–01	2005–06	2010–11	2014–15
Sindh	1,836,019	2,997,989	3,814,398	4,875,542	4,828,670	4,262,858	4,600,108	5,250,428
Pakistan	4,405,037	7,230,927	10,208,708	15,857,729	17,912,815	14,988,128	19,185,600	22,651,899
Share of Sindh (%)	42	41	37	31	27	28	24	23

Source: Hydrocarbon Development Institute of Pakistan, *Pakistan Energy Year Book*, Islamabad, Ministry of Petroleum and Natural Resources, various years.

Figure 12.5: Petroleum Energy Products Consumption by Province (in Million TOE) (1980–2014)

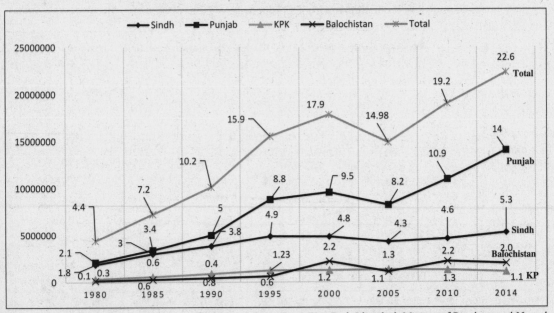

Source: Hydrocarbon Development Institute of Pakistan, *Pakistan Energy Year Book*, Islamabad, Ministry of Petroleum and Natural Resources, various years.

To understand the trends of consumption and production, the time series plots of these two variables are compared with crude oil prices in the world and the GDP of the country. As income per capita and therefore purchasing power rises, the demand—direct and indirect—for petroleum products also rises. But price elasticity does play a key role in consumption. According to Figure 12.8, oil consumption in Pakistan moves roughly along with oil prices. The trend line of the GDP also moves in the same direction, showing positive income elasticity of demand.

Figure 12.6: Petroleum Energy Products Production and Consumption in Sindh
(in Million TOE) (2009–14)

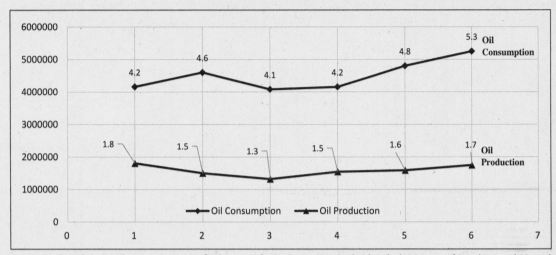

Source: Hydrocarbon Development Institute of Pakistan, *Pakistan Energy Year Book*, Islamabad, Ministry of Petroleum and Natural Resources, Government of Pakistan, various years.

1=2009–10; 2=2010–11; 3=2011–12; 4=2012–13; 5=2013–14; 6= 2014–15

Figure 12.7: Crude Oil Production, GDP of Pakistan, and Crude Oil Price (2007–08 to 2014–15)

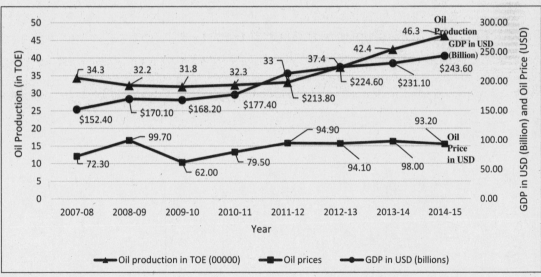

Source: Finance Division, *Pakistan Economic Survey 2013-14*, Islamabad, Ministry of Finance, Government of Pakistan, n.d.; Federal Reserve Bank of St. Louis, 'Crude Oil Prices: Western Texas Intermediate' (WTI), 2017, <https://fred.stlouisfed.org/series/DCOILWTICO#0>; Index Mundi, 'Pakistan-GDP', n.d., <https://www.indexmundi.com/facts/pakistan/gdp>.

Figure 12.8: Oil Consumption, GDP of Pakistan, and Crude Oil Price (1980–2014)

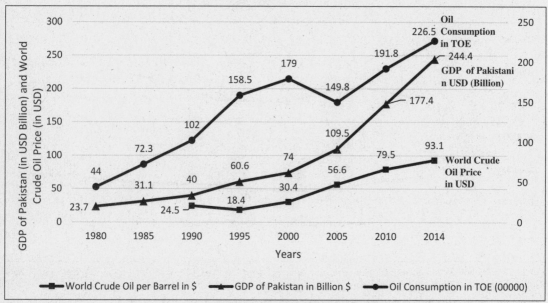

Source: Hydrocarbon Development Institute of Pakistan, *Pakistan Energy Year Book*, Islamabad, Ministry of Petroleum and Natural Resources, Government of Pakistan, various years; World Bank, 'GDP (current $)', 2017, <https://data.worldbank.org/indicator/NY.GDP.MKTP.CD?end=2014&start=1960>.

Federal Reserve Bank of St. Louis, 'Crude Oil Prices: Western Texas Intermediate' (WTI), 2017, <https://fred.stlouisfed.org/series/DCOILWTICO#0>

Production and Consumption of Natural Gas

As pointed out earlier, Sindh has now become a major supplier of natural gas to the country (Table 12.5). From less than 14 per cent of national production in 1980–81 it reached 70 per cent in 2005–06, slighting receding in the last decade. The quantitative expansion during this period 1980–81 to 2014–15 has been quite spectacular—almost twenty-six times in thirty-five years.

The number and proportion of gas consumers in Sindh (Table 12.5) has, however, not kept pace with the rising production levels. The growth in the number of consumer during the last thirty-five years was 6.7 times compared to 10.4 times at the national level. The advantage Sindh offers in attracting gas-intensive industries has not been utilised.

Table 12.5: Natural Gas Production (in MMCFT)
(1980–2015)

	1980–81	1985–86	1990–91	1995–96	2000–01	2005–06	2010–11	2014–15
Sindh	38,150	77,410	177,271	306,972	422,432	982,035	996,913	985,262
Pakistan	285,802	355,354	518,483	666,580	875,433	1,400,026	1,471,591	1,465,760
Share of Sindh (%)	13.4	21.8	34.2	46.1	48.3	70.1	67.7	67.2

Source: Hydrocarbon Development Institute of Pakistan, *Pakistan Energy Year Book*, Karachi, Ministry of Petroleum and Natural Resources, various years.

Figure 12.9 shows the historical time series of gas production by the four provinces. The shift from Balochistan to Sindh and Khyber Pakhtunkhwa is quite perceptible. Unless new discoveries take place in Sindh, it is likely that Khyber Pakhtunkhwa may be able to gain the lead over next decade or so.

Figure 12.9: Natural Gas Production (in MMCFT) by Provinces (1980–81 to 2014–15)

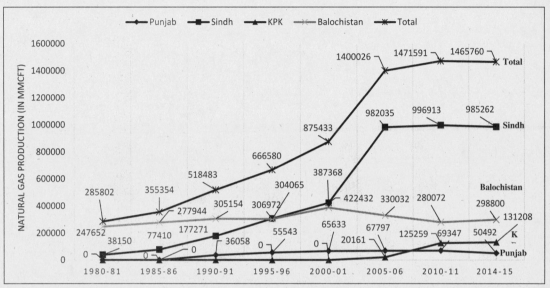

Source: Hydrocarbon Development Institute of Pakistan, *Pakistan Energy Year Book*, Islamabad, Ministry of Petroleum and Natural Resources, various years.

Figure 12.10 shows that in 2015, Sindh consumed 47 per cent of natural gas consumption in the country and is now a major supplier of natural gas to Punjab where domestic consumption is unable to meet the production from within the province.

A comparison of the different usage of gas in Sindh, Punjab, and Pakistan for 2015 is presented in Figure 12.11. Power generation and general industry account for half of the gas consumption in the country,[8] but the usage in Sindh for these two sectors is even higher with 62 per cent of the total consumption in Sindh.[9] Power generation in Sindh itself accounts for 38 per cent of the total consumption of gas in the province.[10] This is higher than the percentage of gas used in power generation in both Punjab (9 per cent) and Pakistan (30 per cent), as plants in the province are based on natural gas as a fuel.[11]

Figure 12.10: Comparison of Natural Gas Consumption and Production by Province
(in MMCFT)
(2014–15)

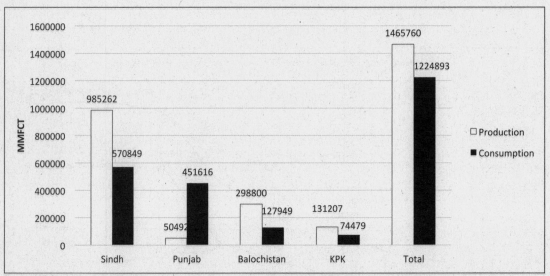

Source: Hydrocarbon Development Institute of Pakistan, *Pakistan Energy Year Book 2015*, Islamabad, Ministry of Petroleum and Natural Resources, 2016.

Table 12.6: Number of Consumers of Natural Gas in Sindh and Pakistan
(1980–2015)

	1980–81*	1985–86*	1990–91*	1995–96*	2000–01	2005–06	2010–11	2014–15
Sindh	369,129	545,938	698,303	1,093,659	1,448,841	1,704,329	2,154,482	2,459,839
Pakistan	740,272	1,111,668	1,533,031	2,616,703	3,591,237	4,549,376	6,332,243	7,692,832
Share of Sindh (%)	49.9	49.1	45.6	41.8	40.3	37.5	34.0	32.0

*Cumulative Number.

Source: Hydrocarbon Development Institute of Pakistan, *Pakistan Energy Year Book*, Karachi, Ministry of Petroleum and Natural Resources, various years.

Policy Issues

When the Eighteenth Amendment was passed in 2010, it caused a temporary hiatus in the much needed progress of the energy sector of Pakistan. It was misconstrued to have awarded provinces the right to construct power houses and grid stations, lay transmission lines, impose taxes, or determine distribution preferences. However, in actuality, this right lay with the provincial governments even before the amendment. The provincial governments had so far lagged in implementing their responsibility due to lack of expertise and resources, inability to provide sovereign guarantees for international funding, and an absence of a national coordination plan. The act was merely a reassurance that the federal government would only take decisions about power generation in any province in concert with the provincial governments. Unfortunately, due to the misinterpretation of the act, the provinces focused their energies in demanding the establishment of provincial regulatory authorities, division of the OGDC and PPL, and direct interaction with exploration and production companies. Regardless of all the hurdles faced by the energy sector as a result of the Eighteenth Amendment, two exploratory and five development wells were drilled for oil and gas in the first half of 2010–11.[12]

To resolve the conundrum, the Ministry of Petroleum and Natural Resources provided marginal field guidelines in 2013, which proved to be successful. After the implementation of these guidelines, the government issued licenses for hydrocarbon exploration in the country. Fifty provisional licenses were granted to eight local and two foreign firms; however, only six of these licenses were implemented in Sindh by ODGC and PPL (Table 12.7).

Figure 12.11: Natural Gas Consumption by Sector in Punjab, Sindh, and Pakistan (%) (2014–15)

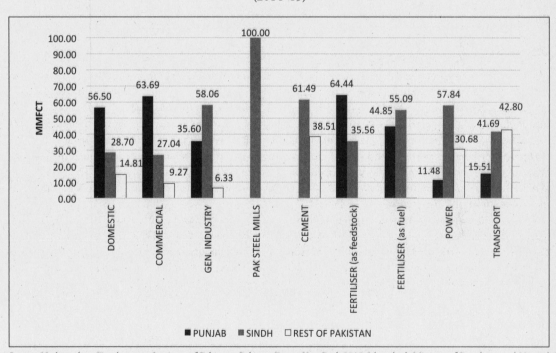

Source: Hydrocarbon Development Institute of Pakistan, *Pakistan Energy Year Book 2015*, Islamabad, Ministry of Petroleum and Natural Resources, 2016.

The situation remains far from satisfactory. A major point of contention is the pricing of natural gas for the fertiliser industry, which is being provided at a concessional rate. The provincial government is also in disagreement with the centre over LNG imports, which lead to substantial losses for Sindh. Moreover, it has declared the Gas Infrastructure Development Cess Ordinance (Act of 2011) illegal and unconstitutional.[13]

Table 12.7: Exploratory On-Shore Licenses in Sindh (2014)

S.No.	Block Name	Districts	Zone	Awarded to
1	2469–9(Armala)	Tharparkar	I	OGDCL
2	2467–13 (Malir)	Karachi and Dadu	II	PPL
3	2569–5 (Khipro East)	Sanghar and Umar Kot	III	PPL
4	2467–16 (Shah Bandar)	Thatta	III	PPL
5	2768–11 (Ranipur)	Larkana, Khairpur, and Naushahro Feroz	III	OGDCL
6	2868–7 (Zorgarh)	Ghotki, Jacobabad, D.G. Khan and Dera Bugti	III	OGDCL

Source: Hydrocarbon Development Institute of Pakistan, *Province-wise Details of Blocks Awarded, Bidding Details of Blocks*, Islamabad, Ministry of Petroleum and Natural Resources, Government of Pakistan, n.d.

Coal

Discovery

The first discovery of coal in Sindh occurred in 1853, when Baloch nomads reportedly struck a coal seam 2.43 meters thick at a depth of 125 meters by sinking a well for water at Lakhra, a village on the western bank of the Indus River in district Dadu, north of Hyderabad. The Burmah Oil Company (1948) and Pak Hunt International (1953) also recorded the presence of coal in this area, while drilling for oil. The Habibullah Mines Ltd. started commercial mining of coal in Lakhra in 1959, while the US Geological Survey carried out exploratory drilling at Lakhra in the 1960s. This area was also intensively explored by the Geological Survey of Pakistan (GSP) and Japan International Cooperation Agency (1981), and in the following years, USAID and WAPDA undertook a mining feasibility study. The Lakhra Coal Mine was considered the largest coal mine of the country until the discovery of coal in Thar.[14]

The second coal field to be discovered in Sindh was the Metting–Jhimpir coalfield in the district of Thatta. Coal production was carried out at both sites, Lakhra and Metting–Jhimpir. This was followed by another discovery in the district of Thatta at Sonda. The Sonda coalfield was discovered in 1981. It is situated in the deltaic area of the lower Indus, approximately 40 kms from Thatta.[15] A modest exploration programme was carried out in Sonda which ended in mid-1980s and was financed by WAPDA, PMDC, and CSP. By 1985, Sonda also began producing coal. Coal at Badin was also discovered around the same time.

In 1991, presence of coal was indicated beneath the Thar Desert, which is located in the south-eastern part of Sindh, during the drilling of water wells by the British Overseas Development Agency (ODA) in coordination with the Sindh Arid Zone Development Authority (SAZDA). Coal was formally discovered there in 1992 by the GSP. It was subsequently deemed the largest coal mine of the country and among the largest in the world. During exploratory drilling at Lakhra–Sonda, it was found that these deposits extend into the Thar Desert.

It was subsequently referred to as a separate coal field called 'Thar Desert' and the deposits are divided into twelve blocks. At the time, the total coal reserves in the field were estimated to be 14.532 billion tonnes (62 per cent of all estimated coal reserves of the country in that year). Only 40 million tonnes of this large reserve was actually measured. Their heating value was said to range between 6,677 and 11,722 Btu/lb. In 2014, Thar Coal Field was estimated to hold 175 billion tons of ignite coal, having the potential to create 100,000 MW of energy. Till 2014, no production of coal was done through this field.

The updated picture of coal reserves of Sindh with its properties is depicted in Tables 12.8 and 12.9. The total reserves in the province are 185,456 million tons, of which 95 per cent are in Thar.

Table 12.8: Sindh Coal Reserves as of June 2015

Area	Seam Thickness Range (Meter)	Measured Reserves (Million Tonnes)	Indicated (Million Tonnes)	Inferred (Million Tonnes)	Hypothetical (Million Tonnes)	Total (Million Tonnes)
Lakhra	0.3–3.3	244	629	455	-	1,328
Sonda-Thatta	0.3–1.5	60	511	2,197	932	3,700
Jherruk	0.3–6.2	106	810	907	-	1,823
Ongar	0.3–1.5	18	77	217	-	312
Indus East	0.3–2.5	51	170	1,556	-	1,777
Meting-Jhimpir	0.3–1.0	10	43	108	-	161
Badin	0.55–3.1	150	0	200	500	850
Thar Coal	0.2–22.81	7,025	17,130	38,650	112,700	175,505
Total	-	7,664	19,370	44,290	114,132	185,456

Source: Hydrocarbon Development Institute of Pakistan, *Pakistan Energy Year Book 2015*, Islamabad, Ministry of Petroleum and Natural Resources, 2016.

Table 12.9: Sindh Coal Quality Proximate Analysis, June 2015

Area	Status	Moisture	Volatile Matter	Fixed Carbon	Ash	Total Sulphur	Rank as per ASTM Classification	Heating Value Range (mmcft)
Lakhra	Dev.	9.7–38.1	18.3–38.6	9.8–38.2	4.3–49.0	1.2–14.8	LigB to SubC	5,503–9,158
Sonda-Thatta	Non-Dev.	22.6–48.0	16.1–36.9	8.9–31.6	2.7–52.0	0.2–15.0	SubC to hvBb	8,878–13,555
Jherruk	Non-Dev.	9.0–39.5	20.0–44.2	15.0–58.8	5.0–39.0	0.4–7.7	SubC to hvCb	8,800–12,846
Ongar	Non-Dev.	9.0–39.5	20.0–44.2	15.0–58.8	5.0–39.0	0.4–7.7	LigB to SubA	5,219–11,172
Indus East	Non-Dev.	9.0–39.5	20.0–44.2	15.0–58.8	5.0–39.0	0.4–7.7	LigA to SubC	7,782–8,660
Meting–Jhimpir	Dev.	26.6–36.6	25.2–34.0	24.1–32.2	8.2–16.8	2.9–5.1	LigA to SubC	7,734–8,612
Badin	Non-Dev.	–	–	–	–	–	–	11,415–11,521
Thar Coal	Non-Dev.	29.6–55.5	23.1–36.6	14.2–34.0	2.9–11.5	0.4–2.9	LigB to SubA	6,244–11,045

Source: Hydrocarbon Development Institute of Pakistan, *Pakistan Energy Year Book 2015*, Islamabad, Ministry of Petroleum and Natural Resources, Government of Pakistan, 2016.

PRODUCTION

The total production of coal in Pakistan in 2014 was 3.71 million tons of which Sindh accounted for one-third as can be seen in Figure 12.12. From 2005 to 2010, overall production of coal showed a drastic decline of 29 per cent in the country followed by a gradual increase of 8 per cent, but it is expected to get a boost with the current mining exploration at several blocks in Thar. The detailed status of activity in Thar is shown in Table 12.11. At the same time, the world is reducing reliance on coal as a source of power generation. Pakistan, which has almost a negligible share of coal, is now engaged in increasing coal-fired power plants. Balochistan still is the highest producer in the country. Coal production levels in Punjab and KP have shown a slight increase during 2008–13; however, production in KP experienced greater fluctuation than Punjab during this period.

Table 12.10: Coal Production in Sindh and Pakistan (in Tonnes) (1980–81 to 2014–15)

	1980–81	1985–86	1990–91	1995–96	2000–01	2005–06	2010–11	2014–15
Sindh	271,114	570,849	914,605	1,277,000	978,540	2,010,000	1,100,500	1,122,313
Pakistan	1,576,922	2,201,607	3,053,908	3,637,825	3,094,652	4,871,159	3,450,091	3,711,561
Share of Sindh (%)	17.2	25.9	29.9	35.1	31.6	41.3	31.90	30.24

Source: Hydrocarbon Development Institute of Pakistan, *Pakistan Energy Year Book*, Islamabad, Ministry of Petroleum and Natural Resources, Government of Pakistan, various years.

Figure 12.12: Coal Production by Province (in Tonnes) (1980–81 to 2014–15)

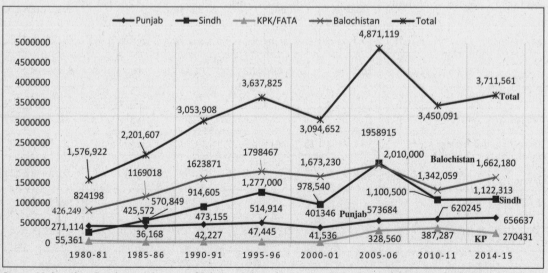

Source: Hydrocarbon Development Institute of Pakistan, *Pakistan Energy Year Book*, Islamabad, Ministry of Petroleum and Natural Resources, Government of Pakistan, various years.

The Sindh Engro Coal Mining Company (SECMC) is actively engaged in coal mining operation of block II of Thar coal reserves while licenses have been issued to other private sector companies. Some of them are foreign investors with technical know-how of the latest techniques which would minimise environmental hazards caused by coal.

Table 12.11: Thar Coal Reserves (in Million Tonnes)—2014

Specific Block/Field	Area (sq. km.)	Drill Holes	Reserves				Total
			Measured	Indicated	Inferred	Hypothetical	
Block-I (Sinhar Vikian Varvia)	122	41	620	1,918	1,028	-	3,566
Block-II (Singharo Bhitro)	55	43	640	944	-	-	1,584
Block-III (Saleh Jo Tar)	99.5	41	411	1,337	258	-	2,006
Block-IV (Sonal Ba)	80	42	637	1,640	282	-	2,559
Sub-Total (Block I-IV)	356.5	167	2,308	5,839	1,568	-	9,715
Rest of Thar coal field	8,643.5	335	4,717	11,291	37,082	112,700	165,790
Total (Thar coal field)	9,000	502	7,025	17,130	38,650	112,700	175,505

Source: Hydrocarbon Development Institute of Pakistan, *Pakistan Energy Year Book 2014*, Islamabad, Ministry of Petroleum and Natural Resources, 2015.

COAL FIRED POWER GENERATION

At the time of Independence, coal's share in the commercial energy of Pakistan was 59 per cent. With the discovery of indigenous oil and gas resources and the increase in oil imports, the share of coal in meeting energy demands fell to 30 per cent in 1963 and by 1993, it was around 5 to 6 per cent.[16] Subsequently, it just fell off the radar screen as the IPPs were mostly allowed to use imported furnace oil for power preservation plans.

In the 1980s, indigenous coal was used mainly in the brick kiln sector and power generation used natural gas in Sindh, Balochistan, and Punjab, and from crude oil in Sindh and Punjab. Imported coal was used mainly by Pakistan Steel Mills, located in Sindh.[17] While coal is cheaper, has a stable international price, and is readily available in Sindh, its environmental costs are high. Besides land surface disturbances, excessive dust concentrations and contaminated mine drainage, and coal burning for power generation and industrial uses releases emissions that contributes to respiratory problems, damage to vegetation, acid rain, and the greenhouse effect. However, proper planning, data collection, clean coal technology, and reclamation and restoration of the mining areas can help to drastically reduce environmental degradation problems attached with coal mining. Pakistan's energy needs had reached a serious crisis level with fewer alternate energy options available. Indigenous energy resources had to be utilised optimally with updated technology, and planning and management techniques, which could mitigate some of the problems with coal fired generation. As Pakistan gears to increase its reliance on coal for power generation, it still pales into insignificance when compared to China and India—the two largest users of coal for thermal power generation—as it is unlikely to exceed 5 to 10 per cent of the total power generation capacity.

Operating and Proposed Coal-fired Power Plants in Sindh

Lakhra Coal Power Station (Partially Operating)

In 1995, WAPDA commissioned three 50-MW coal-fired power plants near Khanot, in the district of Jamshoro in Sindh, with the Dong Fong Electric Corporation of China. These units use fluidised bed combustion technology, most suited for Pakistani coal which is high in sulfur. The power plant consumed 0.5 million tonnes of lignite coal from the Lakhra Mines of PMDC and LCDC annually. The generation cost of the plant was Rs 2.61 per kWh, including the cost of coal and limestone. While operating the plant, WAPDA faced several problems such as boiler tube leakage, air pollution etc. due to supply of coal below the designed specification. The plant was shut down because it was running at de-rated capacity. Unit No. 3 is non-functional since 2009 whereas Unit No. 1 and 2 are running at an underrated load of 30 MW each.[18]

Jamshoro Coal Power Project

The Coal Power Project Jamshoro is being jointly undertaken by the Asian Development Bank, Islamic Development Bank, and the Government of Pakistan to establish a 600MW supercritical coal-fired power generation plant, using an 80/20 blend of imported sub-bituminous coal and domestic lignite. While the loans for this project were obtained in 2014, the construction work has not been initiated as of yet.

Siddiqsons Energy Limited

Siddiqsons Energy Limited (SEL)—formed in September 2014—is engaged in developing a 350 MW[19] supercritical coal fired project in the Eastern Industrial Zone, Port Qasim, Karachi, along with China's state-owned Harbin Electric Corporation. It was anticipated that the construction of the plant will take approximately forty months.[20]

K-Electric Coal Power Plant

In 2014, K-Electric, formerly KESC, signed an MoU with Harbin Electric International (HEI) of China for the setting up of a 660 MW green field coal-fired power plant. This plant is to be the first in the history of Pakistan on the basis of built–operate–transfer. This plant will be operated and maintained by HEI for a limited time and will be then transferred to K-Electric.

Pakistan Port Qasim Power Project

The Pakistan Port Qasim Power Plant—located in Port Qasim Industrial Park, southeast to the city of Karachi—will consist of two 660 MW supercritical units each with one boiler, steam turbine and generator.[21] The boiler will be fuelled by imported sub-bituminous coal which will be transported by ship and unloaded at the dock to be constructed at site. It is a joint venture of China's PowerChina and Qatar's Al-Mirqab Group. Construction began in 2014 and was completed in 2017.

Thar Coal Power Plant

The Private Power and Infrastructure Board (PPIB) and Shanghai Electric Group Company (SEGC) have signed a letter of interest in 2015 for developing two coal-based power projects of 660 MW generation capacity each in

Thar. The project will consume lignite coal, which will be supplied by Sino–Sindh Resources, the lease-holder of Thar block-I. The project is expected to start commercial production in 2018.

UNDERGROUND COAL GASIFICATION

An agreement to carry out the project of underground coal gasification (UCG) at Thar was signed on 23 June, 2010 by the Planning and Commission, Science and Technology, Geological Survey of Pakistan with the approval of the Ministry of Petroleum and Natural Resources. UCG was to develop the process of converting coal to gas. All costs involved for the execution of the project were carried out under the PSDP funded project at Thar.

SECMC POWER PLANT

The Government of Sindh has allocated block II to Sindh Engro Coal Mining Company (SECMC) to excavate 1.57 billion tonnes of coal and build a 660 MW power plant. The plant is expected to dispatch power to the Pakistani national grid by June 2019 and will later be expanded to produce 1,320 MW of power. A state-owned Chinese company, China Machinery & Engineering Corporation (CMEC), is providing the machinery and technical support for the excavation of coal, and for building and running the power plant. The Thar Coal Project was included in the China–Pakistan Economic Corridor and work on the coal field subsequently began in 2015. CPEC includes the creation of eight coal-fired power plants along with other energy and infrastructure related projects. Work on one of these projects has been initiated.

HUB COAL POWER PLANT

Hub Power Company Limited (HUBCO) is a Pakistani power producing company based in Hub, Lasbela district, in Balochistan. Its 1,292 MW plant is located 60 km away from Karachi in Hub; 323 MW oil-fired units generate the electricity that is supplied by 78 km long pipelines from Pakistan State Oil (PSO). In 1994, a loan of USD 425 million was received by HUBCO from the Government of Pakistan via the National Development Finance Corporation. It is considered one of the most successful private–public partnership projects in Pakistan. In January 2015, HUBCO announced that it will set up 1,320 MW coal-based power plants next to its thermal power station at Hub in Balochistan and gradually enhance coal based generation to 3,600 MW. The company's board of directors had formally approved development of two coal-based power plants of 660 MW each. The two plants would be initially run on imported coal for which a coal jetty would also be developed. Hubco reportedly also has enough land available near its 1,292 MW thermal power plant to house six coal plants of 660 MW each and the company has added 1,320 MW capacity in the first phase.

THAL-NOVA COAL POWER PLANT

Thal-Nova Power Thar Private Ltd (TNPTL) is a joint venture between Thal Limited and Novatex Limited. Thal is part of the House of Habib—one of the most respected business houses in Pakistan with investments across banking, auto, retail, building materials, and packaging sectors in Pakistan. Novatex is part of the Gani & Tayub group which is a leading player in the polyester and textile sectors of Pakistan and contributes to a major part of the total exports in the country. It is a 330 MW Thar coal-based power project in Sindh which will be completed by the year 2020. The company would sell power at PKR 3.67 per kilowatt per hour in the first ten years of its operations. The tariff would be reduce to PKR 1.91 per kilowatt per hour for the next twenty years.

Renewable Resources

The oil crises of 1973 and 1979 led to the pursuit of alternative energy sources to fossil fuels. Both the cartelisation of oil producers through OPEC and concerns for damage caused by carbon emissions were the main motivating factors. The dependence on oil was growing at a time when the energy requirements of the world were expanding rapidly. The need for sustainable and renewable energy resources was felt to meet the growing energy requirements as well as to reduce the dependence on oil.

Developed nations were quick to respond with the equipment to harness resources such as solar, wind, geo-thermal, and hydropower. However, developing economies did not have the financial muscle to invest in such ventures owing to the high research and installation costs. Pakistan remains heavily dependent on fossil fuels to meet the country's energy requirements. Oil accounts for 35.2 per cent, hydro-electric 29.9 per cent, gas 29 per cent, and nuclear, solar, wind, and coal six per cent of the total energy requirement. Oil, gas, and nuclear energy fall under the category of non-renewable resources whereas hydro-electric, solar, and wind energy are types of renewable energy resources.

SOLAR ENERGY

Solar energy is derived from the rays of sunlight touching the earth's surface. The solar constant—G_{SC}—is the energy from the sun per unit time, received on a unit area of surface perpendicular to the direction of propagation of the radiation at the earth's mean distance from the sun outside the atmosphere. The value of the solar constant is 1,367 watts/meter^2.[22] The usage of solar energy can be broadly divided into direct and indirect processes; direct processes are technologies which convert sunlight into electricity or heat energy for direct consumption whereas indirect processes convert sunlight into electricity via an intermediate form of energy.

Table 12.12: Daily Insolation Rates for Various Seasons and Regions of Pakistan
(in kwh/m2/day)—2010

Region	Summer	Winter	Fall	Spring	Annual
Southern Sindh Karachi	4.5–5.0	6.0–6.5	5.5–6.0	2.5–3.0	5.5–6.0
Northern Sindh	6.0–6.5	6.5–7.0	6.0–6.5	2.5–3.0	6.0–6.5
Eastern Sindh	6.0–6.5	6.5–7.0	6.0–6.5	2.5–3.0	6.0–6.5
Western Sindh	6.0–6.5	6.0–6.5	5.0–6.65	2.5–3.0	6.0–6.5
Northern Punjab	6.0–6.5	6.0–6.5	5.5–6.0	4.0–4.5	5.5–6.0
Central Punjab	6.0–6.5	6.0–6.5	5.5–6.0	4.0–4.5	5.5–6.0
Lower Punjab	6.0–6.5	6.5–7.0	6.0–6.5	4.0–4.5	6.0–6.5
Northern Balochistan	7.0–7.5	6.5–7.0	7.0–7.5	4.0–4.55	6.0–6.5
Central Balochistan	6.5–7.0	6.5–7.0	6.0–6.5	4.0–4.5	6.0–6.5
Southern Balochistan	4.0–4.5	6.5–7.0	5.5–6.0	2.5–3.0	5.5–6.0
Northern Areas	5.5–6.0	4.5–5.0	5.0–5.5	2.5–3.0	5.0–5.5
Khyber Pakhtunkhwa North	7.0–7.5	4.5–5.0	5.5–6.0	4.0–4.5	5.0–5.5
Khyber Pakhtunkhwa Central	6.0–6.5	6.0–6.5	5.5–6.0	N/A	5.5–6.0
Khyber Pakhtunkhwa South	6.0–6.5	6.0–6.5	5.5–6.0	N/A	5.5–6.0

Source: Ali Akhtar, *Pakistan's energy development: The road ahead*, Karachi, Royal Book Company, 2010.

Sindh, being a sub-tropical and coastal region, faces high temperatures for a major fraction of the year and is rich in solar energy. The world is divided into six solar insolation zones with zone 1 being the highest insolation area (6.0-6.9 kwh/m^2 per day) and zone 6 (1.0-1.9 kwh/m^2 per day) being the lowest. Table 12.12 shows that Sindh falls underÍ zone 1 and zone 2 for a major faction of the year pointing out the availability and sustainability of harnessing solar energy in this region. Keeping this is mind, the government of Pakistan has issued LOIs (letters of intent) with SCATEC, SSJD Bagasse Energy, and Solar Energy Pakistan Ltd. to set up solar power plants in the districts of Sindh, Jhimpur, and Thatta respectively. However, till date, no major solar power plant has been setup in Sindh, but the notion of using this resource is becoming popular in domestic, commercial, and small scale public sector projects. For example, street lights in Karachi are being replaced with solar powered lights so that the dependence on power produced from traditional fuels is gradually reduced.

WIND ENERGY

There is a growing interest to use this source for power generation. Wind energy is used to move turbines which converts kinetic energy of the wind into mechanical energy and subsequently into electrical energy. For instance, a wind blowing at 4.4m/s has approximately 70 watts of power on a surface parallel to sea level. For producing electricity, these systems must be designed at constant angular velocity over a wide range of wind speeds to produce a constant frequency.[23] Although wind energy requires a high installation cost and a low utilisation rate, it will become a major source of energy owing to its zero-fuel cost, abundance and environment friendly nature, and sustainability.[24]

Pakistan, especially the coastal areas of Sindh and Balochistan, receive high speed winds which are ideal and suitable for power generation. The first wind power plant was installed in the Jhimpur district of Sindh in 2009 and has a generation capacity of 56.4 MW today. The Jhimpir Wind Energy Project (FFCEL), with a total installed capacity of 49.5 MW, and Three Gorges First Wind Farm Pakistan Ltd, with an initial installed capacity of 50 MW, have been operational in the same district since December 2012 and December 2014.[25] Jhimpir, Bhambore, Gharo, and Thatta districts offer themselves as attractive locations for installation of wind power plants. Plans are afoot to produce 2,477.5 MW of electricity from this source.

HYDROELECTRIC POWER

Perhaps the most common source of renewable energy in Pakistan and countries across the globe are not wind, solar, or bio-gas but hydroelectric. Hydroelectric power provides almost one-fifth of the world's electricity.[26] It is one of the oldest renewable source of power generation—it was even used by Greek farmers to grind wheat into flour through water wheels.

Hydropower stations convert the kinetic energy of water into mechanical energy which in turn is used to turn turbines and generate electricity. Just like any other renewable energy resource, hydropower uses a renewable source, water, from fast flowing rivers which are fed by rain and snow melting from glaciers. However in order to rotate the turbines, a certain speed of water of considerable magnitude is required, for which dams and reservoirs are created. The water is released to and from the dam and reservoir.

In case of Pakistan, there are eighty-nine dams producing hydropower across the country. However, most of these are located in the northern areas of Pakistan. In areas of Pakistan where dams have not been constructed, hydropower is still a feasible option while in case of Sindh, there is only one hydro plant—Darawat Dam across Nai Baran River near village of Jhangri in Jamshoro district—producing a mere 0.45 MW of electricity. Owing to the absence of dams and the fact that only three barrages exist in Sindh, namely Guddu Barrage, Sukkur Barrage and the Kotri Barrage, it is a challenge to set up a hydro plant in Sindh. Other developing nations such as Vietnam, Cambodia, and India have used other technologies on run-of-the river to generate hydroelectric power.

Pico hydro is a term used for hydroelectric power generation of under 5 KW. It is practical and cost effective for small and remote communities. A Pico-hydro setup is typically run-of-the-river, meaning that dams are not used, but rather pipes divert some of the flow, drop this down a gradient, and through the turbine before returning it to the stream. However, as mentioned earlier, this type of set up is only suitable for a small community. Moreover, it is also highly dependent on the river flow as only a settlement in the immediate vicinity of a river can make use of it.

Sindh, being a coastal area, has another option in the form of tidal hydropower stations. A tidal power station makes use of the daily rise and fall of ocean water due to tides; such sources are highly predictable, and if conditions permit through construction of reservoirs, it can also be dispatched to generate power during high demand periods. However, there are only a small number of locations throughout the world which are suitable for tidal power stations and it is yet to be determined whether our coastal area falls under this category or not.

Electricity

At the time of Pakistan's independence in 1947, the country inherited 60 MW of electricity generation for a population of 31.5 million, thus yielding 4.5 units per capita consumption. During the initial ten years, Pakistan was able to generate electricity through two sources namley hydropower and thermal power.[27] In 1959, when Wapda was established, it undertook projects that increased the power capacity to 119 MW.[28] By 1964–65, electricity generation capacity rose to 636 MW. The momentum accelerated around the 1970s and the commissioning of Tarbela Dam and full utilisation of Mangla Dam hydropower stations doubled capacity to 1,331 MW. The next four decades witnessed considerable expansion, mainly thermal generation, and by 2010, Pakistan's generation capacity had reached 18,467 MW, rising to 20,966 MW in 2015–16.[29] The country has been facing shortages and load shedding for almost nine years. The demand-supply gap is now being tackled through a series of new investments in LNG, coal, wind, solar, and hydroelectric projects. Under CPEC, where China is investing USD 35 billion in power sector projects, it is expected that an additional capacity of 10,000 MW would be added by 2020.

The electricity sector was historically controlled by two public utilities, Wapda and KESC (now known as K-Electric) prior to the creation of PEPCO in 1998. Until its restructuring in 1998, Wapda was responsible for providing electricity to the whole of Pakistan, except for Karachi, while KESC covered the growing demands of the city. It is to be noted that both were fully integrated companies which had to handle not only the generation, but also the transmission and distribution.[30]

The existence of a public monopoly in the form of Wapda and KESC required a regulatory authority to protect the interests of the consumers. The National Electric Power Regulatory Authority (NEPRA) was initiated before the unbundling of Wapda into separate generation, transmission, and dispatch and distribution companies in 1997. In the year 1985, due to lack of funds in the public sector, the government was forced to discontinue its support to Wapda. However, due to the constant increase in the country's energy demands, the government, with the assistance of the World Bank, developed a long-term energy strategy which allowed for the induction of the private sector in the power sector.[31]

An initial framework was established in 1988 that incorporated various incentives to attract the right pool of private investors in the sector that was in dire need of abundant investments.[32] It primarily aimed to cover the following constraints:

- The need of a comprehensive policy framework that fully accounted for the incentives, fiscal treatment, repatriation of profit and capital, and the availability of foreign exchange.
- The absence of long-term financing for various projects.
- The non-existence of efficient institutional arrangements for the needed review and negotiations.

Eventually in 1992, a proper strategic plan was adopted by the Government of Pakistan in order to proceed with the privatisation of the power sector. Under this plan, Wapda, which was the main electricity utility, underwent a major restructuring. The Private Power Infrastructure Board (PPIB) was formed to attract and induct the private sector in power generation. In addition to this, a policy was introduced under which independent power producers (IPPs) were allowed to generate electricity and sell it to NTDC through purchase and sale agreements with guaranteed rate of return by the Benazir government to overcome power shortages in the country. The World Bank and Government of Pakistan created a funding vehicle through which IPPs were financed. This policy, although criticised by the opposition parties and other observers, has continued unabated under successive regimes after revisions and modifications.

The Wapda power wing was unbundled into separate generation, transmission and dispatch, and distribution companies, and four GENCOs, ten DISCOs, and one TransCO (NTDC) were established as distinct, independent corporate entities.[33] A list of GENCOs is shown in Table 12.13 with their location and capacity. As can be seen in Figure 12.13, these ten DISCOs are primarily responsible for the distribution of electricity to their respective end users, while K-Electric met its demand from its own installed generation capacity, plus the purchases from NTDC, IPPs, and from the Karachi Nuclear Power Plant.

Table 12.13: List of GENCOS

Name of Power Station	Province	Installed Capacity MWs
GENCO – I		
Jamshoro	Sindh	850
Kotri	Sindh	174
GENCO – II		
Guddu	Sindh	1655
Sukkur	Sindh	0
Quetta	Balochistan	35
GENCO – III		
Muzaffargarh	Punjab	1350
Faisalabad	Punjab	376
Multan	Punjab	195
Shahdara	Punjab	0
GENCO – IV		
Lakhra Coal 1-3	Sindh	150
Grand Total		4785

Source: National Transmission and Despatch Company, *Power Statistics 2012–13*, Lahore, WAPDA House, n.d.

In the meanwhile, KESC continued to function as an integrated utility with generation, transmission and distribution functions all residing with the same company. Its jurisdiction was, however, limited to Karachi and its environs.

In 2007, KESC, which was suffering huge financial losses, was privatised and sold to a consortium of companies led by a Saudi Arabian investor. The consortium loaded its shares and KESC was acquired by a UAE based private equity company in 2009. Since then, the company has faced many trials and tribulations but has been successful in transforming itself into a profitable company with reliable supply of electricity to the paying consumers. Load-shedding is imposed upon those who fail to pay the bills. There has been expansion and new investment in K-Electric since its privatisation.

Figure 12.13: Current Power Structure

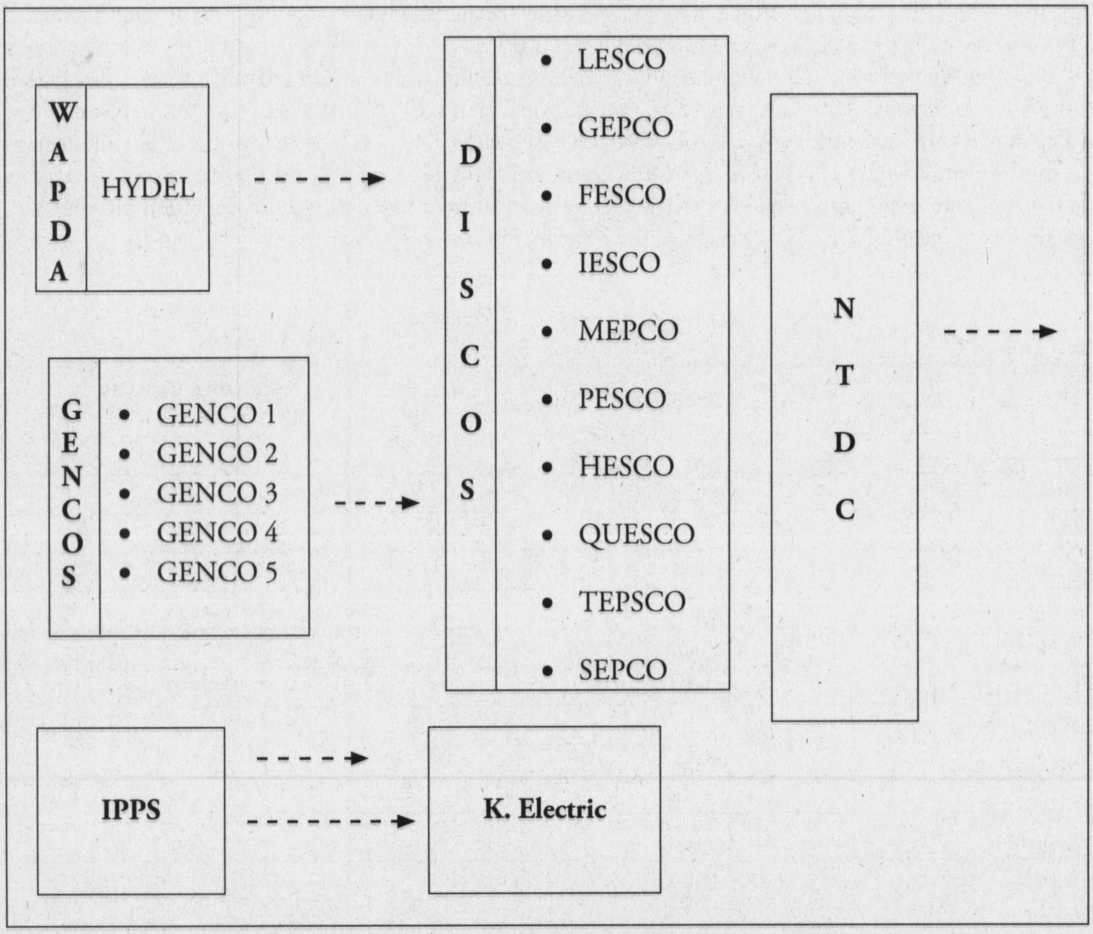

Source: Islamabad Chamber of Commerce and Industry (ICCI), *An Overview of Electricity Sector in Pakistan*. Islamabad, n.d.

Figure 12.14 depicts the two parallel systems that are working in Pakistan. The left side shows the restructured electricity system inherited from Wapda. Black arrows mention the services provided by the different segments of the structure, and the black dotted arrows depict the financial payback of those services. It is to be noted that NTDC is under government control and the hydro projects are under Wapda—a government entity. Although there have been numerous times that Wapda had attempted to attract the private sector for hydro projects, these attempts have not been successful. At this time the private sector remains more willing to participate in thermal generation because of the favourable incentive structure.[34]

Figure 12.14: Reformed Power Sector Structure

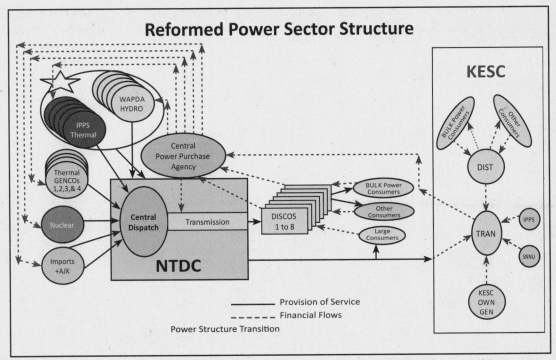

Source: Kafait Ullah, 'Electricity Infrastructure in Pakistan: An Overview', *International Journal of Energy, Information and Communications,* 4/3, 2013.

CURRENT SITUATION

Power Generation

Currently there are three public corporate entities—Wapda, Pakistan Atomic Energy Commission (PAEC), and Pakistan Electric Power Company (PEPCO)—that are responsible for electricity generation. While Wapda generates electricity produced from dams, PAEC handles that produced from nuclear resources, and then there is PEPCO which purchases energy from both the private and public sector thermal generating plants. Private sector operations consist of independent power producers, small power producers (SPPs), and captive power producers (CPPs). Besides Wapda, Pepco and PAEC nuclear generation report to the Ministry of Water and Power.

Power Transmission

The generated electricity is sold by the energy producers to a single buyer, Central Power Purchasing Agency (CPPA), which then sells it to national grid owned by the NTDC.

Power Distribution

There are ten distribution companies in the country organised regionally (Table 12.14). Two of these fall in Sindh province while KE, under private ownership and management, operates as an integrated utility. These DISCOs report to Pepco. Moreover, it is very important to note that while these DISCOs serve their respective cities, K-Electric is an independent entity that is solely responsible for supplying electricity to the city of Karachi.

Table 12.14: List of DISCOS

DISCO Name	DISCOs Full Form
LESCO	Lahore Electric Supply Co.
GEPCO	Gujranwala Electric Supply Co.
FESCO	Faisalabad Electric Supply Co.
HESCO	Hyderabad Electric Supply Co.
IESCO	Islamabad Electric Supply Co.
MEPCO	Multan Electric Supply Co.
PESCO	Peshawar Electric Supply Co.
QESCO	Quetta Electric Supply Co.
TESCO	Tribal Electric Supply Co.
SEPCO	Sukkur Electric Supply Co.

Source: Islamabad Chamber of Commerce and Industry (ICCI), An *Overview of Electricity Sector in Pakistan*, Islamabad, n.d.

INDEPENDENT REGULATORY AUTHORITY

Nepra is an autonomous regulatory body. Established in 1997, it works to improve the efficiency and availability of electric power services by protecting the interests of investors, operators, and consumers with a view to promoting competition and deregulating the power sector.

The Energy Situation in Sindh

Table 12.15 shows the situation of electricity generation in Sindh for 2010–11 and 2015–16. As the generation lagged behind actual demand, consumers had to face severe load-shedding and the industries suffered severe shortages in their supplies. This electricity crisis started in 2006–07 with a gradual widening in the demand and supply gap of electricity. The growth in residential consumers has outpaced that of industrial and commercial consumers, adversely affecting economic activity. Figures 12.15 and 12.16 substantiate this observation.

Table 12.15 Power Generation in Sindh (Plant-wise) (in Kwh)
(2010–11 and 2015–16)

Source	Name, District	2010–11	2015–16
Thermal	TPS Jamshoro, Jamshoro	4,281,000,000	2,655,000,000
	GTPS Kotri, Jamshoro	683,000,000	306,000,000
	TPS Guddu(1–4), Kashmore	2,743,000,000	522,000,000
	TPS Guddu(5–13), Kashmore	4,469,000	3,938,000,000
	Guddu GTPS, Kashmore	0	1,050,000,000
	Lahkra FBC, Jamshoro	116,000,000	103,000,000
IPP Thermal	TNB Liberty Power, Ghotki	1,527,000,000	1,218,000,000
	Engro Energy, Tharparkar	509,000,000	1,427,000,000
	Foundation Power, Daharki	35,000,000	1,321,000,000
IPP Hydro and Others	Zorlu (wind), Thatta	0	156,000,000
	FFCEL(Wind), Thatta	0	139,000,000
	Foundation Power II, Daharki	0	26,000,000
	Foundation Power II, Daharki	0	56,000,000

Source: National Transmission and Dispatch Company, *Power Statistics*, Islamabad, various years.

Figure 12.15: Sectoral Consumption in Sindh (in MW)
(2004–05 to 2007–08)

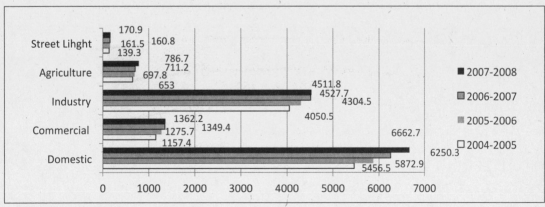

Source: Hydrocarbon Development Institute of Pakistan, *Pakistan Energy Year Book*, Islamabad, Ministry of Petroleum and Natural Resources, various years.

Sindh's electricity consumption is outstripped by Punjab (Figure 12.17). Throughout the years from 1976 to 2013, the share of Punjab has primarily laid within the range from 56 to 63 per cent. Balochistan has also made some gains over the years.

Figure 12.16: Sectoral Consumption in Sindh (in MW) (2010–11 to 2015–16)

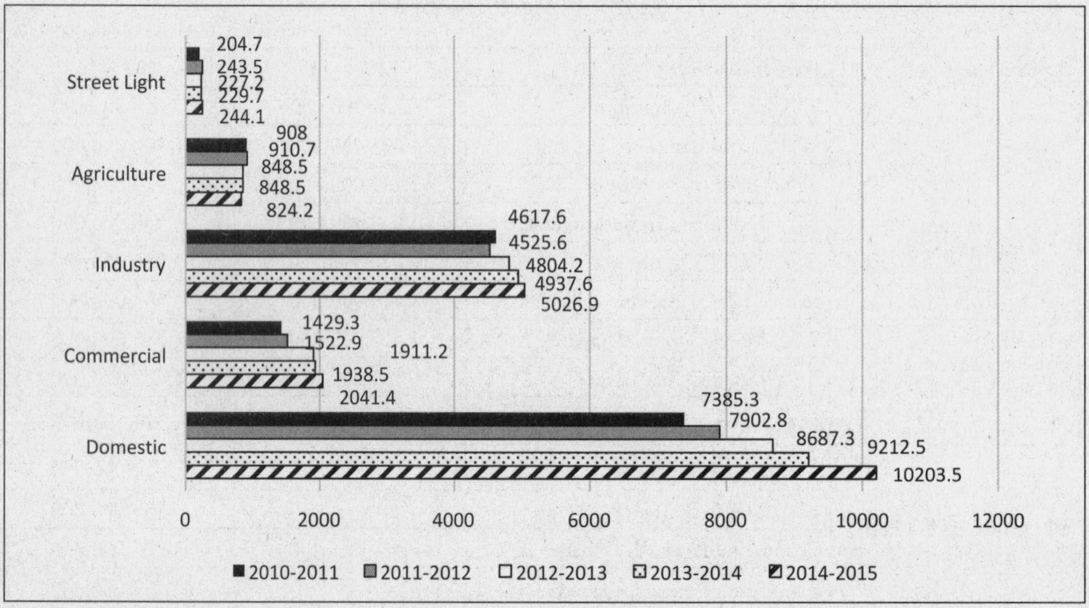

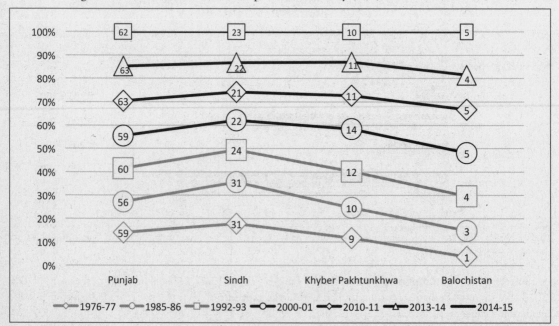

Source: Hydrocarbon Development Institute of Pakistan, *Pakistan Energy Year Book*, Islamabad, Ministry of Petroleum and Natural Resources, various years.

Figure 12.17: Province-wise Consumption of Electricity (%) (1976–77 to 2014–15)

Source: Hydrocarbon Development Institute of Pakistan, *Pakistan Energy Year Book*, Islamabad, Ministry of Petroleum and Natural Resources, various years.

The current energy situation in Sindh can be analysed in terms of electricity consumption, generation, and transmission. The key players involved in the province in the provision of electricity are:

- K-Electric (Karachi only)
- HESCO
- SEPCO
- IPPs

K-ELECTRIC

KESC was established around a hundred years ago on 13 September 1913 as a private limited company, for the purpose of serving the growing needs of the commercial city of Karachi. K-Electric is the only vertically integrated utility company. In 1952, the entity was nationalised by the government, during which the company only owned a diesel and two steam units.[35] Due to poor management issues in the organisation, the city suffered a substantial energy crisis in the late 1980s and 1990s. Since its privatisation in 2009, KE has brought about a major change in its services to its 2.2 million consumers. The distribution system has been sub-divided into twenty-eight integrated business centres, evenly spread throughout the four regions of Karachi.[36] Transmission and distribution losses have been brought down from 35.9 per cent in financial year 2009 to 22.2 per cent in the financial year 2016.[37] The recovery rate ratio has also improved to 90.8 per cent.[38]

Today, K-Electric has increased its electricity generation capacity by 1,010 MW which has eventually led to a fleet efficiency of 24 per cent. K-Electric is generating 52 per cent electricity through its independent power stations. The company generates 2247 MW from its own installed capacity and receives supply of 1,016 MW from the purchase agreements that the company has with different IPPs and NTDC.[39] A brief description of the company's generation capacity can be seen in Table 12.16.

Table 12.16: Generation Capacity of K-Electric (1983–2009)

Power Station	Year	Fuel	Capacity (MW)	Efficiency (%)
Bin Qasim Power Station 1	1983–97	HFO/Gas	50	32.5
Bin Qasim Power Station 2 CCP	2012	Gas	560	45.5
Korangi CCP	2008–09	Gas	247	45
GE Jenbacher SITE and Korangi	2009	Gas	180	36

Source: Generation tab, accessible from KE's official website, <https://www.ke.com.pk/our-business/generation/>.

The company is expanding its generation capacity using LNG as the fuel instead of furnace oil. It has announced a plan to develop 900 MW RLNG based combined cycle power plant at Bin Qasim Power Station Complex at an estimated cost of USD 1 billion. This will enhance its own installed capacity to 3,147 MW. The first unit is targeted to start production in summer 2018 and the second unit by the end of 2019.

KE's transmission system consists of 1,253 km of 220 KV, 132 KV, and 66 KV lines with 64 grid stations and 138 power transformers. KE is implementing a comprehensive and integrated programme to expand the transmission network, including installation of a new grid station which will increase system efficiency.

HESCO

HESCO was previously known as HAEB (Hyderabad Area Electricity Board) that was owned by Wapda. It was eventually incorporated on 23 April 1998. It covers 1,208,550 consumers over an area of 1, 26,758 sq. km in one districts of lower Sindh. Table 12.17 highlights the main features of Hesco. The maximum demand is 1,285 MW and the transmission network extends to 6,536 km with 111 grid stations.

Table 12.17: Distribution and Transmission Network of HESCO

Maximum Demand	1285 MW
Total Consumers	1,208,550
Private Consumers	1,181,391
Government Consumers	27,159
Number of 11 KV Feeders	584
Length of Transmission Lines	6,536 Km
Length of Distribution Lines	57,596 Km
Number of Distribution Transformers	42,052
Number of Grid Stations	111
132 KV	75
66 KV	36

Source: HESCO, 'Distribution System', <http://www.hesco.gov.pk/htmls/mainFrame.asp?req=dsystem>.

Figure 12.18: Service Area of HESCO

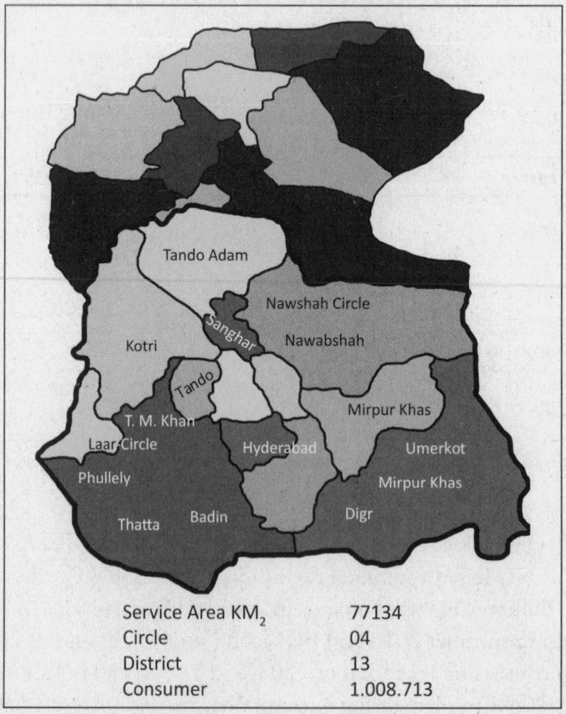

Source: HESCO, 'Organisational Overview', http://hesco.gov.pk/about.asp

The line losses are high, and recovery of bills is quite low. These two variables have made Hesco a loss-making entity relying heavily on government subsidy. If Hesco and SEPCO—both operating in Sindh—are transferred to the government of Sindh, they would create an enormous financial burden on the provincial exchequer.

SEPCO

Sukkur Electric Power Company was formed as a result of Hesco's bifurcation into two entities in August 2010. Sepco covers twelve districts mainly in upper Sindh. Table 12.18 describes the new allotted circles under Sepco and Hesco respectively. Sepco's operational performance is even worse than that of Hesco. Huge line losses and poor recovery of areas has made the company financially unviable.

Table 12.18 Distribution of SEPCO and HESCO

SEPCO	HESCO
Sukkur, Ghotki, Khairpur, Kashmir	Hyderabad I
Larkana, Jacobabad, Shikarpur, Kamber	Hyderabad II
Dadu, Jamshoro, Naushahro Feroz, S.Benazirabad	Nawabshah, S. Benazirabad, Naushahro Feroz

Source: SEPCO, 'About SEPCO', <http://www.sepco.com.pk/index.php/organisation/about-sepco>.

An analysis of the performance of the DISCOs over the last few years, presented in Tables 12.19 and 12.20, shows that the transmission and distribution (T&D) losses and poor recovery of bills have been the main reasons for poor performance of Hesco and Sepco. Their T&D losses and recovery rate are far behind KE and the DISCOs in Punjab. Although there has been some improvement in recent years, it is yet to be seen if it can be sustained over time. Workers' union has assured the authorities that they would make efforts to turn around the companies if their demands are taken off the privatisation agenda.

Table 12.19: DISCO-wise Units Billed and Received
(2005–06 to 2015–16)

Company	2005–6			2010–11			2015–16		
	Units received	Units billed	% Losses	Units received	Units billed	% Losses	Units received	Units billed	% Losses
HESCO	6,756	4,446	34.19	4,581	3,336	27.17	5,085	3,739	26.46
SEPCO	-	-	-	4,204	2,478	41.04	4,197	2,608	37.87
Export K Electric	3,836	3,836	0	5,449	5,449	0	5,059	5,059	0

Source: National Transmission and Despatch Company, Islamabad, various years.

Table 12.20: Company-wise Billing Demand and Collection (in KW)
(2010–2014)

Company			2010–11	2012–13	2014–15
HESCO	Billing	demand in KW	11,966.37	11,803.98	13,961.44
		(in PKR Million)	53,302.00	33,994	45,714
	Collection	(in PKR Million)	31,501.00	27,560	35,768
		Percentage of billing	59%	81%	78%
SEPCO	Billing	demand in KW	8,478.79	11,065.38	11,463.57
		(in PKR Million)	-	33,024	36,706
	Collection	(in PKR Million)	-	17,708	21,222
		Percentage of billing	-	54%	58%
K-Electric	Billing	demand in KW	9,380	9,090	8,530
		(in PKR Million)	44,492	59,026	51,572
	Collection	(in PKR Million)	46,317	84,000	36,000
		Percentage of billing	104%	142%	70%

Source: National Transmission and Despatch Company, *Power Statistics*, Islamabad, various years.

INDEPENDENT POWER PRODUCERS (IPPs)

As discussed earlier, the most significant change in the power sector was the breakup of the bubble of monopoly in power generation through IPPs across Pakistan. There are four IPPS in Sindh with a total installed capacity of 682 MW that are selling power to K-Electric through various electricity purchase agreements. These are listed in Table 12.21 along with their capacity as of 30 June 2015.

Table 12.21: List of IPPS in Sindh as of 2015

Company Name	Capacity (MW)
Tapal Energy (Pvt.) Limited	126
TNP Liberty Power	235
Gul Ahmed Energy	136
Foundation Power Corporation	185

Source: Hydrocarbon Development Institute of Pakistan, *Pakistan Energy Year Book 2015*, Islamabad, Ministry of Petroleum and Natural Resources, Government of Pakistan, 2016, pp. 89–90.

Access to Electricity Generation and Consumption

To fully grasp the position of Pakistan when it comes to electricity access, it is crucial to compare Pakistan with its neighbouring countries. Since India and Bangladesh are among those countries that have shared the same history and legacy as that of Pakistan, economic comparisons turn out to be more meaningful. Figure 12.19

presents a comparative picture of access to electricity in India, Pakistan, and Bangladesh. In 1990, 58.7 per cent of Pakistan's population had access to electricity compared to 45.1 per cent of India's and 7.6 of Bangladesh's. Even though Bangladesh has made significant strides in the twenty-five-year period (1990–2014), it remains behind Pakistan and India in the region. Today, in Pakistan, an impressive 97.5 per cent of the population has access to electricity.

Figure 12.19: Electricity Access as a Percentage of Population (1990–2014)

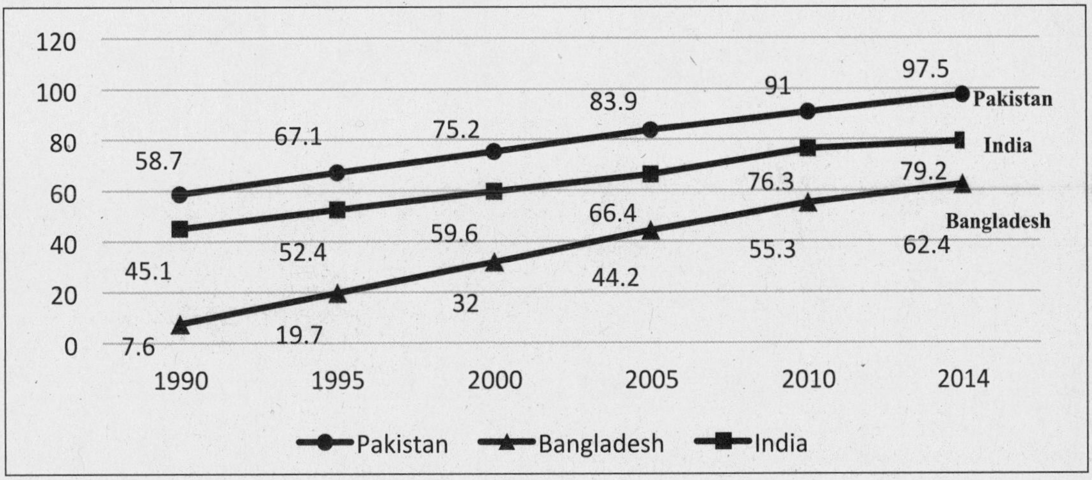

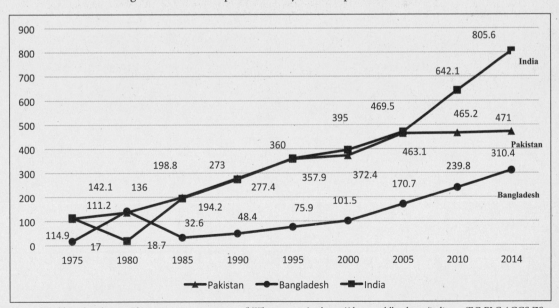

Source: World Development Indicator: Access to electricity, <https://data.worldbank.org/indicator/EG.ELC.ACCS.ZS>.

Figure 12.20: Per Capita Electricity Consumption (1975–2014)

Source: World Bank indicator: Electric power consumption (kWh per capita), <https://data.worldbank.org/indicator/EG.ELC.ACCS.ZS>.

Pakistan's electricity consumption per capita is much lower than India. Although Bangladesh's per capita consumption is lower than that of Pakistan, it can be seen that it is gaining momentum and is definitely trending upwards.

Figure 12.21: Electricity Consumption Growth Rate for Public Utilities (1976–2014)

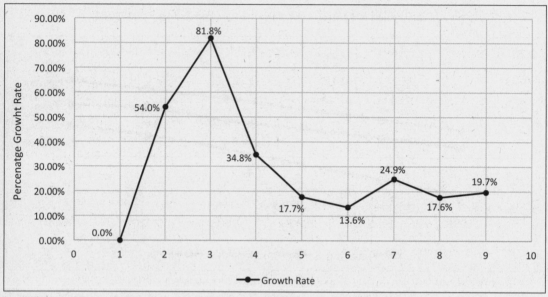

*1=1976–77, 2=1980–81, 3=1985–86, 4=1990–91, 5=1995–96, 6=2000–01, 7=2005–06, 8=2010–11, 9=2014–15

Source: Hydrocarbon Development Institute of Pakistan, Pakistan Energy Year Book, Islamabad, Ministry of Petroleum and Natural Resources, various years.

Figure 12.22: Change in Electricity Consumption of Sindh—Private and Public
(1992–2006)

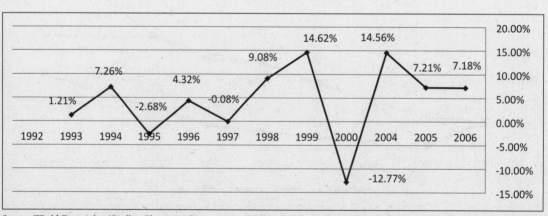

Source: World Data Atlas, 'Sindh – Electricity Consumption (Million kwh)', Knoema (an online statistical database), <https://knoema.com/atlas/Pakistan/Sindh/Electricity-Consumption-Million-Kwh>.

Figure 12.21 shows an interesting trend for growth in electricity consumption in Sindh. As can be seen from the figure, the period from the 1980s to 1985 experienced a striking increase in overall consumption. However, a sharp dip has taken place since then with some growth taking place in the early 2000s.

Since Karachi is the popular and most populous commercial hub of Pakistan, the needs of the city are growing at a rapid rate as depicted in Figure 12.23.

Figure 12.23: Number of Electricity Consumers in Karachi by Type (in Million)
(1980–81 to 2015–16)

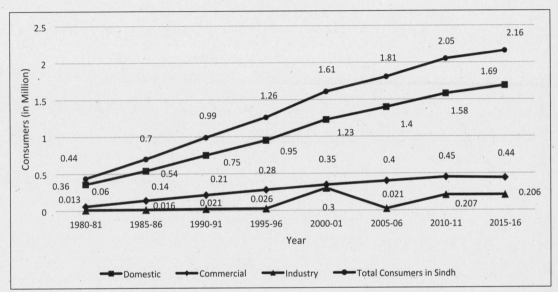

Source: National Transmission and Dispatch Company, Power Statistics, various years, Islamabad, various years.

Mineral Resources

A mineral is a naturally occurring chemical compound. Most often, they are crystalline and abiogenic in origin. A mineral is different from a rock, which can be an aggregate of minerals or non-minerals and does not have one specific chemical composition, as a mineral does. Mankind has been using minerals since pre-historic times, and we have come a long way from cave men using ochre to make drawing and paintings to extracting uranium for nuclear technology.

Pakistan possesses over twenty-three different kinds of minerals such as marble, crude oil, coal, bauxite, chromite, etc. However, possessing a natural resource per se is not as important as its utilisation for economic purposes.

Table 12.22 above shows the minerals found in Pakistan and Sindh. Out of twenty-six minerals extracted in bulk quantities from all over Pakistan, only six are extracted from Sindh in significant quantities. The major minerals extracted in Sindh are China clay and fuller's earth. The production of various minerals over time is given in Annexure Figures 12A to 12D.

Table 12.22: Mineral Resources in Pakistan and Sindh

Pakistan	Sindh
Antimony	N/A
Aragonit/Marble	N/A
Barytes	N/A
Bauxite	N/A
Calcite	N/A
Celestite	N/A
China Clay	China Clay
Chromite	N/A
Coal	Coal
Ebry stone	N/A
Fire clay	N/A
Flourite	N/A
Fuller's earth	Fuller's earth
Gravel	Gravel
Gypsum	N/A
Iron Ore	N/A
Lime stone	Lime stone
Magnesite	N/A
Manganese	N/A
Ochers	N/A
Rock salt	N/A
Salica Sand	Salica Sand
Soap stone	N/A
Sulphur	N/A
Crude oil	Crude oil
Natural gas	Natural gas

Source: Pakistan Bureau of Statistics, *Pakistan Statistical Year Book*, Islamabad, Statistics Division, Government of Pakistan, various years.

CHINA CLAY

China clay, also known as kaolin, is found in significant quantities in Nagar Parkar (Thar Parkar), a town located in the north of the Runn of Kutch at the southern tip of Sindh. Kaolin is an input for numerous industries, such as ceramics, tooth paste, the cosmetic industry, and many more. However, when it comes to Pakistan, it is primarily used in the ceramic industry as the main component of porcelain. Although the overall trend was increasing until 1995–96, there is a downward trend since then.

Fuller's Earth

Fuller's Earth, also known as Natural Bleaching Clay, effectively removes colour and purifies the material from various organic and mineral oils. Mineralogically, Fuller's Earth is mostly Smectite (calcium montmorillonite) mixed with attapulgite and kaolinite. It is famous for its bleaching properties. Annexure Figure 12B shows a constant decrease since 1990 in the output mined in Sindh till 2010, the total decrease of the output being 86 per cent.

Limestone

Limestone is a general name for a wide variety of sedimentary rocks which are composed primarily of calcium carbonate. Limestone is a primary raw material for the cement industry and is also used as a base for roads and foundations, as well as to remove impurities from molten iron amongst several other uses. The data shows that limestone mining has been on the rise and this process gained speed after 2001. However, this pattern can only be seen on an aggregate level, whereas the quantity mined from Sindh could only increase from 1.8 million tons to 6.9 million tons and could not keep pace with that of Pakistan. The reason can be attributed to the increased quarrying of limestone from other regions of Pakistan such as Punjab.

Silica Sand

Silica sand is the sand found on a beach and is also the most commonly used sand. It is made by either crushing sandstone or taken from natural occurring locations, such as beaches and river beds. Silica sand is cheap owing to its high abundance and is used for construction and foundries. It has a high melting point which makes it ideal for foundries.

13

Public Finance: Taxation and Resource Mobilisation

An Overview

PAKISTAN, unlike India and other Asian economies, does not record data of regional income accounts; therefore, the actual composition of provincial economies is not known[1] but Tables 13.1 to 13.3 give us some useful insights to understand the position of Sindh in Pakistan's economy.

Table 13.3 shows that Sindh is the second largest contributor to the economy of Pakistan and contributes approximately 30 per cent to GDP. Over last fifteen years, its share has remained unchanged, at around 30 per cent. Punjab and Sindh together account for 84 per cent of the national economy, almost identical to their share in the population, but the relative share of Sindh at 30 per cent in income is much higher than its share of 23 per cent in the population.

Table 13.1: Estimated PGDP of Sindh by Sector (in PKR Billions at Constant Prices of 2005–06) (1999–2000 to 2014–15)

Sector	1999–2000	Share (%)	2007–08	Share (%)	2012–13	Share (%)	2013–14	Share (%)	2014–15	Share (%)
Agriculture	379.2	22.5	440.3	16.2	480	16.1	498.4	16.2	512.7	16.1
Industry	412.9	24.5	884.6	32.6	864.8	29	903.5	29.30	936.2	29.3
Services	894.6	53	1,387.5	51.1	1,637.8	54.9	1,681.9	54.5	1,743.6	54.6
PGDP	1,686.7	100	2,712.4	100	2,982.6	100	3,083.8	100	3,192.5	100

Source: Hafiz Pasha, 'Growth of the Provincial Economies', *Institute for Policy Reforms*, 2015.

Table 13.2: Share of Provinces in National Economic Sectors (2012–13)

Province	Agriculture (%)	Industry (%)	Services (%)
Punjab	62.3	39.8	55.7
Sindh	23.1	42.2	28.9
Khyber Pakhtunkhwa	10.5	14.2	13.0
Balochistan	4.1	3.8	2.4
Pakistan	100.0	100.0	100.0

Source: Hafiz Pasha, 'Growth of the Provincial Economies', *Institute for Policy Reforms*, 2015.

Table 13.1 indicates that the share of agriculture in provincial GDP has declined while an increasing trend is observed in the remaining two sectors, i.e. services and industry. The share of industry has increased most significantly from 24 per cent in 2000 to approximately 29 per cent in 2015. Moreover, if the national pie in each sector is dissected, Sindh leads in the industrial sector, followed by Punjab, while Punjab is the largest contributor to the agricultural and services sectors as shown in Table 13.2.

Both the size and composition of the economy are consistent with other characteristics—an expanding middle class, rapid urbanisation and large segment of educated and skilled labour force. Karachi, a metropolitan city in Sindh, is regarded as the hub of economic activity which can be gauged from the fact that the province contributes 70 per cent to the total tax collection. Karachi represents a microcosm of Pakistan and also being an economic hub, it has become a melting pot of diverse cultures and ethnicities.

Table 13.3: Size of Provincial Economies (in PKR Billions at Constant Prices of 2005–06)
(1999–2000 and 2014–15)

Province	1999–2000	Share (%)	2014–15	Share (%)
Punjab	3,147.7	55.3	5,757	54.1
Sindh	1,686.7	29.6	3,192.5	30.0
Khyber Pakhtunkhwa	644.2	11.3	1,380.9	13.0
Balochistan	214.5	3.8	313.7	2.9
Pakistan	5,693.1	100	10,644.1	100

Source: Hafiz Pasha, 'Growth of the Provincial Economies', *Institute for Policy Reforms*, 2015.

Public finances play an integral part in the economic dynamics of a region as both taxation proceeds and expenditures are within the control of the provincial governments. In Pakistan, the seventh NFC award of 2009 and the Eighteenth Amendment have brought about a fundamental structural shift in fiscal federalism. Provinces now receive almost 60 per cent of the total divisible tax pool—a big boost to their spending capacity. However, this transfer of resources and decentralisation of authority has stalled at the provincial level and not passed on to the local governments where most of the interaction between a citizen and the government takes place. In fact, the reverse has happened. All the powers devolved to the local governments under the 2001 local government ordinance have once again been centralised at the provincial level and institutions dealing with delivery of basic services have ceased to be local institutions as they have been taken over by the provincial department of local government.

Table 13.4: Sindh Provincial Budgets: Historical Trends (in PKR Million)
(1985–86 to 2015–16)

	1985–86	1990–91	1995–96	2000–01	2005–06	2010–11	2015–16
A. Total Revenue	13,850.7	22,354.0	52,102.2	82,060.3	154,452.0	388,706.8	712,745.3
1. General Revenue Receipts	7,524.2	12,917.6	39,451.1	64,781.2	126,962.6	329,057.0	627,946.1
a. Tax Revenue	4,114.8	9,477.5	35,372.1	54,967.5	108,796.9	257,516.4	547,853.8
Federal Divisible Pool	3,031.2	7,915.9	31,664.5	47,720.2	63,165.1	207,403.0	422,574.0

table continued

	1985–86	1990–91	1995–96	2000–01	2005–06	2010–11	2015–16
Own source tax revenue	1,083.6	1,561.6	3,707.6	7,247.2	45,631.8*	32,748.0	64,279.0
Sindh Sales Tax on Services	–	–	–	–	–	17,365.5	61,000.0
b. Non Tax Revenues	3,409.4	3,440.0	4,078.0	9,813.8	18,165.8	71,540.6	80,092.0
2. Development Revenue	714.1	2,182.3	3,694.0	22.5	10,907.0	3,134.8	9,855.0
3.Capital Revenue	5,612.4	7,255.1	8,957.1	17,256.5	16,582.3	56,515.0	74,943.8
B. Total Expenditure	13,831.7	26,911.2	51,652.7	75,700.3	182,229.0	446,544.1	753,487.6
1. Current Revenue Expenditure	7,397.3	16,285.7	36,826.7	67,657.9	126,184.8	281,237.9	502,771.0
Education	1,896.4	3,834.8	9,508.7	14,207.4	4,350.4	20,424.9	140,393.2
Health	406.2	1,173.7	2,468.2	3,774.1	3,935.4	10,562.1	53,759.6
Police	543.9	1,481.3	4,516.5	6,179.6	15,823.2	33,333.3	65,097.1
Others	4550.8	9,795.9	20,333.3	43,496.8	102,075.8	216,917.6	243,521.1
2. Development Revenue Expenditure	692.7	2,072.6	1,466.6	8,042.4	6,185.5	65,551.3	175,550.0
Education	360.5	153.9	256.9	162.8	873.6	1,494.4	11,380.3
Health	47.5	121.2	334.2	146.0	588.7	2,578.4	14,277.0
Others	284.7	1,797.5	875.5	7,733.6	4,723.2	61,478.5	149,892.7
3 Capital Expenditure	5,741.7	8,552.9	13,359.4	30,064.0	49,858.7	99,755.0	75,165.8
Revenue Deficit/ Surplus	126.9	(3,368.1)	2,624.4	(2,876.7)	777.9	47,819.2	(23,422)

* Includes Federal Excise on Natural Gas amounting to PKR 16,495.6 Million.

Source: Finance Department, *Annual Budget Statement*, Karachi, Government of Sindh, various years.

Table 13.4 shows the increasing dependence of provincial finances on federal divisible pool, and grants and transfers. The only headway that has been made is the collection of sales tax on services by the provinces in place of the FBR. The Sindh Revenue Board (SRB) established for this purpose has done a commendable job in collecting sales tax but the performance of other traditional taxes and non-tax revenues such as land revenue, agriculture income tax, property tax, and abiana (irrigation water charges) has been disappointing. Had the property cadastral surveys been carried out regularly and the valuations updated periodically, the revenue from this source alone could exceed PKR100 billion, annually raising the share of source tax revenues significantly.

Distribution of Financial Resources throughout History and NFC Awards

In order to understand the current fiscal standing of Sindh, it is imperative to look at the following historical events that played a significant role in the distribution of financial resources.

PRE-INDEPENDENCE

In the pre-Partition days, there was no concept of formal provincial or local governments. However, local governments did exist in the form of village 'panchayats' or headman of the village.[2] With the advent of British rule, local governments were introduced. These local governments comprised of native elites, who were not elected by the people they were representing but were directly appointed by the British bureaucracy. With the introduction of Government of India Act 1919, the previously circumscribed power of the local governments was further restricted as provincial government started to assert control over several functions that were previously performed by the local governments. However, the provincial governments did not have financial resources to carry out these functions as they completely relied on the centre, which further strengthened the role of the centre on the provinces and the districts.[3] Under the Government of India Act 1919, Sindh was a district under the Bombay Presidency. Table 13.5 shows the contribution of Sindh in the collection of total tax receipts under the Bombay Presidency. It shows that Sindh was the largest tax contributor amongst all the districts in the Bombay presidency and contributed approximately 57 per cent to the total tax receipts.

Table 13.5: Tax Collection in Bombay Presidency (1925)

Name of Division	Total receipts	Percentage Share
Northern division	10,721,328	21.17
Bombay suburban division	668,735	1.32
Central division	7,488,064	14.78
Southern division	2,709,606	5.35
Sindh	29,054,813	57.37
Total	50,642,546	100

Source: Government of Bombay, *Municipal Taxation and Expenditure in Bombay Presidency (Including Sind)*, 1925, Bombay Presidency, n.d.

Later, the Government of India Act 1935 was introduced, and Sindh became a separate province. Under the Act, the Niemeyer Award was formulated to distribute resources. It established a federal form of government and assigned the jurisdiction of important matters to provincial governments. Under this Award, sales tax was made a provincial subject.[4] Due to the transfer of important subjects to provincial governments, political economists regard the Niemeyer Award as the first step towards fiscal federalism in India.[5]

POST-INDEPENDENCE

In the post-Independence period, the Raisman Award of 1951 was the first attempt at dividing the revenues between the federal and the five provinces. Under the award, the federal government was allocated 50 per cent of the proceeds and the remaining 50 per cent was to be shared among the provinces. After the formation of West Pakistan, Sindh, Punjab, Balochistan, and the then NWFP (now Khyber Pakhtunkhwa) were considered as one single unit of West Pakistan while East Pakistan was declared the other unit. Two awards in 1961 and 1964 were announced under this formula. Under both awards, the share of East Pakistan was 54 per cent and West Pakistan's share was 46 per cent.[6] The divisible pool comprised of 70 per cent of sales tax and other taxes.[7] The duties on agricultural land and capital value tax on immovable property were distributed amongst the provinces based on their collection.[8]

NATIONAL FINANCE COMMITTEE (NFC) (1970)

With the dismemberment of the One Unit scheme and revival of the four provinces in 1970, the need for a distributive formula between the provinces of West Pakistan arose.[9] Hence, the National Finance Committee was set up to address this issue. The terms of reference governing the committee were categorised as (1) the vertical distribution mechanism of revenue between the federation and provinces; and (2) examination of inter-regional inequality.[10]

It was, however, decided that any recommendations would be valid for just 1970–71 and 1971–72—the first two years of the fourth Five-Year Plan.[11] The suggestions put forth by the committee included an increase in 65 per cent share of provinces in the divisible pool to desirably 90 per cent but no less than 80 per cent. In case of horizontal distribution, it was recommended to continue the then formula for a year.

In the case of taxes on income, excise duties, and export duties, East Pakistan receives 54% and Provinces in West Pakistan 46%, while in the case of sales tax 30% is distributed on the basis of collections in each province and the balance in the same ratio as other taxes. The share assigned to West Pakistan is distributed among four provinces as follows[12]: [Table 13.6]

- While the existing grants-in-aid mechanism may persist, efforts should be made to better the distribution process.
- It was categorically stated that the Central government was in no position to forgo the provincial debt in light of external debt 'which was largely utilised for making rupee loans to Provinces'.[13]
- Concerning the issue of inter and intra-regional inequality, it was said that the matter had already been addressed in the formulation of the fourth Five-Year Plan.

Table 13.6: Share of Different Provinces of West Pakistan in the Divisible Pool
(1970–71 and 1971–72)

Punjab	56.5
Sindh	23.5
Khyber Pakhtunkhwa	15.5
Balochistan	4.5
Total	100

Source: Ministry of Finance, 'Working Papers and Minutes of the National Finance Committee', 1970, unpublished report.

Sindh pointed out the error in the revenue distribution formula. Citing examples of the Niemeyer Award of 1937 and the Raisman Award of 1951, the Sindh government emphasised the limitation of just using population as the distribution criterion where the aforementioned awards also took into account tax incidence and backwardness.[14] It was also argued that although Sindh enjoyed the highest per capita income in West Pakistan of PKR 854 (which too was contested by the Planning and Development Department, Government of Sindh) there were nine districts in the province which had a per capita income lower than the provincial average.[15] These included Khairpur, Jacobabad, Sukkur, Larkana, Nawabshah, Dadu, Thatta, Tharparkar, and Sanghar. Of these Dadu, Khairpur, Thatta, and Thar were specifically identified as such by the West Pakistan government to be treated as backward areas. The rising urbanisation of Karachi, and the cost associated, was also presented as a factor to modify the award.

In light of the above, and due to the stress on tackling intra-regional inequality in the fourth Five-Year Plan, the Sindh government argued that it would require extra finances and that the revenue division formula should consider the expenses associated with backwardness.

In terms of recommendations, the Government of Sindh presented the following proposals:[16]

- The share of provinces in divisible pool be raised from 65:35 ratio to 75:25 between federation and provinces.
- Sales tax be devolved to provinces.
- Tax net may be expanded by including excise duty on sugar in the divisible pool.
- Any major changes to tax rates or their scope should not be introduced without compensating the provinces.
- Extend the distribution formula used under the Raisman Award and the then share earmarked for Karachi to Sindh.
- At least half the total debt of Sindh government amounting to Rs. 258 crore be waived and the remaining amount to be treated as 'a single loan repayable over a period of 25 years with 3% rate of interest.'
- Provide Grant to meet 50% of expenditures towards Malaria Eradication Programme and the Rural Works Programme (now transferred to the provincial government). There was also a demand for 'liberal grant-in-aid out of the Road Development Fund for the improvement of roads in Karachi and other areas in Sind'.

After 1973 Constitution

After the separation of East and West Pakistan, the Constitution of 1973 was promulgated. The Constitution made obligatory on the government the formation of the National Finance Commission (NFC) after every five years to ensure efficient distribution of financial resources between the units of West Pakistan.[17] The NFC award has always been a cause of disagreement amongst the provinces. Seven NFC awards have been made following Constitution of 1973, but the path-breaking one was the last award announced in 2009.

First NFC Award 1974

The taxes included in the divisible pool consisted of sales tax, income tax, and export duty. The main criterion for distributing financial resources was population. Resources were distributed vertically among federal and provincial governments with the fixed ratio of 20:80[18] (20 per cent share was given to the federal government and 80 per cent was given to provincial governments). With population being the sole criteria, Punjab's share increased from 56.50 per cent (which was assigned under 1964 award) to 60.25 per cent while those of the other three provinces declined. In addition to that, annual grants of PKR 50 million and PKR 100 million were awarded to Balochistan and the NWFP governments to compensate for their comparatively weak financial situation.[19] As Sindh's financial performance was better compared to Balochistan and the NWFP, no aid or support grants were awarded to Sindh. Under this distribution scheme, Sindh suffered the most because Punjab got the highest share according to the population criteria and Balochistan and the NWFP were supported with additional grants because of their weak financial situations.

Second NFC Award 1979

The second NFC award was constituted by General Ziaul Haq with the chairmanship of Ghulam Ishaq Khan, the then finance minister. Due to the political transition that was taking place in Pakistan at that time, no meetings were held and hence no proposals were made for the Award; therefore, the resource distribution plan of 1974 was followed.[20] However, the political scenario stabilised in the following years and the population census took place in 1981. After the census, the population proportions changed, and resource shares were adjusted accordingly. The adjusted resource allocation improved the financial situation of Sindh and Balochistan and Punjab's share was reduced from 60 per cent to approximately 58 per cent.[21]

Table 13.7: 1983 Presidential Order Specifying Provincial Shares in 2nd NFC

Province	Share (%)
Punjab	57.97
Sindh	23.34
Khyber Pakhtunkhwa	13.39
Balochistan	5.30

Source: Iftikhar Ahmed, Usman Mustafa, Mahmood Khalid, 'National Finance Commission Awards In Pakistan: A Historical Perspective', *PIDE Working Paper 33*, Islamabad, Pakistan Institute of Development Economics, 2007, p. 5.

Third NFC Award 1985

The third NFC was also constituted under Ziaul Haq's regime in 1985. However, Dr Mahbubul Haq was the finance minister and chairman of the finance commission during this time. Dr Mahbubul Haq held nine meetings in three years but despite all these efforts, the commission was not able to finalise its recommendations.[22] The primary reason for not reaching a consensus is attributed to internal and external political instability. Thus, the resource distribution remained unchanged from that of 1974.

The Fourth NFC Award 1990

The fourth NFC award came like a breath of fresh air, breaking the stagnating consistency of following, more or less, the same financial resource distribution formula for the past sixteen years. The commission was headed by the finance minister, Sartaj Aziz, under the democratic government of Nawaz Sharif. The 1990 award is considered as the first positive step towards the decentralisation of powers by granting more autonomy to the provinces.[23] The expansion of the divisible pool is the most salient feature of this award. The divisible pool was expanded by including the excise duties on sugar and tobacco. Other taxes that were in the divisible pool included export duty, sales tax, income tax, and excise duty. However, custom duty still remained with the federal government.[24] In addition to the expansion of the divisible pool, another significant change that was made to the formula was to identify the provinces' right on the revenue generated from the energy sources. Funds from net hydel profit, development surcharge on gas, and excise duty on crude oil were transferred to the provincial governments in the form of straight transfers. Consequently, the transfer to provinces increased from PKR 39 billion (28 per cent) to PKR 64 billion (45 per cent) out of the federal tax revenue. The vertical distribution of financial resources between the federal and provincial respectively, remained unchanged at 20:80.[25]

The horizontal distribution also remained largely unchanged because population was still the sole criteria for resource distribution. However, the volume of money transfer certainly increased because of the inclusion of additional items (excise duties on sugar and tobacco) in the divisible pool along with the increased amount of straight transfers to the provinces. Moreover, special grants were given to the provinces (Table 13.8) to meet their developmental requirements.

Table 13.8: Special Grant to Provinces—1990 NFC Award (in PKR Million)

	Punjab	Sindh	NWFP	Balochistan
Amount	1000	700	200	100
Years	3	5	3	3

Source: Iftikhar Ahmed, Usman Mustafa, Mahmood Khalid, 'National Finance Commission Awards in Pakistan: A Historical Perspective', *PIDE Working Paper 33*, Islamabad, Pakistan Institute of Development Economics, 2007.

Though there was an increase in the amount of funds transferred to the provinces from the divisible pool, the autonomy required to regulate those funds and the motivation to generate own source revenues in the future was certainly lacking.[26]

Fifth NFC Award 1996

The fifth NFC award was constituted by the caretaker prime minister Malik Meraj Khan in December 1996 under the chairmanship of Shahid Javed Burki. The most important features of this award were:

- The scope of the divisible pool was enlarged and all taxes and duties (including custom duty which was under federal jurisdiction until previous awards) were included in the divisible pool under this award. Other taxes/duties included in the divisible pool were income tax, wealth tax, export duties, custom duties, excise duties, capital value tax, sales tax, and any other tax collected by the federal government.[27]
- Incentive of Matching Grants was introduced. Matching Grants are the funds allotted by the state or local government to fund small community development projects. However, to get qualified for the acquisition of matching grants, provincial governments were to exceed their revenue growth target of 14.2 per cent.[28]
- The share of the federal and provincial governments changed drastically under this award. The new vertical allocation was 62.5:37.5 for federal and provincial governments respectively. Previously, the ratio was 20:80, in the same order. This shift in resource distribution was primarily attributed to the inclusion of all the taxes/duties in the divisible pool. However, it is still believed that the contraction in the share of the provinces in the divisible pool was not an advisable policy and the provinces would have been in a better financial position today if the previous award of 1990 still continued to prevail at that time.

Population was still the sole criteria for horizontal distribution of resources amongst the provinces; however, the shares of provinces in the divisible pool were later readjusted in July 2002, owing to the 1998 population census.

Sixth NFC Award 2000

The sixth NFC award faced a fate similar to that of the third NFC award. The recommendations for the implementation of the award could not get finalised despite eleven meetings that were held under the chairmanship of the finance minister, Shaukat Aziz. Provinces were demanding a higher share in the divisible pool and the diversification of resource distribution criteria. Amidst the conflict of ideas, a consensus was never reached.[29]

The formula for the distribution of subvention was one area with which the Government of Sindh was unsatisfied. These subventions, which were increased from PKR 8.7 billion to PKR 20 billion, were to be distributed between Sindh, the NWFP (now Khyber Pakhtunkhwa), and Balochistan.[30] One of Sindh's most important reservation was the underreporting of backwardness in the province for the distribution of subventions.[31] According to the Government of Sindh, the data used to assess the 'backwardness' of a province was based on flawed data of the 1998 Pakistan Integrated Household Survey (PIHS), which did not reflect, or rather underestimated, the true picture of poverty in Sindh. Citing the Applied Economic Research Centre (AERC), the government claimed '35% of the country's poor ... are in Sindh.'[32] This claim then takes on significance since 'the distribution of subvention is overridingly going to be determined on the basis of poverty levels in the provinces.'

Moreover, the Sindh government also pointed out an error in the calculation of the revenue collection percentage which was recorded as 80 per cent in the NFC formula but which should have been 86.3 per cent.[33] The government also objected to the assignment of only 15 per cent weightage to area and collection, as opposed to what the economic advisor of the Government of Pakistan had suggested, i.e. 20 per cent each to area and collection and the remaining 60 per cent to backwardness. According to the economic advisor, the subventions of PKR 20 billion ought to be distributed in the manner laid out in Table 13.9.

Table 13.9: Proposed Subventions to Provinces (in PKR Billion)

Sindh	7.1
NWFP	6.4
Balochistan	6.6
Total	20

Source: NFC Secretariat, 'Government of Sindh's Positon on Distribution of Subvention Under NFC', 2002, unpublished report.

Commenting on the sixth NFC award, the senior minister for finance and cooperation, Government of Sindh, highlighted the significance of Sindh's economy to Pakistan to claim a larger share in the divisible pool. The minister stated:

> Towards the national revenue, Sindh contributes 68 per cent of the income tax, 86 per cent of the customs duties, 70 per cent of sales tax and 31 per cent of federal excise. In spite of such a huge contribution, our redistribution mechanism under the present NFC is such that against PKR 226 billion collected from Sindh in the year 2000–01, merely PKR 32 billion or 14 per cent of the collection was reverted.[34]

This claim assumes importance in light of the information that for the year 1999–2000, Sindh received only 16 per cent of the revenue collected, whereas this figure for Punjab was as high as 90 per cent and for Balochistan and the NWFP was 82 per cent.[35] Hence, 'the absence of weightage of revenue collection in the divisible pool transfers clearly reveals that all the provinces as well as the federal government is effectively being subsidised at the expense of Sindh.'[36]

The most important contention was the population-based revenue sharing formula which was described as 'unfriendly to Sindh'.[37] It has been argued that this system of revenue assignment has prevented Sindh from investing in development and that, 'the per capita development allocations to social and economic infrastructure in Sindh are lower in relation to other provinces' (especially Balochistan and the NWFP).[38] The Sindh minister in his speech stressed, 'No federation of the world distributes its resources on population alone. Even in Pakistan till 1974, population was not the basis of the revenue sharing arrangements. Other time-honoured factors like revenue generation (at least 20 per cent weightage should be given), backwardness, area, and needs should be included in the formula resources distribution.'[39] Sindh's case is highlighted by the data in Table 13.10.

Table 13.10: Share in Tax Collection and Divisible Pool (2000–01)

Name of Province	Share in Tax Collections based on 2000–01 collection (%)	Share in Divisible Pool (%)
Punjab	24.15	57.36
Sindh	68.02	23.71
KP	5.91	13.82
Balochistan	1.92	5.11

Source: Finance Department, Government of Sindh, 'Government of Sindh's Position on 6th National Finance Commission', 2003, unpublished report.

The government argued, 'the maximum gains to Sindh will accrue when the collection (all divisible pool taxes) is included in the distribution formula.'[40] Sindh stands to gain a weightage of 65.07 per cent if collection is adopted as a criterion, and a weightage of 38.07 per cent and 35.24 per cent, if fiscal effort and 'bottom quartile population' are considered (based on the aforementioned AERC study) respectively, whereas with population as a sole criterion, the share of Sindh is only 23.72 per cent.[41] The government went on to acknowledge that such modifications to the revenue sharing formula, while they would benefit the NWFP and Balochistan, would decrease the share of Punjab.

Furthermore, the minister also brought to fore the issues of natural disasters, especially the 2003 monsoon rains which resulted in the loss of PKR 45 billion, as well as the burden of maintaining the law and order situation of the province.[42]

The latter, it was claimed, is the 'moral and constitutional obligation of the federal government'. The deficit in the receipts of GST assignments was also pointed out which was another important contentious issue for Sindh after the distribution formula. The octroi and zila tax, described as 'highly buoyant levies' were removed in 1998–99 and this loss for Sindh (as well as perhaps for other provinces) was to be compensated by an increment of 2.5 per cent on the sales tax.[43] This was to be distributed in two ways: (1) on the basis of historical collection share of the provinces, (2) on the basis of NFC revenue sharing formula, i.e. population.[44] It was claimed that Sindh, taking into account the audited financials, should have received PKR 25.698 billion for the year 1999–2000 as compared to the actual received, i.e. PKR 14.964 billion.[45]

With regard to the distribution of 2.5 per cent GST, Sindh had proposed the following options:

- The first was that now that the historical octroi and zila tax (OZT) incomes have been replaced with the 2.5 per cent GST, Sindh should be given share in accordance with its collection share of GST (which is approximately 64 per cent).
- The second option given was that Sindh should be given the 2.5 per cent GST in accordance with its share in the historical OZT revenues at the time of its abolition which comes to 48 per cent.[46]

Both of these options were rejected, which naturally resulted in Sindh receiving a lower share than it should have. The burden on Karachi due to rising urbanisation and in-migration was also underlined. Especially with regard to the latter, the government made the case that it:

> … creates complex problems of settlement and requires ever increasing resources to support infrastructure facilities. On the contrary, in-migrants working in Karachi [are] responsible for huge resource transfers from this Province resulting in substantial capital formation in their hometowns in other Provinces which are also relieved of the costly responsibility of providing social services and infrastructure for them.[47]

In light of the sixth NFC award, the proposals put forth by the Government of Sindh were:[48]

- Permitting provinces to collect 5 per cent of sales tax (out of 15 per cent) or to dispense 30 per cent of sales tax according to the origin.
- The federal government should divest itself of the tax bases which essentially lie in the provincial ambit to allow for 'financial autonomy and long-run sustainability of the provincial governments'. Moreover, the revenue assignment from coal should be handed over to the provinces as is the case with crude oil and natural gas.
- In the context of devolution of power from federal to provincial governments, the vertical distribution of revenue between the federation and provinces should also be increased from 62.5:37.5 to 40:60.
- Inclusion of petroleum surcharge and other taxes in the divisible pool.
- Revision of revenue sharing formula to include other important factors such as revenue collection, fiscal effort, area, special needs, and backwardness.

SEVENTH NFC AWARD 2006

By 2006, there had been several attempts for reaching consensus which was not achieved. Moreover, the distribution of 2.5 per cent sales tax was further revised via Distribution Order 2006 whereby each province would receive the collection in the ratio mentioned in Table 13.11, which would further be handed over to the district governments and Cantonment Board.[49]

Table 13.11: Distribution Order of 2006

Province	Distribution Order of 2006 (%)	Audited Figures of OZT for 1998–99 (%)
Punjab	50.00	42.63
Sindh	34.85	46.00
KP	9.93	6.04
Balochistan	5.22	5.33

Source: Nawaz Ali Laghari, 'Impact of Distribution of 2.5% GST of Net Sales Tax Under Distribution Order, 2006 in Case of Sindh', 2008, unpublished report.

The seventh National Finance Commission was constituted on 21 July 2005, but it met with a similar fate as that of the previous award and no mutually acceptable mechanism could be decided for distribution of the resources. Resultantly, the chief ministers of all the provinces vested their trust in the then president, Pervez Musharraf, to announce the award. Pervez Musharraf made an amendment to the 'Distribution of revenue and Grants-in-Aid Order, 1997' and the new NFC was put in effect from 1 July 2006. The important features of this award are as follows:

- Provincial share, in total divisible pool and grants, was increased from the previous share of 37.5 to 45 per cent for the first financial year. The share was supposed to increase to 50 per cent, with one per cent subsequent increase in each year.[50]
- The divisible pool consisted of income tax, capital value tax, wealth tax, sales tax, custom duties, export duties, excise duties (excluding excise duty on gas charged at wellhead) and any other tax collected by federal government.[51]
- Furthermore, one-sixth of the sales tax was to be given the provincial governments to transfer it further to the local and district governments, in order to facilitate the resource mobility at ground levels.[52]
- There was also a significant increase in the straight transfers. The royalties on gas and crude oil and excise duties on gas and gas development surcharge were transferred to provincial governments.[53]

The share of provinces under different NFC awards is given in Table 13.12. It can be seen that since population had been the sole criteria to distribute financial resources in all these years, the share of all the provinces have remained same. A slight change in the provincial shares can be seen in the transition from the first NFC in 1974 to the second NFC in 1979. This change can be attributed to the 1981 census. Since then, and until the seventh NFC, Pakistan had neither diversified its portfolio for distribution criteria nor has it conducted a census to make adjustments to the prevalent criteria. Punjab continues to get the highest share from the divisible pool.

Table 13.12: Provincial Percentage Share under NFC Awards (1974–2009)

Year	Punjab (%)	Sindh (%)	KP (%)	Balochistan (%)
1974	60.25	22.50	13.39	3.86
1979	57.97	23.34	13.39	5.30
1990	57.88	23.28	13.54	5.30
1996	57.88	23.28	13.54	5.30
2006	57.36	23.71	13.82	5.11
2009*	51.74	24.55	14.62	9.09

*Usman Mustafa, 'Fiscal Federalism in Pakistan: the 7th National Finance Commission Award and its Implications', *PIDE Working Paper no. 73*, Islamabad, Pakistan Institute of Development Economics, 2011.

Source: Ahmed, Mustafa, and Khalid, 'National Finance Commission Awards In Pakistan: A Historical Perspective', *PIDE Working Paper 33*, Islamabad, Pakistan Institute of Development Economics, 2007.

SEVENTH NFC AWARD 2009

Due to a constitutional obligation, the NFC award is announced only when all of the four provinces have reached a consensus. This problem had halted NFC decisions, especially faced in past meetings. Eventually, after numerous struggles to change allocation methods since 1974, the seventh NFC award's use of multiple indicator criteria for the distribution of resources was a step forward in the right direction. This was especially important for Sindh, as it traditionally claimed its sub-optimal growth and poor development to have been a result of unfair shares allocated in past NFCs.

In 2009, President Asif Ali Zardari approved the release of the seventh NFC papers, which formed the seventh NFC Award and came to affect in July 2010.[54]

The seventh NFC award showed the multiplication and divisional factors and the functions in respect to the following listed issues:

- Inverse population decay and exponential rate
- The derivative change of poverty and societal backwardness
- Provincial GDP growth and revenue collection
- Urban density factor

Following were the recommendations submitted to the President of Pakistan:[55]

a) The divisible pool taxes will consist of the following taxes:
   - Taxes on income, including corporation tax, but not including taxes on income consisting of remuneration paid out of the Federal Consolidated Fund.
   - Taxes on the sales and purchases of goods imported, exported, produced, manufactured, or consumed.
   - Export duties on cotton, and such other export duties as may be specified by the president.
   - Wealth Tax.
   - Capital Value Tax.
   - Customs duties.
   - Federal excise duties, excluding excise duty on gas charged at wellhead.
   - Any other tax which may be levied by the federal government.

b) The net proceeds of the divisible pool taxes shall be derived after deducting one per cent as collection charges.

c) The federal government reiterates its commitment to bear all expenditures incurred on the war on terror in any part of Pakistan. The federal government and all the four provinces recognise the role of Khyber Pakhtunkhwa as a frontline province against the war on terror. As a gesture of support by the federal government and all the provinces, one per cent of the net proceeds of divisible pool taxes will be earmarked for Khyber Pakhtunkhwa as an additional resource for the war on terror during the award period. (This could be equivalent to approximately 1.8 per cent of the provincial share in the divisible pool taxes for the year 2010–11.)

d) After deducting the amounts as prescribed in Paras 2 and 3, of the balance amount of the proceeds of divisible pool taxes, 56 per cent shall be assigned to provinces during the financial year 2010–11 and 57.5 per cent from the financial year 2011–12 onwards. The share of the federal government in the net divisible pool taxes shall be 44 per cent during the financial year 2010–11 and 42.5 per cent from the financial year 2011–12 onwards.

e) It was agreed with consensus for the first time to include multiple indicators in the criterion for horizontal distribution amongst the provinces. The multiple indicators and their respective weights as agreed upon are:
   - Population: 82.0 per cent
   - Poverty/backwardness: 10.3 per cent
   - Revenue collection/generation: 5.0 per cent
   - Inverse population density: 2.7 per cent

f) After giving effect to the special needs of Balochistan and application of the aforesaid multiple indicators, the final percentage share of the provinces for distribution of provincial share in the divisible pool taxes will be as under:
- Punjab 51.74
- Sindh 24.55
- KP 14.62
- Balochistan 9.09

g) The federation and the provinces of Punjab, Sindh, and Khyber Pakhtunkhwa have accepted the special needs of Balochistan and have agreed to provide Balochistan PKR 83 billion (9.09 per cent of the provincial share in the divisible pool taxes) in the first year of the award. Any shortfall in this amount shall be made up by the federal government from its own resources. This arrangement for Balochistan would also remain protected throughout the remaining four years of the award based on annual budgetary projections.

h) Sindh would receive an additional transfer of an amount equivalent to 0.66 per cent of the provincial pool from the federal government.

i) The net proceeds of development surcharge on natural gas shall be distributed amongst the provinces. For the purpose of distribution of development surcharge on natural gas, the royalty on natural gas and development surcharge would be notionally clubbed into one and the average rate per MMBTU would be worked out. Thereafter, royalty on natural gas would be distributed in accordance with Article 161(1) of the constitution whereas the development surcharge on natural gas would be distributed by making adjustments based on this average rate. The rate of excise duty on natural gas will be raised to PKR 10.0 per MMBTU in order to give effect to this formula.

j) The development surcharge on natural gas for Balochistan with effect from 1 July 2002 would be worked out and this amount, subject to maximum of PKR 10.0 billion, would be paid by the federal government in five years in five equal installments.

k) The net amount of royalty on crude oil shall be paid to the provinces according to production in each province as per current practice.

l) NFC recognises that sales tax on services is a provincial subject under the Constitution of Pakistan, and may be collected by respective provinces, if they so desire.

m) The federal and provincial governments should streamline their tax collection systems to reduce leakages and increase their revenues through efforts to improve taxation in order to achieve a 15 per cent tax to GDP ratio by the terminal year, i.e. 2014–15. Provinces would initiate steps to effectively tax the agriculture and real estate sectors.

n) Federal and provincial governments would develop and enforce mechanism for maintaining fiscal discipline at the federal and provincial levels.

o) The federal government may assist the provinces through specific grants in times of unforeseen calamities.

p) The meetings of the NFC would be convened regularly on a quarterly basis to monitor implementation of the award in letter and spirit.

The seventh NFC award represented a major step forward in a number of important ways. Primarily, it made a crucial step in the process of further fiscal decentralisation. This had been Sindh's ultimate concern, which contributed to poor development and rehabilitation of the rural areas. The share of the four provinces combined rose to 56 per cent in the first year to 57.5 per cent thereafter. This represented a substantial increase in transfers when compared with the maximum share of 50 per cent in the Presidential Order of 2006.

Table 13.13: Share of Provinces in Terms of Indicators NFC (2009)

Indicators	Weight	Punjab	Sindh	KP	Balochistan
Population Share (SBP Estimates)	82.0	57.36	23.71	13.82	5.11
Poverty/Backwardness	10.3	23.16	23.41	27.82	25.61
Revenue Generation/Collection	5.0	44.0	50.0	5.0	1.0
Inverse Population Density (SBP Estimates)	2.7	4.34	7.21	6.54	81.92
Total Share	100	51.74	24.55	14.62	9.09

Source: State Bank of Pakistan, *Special Section 2: National Finance Commissions Awards – A Review*, Karachi, 2011.

Furthermore, the fundamental transition was made in the horizontal-sharing formula amongst the provinces. Historically, the distribution was based solely on the basis of population, which had been voiced by Sindh and was agreed upon by Balochistan and Khyber Pakhtunkhwa in the 1994 NFC award. The resentment continued even in 2006, though the award was passed. The seventh NFC award was able to move toward multiple criteria for sharing, with a primary objective of achieving better fiscal equalisation, which led to a higher per capita transfers to the more backward provinces.

The divisible pool of taxes to the provinces consisted of all FBR taxes, excluding tax revenue from remuneration paid out of the Federal Consolidated Fund, and the excise duty on natural gas. Prior to the distribution to the four provinces, a one per cent of the entire pool used to be utilised towards the government of Khyber Pakhtunkhwa to meet the expenses on the war of terror.

In addition to the divisible pool, the transfers made were straight transfers, which were distributed solely on the basis of collection and this improved the resource allocation to the provinces. These straight transfers included the net revenue from the royalty on oil and natural gas, excise duty, and development surcharge on natural gas as mentioned above.

A relatively small special grant-in-aid, equivalent to 0.66 per cent of the revenues in the net proceeds of the divisible pool, was made to Sindh to compensate for the losses due to the abolition of octroi and zila tax.

The federal government guaranteed revenues each year to the Government of Balochistan, based on annual budgetary projections. The seventh NFC award recognised that the sales tax on services is a provincial subject under the constitution and may be collected by respective provinces.

The federal and provincial governments seem to have committed to the development and enforcement of mechanisms—maintaining fiscal discipline. The federal government may assist the provinces through specific grants in time of unforeseen calamities.

The total transfers were estimated at PKR 999 billion in 2010–11—equivalent to 5.5 per cent of the entire GDP. This was an increase of PKR 336 billion, or 53.4 per cent over the transfers in 2009–10, when compared to a year prior to the seventh NFC award. The transfers then increased to PKR 1,862 billion by 2015–16—a growth rate of 12.5 per cent per annum. Currently, only the total transfers represent 6.3 per cent of the GDP. In the absence of the award, the overall growth in transfers in 2010–11 would have been below 16 per cent. It needs to be recognised, however, that the level of grants has fallen in comparison to those of the Presidential Order 2006.[56]

For the economic and financial distribution of the new award under the seventh NFC programme, factors such as an inverse-population density and the rate of change in poverty was ultimately incorporated after numerous calls by Sindh to do so.

A five-indicator index was introduced in order to measure the combined coverage of the different social services. It included primary and secondary enrolment, literacy, immunisation, and provision of tap water to households.

Nationally, the rate of yearly increase of the index of coverage of social services grew all the way from pre-seventh award to post-award period—2004–05 to 2008–09 and 2008–09 to 2014–15. The highest index value of coverage of social services in 2014–15 is in Punjab. However, the biggest increase in the index value was registered in Khyber Pakhtunkhwa, whereas the smallest improvement was in Sindh.[57] A comparison of the criteria for the pre-seventh NFC award and seventh award is presented in Table 13.14, which shows the degree of fiscal decentralisation and shift towards the provinces that took place under the seventh award. For the provincial share in the divisible pool see Table 13.15.

Table 13.14: Criteria for Distribution of National Revenue

	Presidential Order 2006 (%)	7th NFC Award (%)
Provincial Share in Divisible Pool	41.5–46.25	56–57.5
Indicators and Weightage	–	–
Population	100	82.0
Poverty	–	10.3
Revenue Generation	–	5.0
Inverse Population Density	–	2.7

Source: Reports on National Finance Commission, various issues.

Table 13.15: Provincial Share in NFC awards

Provinces	Presidential Order 2006 (%)	7th NFC Award (%)
Punjab	57.36	51.74
Sindh	23.71	24.55
KP	13.82	14.62
Balochistan	5.11	9.09

Source: Reports on National Finance Commission, various issues.

The reduction in the share of the federal government in the divisible pool has enabled the NFC to expand the transfer of funds to all of the provinces giving due regard to the requirements of the most backward province of Balochistan. The increase in the allocation to Balochistan came at the expense of the most advanced province—Punjab (Table 13.16). The recognition of this principle in the allocation criteria is a step forward in harmonious inter provincial fiscal relations. The end of the deadlock, coupled with the transfer of more funds to all the provinces, has led to an almost universal appreciation for the award. The following table shows the gains and losses to the provinces in their shares of divisible pool between 1974 and 2009.

Although the seventh NFC Award has put an end to the deadlock, a key structural issue remains unaddressed: whether there would be deadlocks during the award negotiations.

Table 13:16 Changes in the Provincial Share (%) (1974 and 2009)

Provinces	1974	2009	Percentage Change
Punjab	60.25	51.74	-14.1
Sindh	22.5	24.55	9.1
KP	13.39	14.62	9.2
Balochistan	3.86	9.09	135.5

Source: Reports on National Finance Commission, various issues.

Furthermore, the award has its own flaws too. The distribution design still falls short on various grounds. As the provinces have been reluctant to share the benefit of larger allocation with the local governments, a fixed proportion of the provincial allocation should be assigned by the NFC to the local governments. The weight of 82 per cent for the population share is still on the higher side compared to other Federating Countries. The demographic structure of the population, an important indicator of the expenditure needs, does not fit in the distribution design.[58]

In addition, the basis of weight-allocation, assigned in the four-part revenue distribution, is unknown and no rigorous exercise seems to have been undertaken to determine these weights. Similarly, the matching grants are the key elements of a distribution design, yet they completely remain absent in Pakistan.

Furthermore, the provinces will continue to rely on large transfers from the Centre, despite numerous claims and calls for decentralisation. The reliance that remains, amidst the historic angst and tussle will remove the image of any incentives for the provinces to generate their own revenues or even work to increase it. There is a need to revisit the mechanisms of resource allocation as well as the institutional structure of the NFC itself.

The recent evolution in the provincial share in the divisible pool and actual resources transferred in the two years immediately prior to the seventh award and the post award period is traced in Tables 13.17 and 13.18. Sindh was able to more than double the resources received under the divisible pool by 2015–16 compared to 2009–10.

Table 13.17: Provincial Share in the Divisible Pool Before and After 7th NFC Award (Percentage) (2008–09 to 2015–16)

Year	Punjab	Sindh	KP	Balochistan
Pre 7th NFC				
2008–09	51.51	29.72	12.71	6.06
2009–10	51.04	29.62	13.02	6.32
Post 7th NFC				
2010–11	47.82	27.05	15.51	9.62
2011–12	47.94	26.96	15.94	9.16
2012–13	48.69	25.61	16.57	9.13
2013–14	47.18	26.63	16.74	9.45
2014–15	47.25	26.97	16.49	9.28
2015–16	48.38	26.11	16.25	9.27

Source: Based on the figures from Finance Division, *Annual Budget Statement*, Islamabad, Government of Pakistan, various years.

Table 13.18: Transfers to Provinces and Sindh (in PKR Million)
(2008–09 to 2015–16)

	From Divisible Pool	Straight Transfers	Special Grants/ Subventions	Total Transfer to Provinces*	% of FBR Tax Revenue	To Sindh
Pre 7th NFC						
2008–09	477,418	82,447	40,568	626,786	53.5	174,598
2009–10	574,064	81,213	81,969	753,302	50.4	199,283
Post 7th NFC						
2010–11	834,664	163,037	54,060	1,073,742	67.1	277,878
2011–12	1,063,052	145,564	53,915	1,315,003	66.6	313,476
2012–13	1,117,543	103,479	61,191	1,441,450	65.1	325,777
2013–14	1,287,447	124,388	53,841	1,611,538	64.7	380,342
2014–15	1,476,554	97,415	33,707	1,688,444	64.8	413,511
2015–16	1,751,517	100,361	32,555	1,974,320	61.6	482,956

*Total transfer to provinces also includes Foreign Grants, loans and other aid.

Source: Finance Division, *Budget–in–Brief*, Islamabad, Ministry of Finance, Government of Pakistan, various years.

Fiscal Federalism in Sindh

Sindh's Responsiveness to Fiscal Decentralisation

According to a report on interprovincial comparison, on legislative development after the Eighteenth Amendment, the Sindh Assembly passed 133 laws, which is the highest number followed by Punjab (103). Furthermore, in pursuance the Eighteenth Amendment, the Sindh government formed an organisation, Sindh Revenue Board (SRB) in 2010, to ensure the efficient workings of the taxation system in the province. The organisation is responsible for introducing modern techniques to increase the competitiveness of the overall system and formulate policies to enlarge the tax base in the province. Punjab Revenue Authority and Khyber Pakhtunkhwa Revenue Authority were later formed in 2011 and 2012 respectively.

Resource Mobilisation in Sindh

The revenue mobilisation effort in Sindh remains lacklustre. The province's capacity of generating Own Source Revenue (OSR) is much more than what is collects annually. Lack of a proper tax administration system (outside SRB) has distorted and fragmented tax collection efforts and has resulted in the collection of tax revenues far less than the province's potential. Lack of political initiative to bring those outside the tax net into the tax system has been a major impediment to the broadening of the tax base. Tax effort by the provinces has slackened because of large transfer to resources out of the federal divisible pool. But given the stark regional inequalities in Sindh, it is necessary that the urban metropolitan governments such as in Karachi should be able to raise its own resources, easing the burden on provincial finances. The provincial revenues can then be freed up for utilisation for infrastructure and social services delivery in the rural areas.

Revenue Agencies in Sindh

The provincial government of Sindh has fifteen major taxes and other minor levies under its mandate. The three agencies primarily responsible for collecting these taxes are Sindh Board of Revenue, Board of Revenue (BoR), and Excise, Taxation and Narcotics (ET&N). The taxes that fall under these agencies are presented in Table 13.19. Furthermore, the sector-wise tax revenue collection by the province is given in Table 13.20.

It can be deduced from Table 13.20 that the main burden of provincial taxes is being borne by sales tax on services that constitutes approximately 49 per cent of the provincial tax revenue followed by the other indirect taxes (31 per cent) such as infrastructure cess. Sindh is not doing well in the collection of direct taxes, as is evident from the data. Agriculture income tax, land revenue, and property tax collectively contribute almost 20 per cent to the provincial tax revenues. These figures, which pertain to fiscal year 2015–16, highlight the areas where the provincial government is foregoing substantial amounts of tax revenues.

BoR's contribution to the total provincial tax revenue collection is about 14 per cent, which is significantly low. Agriculture tax, land revenues and stamp duty fall under BoR and the scope of collection from these sources is quite large. Agriculture contributes approximately 16 per cent to the provincial GDP but contributes only 0.5 per cent to the total provincial tax collection. Owners of large land holdings in Sindh are not declaring their full incomes and thus evading agriculture income tax.

ET&N contributes 30 per cent in the generation of the province's own source revenue. Approximately 70 per cent of the tax revenue generated by ET&N comes from infrastructure cess. Other taxes collected by ET&N include property tax and professional tax, which collectively contribute less than 12 per cent to the revenue collected by the agency. Currently, property tax in the province is evaluated on the basis of outdated land valuation tables. Land values have not been updated for the last twelve years and therefore, the lack of up to date valuation data has resulted in the underperformance of the sector.

Table 13.19: Tax Collection Agencies of Sindh by Tax Type

Sindh Revenue Board (SRB)	Board of Revenue (BoR)	Excise, Taxation and Narcotics (ET&N)
Sales tax on services	Registration fee	Property tax
	Stamp duty	Professional tax
	Capital value tax	Infrastructure and development cess
	Agriculture income tax	Entertainment duty
	Land revenue	Excise duty
		Motor vehicle tax

Source: Finance Department, Government of Sindh, *Sindh Tax Revenue Mobilization Plan (STRMP) 2014–2019*, Karachi, Government of Sindh, 2014, p. 5.

Figure 13.1: Contribution of the Major Taxes in the Province's Own Source Revenue

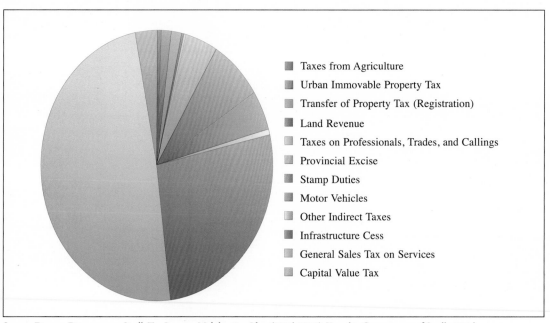

Source: Finance Department, *Sindh Tax Revenue Mobilization Plan (2014-2019)*, Karachi: Government of Sindh, 2014.

Table 13.20: Revised Estimates of Sindh's Provincial Tax Revenue Collection
(in PKR Million)
(1990–91 to 2015–16)

Taxes	1990–91	1995–96	2000–01	2005–06	2010–11	2015–16
Agriculture Income Tax	–	0.32	600.0	300.00	280.5	349.3**
Property Tax	90.6	52.1	322.0	700.0	900.0	3700.0
Land Revenue	29.6	70.6	144.2	110.0	400.0	210.0
Tax–Professions, Trade and Calling	54.3	150.1	200.0	180.0	390.0	380.0
CVT on Immovable Property	60.0	186.4	150.3	337.9	2500.0	3100.0
Provincial Excise	196.9	498.9	900.0	1300.0	2900.0	4000.0
Stamps Duty	502.3	1500.0	2008.7	4308.0	5000.0	7532.5
Motor Vehicles	342.1	513.3	900.1	1850.0	3815.0	5680.0
Other Indirect Taxes	285.5	735.9	2021.9	20050.4	16,562.5	39326.8
Total Tax Collection	1561.6	3707.6	7,247.2	29,136.3*	50,113.5	125,279.0
Tax Collection (Excluding Sales Tax on Services)	1,561.6	3,707.6	7,247.2	29,136.6	32,748.0	64,279.0

* Does not include Federal Excise on Natural Gas.
** Includes recoveries of overpayments

Source: Finance Department, Budget, *Annual Budget Statement*, Karachi, Government of Sindh, various years.

Figure 13.1 depicts that Sindh's Own Source Revenue (OSR) is dominated by sales tax on services which was previously collected by the FBR. There is almost a four-fold increase under this head from 2009 to 2014. Over 51 per cent provincial tax collection was derived from GST on services in 2015–16. Table 13.22 shows that tax revenues collected excluding GST on services increased by over 96 per cent between 2010–11 and 2015–16. The rising trend in overall provincial tax collection is in fact a reflection of the buoyancy in GST on services. To maximise the revenue under the newly devolved structure introduced under the seventh NFC in 2010, the Government of Sindh passed the Sindh Revenue Board (SRB) Act in 2010 and Sindh Sales Tax on Services in 2011.

Table 13.21 compares own source tax revenue collection in the province before and after the seventh NFC Award. An increase of 132.4 per cent, in revenue collection, was recorded in the first year of the implementation of the seventh NFC, followed by a 20.6 per cent increase in the following year. This significant increase was observed due to the transfer of sales tax on services to the province's jurisdiction from the FBR.

Table 13.21: Own Source Tax Revenue Collection Before and After the Implementation of 7th NFC (2009–10 to 2015–16)

Year	Amount (PKR in Million)	Amount (Excluding Sales Tax on Services)	Percentage Change (%)	
			Excluding Sales Tax on Services	Total
2009–10 (Pre 7th NFC)	21,564.9	21,564.9	–	–
2010–11 (First year of 7th NFC)	50,113.5	32,748.0	51.9	132.4
2011–12 (First year of collection by SRB)	60,459.0	36,535.0	11.6	20.6
2012–13	68,697.3	35,031.7	(4.1)	13.6
2013–14	79,836.6	40,329.9	15.1	16.2
2014–15	95,782.6	46,382.9	15.0	20.0
2015–16	125,279.0	64,279.0	38.6	30.8

Source: Finance Department, *Sindh Tax Revenue Mobilization Plan (2014–2019)*, Karachi, Government of Sindh, 2014; Finance Department, Budget 2016–17, *Annual Budget Statement*, Karachi, Government of Sindh, 2016.

Property Tax in Sindh

The Government of Sindh is currently facing numerous challenges in broadening its tax base and increasing its own source revenues, but there are two sources which have not been fully tapped for this purpose. One is the property tax and the other is agriculture income tax. The contribution of property tax in the province's own source revenue is dismally low, approximately 4 per cent of the total revenue receipts. However, it is generally believed that, with concentrated efforts and certain policy adjustments, this tax can substantially augment the province's tax collection.

The primary reason behind the underperformance of the sector is the lack of accurate and updated data on valuation and assessment. ET&N is responsible for handling all the matters related to property, which includes collection of property tax, assessing new properties added, estimating the accurate value/rent of the properties, and updating land valuation tables. However, the land valuation tables in Sindh have not been updated since the last twelve years and thus the figures do not reflect the actual values of the property, which adversely affect tax collection. The Government of Sindh should carry out the cadastral survey and evaluate the current value of the properties to prevent the shrinking of the tax base over time. Furthermore, the Government of Sindh still employs manual methods for keeping data records. This practice encourages rent-seeking behaviour and evasion of the taxes. Although the provincial government is making efforts to automate, the land records by working on the Land Administration and Revenue Management Information System (LARMIS), they need to employ more resources to the project to ensure its speedy completion and effective implementation.

AGRICULTURAL INCOME TAX IN SINDH

Under the 1973 Constitution of Pakistan, fourth schedule, the federal government has the right to collect taxes on the income derived from sources other than agriculture, therefore the right to collect taxes on agriculture income falls solely under provincial jurisdiction. Provinces can collect taxes on agriculture income if they wish.[59]

Like property tax, agriculture income tax is also underperforming. The agricultural sector employs 45 per cent of the country's labour force but when it comes to revenue generation from the levied income taxes, it clearly fails to meet its potential. Agricultural output contributes approximately 16 per cent to the provincial GDP, and 44 per cent of farm area is owned by those with holdings in excess of 25 acres deriving incomes equivalent to the threshold of individual income tax. This problem is not limited to Sindh but is equally applicable throughout Pakistan. The share of the sector in the cumulative tax collection is less than one per cent (Table 13.22). There are 8.26 million farms in Pakistan with an area of 21.41 million hectares and gross sectoral value added of PKR 22.02 billion in 2014–15. The average agriculture tax collection that year was reported to be PKR 2 billion or less than 0.1 per cent of value added. This worked out to be PKR 270 per acre, which is highly inequitable compared to income earners such as salaried workers.[60] This low yield from agriculture can be traced back to historical reasons.

The issue of exempting agricultural income from tax dates back to the British rule in the subcontinent. However in 1860, the British government, attempted to impose income taxes on sectors with wide coverage (which included agricultural sector). But the sector was already heavily taxed through land revenue.[61] It constituted almost 45 per cent of the total federal and provincial tax revenues.[62] Since the agriculture sector already raised a significant amount of tax revenues at that time, the government felt that there was no need to charge tax on income derived from agricultural sources. Hence, the imposed tax on agricultural income was later removed. The Government of India Act 1935 gave provinces complete jurisdiction over agricultural income taxes and barred the central government from collecting any tax on agricultural income.[63] Prior to 1947, some provinces in undivided India used to levy taxes on agricultural income but none of these areas geographically fell in present day Pakistan.

In 1977, the Pakistan Peoples Party enacted the Finance (Supplementary) Act under the government of Zulfikar Ali Bhutto. Under this Act, agricultural income tax was introduced in place of land tax in an attempt to bring the agricultural sector in the tax net.[64] However, things were soon reversed because of transition to military government. After the military coup of 1977, agriculture income was once again exempted from tax through the Income Tax Ordinance of 1979.[65]

In an attempt to bring the sector under the tax net, agricultural income tax ordinances were introduced by each of the four provinces in the 1990s.[66] The first schedule of these ordinances stipulates 'Acreage Tax' or Land Tax rates while the second schedule specifies agriculture income tax rates. Farmers and agriculture landowners are required to pay whichever tax, acreage or agriculture income, is higher.[67] The first and second schedule of the Sindh Agricultural Income Tax Act can be seen in Tables 13.23 and 13.24. The cause of inefficient collection of the taxes in the agriculture sector lies in the policy options given to the farmers who can pay either the tax on acreage or income. Lack of proper monitoring of the system has made it excessively easy for people to deceive the system by not declaring their real agricultural income and instead paying acreage taxes whose burden is significantly lower compared to the tax on agricultural income. There is a need to integrate land revenue and agriculture income tax into a single levy, bringing the rate at par with non-agriculture income tax rates.

Table 13.22: Provincial Agriculture Tax (in PKR Million)
(2000–01 to 2015–16)

Year	Punjab	Sindh	Khyber Pakhtunkhwa	Balochistan	Total Agriculture tax revenue of 4 provinces	Total Tax Revenue of 4 provinces	Total agriculture tax revenue as percentage of total tax revenue	Total provincial revenue	Agriculture tax revenue as a percentage of total provincial revenue
2000–01	2,978	704.8	220	30.5	3,933.26	228,577	1.7	441,526	0.891
2001–02	3,257.3	626.5	250	32.8	4,166.59	231,688	1.8	476,639	0.874
2002–03	3,255.7	319.5	280	43.9	3,899.12	280,192	1.4	555,770	0.702
2003–04	3,923.1	327.4	305	89.6	4,645.13	275,816	1.7	611,456	0.760
2004–05	4162.5*	317.8	365	45.5	4,890.83	338,080	1.5	659,363	0.742
2005–06	4,047.6	320.6	330	268.0	4,966.14	450,342	1.1	752,997	0.660
2006–07	4,261.4	272.1	490.9	74.8	5,099.25	483,421	1.01	889,685	0.573
2007–08	4,879.2	418.8	736.8	83.7	6,118.47	667,199	0.9	1,050,694	0.582
2008–09	5,434.6	320.7	639.7	79.3	6,474.25	1,204,670	0.5	750,475	0.863
2009–10	7,488.1	308.4	592.4	56.4	8,445.24	876,014	1	1,472,821	0.573
2010–11	8,999.1	557	779	40	10,375.06	1,211,291	0.9	1,699,334	0.611
2011–12	10,021.9	450	936	108.2	11,516.02	1,333,951	0.9	2,052,886	0.561
2012–13	10,605.5	611.5	1,082.7	41	12,340.66	1,544,433	0.8	2,199,232	0.561
2013–14	12,048.7	479.2	1,324.0	50.7	13,902.61	1,767,444	0.8	2,564,509	0.542
2014–15	11,962.0	518.3	1,858.6	189.8	14,528.69	1,902,397	0.8	3,017,596	0.481
2015–16	13,396	613.8	1,880.7	245	16,135.51	2,293,852	0.7	3,660,418	0.441

*Value taken from Budget Estimates

Table 13.23: Land Revenue Rates (First Schedule)

Land Ownership (acres)	Tax (Rupees/acre)
Up to 12.5	No tax
12.5–25	100
26–50	250
50 or more	300

Source: Government of Sindh, *The Sindh Land Tax and Agricultural Income Tax Ordinance 2000*, Karachi, Provincial Assembly of Sindh, 2000.

Table 13.24: Progressive Tax Rates Levied By Sindh Agriculture Income Tax Act 2000 (Second Schedule)

Income Level	Tax
If total income is less than Rs. 80,000	No tax
If total income does not exceed Rs. 100,000	5% of the total income
If total income is more than Rs. 100,000 but does not exceed Rs. 200,000	Rs. 5000 + 7.5% on over Rs. 100,000
If total income is more than Rs. 200,000 but does not exceed Rs. 300,000	Rs. 12,500 + 10% on over Rs. 200,000
If total income is more than Rs. 300,000	Rs. 22,500 +15% on over Rs. 300,000

Source: Government of Sindh, *The Sindh Land Tax and Agricultural Income Tax Ordinance 2000*, Karachi, Provincial Assembly of Sindh, 2000.

In 2015–16, the four provinces together collected only PKR 16 billion in the form of agriculture tax compared to PKR 1,217 billion contributed as income tax by the non-agriculture sectors. The ratio of national income received from agriculture and non-agriculture sectors is 20:80. While the ratio of income tax paid by the two sectors is approximately 1:99, the violation of the principle of horizontal equity, therefore, is quite obvious in this case. It is not the ability to pay, but lack of enforcement against those who do not pay. There was some revival of interest in reforming and collecting revenues from agriculture income in early 2000s. In 2001–02, the agriculture tax revenue had reached 1.8 per cent of total provincial tax revenues. But since then there has been a gradual decline and in 2015–16, the agriculture tax yielded only 0.7 per cent of total tax collection.

Table 13.25: Summary of Agro-based Revenues and Agriculture Income Tax (in PKR Million)
(2009–10 to 2012–13)

Year	Agro–Based Tax*	Agricultural Income Tax	Total	Share of Agriculture Income tax as a percentage of total
2009–10	554	4	558	0.72
2010–11	469	4	473	0.84
2011–12	296	5	301	1.66
2012–13	442	7	449	1.56

Source: Author's own calculation based on the data from BOR–Agriculture Tax Reforms.

*The Agro-based tax receipts include Land Tax, Local Cess, Drainage Cess, Water Tax and Misc. Revenue Tax.

In addition to exempting agricultural income from tax, massive amount of subsidies are given to the farm owners each year in the form of tax holidays, support prices, and input subsidisation. Tax subsidies coupled with the farmers' exemption from paying taxes on their income from agriculture, has resulted in the inequitable income tax structure and the burden is transferred to the salaried workers in the business sector.[68]

Public Financial Management Reforms

ONGOING REFORM PROGRAMMES IN SINDH

Sindh has several ongoing reform programmes in public financial management:

1. PIFRA—Project for Improvement of Financial Reporting and Auditing (PIFRA)

PIFRA was initiated in 1997, with the assistance of the World Bank. The project aims towards achieving improved accuracy, increased reliability, and enhanced transparency of public expenditure. The most prominent feature of this project is the introduction and implementation of an IT-based accounting system. Integrated Financial Management Information System (IFMIS) and Accounting Policy and Procedural Methods (APPM), which are implemented all across Pakistan, are a product of the project. The concept of performance and risk-based audit was also introduced under PIFRA.

Although PIFRA is a welcome move, the present processes of authorisation, approval, and releases of funds are highly cumbersome and confer enormous discretionary process to low level officials of the provincial departments and the accountant general's office. The business processes have to be revamped and simplified and the opportunities for rent-seeking minimised.

2. Procurement and Regulatory Authority support

The Government of Sindh has set up the Sindh Public Procurement and Regulatory Authority (SPPRA), to streamline procurements procedures including a dispute resolution mechanism. In addition to harmonising and facilitating the collection process at the procurement agencies, the objectives for SPPRA also include the introduction of the use of technology in procurement processes to facilitate transparency, fairness, and to achieve value for money. In actual practice, the procurement process has become an impediment in utilisation of funds and implementation of projects.

In 2013, the Government of Sindh held a Public Financial Management and Accountability Assessment (PFMAA) to assess the province's performance. It was a follow-up to the 2009 assessment and was conducted against thirty-two PFM performance management indicators. Based on the assessment findings, the Government of Sindh prioritised the area reforms amongst short-, medium-, and long-term plans. In short- to medium-term plan, the government planned on consolidating previous reforms rather than introducing new ones, while the objective in medium-long term horizon is to develop new systems as required. The PEFA rating shows that for twenty-two out of thirty-two indicators, Sindh falls in either the C or D category.

On comparing the PEFA Assessment scores for the years 2009 and 2013, the indicators largely exhibit a deteriorating trend. Some scores remained unchanged or slightly improved, indicating that little progress has been made in the financial sector of the province. Some of the important indicators of the assessment and their performance are discussed below.

There can be two approaches to PFM reforms; expenditure based and revenue based. The revenue-based approach primarily focuses on broadening the revenue base by improving the tax administration, whereas, expenditure management approach focuses on improving the budget functions. Other reforms needed in this area are credibility, transparency, and predictability of the budgetary process.

Table 13.26: PEFA Ratings for PFM Assessment

Core dimensions of performance	Ratings			Total Indicators
	A/B	C/D	Not Rated	
Credibility	–	3	1	4
Comprehensiveness and Transparency	3	3	–	6
Policy–based budgeting	1	1	–	2
Predictability and control in budget execution	2	6	1	9
Accounting, recording and reporting	1	3	–	4
External scrutiny and audit	–	3	–	3
Donor practices	1	2	–	3
Higher level of Government	–	1	–	1
Total	8	22	2	32

Source: Government of Sindh and Development Partners, *Pakistan Sindh Province—Public Financial Management and Accountability Assessment*, Karachi, PEFA, 2013.

Credibility of the budget

Practices, which reduce the credibility of the budget, include granting unlimited power to the executives to control and change the budget. Moreover, since the last couple of years, the budget estimates for revenue collection estimated are highly inflated than the actual collections while expenditures are understated. The actual outcomes show significant deviations from the budget approved by the legislature. This raises questions about the credibility of the mechanisms that are employed in estimating the revenues and expenditures. In addition, there is no consolidated record of public expenditures that results in poor control of expenditure. According to a PEFA report, during the years 2009–13, the budgeted expenditure exceeded the aggregate expenditure. Inability to increase OSR, lacklustre efforts in collecting taxes and poor forecasting tools are attributed as the probable causes.

Transparency and Comprehensiveness of the budget

PFM assessments indicators have shown some improvement in inter-governmental fiscal relations. Announcement of budget has also improved but the launching of releases in the fourth quarter in order to meet the targets introduces inefficiencies lapses of funds and leakages. Delivery of public services such as education and health suffer consequently.

Policy-Based Budgeting

The government's performance in this domain has deteriorated since 2009. The assessment indicators reveal that there is room for massive improvement in areas pertaining to long-term fiscal planning (of budget and public expenditure).

Accounting and Reporting

The government, in the recent years, has started to emphasise the use of IT-based processes in reporting and recording of activities related to public finance but the indicators have also shown deterioration.

Predictability

Majority of the indicators in this domain have declined and the primary reason is the absence of internal and external audit.

DECENTRALISATION TO LOCAL GOVERNMENTS

As pointed out earlier, the seventh NFC award has considerably strengthened the financial situation of the provinces compared to the pre-seventh NFC periods. But additional resources have not been shared with the local governments, where most of the interaction between an ordinary citizen and the state takes place for accessing basic public goods and services. The latest Sindh Local Government Act has in fact reversed the fiscal decentralisation trend set in the 2001 law, and local governments have in fact weakened.

The Provincial Finance Commission (PFC) has similar obligations to that of a National Finance Commission, in respect to distribution between provincial and local governments. The finance minister of the province heads the PFC. The sharing formula followed for distributing resources amongst different tiers of local government is based on differential need assessments. PFC was constituted in 2001 and the primary objective of the commission was to devise a formula for sharing resources among the districts of Sindh to help local governments work smoothly and minimise poverty by efficient and effective mobilisation of resources at the grassroots level.

The announcement of a fair and equitable PFC award is critical for meeting the development needs of the population at the local level. However, this issue has been on the backburner for more than a decade and poor public amenities in both, large urban centres and rural districts, reflect this neglect. Qazi Masood Ahmed and Akhter Lodhi (2006) have analysed the revenue sharing formulas used by the provinces. By computing the rank correlation, they studied the extent to which the development transfers are based on the existing level of deprivation in the districts. On comparing the statistics obtained from different provinces, the paper concluded that Punjab and the NWFP allocate their resources based on their deprivation index. In contrast, statistics from Sindh did not reveal any correlation between resource distribution and the deprivation index.

The provincial government should constitute the provincial finance commission which would determine revenue sharing arrangements between provincial and local governments. Revenues ought to be distributed amongst district governments through a composite index that takes into account population, service infrastructure, development needs, the deprivation index, and the local tax effort made.

The weightage allotted to each domain under the last PFC award was as follows:

- Population – 40 per cent
- Service infrastructure – 35 per cent
- Deprivation index – 5 per cent
- Development needs – 10 per cent
- Previous progress – 10 per cent

The above formula needs to be revisited once further devolution of administrative powers and authority to the district governments is completed. The Eighteenth Amendment to the constitution has devolved powers from federal government to the provincial governments and it is high time that the provinces devolve further to the local governments; 210 million people cannot be governed effectively by four provincial headquarters. According to Article 140(A), it has been made mandatory that, 'Each province shall, by law, establish a local government system and devolve political, administrative, and financial responsibility and authority to the elected representatives of the Local Governments.' Inclusive growth would evade us until further fiscal decentralisation to fund water supply, sanitation, solid waste disposal, education, and health for citizens is undertaken.

Development Expenditure

One of the expectations implicit in the transfer of revenues from the federal to the provincial governments was that the latter would increase their spending on development programmes and projects, and sustain the well-being of the citizens by investing in infrastructure and social sectors. The unfulfilled demands for funds to reach the goals of universal primary education, affordable health care for all, provision of portable drinking water, and sanitation is now within easy reach of the provinces as the volume of financial resources available to them have multiplied several-fold compared to the earlier periods. Some increase in expenditure has been discerned but the outcome indicators do not reflect their impact. Additional measures that are being taken such as private–public partnership (PPP mode) can perhaps make some difference. Sindh has already taken some steps in forging PPP relationships in roads, schools, and hospitals in some districts on pilot basis with favourable results. It is hoped that the initiative would be extended and cover a large segment of the population.

The Annual Development Programme (ADP) is the instrument through which the provincial government allocates resources for public expenditure on development. ADP is a comprehensive list of all development projects that indicates the physical targets to be achieved during a single financial year by each department or executing agency along with an allocation of the requisite financial allocations that would be released.

Table 13.27 shows the reported ADP budgets and total development expenditures over the course of the the last forty-five years with a five-year interval between successive years; we can see that some ADP allocations have substantially increased or decreased spending. The possible reasons for over- and under-spending of ADP allocations are given below.

Table 13.27: Annual Development Programme (ADP) Allocations and Expenditure (in PKR Million)
(1970–71 to 2015–16)

Year	ADP Allocation	ADP Expenditure
1970–71	227.3	192.8
1975–76	760.0	788.0
1980–81	972.0	1,112.4
1985–86	2,090.0	2,339.9
1990–91	3,113.4	3,782.8
1995–96	14,394.0	16,445.0
2000–01	11,253.0	8,842.0
2005–06	38,224.0	36,545.1*
2010–11	135,085.0	91,487.0*
2015–16	177,000.0	134,405.8*

* Taken from *Accounts*.

Source: Finance Department, *Annual Budget Statement*, Karachi, Government of Sindh, various years.

OVER-SPENDING

1. Supplementary budgets in selected cases due to prime minister's/chief minister's/chief martial law administrator's directives.
2. Emergency expenses due to floods, cyclones, droughts, and other natural calamities.
3. Belated adjustments by auditor/account general's office.

UNDER-SPENDING

Various reasons can be attributed to the under-spending including, but not limited to the following: (1) short releases by federal government; from divisible pool/direct transfers, project commitments through federal Public Sector Development Programme (PSDP); (2) non-utilisation of foreign assistance; (3) capacity constraints of provincial departments; and (4) belated releases from the finance department to the concerned departments.

According to Table 13.27, ADP expenditures have increased from PKR 36.5 billion in 2005–06 to PKR 134 billion in 2015–16—almost four times. The question arises whether the provincial departments and agencies had the capacity to manage such a heavy workload in an effective manner. In order to get a clearer picture of how the ADP has changed over the years and the economic implications of this transformation, it would be pertinent to go through a department-wise analysis of the expenditures. More particularly, three major departments will be analysed due to their centrality in the economic growth of the province, namely education, health, water supply, and sanitation.

There is a widely held perception that the results of such huge expenditures are not visible either in form of infrastructure improvement or better social indicators. Poor governance, inadequate monitoring, and lack of accountability are the main factors responsible for the disconnect between resource utilisation and economic and social outcomes. The ADP allocation process itself has been found to be flawed. A large number of projects are included at the insistence of the political leaders in the ADP, creating a huge gap between the demand and financing available for the ADP; therefore, some allocated amount is provided against each of the projects, irrespective of whether it is near completion or completely new. Incomplete projects, cost overruns, and time delays create a wedge between the promised benefit stream and the actual outcomes. Unless strict discipline is introduced both in the ADP formulation as well as monitoring, the wait for the population in the province for the improvement of their lives would be endless.

Education

In contemporary literature on human capital and human development, there is evidence to support the claim that education attainment plays an integral part in improving social and economic conditions of any society. Of course, it is obvious that developed nations as compared to developing ones show higher literacy rates as well as generally higher levels of education attainment. There also exists evidence that as levels of literacy rise, there are externalities generated that maximise social returns while also increasing private benefits to the individual. Recent research on the relationship between crime rates and literacy finds a negative relationship between the two.[69] A positive relationship is found between maternal education and the health of the child.[70] In summary, given all types of investments in human capital, investment in education gives holistic returns that affect societies at multiple levels. Therefore, investment in education to improve quality and outreach of education is of the utmost importance from a governmental point of view.

Table 13.28: ADP Allocations to Education (in PKR Million)
(1990–91 to 2015–16)

Year	Allocations for Education	Total ADP Allocations	Allocation as Percentage of Total ADP (%)
1990–91	669.0	3,113.4	21.5
2000–01	877.0	11,253.0	7.8
2005–06	1,600.0	38,224.0	4.2
2015–16	12,616.0	177,000	7.1

Source: Finance Department, *Annual Budget Statement*, Karachi, Government of Sindh, various years.

Table 13.28 shows the allocations made for education in the overall ADP. It can be seen that over the years the absolute allocation to education in the ADP has increased; however, the share of expenditure in the total allocation has fallen. This is contrary to the expectations that larger resources transferred to the provinces out of the divisible pool would, inter alia, raise spending on education and fill in the financing gap overtime. The challenge of the education sector does not remain confined to formal education but also to vocational and technical training that can upgrade the skills of the employed labour force.

As of 2013–14, in Sindh, 40.8 per cent of the total labour force was employed in the agricultural sector, 13.8 per cent in the manufacturing sector and 15.9 per cent were engaged in wholesale and retail trade and the remaining 30 per cent worked in other services (Table 13.31). A large majority of the labour force is either unskilled or is semi-skilled, implying that there exists a need to train them so that they can pursue self-employment and entrepreneurship or get absorbed in the domestic labour market for employment. Investments in skill formation is imperative for a variety of reasons: (a) we have a youthful population that needs jobs; (b) there is a mismatch between the output of our universities and colleges and the demand for marketable skills; and (c) the employment prospects overseas are much promising for those who possess skills and are adequately trained compared to the unskilled or semi-skilled labour force.

Table 13.29: Sectoral Breakdown of Employment (2013–14)

Sectors	Employment share (%)
Agriculture	40.8
Manufacturing	13.8
Whole sale, Retail Trade, Repair of vehicles	15.9
Professional, Scientific and Technical Activities	0.2
Education	3.5
Human Health and Social Work	1.5

Source: Percentage Distribution of Employed Person 10 Years of Age and Over By major industry Division, Sex and Area Pakistan Bureau of Statistics Labour Force Statistics 2013–2014, <http://www.pbs.gov.pk/sites/default/files//Labour%20Force/publications/lfs2013–14/t20–pak–fin.pdf>.

The partnership with the private sector in identifying the trades, developing the curriculum and contents of training, pedagogical tools and assessment methods would go a long way in filling in this gap of skilled manpower. ADP allocations for technical and vocational (T&V) education would have to be raised very significantly. At the same time, attention should be focused on the whole educational value chain for pre-primary to university as the literacy rates in the country are far from satisfactory.

Health

Investments in health are positively correlated with poverty reduction. As workers remain healthy and do not suffer from various illnesses, the absenteeism from work is reduced and productivity is enhanced. Their incomes are steady as they do not fall back below the poverty line due to prolonged absences from work. Table 13.30 shows the pattern of health expenditure under ADP over the years. The jump in health allocation in the last decade is highly welcome but the proportion is still relatively low compared to the requirements as well as the norms. Table 5.10 ('Chapter 5') reinforces this point by showing that the ratios of patients to doctors or patients per nurses or patients per bed have not shown any upward movement in the years when the provinces were flush with excess cash flows.

Table 13.30: ADP Allocations to Health (in PKR Million) (1990–91 to 2015–16)

Year	Allocation to Health	Allocation as Percentage of Total ADP (%)
1990–91	371	11.9
2000–01	393	3.5
2005–06	980	2.6
2015–16	15,385	8.7

Source: Finance Department, *Annual Budget Statement*, Karachi, Government of Sindh, various years.

Water Supply and Sanitation

Adequate drinking water and sanitation facilities are of immense importance for an individual. Improving these does not only bring economic gain for a country but also helps build resilience, given increasing climate variability. Many developing countries today are struggling due to chronic water shortages and inadequacies of the existing water supplies. The human right to water and sanitation remains unmet and unrealised for billions of people worldwide.

Poor sanitation and hygiene have many serious consequences. Children die from preventable illnesses, and mainly girls are denied their basic right of education because of poor sanitation facilities in public schools; health systems are overwhelmed, and the economy suffers on a whole. Due to its significance, a host of water utilities have been established in many developing countries, both in urban and rural areas, mostly covering water supply schemes and sanitation infrastructure. These schemes are either financed by international agencies, central governments, or the provincial or local governments. Despite the substantial support, the fact remains that many water supply schemes have resulted in limited level of service delivery. The situation in Sindh is no different.

It can be seen from Table 13.31 that over the years, ADP allocations to water supply and sanitation has risen. However, the same has not been translated in building long-term sustainable projects, as 582 water supply and sanitation ADP schemes (out of 1,337) remained non-functional from 2010–11 to 2015–16.[71]

Table 13.31: ADP Allocations to Water Supply and Drainage (Approved Schemes) (in PKR Million)
(1990–91 to 2015–16)

Years	Urban	Rural	Total Water Supply and Sanitation	Percentage of Total ADP Allocations (%)
1990–91	120.5	284	404.5	13.0
2000–01	145.0	444.4	589.4	5.2
2010–11	269.9	647.7	917.6	0.8
2015–16*	3,753	1297.3	5050.3	2.9

*Water Supply and Sanitation.

Source: Finance Department, 'Public Sector Development Programme', *Annual Budget*, Vol. V, various years.

A substantial proportion of Sindh's population is suffering from waterborne diseases. Infants are suffering more than adults from preventable diseases like cholera, diarrhoea, typhoid, and other diseases. Thar is the most affected part of Sindh where many children have lost their lives owing to the scarcity of water and unhygienic food.

Sanitation coverage is poor in most parts of the province, 16 per cent of Sindh's population has no access to toilet facilities—5 per cent in urban areas and 27 per cent in rural areas—whereas an overall 32 per cent population has non-flush toilets, 56 per cent in rural and 7 per cent in urban areas.[72] In urban areas, underground drains serve only 69 per cent of households and in rural areas 85 per cent of households have no system at all.

Water supply and sanitation conditions are deteriorating in rural as well as urban areas of Sindh. Karachi, the largest city of Pakistan, has been affected immensely. The population of Karachi grew at an average annual growth rate of 2.6 from 1998–17,[73] but the water supply does not correspond accordingly. The Karachi Water and Sewerage Board (KWSB) has failed to meet the demands of the residents of Karachi. Once very effective, KWSB is now facing an overall institutional decay. Some of the major problems that it is facing[74] are (1) acute shortage in the bulk supply level; (2) increase in water theft and leakages (3) ageing and crumbling pipeline networks; (4) lack of a comprehensive maintenance and network rehabilitation plan for older neighbourhoods; and (5) inability of KWSB to add more freshwater connections in suburbs and elsewhere.

More than half of Karachi's population resides in sub-urban neighbourhoods or slums. People in these areas are bound to purchase expensive water tankers, setting aside other necessities, and hence are trapped in the poverty spiral.

Rural areas are in far worse condition than the urban areas. For example, 88 per cent of Thar's population does not have toilets; 90 per cent of the schools do not have toilets, and more than 90 per cent of people do not have access to safe water. In the other rural areas of Sindh, access to safe water and sanitation is low and hygiene is nowhere to be found. This has serious implications for the people in Sindh and the main victims are women and children. People in rural Sindh and urban slums are poor and cannot build water or sanitation facilities on their own. Majority of them are not even aware of the need of it because of high illiteracy rates.

Summing Up

Sindh's tax and non-tax collection efforts have remained sub-optimal and can be easily stepped up. The two possible sources that can yield considerable revenues are urban property tax and agriculture income tax. There is also a need to consolidate and simplify various tax levies. As an urbanised, literate, and modern province contributing as much as 30 per cent to the national GDP, Sindh is underperforming in relation to its potential.

It can, in fact, help the country as far as fiscal resource mobilisation is concerned. Pakistan has faced fiscal crises several times and had to approach the IMF and external donors for bail out. The reasons behind these frequent recurring crises are the rigid structure of our public finances and lack of political will to mobilise revenues. Recurrent expenditures such as defence, large interest payments on public debt, and huge amount of subsidies given to publicly owned enterprises make up most of the public expenditure in Pakistan and the government is left with insufficient resources to finance the development sector. Low tax-to-GDP ratio forces successive governments to finance the gap between expenditures and revenues by reverting to external and domestic borrowing. In Sindh, a former provincial finance minister is on record that the province has the capacity to increase its revenue four times the current level. This can be accomplished by accurate assessments and intensified efforts to record property tax, agriculture income tax and abiana. By 2014, Pakistan's public debt stood at 63 per cent of the GDP, (exceeding the limits laid down in the Fiscal Responsibility and Debt Limitation Act), of which two-thirds was the domestic debt. According to the IMF and other studies, Pakistan can tap 50 per cent additional revenues by widening the tax net.

Ninety-nine per cent of the provincial tax revenue is generated only from nine of the fifteen tax levies that lie under Sindh's jurisdiction. Other six tax domains contribute to the remaining one per cent. These can either be consolidated or eliminated altogether except for the taxes on agriculture that need to be redesigned and revamped The primary objectives of PFM systems are to provide an aggregated financial system and uniformly manage its operation at different levels of government within a country. It increases the accountability between various stakeholders such as state and development agencies, ministries, donor agencies, the government, and citizens. The following specific reforms can help achieve this goal of realising the tax potential:

- SRB's performance has improved after the Eighteenth Amendment and it is collecting the most revenue amongst the three revenue-collecting agencies. Following Punjab's example, Sindh government should consider the possibility of gradual merger of ET&N, BOR, and SRB into one entity, so as to reduce the operational costs, provide convenience to tax payers, improve communication and reconciliation among the tax base, and enable a comprehensive compilation of public finance records. This new entity would have an integrated automated IT system that would improve vigilance and compliance. At present, all the data is sent to the Pakistan Revenue Automation Limited Company (PRAL) for compilation and processing of data.
- The government's lack of predictability about the budget and public expenditure can be improved by a robust system of internal and external audit. Therefore, the audit capacity of the major spending departments such as works and buildings, irrigation, etc. should be strengthened.
- There is a large informal service sector currently operating in Sindh. Efforts should be made to bring them into the tax net by introducing a simplified process of filing and facilitation with built in incentives.
- Land records in the province are not updated and, therefore, the agriculture sector is underperforming. Land records should be computerised, updated, and easily accessed with land title clearly defined so that tax is collected on the actual value rather than outdated, undervalued records.
- Rates for property tax assessment must be revised, updated, and put on the website for public information. Property registration should be automated as the manual process is prone to large scale misuse and rent-seeking by lower functionaries of the government. The government should complete Land Administration and Revenue Management Information System as expeditiously as possible as Punjab has successfully transformed its land record system.
- Infrastructure cess is collected to maintain and develop the infrastructure. Although the sector is performing well and is the largest revenue yielding tax collected by ET&N, there is scope for expansion. Petroleum and goods for Afghan transit trade are two areas that have maximum potential for revenue

generation but they are outside the scope of this tax. Many cases such as these, currently exempted from paying infrastructure cess, should be reconsidered and added to the tax's scope.

On the expenditure side, waste inefficiency and leakages can be plugged in and cost effectiveness ensured by following a robust Public Financial Management (PFM) system. The primary objective of PFM is to improve accountability of the government, i.e. its departments, development agencies, ministries, corporations, and autonomous bodies, on the citizens.

Conclusion

SINDH is the most urbanised and educated province of Pakistan with the highest per capita income in the country. However, over time, Punjab has improved its economic standing and is catching up with Sindh, while the gap between the latter and the national average has narrowed down. On the whole, the province enjoys certain advantages that are not shared by the other three provinces; two major seaports of the country, a rich pool of talent produced by high quality educational institutions, vast tracts of irrigated land that can be tapped to reach their potential, significant reserves of natural gas, coal, and minerals, a dynamic private sector, strong financial and industrial infrastructure, and the wherewithal to mobilise revenues for its development and public services make it an attractive place for private investment.

At the same time, Sindh is also the most unequal and diverse province as the per capita income of the rural inhabitants is one half of that of their urban counterparts. Social indicators in the rural districts are dismally low while those of the urban areas are among the top. The social gap between urban males and rural females is quite wide. Almost half of the population is not a part of the labour force, with 72 per cent of females being outside the workforce, and hence the labour force participation rate is only 43 per cent.[1] Agricultural productivity is on a downward moving path and the share of employment in agriculture is also shrinking, affecting rural income formation. The intra provincial disparities thus get accentuated.

Given these stark disparities, a sensible policy initiative was to empower the local governments to address the specific challenges faced by each of the districts. The devolution of powers and decentralisation of resources from the federal to provincial governments should have been taken to its culmination point, i.e. the local governments. What has happened after 2008 is completely the opposite.

The new law enacted has enabled the provincial government to resume and centralise the powers and functions previously allocated to the local government system under the 2001 law. This concentration of powers and financial resources has weakened the system of delivery of public services to the citizens especially in the backward districts which require more attention.

Poor supervision and monitoring and lack of accountability have led to under-provision of services particularly to the poorest and most vulnerable sections of the society, and have undermined incentives for firm investment. According to public opinion polls, the situation has deteriorated in recent years. Politics is dominated by patron–client relationships where loyalty to the two major political parties and payments in exchange for favours or rent sharing are the sole criteria for the award of state contracts, licenses, permits, NOCs, state land, appointments, postings, and transfers. Businesses who want to take advantage of Karachi's location are stymied by an intrusive, obstructive, and corrupt bureaucracy.

The cost of business has also shot up due to multiple claims of extortion by criminal gangs, who are supported by some elements within the political parties. Land and water mafias have hiked the prices of public goods and services. Kidnapping of businessmen for ransom had become quite common. Lack of security and poor governance have therefore neutralised the advantages that Karachi enjoyed and has led to the industries and business hubs shifting from Karachi to the north. The action taken by the Rangers in the last two years has, to a large extent, put an end to these nefarious activities and restored peace, but what is really needed for sustained growth is to improve the governance environment with particular attention to enhancing state effectiveness and accountability

The deep divide among the two large communities living in the province remains a matter of serious concern for realising the future prospects of Sindh's economic and social development. The continuous tussle for control of local governments between the two political parties illustrates the gravity of this problem. A dysfunctional system for the delivery of public services is creating disaffection and frustration among the public at large. This is most apparent in case of the largest city of the country, Karachi.

With more people getting added to Karachi's population every year, the city's infrastructure is creaking under population overload. Severe water shortages, leaking sewerage, piles of garbage in the main streets and residential areas, traffic congestion, and poor maintenance of roads, absence of a reliable public transport system, and a highly unsatisfactory security situation had turned businesses away from Karachi. Institutional frailty with multiple agencies working in an uncoordinated manner have added to the plethora of problems. Other secondary cities such as Hyderabad, Sukkur, Larkana, Nawabshah, and Mirpurkhas have also been neglected despite huge public sector development allocations and expenditure. These cities have to become competitive. A World Bank study of 750 cities across the world defined the concept of competitive city as '… one that successfully facilitates its firms and industries to create jobs, raise productivity, and increase incomes of citizens over time.'[2]

For the uplift of the rural economy, promised additional facilities such as a water distribution system, proper storage, and warehousing etc. should be developed. Productivity growth has slowed mainly due to political interference and governance weaknesses. It is estimated that more than 40 per cent of irrigation water is lost because of inefficiencies, leakages, and thefts in the distribution and conveyance system.[3] Existence of multiple agencies for managing the resource has compounded the problem. Water pricing is causing misallocation and excessive use of this scarce resource. Recovery of water charges from the users accounts for only 20–25 per cent of the operation and management expenses. In areas where the water courses have been brick-lined, the conveyance losses have been reduced.[4]

Given the weakening irrigation system, increasing droughts, and effects of global warming on the economy, there is a need to seriously explore the rural economy's potentials in order to absorb the increasing labour force supply and ease the pressure on the existent urban infrastructure. There are certain sectors in both the rural and urban economy whereby substantial investments can not only help alleviate poverty but also build infrastructure and provide economic opportunities. The sectors—fisheries, livestock, tourism, and ecotourism—have huge growth potential and currently have limited funding from the public and private sectors. If explored, these sectors can prove to be reliable in addressing the concerns cited above and provide room for economic growth in the mid and long term.

Sindh is blessed with a 352 km long coastline, which contains around 71 per cent of Pakistan's fishery resources. This sector needs to be improved.[5] The fisheries sector produces merely 0.7 million tonnes of fish, which is valued at USD300 million while the overall catch is estimated to be at 400,000 metric tonnes, of which only twenty per cent is exported; it is worth around USD200 million.[6] This means that we have yet to tap into a potential of USD800 million, which will help increase the worth of our fisheries export from USD200 million to USD1 billion.[7] This is achievable mainly due to Pakistan's low per capita fish consumption—under two kilos—compared to that of the Far East—twelve to thirteen kilos.[8] This target is also realistic because the total world fisheries market is valued at over USD95 billion.[9] Despite the potential and supporting natural environment in the country and province, especially in the Indus Delta and coastal belt of Sindh, fisheries contribute a meagre one per cent to the GDP, although it employs one million people in the country—two-fifths directly and three-fifths indirectly.[10] This means that if the full potential were to be realised, then the labour employed can be expected to increase three-fold, given that the levels of technology, efficiency, and output remain the same.

To better understand the level of employment of this sector, as of 2014, more than 37 per cent of Pakistan's labour force is associated with agriculture, fisheries, and forestry while overall, 42 per cent of it is composed of in the same sector compared to 39 per cent in Sindh and almost 45 per cent in Punjab. This uniquely situated province has a lot of marine potential for which there is a need to implement efficient and sustainable measures to tap into export potential and trade competitiveness.

There are certain areas of potential and interest for the livestock sector as well, which can help Sindh grow economically and create infrastructure and jobs—both in the urban and rural economy. Similarly, in spite of the fact that Sindh's domesticated animals populace is of superb quality, changes in the execution of breeds and misuse of their hereditary potential have reduced profitability.[11] The accessibility to feed materials is declining instead of expanding, attributable to the steady weight of expanding the domesticated animals populace, frequent dry spells, and more noteworthy weight on cultivable land for agricultural produce.[12] There is also a need for an expansion of facilities offered to domesticated animals which incorporate access to present-day information sources, innovation, and domesticated animal wellbeing administrations.

There is a system of veterinary healing centres and dispensaries at the dehi and tehsil levels, which provide health facilities and preventive immunisation to livestock as well as domesticated animals. These facilities must be improved further so as to ensure healthy livestock that is free of diseases. Furthermore, dairy towns ought to be set up on barren rural lands for raising of dairy wild oxen, with adequate access to business sectors through dairy associations and ensuring satisfactory setups for commerce and support in territories that have no dairy support centres.

The vast coastline of Sindh is not only well-suited for fish-farming, it can also revive the tourism industry and improve the image of Pakistan all over the world. It is also ideal for marine life because of its salinity and temperature characteristics.[13] Moreover, the coastline and the high temperatures make Sindh suitable for establishment of resorts, which will not only help increase foreign exchange, but also create jobs and sustain the economy. The revival of the tourism industry is indeed possible because the province has internationally renowned historic sites such as Mohenjo Daro, Kahujo Daro, Ratto Kot, Ranikot, mangrove forests, etc.

While the hot and humid climate of Sindh is good for attracting tourism, it should be noted that the increasing temperatures are a result of global warming. They not only present a risk to marine life, but can also prove to have an adverse effect on urban communities. This makes the nearness of woodlands and wetlands considerably more essential for the sustenance of the marine economy and that of the traditional economy too.

While Sindh is a resource-rich and an all-terrain region, it is likewise subject to a plethora of problems. There is a serious water deficiency in the province, particularly in the dry and desert regions, owing to the lack of infrastructure and scanty population in such terrains. Land is likewise beset by desertification, waterlogging, and salinity. Woodlands involve just 2.5 per cent of the aggregate land region and this has been quickly diminishing because of overgrazing and cutting down of trees. In addition, lately there has been ocean-water intrusion into the Indus Delta, which has devastated a vast part of the farming area and cost the nearby people their vocation.

Inferable from these variables and different issues, for example, poor monetary and social advancement, the region has a high occurrence of poverty and rural-urban migration. Continued dry seasons further intensify the issues. It is important that maintainable advancement and administrative action be taken in the region.

New firms are most likely to enter the rural areas and product markets if education levels, quality of physical infrastructure such as electricity, roads, water and sanitation, and telecom become available as the relative margins in these untapped markets are high. Small scale agro-processing and marketing firms would be able to take advantage of better connectivity and higher volumes of output and thus absorb some of the incremental labour supply. This may diminish, to some extent, the push factors for migration to urban areas.

Looking at the future, the urban population of Pakistan is estimated to exceed 60 per cent, while that of Sindh is expected to be even higher. The population of Karachi would rise by 50 per cent in the next fifteen years or so. The principal challenge facing the province is how to absorb over 382,000 new entrants to the labour force so that they are gainfully and productively employed.[14]

The demographics of the youth bulge can prove to be a boon if these younger cohorts can be educated, trained, and skilled to meet the demands of the economy or those of the labour deficient countries in the Gulf. The same cohorts can become an explosive time bomb if they remain illiterate, unemployed, and economically and socially disadvantaged. In the absence of an adequate number of job openings available and equitable sharing of economic opportunities by both the urban and rural youth, the existing ethno-linguistic division is likely to deepen adding to mistrust, social disharmony, and political fragmentation.

To rule out the possibility of this scenario, it is imperative that economic growth should be balanced lifting the fortunes of both the urban and rural segments of the population and at the same time rapid enough, so that it can create jobs, businesses, and livelihoods on a sustained basis. The sharing of prosperity by these two segments of the population and equitable access to public goods and services by the majority, particularly the poor and the disadvantaged, is the only sure way of keeping harmony and social cohesion in the province. That social capital, in turn, would reinforce the impulses for higher growth rates.

The second big challenge has to do with the problems of food insecurity, irrigation water shortages, and lower crop yields arising from global warming in the face of increasing demand from the urban middle class for meat, poultry, marine products, vegetables, and fruits. Water requirements could therefore register a steep rise in the coming decades. Improvement in water use efficiency, rationalisation of water pricing, water conservation techniques, substitution of flood irrigation by drips or sprinklers, drought resilient and high yielding varieties, rainwater harvest, construction of storage dams and reservoirs, better animal husbandry, and use of genetics and biotechnology could help in boosting the agriculture sector and the overall economy of Sindh. But governance reforms, greater use of private economic agents, and capacity building of research and development institutions are the sine qua non for the success of this approach.

If the aforementioned sectors are concentrated upon and funded by the government and private sector, along with better fisheries and livestock research and support centres, then food insecurity can be curbed along with high unemployment and low standards of living. The exports from the revived sectors will improve the cash flows of the country and curtail the already bleak foreign exchange reserves. This will further help bridge the rural–urban divide and lower migration by reducing the inter-dependency of the rural population on the urban centres as the only job markets.

The main objective of the future development strategy should therefore, be to cement the existing gaps between the rural and urban areas in the province. Consequently, it should avoid a uniform 'one shoe fits all' approach. There should be specifically targeted interventions for the urban and rural segments with the aim of maximising the synergies and interdependencies among the two.

It is fortuitous that the congruence of sectoral, ethnic, linguistic, and gender dimensions with the geographical division makes it easy to sharpen the impact of policy instruments and investments.

A provincial economy faces many more constraints than the national economy as its degrees of freedom are more limited. Macroeconomic stability, and prudent fiscal, monetary, trade, and exchange rate policies fall within the domain of the federal government but have a powerful impact on the economic outcomes in the province. Another important interdependency is the mobilisation of tax revenues by the Federal Board of Revenue which are then distributed among the provinces. Sindh derives 80 per cent of its revenues from the divisible tax pool and therefore the collection effort of FBR is a critical determinant of the fiscal management of Sindh. As these variables are taken as given, the province has to design and adapt its development strategy within these given parameters. The province has, however, control over land, labour, and agriculture output markets. It can facilitate farmers and firms in doing business, reducing inefficiencies, waste, and leakages, and allocating public sector development expenditures to overcome infrastructure and human development deficiencies.

The future strategy for economic and social development of Sindh has to therefore be carefully charted out, as any linear derivation from the national strategy, without careful adaptation in the light of the sharp urban–rural, ethno-linguistic, agriculture–non agriculture income divide, with the attendant political polarisation, would prove to be counterproductive. The Provincial Finance Commission should give higher allocations to the backward districts of the province while provide incentives to advanced districts to mobilise resources on their own. Public–private partnership should be encouraged for investment in infrastructure and human development.

Within those given constraints, the strategy proposed here focuses on levers under the control of the province. The past practices of blaming the federal government for all the ills and shortcomings have not been conducive and a different tack needs to be adopted. Without compromising or sacrificing the rights of the province the emphasis should be to influence federal policies so that they do not harm Sindh. A more conciliatory and cooperative path may perhaps produce better results rather than an adversarial and confrontational avenue that has not worked in the past.

The six pillars of the proposed growth strategy for Sindh should consist of:

(a) Improving the governance and institutional capacity of the provincial and district governments by enhancing accountability, transparency, and rule of law.
(b) Introducing a citizens' feedback system and a robust freedom of information law.
(c) Making the urban economy more competitive and efficient by removing distortions in land, labour, and goods markets and removing infrastructural bottlenecks.
(d) Raising the productivity of water, livestock, and agricultural land through water course lining, precision land levelling, new varieties of seeds, improved crop and animal husbandry practices, promotion of fisheries and marine products, and value-added horticulture, vegetables, and oilseeds.
(e) Mobilising province's own revenues by reforming urban property tax, agriculture income tax, local cesses, and user charges on irrigation water.
(f) Improving access of the poor, particularly the rural female population and those living in the backward districts, to basic services such as education and health by giving scholarships, free lunches, and conditional cash grants for female students, subsidies, free medicines etc.

The synergies and interdependence in this strategy are woven in so far as the provincial finances would be largely channelled to the poor and backward districts while the urban and better off districts would be incentivised to mobilise their own resources, reducing the demands on the province. Sales tax on services used to be collected by the FBR and the actual yields were quite low. Since the province has taken over this function, there has been a tremendous jump in the amounts collected. This example should convince the decision makers that the closer the authority is to the payers, the larger the yield (tax revenue) will be.

Therefore, urban areas would be in a position to mobilise additional revenues which are evaded at present and not at the cost of the rural areas as the beneficiaries would be able to see for themselves the impact their taxes would be making in their communities and districts. The success of this strategy depends upon the following critical question: how quickly and responsibly the two major ethnic communities can come to realise that, given their interdependence and strong linkages between the urban and rural economies of Sindh, a more symbiotic relationship between them would help in maximising economic potential of the province and thus derive benefits for the constituents of both the groups? Their leaders have to forego narrow parochial considerations and take bold initiatives to work together in removing the political fragmentation, social polarisation, and economic distance that have resulted in underperformance. A common bright future is ahead for the province only if they can get their act together.

ANNEXURES

List of Annexure Tables

Chapter 1: Land and People

Table 1A:	Administrative Units of Sindh—Divisions, Districts, and Talukas/Tehsils/Towns	340

Chapter 3: Population

Table 3A:	Number of Urban Localities by Size, Urban Population, and Average Annual Growth Rate 1961, 1972, and 1981 Censuses)	344
Table 3B:	Divisional Population of Sindh—2017	344
Table 3C:	Proportion of Muhajirs in Population—1951	345
Table 3D:	Number of People Speaking Urdu—1951	345
Table 3E:	Number of Rural Localities by Population Size, District and Taluka (1981 and 1998 Censuses)	346
Table 3F:	Number of Urban Localities by Size and Type (1951–81)	346
Table 3G:	Population Distribution (15 Years and Over) by Marital Status, Sex and Rural/Urban (1972–98 Censuses)	347
Table 3H:	Rural and Urban Distribution of Districts of Sindh (in Thousand) (1981–98 Censuses)	348
Table 3I:	Sindh Language Groups (in Thousand) (1931–98 Censuses)	349
Table 3J:	Sindh–Karachi Comparison and Percentage Shares (in Bracket) (in Million) (1931–2017 Censuses)	
Table 3K:	Sindh Urban-Hindu/Muslim population (in Lacs) (1941 and 1951 Censuses)	350
Table 3L:	Religion—Sindh Urban/Rural (in Lacs) (1941)	351
Table 3M:	Province-wise Population Size, Percentage Share (in brackets) and Inter-Census Annual Growth (in Lacs)	351
Table 3N:	Sindh and Pakistan Rural/Urban Population (in Lacs) (1951 to 2017 Censuses)	352
Table 3O:	Comparative Census of Pakistan and Regions (in Million) (1951 and 2017 Censuses)	352
Table 3P:	Percentage Distribution of Male and Female Population in Sindh (1998 and 2017 Censuses)	352
Table 3Q:	Provincial, Rural, and Urban Population Share by Mother Tongue (in Million) (1998)	353
Table 3R:	Sex Ratio by Age Groups and Rural/Urban Areas—1998	353
Table 3S:	Population of Females by Age, Area, Marital Status (in Percentage)—1998	354

Chapter 4: Education

Table 4A:	District and Level-wise Schools (2015–16)	355
Table 4B:	District and Level-wise Schools (2010–11)	356
Table 4C:	Schools by Level (2005–06)	357
Table 4D:	Schools by Level (2001–02)	358
Table 4E:	Schools by Gender (2015–16)	358
Table 4F:	Schools by Gender (2010–11)	359
Table 4G:	Schools by Gender (2005–06)	360

Table 4H: Level-wise Boys Enrolment (2015–16)   361
Table 4I: Boys Enrolment (2010–11)   362
Table 4J: Boys Enrolment (2005–06)   363
Table 4K: Boys Enrolment (2001–02)   364
Table 4L: Level-Wise Girls Enrolment (2015–16)   364
Table 4M: Girls Enrolment (2010–11)   365
Table 4N: Girls Enrolment (2005–06)   366
Table 4O: Girls Enrolment (2001–02)   367
Table 4P: Sindh—Urban–Rural Education Statistics (2001–02 to 2015–16)   368
Table 4Q: District-Wise Number of Teachers (2001–15)   368
Table 4R: District-Wise Students–Teacher Ratio (STR) (2015–16)   369
Table 4S: Number of Primary Schools Merged into Campus Schools (Up to 2015–16)   370
Table 4T: Gender-Wise Enrolment across Different Grades (2015–16)   371
Table 4U: Transition Rates from Primary to Middle (2014–15)   372

Chapter 5: Health

Table 5A: Medical & Paramedical Personnel (Government) by Category in Sindh (2008–15)   374
Table 5B: Government Hospitals, Dispensaries, Rural Health Centres, TB Clinics, Basic Health Units   374
              and Mother Child Health Centres with Bed Capacity in Sindh (2008–12)
Table 5C: Allocated and Revised Estimates of Health Budget (in PKR Million) (1970–2015)   375
Table 5D: Medical Personnel of Sindh (Government) (1975–2015)   376
Table 5E: Trained Medical Staff at the Sindh Medical Centres and Units (Public) (1975–2015)   376
Table 5F: Trained Technical Staff at the Sindh Medical Centres and Units (Public) (1975–2015)   377
Table 5G: Indoor and Outdoor Patients in Centres or Units (1965–1995)   377
Table 5H: Medical Centres and Units (Government) (1965–2015)   378
Table 5I: Beds in Medical Centres and Units (1965–2010)   378
Table 5J: Health Indicators of Sindh (1952–56)   379
Table 5K: Health Indicators—2015   379
Table 5L: Diseases (1952–56)   379

Chapter 6: Labour and Employment

Table 6A: Labour Force Participation Rates and Unemployment Rates for Pakistan for Different   380
              Age Groups (2014–15)
Table 6B: Labour Force Participation Rates and Unemployment Rates for Punjab for Different   380
              Age Groups (2014–15)
Table 6C: Percentage Distribution of Unemployed Persons 10 Years of Age and Over Who Were Not   381
              Available for Work Due to Certain Reasons (1997–98 and 2014–15)
Table 6D: Percentage Distribution of Employed Persons 10 Years of Age and Over Who Worked   382
              Less than 35 Hours during Reference Week by Reasons (Pakistan) (2014–15)
Table 6E: Sindh's Share in Percentage Distribution of Employed Persons 10 Years of Age and   383
              Over Who Worked Less than 35 Hours during Reference Week by Reasons (2014–15)
Table 6F: Punjab's Share in Percentage Distribution of Employed Persons 10 Years of Age and Over   383
              Who Worked Less than 35 Hours during Reference Week by Reasons (2014–15)
Table 6G: Distribution of Population by Age, Literacy, and Level of Education for Pakistan (2014–15)   384
Table 6H: Distribution of Population by Age, Literacy, and Level of Education for Sindh (2014–15)   384
Table 6I: Distribution of Population by Age, Literacy, and Level of Education for Punjab (2014–15)   385
Table 6J: Trends in the Population 10 Years of Age and Over by Level of Education (2005–06 to 2014–15)   386

Table 6K: Percentage Distribution of Migrant Population 10 Years of Age and Over by Main Reasons   386
             of Migration (2014–15)
Table 6L: Distribution of Employment by Industries (Pakistan) (1990–91 and 2014–15)   387
Table 6M: Distribution of Employment by Industries (Sindh) (1990–91 and 2014–15)   387
Table 6N: Distribution of Employment by Industries (Punjab) (1990–91 and 2014–15)   388
Table 6O: Percentage Distribution of Employed Persons 10 Years of Age and Over by Major Industry   389
             Division (1982–83 to 1997–98)
Table 6P: Percentage Distribution of Employed Persons 10 Years of Age and Over by Major Industry   391
             Division (2005–06 to 2014–15)
Table 6Q: Percentage Distribution of Employed Persons 10 Years of Age and Over by Major Industry   392
             Division (1982–83 to 1997–98)
Table 6R: Percentage Distribution of Employed Persons 10 Years of Age and Over by Major Industry   393
             Division (Sindh) (2014–15)
Table 6S: Percentage Distribution of Employed Persons 10 Years of Age and Over by Major Industry   393
             Division (Punjab) (2014–15)
Table 6T: Percentage of Employed Persons Who Worked for at least 35 Hours (Pakistan) (1997–98 to 2014–15)   394
Table 6U: Percentage of Employed Persons Who Worked for at least 35 Hours (Sindh) (1997–98 to 2014–15)   394

Chapter 7: Poverty and Inequality

Table 7A: Distribution of Monthly Consumption Expenditure in Sindh (Rural/Urban) (2007–08 to 2013–14)   395
Table 7B: Average Per Capita Income Estimates (in PKR Thousand) (2010–11)   395

Chapter 8: Agriculture

Table 8A: Area of Major Crops in Pakistan, Punjab, and Sindh (in Thousand Hectare) (1947–48 to 2015–16)   396
Table 8B: Yield of Major Crops in Pakistan, Punjab, Sindh (Kgs Per Hectare) (1947–48 to 2015–16)   397
Table 8C: Production of Major Crops in Pakistan, Punjab, and Sindh (in Thousand Tonne)   398
             (1947–48 to 2015–16)
Table 8D: Area of Fruits in Pakistan, Punjab and Sindh (in Thousand Hectare) (1947–48 to 2015–16)   399
Table 8E: Production of Fruits in Pakistan, Punjab, and Sindh (in Thousand Tonne) (1947–48 to 2015–16)   399
Table 8F: Area of Vegetables in Pakistan, Punjab, and Sindh (in Thousand Hectare) (1947–48 to 2015–16)   400
Table 8G: Production of Vegetables in Pakistan, Punjab, and Sindh (in Thousand Tonne) (1947–48 to 2015–16)   401
Table 8H: Area of Vegetables in Pakistan, Punjab, and Sindh (in Thousand Hectare) (1947–48 to 2015–16)   401
Table 8 I: Production of Vegetables in Pakistan, Punjab and Sindh (in Thousand Tonne) (1947–48 to 2015–16)   402
Table 8J: Area of Lentils in Pakistan, Punjab, and Sindh (in Thousand Hectare) (1947–48 to 2015–16)   403
Table 8K: Production of Lentils in Pakistan, Punjab, and Sindh (in Thousand Tonne) (1947–48 to 2015–16)   403
Table 8L: Consumption of Fertiliser (in Thousand Tonne) (1957–58 to 2015–16)   404
Table 8M: Production of Chemical Fertilisers (Pakistan) (1957–58 to 2015–16)   405
Table 8N: Usage of Fertilisers, Manures, Pesticides and Herbicides by Size of Farm in Pakistan (2011–12)   405
Table 8O: Usage of Fertilisers, Manures, Pesticides and Herbicides by Size of Farm in Punjab (2011–12)   406
Table 8P: Usage of Fertilisers, Manures, Pesticides and Herbicides by Size of Farm in Sindh (2011–12)   406
Table 8Q: Sindh's Relative Percentage Share in Agriculture (1947–48 to 2015–16)   407
Table 8R: Percentage Change in Area of Major Crops in Pakistan, Punjab, and Sindh (1970–2015)   408
Table 8S: Percentage Change in Production of Majors Crops in Pakistan, Punjab, and Sindh (1970–2015)   408
Table 8T: Percentage Change in Yield of Major Crops in Pakistan, Punjab, and Sindh (1970–2015)   409
Table 8U: Average Annual Growth Rate (Sindh) (1947–48 to 2014–15)   409

Chapter 12: Energy and Mineral Resources

Table 12A: Output of China Clay in Pakistan and Sindh (in Tonne) (1970–71 to 2014–15)   410

Table 12B: Output of Fuller's Earth in Pakistan and Sindh (in Tonne) (1970–71 to 2014–15)   410

Table 12C: Output of Limestone in Pakistan and Sindh (in Tonne) (1970–71 to 2014–15)   411

Table 12D: Output of Silica Sand in Pakistan and Sindh (in Tonne) (1970–71 to 2014–15)   411

List of Annexure Figures

Chapter 4
Figure 4A: Transition from Primary to Middle School (2015–16)   412

Chapter 11
Figure 11A: Method of Projection   414
Figure 11B: Map of Industrial Zones and Clusters   415

Chapter 12
Figure 12A: Output of China Clay in Pakistan and Sindh (1970–71 to 2014–15)   416
Figure 12B: Output of Fuller's Earth in Pakistan and Sindh (1970–71 to 2014–15)   417
Figure 12C: Output of Silica Sand in Pakistan and Sindh (1970–71 to 2014–15)   417
Figure 12D: Output of Limestone in Pakistan and Sindh (1970–71 to 2014–15)   418

Annexure Tables

Chapter 1

Table 1A: Administrative Units of Sindh—Divisions, Districts, and Talukas/Tehsils/Towns

Division	District	Taluka/Tehsil/Town
Hyderabad	Dadu	Dadu
		Johi
		Khairpur Nathan Shah
		Mehar
	Hyderabad	Hyderabad
		Hyderabad City
		Latifabad
		Qasimabad
	Thatta	Ghorabari
		Keti Bundar
		Mirpur Sakro
		Thatta
	Sujawal	Jati
		Kharo Chann
		Mirpur Bathoro
		Shah Bunder
		Sujawal
	Jamshoro	Kotri
		Sehwan
		Thano Bula Khan
		Manjhand
	Matiari	Hala
		Matiari
		Saeedabad
	Tando Allah Yar	Tando Allah Yar
		Jhando Mari
		Chamber
	Tando Muhammad Khan	Tando Muhammad Khan
		Bulri Shah Karim
		Tando Ghulam Hyder
	Badin	Badin
		Golarchi (Shaheed Fazil Rahu)
		Matli
		Tando Bago
		Talhar

Division	District	Taluka/Tehsil/Town
Karachi	Karachi West	SITE Town
		Baldia Town
		Orangi Town
	Karachi South	Lyari Town
		Kemari Town
		Saddar Town
	Karachi East	Jamshed Town
		Gulshan-E-Iqbal Town
	Korangi Karachi	Shah Faisal Town
		Landhi Town
		Korangi Town
		Malir Town
	Karachi Central	North Nazimabad Town
		New Karachi Town
		Gulberg Town
		Liaquatabad Town
	Malir Karachi	Bin Qasim Town
		Gadap Town
Larkana	Jacobabad	Garhi Khairo
		Jacobabad
		Thull
	Larkana	Dokri
		Larkana
		Rato Dero
		Bakrani
	Shikarpur	Garhi Yasin
		Khanpur
		Lakhi
		Shikarpur
	Kashmor	Kandhkot
		Kashmore
		Tangwani
	Kambar-Shahdadkot	Kambar Ali Khan
		Miro Khan
		Shahdadkot
		Warah
		Qubo Saeed Khan
		Naseerabad
		Sujawal Junejo

Division	District	Taluka/Tehsil/Town
Mirpurkhas	Mirpurkhas	Digri
		Kot Ghulam Mohd
		Mirpurkhas
		Jhudo
		Sindhri
		Hussain Bux Mari
		Shujaabad
	Tharparkar	Chachro
		Diplo
		Mithi
		Nagarparkar
		Islamkot
		Dahli
		Kaloi
	Umer Kot	Samaro
		Umer Kot
		Pithoro
		Kunri
Shaheed Benazirabad (SBA)	Naushahro Feroze	Bhiria
		Kandiaro
		Moro
		Naushahro Feroze
		Mehrabpur
	Sanghar	Jam Nawaz Ali
		Khipro
		Sanghar
		Shahdadpur
		Sinjhoro
		Tando Adam
	Shaheed Benazirabad	Kazi Ahmed
		Nawabshah
		Sakrand
		Daur

Division	District	Taluka/Tehsil/Town
Sukkur	Khairpur Mirs	Faiz Ganj
		Gambat
		Khairpur Mirs
		Kingri
		Kot Diji
		Mirwah
		Nara
		Sobhodero
	Sukkur	Pano Aqil
		Rohri
		Sukkur City
		Salehpat
		New Sukkur
	Ghotki	Ghotki
		Mirpur Mathelo
		Ubauro
		Khangarh
		Daharki

Source: Local Government Commission, Government of Sindh, Karachi.

Chapter 3

Table 3A: Number of Urban Localities by Size, Urban Population, and Average Annual Growth Rate (1961, 1972, and 1981 Censuses)

Year	Number of Urban Localities by Size					Urban Population		Inter-censal Average Annual Growth Rate of Urban Population
	Total	Less Than 25,000	25,000 to 49,999	50,000 to 99,999	One Lakh and Over	Number	Percent	
1961	68	55	5	4	4	3,167,018	37.9	
1972	121	96	11	8	6	5,725,776	40.5	5.2
1981	125	99	14	5	7	8,243,036	43.3	4.4

Source: Population Census Organisation, *1981 Population Census Report of Sindh*, Islamabad, Statistics Division, Government of Pakistan, 1984.

Table 3B: Population of Main Districts of Sindh—2017

Division	Population (in Thousand)
Hyderabad	2,892
Dadu	1,689
Khairpur	1,547
Sanghar	1,453
Jacobabad	1,426
Badin	1,136
Thatta	1,113
Naushahro Feroze	1,088
Shaheed Benazirabad (Nawabshah)	1,072
Ghotki	970
Tharparkar	914
Sukkur	908
Mirpurkhas	906
Shikarpur	880
Umer Kot	663

Source: Pakistan Bureau of Statistics, *District-wise Census Results 2017*, Islamabad, Statistics Division, Government of Pakistan, n.d.

Table 3C: Proportion of Muhajirs in Population—1951

Province and State	Population (in 1000)	Muhajirs (in 1000)	Percentage of Muhajirs	Males Per 1,000 Females	
				Total	Muhajirs
Pakistan	73,880	7,226	9.8	1,127	1,187
Balochistan and State Union	1,154	28	2.4	1,215	1,800
Districts	602	28	4.7	1,239	1,300
States Union	551	-	-	1,139	-
East Bengal	41,932	699	1.7	1,097	1,205
Federal Capital Area Karachi	1,122	617	55	1,342	1,320
NWFP	3,222	51	1.6	1,117	1,429
Punjab and Bahawalpur State	20,636	5,281	25.6	1,152	1,167
Districts	18,814	4,908	26.1	1,149	1,164
Bahawalpur State	1,822	372	20.4	1,189	1,207
Sindh and Khairpur State	4,925	550	11.2	1,220	1,165
Districts	4,665	540	11.7	1,218	1,169
Khairpur State	319	10	3.1	1,246	1,133

Source: Population Census Organisation, *Census of Pakistan, 1951*, Karachi, Government of Pakistan, n.d.

Table 3D: Number of People Speaking Urdu—1951

Province	Total Population (in Lacs)	Mother Tongue (in Lacs)		Urdu Speakers (in Lacs)	Persons Speaking Urdu as Additional Language (in Lacs)	Ratio (A)
		Urdu	Other			
Balochistan	11.5	0.2	11.3	0.8	0.6	5.3
East Bengal	419.3	2.7	416.6	4.6	1.9	0.5
Karachi	11.2	5.7	5.5	7.6	1.9	34.5
NWFP	41.1	0.5	40.6	2	1.5	3.7
Punjab	206.4	10.7	195.7	32.3	21.6	11
Sindh	49.3	4.8	44.5	6.8	2	4.5
Total	738.8	24.6	714.2	54.2	29.5	4.1

(a) Per cent of persons who do not claim under to be their mother tongue.

Source: Population Census Organisation, *Census of Pakistan, 1951*, Karachi, Government of Pakistan, n.d.

Table 3E: Number of Rural Localities by Population Size, District, and Taluka
(1981 and 1998 Censuses)

District/ Taluka	Rural Localities by Population Size								Rural Population	
	Total	5000 and Over	2000 to 4999	1000 to 1999	500 to 999	200 to 499	Under 200	Uninhabited	Number	Percentage
1981										
Total	5,848	264	1,705	1,916	1,105	483	287	88	10,785,630	56.7
1998										
Total	5871	709	2,251	1,617	657	312	234	91	15,600,031	51.2

Source: Population Census Organisation, *Handbook of Population Census Data Sindh*, Islamabad, Statistics Division, Government of Pakistan, 1988.

Table 3F: Number of Urban Localities by Size and Type
(1951–81)

Year/Population Size	Urban Localities				
	Total	Municipal Corporation	Municipal Committee	Town Committee	Cantonment
1951					
Under 10,000	13	-	4	9	-
10,000 to 24,999	10	-	9	-	1
25,000 to 49,999	4	-	4	-	-
50,000 to 99,999	2	-	1	-	1
100,000 and Over	3	1	1	-	1
	32	1	19	9	3
1961					
Under 10,000	41	-	5	36	-
10,000 to 24,999	14	-	9	4	1
25,000 to 49,999	5	-	5	-	-
50,000 to 99,999	4	-	2	-	2
100,000 and Over	4	2	2	-	-
	68	2	23	40	3
1971					
Under 10,000	66	-	-	64	2
10,000 to 24,999	30	-	3	25	2
25,000 to 49,999	11	-	8	-	3
50,000 to 99,999	8	-	5	3	-

Year/Population Size	Urban Localities				
	Total	Municipal Corporation	Municipal Committee	Town Committee	Cantonment
100,000 and Over	6	1	3	1	1
	121	1	19	93	8
1981					
Under 10,000	51	-	-	50	1
10,000 to 24,999	47	-	4	42	1
25,000 to 49,999	14	-	11	1	2
50,000 to 99,999	5	-	4	-	1
100,000 and Over	7	3	3	-	1
	124	3	22	93	6

Source: Population Census Organisation, *Handbook of Population Census Data Sindh*, Islamabad, Statistics Division, Government of Pakistan, 1988.

Table 3G: Population Distribution (15 Years and Over) by Marital Status, Sex, and Rural/Urban (1972–98 Censuses)

Sex	Total Population	Marital Status (Percentage)			
		Never Married	Currently Married	Widowed	Divorced
Total – 1998					
Both Sexes	30,400,000	30.6	64.1	5.0	0.2
Male	16,100,000	36.2	61.1	2.6	0.1
Female	14,300,000	24.4	67.5	7.8	0.3
Total – 1981					
Both Sexes	10,448,780	24.8	69.1	5.9	0.2
Male	5,658,773	31.9	65.3	2.7	0.1
Female	4,790,007	16.4	73.7	9.7	0.2
Rural – 1981					
Both Sexes	5,713,852	20.2	73.5	6.2	0.1
Male	3,035,199	28.0	69.1	2.8	0.1
Female	2,678,653	11.3	78.5	10.1	0.2
Urban – 1981					
Both Sexes	4,734,928	30.4	63.9	5.5	0.2
Male	2,623,574	36.5	60.8	2.6	0.1
Female	2,111,354	22.9	67.7	9.2	0.2

Sex	Total Population	Marital Status (Percentage)			
		Never Married	Currently Married	Widowed	Divorced
Total – 1972					
Both Sexes	7,944,650	22.7	69.9	7.2	0.1
Male	4,357,645	31.4	64.3	4.2	0.1
Female	3,587,005	12.2	76.8	10.9	0.2
Rural – 1972					
Both Sexes	4,614,625	18.6	74.07	7.25	0.1
Male	2,471,475	27.6	68.19	4.17	0.1
Female	2,143,150	8.2	80.85	10.81	0.1
Urban – 1972					
Both Sexes	3,330,025	28.4	64.2	7.2	0.2
Male	1,886,170	36.4	59.3	4.2	0.2
Female	1,443,855	18.0	70.7	11.1	0.2

Source: Population Census Organisation, *Handbook of Population Census Data Sindh*, Islamabad, Statistics Division, Government of Pakistan, 1988.

Table 3H: Rural and Urban Distribution of Districts of Sindh (in Thousand)
(1981–98 Censuses)

No.	Districts	1981			1998			2017		
		Rural	Urban	Total	Rural	Urban	Total	Rural	Urban	Total
1	Sukkur	779	320	1,099	446	462	908	768	720	1,488
2	Khairpur	734	246	980	1,182	365	1,547	1,623	776	2,399
3	S.B.Abad	1,381	266	1,647	789	283	1,072	-	-	-
4	N. Feroze **	-	-	-	895	193	1,088	1,124	489	1,613
5	Ghotki *	-	-	-	812	158	970	1,242	404	1,646
6	Larkana	882	257	1,139	1,370	557	1,927	-	-	-
7	Jacobabad	854	158	1,012	1,079	347	1,426	7,09	297	1,006
8	Kashmor ***	-	-	-	-	-	-	836	254	1,090
9	Kambar Shahdad Kot ***	-	-	-	-	-	-	943	398	1,341
10	Jamshoro ***	-	-	-	-	-	-	559	434	993
11	Matiari ***	-	-	-	-	-	-	587	183	770
12	Sajawal ***	-	-	-	-	-	-	696	86	782
13	Tando Allahyar ***	-	-	-	-	-	-	575	262	837
14	Tando Muhammad Khan ***	-	-	-	-	-	-	535	142	677

No.	Districts	1981			1998			2017		
		Rural	Urban	Total	Rural	Urban	Total	Rural	Urban	Total
15	Shikarpur	504	116	620	668	212	880	928	303	1,231
16	Hyderabad	1,143	912	2,055	1,423	1,469	2,892	366	1,833	2,199
17	Dadu	926	151	1,077	1,328	361	1,689	1,167	383	1,550
18	Badin	694	82	776	950	186	1,136	1,414	390	1,804
19	Thatta	688	73	761	988	125	1,113	804	176	980
20	Mirpurkhas*	-	-	-	606	300	906	1,080	426	1,506
21	Sanghar	725	198	923	1,122	331	1,453	1,469	588	2,057
22	Tharparkar	1,245	257	1,502	874	40	914	1,517	132	1,649
23	Umerkot*	-	-	-	551	112	663	830	243	1,073
24	Karachi Central*	-	-	-	0	2,278	2,278	-	2,972	2,972
25	Karachi West	-	-	2,156	185	1,910	2,095	283	3,632	3,915
26	Karachi East	-	-	1,886	0	2,746	2,746	0	2,907	2,907
27	Karachi South	-	-	1,396	0	1,745	1,745	0	1,792	1,792
28	Malir*	-	-	-	321	660	981	858	1,151	2,009
29	Korangi***	-	-	-	-	-	-	-	2,457	2,457

* Newly formed districts introduced in the census of 1998
** Renamed to Shaheed Benazirabad and introduced as in the 2017 census.
*** Newly formed districts introduced in the census of 2017.
**** Territorial boundaries of some of the districts has altered over the years.

Source: Bureau of Statistics, *Development Statistics Report 2011*, Karachi, Planning and Development Department, Government of Sindh, n.d.; Pakistan Bureau of Statistics, *District-wise Census Results 2017*, Islamabad, Statistics Division, Government of Pakistan, n.d.

Table 3I: Sindh Language Groups (in Thousand)
(1931–98 Censuses)

Year	Sindhi	Urdu	Seraiki	Pushto	Punjabi	Others	Total
1931	2,874	73	631	17	72	447	4,114
Percentage	70	2	15	0.4	1.8	11	100
1941	3,175	234**	732*	17	87	277	4,522
Percentage	70	5	16	0.4	2	6.1	100
1951	-	-	-	-	-	-	-
1961*	4,850	1,755	750	172	361	491	8,370
Percentage	58	21	9	2	4	6	100
1981**	1,422	614	213	83	209	163	2,714
Percentage	53	23	8	3	8	6	100

Year	Sindhi	Urdu	Seraiki	Pushto	Punjabi	Others	Total
1998	18,181	6,409	944	1,276	2,128	1,501	30,439
Percentage	60	21	3	4	7	5	100
31–98 (67 Years Growth)	6 Times	88 Times	1.5 Times	75 Times	30 Times	3 Times	7 Times

*Including Thari/Dhatki, Jatki and Balochi/Brahwi
** Including Hindustani, Western Hindi, and Rajastani

Source: Government of India, *Census of India 1931*, Vol. 8, Bombay, n.d.; Government of India, *Census of India 1941*, Vol. 12, Sindh, n.d.; Population Census Organisation, *Population Census Report*, Karachi/Islamabad, Government of Pakistan, various years.

Table 3J: Sindh–Karachi Comparison and Percentage Shares (in Bracket)
(in Million)
(1931–2017 Censuses)

Year	Sindh	Karachi	Rest of the Sindh
1931*	4.1 (100)	0.26 (6.4)	3.8 (93.6)
1941**	4.5 (100)	0.4 (9.7)	4.1 (90.3)
1951	6.1 (100)	1.1 (18.7)	4.9 (81.3)
1961	8.4 (100)	2.0 (24.3)	6.3 (75.7)
1972	14.2 (100)	3.6 (25.5)	10.6 (74.5)
1983	19.0 (100)	5.4 (28.6)	13.6 (71.4)
1998	30.4 (100)	9.9 (32.4)	20.6 (67.6)
2017	47.9 (100)	14.9 (31.1)	33.0 (68.9)

* Government of India, *Census of India 1931*, 8 Vol. 8, Bombay, n.d.
**Government of India, *Census of India 1941*, Vol. 12, Sindh, n.d.

Source: Population Census Organisation, *Population Census Report*, Karachi/Islamabad, Government of Pakistan, various years; Pakistan Bureau of Statistics, *Population Census 2017*, Islamabad, Statistics Division, Government of Pakistan, 2017.

Table 3K: Sindh Urban-Hindu/Muslim Population (in Lacs)
(1941 and 1951 Censuses)

Urban Dist.	Hindu	Muslim	Others*	Total 1941	Total 1951
Karachi	1.97	1.67	0.31	3.95	10.7
Hyderabad	1.13	0.53	0.03	1.69	2.9
Sukkur	1.07	0.49	0.02	1.58	1.5
Sub Total	4.17	2.69	0.36	7.22	15.1
Rest Sindh Ex: Khairpur	1.13	0.54	0.03	1.70	2.4
Sub Total Sindh	5.30	3.23	0.39	8.92	17.5

Urban Dist.	Hindu	Muslim	Others*	Total 1941	Total 1951
Khairpur	0.10	0.11	0.01	0.22	0.2
Total Sindh (U)	5.40	3.34	0.40	9.14	17.7
Percentage Share	59	37	4	100	100

*Christians, Jains, Sikhs, and Others

Source: Government of India, *Census of India 1941,* Vol. 12, Sindh, n.d.; Population Census Organisation, *Census of Pakistan, 1951,* Karachi, Government of Pakistan, n.d.

Table 3L: Religion—Sindh Urban/Rural (in Lacs)
(1941)

Total %Age	Urban (Mes, Tcs, and Cant)			Rural		
	Muslims	Hindus	Others	Muslims	Hindu	Others
100	36.2	59.4	4.4	79.8	19.2	1.0
Sindh in Lacs	**Total**			**Total**		
45.35	8.92			36.43		
Percentage	19.7			80.3		

Source: Government of India, *Census of India 1941,* Vol. 12, Sindh, n.d.

Table 3M: Province-wise Population Size, Percentage Share (in Brackets), and Inter-Census Annual Growth (in Lacs)

Province	1951	GR	1961	GR	1972	GR	1981	GR	1998	GR	2017
Pakistan	338 (100)	2.4	429 (100)	3.7	653 (100)	3.1	843 (100)	3.3	1323 (100)	3.0	2077 (100)
Punjab	206 (60.9)	2.2	255 (59.3)	3.4	376 (57.6)	2.7	473 (56.1)	3.3	736 (55.7)	2.6	1100 (53)
Sindh	61 (17.9)	3.3	84 (19.5)	4.6	142 (21.7)	3.6	190 (22.6)	3.5	304 (23.0)	3.0	478 (23)
NWFP*	46 (13.6)	2.3	58 (59.3)	3.3	84 (12.8)	3.3	111 (13.1)	3.5	177 (13.4)	6.7	305 (15.1)
Balochistan	12 (3.5)	1.6	14 (3.2)	5.0	24 (3.7)	7.1	43 (5.2)	3.1	66 (4.9)	3	123 (5.9)
FATA	13 (3.9)	3.3	18 (4.3)	2.6	25 (3.8)	-1.5	22 (2.6)	2.7	32 (2.4)	9.5	50 (2.4)
Islamabad	-	-	1.2 (0.3)	6.0	2.4 (0.4)	4.5	3.4 (0.4)	0.04	08 (0.6)	7.9	20 (0.01)

*Renamed Khyber Pakhtunkhwa in the 2017 Census.

Source: Pakistan Bureau of Statistics, *Population,* Islamabad, Government of Pakistan, n.d.; Population Census Organisation, *1998 Census Report of Sindh,* Islamabad, Statistics Division, Government of Pakistan, 2000.

Table 3N: Sindh and Pakistan Rural/Urban Population (in Lacs)
(1951 to 2017 Censuses)

Census Year	Pakistan and %Age Share			Sindh and %Age Share		
	Urban	Rural	Total	Urban	Rural	Total
1951	60 (18)	277 (82)	337 (100)	18 (30)	43(70)	61(100)
1961	97 (23)	332 (77)	429 (100)	32(38)	52(62)	84(100)
1972	166 (25)	487 (75)	653 (100)	57(40)	84(60)	141(100)
1981	238 (28)	604 (72)	842 (100)	82(43)	108(57)	190(100)
1998	430 (33)	893 (67)	1323 (100)	148(49)	156(51)	304(100)
2017	76 (37)	132 (64)	208 (100)	230 (48)	250(52)	480 (100)

Source: Population Census Organisation, *1998 Census Report of Sindh*, Islamabad, Statistics Division, Government of Pakistan, 2000.

Table 3O: Comparative Census of Pakistan and Regions (in Million)
(1951 and 2017 Censuses)

Province/Region	Population Shares (%)		Growth		
	1951	2017	Number	Percentage	Ave/Year
Pakistan**	33.7 (100)	207.7 (100)	98.6	292	5.1
Sindh	6.1 (17.9)	47.9 (23.04)	24.4	403	7.1
Punjab	20.5 (60.9)	110.0 (52.9)	53.1	258	4.5
NWFP*	4.6 (13.5)	30.5 (14.7)	13.2	289	5.1
Balochistan	1.2 (3.5)	12.3 (5.94)	5.4	263	4.6
FATA	1.3 (4.0)	5.0 (2.41)	1.9	139	2.4
Islamabad	0.1 (0.3)	2.0 (0.096)	0.7	710	12.5
Languages	Total	Urdu	Punjabi	Sindhi	Pushto
Total 1998 Census	132 (100)	10 (7.6)	58 (43.9)	19 (14.4)	20 (15.2)

* Now Khyber Pakhtunkhwa (KP)

**East Pakistan (Bangladesh) 42 million (55%), West Pakistan (Pakistan) 34 million (45%), Total 76 million (100%)

Source: Population Census Organisation, *1998 Census Report of Sindh*, Islamabad, Statistics Division, Government of Pakistan, 2000.

Table 3P: Percentage Distribution of Male and Female Population in Sindh
(1998 and 2017 Censuses)

Year	1998	2017
Male	52.9	51.2
Female	47.1	48.8

Source: Bureau of Statistics, *Development Statistics Report 2011*, Karachi, Planning and Development Department, Government of Sindh, n.d.; Bureau of Statistics, *District-wise Census Results 2017*, Karachi, Statistics Division, Government of Sindh, n.d.

Table 3Q: Provincial, Rural, and Urban Population Share by Mother Tongue (in Million) (1998)

Province	Punjabi	Sindhi	Pushto	Baluchi	Seraiki	Urdu	Others	Total
Punjab	55.4	0.1	0.9	0.5	12.8	3.3	0.7	73.6
Percentage	75.3	0.1	1.2	0.7	17.4	4.4	0.9	100
Sindh	2.1	18.2	1.3	0.6	0.3	6.4	1.5	30.4
Percentage	6.9	59.9	4.3	2.0	1.0	21.0	4.9	100
NWFP	0.2	-	13.1	-	0.7	0.1	3.6	17.7
Percentage	1.1	-	74.0	-	4.0	0.6	20.3	100
Balochistan	0.2	0.4	1.9	3.6	0.2	-	0.3	6.6
Percentage	3.0	6.0	28.9	54.6	3.0	-	4.5	100
FATA	-	-	3.1	-	-	-	-	3.1
Percentage	-	-	100	-	-	-	-	100
Islamabad	0.6	-	-	-	-	0.1	0.1	0.8
Percentage	75	-	-	-	-	12.5	12.5	100
Total	58.5	18.7	20.3	4.7	14.0	9.9	6.2	132.3
Percentage	44.2	14.1	15.3	3.6	10.6	7.5	4.7	100
Sindh Urban	1.7	3.8	1.2	0.4	0.3	6.1	1.3	14.8
Percentage	11.5	25.7	8.1	2.8	2.0	41.2	8.7	100
Karachi Div	1.4	7	1.1	0.4	0.2	4.8	1.2	9.8
Percentage	14.3	7.1	11.2	4.1	2.0	49.0	12.3	100
Sindh Rural	0.4	14.3	0.1	0.2	0.1	0.3	0.2	15.6
Percentage	2.7	91.6	0.6	1.3	0.6	1.9	1.3	100

Source: Population Census Organisation, *1998 Census Report of Sindh*, Islamabad, Statistics Division, Government of Pakistan, 2000.

Table 3R: Sex Ratio by Age Groups and Rural/Urban Areas—1998

Age Groups	Sex Ratio		
	All Areas	Rural	Urban
0–4	104.4	104.3	104.5
5–9	112	115.9	107.1
10–14	120	131.1	110
15–19	107.4	105.7	108.8
20–24	104.2	94.1	114.8
25–29	115	107.3	123.1
30–34	122.2	116.4	127.6
35–39	117.6	111	123.4
40–44	108.2	98.4	117.9

Age Groups	Sex Ratio		
	All Areas	Rural	Urban
45–49	117.4	110.6	124.3
50–54	119.1	116.9	121.2
55–59	123.7	120	127
60–64	116.8	117.9	115.5
65–69	120.6	117.1	124.1
70–74	116.4	114.1	119.4
75+	107.2	108.3	107.5
All Age Group	112.2	110.6	113.9

Source: Population Census Organisation, *1998 Census Report of Sindh*, Islamabad, Statistics Division, Government of Pakistan, 2000).

Table 3S: Population of Females by Age, Area, Marital Status (in Percentage)—1998

Age Group	All Areas				Rural				Urban			
All Group	Never Married	Currently Married	Widowed	Divorced	Never Married	Currently Married	Widowed	Divorced	Never Married	Currently Married	Widowed	Divorced
All Ages	28.05	69.05	2.61	0.29	20.11	77.15	2.58	0.16	35.75	61.19	2.64	0.42
15–19	73.32	27.13	0.46	0.09	58.66	40.69	0.57	0.08	84.53	15.02	0.36	0.10
20–24	34.40	64.79	0.64	0.18	21.46	77.72	0.70	0.11	47.99	51.20	0.56	0.25
25–29	14.68	83.85	1.16	0.31	8.10	90.48	1.27	0.15	21.55	76.94	1.05	0.46
30–34	8.28	89.22	2.08	0.42	5.11	92.48	2.22	0.19	11.22	86.21	1.94	0.63
35–39	4.92	90.85	3.71	0.51	3.20	92.91	3.66	0.23	6.45	89.02	3.76	0.77
40–44	3.97	88.47	7.09	0.47	3.08	89.76	6.90	0.26	4.85	87.19	7.28	0.68
45–49	2.76	85.22	11.59	0.44	2.17	87.27	10.34	0.23	3.35	83.13	12.86	0.65

Source: Population Census Organisation, *1998 Census Report of Sindh*, Islamabad, Statistics Division, Government of Pakistan, 2000.

Chapter 4

Table 4A: District and Level-wise Schools (2015–16)

District	Primary	Middle	Elementary	Secondary	Higher Secondary	Total Schools	Percentage of Primary Schools	Total Post-Primary	
								Number	%
Badin	2,820	82	19	60	10	2,991	94	171	6
Dadu	1,795	45	11	69	15	1,935	93	140	7
Hyderabad	722	71	1	66	16	876	82	154	18
Thatta	1,413	42	5	38	7	1,505	94	92	6
Mirpurkhas	1,973	100	11	74	16	2,174	91	201	9
Tharparkar	3,716	244	3	40	7	4,010	93	294	7
Sanghar	2,935	104	5	61	19	3,124	94	189	6
Karachi Central	372	44	56	134	9	615	60	243	40
Karachi East	169	21	9	62	6	267	63	98	37
Karachi South	331	36	39	88	5	499	66	168	34
Karachi West	280	25	17	47	3	372	75	92	25
Jacobabad	1,328	65	4	37	9	1,443	92	115	8
Larkana	1,028	58	7	59	14	1,166	88	138	12
Shikarpur	1,171	60	4	54	12	1,301	90	130	10
Khairpur Mirs	3,132	70	119	118	21	3,460	91	328	9
Naushahro Feroze	2,105	126	31	52	20	2,334	90	229	10
Shaheed Benazirabad	2,309	63	63	85	12	2,532	91	223	9
Sukkur	1,071	35	48	61	12	1,227	87	156	13
Ghotki	1,828	86	10	32	7	1,963	93	135	7
Umerkot	2,080	77	7	57	13	2,234	93	154	7
Malir Karachi	488	52	23	43	7	613	80	125	20
Jamshoro	707	20	9	39	8	783	90	76	10
Mitiari	813	18	2	38	3	874	93	61	7
Tando Allahyar	723	49	1	32	5	810	89	87	11
Tando M.K.	951	20	12	36	2	1,021	93	70	7
Kashmore	1,393	53	1	38	12	1,497	93	104	7
Kambar-Shahdadkot	1,515	56	4	46	10	1,631	93	116	7
Sujawal	1,586	29	-	18	6	1,639	97	53	3
Korangi Karachi	377	32	25	112	5	551	68	174	32
Total	41,131	1,783	546	1,696	291	45,447		4,316	

Source: Sindh Education Management Information System (SEMIS), Reform Support Unit, Karachi, Education and Literacy Department, Government of Sindh.

Table 4B: District and Level-wise Schools (2010–11)

District	Primary	Middle	Elementary	Secondary	Higher Secondary
Badin	2,967	121	12	50	9
Dadu	2,004	70	2	50	10
Ghotki	1,866	85	13	33	4
Hyderabad	904	81	-	82	13
Jacobabad	1,456	62	7	27	9
Jamshoro	820	30	-	34	5
Kambar-Shahdadkot	1,572	67	-	32	9
Karachi City	2,530	253	203	583	40
Kashmore	1,423	47	-	23	9
Khairpur Mirs	3,370	166	29	97	17
Larkana	1,223	67	-	51	10
Matiari	947	45	-	32	2
Mirpurkhas	2,053	119	4	61	14
Naushahro Feroze	-	154	35	48	17
Sanghar	3,153	106	7	62	17
Shaheed Benazirabad	2,546	109	12	59	10
Shikarpur	1,256	66	2	47	9
Sukkur	1,227	36	38	63	9
Tando Allah Yar	774	36	1	22	4
Tando Muhammad Khan	986	15	16	37	2
Tharparkar	3,873	233	1	40	5
Thatta	3,162	68	4	62	10
Umerkot	2,188	73	10	46	12

Source: Sindh Education Management Information System (SEMIS), Reform Support Unit, Karachi, Education and Literacy Department, Government of Sindh.

Table 4C: Schools by Level (2005–06)

District	Primary	Middle	Elementary	Secondary	Higher Secondary
Badin	3,120	145	5	55	5
Dadu	1,934	74	7	54	9
Hyderabad	887	80	-	85	9
Thatta	2,971	86	7	61	11
Mirpurkhas	1,919	67	2	60	8
Tharparkar	3,702	292	5	33	1
Sanghar	3,116	152	12	74	10
Karachi City	2,642	322	228	537	33
Jacobabad	1,471	62	-	32	4
Larkana	1,214	68	-	51	8
Shikarpur	1,284	64	-	49	7
Khairpur Mirs	3,362	176	18	101	11
Naushahro Feroze	2,181	138	14	62	7
Nawab Shah	2,397	93	18	52	6
Sukkur	1,044	50	22	53	6
Ghotki	1,633	89	-	32	4
Umerkot	1,845	83	5	31	7
Jamshoro	803	28	2	31	6
Mitiari	932	37	-	30	3
Tando Allah Yar	687	41	2	22	3
Tando Muhammad Khan	953	23	1	21	-
Kashmore	1,409	58	1	29	3
Shahdadkot	1,512	67	4	33	7

Source: Sindh Education Management Information System (SEMIS), Reform Support Unit, Karachi, Education and Literacy Department, Government of Sindh.

Table 4D: Schools by Level (2001–02)

District	Mosque	Mohalla	Primary	Middle	Elementary	Secondary	Higher Secondary
Badin	1,176	35	1,559	118	2	51	1
Dadu	941	2	1,734	96	1	84	13
Hyderabad	1,077	2	2,085	168	2	139	18
Thatta	1,158	8	1,406	82	2	54	7
Mirpurkhas	637	37	2,774	114	4	89	11
Mithi	668	4	2,354	260	2	29	-
Sanghar	964	9	2,058	152	7	71	6
Karachi	463	69	1,795	283	172	486	34
Jacobabad	1,025	22	1,587	113	-	56	7
Larkana	929	3	1,754	122	1	84	11
Shikarpur	531	16	688	63	-	50	2
Khairpur Mirs	1,003	30	2,082	156	9	99	11
Naushahro Feroze	692	8	1,288	118	-	57	6
Nawab Shah	648	11	1,406	63	-	49	5
Sukkur	381	16	647	54	5	50	5
Ghotki	566	3	825	71	-	32	2

Mohalla and madrassa schools existed as per the government poll

Source: Sindh Education Management Information System (SEMIS), Reform Support Unit, Karachi, Education and Literacy Department, Government of Sindh.

Table 4E: Schools by Gender (2015–16)

District	Boys	Girls	Mixed
Badin	766	364	1,861
Dadu	632	352	951
Hyderabad	187	153	536
Thatta	744	199	562
Mirpurkhas	421	344	1,359
Tharparkar	733	608	2,669
Sanghar	507	337	2,280
Karachi Central	197	142	276
Karachi East	78	61	128
Karachi South	170	105	224
Karachi West	105	72	195
Jacobabad	389	223	831
Larkana	129	184	853

District	Boys	Girls	Mixed
Shikarpur	516	226	559
Khairpur Mirs	338	562	2,560
Naushahro Feroze	182	238	1,914
Shaheed Benazirabad	552	402	1,578
Sukkur	172	199	856
Ghotki	789	244	930
Umerkot	575	435	1,224
Malir Karachi	176	108	329
Jamshoro	44	115	624
Mitiari	81	113	680
Tando Allah Yar	96	102	612
Tando Mohammad Khan	419	127	475
Kashmore	453	217	827
Kambar - Shahdadkot	541	293	797
Sujawal	262	191	1,186
Korangi Karachi	181	152	218

Source: Sindh Education Management Information System (SEMIS), Reform Support Unit, Karachi, Education and Literacy Department, Government of Sindh.

Table 4F: Schools by Gender (2010–11)

District	Boys	Girls	Mixed
Badin	472	449	2,238
Dadu	508	396	1,232
Hyderabad	263	235	582
Thatta	1394	507	1,405
Mirpurkhas	497	418	1,336
Tharparkar	620	629	2,903
Sanghar	780	437	2,128
Karachi City	1078	908	1,623
Jacobabad	448	278	835
Larkana	218	292	841
Shikarpur	563	255	562
Khairpur Mirs	1424	617	1,638
Naushahro Feroze	734	401	1,341
Shaheed Benazirabad	482	475	1,779
Sukkur	430	263	680

District	Boys	Girls	Mixed
Ghotki	742	257	1,002
Umerkot	623	479	1,227
Jamshoro	212	198	479
Matiari	131	154	741
Tando Allah Yar	157	139	541
Tando Muhammad Khan	244	157	655
Kashmore	430	208	864
Kambar-Shahdadkot	377	306	997

Source: Sindh Education Management Information System (SEMIS), Reform Support Unit, Karachi, Education and Literacy Department, Government of Sindh.

Table 4G: Schools by Gender (2005–06)

District	Boys	Girls	Mixed
Badin	591	531	2,208
Dadu	410	375	1,293
Hyderabad	392	317	352
Thatta	1,588	437	1,111
Mirpurkhas	722	365	969
Tharparkar	2,592	588	853
Sanghar	1,308	442	1,614
Karachi City	1,312	1107	1,343
Jacobabad	678	274	617
Larkana	649	289	403
Shikarpur	749	270	385
Khairpur Mirs	1,688	647	1,333
Naushahro Feroze	1,228	385	789
Nawab Shah	1,186	434	946
Sukkur	491	224	460
Ghotki	1,047	248	463
Umerkot	1,136	343	492
Jamshoro	258	172	440
Mitiari	141	170	691
Tando Allah Yar	144	144	467
Tando Muhammad Khan	259	130	609
Kashmore	734	267	499
Shahdadkot	1,131	298	194

Source: Sindh Education Management Information System (SEMIS), Reform Support Unit, Karachi, Education and Literacy Department, Government of Sindh.

Table 4H: Level-wise Boys Enrolment (2015–16)

District	Primary	Middle	Elementary	Secondary	Higher Secondary
Badin	89,664	3,966	2,101	22,862	8,834
Dadu	99,229	4,500	1,341	24,880	9,732
Hyderabad	37,067	10,382	261	21,378	11,843
Thatta	36,083	1,002	676	6,095	3,598
Mirpurkhas	70,304	3,200	2,197	16,462	11,031
Tharparkar	74,668	8,638	242	9,503	6,382
Sanghar	111,108	3,754	298	25,063	16,648
Karachi Central	20,684	941	3,754	19,656	2,775
Karachi East	9,287	570	304	10,805	1,122
Karachi South	13,060	1,817	2,035	14,691	2,571
Karachi West	13,355	934	1,032	8,362	792
Jacobabad	63,132	4,119	333	11,660	7,414
Larkana	80,550	3,757	1,227	30,432	15,438
Shikarpur	63,083	2,464	614	17,582	9,980
Khairpur Mirs	121,460	3,247	15,357	40,916	20,347
Naushahro Feroze	96,009	8,581	4,623	23,623	17,393
Shaheed Benazirabad	97,389	2,404	6,299	26,651	13,985
Sukkur	56,811	2,253	6,895	22,168	9,217
Ghotki	99,796	5,438	1431	15,875	10,053
Umerkot	56,698	3,015	453	6,704	10,623
Malir Karachi	18,249	850	2799	7,065	2,447
Jamshoro	28,325	1,456	1395	12,579	6,547
Mitiari	36,089	1,383	375	14,775	2,402
Tando Allah Yar	34,537	1,722	263	10,399	4,252
Tando Muhammad Khan	28,963	550	1723	8,725	1,496
Kashmore	58,187	3,261	15	12,662	13,106
Kambar-Shahdadkot	76,150	2,917	19	22,243	6,603
Sujawal	38,560	700		5,756	3,782
Korangi Karachi	20,110	1,038	977	20,719	1,971

Source: Sindh Education Management Information System (SEMIS), Reform Support Unit, Karachi, Education and Literacy Department, Government of Sindh.

Table 4I: Boys Enrolment (2010–11)

District	Primary	Middle	Elementary	Secondary	Higher Secondary
Badin	84,347	4,516	1,396	14,104	8,005
Dadu	124,006	2,717	0	17,901	7,148
Hyderabad	56,673	4,129		18,232	6,365
Thatta	79,366	945	520	9,329	5,351
Mirpurkhas	74,961	3,737	68	12,568	9,205
Tharparkar	105,494	8,587	0	7,833	3,275
Sanghar	128,578	3,917	381	20,860	11,859
Karachi City	154,447	8,712	14,278	6,4651	8,098
Jacobabad	81,001	2,380	934	8,896	6,742
Larkana	94,449	3,789	-+	20,986	11,704
Shikarpur	60,578	1,262	222	14,305	7,408
Khairpur Mirs	145,593	6,723	5,002	30,229	13,861
Naushahro Feroze	107,361	7,981	3,999	20,937	12,056
Shaheed Benazirabad	99,808	3,931	1,793	16,801	7,126
Sukkur	64,404	1,335	3,596	17,429	6,694
Ghotki	116,782	5,913	1,799	18,513	3,822
Umerkot	61,763	1,721	498	5,834	11,375
Jamshoro	36,873	1,882	-	6,532	3,280
Matiari	41,851	1,595	-	11,254	1,159
Tando Allah Yar	32,773	1,721	260	6,439	2,743
Tando Muhammad Khan	31,958	455	1,810	3,564	783
Kashmore	61,035	2,029	-	5,602	7,900
Kambar-Shahdadkot	98,375	2,694	-	13,275	5,412

Source: Sindh Education Management Information System (SEMIS), Reform Support Unit, Karachi, Education and Literacy Department, Government of Sindh.

Table 4J: Boys Enrolment (2005–06)

District	Primary	Middle	Elementary	Secondary	Higher Secondary
Badin	102,259	3,589	483	12,986	1,794
Dadu	127,908	2,511	190	18,251	5,496
Hyderabad	63,585	3,443	-	17,917	3,992
Thatta	96,858	1,005	627	7,825	3,803
Mirpurkhas	67,966	1,530	-	15,899	3,539
Tharparkar	70,522	6,165	44	5,844	333
Sanghar	120,407	5,003	313	22,386	5,758
Karachi City	181,033	14,684	14,295	69,111	6,237
Jacobabad	65,585	2,229	-	10,781	2,137
Larkana	92,828	2,865	-	16,197	8,247
Shikarpur	64,495	1,319	-	13,929	4,533
Khairpur Mirs	149,845	6,861	1,845	25,789	8,163
Naushahro Feroze	115,854	8,232	2,254	21,923	5,132
Nawab Shah	94,398	3,108	1,309	15,789	5,366
Sukkur	63,464	2,514	2,737	13,024	3,744
Ghotki	111,436	4,679	-	12,763	2,478
Umerkot	49,096	1,562	64	5,990	5,877
Jamshoro	44,679	1,504	-	5,761	2,443
Mitiari	53,133	1,212	-	8,342	1,720
Tando Allah Yar	34,339	1,417	403	6,013	1,613
Tando Muhammad Khan	33,472	1,422	20	3,681	-
Kashmore	75,591	1,853	-	8,826	1,822
Shahdadkot	72,543	2,001	108	11,931	3,379

Source: Sindh Education Management Information System (SEMIS), Reform Support Unit, Karachi, Education and Literacy Department, Government of Sindh.

Table 4K: Boys Enrolment (2001–02)

District	Mosque	Mohalla	Primary	Middle	Elementary	Secondary	Higher Secondary
Badin	24,204	194	45,041	2,796	-	7,590	-
Dadu	19,633	87	66,224	2,025	83	19,138	5,372
Hyderabad	34,562	28	109,640	4,980	149	31,899	6,313
Thatta	25,216	113	51,890	1,019	16	7,652	1,626
Mirpurkhas	14,099	414	80,219	2,510	70	17,460	4,626
Mithi	12,325	146	49,946	4,158	-	4,374	-
Sanghar	26,921	315	80,048	3,927	96	18,168	1,841
Karachi	19,850	743	121,942	12,208	11,748	75,323	7,417
Jacobabad	32,045	384	64,912	3,806	-	11,954	2,292
Larkana	30,333	-	97,946	3,851	88	26,077	9,548
Shikarpur	14,100	25	36,189	1,302	-	12,184	643
Khairpur Mirs	35,493	735	109,087	4,695	751	23,996	7,123
Naushahro Feroze	22,777	156	67,380	5,602	-	19,859	2,911
Nawab Shah	21,058	475	56,303	2,402	-	10,709	1,949
Sukkur	12,458	8	36,527	1,933	1,093	13,908	3,025
Ghotki	23,836	-	54,120	3,150	-	10,751	1,605

Source: Sindh Education Management Information System (SEMIS), Reform Support Unit, Karachi, Education and Literacy Department, Government of Sindh.

Table 4L: Level-wise Girls Enrolment (2015–16)

District	Primary	Middle	Elementary	Secondary	Higher Secondary
Badin	47,480	2,129	1,104	10,617	3,203
Dadu	71,237	3,663	1,076	13,720	4,968
Hyderabad	29,108	9,258	54	25,594	10,099
Thatta	21,759	740	494	3,139	1,371
Mirpurkhas	34,341	1990	502	9,922	7,404
Tharparkar	45,112	4,760	75	4,039	1,260
Sanghar	60,664	4,704	876	11,440	8,077
Karachi Central	20,928	903	6,559	25,887	4,096
Karachi East	10,257	375	748	16,382	2,489
Karachi South	13,967	1,429	4,689	24,459	1,609
Karachi West	16,876	627	1,424	13,902	519
Jacobabad	43,048	3,897	389	7,882	4,057
Larkana	59,993	3,382	796	16,486	10,165

District	Primary	Middle	Elementary	Secondary	Higher Secondary
Shikarpur	36,341	2,292	226	9,237	4,136
Khairpur Mirs	80,594	2,723	10,050	22,617	6,678
Naushahro Feroze	67,170	6,371	2,203	11,629	8,801
Shaheed Benazirabad	62,601	1,854	4,469	15,350	5,339
Sukkur	36,170	2,014	5,472	12,401	7,292
Ghotki	44,849	3,299	744	5,506	3,924
Umerkot	27,290	1,599	179	4,610	1,786
Malir Karachi	15,192	1,336	2,239	6,124	1,329
Jamshoro	18,770	952	717	8,040	4,597
Mitiari	20,923	730	201	7,678	933
Tando Allah Yar	18,076	1,322	35	4,698	4,706
Tando Muhammad Khan	15,297	312	572	4,809	363
Kashmore	26,288	1,716	0	4,944	3,761
Kambar-Shahdad Kot	51,536	2,400	249	10,820	5,796
Sujawal	22,749	663	-	1,904	1,518
Korangi Karachi	21,178	1,668	2,698	32,267	1,918

Source: Sindh Education Management Information System (SEMIS), Reform Support Unit. Karachi, Education and Literacy Department, Government of Sindh.

Table 4M: Girls Enrolment (2010–11)

District	Primary	Middle	Elementary	Secondary	Higher Secondary
Badin	61,221	3,222	793	6,810	1,414
Dadu	84,825	2,431	72	8,407	4,027
Hyderabad	52,487	4,476	-	20,460	6,645
Thatta	60,258	1,298	225	3,989	1,382
Mirpurkhas	42,608	2,742	200	7,715	6,886
Tharparkar	84,876	6,259	206	4,297	376
Sanghar	77,507	3,172	1,179	8,685	6,200
Karachi City	168,707	8,892	26,089	101,947	12,076
Jacobabad	51,757	3,375	521	3,417	3,785
Larkana	71,892	4,331	-	10,772	7,996
Shikarpur	35,650	2,321	90	6,717	1,802
Khairpur Mirs	102,053	6,442	2,842	14,758	4,381
Naushahro Feroze	77,436	7,756	2,960	7,485	8,002

District	Primary	Middle	Elementary	Secondary	Higher Secondary
Shaheed Benazirabad	60,385	2,325	2,098	7,964	4,473
Sukkur	43,153	1,711	4,411	8,085	5,742
Ghotki	57,226	4,145	824	5,075	2,802
Umerkot	38,456	1,394	192	4,163	1,823
Jamshoro	27,016	1,037	-	3,356	1,898
Matiari	28,141	922	-	6,334	92
Tando Allah Yar	19,611	1,237	48	1,884	2,575
Tando Muhammad Khan	17,836	243	781	3,401	159
Kashmore	24,773	1,714	-	2,089	2,631
Kambar-Shahdadkot	61,624	2,800	-	7,067	4,527

Source: Sindh Education Management Information System (SEMIS), Reform Support Unit, Karachi, Education and Literacy Department, Government of Sindh.

Table 4N: Girls Enrolment (2005–06)

District	Primary	Middle	Elementary	Secondary	Higher Secondary
Badin	72,482	1,854	208	4,630	846
Dadu	72,423	1,861	14	4,244	2,403
Hyderabad	60,307	3,401	-	21,590	2,757
Thatta	63,465	728	769	3,223	1,038
Mirpurkhas	37,984	1,945	49	7,133	4,574
Tharparkar	54,503	2,604	19	1,821	34
Sanghar	60,727	2,953	116	7,586	3,095
Karachi City	198,366	11,545	28,663	100,005	11,764
Jacobabad	33,309	1,392	-	2,943	1,192
Larkana	61,030	2,016	-	5,907	6,162
Shikarpur	33,586	1,398	-	2,999	775
Khairpur Mirs	90,854	5,289	940	9,119	2,420
Naushahro Feroze	79,485	4,947	1,100	6,728	2,453
Nawab Shah	49,235	2,274	951	4,399	1,554
Sukkur	41,741	2,057	2,268	7,292	2,321
Ghotki	52,156	1,725	-	2,176	1,857
Umerkot	26,807	1,314	56	2,014	1,061

District	Primary	Middle	Elementary	Secondary	Higher Secondary
Jamshoro	27,219	953	61	1,760	2,439
Mitiari	33,321	377	-	3,673	149
Tando Allah Yar	21,317	959	208	1,140	2,311
Tando Muhammad Khan	19,399	585	2	2,056	-
Kashmore	29,128	1,841	715	1,086	1,371
Shahdadkot	42,922	1,136	53	4,230	1,363

Source: Sindh Education Management Information System (SEMIS), Reform Support Unit, Karachi, Education and Literacy Department, Government of Sindh.

Table 4O: Girls Enrolment (2001–02)

District	Mosque	Mohalla	Primary	Middle	Elementary	Secondary	Higher Secondary
Badin	8,199	86	22,430	1,189	33	2,020	144
Dadu	8,456	34	34,900	370	-	663	4,091
Hyderabad	14,349	177	73,496	4,752	25	23,708	5,920
Thatta	8,865	155	25,167	599	1	1,538	239
Mirpurkhas	3,874	153	42,671	2,534	599	7,387	4,463
Mithi	5,354	43	25,994	902	46	926	-
Sanghar	8,862	112	37,387	1,700	71	6,041	2,835
Karachi	14,755	1,403	145,281	9,421	19,109	120,578	14,167
Jacobabad	8,658	81	29,171	1,333	-	2,942	1,525
Larkana	9,953	13	57,452	2,591	14	7,944	5,591
Shikarpur	3,240	78	20,316	1,095	-	3,625	298
Khairpur Mirs	13,142	506	50,316	3,116	313	6,708	1,853
Naushahro Feroze	10,677	118	43,069	2,240	-	5,562	1,735
Nawab Shah	5,603	240	25,692	1,245	-	3,461	3,069
Sukkur	4,836	455	22,974	1,639	98	5,405	3,146
Ghotki	4,861	58	15,363	979	-	2,008	550

Source: Sindh Education Management Information System (SEMIS), Reform Support Unit, Karachi, Education and Literacy Department, Government of Sindh.

Table 4P: Sindh—Urban–Rural Education Statistics
(2001–02 to 2015–16)

Location	No of Schools				Enrolment				Teachers			
	2001–02	2005–06	2010–11	2015–16	2001–02	2005–06	2010–11	2015–16	2001–02	2005–06	2010–11	2015–16
Urban	5,932	6,513	5,765	4,498	1,284,788	1,508,874	10,262,716	1,083,230	67,674	61,104	55,356	54,751
Rural	37,103	40,909	43,149	40,949	1,772,381	2,601,191	3,140,277	3,061,989	73,657	70,271	89,254	101,465

Sources: Sindh Education Management Information System (SEMIS), *Sindh Education Profile 2001–02*, Karachi, Education and Literacy Department, Government of Sindh, n.d.; *Sindh Education Profile 2005–06*, Karachi; *Sindh Education Profile 2010–11*, Karachi; *Sindh Education Profile 2015–16*, Karachi.

Table 4Q: District-wise Number of Teachers
(2001–15)

2001–02		2005–06		2010–11		2015–16	
District	Teachers	District	Teachers	District	Teachers	District	Teachers
Badin	5,242	Badin	5,082	Badin	6,120	Badin	6,805
Dadu	6,671	Dadu	6,689	Dadu	7,207	Dadu	7,271
Hyderabad	16,426	Hyderabad	8,584	Hyderabad	8,633	Hyderabad	8,862
Thatta	6,003	Thatta	5,293	Thatta	5,586	Thatta	3,095
Mirpurkhas	9,257	Mirpur Khan	5,296	Mirpurkhas	5,912	Mirpur Khan	5,818
Mithi	4,558	Tharparkar	4,588	Tharparkar	5,469	Mirpurkhas	457
Sanghar	10,098	Sanghar	8,835	Sanghar	9,092	Tharparkar	6,010
Karachi	30,614	Karachi City	27,791	Karachi City	27,037	Sanghar	8,980
Jacobabad	7,164	Jacobabad	4,164	Jacobabad	4,774	Karachi Central	7,350
Larkana	9,679	Larkana	5,833	Larkana	6,843	Karachi East	3,430
Shikarpur	4,443	Shikarpur	4,460	Shikarpur	4,428	Karachi South	4,426
Khairpur Mirs	9,295	Khairpur Mirs	7,554	Khairpur Mirs	9,325	Karachi West	2,536
Naushahro Feroze	7,557	Naushahro Feroze	6,497	Naushahro Feroze	6,734	Jacobabad	5,160
Nawab Shah	4,700	Nawab Shah	4,928	Shaheed Benazirabad	6,174	Larkana	7,654
Sukkur	5,724	Sukkur	3,770	Sukkur	5,186	Shikarpur	5,069
Ghotki	3,900	Ghotki	3,869	Ghotki	4,552	Khairpur Mirs	10,389

2001–02		2005–06		2010–11		2015–16	
District	**Teachers**	**District**	**Teachers**	**District**	**Teachers**	**District**	**Teachers**
		Umerkot	3,136	Umerkot	3,851	Naushahro Feroze	8,092
		Jamshoro	2,444	Jamshoro	2,786	Shaheed Benazirabad	7,269
		Mitiari	3,190	Matiari	3,492	Sukkur	5,504
		Tando Allah Yar	1,733	Tando Allah Yar	1,933	Ghotki	5,196
		Tando M. Khan	1,757	Tando M. Khan	2,186	Umerkot	4,634
		Kashmore	2,626	Kashmore	3,051	Malir Karachi	2,362
		Shandadkot	3,201	Kambar-Shandadkot	423	Jamshoro	3,107
						Mitiari	3,535
						Tando Allah Yar	2,249
						Tando M. Khan	2,579
						Kashmore	3,898
						Kambar-Shandadkot	5,951
						Sujawal	2,912
						Korangi Karachi	5,616

Source: Sindh Education Management Information System (SEMIS), *Sindh Education Profile 2000–01*, Karachi, Education and Literacy Department, Government of Sindh, n.d.; *Sindh Education Profile 2005–06*, Karachi; *Sindh Education Profile 2010–11*, Karachi; *Sindh Education Profile 2015–16*, Karachi.

Table 4R: District-wise Students–Teacher Ratio (STR)
(2015–16)

Region	District	Students Per Teacher
Hyderabad	Badin	28
	Dadu	32
	Hyderabad	17
	Jamshoro	27
	Mitiari	24
	Sujawal	26
	Tando Allah Yar	36
	Tando Muhammad Khan	24
	Thatta	24

Region	District	Students Per Teacher
Karachi	Central	14
	East	15
	Korangi	19
	Malir	24
	South	18
	West	23
Larkana	Jacobabad	28
	Kambar-Shahdadkot	30
	Kashmore	32
	Larkana	29
	Shikarpur	29
Mirpurkhas	Mirpurkhas	25
	Tharparkar	26
	Umerkot	24
Shaheed Benazirabad	Naushahro Feroze	30
	Sanghar	27
	Shaheed Benazirabad	33
Sukkur	Ghotki	37
	Khairpur Mirs	31
	Sukkur	29

Source: Sindh Education Management Information System (SEMIS), *Sindh Education Profile 2015–16*, Karachi, Education and Literacy Department, Government of Sindh, n.d.

Table 4S: Number of Primary Schools Merged into Campus Schools
(Up to 2015–16)

District	Total No. of Campus School	No. of Merged Primary Schools
Badin	57	119
Karachi Central	36	78
Dadu	37	209
Karachi East	42	72
Ghotki	21	33
Hyderabad	112	187
Jacobabad	23	29
Jamshoro	52	100
Kambar Shadadkot	10	17
Kashmore	25	32

District	Total No. of Campus School	No. of Merged Primary Schools
Khairpur	130	136
Korangi	57	101
Larkana	112	192
Malir	29	41
Matiari	34	79
Mirpurkhas	36	39
Naushahro Feroz	51	84
Sanghar	54	68
Shaheed Benazirabad	99	163
Shikarpur	28	38
Karachi South	70	192
Sujawal	16	33
Sukkur	62	69
Tando Allahyar	23	45
Tando Muhammad Khan	30	39
Tharparkar	33	68
Thatta	20	39
Umerkot	33	100
Karachi West	18	37
Total	1350	2439

Source: Sindh Education Management Information System (SEMIS), Reform Support Unit, Karachi, Education and Literacy Department, Government of Sindh.

Table 4T: Gender-wise Enrolment Across Different Grades (2015–16)

Classes	Enrolment	Percentage (%)	Total
Boys Kachi	372,057	58	641,038
Girls Kachi	268,981	42	
Boys-1	406,402	61	671,004
Girls-1	264,602	39	
Boys-2	343,045	62	552,627
Girls-2	209,582	38	
Boys-3	288,586	61	469,739
Girls-3	181,153	39	
Boys-4	254,403	61	420,145
Girls-4	165,742	39	

Classes	Enrolment	Percentage (%)	Total
Boys-5	193,098	61	316,406
Girls-5	123,308	39	
Boys-6	126,758	61	209,122
Girls-6	82,364	39	
Boys-7	124,819	61	205,555
Girls-7	80,736	39	
Boys-8	109,965	59	187,753
Girls-8	77,788	41	
Boys-9	116,814	62	187,721
Girls-9	70,907	38	
Boys-10	111,423	62	179,980
Girls-10	68,557	38	
Boys-11	38,246	70	55,013
Girls-11	16,767	30	
Boys-12	33,564	68	49,116
Girls-12	15,552	32	
Total			4,145,219

Source: Sindh Education Management Information System (SEMIS), *Sindh Education Profile 2015–16*, Karachi, Education and Literacy Department, Government of Sindh, n.d.

Table 4U: Transition Rates from Primary to Middle (2014–15)

District	Boys	Girls	Total
Badin	71	43	61
Dadu	48	35	43
Hyderabad	71	82	76
Thatta	55	36	47
Jamshoro	64	59	62
Mitiari	72	47	62
Tando Allah Yar	79	57	71
Tando Muhammad Khan	54	42	49
Sujawal	44	19	33
Karachi Central	98	100	99
Karachi East	103	97	100
Karachi South	80	102	92
Karachi West	62	76	70
Malir Karachi	84	88	86

District	Boys	Girls	Total
Korangi Karachi	77	93	86
Jacobabad	45	43	44
Larkana	60	48	55
Shikarpur	60	48	56
Kashmore	44	44	44
Kambar-Shahdadkot	61	40	53
Khairpur Mirs	72	56	65
Sukkur	69	54	63
Ghotki	62	50	58
Mirpurkhas	53	53	53
Tharparkar	44	38	42
Umerkot	61	60	61
Sanghar	48	32	41
Naushahro Feroze	53	48	51
Shaheed Benazirabad	58	43	53
All Sindh	60	55	58

Source: Sindh Education Management Information System (SEMIS), *Sindh Education Profile 2015–16*, Karachi, Education and Literacy Department, Government of Sindh, n.d.

Chapter 5

Table 5A: Medical and Paramedical Personnel (Government) by Category in Sindh
(2008–15)

Categories	2008	2009	2010	2011	2012	2013	2014	2015
Doctors	8,587	8,535	8,804	7,405	7,549	7,577	7,768	7,990
Nurses	2,670	2,637	2,388	1,565	1,587	1,619	1,649	1,630
LHV Technicians	609	584	589	464	675	705	740	786
Dispenser/Dresser	3,955	3,783	3,935	1,669	1,681	1,768	1,843	1,915
X-Ray Technicians	278	276	276	238	249	265	279	282
Lab Technicians	317	324	342	242	243	257	266	278
OT Technicians	289	282	282	218	228	233	241	249
X-Ray Assistant	65	63	74	66	64	67	69	80
Lab Assistant	292	286	303	254	250	261	283	286
OT Assistant	192	191	199	147	146	159	164	172
Midwives	1,264	1,241	1,241	915	1,020	1,097	1,138	1,151

Source: Bureau of Statistics, *Development Statistics of Sindh*, Karachi, Planning and Development Department, Government of Sindh, various years.

Table 5B: Government Hospitals, Dispensaries, Rural Health Centres, TB Clinics, Basic Health Units and
Mother Child Health Centres with Bed Capacity in Sindh
(2008–12)

Items	2008	2009	2010	2011	2012
Hospitals					
Teaching	6	6	6	6	6
Civil, Major Specialised and Taluka	82	82	82	82	86
Beds					
Teaching	5,799	5,799	5,799	5,799	5,799
Civil, Major Specialised and Taluka	5,789	5,789	5,878	5,878	6,123
Dispensaries					
Numbers	420	399	444	420	520
Beds	6	6	6	6	6
Rural Health Centres					
Numbers	106	106	106	108	124
Beds	1,582	1,582	1,582	1,600	1,625
T.B Clinics					
Numbers	186	186	186	186	186
Beds	-	-	-	-	-

Items	2008	2009	2010	2011	2012
Basic Health Units					
Numbers	772	772	772	308	789
Beds	1,586	1,586	1,586	1,648	1,580
Mother Child Health Centres					
Numbers	40	40	40	40	40
Beds	20	20	20	20	20

Source: Bureau of Statistics, *Development Statistics of Sindh*, Karachi, Planning and Development Department, Government of Sindh, various years.

Table 5C: Allocated and Revised Estimates of Health Budget
(in PKR Million)
(1970–2015)

Budget Allocated to Health (During the Year)	Budget Estimate	Revised Estimate
1970	26.9	-
1975	67.5	67.9
1980	70.4	61.9
1985	223.3	226.9
1990	371	411.7
1995	762.9	637.9
2000	393.3	276.4
2005	795	581.8
2010	6,300	4536.6
2015	54,000	-

Source: Sindh Directorate General of Health, *Health Statistics Sindh*, Karachi, Health Department, Government of Sindh, 2010.

Table 5D: Medical Personnel of Sindh (Government)
(1975–2015)

	Dispenser/ Dresser	X-Ray Asst.	OT Asst.	Midwives	Dais	OT Techs	Lab Asst.
1975	416	5	-	106	89	-	100
1980	541	18	46	128	149	33	124
1985	878	78	72	91	346	41	198
1990	1,393	34	122	149	751	143	320
1995	1,569	27	123	488	797	203	353
2000	1,989	36	137	653	987	137	371
2005	1,667	42	129	900	-	213	225
2010	1,669	238	218	915	-	218	254
2015	1,915	80	172	1151	-	249	278

Source: Bureau of Statistics, *Development Statistics of Sindh*, Karachi, Planning and Development Department, Government of Sindh, various years); Bureau of Statistics, *Health Profile*, Karachi, Planning and Development Department, Government of Sindh, various years.

Table 5E: Trained Medical Staff at the Sindh Medical Centres and Units (Public*)
(1975–2015)

Year	Doctors	Nurses	X-Ray Tech.	LHV Techs	Lab Techs	Radio- Graphers	Health Tech	Compounders
1975	926	415	46	107	100	14	95	283
1980	969	436	54	135	105	15	105	395
1985	1,758	607	66	158	190	13	82	-
1990	7,213	837	147	220	282	13	295	-
1995	7702	1,343	218	300	326	11	1,027	-
2000	7,953	1,639	254	322	355	11	1,382	-
2005	6,767	1,581	235	406	212	-	-	-
2010	8,632	2,398	284	614	355	-	-	-
2015	9744	2499	344	950	404	-	-	-

*Includes figures for government, semi-government and local bodies.

Source: Bureau of Statistics, *Development Statistics of Sindh*, Karachi, Planning and Development Department, Government of Sindh, various years; Bureau of Statistics, *Health Profile*, Karachi, Planning and Development Department, Government of Sindh, various years.

Table 5F: Trained Technical Staff at the Sindh Medical Centres and Units (Public*)
(1975–2015)

Year	Dispenser/ Dressers	X-Ray Assistants	Lab Assistants	OT Assistants	Midwives	Dais/Ayas	OT Techs.
1975	145	5	100	17	106	89	-
1980	142	18	124	46	128	149	33
1985	792	10	176	67	80	302	63
1990	1,360	22	269	120	169	659	134
1995	1,569	27	353	123	488	797	203
2000	1,989	36	371	137	653	987	227
2005	3871	58	296	186	1229	-	283
2010	3,942	82	327	199	1,241	-	288
2015	4,777	113	367	465	1,505	-	326

*Includes figures for government, semi-government and local bodies

Source: Bureau of Statistics, *Development Statistics of Sindh*, Karachi, Planning and Development Department, Government of Sindh, various years; Bureau of Statistics, *Health Profile*, Karachi, Planning and Development Department, Government of Sindh, various years.

Table 5G: Indoor and Outdoor Patients in Centres or Units
(1965–95)

Year	Hospitals		Dispensaries	Rural Health Centres	Basic Health Units
	Indoor Patients	Outdoor Patients	Total Patients	Total Patients	Total Patients
1965	83,598	1,159,296	401,558	1,054,469	-
1970	127,780	5254393	2,287,527	408,872	-
1975	190,436	5,094,156	727,464	634,712	-
1980	129,145	5,420,791	817,326	593,514	-
1985	182911	4,382,500	544,345	565,243	-
1990	237,943	6,931,621	584,230	998,393	2,213,363
1995	292,693	10,149,336	1,227,879	1,767,916	3,525,498

Source: Bureau of Statistics, *Development Statistics of Sindh*, Karachi, Planning and Development Department, Government of Sindh, various years.

Table 5H: Medical Centres and Units (Government)
(1965–2015)

Centre/Unit	1965	1970	1975	1980	1985	1990	1995	2000	2005	2010	2015
General and Training Hospitals	2	2	2	6	6	6	7	5	5	6	7
Civil, Specialised, Taluka and Others	20	21	29	51	65	73	78	80	83	82	99
Dispensaries	48	44	47	85	100	94	147	238	350	444	865
Rural Health Centres	19	19	27	52	60	67	84	97	103	106	129
TB Clinics/Centres	10	12	13	14	13	13	159	174	180	186	187
Sub-Rural Health Centres	-	-	-	-	55	-	-				
Basic Health Units	-	-	-	-	33	372	644	712	757	773	798
Mother Child Health Centres	-	-	-	-	-	-	-	37	40	40	94

Source: Bureau of Statistics, *Development Statistics of Sindh*, Karachi, Planning and Development Department, Government of Sindh, various years; Bureau of Statistics, *Health Profile*, Karachi, Planning and Development Department, Government of Sindh, various years.

Table 5I: Beds in Medical Centres and Units
(1965–2010)

Centre/Unit	1965	1970	1975	1980	1985	1990	1995	2000	2005	2010	2015
General and Training Hospitals	1,408	1,775	2,205	4,195	3,402	4,384	5018	5085	5,474	5,799	6017
Civil, Specialised, Taluka, and Others	1,677	2,084	2,715	5,615	4,079	4833	5082	5659	6040	5,878	6499
Dispensaries	53	49	60	60	14	14	12	6	6	6	6
Rural Health Centres	82	82	108	640	700	814	1,262	1,364	1,540	1,580	1,629
Basic Health Units	-	-	-	-	-	952	1341	1,450	1,556	1,588	1,598
Mother Child Health Centres		-	-	-	-	-	-	-	-	20	24

Source: Bureau of Statistics, *Development Statistics of Sindh*, Karachi, Planning and Development Department, Government of Sindh, various years; Bureau of Statistics, *Health Profile*, Karachi, Planning and Development Department, Government of Sindh, various years.

Table 5J: Health Indicators of Sindh
(1952–56)

Years	Birth Rate Per 1000 Population	Death Rate Per 1000 Population	Infant Mortality Per 1000 of Live Births
1952	5.59	3.46	85
1953	5.74	3.01	74
1954	4.31	2.05	75
1955	4.19	2.24	74
1956	5.31	3.02	86

Source: H.T. Sorley, *The Gazetteer of West Pakistan: The Former Province of Sind Including Khairpur State*, Lahore, Gazeteer Cell, Board of Revenue, 1968.

Table 5K: Health Indicators—2015

Health Indicator	Value
Life Expectancy at Birth (Years)	66.4
Public Health Expenditure (% of GDP)	0.9
Child Mortality (Under-Five) Rate (Per 1,000 Live Births)	81.1
Adult Mortality Rate, Male (Per 1,000 People)	179
Adult Mortality Rate, Female (Per 1,000 People)	143
Deaths Due to Malaria (Per 100,000 People)	1.8
Deaths Due to Tuberculosis (Per 100,000 People)	26
HIV Prevalence, Adult (% Ages 15–49), (Total)	0.1
Infant Mortality Rate (Per 1,000 Live Births)	65.8
Infants Lacking Immunisation, DTP (% of One-Year-Olds)	21
Infants Lacking Immunisation, Measles (% of One-Year-Olds)	37
Stunting (Moderate or Severe) (% Under Age 5)	45

Sources: United Nations Development Programme, *Human Development Report 2016*, New York, 2016; World Bank Open Data <https://data.worldbank.org/>

Table 5L: Diseases
(1952–56)

Years	Smallpox	Fevers	Dysentery and Diarrhoea	Respiratory Diseases	Injuries	Others
1952	263	11,200	217	2,207	-	2,322
1953	19	10,803	231	1,077	-	2,144
1954	14	5,656	88	1,217	89	2,750
1955	66	6,748	136	2,108	71	1,747
1956	95	9,970	162	2,404	113	2,104

Source: H.T. Sorley, *The Gazetteer of West Pakistan: the Former Province of Sindh Including Khairpur State*, Lahore, Gazeteer Cell, Board of Revenue, 1968.

Chapter 6

Table 6A: Labour Force Participation Rates and Unemployment Rates for Pakistan for Different Age Groups (2014–15)

Age Groups	Labour Force Participation Rates					Unemployment Rates				
	Total	Male		Female		Total	Male		Female	
		Rural	Urban	Rural	Urban		Rural	Urban	Rural	Urban
Total (All Ages)	32.3	47.4	49.4	20.2	7.5	-	-	-	-	-
Total (10 Years and Over)	45.3	69.0	65.7	28.8	10.0	5.9	4.3	6.2	6.7	20.4
10–14	9.6	13.8	6.0	11.2	1.3	9.9	10.0	22.2	5	21.8
15–19	33.5	53.6	37.0	24.1	7.7	10.1	8.4	14.2	7.9	23.4
20–24	52.6	86.6	76.0	31.7	15.3	11	8.3	10.6	12.2	31.5
25–29	58.6	97.2	95.8	33.4	14.4	6.1	3.1	4.7	10.2	26.4
30–34	60.1	98.3	97.8	35.9	13.7	3.5	1.6	2.1	6.6	17.7
35–39	62.6	98.2	98.3	38.7	12.3	1.9	1.3	1.2	2.8	10.3
40–44	64.4	98.4	98.5	39.6	13.8	2.0	1.4	1.5	3.0	7.5
45–49	66.0	98.2	97.0	43.5	11.6	1.8	1.4	1.8	1.9	6.1
50–54	65.3	97.3	95.6	40.2	11.0	3.6	2.9	3.8	3.7	13.4
55–59	63.8	94.5	92.8	36.2	10.94	5.8	4.8	4.7	8.0	22.9
60–64	51.2	82.3	65.4	26.0	5.6	9	5.3	16.1	9.6	29.7
65 Years and Over	27.6	46.1	35.5	9.3	3.3	11.1	4.0	31.7	5.7	38.2

Source: Pakistan Bureau of Statistics, *Labour Force Survey 2014–15*, Islamabad, Statistics Division, Government of Pakistan, 2015.

Table 6B: Labour Force Participation Rates and Unemployment Rates for Punjab for Different Age Groups (2014–15)

Age Groups	Labour Force Participation Rates					Unemployment Rates				
	Total	Male		Female		Total	Male		Female	
		Rural	Urban	Rural	Urban		Rural	Urban	Rural	Urban
Total (All Ages)	35.4	50.0	50.4	25.8	9.7	-	-	-	-	-
Total (10 Years and Over)	48.5	70.9	66.7	35.5	12.8	6.3	5.2	6.7	6.1	17.0
10–14	11.5	14.3	8.3	14.9	2.0	14.4	17.2	32.1	5.9	18.2
15–19	36.7	54.6	39.6	30.8	10.2	12.4	11.7	20.1	6.4	23.9
20–24	55.1	88.1	76.8	37.6	17.9	11.0	9	11.2	10.4	28.2
25–29	62.1	97.3	95.5	41.1	16.7	5.7	3.1	4.6	9.2	18.2
30–34	64.5	98.3	96.8	44.2	18.4	3.6	1.7	2.5	5.7	15.3
35–39	65.6	97.9	97.4	48.3	15.1	1.9	1.4	1.2	2.6	8.4
40–44	67.9	98.4	98.0	49.1	19.6	2.2	1.4	2.2	3.1	4.5
45–49	68.2	98.3	95.8	52.8	15.4	1.7	1.5	1.5	1.7	4.6

Age Groups	Labour Force Participation Rates					Unemployment Rates				
	Total	Male		Female		Total	Male		Female	
		Rural	Urban	Rural	Urban		Rural	Urban	Rural	Urban
50–54	68.6	97.9	94.3	49	14.8	3.9	3.6	3.9	3.1	12.2
55–59	64.7	94.5	90.7	42.6	14.2	6.6	5.6	5.2	7.9	23.0
60–64	53.1	84.4	64.4	30.7	6.7	7.2	5.1	9.6	9.6	22.9
65 Years and Over	28.2	47.7	32.0	10.1	3.4	6.1	3.5	14.8	6.0	14.2

Source: Pakistan Bureau of Statistics, *Labour Force Survey 2014–15*, Islamabad, Statistics Division, Government of Pakistan, 2015.

Table 6C: Percentage Distribution of Unemployed Persons 10 Years of Age and Over Who Were Not Available for Work Due to Certain Reasons
(1997–98 and 2014–15)

Region	Reasons	1997–98					2014–15				
		Rural		Urban		Total	Rural		Urban		Total
		Male	Female	Male	Female		Male	Female	Male	Female	
Pakistan	Illness	18.1	30.5	11.5	10.7	70.8	16.9	12.7	9.1	5.3	44.0
	Will Take a Job Within a Month	1.7	0.3	2.2	0.5	4.7	2.8	0.2	1.5	0.4	5.0
	Temporarily Laid Off	0.4	1.3	0.9	0.5	3.1	2.0	1.4	1.0	0.5	4.9
	Apprentice and Not Willing to Work	8.0	1.8	9.9	1.8	21.4	22.2	6.6	13.7	3.8	46.2
						100					100
Sindh*	Illness	5.4	8.0	16.2	17.4		4.2	13.0	24.3	36.2	
	Will Take a Job Within a Month	15.2	0.00	23.9	10.6		6.0	0.00	0.00	0.00	
	Temporarily Laid Off	0.00	21.3	0.00	0.00		2.6	9.0	37.6	15.2	
	Apprentice and Not Willing to Work	2.0	3.9	6.1	27.8		4.5	0.2	0.00	2.7	

Region	Reasons	1997–98					2014–15				
		Rural		Urban		Total	Rural		Urban		Total
		Male	Female	Male	Female		Male	Female	Male	Female	
Punjab*	Illness	63.4	53.7	75.0	70.0		83.4	70.3	66.6	57.0	
	Will Take a Job Within a Month	64.9	100.0	68.0	78.7		76.2	85.7	92.2	87.8	
	Temporarily Laid Off	44.4	72.4	96.8	93.8		70.9	65.3	45.5	71.7	
	Apprentice and Not Willing to Work	91.7	76.4	93.3	71.0		93.6	99.5	99.0	96.0	

*The values for provinces are percentages of the national for each category.

Source: Pakistan Bureau of Statistics, *Labour Force Survey*, Islamabad, Statistics Division, Government of Pakistan, various years.

Table 6D: Percentage Distribution of Employed Persons 10 Years of Age and Over Who Worked Less than 35 Hours during Reference Week by Reasons (Pakistan)
(2014–15)

Reasons for Underemployment	2014–15								
	All Areas			Rural			Urban		
	Total	Male	Female	Total	Male	Female	Total	Male	Female
Normally Works the Same Number of Hours	86.4	25.6	60.8	88.1	24.6	63.5	73.5	32.6	40.9
Illness or Injury	1.2	0.8	0.4	1.1	0.8	0.4	1.6	1.2	0.3
Strike or Lockout or Layoff	0.1	0.03	0.05	0.09	0.04	0.05	-	-	-
Holiday, Ramzan, Vacation or Leave of Absence	1.7	1.3	0.4	0.6	0.4	0.17	9.6	7.7	1.9
Educational and Training Leave	0.7	0.5	0.2	0.8	0.5	0.2	0.2	0.2	-
Involuntary Reasons	7.7	4.1	3.5	7.5	3.9	3.7	8.7	6.1	2.7
Supply-Side Issues	0.3	0.3	0.06	0.2	0.2	0.04	1.19	1	0.19
Economic Issues (External)	0.65	0.37	0.28	0.51	0.26	0.25	1.75	1.25	0.51
Voluntary Reasons	1.4	0.9	0.5	1.1	0.7	0.4	3.5	2.5	1.1

Source: Pakistan Bureau of Statistics, *Labour Force Survey 2014–15*, Islamabad, Statistics Division, Government of Pakistan, 2015.

Table 6E: Sindh's Share in Percentage Distribution of Employed Persons 10 Years of Age and Over Who Worked Less than 35 Hours during Reference Week by Reasons
(2014–15)

| Reasons for Unemployment | 2014–15 | | | | | | | | |
| | All Areas | | | Rural | | | Urban | | |
	Total	Male	Female	Total	Male	Female	Total	Male	Female
Normally Works the Same Number of Hours	12.0	7.1	4.9	11.5	6.5	5.0	15.4	11.1	4.3
Illness or Injury	0.16	0.09	0.07	0.16	0.08	0.08	0.17	0.17	
Strike or Lockout or Layoff	-	-	-	-	-	-	-	-	-
Holiday, Ramzan, Vacation or Leave of Absence	0.14	0.14		0.13	0.13		0.27	0.27	
Educational and Training Leave	0.01	0.01		0.01	0.01				
Involuntary Reasons	0.51	0.33	0.18	0.46	0.32	0.14	0.99	0.49	0.5
Supply-Side Issues	0.13	0.12	0.02	0.07	0.07		0.63	0.47	0.16
Economic Issues (External)	0.18	0.08	0.1	0.21	0.09	0.11			
Voluntary Reasons	0.08	0.04	0.04	0.09	0.05	0.04			

Source: Pakistan Bureau of Statistics, *Labour Force Survey 2014–15*, Islamabad, Statistics Division, Government of Pakistan, 2015.

Table 6F: Punjab's Share in Percentage Distribution of Employed Persons 10 Years of Age and Over Who Worked Less than 35 Hours during Reference Week by Reasons
(2014–15)

| Reasons for Unemployment | 2014–15 | | | | | | | | |
| | All Areas | | | Rural | | | Urban | | |
	Total	Male	Female	Total	Male	Female	Total	Male	Female
Normally Works the Same Number of Hours	59.3	12.5	46.8	60.9	12.1	48.8	47.2	15.6	31.5
Illness or Injury	0.93	0.69	0.24	0.87	0.64	0.23	1.36	1.03	0.33
Strike or Lockout or Layoff	0.08	0.03	0.05	0.09	0.04	0.05	-	-	-
Holiday, Ramzan, Vacation or Leave of Absence	1.3	0.92	0.36	0.37	0.2	0.17	8.2	6.4	1.8
Educational and Training Leave	0.6	0.4	0.18	0.6	0.4	0.2	0.09	0.09	-
Involuntary Reasons	5.5	2.5	3.1	5.5	2.3	3.2	6.2	4.1	2.1
Supply-Side Issues	0.11	0.1	0.01	0.08	0.07	0.01	0.31	0.31	-
Economic Issues (External)	0.45	0.27	0.18	0.27	0.14	0.14	1.8	1.3	0.5
Voluntary Reasons	1.2	0.75	0.42	0.88	0.54	0.33	3.4	2.3	1.1

Source: Pakistan Bureau of Statistics, *Labour Force Survey 2014–15*, Islamabad, Statistics Division, Government of Pakistan, 2015.

Table 6G: Distribution of Population by Age, Literacy, and Level of Education for Pakistan (2014–15)

Age Groups	Total	Illiterate	Literate	No Formal Education	Formal Education	Less Than KG	Less Than Primary	Less Than Middle School	Less Than Matric	Less Than Inter	Less Than Degree	Degree, Post Graduate and Phds
Total 10+ Years	100	39.3	60.7	0.4	60.3	0.04	6	19.4	12.1	11.6	5.6	5.5
10–14	15.2	3.5	11.7	0.02	11.62	0.01	4.12	6.7	0.8	-	-	-
15–19	12.7	3.1	9.6	0.02	9.6	0.01	0.22	2.3	3.8	2.6	0.75	
20–24	10.4	3.3	7.1	0.04	7.0		0.13	1.5	1.3	1.7	1.5	1
25–29	8.2	3.2	5.0	0.03	5.0		0.11	1.2	1.0	1.2	0.6	0.96
30–34	7	2.9	4.1	0.04	4.0		0.08	1.02	0.83	0.98	0.45	0.65
35–39	6.4	3.0	3.4	0.04	3.4		0.06	0.86	0.66	0.85	0.42	0.5
40–44	5.7	2.9	2.8	0.03	2.8		0.06	0.67	0.49	0.71	0.33	0.5
45–49	4.9	2.8	2.2	0.04	2.1		0.05	0.6	0.41	0.51	0.21	0.35
50–54	3.7	2.2	1.5	0.02	1.5		0.03	0.4	0.29	0.4	0.15	0.24
55–59	2.8	1.7	1.14	0.02	1.12		0.03	0.32	0.22	0.28	0.12	0.15
60–64	2.1	1.4	0.74	0.02	0.72		0.02	0.21	0.13	0.2	0.06	0.11
65 and Above	3.5	2.6	0.96	0.02	0.94		0.04	0.3	0.19	0.23	0.06	0.11

Source: Pakistan Bureau of Statistics, *Labour Force Survey 2014–15*, Islamabad, Statistics Division, Government of Pakistan, 2015.

Table 6H: Distribution of Population by Age, Literacy, and Level of Education for Sindh (2014–15)

Age Groups	Total	Illiterate	Literate	No Formal Education	Formal Education	Less Than K.G	Less Than Primary	Less Than Middle School	Less Than Matric	Less Than Inter	Less Than Degree	Degree, Post Graduate and Phds
Total 10+ Years	100	37.0	63.0	0.25	62.7	0.07	6.5	19.6	10.3	12.0	7.6	6.6
10–14	16.6	4.1	12.5	0.03	12.5		4.9	7.0	0.63			
15–19	12.9	3.5	9.4	0.02	9.4		0.1	2.2	3.4	2.8	0.93	
20–24	9.7	3.3	6.5	0.03	6.4	0.01	0.05	1.3	0.89	1.52	1.9	0.8
25–29	7.6	3.0	4.6	0.01	4.5	0.01	0.05	1.04	0.72	1.1	0.7	0.89
30–34	7.3	3.0	4.4	0.03	4.3	0.01	0.03	0.99	0.74	1.2	0.66	0.73

Age Groups	Total	Illiterate	Literate	No Formal Education	Formal Education	Less Than K.G	Less Than Primary	Less Than Middle School	Less Than Matric	Less Than Inter	Less Than Degree	Degree, Post Graduate and Phds
35–39	6.6	2.9	3.7	0.02	3.7		0.03	0.88	0.57	0.87	0.68	0.67
40–44	6.4	2.8	3.4	0.02	3.5	0.01	0.07	0.8	0.49	0.8	0.55	0.81
45–49	4.8	2.2	2.6	0.02	2.6	0.01	0.03	0.65	0.43	0.55	0.28	0.66
50–54	3.6	1.9	1.7	0.01	1.7		0.03	0.44	0.23	0.38	0.23	0.4
55–59	2.7	1.4	1.3	0.01	1.29		0.03	0.37	0.2	0.27	0.16	0.25
60–64	1.7	1.0	0.72		0.71		0.01	0.25	0.09	0.17	0.08	0.12
65 and Above	2.0	1.3	0.65		0.64		0.01	0.21	0.09	0.17	0.05	0.1

Source: Pakistan Bureau of Statistics, *Labour Force Survey 2014–15*, Islamabad, Statistics Division, Government of Pakistan, 2015.

Table 6I: Distribution of Population by Age, Literacy, and Level of Education for Punjab (2014–15)

Age Groups	Total	Illiterate	Literate	No Formal Education	Formal Education	Less Than K.G	Less Than Primary	Less Than Middle School	Less Than Matric	Less Than Inter	Less Than Degree	Degree, Post Graduate and Phds
Total 10+ Years	100	38.1	61.9	0.32	61.6	0.04	5.4	19.7	13.6	12.2	5.2	5.5
10–14	14.0	3.2	10.9	0.02	10.9	0.01	3.4	6.4	1.1			
15–19	12.6	2.8	9.8	0.02	9.8	0.01	0.29	2.3	3.9	2.6	0.8	
20–24	11.1	3.2	7.9	0.04	7.9		0.19	1.7	1.6	1.9	1.4	1.2
25–29	8.7	3.0	5.7	0.02	5.6		0.14	1.4	1.2	1.3	0.58	1.08
30–34	6.9	2.7	4.2	0.02	4.2		0.11	1.09	0.94	0.98	0.39	0.67
35–39	6.3	2.8	3.5	0.02	3.5		0.08	0.92	0.76	0.9	0.36	0.45
40–44	5.5	2.7	2.8	0.02	2.8		0.07	0.7	0.53	0.75	0.29	0.43
45–49	5.2	3.0	2.2	0.03	2.2		0.06	0.67	0.46	0.57	0.2	0.26
50–54	3.9	2.3	1.7	0.01	1.7		0.04	0.44	0.37	0.47	0.15	0.18
55–59	3.0	1.8	1.2	0.01	1.2		0.03	0.34	0.26	0.33	0.11	0.13
60–64	2.4	1.5	0.9	0.02	0.83		0.03	0.23	0.16	0.23	0.07	0.12
65 and Above	4.5	3.3	1.3	0.03	1.24		0.06	0.4	0.27	0.31	0.08	0.13

Source: Pakistan Bureau of Statistics, *Labour Force Survey 2014–15*, Islamabad, Statistics Division, Government of Pakistan, 2015.

Table 6J: Trends in the Population 10 Years of Age and Over by Level of Education
(2005–06 to 2014–15)

Region		Employed (%)						
	Year	Illiterate	Literate	No Formal Education	Pre-Matric	Matric	Inter	Degree, Post-Grad and Phd
Pakistan	2005–06	47.2	52.9	0.7	58.1	22.5	8.4	10.4
	2010–11	45.4	54.6	1.0	56.4	22.2	9.0	11.5
	2014–15	44.2	55.8	0.7	53.6	22.4	9.9	13.4
Sindh	2005–06	41.8	58.2	1.1	49.2	21.2	11.7	16.9
	2010–11	42.4	57.7	0.9	48.3	20.5	12.5	17.8
	2014–15	39.4	60.6	0.5	46.1	21.7	14.0	17.6
Punjab	2005–06	48.2	51.8	0.6	61.5	22.9	7.1	7.9
	2010–11	46.8	53.2	1.1	60.3	22.5	7.3	8.8
	2014–15	46.0	54.0	0.7	57.5	22.3	8.0	11.5

Source: Pakistan Bureau of Statistics, *Labour Force Survey*, Islamabad, Statistics Division, Government of Pakistan, various years.

Table 6K: Percentage Distribution of Migrant Population 10 Years of Age and Over by
Main Reasons of Migration (2014–15)

Region	Main Reason for Migration	All Areas	Rural		Urban	
		Total	Male	Female	Male	Female
Pakistan	Job/Employment	13.3	3.9	0.23	8.9	0.37
	Family	79.1	13.4	27.1	11.3	27.3
	Other	7.7	2.6	1.0	2.9	1.2
Sindh	Job/Employment	17.2	1.1	0.07	15.5	0.55
	Family	75.4	3.1	9.1	20.8	42.4
	Other	7.4	0.7	0.14	3.7	2.8
Punjab	Job/Employment	12.2	3.8	0.29	7.7	0.35
	Family	80.6	12.9	33.6	8.8	25.3
	Other	7.2	2.8	0.96	2.7	0.76

Source: Pakistan Bureau of Statistics, *Labour Force Survey 2014–15*, Islamabad, Statistics Division, Government of Pakistan, 2015.

Table 6L: Distribution of Employment by Industries (Pakistan)
(1990–91 and 2014–15)

Major Industry Division	1990–91			2014–15		
	All Areas	Rural	Urban	All Areas	Rural	Urban
Agriculture, Forestry, Hunting, and Fishing	47.5	45.2	2.2	42.3	40.7	1.6
Mining and Quarrying	0.2	0.1	0.1	0.2	0.1	0.0
Manufacturing	12.2	5.7	6.5	15.3	7.4	8.0
Electricity, Gas, and Water	0.8	0.4	0.5	0.8	0.3	0.5
Construction	6.6	4.7	1.9	7.3	4.9	2.4
Wholesale, Retail Trade, Restaurants, and Hotels	13.2	5.5	7.7	14.6	6.4	8.2
Transport, Storage, and Communication	5.3	2.6	2.6	7.0	3.7	3.3
Financing, Insurance, Real Estate, and Business Services	0.9	0.2	0.7	1.4	0.4	1.0
Community, Social, and Personal Services	13.3	6.4	6.9	11.1	5.5	5.6
Activities Extraterritorial Organisations and Bodies	0.1	0.0	0.0	0.0	0.0	0.0

Source: Pakistan Bureau of Statistics, *Labour Force Survey*, Islamabad, Statistics Division, Government of Pakistan, various years.

Table 6M: Distribution of Employment by Industries (Sindh)
(1990–91 and 2014–15)

Major Industry Division	1990–91			2014–15		
	All Areas	Rural	Urban	All Areas	Rural	Urban
Agriculture, Forestry, Hunting, and Fishing	40.2	37.8	2.3	39.3	37.5	1.8
Mining and Quarrying	0.15	0.13	0.02	0.11	0.09	0.02
Manufacturing	14.4	2.3	12.2	15.2	3.3	11.9
Electricity, Gas, and Water	1.09	0.39	0.70	1.4	0.42	0.98
Construction	5.9	2.6	3.3	7.00	3.5	3.5
Wholesale and Retail Trade and Restaurants and Hotels	15.8	3.6	12.1	15.8	4.0	11.8
Transport, Storage and Communication	6.1	1.6	4.5	8.4	3.1	5.3
Financing, Insurance, Real Estate and Business Services	1.6	0.23	1.40	1.8	0.15	1.6
Community, Social, and Personal Services	14.7	4.01	10.7	11.0	4.0	7.1
Activities Extraterritorial Organisations and Bodies	0.06	0.00	0.06	0.01	0.00	0.01

Source: Pakistan Bureau of Statistics, *Labour Force Survey*, Islamabad, Statistics Division, Government of Pakistan, various years)

Table 6N: Distribution of Employment by Industries (Punjab)
(1990–91 and 2014–15)

Major Industry Division	1990–91			2014–15		
	All Areas	Rural	Urban	All Areas	Rural	Urban
Agriculture, Forestry, Hunting, and Fishing	48.9	46.5	2.4	44.7	43.1	1.6
Mining and Quarrying	0.12	0.06	0.07	0.07	0.05	0.02
Manufacturing	13.0	7.5	5.5	16.5	8.7	7.7
Electricity, Gas, and Water	0.68	0.31	0.37	0.56	0.26	0.31
Construction	6.7	5.1	1.6	6.6	4.4	2.2
Wholesale, Retail Trade, Restaurants, and Hotels	12.4	5.4	7.00	13.9	6.4	7.5
Transport, Storage, and Communication	4.8	2.6	2.3	5.9	3.1	2.8
Financing, Insurance, Real Estate, and Business Services	0.68	0.22	0.46	1.43	0.52	0.89
Community, Social, and Personal Services	12.7	6.6	6.1	10.4	5.1	5.3
Activities Extraterritorial Organisations and Bodies	0.06	0.05	0.01	0.02	0.02	0.01

Source: Pakistan Bureau of Statistics, *Labour Force Survey*, Islamabad, Statistics Division, Government of Pakistan, various years.

Table 6O: Percentage Distribution of Employed Persons 10 Years of Age and Over by
Major Industry Division
(1982–83 to 1997–98)

Region	Major Industry Division	1982–83			1990–91			1997–98		
		All Areas	Rural	Urban	All Areas	Rural	Urban	All Areas	Rural	Urban
		Total	Total	Total	Total	Total	Total	Total	Total	Total
Pakistan	Total	100	100	100	100	70.9	29.1	100	70.0	30.0
	Agriculture, Forestry, Hunting, and Fishing	52.7	67.7	6.7	47.5	45.2	2.2	47.3	45.6	1.7
	Mining and Quarrying	0.1	0.11	0.08	0.15	0.1	0.05	0.19	0.17	0.02
	Manufacturing	13.3	9.4	25.9	12.2	5.7	6.5	10.0	4.0	5.9
	Electricity, Gas, and Water	1.13	0.96	1.7	0.8	0.4	0.5	0.7	0.27	0.43
	Construction	4.8	4.1	6.9	6.6	4.7	1.9	6.3	4.1	2.2
	Wholesale, Retail Trade, Restaurants, and Hotels	11.9	7.1	26.7	13.2	5.5	7.7	13.9	5.3	8.5
	Transport, Storage, and Communication	4.6	3.1	9.2	5.2	2.6	2.6	5.5	2.5	3.0
	Financing, Insurance, Real Estate and Business Services	0.82	0.26	2.5	0.89	0.24	0.66	0.87	0.16	0.71
	Community, Social, and Personal Services	10.2	6.9	20.2	13.3	6.4	6.9	15.4	7.9	7.5
	Activities Extraterritorial Organisations and Bodies	0.27	0.31	0.13	0.06	0.04	0.02	0.05	0.04	0.01
Sindh	Total	100	100	100	100	52.7	47.3	100	52.2	47.8
	Agriculture, Forestry, Hunting, and Fishing	51.6	81	4.4	40.2	37.8	2.3	43.1	41.0	2.13
	Mining and Quarrying				0.15	0.13	0.03	0.06	-	0.06
	Manufacturing	13.5	4.6	27.9	14.4	2.3	12.2	10.2	0.9	9.3
	Electricity, Gas, and Water	1.16	0.91	1.55	1.09	0.39	0.7	1.13	0.32	0.81
	Construction	4.2	2.6	6.8	5.9	2.6	3.3	6.1	2.4	3.7
	Wholesale and Retail Trade and Restaurants and Hotels	12.5	4.6	25.3	15.8	3.6	12.1	17.4	3	14.4
	Transport, Storage, and Communication	5.0	1.7	10.5	6.1	1.6	4.5	5.6	1.3	4.3
	Financing, Insurance, Real Estate, and Business Services	1.4	0.07	3.4	1.6	0.23	1.4	1.6	0.03	1.6
	Community, Social, and Personal Services	10.5	4.6	20.1	14.7	4.01	10.7	14.8	3.3	11.5
	Activities Extraterritorial Organisations and Bodies	0.09	0.02	0.22	0.06	-	0.06	0.04	0.04	-

Region	Major Industry Division	1982–83			1990–91			1997–98		
		All Areas	Rural	Urban	All Areas	Rural	Urban	All Areas	Rural	Urban
		Total	Total	Total	Total	Total	Total	Total	Total	Total
Punjab	Total	100	100	100	100	74.2	25.8	100	72.7	27.3
	Agriculture, Forestry, Hunting, and Fishing	53.1	65.3	7.6	48.9	46.5	2.4	47.9	46.3	1.6
	Mining and Quarrying	0.1	0.1	0.13	0.12	0.06	0.07	0.25	0.24	0.01
	Manufacturing	14.7	11.4	26.7	13.0	7.5	5.5	11	5.2	5.8
	Electricity, Gas, and Water	0.95	0.81	1.5	0.68	0.31	0.37	0.55	0.21	0.34
	Construction	4.8	4.3	6.8	6.7	5.1	1.6	5.9	4.0	1.9
	Wholesale, Retail Trade, Restaurants, and Hotels	11.6	7.3	27.6	12.4	5.4	7	12.9	5.4	7.6
	Transport, Storage, and Communication	4.3	3.1	8.5	4.8	2.6	2.3	5.2	2.3	2.8
	Financing, Insurance, Real Estate, and Business Services	0.65	0.27	2.07	0.68	0.22	0.46	0.66	0.16	0.5
	Community, Social, and Personal Services	0.7	7.2	19	12.7	6.6	6.13	15.7	8.9	6.8
	Activities Extraterritorial Organisations and Bodies	0.14	0.17	0.03	0.06	0.05	0.01	0.05	0.04	0.01

Source: Pakistan Bureau of Statistics, *Labour Force Survey*, Islamabad, Statistics Division, Government of Pakistan, various years.

Table 6P: Percentage Distribution of Employed Persons 10 Years of Age and Over by
Major Industry Division
(2005–06 to 2014–15)

Region	Major Industry Division	2005–06			2010–11			2014–15		
		All Areas	Rural	Urban	All Areas	Rural	Urban	All Areas	Rural	Urban
		Total	Total	Total	Total	Total	Total	Total	Total	Total
Pakistan	Total	100	69.2	30.8	100	70.3	29.7	100	69.4	30.6
	Agriculture, Forestry, Hunting, and Fishing	43.4	41.4	2.0	45.05	43.2	1.9	42.3	40.7	1.6
	Mining and Quarrying	0.09	0.08	0.01	0.15	0.12	0.03	0.16	0.13	0.03
	Manufacturing	13.8	6.2	7.6	13.7	6.2	7.5	15.4	7.4	8.0
	Electricity, Gas, and Water	0.7	0.3	0.4	0.5	0.2	0.3	0.79	0.32	0.5
	Construction	6.1	4.3	1.8	7.0	5.0	2.0	7.3	4.9	2.4
	Wholesale, Retail Trade, Restaurants, and Hotels	14.6	6.4	8.2	16.2	7.0	9.2	14.6	6.4	8.2
	Transport, Storage and Communication	5.7	3.2	2.5	5.1	2.8	2.3	7.0	3.7	3.3
	Financing, Insurance, Real Estate and Business Services	1.1	0.2	0.9	1.5	0.4	1.1	1.4	0.4	1.0
	Community, Social, and Personal Services	14.4	7.0	7.4	11.0	5.5	5.5	8.5	4.4	4.1
	Activities Extraterritorial Organisations and Bodies	0.04	0.02	0.02	0.01	-	0.01	0.03	0.02	0.01
Sindh	Total	100	53.1	46.9	100	58.7	41.3	100	55.9	44.1
	Agriculture, Forestry, Hunting, and Fishing	37.3	35.1	2.2	45.8	44.3	1.5	39.3	37.5	1.8
	Mining and Quarrying	-	-	-	0.18	0.12	0.05	0.11	0.09	0.02
	Manufacturing	15.0	2.8	12.2	12.5	2.0	10.5	15.3	3.3	12.0
	Electricity, Gas, and Water	1.1	0.3	0.8	0.62	0.12	0.5	1.42	0.42	0.98
	Construction	5.8	2.8	3.0	4.9	2.4	2.5	7	3.5	3.5
	Wholesale, Retail Trade, Restaurants, and Hotels	17.81	5.1	12.8	16.8	4	12.8	15.8	4.0	11.8
	Transport, Storage, and Communication	5.73	2.2	3.6	5.2	1.6	3.6	8.4	3.1	5.3
	Financing, Insurance, Real Estate, and Business Services	1.7	0.1	1.6	2.17	0.14	2.03	1.8	0.2	1.6
	Community, Social, and Personal Services	15.5	4.8	10.7	11.9	4.1	7.8	11.1	4.0	7.1
	Activities Extraterritorial Organisations and Bodies	0.05	0.01	0.04	0.01	-	0.01	0.01	-	0.01

Region	Major Industry Division	2005–06			2010–11			2014–15		
		All Areas Total	Rural Total	Urban Total	All Areas Total	Rural Total	Urban Total	All Areas Total	Rural Total	Urban Total
Punjab	Total	100	71.8	28.2	100	72.0	28.0	100	71.7	28.3
	Agriculture, Forestry, Hunting, and Fishing	44.3	42.3	2.0	45.4	43.3	2.1	44.7	43.1	1.6
	Mining and Quarrying	0.07	0.07	-	0.05	0.03	0.03	0.07	0.05	0.02
	Manufacturing	15.4	8.1	7.3	15.5	8.0	7.5	16.4	8.7	7.7
	Electricity, Gas, and Water	0.5	0.2	0.2	0.4	0.2	0.2	0.56	0.26	0.3
	Construction	5.5	4.0	1.5	6.7	4.9	1.8	6.6	4.4	2.2
	Wholesale, Retail Trade, Restaurants, and Hotels	14.1	6.6	7.5	16.0	7.4	8.6	13.9	6.4	7.5
	Transport, Storage, and Communication	5.3	3.0	2.3	4.8	2.8	2.0	5.9	3.1	2.8
	Financing, Insurance, Real Estate, and Business Services	1.0	0.3	0.7	1.2	0.4	0.8	1.4	0.5	0.9
	Community, Social, and Personal Services	13.7	7.0	6.7	10.1	5.1	5.0	10.4	5.1	5.3
	Activities Extraterritorial Organisations and Bodies	0.04	0.03	0.01	0.01	-	0.01	0.02	0.02	0.01

Source: Pakistan Bureau of Statistics, *Labour Force Survey*, Islamabad, Statistics Division, Government of Pakistan, various years.

Table 6Q: Percentage Distribution of Employed Persons 10 Years of Age and Over by Major Industry Division (1982–83 to 1997–98)

Major Industry Division	2014–15				
	All Areas	Rural		Urban	
	Total	Male	Female	Male	Female
Agriculture, Forestry, Hunting, and Fishing	42.3	24.2	16.5	1.2	0.4
Mining and Quarrying	0.16	0.13	-	0.03	-
Manufacturing	15.3	5.3	2.1	6.8	1.2
Electricity, Gas, and Water	0.81	0.3	0	0.5	0.01
Construction	7.31	4.89	0.04	2.37	0.01
Wholesale, Retail Trade, Restaurants, and Hotels	14.64	6.25	0.17	8.07	0.15
Transport, Storage, and Communication	7.01	3.67	0.02	3.28	0.04
Financing, Insurance, Real Estate, and Business Services	1.42	0.4	0.01	0.96	0.03
Community, Social, and Personal Services	11.05	4.38	1.06	4.1	1.51
Activities by Extraterritorial Organisations and Bodies	0.02	0.02	-	0.01	-

Source: Pakistan Bureau of Statistics, *Labour Force Survey 2014–15*, Islamabad, Statistics Division, Government of Pakistan, 2015.

Table 6R: Percentage Distribution of Employed Persons 10 Years of Age and Over by
Major Industry Division (Sindh)
(2014–15)

| Major Industry Division | 2014–15 | | | | |
| | All Areas | Rural | | Urban | |
	Total	Male	Female	Male	Female
Agriculture, Forestry, Hunting, and Fishing	39.3	27.2	10.2	1.6	0.27
Mining and Quarrying	0.11	0.09	-	0.01	0.01
Manufacturing	15.2	2.7	0.61	11.0	0.89
Electricity, Gas, and Water	1.4	0.42	0.01	0.94	0.04
Construction	7.00	3.5	0.01	3.5	0.02
Wholesale, Retail Trade, Restaurants, and Hotels	15.8	4.0	0.04	11.8	0.03
Transport, Storage, and Communication	8.4	3.1	0.02	5.3	0.06
Financing, Insurance, Real Estate and Business Services	1.8	0.14	0	1.6	0.06
Community, Social, and Personal Services	11.0	3.7	0.3	5.8	1.3
Activities Extraterritorial Organisations and Bodies	0.01	-	-	0.01	-

Source: Pakistan Bureau of Statistics, *Labour Force Survey 2014–15*, Islamabad, Statistics Division, Government of Pakistan, 2015.

Table 6S: Percentage Distribution of Employed Persons 10 Years of Age and Over by
Major Industry Division (Punjab)
(2014–15)

| Major Industry Division | All Areas | Rural | | Urban | |
	Total	Male	Female	Male	Female
Agriculture, Forestry, Hunting, and Fishing	44.7	22.9	20.3	1.12	0.44
Mining and Quarrying	0.07	0.05	-	0.02	-
Manufacturing	16.5	6.4	2.4	6.2	1.5
Electricity, Gas, and Water	0.56	0.26	0.01	0.3	0
Construction	6.6	4.4	0.04	2.2	0.01
Wholesale, Retail Trade, Restaurants, and Hotels	13.9	6.1	0.24	7.3	0.22
Transport, Storage, and Communication	5.9	3.0	0.03	2.8	0.04
Financing, Insurance, Real Estate, and Business Services	1.4	0.52	0.01	0.9	0.04
Community, Social, and Personal Services	10.4	3.8	1.4	3.6	1.8
Activities Extraterritorial Organisations and Bodies	0.02	0.02	-	0.01	-

Source: Pakistan Bureau of Statistics, *Labour Force Survey 2014–15*, Islamabad, Statistics Division, Government of Pakistan, 2015.

Table 6T: Percentage of Employed Persons Who Worked for at least 35 Hours (Pakistan)
(1997–98 to 2014–15)

	All Areas			Rural			Urban		
	Total	Male	Female	Total	Male	Female	Total	Male	Female
1997–98	86.5	78.9	7.5	83.7	75.0	8.7	92.3	88.0	4.7
2005–06	83.7	72.7	11.0	80.3	67.7	12.6	91.1	83.9	7.2
2010–11	84.8	62.4	13.5	81.7	65.8	16.0	92.3	84.7	7.6
2014–15	86.5	72	14.5	82.9	65.8	17.1	94.5	86.1	8.3

Source: Pakistan Bureau of Statistics, *Labour Force Survey*, Islamabad, Statistics Division, Government of Pakistan, various years.

Table 6U: Percentage of Employed Persons Who Worked for at least 35 Hours (Sindh)
(1997–98 to 2014–15)

	All Areas			Rural			Urban		
	Total	Male	Female	Total	Male	Female	Total	Male	Female
1997–98	85.0	75.2	9.8	82.4	71.1	11.2	92.0	86.1	5.9
2005–06	81.8	68.2	13.6	78.8	63.5	15.3	89.6	80.4	9.3
2010–11	83.3	67.6	15.7	80.4	62.2	18.2	90.7	81.5	9.2
2014–15	84.5	58.4	17.1	81.0	61.4	10.6	93.1	82.6	10.6

Source: Pakistan Bureau of Statistics, *Labour Force Survey*, Islamabad, Statistics Division, Government of Pakistan, various years.

Chapter 7

Table 7A: Distribution of Monthly Consumption Expenditure in Sindh (Rural/Urban) (2007–08 to 2013–14)

	Years	Bottom 20%	Second 20%	Third 20%	Fourth 20%	Top 20%
Rural	2007–08	20.2	25.0	22.9	19.8	12.1
	2010–11	18.8	21.8	24.2	19.1	16.1
	2011–12	21.1	23.9	21.1	18.2	15.8
	2013–14	25.4	27.2	20.1	16.2	11.0
Urban	2007–08	2.8	7.5	11.0	17.9	60.9
	2010–11	3.4	6.9	11.2	20.4	58.2
	2011–12	2.3	5.9	12.1	20.5	59.3
	2013–14	3.8	8.4	13.6	24.2	50.1

Source: Pakistan Bureau of Statistics, *Household Integrated Economic Survey*, Islamabad, Government of Pakistan, various years.

Table 7B: Average Per Capita Income Estimates (in PKR Thousand) (2010–11)

	Per Capita Income	Ratios of Urban to Rural Per Capita Incomes
Pakistan	21,785.4	1.5
Urban	27,663.8	
Rural	18,712.7	
Punjab	22,859.3	1.5
Urban	29,492.0	
Rural	19,778.3	
Sindh	20,606.2	1.6
Urban	25,253.1	
Rural	15,499.7	

Source: Pakistan Bureau of Statistics, *Household Integrated Economic Survey 2010–11*, Islamabad, Statistics Division, Government of Pakistan, 2011.

Chapter 8

Table 8A: Area of Major Crops in Pakistan, Punjab, and Sindh (in Thousand Hectare)
(1947–48 to 2015–16)

Year	Pakistan				Punjab				Sindh			
	Wheat	Sugarcane	Rice	Cotton	Wheat	Sugarcane	Rice	Cotton	Wheat	Sugarcane	Rice	Cotton
1947–48	3953.7	189.4	789.9	1236.7	2900.7	133.5	268.7	897.2	538.2	6.9	486.4	337.1
1957–58	4608.5	397.4	1073.2	1407.1	3483.1	318.1	406.3	978.9	529.7	18.6	626.4	423.7
1967–68	5983.2	503.8	1419.6	1785.0	4292.4	367.5	667.7	1329.8	845.8	60.3	660.4	452.0
1970–71	5977.5	636.2	1503.4	1733.2	4389.5	475.9	738.1	1308.3	837.3	79.3	671.4	422.9
1975–76	6110.6	699.8	1709.7	1851.6	4471.7	499.8	877.3	1384.0	797.4	105.6	731.1	464.8
1980–81	6983.7	824.7	1933.1	2108.5	4978.0	597.5	1061.9	1506.2	1030.0	136.0	763.8	599.0
1985–86	7403.3	779.8	1863.2	2364.1	5343.0	510.6	1113.3	1745.8	1030.8	177.4	585.7	615.4
1990–91	7911.4	883.8	2112.7	2662.2	5711.7	525.6	1261.8	2124.6	1053.5	253.1	679.9	536.6
1995–96	8376.5	963.1	2161.8	2997.3	5973.5	605.6	1327.8	2463.3	1106.4	254.4	642.3	529.3
2000–01	8180.8	960.8	2376.6	2927.5	6255.5	615.5	1627.2	2386.9	810.7	238.8	540.1	523.6
2005–06	8447.9	907.3	2621.4	3103.0	6483.4	625.2	1762.4	2426.0	933.2	183.2	593.2	637.1
2010–11	8900.7	987.6	2365.3	2689.1	6691.0	672.2	1766.8	2200.6	1144.4	226.4	361.2	457.0
2015–16	9224**	1131**	2739**	2902**	6981*	710.6*	1877.7*	2323*	1106.9*	316.7*	781.7*	596.2*

* Provincial figures have been taken for 2014–15 and are from Ministry of National Food Security and Research, *Agricultural Statistics 2014–15*, Islamabad, Government of Pakistan, n.d.

** National figures were taken from Finance Division, *Pakistan Economic Survey 2016–17*, Islamabad, Ministry of Finance, Government of Pakistan, 2017.

Source: Bureau of Statistics, *Development Statistics of Sindh*, Karachi, Planning and Development Department, Government of Sindh, various years; Ministry of Food, Agriculture and Livestock, *50 Years of Agricultural Statistics in Pakistan (1947–2000)*, Islamabad, Government of Pakistan, 2007; Pakistan Bureau of Statistics, *Agricultural Statistics of Pakistan (2011–2012)*, Islamabad, Statistics Division, Government of Sindh, 2013.

Table 8B: Yield of Major Crops in Pakistan, Punjab, Sindh (Kgs Per Hectare)
(1947–48 to 2015–16)

Year	Pakistan				Punjab				Sindh			
	Wheat	Sugarcane	Rice	Cotton	Wheat	Sugarcane	Rice	Cotton	Wheat	Sugarcane	Rice	Cotton
1947–48	848.5	28,776.2	867.0	312.9	903.9	29,237.3	922.3	286.5	719.4	27,946.1	848.5	382.7
1957–58	774.7	27,946.1	802.4	411.6	802.4	25,917.0	747.1	392.3	811.6	52,664.1	839.3	456.7
1967–68	1,055.8	37,077.0	1,042.2	285.9	1,156.9	35,509.1	1,152.9	295.1	983.7	39,198.3	950.0	285.9
1970–71	1,079.0	36,400.0	1,466.0	314.0	1,125.0	35,300.0	1,328.0	304.0	1,337.0	40,900.0	1,669.0	341.0
1975–76	1,420.0	36,400.0	1,531.0	277.0	1,467.0	36,600.0	1,374.0	249.0	1,568.0	33,900.0	1,762.0	360.0
1980–81	1,643.0	39,200.0	1,616.0	339.0	1,677.0	39,700.0	1,282.0	315.0	1,889.0	36,800.0	2,029.0	399.0
1985–86	1,881.0	35,700.0	1,567.0	515.0	1,952.0	32,800.0	1,328.0	555.0	2,107.0	42,500.0	1,830.0	401.0
1990–91	1,841.0	40,700.0	1,546.0	615.0	1,841.0	37,400.0	1,089.0	681.0	2,159.0	46,700.0	2,148.0	356.0
1995–96	2,018.0	47,000.0	1,835.0	601.0	2,081.0	44,400.0	1,358.0	602.0	2,119.0	54,000.0	2,642.0	598.0
2000–01	2,325.0	45,400.0	2,021.0	624.0	2,465.0	43,400.0	1,584.0	609.0	2,746.0	50,500.0	3,115.0	696.0
2005–06	2,519.0	49,200.0	2,116.0	714.0	2,588.0	46,300.0	1,804.0	720.0	2,947.0	61,400.0	2,901.0	707.0
2010–11	2,833.0	56,000.0	2,039.0	725.0	2,846.0	55,800.0	1,915.0	607.0	3,747.0	60,800.0	3,406.0	1,316.0
2015–16	2,779.0**	57,897.0**	2,483.0**	582.0**	2,762.0*	57,800.0*	1,943.0*	752.0*	3,318.0*	52,500.0*	3,393.0*	1019*

*Provincial figures have been taken for 2014–15 and are from Ministry of National Food Security and Research, *Agricultural Statistics 2014–15*, Islamabad, Government of Pakistan, n.d.

** National Figures Were Taken from Finance Division, *Pakistan Economic Survey 2016–17*, Islamabad, Ministry of Finance, Government of Pakistan, 2017.

Source: Bureau of Statistics, *Development Statistics of Sindh*, Karachi, Planning and Development Department, Government of Sindh, various years; Ministry of Food, Agriculture and Livestock, *50 Years of Agricultural Statistics in Pakistan (1947–2000)*, Islamabad, Government of Pakistan, 2007; Pakistan Bureau of Statistics, *Agricultural Statistics of Pakistan (2011–2012)*, Islamabad, Statistics Division, Government of Sindh, 2013.

Table 8C: Production of Major Crops in Pakistan, Punjab, and Sindh (in Thousand Tonne)
(1947–48 to 2015–16)

Year	Pakistan				Punjab				Sindh			
	Wheat	Sugarcane	Rice	Cotton	Wheat	Sugarcane	Rice	Cotton	Wheat	Sugarcane	Rice	Cotton
1947–48	3,301.0	5,442.0	682.0	188.1	2,595.0	3,909.0	249.0	125.0	381.0	192.0	412.0	62.6
1957–58	3,508.0	11,116.0	862.0	290.5	2,750.0	8,243.0	303.0	192.2	422.0	985.0	524.0	98.0
1967–68	6,317.0	18,365.0	1,475.0	495.1	4,966.0	13,040.0	770.0	368.5	832.0	2,362.0	629.0	126.0
1970–71	6,476.3	23,167.0	2,199.7	542.4	4,948.2	16,834.0	982.5	396.3	1,120.7	3,239.2	1,122.7	145.7
1975–76	8,690.7	25,546.7	2,617.5	513.8	6,571.6	18,267.7	1,207.2	344.4	1,320.9	3,586.4	1,286.1	168.8
1980–81	11,474.6	32,359.4	3,123.2	714.6	8,350.0	23,733.0	1,361.7	474.4	1,945.8	5,007.3	1,549.9	239.3
1985–86	13,923.0	27,856.3	2,918.9	1,216.9	10,431.6	16,755.1	1,478.2	969.7	2,172.2	7,533.2	1,071.7	246.5
1990–91	14,565.0	35,988.7	3,260.8	1,637.6	10,513.8	19,633.4	1,422.3	1,446.0	2,274.5	11,815.6	1,433.4	191.3
1995–96	16,907.4	45,229.7	3,966.5	1,802.1	12,430.0	26,880.0	1,803.0	1,483.2	2,344.8	13,737.2	1,697.2	316.6
2000–01	19,023.7	43,606.3	4,802.6	1,825.4	15,419.0	26,740.0	2,577.0	1,452.6	2,226.5	12,049.7	1,682.3	364.2
2005–06	21,276.8	44,665.5	5,547.2	2,214.4	16,776.0	28,968.6	3,179.6	1,746.5	2,750.3	11,243.4	1,721.0	450.4
2010–11	25,213.8	55,308.5	4,823.3	1,949.3	19,041.0	37,481.0	3,384.0	1,335.9	4,287.9	13,766.4	1,230.3	601.6
2015–16	25,633.0**	65,482.0**	68,01.0**	1,686.78**	19,281.9*	41,074.3*	3,648*	1,748*	3,672.2*	16,613.8*	2,652.6*	607.6*

*Provincial figures have been taken for 2014–15 and are from Ministry of National Food Security and Research, *Agricultural Statistics 2014–15*, Islamabad, Government of Pakistan, n.d.

** National figures were taken from Finance Division, *Pakistan Economic Survey 2016–17*, Islamabad, Ministry of Finance, Government of Pakistan, 2017.

Source: Sindh Bureau of Statistics, *Development Statistics of Sindh*, Karachi, Planning and Development Department, Government of Sindh, various years; Ministry of Food, Agriculture and Livestock, *50 Years of Agricultural Statistics in Pakistan (1947–2000)*, Islamabad, Government of Pakistan, 2007; Pakistan Bureau of Statistics, *Agricultural Statistics of Pakistan (2011–2012)*, Islamabad, Statistics Division, Government of Sindh, 2013; Ministry of National Food Security and Research, *Agricultural Year Book 2015–16*, Islamabad, Government of Pakistan, p. 20.

Table 8D: Area of Fruits in Pakistan, Punjab, and Sindh (in Thousand Hectare)
(1947–48 to 2015–16)

Year	Pakistan					Punjab					Sindh				
	Mango	Citrus	Dates	Guava	Banana	Mango	Citrus	Dates	Guava	Banana	Mango	Citrus	Dates	Guava	Banana
1947–48	-	-	-	-	-	-	-	-	-	-	-	-	-	-	-
1957–58	20.6	14.3	-	3.2	1.2	6.1	10.8	-	1.8	0.10	14.6	2.6	-	0.97	1.2
1967–68	53.0	49.1	18.6	13.4	4.9	19.4	42.9	4.1	9.3	0.10	33.2	3.8	5.6	3.2	4.5
1970–71	55.4	43.6	18.5	11.3	9.1	24.3	39.0	4.0	6.2	0.20	30.7	1.8	5.7	3.6	8.4
1975–76	54.0	63.1	22.5	16.9	14.1	21.8	58.4	7.7	12.7	0.80	31.7	2.1	5.5	2.7	12.8
1980–81	57.5	94.5	24.2	17.3	14.8	22.2	87.7	5.6	13.4	1.1	34.4	3.3	9.0	2.0	13.2
1985–86	75.3	147.9	38.7	42.1	16.1	41.0	141.9	13.0	37.1	2.2	33.5	3.8	15.4	2.7	13.3
1990–91	85.4	173.3	42.0	46.9	22.7	47.7	164.8	14.3	41.1	2.3	36.7	4.1	17.2	2.9	19.8
1995–96	89.5	193.6	73.9	55.5	24.7	48.0	183.3	11.1	48.1	2.6	39.5	4.2	19.7	3.5	21.3
2000–01	97.0	198.7	78.6	63.4	30.3	49.5	187.6	11.4	51.6	2.6	45.0	3.9	23.1	6.9	26.3
2005–06	156.6	192.3	82.0	61.8	32.5	104.9	182.1	5.8	49.4	1.7	50.0	4.4	26.7	8.1	29.7
2010–11	171.9	194.5	90.1	64.0	29.6	111.9	184.2	5.8	49.3	1.2	59.2	4.9	32.7	9.8	26.8
2015–16	170.2	458.8	97.1	70.0	48.7	107.0	448.4	5.8	57.6	0.2	62.3	4.9	36.5	8.5	26.7

Source: Bureau of Statistics, *Development Statistics of Sindh*, Karachi, Planning and Development Department, Government of Sindh, various years; Ministry of Food, Agriculture and Livestock, *50 Years of Agricultural Statistics in Pakistan (1947–2000)*, Islamabad, Government of Pakistan, 2007; Pakistan Bureau of Statistics, *Agricultural Statistics of Pakistan (2011–2012)*, Islamabad, Statistics Division, Government of Sindh, 2013.

Table 8E: Production of Fruits in Pakistan, Punjab, and Sindh (in Thousand Tonne)
(1947–48 to 2015–16)

Year	Pakistan					Punjab					Sindh				
	Mango	Citrus	Dates	Guava	Banana	Mango	Citrus	Dates	Guava	Banana	Mango	Citrus	Dates	Guava	Banana
1947–48	-	-	-	-	-	-	-	-	-	-	-	-	-	-	-
1957–58	130.0	-	-	-	-	102.0	-	-	-	-	28.0	-	-	-	-
1958–59	-	106.0	16.0	16.0	2.0	-	89.0	11.0	10.0	1.0	-	4.0	2.0	4.0	1.0
1967–68	608.0	-	-	-	-	249.0	-	-	-	-	356.0	-	-	-	-
1968–69	-	484.8	148.4	30.5	51.0	-	456.2	17.9	21.9	1.0	-	11.6	49.4	7.2	48.0
1970–71	519.2	445.3	157.3	88.3	88.6	320.1	399.7	30.3	51.8	1.2	197.1	22.7	51.5	25.7	74.3
1975–76	595.7	671.1	168.3	136.1	126.4	350.7	625.7	35.3	81.4	3.9	241.7	25.1	50.1	45.8	114.4
1980–81	546.6	926.2	194.1	123.6	130.8	273.9	864.3	41.4	95.4	5.8	267.4	34.3	68.7	12.2	117.5
1985–86	713.4	1,434.4	268.6	312.7	139.9	450.6	1,368.8	87.1	274.6	11.4	257.2	34.2	90.4	16.3	118.2

Year	Pakistan					Punjab					Sindh				
	Mango	Citrus	Dates	Guava	Banana	Mango	Citrus	Dates	Guava	Banana	Mango	Citrus	Dates	Guava	Banana
1990–91	776.0	1,609.1	287.3	115.9	201.8	501.0	1,538.5	96.2	101.3	12.1	267.1	34.8	97.6	7.2	179.2
1995–96	907.8	1,959.5	532.5	136.7	81.7	598.8	1,872.3	91.5	118.9	16.1	291.7	35.1	31.5	8.7	51.5
2000–01	989.8	1,897.7	612.5	525.5	139.5	634.9	1,813.0	97.9	438.4	17.4	340.3	30.9	266.0	47.3	101.7
2005–06	1,753.9	2,458.4	496.6	552.2	163.5	1,391.8	2,385.2	42.6	446.0	11.4	352.4	29.5	192.8	60.2	134.7
2010–11	1,885.9	1,982.2	522.2	546.6	141.2	1,503.2	1,912.0	42.5	420.1	10.3	381.3	30.9	268.6	75.4	113.4
2015–16	1,645.8	2,341.7	467.7	522.7	134.7	1,228.0	2,273.7	42.9	414.7	1.4	404.2	29.5	201.2	63.6	112.4

Source: Sindh Bureau of Statistics, *Development Statistics of Sindh*, Karachi, Planning and Development Department, Government of Sindh, various years; Ministry of Food, Agriculture and Livestock, *50 Years of Agricultural Statistics in Pakistan (1947–2000)*, Islamabad, Government of Pakistan, 2007; Pakistan Bureau of Statistics, *Agricultural Statistics of Pakistan (2011–2012)*, Islamabad, Statistics Division, Government of Sindh, 2013; Ministry of National Food Security and Research, *Agricultural Year Book 2015–16*, Islamabad, Government of Pakistan, 2017.

Table 8F: Area of Vegetables in Pakistan, Punjab, and Sindh (in Thousand Hectare)
(1947–48 to 2015–16)

Year	Pakistan			Punjab			Sindh		
	Chillies	Onion	Tomatoes	Chillies	Onion	Tomatoes	Chillies	Onion	Tomatoes
1947–48	8.9	7.3	-	7.7	4.5	-	0.4	2.0	-
1957–58	28.7	10.1	-	21.9	5.7	-	1.2	2.8	-
1967–68	24.3	22.3	-	17.8	10.5	-	4.1	7.7	-
1970–71	30.8	23.4	-	15.8	10.1	-	12.6	8.1	-
1975–76	51.4	30.8	-	27.0	9.7	-	22.1	16.0	-
1980–81	64.0	43.2	11.6	19.0	12.2	1.5	43.1	23.5	5.4
1985–86	68.4	49.4	15.8	18.9	14.1	1.3	45.6	26.1	6.0
1990–91	61.6	58.6	20.8	17.1	16.1	3.4	40.6	26.1	5.8
1995–96	86.2	77.9	28.1	13.8	20.0	4.4	67.9	32.8	6.3
2000–01	84.5	105.6	27.9	10.3	23.1	4.4	72.1	51.8	6.1
2005–06	64.6	148.7	46.2	5.8	32.6	5.3	55.4	66.1	9.4
2010–11	63.6	147.6	52.3	5.1	44.7	6.7	52.8	63.2	14.6
2015–16	63.1	136	61.9	5.7	44.7	7.4	52.8	51.7	27.9

Source: Bureau of Statistics, *Development Statistics of Sindh*, Karachi, Planning and Development Department, Government of Sindh, various years; Ministry of Food, Agriculture and Livestock, *50 Years of Agricultural Statistics in Pakistan (1947–2000)*, Islamabad, Government of Pakistan, 2007; Pakistan Bureau of Statistics, *Agricultural Statistics of Pakistan (2011–2012)*, Islamabad, Statistics Division, Government of Sindh, 2013; Ministry of National Food Security and Research, *Agricultural Year Book 2015–16*, Islamabad, Government of Pakistan, 2017.

Table 8G: Production of Vegetables in Pakistan, Punjab, and Sindh (in Thousand Tonne)
(1947–48 to 2015–16)

Year	Pakistan			Punjab			Sindh		
	Chillies	Onion	Tomatoes	Chillies	Onion	Tomatoes	Chillies	Onion	Tomatoes
1947–48	8.2	56.0	-	7.0	46.0	-	0.2	5.0	-
1957–58	26.0	80.0	-	20.6	58.0	-	1.3	12.0	-
1967–68	31.0	209.0	-	24.0	118.0	-	4.0	53.0	-
1970–71	42.2	246.9	-	22.0	121.9	-	18.1	61.0	-
1975–76	79.3	322.7	-	40.8	118.3	-	36.2	135.6	-
1980–81	106.2	447.6	92.1	30.8	140.2	19.0	73.0	206.1	22.4
1985–86	98.8	558.5	150.0	31.8	163.3	15.8	61.6	270.4	27.4
1990–91	100.9	702.4	213.5	27.7	157.9	49.5	67.0	270.4	28.3
1995–96	135.8	1,097.6	304.6	22.0	212.1	64.1	107.0	425.2	32.2
2000–01	174.6	1,563.3	268.6	18.6	251.3	60.8	153.0	739.3	32.9
2005–06	122.9	2,055.7	468.1	9.3	306.4	64.6	108.8	833.5	48.3
2010–11	171.8	1,939.6	529.6	8.0	367.9	87.8	158.2	861.5	114.8
2015–16	140.0	1,736.5	587.1	9.1	328.2	106.2	124.3	692.3	206.5

Source: Sindh Bureau of Statistics, *Development Statistics of Sindh*, Karachi, Planning and Development Department, Government of Sindh, various years; Ministry of Food, Agriculture and Livestock, *50 Years of Agricultural Statistics in Pakistan (1947–2000)*, Islamabad, Government of Pakistan, 2007; Pakistan Bureau of Statistics, *Agricultural Statistics of Pakistan (2011–2012)*, Islamabad, Statistics Division, Government of Sindh, 2013; Ministry of National Food Security and Research, *Agricultural Year Book 2015–16*, Islamabad, Government of Pakistan, 2017.

Table 8H: Area of Vegetables in Pakistan, Punjab, and Sindh (in Thousand Hectare)
(1947–48 to 2015–16)

Year	Pakistan		Punjab		Sindh	
	Garlic	Potato	Garlic	Potato	Garlic	Potato
1947–48	0.40	2.8	0.30	2.4	0.10	-
1957–58	1.2	12.6	0.90	6.9	0.10	0.40
1967–68	2.0	20.2	0.80	11.7	0.40	1.6
1970–71	1.9	20.2	0.90	12.1	0.20	1.6
1975–76	1.8	28.6	0.80	17.6	0.20	1.4
1980–81	4.9	38.0	0.90	25.6	2.4	0.90
1985–86	6.6	62.9	1.8	45.9	2.5	1.0
1990–91	6.3	72.0	1.9	56.5	2.2	0.60

Year	Pakistan		Punjab		Sindh	
	Garlic	Potato	Garlic	Potato	Garlic	Potato
1995–96	9.1	78.9	2.6	63.1	2.8	0.60
2000–01	7.9	101.5	2.6	87.1	2.4	0.80
2005–06	7.0	117.4	2.8	104.5	2.0	0.30
2010–11	6.6	159.4	3.1	148.1	0.90	0.40
2015–16	8.1	175.8	3.1	165.5	1.3	0.60

Source: Bureau of Statistics, *Development Statistics of Sindh*, Karachi, Planning and Development Department, Government of Sindh, various years; Ministry of Food, Agriculture and Livestock, *50 Years of Agricultural Statistics in Pakistan (1947–2000)*, Islamabad, Government of Pakistan, 2007; Pakistan Bureau of Statistics, *Agricultural Statistics of Pakistan (2011–2012)*, Islamabad, Statistics Division, Government of Sindh, 2013; Ministry of National Food Security and Research, *Agricultural Year Book 2015–16*, Islamabad, Government of Pakistan, 2017.

Table 8I: Production of Vegetables in Pakistan, Punjab, and Sindh (in Thousand Tonne)
(1947–48 to 2015–16)

Year	Pakistan		Punjab		Sindh	
	Garlic	Potato	Garlic	Potato	Garlic	Potato
1947–48	3.0	28.0	2.5	24.0	0.10	1.0
1957–58	8.0	99.0	5.5	79.0	0.90	1.0
1967–68	21.0	186.0	8.2	116.0	4.3	11.0
1970–71	17.6	228.6	10.8	134.1	1.9	13.2
1975–76	16.7	320.8	9.8	223.9	1.7	11.8
1980–81	36.9	394.3	10.0	277.4	14.8	7.9
1985–86	54.4	618.4	20.3	427.8	15.1	8.6
1990–91	53.4	751.3	18.5	571.7	13.9	5.1
1995–96	82.5	1,063.5	26.8	851.6	17.0	6.1
2000–01	63.9	1,665.7	22.2	1,479.7	12.0	7.5
2005–06	57.3	1,567.9	22.9	1,389.6	10.4	2.6
2010–11	55.3	3,491.7	24.3	3,339.9	4.6	3.9
2015–16	70.9	3962.4	24.1	3,811.1	6.8	4.9

Source: Bureau of Statistics, *Development Statistics of Sindh*, Karachi, Planning and Development Department, Government of Sindh, various years; Ministry of Food, Agriculture and Livestock, *50 Years of Agricultural Statistics in Pakistan (1947–2000)*, Islamabad, Government of Pakistan, 2007; Pakistan Bureau of Statistics, *Agricultural Statistics of Pakistan (2011–2012)*, Islamabad, Statistics Division, Government of Sindh, 2013; Ministry of National Food Security and Research, *Agricultural Year Book 2015–16*, Islamabad, Government of Pakistan, 2017.

Table 8J: Area of Lentils in Pakistan, Punjab, and Sindh (in Thousand Hectare)
(1947–48 to 2015–16)

Year	Pakistan				Punjab				Sindh			
	Gram	Mash	Masoor	Moong	Gram	Mash	Masoor	Moong	Gram	Mash	Masoor	Moong
1947–48	881.8	53.1	68.3	86.0	631.3	49.9	65.6	73.0	182.1	1.4	2.7	4.2
1957–58	1,213.3	33.2	79.7	66.3	887.5	29.8	71.5	56.5	211.7	0.89	6.2	2.0
1967–68	1,120.6	45.4	78.3	81.0	796.8	40.2	66.5	54.0	212.1	1.5	7.2	11.7
1970–71	914.2	39.9	61.0	70.0	634.9	34.3	50.5	45.9	196.3	1.7	6.6	9.2
1975–76	1,068.4	58.4	72.9	67.3	759.7	49.4	55.9	45.8	201.1	3.6	12.1	10.9
1980–81	842.9	68.2	72.7	67.0	642.1	61.3	57.6	43.7	127.3	1.9	12.3	11.1
1985–86	1,033.3	79.2	57.4	104.2	821.1	72.7	44.7	74.4	94.1	2.4	9.9	14.8
1990–91	1,091.5	79.1	63.4	141.6	863.5	72.1	46.2	118.9	84.4	1.9	9.8	9.7
1995–96	1,118.9	58.2	63.5	199.1	896.6	52.3	43.9	174.1	87.0	1.9	11.7	9.8
2000–01	905.0	45.8	46.1	219.2	780.1	40.4	28.2	198.5	51.9	2.0	10.2	8.1
2005–06	1,028.9	34.6	33.9	208.5	900.1	30.4	20.7	189.3	51.4	1.4	4.8	5.5
2010–11	1,053.8	24.5	26.1	137.4	964.6	18.0	16.5	105.5	19.7	0.50	3.3	10.8
2015–16	940.3	19.2	49.4	146.2	854.9	15.3	11.3	133.1	15.6	0.30	1.4	2.2

Source: Bureau of Statistics, *Development Statistics of Sindh*, Karachi, Planning and Development Department, Government of Sindh, various years; Ministry of Food, Agriculture and Livestock, *50 Years of Agricultural Statistics in Pakistan (1947–2000)*, Islamabad, Government of Pakistan, 2007; Pakistan Bureau of Statistics, *Agricultural Statistics of Pakistan (2011–2012)*, Islamabad, Statistics Division, Government of Sindh, 2013; Ministry of National Food Security and Research, *Agricultural Year Book 2015–16*, Islamabad, Government of Pakistan, 2017.

Table 8K: Production of Lentils in Pakistan, Punjab, and Sindh (in Thousand Tonne)
(1947–48 to 2015–16)

Year	Pakistan				Punjab				Sindh			
	Gram	Mash	Masoor	Moong	Gram	Mash	Masoor	Moong	Gram	Mash	Masoor	Moong
1947–48	465.0	25.0	35.9	30.4	351.0	23.5	33.0	25.0	86.0	0.70	2.9	1.1
1957–58	653.0	11.9	30.6	21.2	516.0	10.6	27.8	18.0	111.0	0.30	2.2	0.90
1967–68	473.0	22.3	25.1	34.9	340.0	19.8	21.4	25.2	116.0	0.50	2.8	3.6
1970–71	493.8	19.6	21.1	32.8	343.4	17.2	17.3	21.2	130.1	0.60	2.9	4.1
1975–76	601.4	29.8	28.3	31.9	427.5	25.8	21.0	22.0	136.5	1.5	5.2	4.9
1980–81	336.9	33.9	29.5	31.8	240.1	29.1	22.8	20.6	88.7	0.80	5.4	4.8
1985–86	586.2	48.8	31.3	48.8	440.2	42.7	25.2	33.2	76.0	1.0	4.5	6.3
1990–91	531.0	36.8	27.2	56.5	403.0	32.1	18.8	45.3	67.2	0.80	4.5	4.0
1995–96	679.6	28.4	34.0	90.6	537.5	24.6	22.7	77.2	72.8	0.80	5.6	4.0

Year	Pakistan				Punjab				Sindh			
	Gram	Mash	Masoor	Moong	Gram	Mash	Masoor	Moong	Gram	Mash	Masoor	Moong
2000–01	397.0	25.7	26.9	104.5	334.8	22.0	17.9	92.7	42.3	0.90	5.5	3.7
2005–06	479.5	16.5	17.9	113.9	382.5	13.6	10.1	101.8	45.8	0.80	3.0	3.2
2010–11	496.0	11.3	13.3	76.2	429.1	6.5	7.7	60.0	20.5	0.30	2.0	4.4
2015–16	286.2	8.5	7.9	102.1	227.2	4.9	4.1	93.9	14.4	0.10	0.9	0.9

Source: Bureau of Statistics, *Development Statistics of Sindh*, Karachi, Planning and Development Department, Government of Sindh, various years; Ministry of Food, Agriculture and Livestock, *50 Years of Agricultural Statistics in Pakistan (1947–2000)*, Islamabad, Government of Pakistan, 2007; Pakistan Bureau of Statistics, *Agricultural Statistics of Pakistan (2011–2012)*, Islamabad, Statistics Division, Government of Sindh, 2013; Ministry of National Food Security and Research, *Agricultural Year Book 2015–16*, Islamabad, Government of Pakistan, 2017.

Table 8L: Consumption of Fertiliser (in Thousand Tonne)
(1957–58 to 2015–16)

Year	Pakistan	Punjab	Sindh
1957–58	16.4	N/A	N/A
1967–68	190.4	130.9	36.8
1970–71	283.2	253.0	35.9
1975–76	543.8	370.1	137.9
1980–81	1,079.5	697.7	303.3
1985–86	1,511.7	1,050.9	368.8
1990–91	1,892.9	1,347.6	423.6
1995–96	2,515.0	1,836.5	520.5
2000–01	2,964.0	2,060.1	667.5
2005–06	3,804.1	2,672.4	799.7
2010–11	3,932.8	2,803.6	761.3
20115–16	3,699.3	2,502.6	947.3

Source: Bureau of Statistics, *Development Statistics of Sindh*, Karachi, Planning and Development Department, Government of Sindh, various years; Ministry of Food, Agriculture and Livestock, *50 Years of Agricultural Statistics in Pakistan (1947–2000)*, Islamabad, Government of Pakistan, 2007; Pakistan Bureau of Statistics, *Agricultural Statistics of Pakistan (2011–2012)*, Islamabad, Statistics Division, Government of Sindh, 2013; Ministry of National Food Security and Research, *Agricultural Year Book 2015–16*, Islamabad, Government of Pakistan, 2017.

Table 8M: Production of Chemical Fertilisers (Pakistan)
(1957–58 to 2015–16)

Year	Tonnes
1957–58	7,958
1967–68	182,217
1970–71	374,826
1975–76	830,588
1980–81	1,623,000
1985–86	2,749,000
1990–91	2,964,000
1995–96	4,166,000
2000–01	5,127,000
2005–06	6,227,000
2010–11	6,797,000
2015–16	8,015,000

Source: Bureau of Statistics, *Development Statistics of Sindh*, Karachi, Planning and Development Department, Government of Sindh, various years; Ministry of Food, Agriculture and Livestock, *50 Years of Agricultural Statistics in Pakistan (1947–2000)*, Islamabad, Government of Pakistan, 2007; Pakistan Bureau of Statistics, *Agricultural Statistics of Pakistan (2011–2012)*, Islamabad, Statistics Division, Government of Pakistan, 2013; Ministry of National Food Security and Research, *Agricultural Year Book 2015–16*, Islamabad, Government of Pakistan, 2017.

Table 8N: Usage of Fertilisers, Manures, Pesticides, and Herbicides, by Size of Farm in Pakistan (2011–12)

Size of Farm (Acres)	Total Farms	Fertilisers and Manure		Fertilisers Only		Manure Only		Pesticides		Herbicides	
		Number	Percentage of Total	Number	Percentage of Total	Number	Percentage of Total	Number	Percentage of Total	Number	Percentage of Total
Private Farms – Total	8264,480	2,445,133	30	3,350,976	41	222,983	3	2,752,139	33	2,452,938	30
Under 1.0	1,254,718	318,929	25	287,162	23	74,735	6	181,169	14	168,305	13
1.0 to Under 2.5	2,342,233	734,465	31	967,757	41	64,803	3	768,083	33	685,695	29
2.5 to Under 5.0	1,753,995	550,442	31	782,128	45	40,878	2	650,289	37	574,463	33
5.0 to Under 7.5	1,131,990	332,211	29	520,675	46	18,578	2	441,547	39	399,568	35
7.5 to Under 12.5	917,007	268,870	29	421,638	46	14,437	3	374,874	41	333,752	36
12.5 to Under 25	560,748	157,582	28	246,406	44	7,027	1	225,734	40	201,502	36
25 to Under 50	210,907	57,421	27	90,342	43	1,852	1	79,105	38	65,536	31
500 to Under 100	66,874	18,597	28	26,225	39	472	1	23,780	36	17,608	26
100 to Under 150	12,607	3,849	31	4,753	38	87	1	3,982	32	3,393	27
150 and Above	13,438	2,788	21	3,902	29	117	1	3,567	27	3,133	23

Source: Pakistan Bureau of Statistics, *Agricultural Statistics of Pakistan (2011–2012)*, Islamabad, Statistics Division, Government of Pakistan, 2013.

Table 8O: Usage of Fertilisers, Manures, Pesticides, and Herbicides by Size of Farm in Punjab (2011–12)

Size of Farms	Total Farms	Fertilisers and Manure		Fertilisers Only		Manure Only		Pesticides		Herbicides	
		Number	Percentage of Total	Number	Percentage of Total	Number	Percentage of Total	Number	Percentage of Total	Number	Percentage of Total
Private Farms – Total	5,249,804	1,558,007	30	2,378,435	45	85,660	2	2,166,626	41	2,110,697	40
Under 1.0	729,981	143,911	20	207,849	28	31,492	4	142,198	19	139,794	19
1.0 to Under 2.5	1,473,113	451,323	31	680,476	46	19,926	1	606,149	41	581,969	40
2.5 to Under 5.0	1,144,394	365,343	32	544,367	48	16,293	1	503,817	44	493,171	43
5.0 to Under 7.5	792,342	243,387	31	396,533	50	8,957	1	365,046	46	360,607	46
7.5 to Under 12.5	620,261	199,128	32	309,827	50	6,195	1	303,073	49	295,040	48
12.5 to Under 25	359,408	112,984	31	173,351	48	2,307	1	178,407	50	173,503	48
25 to Under 50	96,590	31,149	32	48,880	51	380	-	49,835	52	49,692	51
500 to Under 100	25,015	7,940	32	12,298	49	104	-	13,399	54	12,192	49

Source: Pakistan Bureau of Statistics, *Agricultural Statistics of Pakistan (2011–2012)*, Islamabad, Statistics Division, Government of Pakistan, 2013.

Table 8P: Usage of Fertilisers, Manures, Pesticides, and Herbicides by Size of Farm in Sindh (2011–12)

Size of Farm (Acres)	Total Farms	Fertilisers and Manure		Fertilisers Only		Manure Only		Pesticides		Herbicides	
		Number	Percentage of Total	Number	Percentage of Total	Number	Percentage of Total	Number	Percentage of Total	Number	Percentage of Total
Private Farms – Total	1,115,285	187,513	17	671,206	60	13,587	1	412,430	37	196,495	18
Under 1.0	41,640	3,344	8	18,616	45	1,366	3	11,364	27	5,279	13
1.0 to Under 2.5	305,589	47,283	15	195,751	64	4,391	1	115,457	38	64,223	21
2.5 to Under 5.0	282,248	47,224	17	181,502	64	4,019	1	110,336	39	51,368	18
5.0 to Under 7.5	159,335	24,860	16	93,746	59	1,572	1	53,187	33	22,521	14
7.5 to Under 12.5	138,060	21,819	16	82,088	59	1,105	1	51,692	37	21,448	16
12.5 to Under 25	97,700	19,943	20	53,253	55	657	1	35,701	37	16,281	17
25 to Under 50	64,040	15,419	24	32,545	51	412	1	24,435	38	10,492	16
500 to Under 100	21,102	5,939	28	11,192	53	57	-	8,212	39	3,636	17
100 to Under 150	3,182	957	30	1,348	42	7	-	1,069	34	508	16
150 and Above	2,393	732	31	1,158	48	3	-	971	41	748	31

Source: Pakistan Bureau of Statistics, *Agricultural Statistics of Pakistan (2011–2012)*, Islamabad, Statistics Division, Government of Pakistan, 2013.

Table 8Q: Sindh's Relative Percentage Share in Agriculture
(1947–48 to 2015–16)

	1947–48	1954–55	1970–71	1990–91	2000–01	2015–16	1947-48	1954-55	1970-71	1990-91	2000-01	2015/16
	Wheat						Cotton					
Area as a % of Pakistan's Total Area	13.6	11.7	14.0	13.3	12.9	12.2	27.3	30.1	24.4	20.2	17.0	24.2
Production as a % of Pakistan's Total Production	11.5	12.3	17.3	15.6	17.0	13.8	33.3	34.9	26.9	11.7	30.9	36.0
Yield as a % of Pakistan's Average Yield	84.8	104.9	123.9	117.3	132.3	119.4	122.1	116.1	108.6	57.9	140.1	175.1

	1947–48	1954–55	1970–71	1990–91	2000–01	2015–16	1947-48	1954-55	1970-71	1990-91	2000-01	2015-16
	Sugarcane						Rice					
Area as a % of Pakistan's Total Area	3.6	4.3	12.5	28.6	23.0	23.8	61.6	59.0	44.7	32.2	15.3	24.2
Production as a % of Pakistan's Total Production	3.5	4.7	14.0	32.8	24.9	21.0	60.4	62.3	51.0	44.0	25.5	39.0
Yield as a % of Pakistan's Average Yield	97.1	111.3	112.4	114.7	92.1	110.3	97.9	106.5	113.9	147.5	167.0	72.9

Source: Bureau of Statistics, *Development Statistics of Sindh*, Karachi, Planning and Development Department, Government of Sindh, various years; Ministry of Food, Agriculture and Livestock, *50 Years of Agricultural Statistics in Pakistan (1947–2000)*, Islamabad, Government of Pakistan, 2007; Pakistan Bureau of Statistics, *Agricultural Statistics of Pakistan (2011–2012)*, Islamabad, Statistics Division, Government of Sindh, 2013; Ministry of National Food Security and Research, *Agricultural Year Book 2015–16*, Islamabad, Government of Pakistan, 2017.

Table 8R: Percentage Change in Area of Major Crops in Pakistan, Punjab, and Sindh (1970–2015)

	Pakistan				Punjab				Sindh			
	Wheat	Sugarcane	Rice	Cotton	Wheat	Sugarcane	Rice	Cotton	Wheat	Sugarcane	Rice	Cotton
Percentage Increase 1970–90	32	39	41	54	30	10	71	62	26	219	1	27
Percentage Increase 1990–2010	13	12	12	1	17	28	40	4	9	-11	-47	-15
Percentage Increase 2010–15	4	15	16	8	4	6	6	6	-3	40	116	30
Percentage Increase 1947–2015	133	497	247	135	141	432	599	159	106	4,503	61	77
Percentage Increase 1970–2015	54	78	82	67	59	49	154	78	32	299	16	41

Source: Bureau of Statistics, *Development Statistics of Sindh*, Karachi, Planning and Development Department, Government of Sindh, various years; Ministry of Food, Agriculture and livestock, *50 Years of Agricultural Statistics in Pakistan (1947–2000)*, Islamabad, Government of Pakistan, 2007; Pakistan Bureau of Statistics, *Agricultural Statistics of Pakistan (2011–2012)*, Islamabad, Statistics Division, Government of Sindh, 2013; Ministry of National Food Security and Research, *Agricultural Year Book 2015–16*, Islamabad, Government of Pakistan, 2017.

Table 8S: Percentage Change in Production of Major Crops in Pakistan, Punjab, and Sindh (1970–2015)

	Pakistan				Punjab				Sindh			
	Wheat	Sugarcane	Rice	Cotton	Wheat	Sugarcane	Rice	Cotton	Wheat	Sugarcane	Rice	Cotton
Percentage Increase 1970–90	125	55	48	202	112	17	45	265	103	265	28	31
Percentage Increase 1990–2010	73	54	48	19	81	91	138	-8	89	17	-14	214
Percentage Increase 2010–15	2	18	41	-13	1	10	8	31	-14	21	116	1
Percentage Increase 1947–2015	677	1,103	897	797	643	951	1,365	1,298	864	8,553	544	871
Percentage Increase 1970–2015	296	183	209	211	290	144	271	341	228	413	136	317

Source: Bureau of Statistics, *Development Statistics of Sindh*, Karachi, Planning and Development Department, Government of Sindh, various years; Ministry of Food, Agriculture and Livestock, *50 Years of Agricultural Statistics in Pakistan (1947–2000)*, Islamabad, Government of Pakistan, 2007; Pakistan Bureau of Statistics, *Agricultural Statistics of Pakistan (2011–2012)*, Islamabad, Statistics Division, Government of Sindh, 2013; Ministry of National Food Security and Research, *Agricultural Year Book 2015–16*, Islamabad, Government of Pakistan, 2017.

Table 8T: Percentage Change in Yield of Major Crops in Pakistan, Punjab, and Sindh
(1970–2015)

	Pakistan				Punjab				Sindh			
	Wheat	Sugarcane	Rice	Cotton	Wheat	Sugarcane	Rice	Cotton	Wheat	Sugarcane	Rice	Cotton
Percentage Increase 1970–90	71	12	5	96	64	6	-18	124	61	14	29	4
Percentage Increase 1990–2010	54	38	32	18	55	49	76	-11	74	30	59	270
Percentage Increase 2010–15	-2	3	22	-20	-3	4	1	24	-11	-14	0	-23
Percentage Increase 1947–2015	228	101	186	86	206	98	111	163	361	88	300	166
Percentage Increase 1970–2015	158	59	69	85	146	64	46	147	148	28	103	199

Source: Bureau of Statistics, *Development Statistics of Sindh*, Karachi, Planning and Development Department, Government of Sindh, various years; Ministry of Food, Agriculture and Livestock, *50 Years of Agricultural Statistics in Pakistan (1947–2000)*, Islamabad, Government of Pakistan, 2007; Pakistan Bureau of Statistics, *Agricultural Statistics of Pakistan (2011–2012)*, Islamabad, Statistics Division, Government of Sindh, 2013; Ministry of National Food Security and Research, *Agricultural Year Book 2015–16*, Islamabad, Government of Pakistan, 2017.

Table 8U: Average Annual Growth Rate (Sindh)
(1947–48 to 2014–15)

Year	Rice			Wheat			Cotton			Sugarcane		
	Area	Production	Yield	Area	Production	Yield	Area	Production	Yield	Area	Production	Yield
1947–48 to 2014–15	60.7	543.8	299.9	105.7	863.8	361.2	76.9	870.7	166.3	4489.9	8553.0	88.2
1947–48 to 1954–55	16.2	24.8	7.6	-7.2	1.3	9.0	13.3	50.3	32.6	87.0	114.6	14.0
1954–55 to 1970–71	18.8	118.4	82.8	67.7	190.3	70.5	10.7	321.1	-32.8	514.7	686.2	28.6
1970–71 to 1989–90	-2.4	19.4	22.5	24.8	90.1	52.6	32.7	-52.6	-2.1	216.1	281.6	20.5
1990–91 to 2014–15	15.0	85.1	58.0	5.1	61.5	53.7	11.1	217.7	186.2	25.1	40.6	12.4

Source: Bureau of Statistics, *Development Statistics of Sindh*, Karachi, Planning and Development Department, Government of Sindh, various years; Ministry of Food, Agriculture and Livestock, *50 Years of Agricultural Statistics in Pakistan (1947–2000)*, Islamabad, Government of Pakistan, 2007; Pakistan Bureau of Statistics, *Agricultural Statistics of Pakistan (2011–2012)*, Islamabad, Statistics Division, Government of Sindh, 2013; Ministry of National Food Security and Research, *Agricultural Year Book 2015–16*, Islamabad, Government of Pakistan, 2017.

Chapter 12

Table 12A: Output of China Clay in Pakistan and Sindh (in Tonne)
(1970–71 to 2014–15)

Year	Pakistan	Sindh
1970–71	8,067	4,333
1975–76	N/A	N/A
1980–81	40,022	N/A
1985–86	21,288	443
1990–91	43,620	9,856
1995–96	43,031	20,916
2000–01	46,574	12,775
2005–06	53,051	10,071
2010–11	16,055	13,025
2014–15	18,956	6,744

Source: Pakistan Bureau of Statistics, *Pakistan Statistical Year Book*, Islamabad, Statistics Division, Government of Pakistan, various years.

Table 12B: Output of Fuller's Earth in Pakistan and Sindh (in Tonne)
(1970–71 to 2014–15)

Year	Pakistan	Sindh
1970–71	N/A	N/A
1975–76	22,643	17,501
1980–81	21,285	18,331
1985–86	10,222	6,299
1990–91	22,743	18,757
1995–96	18,033	10,666
2000–01	12,926	9,363
2005–06	16,209	9,486
2010–11	4,180	2,690
2014–15	8,005	4,219

Source: Pakistan Bureau of Statistics, *Pakistan Statistical Year Book*, Islamabad, Statistics Division, Government of Pakistan, various years.

Table 12C: Output of Limestone in Pakistan and Sindh (in Tonne)
(1970–71 to 2014–15)

Year	Pakistan	Sindh
1970–71	2,896,830	1,863,755
1975–76	2,968,382	2,110,671
1980–81	3,464,159	2,287,551
1985–86	6,312,512	2,815,733
1990–91	9,008,941	3,249,934
1995–96	9,739,869	3,329,502
2000–01	10,871,767	1,624,295
2005–06	18,391,364	2,573,266
2010–11	32,020,996	5,576,390
2014–15	39,819,401	6,921,736

Source: Pakistan Bureau of Statistics, *Pakistan Statistical Year Book*, Islamabad, Statistics Division, Government of Pakistan, various years.

Table 12D: Output of Silica Sand in Pakistan and Sindh (in Tonne)
(1970–71 to 2014–15)

Year	Pakistan	Sindh
1970–71	34,150	8,356
1975–76	43,135	28,457
1980–81	83,514	23,215
1985–86	193,408	136,406
1990–91	142,557	47,766
1995–96	184,203	57,139
2000–01	154,867	59,160
2005–06	411,047	66,823
2010–11	300,501	40,121
2014–15	269,156	22,607

Source: Pakistan Bureau of Statistics, *Pakistan Statistical Year Book*, Islamabad, Statistics Division, Government of Pakistan, various years.

Annexure Figures

Chapter 4

Figure 4A: Transition from Primary to Middle School (2015–16)

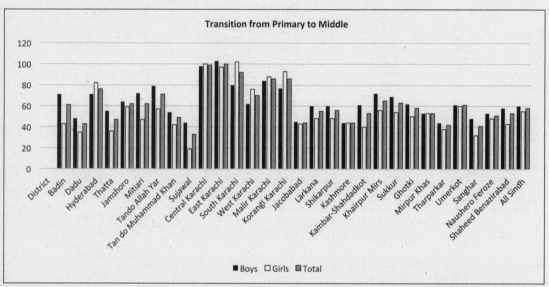

Source: Sindh Education Management Information System (SEMIS), *Sindh Education Profile 2015–16*, Karachi, Government of Sindh, n.d.

Chapter 11

Year	Y	Ln_Y
1970	109.28	4.694
1975	113.29	4.730
1980	139.23	4.936
1985	168.17	5.125
1990	161.66	5.085
1995	171.53	5.145
2000	174.83	5.164
2005	247.17	5.510
2010	279.81	5.634
2015*		

Method of forecasting used is that of *Average Growth Rate*, for example, there is some interval 'T' as shown below and we have to find the projected value for 2015 (denoted by *).

We first take the natural logarithm of the value y. Now, a scatter plot will be made between time and a trend-line will be made (using normal least square estimates).

Figure 11A:

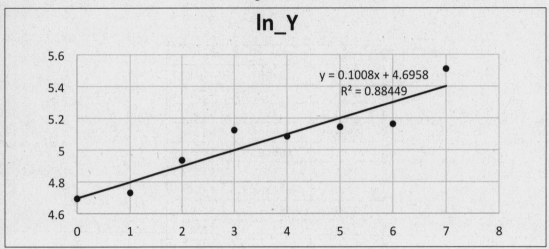

Now, best-fit average growth rate can be found from the slope i.e. 0.1008.

$$Avg.\,Growth\,Rate = e^{0.1008} - 1 = 0.1061$$

the missing value is found by multiplying the last known value of y with the (avg. growth rate + 1). in this case the last known value is for the year 2010 and is equal to 279.81. Hence, the value for 2015 can be found by the following equation:

$$Missing\,Value\,Y\,for\,2015 = 279.81(1 + 0.1061) = 309.5$$

Calculation for Compound Annual Growth Rate (CAGR):

$$CAGR = \left(\left(\frac{Ending\,Value}{Beginning\,Value}\right)^{\frac{1}{No.\,of\,years}} - 1\right) \times 100$$

Figure 11B: Industrial Zones and Clusters

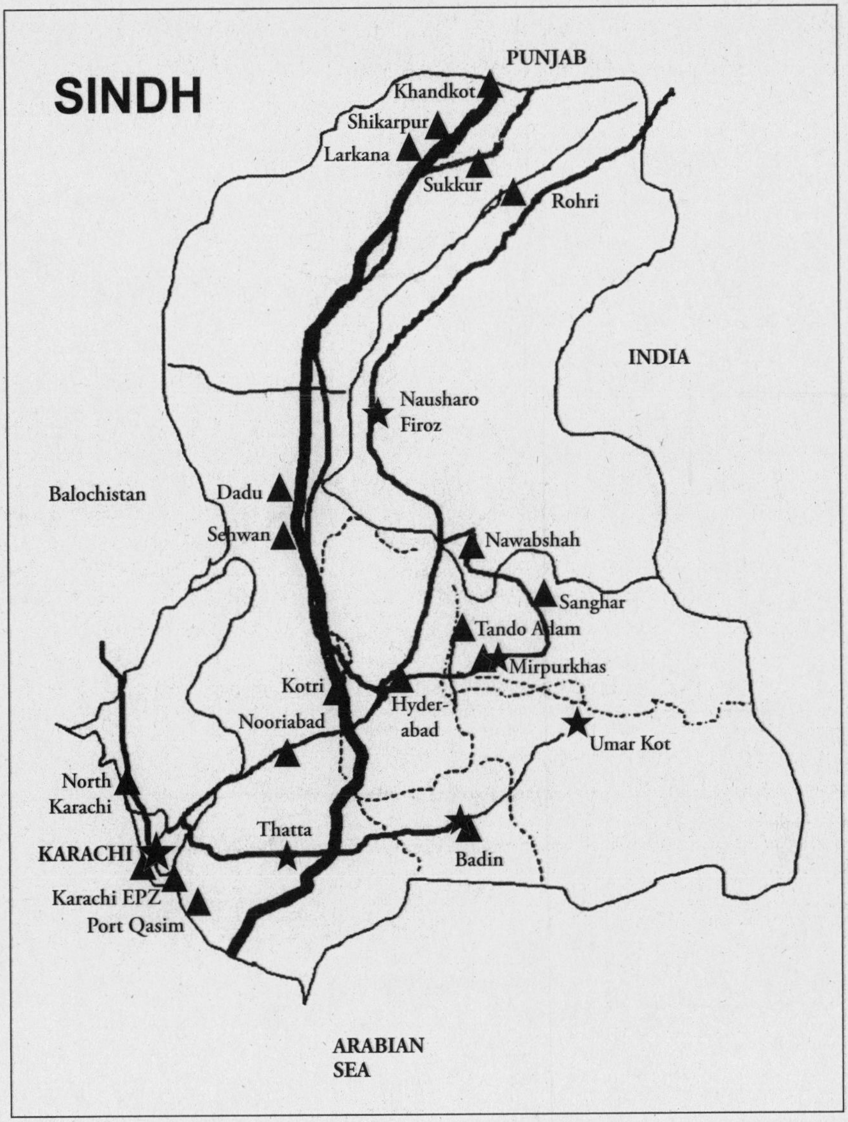

SINDH

PUNJAB

Khandkot
Shikarpur
Larkana
Sukkur
Rohri

INDIA

Nausharo
Firoz

Balochistan

Dadu
Sehwan

Nawabshah

Sanghar
Tando Adam
Mirpurkhas

Kotri
Nooriabad
Hyder-abad

Umar Kot

North
Karachi

KARACHI

Thatta

Badin

Karachi EPZ
Port Qasim

ARABIAN
SEA

Source: SMEDA and Pakistan Business Guide

Chapter 12

Figure 12A: Output of China Clay in Pakistan and Sindh (1970–71 to 2014–15)

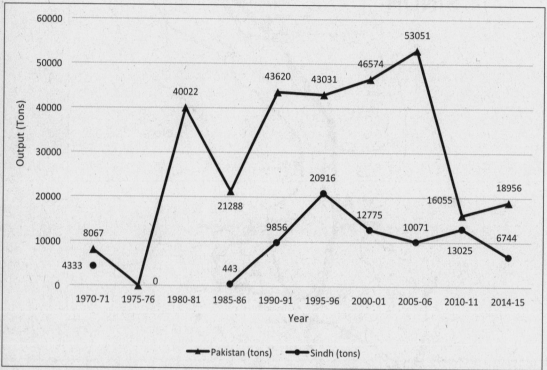

Source: Pakistan Bureau of Statistics, *Pakistan Statistical Year Book*, Islamabad, Statistics Division, Government of Pakistan, various years.

Figure 12B: Output of Fuller's Earth in Pakistan and Sindh (1970–71 to 2014–15)

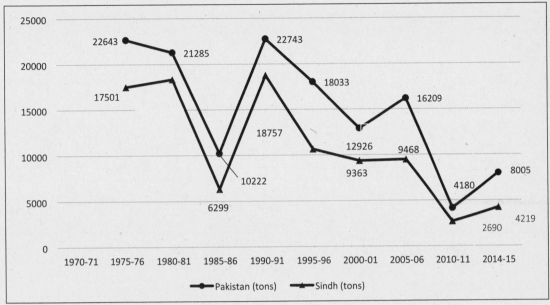

Source: Pakistan Bureau of Statistics, *Pakistan Statistical Year Book*, Islamabad, Statistics Division, Government of Pakistan, various years)

Figure12C: Output of Silica Sand in Pakistan and Sindh (1970–71 to 2014–15)

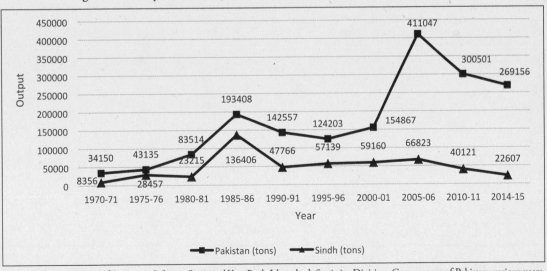

Source: Pakistan Bureau of Statistics, *Pakistan Statistical Year Book*, Islamabad, Statistics Division, Government of Pakistan, various years.

Figure 12D: Output of Limestone in Pakistan and Sindh (1970–71 to 2014–15)

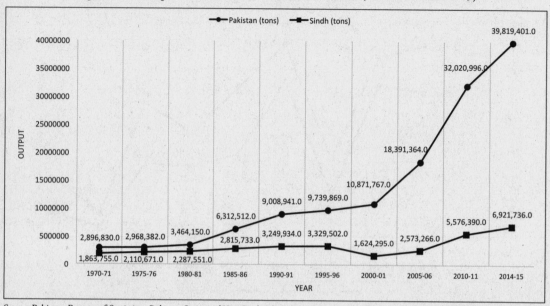

Soure: Pakistan Bureau of Statistics, *Pakistan Statistical Year Book*, Islamabad, Statistics Division, Government of Pakistan, various years.

Notes

Introduction

1. U. Mustafa, 'Fiscal Federalism in Pakistan: the 7th National Finance Commission Award and its Implications', *PIDE Working Paper* no. 73, Islamabad, Pakistan Institute of Development Economics, 2011, p. 2.
2. Government of Pakistan, '18th Amendment to the Constitution of Pakistan 1973', Islamabad, Senate Secretariat, 2010, accessed at: <http://www.na.gov.pk/uploads/documents/1302138356_934.pdf>.
3. Ibid.
4. For population demographics as of 2017: Pakistan Bureau of Statistics, *Provisional Summary Results of 6th Population and Housing Census*, Islamabad, Statistics Division, 2017, <http://www.pbscensus.gov.pk/sites/default/files/DISTRICT_WISE_CENSUS_RESULTS_CENSUS_2017.pdf> accessed 10 November 2017. For Information on the livelihood aspects, see Statistical Table 20: Pakistan Bureau of Statistics, 'Statistical Table', *Labour Force Survey 2014–15*, Islamabad, Statistics Division, Government of Pakistan, 2015, accessed at: <http://www.pbs.gov.pk/sites/default/files/Labour%20Force/publications/lfs2014_15/t20-pak.pdf>.
5. Ibid. The following figures will help provide an elaborate understanding on how little manufacturing and services sectors contribute to in rural Sindh: Manufacturing 3.27%, Construction 3.53%, Wholesale and Retail Trade 4.05%, Transport and Storage 2.22%, and Education 1.57%.
6. Pakistan Bureau of Statistics, *Provisional Summary Results of 6th Population And Housing Census*, Islamabad, Statistics Division, 2017, accessed at <http://www.pbscensus.gov.pk/sites/default/files/DISTRICT_WISE_CENSUS_RESULTS_CENSUS_2017.pdf>, 10 November 2017.
7. Ibid.
8. Pakistan Bureau of Statistics, 'Highlights', *Pakistan Economic Survey 2014–15*, Islamabad, Statistics Division, Government of Pakistan, 2015, p. VI.
9. Labour force of Sindh for the years 1998 and 2014 was 14.3 and 7.8 million respectively. The average increase in Sindh's labour force was 382,353 and the following formula was used: Labour force/number of years = (14.3-7.8)/17 = 382,352. Pakistan Bureau of Statistics, *Labour Force Survey*, Islamabad, Statistics Division, Government of Pakistan, various years; Labour force of Pakistan for the years 1998 and 2014 was 61.04 and 29.4 million respectively. Similarly, the annual average increase to the labour force of Pakistan was 1.44 million and the following calculations were made: Labour force/number of years = (61.04-29.4)/17 = 1.44 million. Source: For 2014 values: Pakistan Bureau of Statistics, *Pakistan Economic Survey 2014–15*, Islamabad, Statistics Division, Government of Pakistan, 2015; For 1998 values, Table 12.1. Pakistan Bureau of Statistics, *Statistical Supplement Economic Survey 1999–2000*, Islamabad, Statistics Division, Government of Pakistan, 1999) p. 253.
10. Table—Distribution of Employed Persons by Formal and Informal Sectors, Pakistan Bureau of Statistics, *Labour Force Survey*, Islamabad, Statistics Division, Government of Pakistan, 2015.
11. Table—Distribution of Employed Persons By Agriculture And Non-Agriculture Sector, Pakistan Bureau of Statistics, *Labour Force Survey*, Islamabad, Statistics Division, Government of Pakistan, various years.
12. Table—Labour Force Participation Rates and Unemployment Rates (Sindh). Ibid.
13. Dependents (2014–15) => Population out of labour force/total workforce = (191.71-61.04)/61.04=2.15 (Pakistan).
14. Table—Unemployment Rates, Ibid.

15. For Population: Pakistan Bureau of Statistics, *Provisional Summary Results of 6th Population And Housing Census*, Islamabad, Statistics Division, 2017, accessed 10 November 2017 <http://www.pbscensus.gov.pk/sites/default/files/DISTRICT_WISE_CENSUS_RESULTS_CENSUS_2017.pdf>; Source: Finance Division, *Annual Budget Statement*, Islamabad, Government of Pakistan, 2015.

16. Calculations pertaining to the fiscal year 2005 by Dr Hafiz Pasha in *Growth of the Provincial Economies*, Lahore, Institute for Policy Reforms, 2015.

17. Ibid.

18. According to the new poverty line of $1.9 a day, introduced by the World Bank Group; Household Integrated Economic Survey (HIES) and the World Bank staff calculations; Oxford Poverty and Development Initiative and the United Nations Development Programme, *Multidimensional Poverty in Pakistan*, 2016, Oxford Poverty and Development Initiative and the United Nations Development Programme, Islamabad.

19. Ibid.

20. For distribution of employed persons by agriculture and non-agriculture sector: Pakistan Bureau of Statistics, *Labour Force Survey*, Islamabad, Statistics Division, Government of Pakistan, various years; For an estimated PGDP of Sindh by Sector (1999–2000 to 2014–15): Pasha Hafiz, *Growth of The Provincial Economies*, Lahore, Institute for Policy Reforms, 2015.

21. The agriculture sector, as per the budget book definition, includes crop cultivation, forestry, fishing, and livestock.

22. *Report of the Land Reforms Commission for West Pakistan: January 1959*, Lahore, Superintendent Government Printing, West Pakistan, 1961.

23. Percentages have been calculated using the data under the following assumptions and limitations.
* Provincial figures have been taken from Ministry of National Food Security and Research, *Agricultural statistics 2014–15*, Islamabad, Government of Pakistan, n.d.
** National figures were taken from Finance Division, *Pakistan Economic Survey 2016–17*, Islamabad, Ministry of Finance, Government of Pakistan, 2017. Source: Bureau of Statistics, *Development Statistics of Sindh*, Karachi: Planning and Development Department, Government of Sindh, various years; Ministry of Food, Agriculture and Livestock, *50 Years of Agricultural Statistics in Pakistan (1947–2000)* Islamabad, Government of Pakistan, 2007; Pakistan Bureau of Statistics, *Agricultural Statistics of Pakistan (2011–2012)* Islamabad, Statistics of Division, Government of Sindh, 2013.

24. The latest data on roads, as of November 2017, is from 2012 and is available in the latest Development Statistics of Sindh. See Tables 12.04 and 12.05. Sindh Bureau of Statistics, *Development Statistics 2014*, Karachi, Government of Sindh, n.d.

25. A part of this deterioration comes from the fact that the impact of the 1999–2000 and 2001–02 droughts on agriculture was more severe in Sindh than elsewhere in the country.

26. Actual budget expenditure, Ministry of Finance, Pakistan, *Annual Budget Statement*, Government of Sindh, Finance Department, various years.

27. Pakistan Bureau of Statistics, *Population Census 2017*, Islamabad, Statistics Division, Government of Pakistan, 2017.

28. Sindh Bureau of Statistics and United Nations Children's Fund, *Multiple Indicator Cluster Survey 2015*, Karachi, Sindh Bureau of Statistics and United Nations Children's Fund.

29. Table 4.10, Sindh Education Management Information System (SEMIS), Reform Support Unit. n.d.; 'Sindh Education Profile 2015–16', Karachi, Education & Literacy Department, Government of Sindh.

Chapter 1
Land and People

1. Mumtaz Husain Pathan, *Arab Kingdom of Al-Mansurah in Sind*, Hyderabad, Institute of Sindhology, University of Sindh, 1974.

2. Maneckji B. Pithawalla, *Historical Geography of Sind*, Jamshoro, Institute of Sindhology, University of Sindh, 1978, p. 8.

3. H. T. Sorley, *The Gazetteer of West Pakistan: The Former Province of Sind Including Khairpur State*, Lahore, Gazetteer Cell, Board of Revenue, 1968, p. 1.

4. Ibid., p. 2.

5. A. W. Hughes, *A Gazetteer of the Province of Sindh*, London, George Bell and Sons, 1876.

6. Indus Ecoregion Programme, World Wildlife Fund, accessed at <http://foreverindus.org/>.

7. Mushtaqur Rahman, *A Geography of Sind Province, Pakistan*, Karachi, Oxford University Press, 1975, p. 332.

8. Sorley, *The Gazetteer of West Pakistan*.

9. Ibid., p. 5.

10. Ghulam Rasul, *Impacts of Climate Change*, Islamabad, Pakistan Meterological Department, Research and Development Division.
11. Sorley, *The Gazetteer of West Pakistan*, p. 273.
12. Ibid., p. 274.
13. Ibid., p. 288.
14. Rehman, *A Geography of Sind Province*, p. 54.

Chapter 2
Administrative and Economic History

1. S. Akbar Zaidi, *Issues in Pakistan's Economy: A Political Economy Perspective*, Karachi, Oxford University Press, p. 21.
2. C. L. Mariwalla, *Essays on British Policy Towards Sind up to the First Afghan War 1839*, Karachi, Indus Publications, 1982, p. 34.
3. H. T. Sorley, *The Gazetteer of West Pakistan: The Former Province of Sind Including Khairpur State*, Lahore, Gazetteer Cell, Board of Revenue, 1968, p. 141.
4. Ibid., p. 141.
5. Ibid., p. 155.
6. Ibid., p. 158.
7. Hamida Khuhro, *The Making of Modern Sindh: British Policy and Social Change in the Nineteenth Century*, GB, Indus Publications, 1978, p. 23.
8. Sorley, *The Gazetteer of West Pakistan*, p. 163.
9. Khuhro, *The Making of Modern Sindh*, p. 195.
10. Sorley, *The Gazetteer of West Pakistan*, p. 165.
11. Ibid., p. 168.
12. Ibid., p. 170.
13. Ibid., p. 171.
14. Mubarak Ali (ed.), *The English Factory in Sindh*, Lahore, Fiction House, 2005, p. 6.
15. Ibid., p. 7.
16. Ibid., p. 6.
17. Ibid., p. 7.
18. Ibid., p. 9.
19. Ibid., p. 11.
20. Ibid.
21. Ibid.
22. Ibid.
23. Ibid., p. 12.
24. Ibid., p. 13.
25. Ibid., p. 2.
26. Sorley, *The Gazetteer of West Pakistan*, p. 161.
27. Robert A. Huttenback, *British Relations with Sind 1799–1843: An Anatomy of Imperialism*, Karachi, Oxford University Press, 2007, p. xv.
28. Ibid., p. 2.
29. Ibid.
30. Sorley, *The Gazetteer of West Pakistan*, p. 175.
31. Albert Hughes, *A Gazetteer of the Province of Sind*, 2nd edn, London, George Bell and Sons, 1876, p. 85.
32. Hughes, *A Gazetteer of the Province of Sind*, p. 85.
33. Ibid., p. 86.
34. Mubarak Ali, *The English Factory*, p. 173.
35. Ibid.
36. Ibid., p. 174.
37. Sorley, *The Gazetteer of West Pakistan*, p. 213.
38. Ibid.
39. Ibid., p. 214.
40. Khuhro, *The Making of Modern Sindh*, p. 24.
41. Ibid.
42. Ibid., p. 23.
43. Ibid., p. 25.
44. Ibid., p. 54.
45. Zaidi, *Issues in Pakistan's Economy*, p. 15.
46. Khuhro, *The Making of Modern Sindh*, p. 55.
47. Ibid., p. 75.
48. Ibid., p. 64.
49. Ibid., p. 76.
50. Ibid., p. 107.
51. Sir Henry Bartle Edward Frere was a British colonial administrator who succeeded Pringle to become the second Commissioner of Sindh (1851–59).
52. Ibid., 58; using conversion 1 *biga* = 2,530 sq meters = 0.000977 sq mile; total area from Choksey, *The Story of Sind*, 46 being 23,500 sq miles in which only half is considered cultivable land.
53. Ibid., p. 80.
54. Ibid., p. 67.
55. Ibid., p. 71.
56. Richard Keith Pringle was a civil servant in the Bombay Presidency who assumed control of Sindh, following Napier's resignation, in a new office of 'Commissioner of Sindh' (1847–51).
57. Sorley, *The Gazetteer of West Pakistan*, p. 381.
58. Dayaram Gidumal, *History of Alienations in the Province of Sind: Compiled from the Jagir and Other Records in the Commissioner's Office on the Authority of Bombay Government, Resolution No. 12, Dated 2nd January 1878, Revenue Department*, vol. 1, Karachi, Commissioner's Press, 1886, p. 316.
59. Sorley, *The Gazetteer of West Pakistan*, p. 381.
60. Khuhro, *The Making of Modern Sindh*, p. 102.
61. Ibid., p. 106.
62. Sorley, *The Gazetteer of West Pakistan*, p. 382.

63. Ibid., p. 370.
64. Ibid.
65. Ibid., p. 371.
66. Ibid.
67. Ibid., p. 373.
68. Ibid., p. 527.
69. Ibid., p. 539.
70. Ibid., p. 540.
71. Ibid.
72. Ibid., p. 541.
73. Khuhro, *The Making of Modern Sindh*, p. 115.
74. R. D. Choksey, *The Story of Sind: An Economic and Social Survey (1843–1933)*, Karachi, Indus Publications, 2003, p. 25.
75. Sorley, *The Gazetteer of West Pakistan*, p. 362.
76. Khuhro, *The Making of Modern Sindh*, p. 117.
77. Choksey, *The Story of Sind*, p. 25.
78. Sorley, *The Gazetteer of West Pakistan*, p. 362.
79. Khuhro, *The Making of Modern Sindh*, p. 118.
80. Ibid., p. 117.
81. Sorley, *The Gazetteer of West Pakistan*, p. 363.
82. Ibid., p. 42.
83. Ibid., p. 131.
84. Ibid., p. 363.
85. David Cheesman, *Landlord Power and Rural Indebtedness in Colonial Sind, (1865–1901)*, Oxford, Routledge, 2013, p. 125.
86. Khuhro, *The Making of Modern Sindh*, p. 144.
87. Ibid., pp. 148–9.
88. Ibid., p. 153.
89. Sorley, *The Gazetteer of West Pakistan*, p. 364.
90. Ibid.
91. Ibid.
92. Ibid., p. 365.
93. Ibid.
94. Ibid.
95. Siddique G. Memon, *Sukkur Then and Now*, Oxford, Oxford University Press, 2000, p. 72.
96. Sorley, *The Gazetteer of West Pakistan*.
97. Ibid., p. 449.
98. Ibid., p. 467.
99. Ibid.
100. Mumtaz Hussain Pathan, *Sind: Arab Period (History of Sind series)*, n.p., Oxford University Press, 1978, p. 179.
101. Ibid.
102. Del Hoste quoted in Sorley, *The Gazetteer of West Pakistan*.
103. Ibid.
104. The then chief engineer Sukkur Barrage; the Barrage was completed during his tenure and his supervision. Later, he became Sir Arnold A. Musto.
105. 'Indus Basin Working Party', draft outline as prepared by the Indian Designer, comprehensive long-range plane for most effective utilisation of water resources of the Indus Basin, presented to the working party on October 6, 1953 at New Delhi.
      The Manager, Government of India Press, 1954, Annexure I Engineering Data, p.30 and Hundred Years of PWD p.35, quoted in Alloys Arthur Michel, *The Indus Rivers: A Study of Effects of Partition*, New Haven, Connecticut, Yale University Press, 1967, p. 119.
106. Ibid., p. 120.
107. Ibid., p. 121–2.
108. Sorley, *The Gazetteer of West Pakistan*, p. 447.
109. Ibid., p. 449.
110. Ibid.
111. Ibid.
112. Khuhro, *The Making of Modern Sindh*, p. 169.
113. Ibid.
114. Ibid, p. 170.
115. Sorley, *The Gazetteer of West Pakistan*, p. 453.
116. Khuhro, *The Making of Modern Sindh*, p. 171.
117. Sorley, *The Gazetteer of West Pakistan*, pp. 450–2.
118. Khuhro, *The Making of Modern Sindh*, p. 172.
119. Ibid., p. 173.
120. Ibid., p. 174.
121. Ibid., p. 176.
122. Ibid., p. 180.
123. Ibid., p. 184.
124. Ibid.
125. Ibid., p. 187; Choksey, *The Story of Sindh*, p. 58.
126. Khuhro, *The Making of Modern Sindh*, pp. 187–8.
127. Ibid., p. 189.
128. Sorley, *The Gazetteer of West Pakistan*, p. 456.
129. Khuhro, *The Making of Modern Sindh*, p. 190.
130. Sorley, *The Gazetteer of West Pakistan*, p. 455.
131. Ibid., p. 458.
132. Ibid.
133. Ibid., p. 471.
134. Sorley, *The Gazetteer of West Pakistan*, p. 532.
135. Ibid., p. 407.
136. Ibid., p. 408.
137. Choksey, *The Story of Sind*, p. 96.
138. Ibid., p. 91.
139. Ibid.
140. Ibid., p. 92.
141. Ibid., p. 93.

142. Ibid., p. 94.
143. Ibid.
144. Ibid.
145. Sorley, *The Gazetteer of West Pakistan*, p. 416.
146. Ibid.
147. Choksey, *The Story of Sind*, p. 97.
148. Ibid., p. 98.
149. Ibid., p. 97.
150. Ibid.
151. Ibid., pp. 97–8.
152. Ibid.
153. Ibid., p. 97.
154. Sorley, *The Gazetteer of West Pakistan*, p. 431.
155. Choksey, *The Story of Sind*, p. 97.
156. W. P. Andrew, *The Indus and its Provinces: Their Political and Commercial Importance Considered in Connexion with Improved Means of Communication*, Karachi, Indus Publications, 1986, p. 6.
157. Siddique Memon, *Sukkur Then and Now*, p. 101.
158. Khuhro, *The Making of Modern Sindh*, p. 208.
159. Ibid.
160. Ibid., p. 209.
161. Ibid., p. 210.
162. Ibid., p. 212.
163. Ibid., p. 214.
164. Ibid., p. 218.
165. Ibid., p. 214.
166. Ibid., p. 215.
167. Ibid.
168. Ibid., p. 216.
169. Ibid., p. 217.
170. Ibid.
171. Ibid., p. 219.
172. Ibid., p. 58.
173. Ibid., p. 65.
174. Ibid., p. 69.
175. Ibid.
176. Ibid., p. 58–9.
177. Ibid., p. 59.
178. Khuhro, *The Making of Modern Sindh*, p. 218.
179. Ibid., p. 219.
180. Ibid.
181. Ibid.
182. Andrew, *The Indus and its Provinces*, p. 67.
183. Khuhro, *The Making of Modern Sindh*, p. 220.
184. Ibid.
185. Ibid., p. 221.
186. Ibid., p. 229.
187. Ibid.
188. Ibid.
189. Ibid., p. 232
190. Ibid.
191. Ibid., p. 237.
192. Ibid.
193. Ibid., p. 234; from Rs. 8,000,000 in 1853–54 to Rs. 66, 628, 106 in 1863–64.
194. Sorley, *The Gazetteer of West Pakistan*, p. 648.
195. Ibid., p. 649.
196. Ibid., p. 648.
197. Ibid., p. 649.
198. Ibid.
199. Ibid., pp. 649–50.
200. Ibid., p. 650.
201. Ibid., p. 657.
202. Ibid., p. 658.
203. Ibid., p. 659.
204. Ibid.
205. Ibid.
206. Ibid., p. 660.
207. Ibid., p. 668.
208. Ibid.

Chapter 3
Population

1. Pakistan Bureau of Statistics, *District-wise Census Results 2017*, Islamabad, Statistics Division, Government of Pakistan, 2017, p. 1, accessed at: <http://www.pbscensus.gov.pk/sites/default/files/district_wise_census_results_census_2017.pdf>.
2. Ibid.
3. Ibid.
4. Population Census Organization, *1998 Population Census Report of Sindh*, Islamabad, Statistics Division, Government of Pakistan, 2000, p. 46.
5. Ibid., p. 73.
6. Agglomeration, in economics, pertains to benefits achieved due to the concentration of economic activities within a geographic region, usually cities, and the concentration of population as a result of it. Diseconomy of agglomeration is largely attributed to unplanned urbanization and migration and an uncontrolled sprawl caused by the economic activities.
7. Ibid., p. 89.
8. Ibid., p. 79.
9. Population Census Organization, *1981 Population Census Report of Sindh*, Islamabad, Statistics Division, Government of Pakistan, 1984; Pakistan Bureau of Statistics, *Demographic Indicators—Census 1998*,

Islamabad, Statistics Division, Government of Pakistan, n.d., p. 1.

10. Population Census Organization, *1998 Population Census Report of Sindh*, p. 90.

11. Ibid. As per the official definition by the Pakistan Bureau of Statistics: 'Crude activity rate is the currently active population expressed as a percentage of the total population in Pakistan, while a Refined activity rate is the currently active population expressed as a percentage of the population 10 years and above.' Source: Pakistan Bureau of Statistics <http://www.pbs.gov.pk/sites/default/files/Labour%20Force/publications/lfs2005_06/definitions.pdf>.

12. Ishrat Husain, *Pakistan: The Economy of an Elitist State*, Karachi, Oxford University Press, 1999, p. 4.

13. Hanif Samoon, *14-Year-Old Hindu Girl Married off to 55-Year Old Man Recovered by Thar Police*, Dawn, 10 March 2018, accessed at: <https://www.dawn.com/news/1394399>.

14. World Bank, 'What five Sahel countries learned from Bangladesh about strengthening population policies', 2016, accessed at <http://www.worldbank.org/en/news/feature/2016/06/23/what-five-sahel-countries-learned-from-bangladesh-about-strengthening-population-policies>.

15. According the Malthusian Theory by Thomas Robert Malthus.

16. Bureau of Statistics, *Development Statistics Report 2011*, Karachi, Planning and Development Department, Government of Sindh, p. 25.

17. Ibid.

Chapter 4
Education

1. Habibullah Siddiqui, *Education in Sindh Past, Present and Future*, Jamshoro, Institute of Sindhology, 1987, p. 308.

2. Ministry of Federal Education and Professional Training, *Pakistan Education Statistics 2015–16*, Islamabad, Government of Pakistan, 2017.

3. Sindh Education Management Information System (SEMIS), *Sindh Education Profile 2015–16*, Karachi, Government of Sindh, n.d., p. 9.

4. Ibid., p. 6.

5. United Nations Children's Education Fund (UNICEF), *Defining Quality in Education* (a paper presented by UNICEF at the International Working Group on education), Florence, 2000.

6. SEMIS, *Education Profile*, p. 24.

7. Ibid., pp. 30–3.

8. Ibid., p. 5.

9. Ministry of Federal Education and Professional Training, *Pakistan Education Statistics 2015–16*, Islamabad, Government of Pakistan, 2017.

10. Reform Support Unit (RSU), *Student Achievement Test (I to IV)*, Karachi, Government of Sindh, n.d.

11. SEMIS, *Education Profile*, p. 1.

12. 'Sukkur education dept gets biometric system', *Dawn*, 13 May 2015, accessed at <https://www.dawn.com/news/1181548>.

13. Reform Support Unit, Education and Literacy Department, Government of Sindh.

14. Tahir Andrabi, Jishnu Das, and Asim Khawaja, *The Rise of Private Schooling in Pakistan: Catering to the Urban Elite or Educating the Rural Poor* (World Bank and Harvard University, 2002) cited in Monazza Aslam, 'The Determinants of Student Achievement in Government and Private Schools in Pakistan', *The Pakistan Development Review*, 42/4, 2003, p. 841.

15. Ministry of Federal Education and Professional Training, *Education Statistics*, pp. 61–3.

16. Adam Curle, *Planning for education in Pakistan: a personal case study*, Harvard University Press, p. 69, quoted in Akhtar Hassan Malik, 'A Comparative Study of Elite English-Medium Schools, Public Schools and Islamic Madaris in Contemporary Pakistan', PhD thesis, University of Toronto, 2012, p. 4.

17. Malik, *Contemporary Pakistan*, p. 3.

18. Dawn E. Jones and Rodney. W. Jones, 'Nationalizing Education in Pakistan: Teacher's Associations and the People's Party', *Pacific Affairs*, 50/4, 1977–1978, p. 582 cited in Malik, *Contemporary Pakistan*, p. 4.

19. Ibid.

20. Education and Literacy Department, *Sindh Basic Education Program (SBEP)—Monitoring and Evaluation Manual*, Karachi, Government of Sindh, 2013.

21. Ravish Amjad, *A Comparative Analysis of the Role of the Private Sector as Education Providers in Improving Issues of Access and Quality*, Lahore, Development Policy Research Center, p. 7.

22. W. Steven Barnett, 'Long Term Effects of Early Childhood Programs on Cognitive and School Outcomes', *The Future of Children* 5/3, 1995, pp. 25–50.

23. Ibid.

24. SEMIS, *Education Profile*, p. 6 and p. 15.

25. The percentage of schools having less than five classrooms has been calculated from the figures for number of schools having classrooms in *Education Profile*, p. 27.

26. SEMIS, *Education Profile*, p. 44. Also, refer to table 4U in the annexure.

27. SEMIS, *Education Profile*, p. 46.

28. Ibid., p. 44.

29. Sindh Education Management Information System (SEMIS), *Sindh Education Profile* (various years), Karachi, Government of Sindh.

30. SEMIS, *Education Profile*, p. 1.

31. Ministry of Finance, *Economic Survey of Pakistan 2016–17*, Islamabad, Government of Pakistan, 2017, p. 172.

32. The total figure of Technical and Vocational institutions includes numbers of Azad Jammu and Kashmir, Gilgit-Baltistan, FATA and Islamabad. *See*, Ministry of Federal Education and Professional Training, *Education Statistics*, 55

33. Ibid.

34. Ibid., p. 67.

35. Ibid., p. 61.

36. SEMIS, *Education Profile*, p. 39.

37. Ministry of Federal Education and Professional Training, *Education Statistics*, p. 51.

Chapter 5
Health

1. World Health Organization, *Constitution of the World Health Organization*, Geneva, WHO, 1948.

2. United Nations System Standing Committee on Nutrition, *5th Report on the World Nutrition Situation: Nutrition for Improved Development Outcome*, Geneva, WHO, 2004.

3. Finance Division, 'Annual Budget Statement 2017–2018', Sindh Budget 2017–2018 Volume I, Karachi, Government of Sindh, 2017; Finance Division, 'Annual Budget Statement 2017–2018', Punjab Budget 2017–2018 Volume I, Lahore, Government of Punjab, 2017.

4. Z. A. Sathar, M. A. Wazir and M. Sadiq, *Prioritizing Family Planning for Achieving Provincial Maternal Child Health and Development Goals*, Islamabad, Population Council, 2014.

5. Ibid.

6. Ibid.

7. Bureau of Statistics, *Health Profile of Sindh: As on 01.01.2016*, Karachi, Planning and Development, Government of Sindh, 2016.

8. Ibid.

9. Government of Sindh, *Post War Development Schemes (1947–1952)*, Karachi, Government of Sindh, n.d.

10. According to 2014–15 Pakistan Standard of Living Measurement Survey (PSLM), in Sindh, total pre-natal consultation (percentage of married women aged 15–49 years) is 72 out of which 59 were in the rural areas and 87 in the urban areas.

11. Pakistan Standard of Living Measurement Survey (PSLM) Results: Percentage of pregnant women who had received at least one tetanus toxoid injection: Urban Areas: 68 (2004–05) 73 (2006–07) 81 (2008–09); Rural Areas: 34 (2004–05), 28 (2006–07), 39 (2008–09).

12. Narjis Rizvi and Sania Nishtar, 'Pakistan's Health Policy: Appropriateness and Relevance to Women's Health Needs', *Health Policy*, 88/2–3, 2008, pp. 269–81.

13. Sindh Health Budget Analysis and Budget Statements 2015.

14. Khawar Ghumman, 'One in Three Pakistanis Lacks Access to Adequately Nutritious Food', *Dawn*, 22 December 2015.

15. Ibid.

16. Planning and Development Department, *Development Initiatives and Achievements—Four Year Performance*, Karachi, Government of Sindh, 2010, p. 4.

17. 'Nutrition Landscape Information System (NLiS),' *World Health Organization*, 2017.

18. The figure for Karachi is an average of the city's five districts. Sindh Bureau of Statistics and United Nations International Children's Fund, *Multiple Indicator Cluster Survey 2014*, Karachi, Planning and Development Department, Government of Sindh, 2015, p. 219.

19. Ibid., p. 27.

20. Sindh Bureau of Statistics and United Nations International Children's Fund, *Multiple Indicator Cluster Survey 2014*, p. 110.

21. Ibid., p. 124.

22. Shehla Zaidi et al., 'Situation Analysis for Post Devolution,' *Researchgate.net*, 13, accessed 27 May 2017, <https://www.researchgate.net/publication/299391057_Situation_Analysis_for_Post_Devolution_Health_Sector_Strategy_of_Sindh_Province>.

23. Ibid.

24. Ibid., p. 194.
25. Ministry of National Health Services, *Sindh AIDS Control Programme 2014*, n.p., Government of Pakistan, 2014.
26. Hasan Mansoor, '994 new cases of HIV/Aids detected in Sindh this year', *Dawn.com*, 28 November 2014, <https://www.dawn.com/news/1147347>.
27. Zaidi et al., 'Situation Analysis for Post Devolution', p. 14.
28. Ibid., p. 16.
29. HANDS, *1st Situation Analysis Survey – Tharparkar*, Karachi, HANDS Pakistan Head Office, 2014.
30. Ibid.
31. United States Agency for International Development, *Pakistan Emergency Situational Analysis—A Profile of Tharparkar*, Washington DC, iMMAP, 2014.
32. Ibid.
33. World Health Organisation, *Pakistan—Tharparkar Crisis: Overview, Response, Damages*, Islamabad, WHO, 2014.
34. Zaidi et al., 'Situation Analysis for Post Devolution,' p. 16.
35. Ibid., p. 12.
36. Ikram Junaidi, 'Conditions in Teaching Hospitals Unsatisfactory, Says PMDC President', accessed 27 May 2017 <https://www.dawn.com/news/1240329>.
37. Technical Resource Facility, *Health Facility Assessment—Sindh Provincial Report, June 2012* <http://www.trfpakistan.org/LinkClick.aspx?filetick et=DVWqxBDJs6s%3D&tabid=2618>, accessed 4 November 2017.
38. World Health Organization, 'Pakistan, Tharparkar Crisis: Overview, Response, Damages', p. 39.
39. Annual Budget Statements 2007 and 2017.
40. Government of Sindh and United Nations Development Programme, 'Report on the status of the Millennium Development Goals Sindh', United Nations Development Programme Nepal, accessed 28 April 2017 <http://www.np.undp.org/content/dam/pakistan/docs/MDGs/UNDP-PK-MDG-SindhReport-2012.pdf>.

Chapter 6 ̇
Labour and Employment

1. Pakistan Bureau of Statistics, *Labour Force Survey 2014–15*, Islamabad, Statistics Division, Government of Pakistan, p. 10.
2. Zeenat Hisam, 'Labor Conditions', in *Status of Labor Rights in Pakistan 2015*, Karachi, Pakistan Institute of Labour Education and Research (PILER), 2016, p. 24.
3. Habib Khan Ghori, 'Sindh Assembly Bans Employment of Children Under 14', *Dawn*, 26 January 2017.
4. International Labour Organization (ILO), *Key Indicators of the Labour Market*, Geneva, 2016, p. 16.
5. Pakistan Bureau of Statistics, *Labour Force Survey 2014–15*, p. 12.
6. ILO, *Key Indicators*, p. 16.
7. Ibid., p. 17.
8. Pakistan Bureau of Statistics, *Labour Force Survey 2014–15*, p. 12.
9. Ibid., p. 115.
10. ILO, *Key Indicators*, p. 15.
11. Ibid., p. 16.
12. Hisam, *Labour Conditions*, p. 26.
13. Pakistan Bureau of Statistics, *Labour Force Survey 2014–15*, p. 261.
14. Hisam, *Labour Conditions*, p. 27.
15. Mi Zhou, *Minimum Wage Setting, Implementation and Working Conditions in the Formal and Informal Sectors of the Garment Industry in Pakistan, Key Indicators of the Labour Market*, Geneva, ILO, 2016, p. ix.
16. Provincial Assembly of Sindh, 'Sindh Minimum Wages Act', [website] (April 2016). <http://www.pas.gov.pk/uploads/acts/Sindh%20Act%20No.VIII%20of%202016.pdf>, accessed September 2016.
17. Zhou, *Minimum Wage Setting*, p. x.
18. Ibid.
19. Hisam, *Labour Conditions*, p. 27.
20. Ibid.
21. Ibid., p. 19.
22. Ibid., p. 20.
23. Ibid., pp. 19–20.
24. ILO, 'WOMEN—Only 2 per cent trade union members in the formal and invisible in the informal economy', *ILO.org* [website], August 2012. <http://www.ilo.org/islamabad/info/public/pr/WCMS_187903/lang--en/index.htm?ssSourceSiteId=asia/lang--en/index.htm>, accessed 5 March 2017.
25. Nadia Tahir, 'Gender Wage Differential in Pakistan', in *Status of Labour Rights in Pakistan 2015*, Karachi, PILER, 2016, p. 55.
26. Ministry of Finance, 'Population, Labour Force and Employment', in *Pakistan Economic Survey 2007–2008*, p. 195.
27. Ibid., p. 211.

28. Maliha H. Hussein et al., *Bonded Labour in Agriculture: A Rapid Assessment in Sindh and Balochistan*, Working Paper no. 26, Geneva, ILO, 2004, p. 4.

29. G. M. Arif, *Bonded Labour in Agriculture: A Rapid Assessment in Punjab and North West Frontier Province, Pakistan*, Geneva, ILO, 2004, p. 6.

30. Hussein et al., *A Rapid Assessment in Sindh and Balochistan*, p. 5.

31. Arif, *A Rapid Assessment in Punjab and North West Frontier Province, Pakistan*, p. 6.

32. Ibid.

33. Ibid., p. 30.

34. Ibid.

35. Ibid.

36. Hussein et al., *A Rapid Assessment in Sindh and Balochistan*, p. 17.

37. Arif, *A Rapid Assessment in Punjab and North West Frontier Province, Pakistan*, p. 29.

38. ILO, 'C029 - Forced Labour Convention, 1930 (No. 29)', *ILO.org* [website], <http://www.ilo.org/dyn/normlex/en/f?p=NORMLEXPUB:12100:0::NO::P12100_ILO_CODE:C029>, accessed 2 October 2016.

39. Ayaz Qureshi and Ali Khan, 'Introduction', *Bonded Labour in Pakistan*, Karachi, Oxford University Press, 2016, p. vii.

40. Walk Free Foundation, 'Global Slavery Index 2016', *Walk Free Foundation* (2017), <https://www.globalslaveryindex.org/index/> accessed 17 January 2017.

41. Ali Qazilbash, 'Beyond Setting at Liberty: a Legal Study of Bonded Labour in Pakistan', *Bonded Labour in Pakistan*, eds. Ayaz Quershi and Ali Khan, Karachi, Oxford University Press, 2016, p. 2.

42. Ibid., p. 1.

43. Ibid.

44. Ibid., p. 19.

45. Free Foundation, 'Global Slavery Index 2016'.

46. Qureshi and Khan, 'Introduction', p. xi.

47. Ibid.

48. Ibid., p. xiii.

49. Ibid., p. xi.

50. Ibid., p. xii.

51. Ali Khan, 'Bonded Labour without Bondage: Reconsidering the Links between Debt and Peshgi', *Bonded Labour in Pakistan*, eds. Ayaz Quershi and Ali Khan, Karachi, Oxford University Press, 2016, p. 163.

52. Ibid.

53. Ibid., pp. 182–3.

54. Ahmed Saleem, '*Peshgis* in the Mining Sector', *Bonded Labour in Pakistan*, eds. Ayaz Qurshi and Ali Khan, Karachi, Oxford University Press, 2016, pp. 52–3.

55. Sadaf Ahmed, 'Constructing a Culture of Fear: The Role of Gender Based Violence in Controlling Bonded Labour in Pakistan', *Bonded Labour in Pakistan*, eds. Ayaz Quershi and Ali Khan, Karachi, Oxford University Press, 2016, p. 147.

56. Hussein et al., *A Rapid Assessment in Sindh and Balochistan*, p. 15.

57. Ibid.

58. Ibid., p. 34.

59. Ibid., p. 16.

60. Ibid.

61. Ibid., p. 17.

62. Ibid., p. 16.

63. Ibid., p. 17.

64. Ibid., p. 19.

65. Ibid., p. 19.

66. Ibid.

67. Ibid., p. 37.

68. Ahmed, 'Constructing a Culture of Fear', p. 145.

69. Ibid.

70. Ibid., 150.

71. Ibid., 155.

72. Ibid., 15.

73. Ibid.

74. Ibid.

75. Ibid., pp. 159–60.

76. Radio Pakistan, 'Sindh Governor Accords Assent to 'Sindh Bonded Labour System' (Abolition) Act 2015,' Radio Pakistan [website], (June 2016), http://www.radio.gov.pk/23Jun-2016/sindh-governor-accords-assent-to-sindh-bonded-labour-system-act-2015, accessed 3 March 2017.

77. ILO, 'Observation (CEACR)—adopted 2013, published 103rd ILC session (2014): Freedom of Association and Protection of the Right to Organise Convention, 1948 (No. 87)', *ILO* [website], <http://www.ilo.org/dyn/normlex/en/f?p=1000:13100:0::NO:13100:P13100_COMMENT_ID:3149517>.

78. Provincial Assembly of Sindh, 'The Sindh Bonded Labour Abolition Act, 2015', *Open Parliament* [website].

Chapter 7
Poverty and Inequality

1. United Nations, Economic and Social Council, 'ACC Statement of Commitment for Action to Eradicate

Poverty (22 June 1998)', <https://www.unsceb.org/CEBPublicFiles/press/9818151e.pdf> accessed 22 June 2017.

2. Department of Economic and Social Affairs, 'World Summit for Social Development Programme of Action—Chapter 2', Copenhagen, United Nations, 1995, <http://www.un.org/esa/socdev/wssd/text-version/agreements/poach2.htm>, accessed 22 June 2017.

3. Michael B. Todaro and Stephen C. Smith, 'Poverty, Inequality, and Development,' *Economic Development*, Boston, Pearson Addison Wesley, 2012, p. 212.

4. The World Bank, *World Bank Forecasts Global Poverty to Fall Below 10% for First Time; Major Hurdles Remain in Goal to End Poverty by 2030*, 4 October 2015, <http://www.worldbank.org/en/news/press-release/2015/10/04/world-bank-forecasts-global-poverty-to-fall-below-10-for-first-time-major-hurdles-remain-in-goal-to-end-poverty-by-2030>, accessed 22 June 2017.

5. United Nations Development Programme, 'Eradicate Extreme Hunger and Poverty', <http://www.pk.undp.org/content/pakistan/en/home/post-2015/mdgoverview/overview/mdg1/>, accessed 22 June 2017.

6. Ali Raza Rizvi et al., *Sindh Strategy for Sustainable Development*, Karachi, International Union for Conservation of Nature and Natural Resources Pakistan, 2007, p. 14 <http://cmsdata.iucn.org/downloads/sssd.pdf>, accessed 22 June 2017.

7. Irfan Ghauri, 'Poverty Afflicts 75% People in Rural Sindh', *Express Tribune*, <https://tribune.com.pk/story/1135227/alarming-stats-poverty-afflicts-75-people-rural-sindh/>.

8. Oxford Poverty and Human Development Initiative and United Nations Development Program, *Multidimensional Poverty in Pakistan*, Islamabad, Planning Commision of Pakistan, 2015, p. 9, <http://www.pk.undp.org/content/dam/pakistan/docs/MPI/Multidimensional%20Poverty%20in%20Pakistan.pdf>, accessed 6 June 2017.

9. Ibid., p. 10.

10. Ibid., p. 9.

11. Ibid.

12. Ibid.

13. Ibid.

14. Oxford Poverty and Human Development Initiative and United Nations Development Program, *Multidimensional Poverty in Pakistan*, p. 9.

15. United Nations Development Program Pakistan, *Pakistan Human Development Index Report 2017*, <http://www.pk.undp.org/content/dam/pakistan/docs/HDR/HDI%20Report_2017.pdf>, accessed 20 January 2018.

16. Ibid.

17. Institute for Policy Reforms, *Human Development Index of the Provinces*, December 2017, <http://ipr.org.pk/wp-content/uploads/2017/03/HDI-of-Provinces.pdf>, accessed 20 January 2018.

18. Ibid., pp. 43–8.

19. Arif Naveed, Nazim Ali, *Clustered Deprivation: District Profile of Poverty in Pakistan*, Islamabad, SDPI, 2012, p. 26, <https://www.sdpi.org/publications/files/Clustered%20Deprivationdistrict%20profile%20of%20poverty%20in%20pakistan.pdf>, accessed 22 June 2017.

20. Social Policy and Development Centre, 'Poverty, Inequality and Social Inclusion', *The State of Social Development in Rural Pakistan 2012–13*, Karachi, 2014, p. 87, <http://www.spdc.org.pk/Data/Publication/PDF/AR%2012.pdf>, accessed 22 June 2017.

21. Ibid., p. 89.

22. Stephen Jenkins, 'The Measurement of Income Inequality,' *Economic Inequality and Poverty: International Perspectives*, New York, ME Sharpe, 1991, p. 4.

23. Amartya Sen, *On Economic Inequality*, New York, Oxford University Press, 1973, p. 1.

24. United Soviet Socialist Republics. Modern day Russia existed as USSR from 1917–89 and functioned under Communist principles laid out by Marx. The Soviets were particularly concerned with eradicating inequality.

25. The World Bank, *Poverty and Equity Database*, <http://databank.worldbank.org/data/reports.aspx?source=poverty-and-equity-database>.

26. Michael B. Todaro and Stephen C. Smith, 'Poverty, Inequality, and Development', p. 208.

27. Pakistan Bureau of Statistics, *Household Integrated Economic Survey*, Islamabad, Government of Pakistan, 2005–06, 2007–08, 2011–12, 2013–14.

28. *Household Integrated Economic Survey 2013–2014.*

29. *Household Integrated Economic Survey 2007–2008.*

30. Michael B. Todaro and Stephen C. Smith, 'Poverty, Inequality, and Development', p. 228.

31. Ishrat Husain, 'Poverty Reduction Strategy of Pakistan', <https://ishrathusain.iba.edu.pk/speeches/

povertyReduction/PovertyReduction-13-Oct-05.pdf>, accessed 22 June 2017.

32. Daron Acemoglu, Simon Johnson, and James Robinson, *Understanding Prosperity and Poverty: Geography, Institutions and the Reversal of Fortune*, New York, Oxford University Press, 2006, <http://www.econ.yale.edu/~cru2/book/Acemoglu-Johnson-Robinson-understanding%20poverty%20and%20 prosperi.pdf>, accessed 22 June 2017.

33. Muhammad Irfan, 'Poverty and Natural Resource Management in Pakistan', *The Pakistan Development Review* (46), p. 697.

34. Ibid.

Chapter 8
Agriculture

1. Agricultural Census Organization, *Agriculture Census 2010*, Islamabad, Statistics Division, Government of Pakistan, n.d.

2. Ibid.

3. Where cotton, wheat, rice and sugarcane are cash crops, the latter three, alongside chilies, onions, tomatoes, mangoes and dates, are also food crops.

4. Oxford Poverty and Human Development Initiative and United Nations Development Program, *Multidimensional Poverty in Pakistan*, Karachi, Planning Commission of Pakistan, 2015, pp. 66–7.

5. I. M. Bhatti and Atta H. Soomro, 'Agriculture in Sindh', *Agricultural Inputs and Field Crop Production in Sindh*, Hyderabad, Directorate General Agricultural Research Sindh, 1994, p. 2.

6. Rabi crops are crops grown in the winter months of October up until March.

7. Kharif crops are also referred to as monsoon crops and are cultivated and harvested during rainy (or monsoon) season, which lasts from April to October.

8. See tables summarising how and when crops are planted in Sindh, Pakistan Bureau of Statistics, *Approved Crop Calendar*, Karachi, Planning and Development Department, 2011.

9. H. T. Sorley, *The Gazetteer of West Pakistan: The Former Province of Sind Including Khairpur State*, Lahore, Gazetteer Cell, Board of Revenue, 1968.

10. Salim Ahmed, *Peasant Land Rights Movements of Pakistan*, Preliminary Draft Version, Islamabad, Sustainable Development Policy Institute, 2008, pp. 28–32.

11. Muhammad Ali Shaikh, *Report on Agriculture in Sindh—Issues and Options*, Karachi, SZABIST Centre for Information and Research, 2001.

12. Ahmed Feroz, 'Agrarian Change and Class Formation in Sindh', *Economic and Political Weekly*, 19/39, 1984, pp. 149–64.

13. A share labourer may be one who migrates, or is a nomad who helps on the farm during peak seasons. Often, such people are Baloch, Brohis, Kolis, Kacchi, Samat, Bugti, and Bhils from Sukkur and Guudu barrages, Kachhi plain, Bugti plain, Thar Desert, Rohri canal.

14. Ishrat Husain, 'Agriculture', *Economy of Modern Sind*, Jamshoro, Institute of Sindhology, 1981, p. 139.

15. Ibid.

16. Ibid., p. 132.

17. Husain, *Economy of Modern Sindh*, p. 135.

18. Ibid.

19. Ibid.

20. Dubari crop is grown on residual moisture of rice crop in kharif, e.g. oil seeds, peas, beans, wheat, and barley.

21. Wapda, 'Water Availability and Future Projections', *Lower Indus Development Study*, Hyderabad, Wapda, 1966.

22. Sindh Water Sector Improvement Project (WISP), *The Irrigation Management Strategy for Irrigated Agriculture of Sindh Province (Pakistan)*, Karachi, Planning and Development Department, Government of Sindh, 2016; Sindh Irrigation Management Strategy 2016.

23. Hydraulic data obtained from the Department of Irrigation, Government of Sindh.

24. Sindh Water Sector Improvement Project (WISP), *The Irrigation Management Strategy for Irrigated Agriculture of Sindh Province (Pakistan)*, Karachi, Planning and Development Department, Government of Sindh, 2016; Sindh Irrigation Management Strategy 2016.

25. Sindh Irrigation and Drainage Authority, *Master Plan for Left Bank of River Indus, Delta & Coastal Zone*, Karachi, Water Sector Improvement Project (WSIP), 2013.

26. 'Sindh Act No. XX of 1950,' *Sindh Laws* [Website], <http://sindhlaws.gov.pk/setup/publications/PUB-14-000123.pdf>, accessed 15 July 2017.

27. S. Akbar Zaidi, *Issues in Pakistan's Economy*, 3rd edition, Karachi, Oxford University Press, 2015, p. 36.

28. Ibid.

29. Sorley, *The Gazetteer of West Pakistan*, p. 738.

30. Mohammad, Aslam Chuadhary, 'Regional Agricultural Underdevelopment in Pakistan', *The Pakistan Development Review*, 33/4, 1994, pp. 889–98.

31. Mohammad Ghaffar Chaudhary and Ghulam Mustafa Chaudhry, 'Pakistan's Agricultural Development since Independence: Intertemporal Trends and Explanations', *Pakistan Institute of Development Economics*, 36/4, 1997, pp. 593–612.

32. Husain, *Economy of Modern Sindh*, p. 135.

33. Shaikh, *Report on Agriculture in Sindh—Issues and Options.*

34. Benami transfers were done by manoeuvring alterations in the revenue record.

35. Ahmed, *Agrarian Change and Class Formation in Sindh*, 149–64.

36. Shaikh, *Report on Agriculture in Sindh—Issues and Options.*

37. Ibid.

38. Leslie Nulty, *The Green Revolution in West Pakistan—Implications of Technological Change*, New York, Praeger Publishers, 1972.

39. The sharecropping system involves the total produce being divided into two equal parts—one for the farmers and their families, and one for the feudal lord. In practice the cultivator is given just enough yield to help him survive; if the farmer and his family ask for any assistance, the landlord provides it willingly creating the impression of generosity and grace further tying down the farmer in the traditions of favour and respect.

40. Husain, *Economy of Modern Sindh*, p. 138.

41. N. Hamid, A. Hussain, 'Regional Inequalities and Capitalist Development', *Pakistan Economic and Social Review*, 12/3, 1974, pp. 255–88.

42. S. Salma, S. Rehman, M. A. Shah, 'Rainfall Trends in Different Climate Zones of Pakistan', *Pakistan Journal of Meteorology*, 9/17, 2012, pp. 37–47.

43. Finance Division, *Pakistan Economic Survey 2016–7*, Islamabad, Ministry of Finance, Government of Pakistan, 2017, p. 34.

44. I. M. Bhatti and A. H. Soomro, 'Wheat', *Agricultural Inputs and Field Crop Production in Sindh*, Hyderabad, Directorate General Agricultural Research Sindh, 1994, pp. 109–22.

45. Karim Dino Jamali, 'Crops', *Nuclear Institute of Agriculture*, n.d., <http://www.nia.org.pk/crop.html>, accessed 15 June 2017.

46. Directorate of Agriculture, *Cotton Production, Marketing and Export*, Lahore, Government of Punjab, 2006, pp. 6–7.

47. I. M. Bhatti and A. H. Soomro, 'Cotton', *Agricultural Inputs and Field Crop Production in Sindh*, Hyderabad, Directorate General Agricultural Research Sindh, 1994, pp. 233–58.

48. Muzaffar Qureshi, 'Cotton production may fall in Sindh', *Dawn*, 10 August 2010.

49. Javed Hussain, and Jan Khaskheli, *Issues & Problems of Women Cotton Pickers in Sindh—Baseline Study of Matiari District*, Hyderabad, Sindh Community Foundation, n.d.

50. Ashfak Bukhari, 'Preventing decline of rice exports', *Dawn*, 8 August 2016, <https://www.dawn.com/news/1276077>.

51. Finance Division, *Pakistan Economic Survey 2016–17*, Islamabad, Government of Pakistan, 2017, p. 27.

52. Hussain and Khaskheli, *Issues & Problems of Women Cotton Pickers in Sindh*, pp. 177–91.

53. Agriculture Department, 'History', *Sindh Agriculture Department*, n.d., <http://sindhagri.gov.pk/history.html>, accessed 2 June 2017.

54. Jamali, 'Crops', *Nuclear Institute of Agriculture*.

55. For details on how area cultivated explains rice yield and production, see Khurshid Ali Qureshi et al. 'Contribution of area and yield of total rice production in Pakistan: an analysis', *Pakistan Journal of Agricultural Sciences*, 30/1, 1993, pp. 4–6.

56. I. M. Bhatti and A. H. Soomro, 'Sugarcane', *Agricultural Inputs and Field Crop Production in Sindh*, Hyderabad, Directorate General Agricultural Research Sindh, 1994, pp. 259–76.

57. Mohammad Hussain Khan, 'Sindh's Irrational Sugarcane Pricing Policy', *Dawn*, 11 January 2016.

58. Sindh Board of Investment, Mango, *Sindh Enterprise Development Fund*, <http://www.sedf.gos.pk/pdf/sectors/mango.pdf> accessed 17 June 2017. For a further analysis of investment opportunities in Pakistan's mango industry, see: Islamabad Chamber of Commerce, *Report on Mangoes from Pakistan*, Islamabad, n.d., pp. 1–17. For details specific to Sindh, see *Pre-Feasibility—Mango Pulping Unit and Dry Mango Products*, pp. 1–17, <http://www.sbi.gos.pk/pdf/mango.pdf/>, accessed 11 June 2017.

59. The most popular and important ones are *Sindhri, Chaunsa, Langra, Dasehri, Anwar ratol, Bangan Palli, Alphonso*, and *Neelam*.

60. Mohammad Hussain Khan, 'Sindh to Produce Less Mangoes This Season', *Dawn*, 11 April 2016.

61. Momin Bullo, 'Date Crop of Khairpur', *Sindh Enterprise Development Fund*, <http://sedf.gos.pk/pdf/Date Crop of Khairpur.pdf>, accessed 17 June 2017.

62. Sindh Board of Investment, *Sector Brief Dates*, Karachi, n.d.

63. Sarfaraz Memon, 'In Khairpur, a tutorial benefits date growers', *Express Tribune*, 4 September 2012.

64. Ministry of Food Security and Research, *Fruit, Vegetables and Condiments Statistics of Pakistan*, Islamabad, Government of Pakistan, 2016, p. 15.

65. Ibid., p. 16.

66. Taken from in-paper magazine, see 'Salinity problem in vegetable crops', *Dawn*, 4 March 2012.

67. Sindh Board of Investment, *Red Chilli De-Hydration Plant-Kunri, Sindh*, Karachi, Government of Sindh, 2010.

68. Agriculture Marketing Information Service, *Marketing of Garlic: Problems and Prospects*, Lahore: Directorate of Agriculture, Government of Punjab, n.d.

69. *Dawn*, 'Sindh forests', 15 February 2016.

70. *Dawn*, 'Riverine Forests Fast Disappearing', 18 February 2008.

71. *Dawn*, 'Mangroves Worst Hit by Deforestation: Study', 20 June 2012.

72. Faiza Ilyas, 'Drafts on Forest, Wildlife Laws Await Govt Approval for Four Years', *Dawn*, 17 January 2015.

73. Livestock and Fisheries Department, *Livestock Sindh Website*, <http://www.livestocksindh.gov.pk/>, accessed 10 August 2017.

74. *Dawn*, 'Extending Poultry Farming to Rural Areas', 3 September 2007.

75. Ibid.

76. Aamir Shafaat Khan, 'Poultry Rates Continue to Rise Unabated', *Dawn*, 2 April 2016.

77. Sindh Board of Investment, 'Sector Brief Poultry', *Sindh Board of Investment*, <http://www.sbi.gos.pk/pdf/sector-brief-poultry.pdf>, accessed 1 June 2017.

78. Bureau of Statistics, *Development Statistics of Sindh 2016*, Karachi, Planning and Development Department, Government of Sindh, 2016.

79. *Dawn*, 'Sindh has over 5,200 poultry farms, PA told', 1 March 2011, <https://www.dawn.com/news/609865>.

80. Ibid.

81. Agricultural Census Organization, *Agricultural Census 2010*, Islamabad, Statistics Division, Pakistan Bureau of Statistics, Government of Pakistan, 2012. For a more scholarly understanding of how fertiliser production affects manure usage, *see* Praveen Mohil, and Usha Jain, 'Influence of Inorganic and Organic Fertilisers on Biomass Production of Amaranthus', *European Journal of Experimental Biology*, 6/4, 2016, pp. 33–7.

82. Muhammad Hanif, Shakeel Ahmed Khan, and Fayyaz Ahmed Nouman, *Agricultural Perspective and Policy*, Islamabad, Ministry of Food, Agriculture and Livestock, Government of Pakistan, 2004, pp. 28–30.

83. For a description of national fertiliser policies, see Ministry of Industries and Production, *Fertiliser Policy*, Islamabad, Government of Pakistan, n.d.

84. Natural Resources Management and Environment Department, *Fertiliser use by crop in Pakistan*, Rome, Food and Agriculture Organization of the United Nations, 2004.

85. Government of Sindh, 'The Sindh Fertiliser (Control) Act, 1994', *Sindh Laws* [Website], 1994, <http://sindhlaws.gov.pk/setup/Publications_SindhCode/PUB-15-000810.pdf>, accessed 17 June 2017.

86. Government of Sindh, 'The Sindh Fertiliser (Control) Rules 1999', *Sindh Laws* [Website], 1999, <http://sindhlaws.gov.pk/setup/Publications_SindhCode/PUB-15-000555.pdf>, accessed 17 June 2017.

87. Hafiz Ghufran Ali Khan, Arif Ahmed and Awais e Siraj, 'Impact of Rising Prices of Fertilisers on Crops Production in Pakistan', *Global Journal of Management and Business Research*, 10/9, 2010, pp. 54–61.

88. *Dawn*, 'Hyderabad: Fertiliser Samples Found Substandard', 30 May 2002.

89. *Dawn*, 'Hyderabad: Cut in Sindh's Fertiliser Share Slated', 29 March 2003.

90. *Dawn*, 'Sukkur: Spurious Pesticides, Fertilisers Seized', 4 August 2004; *Dawn*, 'Hyderabad: Samples of 10 Fertilisers Found Substandard', 16 April 2003.

91. Ibid.

92. Calculated from the table on use of fertilisers, manures, pesticides and herbicides by size of farm in Agriculture Census 2010.

93. Brief content analysis of Dawn newspaper articles available online from the year 2008 to 2011.

94. Ahmad Fraz Khan, 'Farms Without Subsidies', *Dawn*, 4 August 2008.

95. *Dawn*, 'Subsidized Tractor Scheme and Farm Mechanisation', 29 March 2010.

96. *Dawn*, 'Farmers in Sindh Get Free Sunflower Seeds', 25 March 2011.

97. Aamir Shafaat Khan, 'Sharp Decline in Tractor Sales', *Dawn*, 6 August 2011; Aamir Shafaat Khan, 'Makers Halt Tractor Production', *Dawn,* 27 December 2011.

98. *Dawn*, 'Farmers Plan Protest across Sindh', 15 March 2012; *Dawn*, 'Peasants, Rights Activists Protest Against Water Shortage', *Dawn*, 25 July 2011.

99. Mohiuddin Aazim, 'Towards Agricultural Mechanization', *Dawn*, 13 January 2014; Mohiuddin Aazim, 'Issues in Farm Mechanization', *Dawn*, 8 December 2014.

100. Shaikh, *Report on Agriculture in Sindh*, pp. 93–4.

101. Akmal Hussain, 'Agrarian Structure and Social Change', *The Oxford Companion to Pakistani History*, ed. Ayesha Jalal, Karachi, Oxford University Press, 2012, pp. 1–5.

102. Arif Hasan, 'Eclipse of Feudalism', *Dawn*, 8 December 2015.

103. For a psychological perspective on the effects of feudalism on peasants, see Rob J. F. Burton, 'Reconceptualising the "Behavioural Approach" in Agricultural Studies: A Socio-Psychological Perspective', *Journal of Rural Studies* 20, 2004, pp. 359–71.

104. Shehryar Rashid and Asjad Tariq Sheikh, *Farmers' Perceptions of Agricultural Land Values in Rural Pakistan*, Islamabad, Pakistan Institute of Development Economics, n.d.

105. Calculated from table on number and area of farms by size of farm in the province of Sindh. See Agriculture Census 2010.

Chapter 9
Irrigation

1. H. T. Sorley, *The Gazetteer of West Pakistan: The Former Province of Sind Including Khairpur State*, Lahore, Gazetteer Cell, Board of Revenue, p. 459.

2. Government of Sindh, 'Sukkur Barrage', <http://sindh.gov.pk/dpt/Irrigation/sukkur%20barrage.htm>, accessed 3 August 2016.

3. Sorley, *The Gazetteer of West Pakistan*, p. 464.

4. Ibid., p. 459.

5. Department of Irrigation, Government of Sindh, Karachi.

6. Ibid.

7. Muhammad Idris Rajput, *Inter-Provincial Water Issues in Pakistan*, Islamabad, PILDAT, 2011, p. 14.

8. Muhammad Idris Rajput, *Kalabagh Dam and Sind: A View Point*, Karachi, Sindh Graduates Association, 2005, p. 130.

9. Ahmed Hayat Khan, 'Water Sharing Disputes in Pakistan: Standpoint of Provinces', *Berkeley Journal of Social Sciences*, vol. 4, 2014.

10. Muhammad Idris Rajput, *Kalabagh Dam and Sind: A View Point*.

11. Ibid.

12. Ibid.

13. Karim, Muhammad Umer, Project Coordination and Monitoring Unit (PCMU), Karachi, Water Sector Improvement Project, Planning and Development Department, Government of Sindh, 2011.

14. Ibid.

15. Ibid.

16. *The Irrigation Management Strategy for Irrigated Agriculture of Sindh Province (Pakistan)*.

17. Finding of consultative sessions with the irrigation department for formulation of Irrigation Strategy 2015.

18. Friends of Democratic Pakistan Forum, *A Productive and Secure Pakistan*, Islamabad, Water Sector Task Force, Ministry of Water and Power, Government of Pakistan, 2012.

19. Unlike Punjab, Sindh's groundwater cannot be used for agriculture because as many as 70 per cent of the aquifer is already saline.

Chapter 10
Infrastructure

1. Klaus Schwab, *The Global Competitiveness Report 2017–2018*, Geneva, World Economic Forum, 2017, <http://www3.weforum.org/docs/GCR2017–2018/05FullReport/TheGlobalCompetitivenessReport2017%E2%80%932018.pdf>.

2. Government of Sindh, 'Highways Department', *Government of Sindh* [Website], n.d., <http://www.sindh.gov.pk/dpt/worksandservices/highway.htm>, accessed 25 February 2017.

3. Bureau of Statistics, *Development Statistics 2016*, Karachi, Planning and Development Department, 2016.

4. Planning Commission, 'Transport', *The First Five-Year Plan 1955–60*, Karachi, Government of Pakistan, 1957, p. 485.

5. Ibid., p. 2.

6. Planning Commission, 'Transport and Communications', *The Third Five-Year Plan 1965–70*, Islamabad, Ministry of Planning, Development and Reforms, Government of Pakistan, 1965, pp. 326–7.

7. Planning Commission, 'Transport and Communications', *The Fourth Five-Year Plan 1970–75*, Islamabad, Ministry of Planning, Development and Reforms, Government of Pakistan, 1970, p. 447.

8. Ibid., p. 449.

9. Planning Commission, 'Transport and Communications', *The Fifth Five-Year Plan 1978–83 Sectoral Pro-*

grammes (Part II), Islamabad, Ministry of Planning, Development and Reforms, Government of Pakistan, 1978, p. 212.

10. Ibid., p. 228.
11. 'Transports and Communications: Providing the Missing Infrastructure', *The Sixth Five-Year Plan 1983–88*, p. 237.
12. 'Transport and Communications', *Pakistan Economic Survey 1990–91*, p. 113.
13. 'Transport and Communications', *Pakistan Economic Survey 1995–96*, pp. 73, 75–6.
14. 'Transport and Communications', *Pakistan Economic Survey 2000–01*, pp. 201–2.
15. 'Transport and Communications', *Pakistan Economic Survey 2005–06*, p. 203.
16. Planning Commission, 'Infrastructure Development through Public–Private Partnership', *The Tenth Five-Year Plan 2010–15*, Islamabad, Ministry of Planning, Development and Reforms, 2010, p. 304.
17. Ibid., p. 305.
18. Ibid., p. 312.
19. Ibid., p. 311.
20. Ibid., p. 313.
21. Ibid., p. 312.
22. Ibid., p. 491.
23. 'Transport and Communications', *The Third Five-Year Plan 1965–70*, p. 314.
24. Ibid., pp. 320–321.
25. 'Transport and Communications', *The Fourth Five-Year Plan 1970–75*, p. 448.
26. 'Transports and Communications', *The Fifth Five-Year Plan 1978–83*, pp. 219–220.
27. Ibid., p. 213.
28. 'Transports and Communications: Providing the Missing Infrastructure', *The Sixth Five-Year Plan 1983–88*, p. 232.
29. Ibid., p. 235.
30. Planning Commission, 'Transport and Communications', *The Seventh Five-Year Plan 1988–93 Federal/Provincial Projects and Programme*, Islamabad, Ministry of Planning, Development and Reforms, Government of Pakistan, 1989, p. 266.
31. 'Transport and Communications', *Pakistan Economic Survey 2000–01*, p. 203.
32. 'Transport and Communications', *Pakistan Economic Survey 2005–06*, p. 205.
33. 'Infrastructure Development through Public–Private Partnership', *The Tenth Five-Year Plan 2010–15*, p. 314.
34. Ibid., p. 315.

35. Planning Commission, 'Transport and Logistics', *The Eleventh Five-Year Plan 2013–2018*, Islamabad, Ministry of Planning, Development and Reforms, Government of Pakistan, p. 341.
36. Ibid., p. 344.
37. Ibid., p. 351.
38. Planning Commission, 'Transport', *The First Five Year Plan 1955–60*, p. 497.
39. Planning Commission, 'Transport and Communications', *The Third Five-Year Plan 1965–70*, p. 335.
40. Ibid., p. 334.
41. Ibid., p. 336.
42. Planning Commission, 'Transport and Communications', *The Fourth Five-Year Plan 1970–75*, p. 458.
43. Ibid., p. 232.
44. Ibid.
45. Planning Commission, 'Transports and Communications: Providing the Missing Infrastructure', *The Sixth Five-Year Plan 1983–88*, p. 234.
46. Ibid., pp. 240–1.
47. Planning Commission, 'Transport and Communications', *The Eighth Five-Year Plan 1993–98*, Islamabad, Ministry of Planning, Development and Reforms, Government of Pakistan, 1994, p. 267.
48. Ibid., pp. 267–8.
49. Finance Division, 'Transport and Communications', *Pakistan Economic Survey 1995–96*, p. 79.
50. Salman Siddiqui, 'Trade via Karachi records 15% increase', *Express Tribune*, 5 July 2016, <https://tribune.com.pk/story/1136469/imports–exports–trade–via–karachi–port–records–15–increase/>.
51. Planning Commission, 'Infrastructure Development through Public–Private Partnership', *The Tenth Five-Year Plan 2010–15*, p. 305.
52. Ibid., p. 309.
53. Planning Commission, 'Transport and Logistics', *The Eleventh Five-Year Plan 2013–2018*, p. 346.
54. Ernesto Sánchez-Triana, et al., 'Infrastructure Modernisation', *Revitalizing Industrial Growth in Pakistan: Trade, Infrastructure, and Environmental Performance*, Washington DC, World Bank, 2014.
55. Planning Commission, 'Transport', *The First Five-Year Plan 1955–60*, p. 486.
56. Ibid., p. 507.
57. Ibid.
58. Planning Commission, 'Transport and Communications', *The Third Five-Year Plan 1965–70*, p. 314.

59. Ibid., p. 340.
60. Planning Commission, 'Transport and Communications', *The Fourth Five Year Plan 1970–75*, p. 461.
61. Ibid., p. 454.
62. Ibid., p. 238.
63. Planning Commission, 'Transports and Communications: Providing the Missing Infrastructure', *The Sixth Five-Year Plan 1983–88*, p. 242.
64. Ibid., pp. 242–3.
65. Planning Commission, 'Transport and Communications', *The Seventh Five-Year Plan 1988–93 Federal/Provincial Projects and Programmes*, p. 79.
66. Ibid., p. 317.
67. Planning Commission, 'Transport and Logistics', *The Eleventh Five-Year Plan 2013–2018*, p. 353.
68. IUCUN, *Sindh State of Environment and Development*, Karachi, IUCUN Pakistan, 2004, p. 305.
69. Ibid., pp. 305–6.
70. Planning Commission, 'Transport and Communications', *The Third Five-Year Plan 1965–70*, p. 349.
71. Planning Commission, 'Transport and Communications', *The Seventh Five-Year Plan 1988–93 Federal/Provincial Projects and Programmes*, pp. 91–3.
72. Planning Commission, 'Transport and Communications', *The Eighth Five-Year Plan 1993–98*, p. 404.
73. Planning Commission, 'Physical Planning and Housing', *The Third Five-Year Plan 1965–70*, p. 371.
74. Ibid., p. 366.
75. Ibid., p. 365.
76. Ibid., p. 377.
77. Planning Commission, 'Physical Planning and Housing', *The Fourth Five-Year Plan 1970–75*, p. 476.
78. Ibid., p. 489.
79. Ibid., p. 491.
80. Ibid.
81. Ibid., p. 271.
82. Ibid., p. 276.
83. Ibid., p. 278.
84. Ibid., p. 280.
85. Planning Commission, 'Housing: Shelter for the Poor', *The Sixth Five-Year Plan 1983–88*, p. 393.
86. Arif Hasan, 'The Causes of Land Contestation in Karachi and How These Impact on Housing and Urban Development', International Institute for Environment and Development (IIED), 27/1, 2015, p. 222.
87. Planning Commission, 'Water Supply: Farewell to Polluted Water', *The Sixth Five-Year Plan 1983–88*, p. 398.
88. Government of Sindh, 'Katchi Abadis Government of Sindh—Profile of Katchi Abadis', Government of Sindh [Website], n.d., <http://sindh.gov.pk/dpt/SKAA/status%20of%20katchi.htm>, accessed 20 April 2017.
89. Planning Commission, 'Physical Planning and Housing', *The Seventh Five-Year Plan 1988–93 Federal/Provincial Projects and Programmes*, pp. 272–3.
90. Planning Commission, 'Physical Planning and Housing', *The Eighth Five-Year Plan 1993–98*, p. 291.
91. Population Census Organization, 'Broad Analysis of Housing Data', *1998 Provincial Census Report of Sindh*, Islamabad, Statistics Division, Government of Pakistan, 2000.
92. IUCN, *Sindh State of Environment and Development*, p. 200.
93. Ibid., p. 200.
94. Arif Hasan, 'Urban Land Reform', *Dawn*, 15 July 2015.
95. Arif Hasan, 'Ugly Karachi', *Dawn*, 6 November 2016.
96. ICUN, *Sindh State of Environment and Development*, p. 201.
97. Arif Hasan, 'Ugly Karachi', *Dawn*, 6 November 2016.
98. Ibid.
99. Arif Hasan, 'The Water and Sanitation Challenge: The Conflict Between Reality and Planning Paradigms', 27 October 2009, <http://arifhasan.org/seminars/the–water–and–sanitation–challenge–the–conflict–between–reality–and–planning–paradigms> accessed 10 April 2017.

Chapter 11
Sindh's Industrial Structure: Past and Present

1. Sahar S. Hussain and Viqar Ahmed, 'Experiments with Industrial Policy: The Case of Pakistan', Islamabad, Sustainable Development Policy Institute, 2011, p. 6.
2. Ishrat Husain, *Economy of Modern Sindh*, Hyderabad, Institute of Sindhology, Sindh University Press, 1981, p. 218.
3. Ahmed and Hussain, 'Experiments with Industrial Policy', p. 8.
4. Ibid., 9.

5. IUCN Pakistan, *Sindh Strategy for Sustainable Development*, Karachi, IUCN Pakistan, Sindh Programme, 2007, p. 103.
6. Ibid.
7. *Unlocking the Economic Potential of Sindh: An Enhanced Framework for Competitiveness*, n.p., Competitiveness Support Fund, n.d., p. 41.
8. Ibid., p. 45.
9. 'Company profile', *Pakistan Refinery Limited* [website] <http://www.prl.com.pk/about/companyprofile.php>, accessed 31 July 2017.
10. 'Production and Capacity', *National Refinery Limited* [website] <www.nrlpak.com/ProductionCapacity.aspx>, accessed 1 August 2017.
11. 'Byco in Brief,' *Byco* [website] <http://www.byco.com.pk/index.php?option=com_content&view=article&id=2&Itemid=3>, accessed 1 August 2017.
12. Hussain, *Modern Sindh*, p. 231.
13. *Unlocking the Economic Potential of Sindh*, pp. 48–9.
14. Ibid., p. 230.
15. Sindh Economy, *Sindh Board of Investment*, 2016, accessed at <http://www.sbi.gos.pk/>.
16. 'Sugar Industry of Pakistan—An Academic Report', *Ravi Magazine* [online magazine], May 2015, <https://www.ravimagazine.com/sugar-industry-of-pakistan-an-academic-report/>, accessed 20 June 2017.
17. Ibid.
18. Ibid.
19. 'Analysis of Pakistani Fertiliser Industry—A Report', *Ravi Magazine* [online magazine], April 2015, <https://www.ravimagazine.com/analysis-of-pakistani-fertiliser-industry-a-report/>, accessed 18 June 2017.
20. Ibid.
21. Hussain, *Modern Sindh*, p. 231.
22. Ibid.
23. Ibid., pp. 46–8.
24. Ibid., p. 54.
25. Subuk Hasnain, 'The Demise of Pakistan Steel Mills', *Herald*, Dawn Online, 31 October 2016, <https://herald.dawn.com/news/1153574>.
26. Ibid.
27. Ibid. According to the Pakistan Steel Mills website, the Pakistan Steel Mill project was first proposed in the First Five-Year Plan (1955–60).
28. Ibid.
29. Ibid.
30. Ibid.
31. *About Us*, Pakistan Steel, <http://www.paksteel.com.pk/organ_about_us.html>.
32. The township of Pakistan Steel Mills has its own schools, markets, recreational facilities, a dispensary, a mosque, a church, and a temple. Many of the Mill's existing and former employees live here.
33. Subuk Hasnain, 'The Demise of Pakistan Steel Mills'; *About Us*, Pakistan Steel, <http://www.paksteel.com.pk/organ_about_us.html>
34. A requirement for members of the world steel association is that a country should produce at least 2 million metric tons of iron and/steel per annum.
35. World Steel Association, *Statistical Year Book 2017*, Brussels, World Steel Association, 2017, <https://www.worldsteel.org/en/dam/jcr:3e275c73-6f11-4e7f-a5d8-23d9bc5c508f/Steel%2520Statistical%2520Yearbook%25202017_updated%2520version090518.pdf>.
36. *About Us*, Pakistan Steel.
37. Zafar Bhutta, 'Pakistan Steel Mills in further trouble as losses swell to Rs200b', *Express Tribune*, Karachi, 2018. <https://tribune.com.pk/story/1748016/2-pakistan-steel-mills-trouble-losses-swell-rs200b/>.
38. Ibid.
39. Aamir Sharafat Khan, 'Pakistan Steel Mills Financial Woes Continue', *Dawn*, Karachi, 2016, <https://www.dawn.com/news/1305421>.
40. Ibid.
41. *About Us*, Pakistan Steel.
42. Zafar Bhutta, 'Pakistan Steel Mills in further trouble as losses swell to Rs200b'.
43. Ibid.
44. Ibid.
45. Hussain, *Modern Sindh*, pp. 243–5.
46. Ibid., pp. 243–4.
47. 'Sindh Economy'.
48. *Unlocking the Economic Potential of Sindh*, p. 41.
49. Ibid., pp. 48–9.
50. Ibid.
51. Ibid.
52. Ibid., p. 44.
53. Saleem Sheikh, 'Sindh's Sagging Handicraft Business', *Dawn* [online newspaper], March 2010, <https://www.dawn.com/news/839308> accessed 1 July 2017.
54. Ibid.
55. Ibid.
56. 'Rich Heritage of Handicraft', *Pakistan Economist*, 1975.
57. *Unlocking the Economic Potential of Sindh*, p. 55.
58. Ibid.

59. Ibid.
60. Ibid.
61. Ibid.
62. Ibid.
63. Ibid.

Chapter 12
Energy and Mineral Resources

1. Ministry of Petroleum and Natural Resources, *Investment Opportunities in Pakistan's Upstream Oil and Gas Sector*, Islamabad, Government of Pakistan, 2015, p. 13.
2. Ibid.
3. Verneze James, Niazi Kabalan, *Oil and Gas*, London, Clyde & Co, 2012, <https://www.clydeco.com/uploads/Files/Publications/2012/CC000606_Oil%20&%20gas_Pakistan_Overview_06_02_ 12.pdf>.
4. 'Six new oil, gas discoveries in Sindh, KP', *The News*, Karachi, 29 June 2016.
5. Zafar Bhutta, 'Pakistan's oil and gas discoveries touch record', *The Express Tribune*, 29 June 2016.
6. Ibid.
7. Ibid.
8. 'Hydrocarbon', *Pakistan Energy Year Book 2014–15*, Institute of Pakistan, Islamabad, Ministry of Petroleum and Natural Resources, Government of Pakistan, 2016, p. 78.
9. Ibid.
10. Ibid.
11. Ibid
12. Finance Division, *Pakistan Economic Survey 2011–12*, Islamabad, Ministry of Finance, Government of Pakistan, 2012, p. 211.
13. 'Sindh withholds its assent to energy policy', *Dawn*, 7 April 2015, <https://www.dawn.com/news/1174375>.
14. Private Power and Infrastructural Board, *Pakistan Coal Power Generational Potential*, Islamabad, Ministry of Water and Power, Government of Pakistan, 2004.
15. I. Siddiqui and M.T. Shah, 'Environmental Impact Assessment of the Thar, Sonda and Meting–Jhimpir Coalfields of Sindh', *Journal of Chemical Society Pakistan*, 29/3, 2007, pp. 222–30, <http://www.jcsp.org.pk/ArticleUpload/1182-5246-1-CE.pdf>.
16. Energy/Development International Price Waterhouse, *The Coal Industry in Pakistan: Requirements for Growth*, prepared under USAID, 4 February 1985, <http://pdf.usaid.gov/pdf_docs/PNAAZ147.pdf>, accessed 25 September 2017.
17. 'Hydrocarbon', *Pakistan Energy Year Book 1983*, Development Institute of Pakistan, Islamabad, Ministry of Petroleum and Natural Resources, Government of Pakistan, n.d.
18. Private Power and Infrastructural Board, *Pakistan Coal Power*, p. 35.
19. Coal, Siddiqsons Power, <http://www.thesiddiqsonsgroup.com/siddiqsons-power-coal>, accessed 22 September 2017.
20. Siddiqsons Energy Limited, 'Application for the grant of a generational power license under section 15 of the regulation of generation, transmission and distribution Act 1997: In respect of 350 MW coal power project at Port Qasim, Sindh', The National Electric Power Regulatory Authority, Islamabad, 2015.
21. Mian Abrar, 'Port Qasim Coal- Fired Power Project: CPEC's first project witnesses emphatic progress on ground', *Pakistan Today*, 7 March 2016, <https://www.pakistantoday.com.pk/2016/03/07/port-qasim-coal-fired-power-project-cpecs-first-project-witnesses-emphatic-progress-on-ground/>, accessed 7 August 2017.
22. Akhtar Ali, *Pakistan's Energy Development: The Road Ahead*, Karachi, Royal Book Company, 2010.
23. Ibid.
24. Nasim A. Khan, *Energy Resources and Their Utilization in Pakistan*, Karachi, Hamdard University Press, 2010.
25. FFC Energy Limited, 'About Us', <https://www.ffcel.com.pk/about-us.php>, accessed 22 September 2017.
26. 'Hydropower', National Geographic, <http://www.nationalgeographic.com/environment/global-warming/hydropower/>, accessed 22 September 2017.
27. Jawad Rizvi, 'Demystifying Pakistan's Energy Crisis', *MIT Technology Review Pakistan*, 2015, <http://www.technologyreview.pk/demystifying-pakistans-energy-crisis/>.
28. Shakeel Khan and Hafiz Farhan, *Analysis of Pakistan's Electric Power Sector*, Blekinge Institute of Technology, Department of Electrical Engineering, March 2015, <https://www.diva-portal.org/smash/get/diva2:917526/FULLTEXT01.pdf>.
29. National Transmission and Dispatch Company, Power System Statistics 2016, Islamabad, National Transmission and Dispatch Company, 2016.
30. Usama Siddiqui, 'Pakistan Power Sector Reforms: Pakistan Struggles to Overcome the Power Crisis', *The Express Tribune*, 25 April 2011, accessed 30 August 2016, <http://tribune.com.pk/story/155979/power-

sector-reforms-pakistan-struggles-to-overcome-the-power-crisis/>.

31. Fahd Ali and Fatima Beg, 'The History of Private Power in Pakistan', Working Paper 106, Karachi, Sustainable Development Policy Institute, 2007.

32. J. M. Fraser, 'Lessons from the Independent Private Power Experience in Pakistan', *Energy and Mining Sector Board Discussion Paper*, Discussion Paper No. 14, 5, 2005.

33. Ibid.

34. Kafait Ullah, 'Electricity Infrastructure in Pakistan: an Overview', *International Journal of Energy, Information and Communications* 4/3, 2013.

35. Shakeel Khan and Hafiz Farhan, *Analysis of Pakistan's Electric Power Sector*, Blekinge Institute of Technology, Department of Electrical Engineering, 2015.

36. K-Electric, *Financial Data—Analyst Breifing*, 2015, <http://www.ke.com.pk/pdf/financialdata/KE%20 Analyst%20Briefing%20FY-2015.pdf>, accessed 5 September 2016.

37. K-Electric, *KE Annual Report 2016*, Karachi, n.d., p. 31.

38. K-Electric, *Business Distribution*, <https://www. ke.com.pk/our-business/distribution/>.

39. K-Electric, *Financial Data—Analyst Breifing*, 2015, <http://www.ke.com.pk/pdf/financialdata/KE%20 Analyst%20Briefing%20FY-2015.pdf>, accessed 5 September 2016.

Chapter 13
Public Finance: Taxation and Resource Mobilisation

1. Hafiz Pasha, 'Growth of The Provincial Economies', Institute for Policy Reforms, 2015.

2. Ali Cheema, Asim Ijaz Khwaja, and Adnan Khan, 'Decentralization in Pakistan: Context, Content and Causes', KSG Working Paper No. RWP05-034, 2005.

3. Ibid.

4. Iftikhar Ahmed, Usman Mustafa, Mahmood Khalid, 'National Finance Commission Awards in Pakistan: A Historical Perspective', *PIDE Working Paper 33*, Islamabad, Pakistan Institute of Development Economics, 2007, p. 3, <http://www.pide.org.pk/ pdf/Working%20Paper/WorkingPaper-33.pdf>.

5. Ali Cheema, Asim Ijaz Khwaja, and Adnan Khan, 'Decentralization in Pakistan: Context, Content and Causes', *KSG Working Paper No. RWP05–034*, 2005, p. 3.

6. Ahmed, Mustafa, and Khalid, 'National Finance Commission Awards in Pakistan', p. 3.

7. Ibid., p. 4.

8. Ibid.

9. Ministry of Finance, 'Working Papers and Minutes of the National Finance Committee', unpublished report, 1970, p. 135.

10. Ibid., p. 1.

11. Ibid., p. 4.

12. Ibid.

13. Ibid.

14. Ibid., p. 135.

15. Ibid., p. 138.

16. Ibid., p. 139.

17. Nighat Jaffery Bilgrami and Mahapara Sadaqat, 'NFC Awards-Commentary and Agenda', *Pakistan Economic and Social Review*, 44/2, 2006, p. 209.

18. Ahmed, Mustafa, and Khalid, 'National Finance Commission Awards in Pakistan', p. 5.

19. Ibid.

20. Ibid.

21. Ibid

22. Ibid., p. 6.

23. Ibid.

24. Ibid.

25. Ibid., p. 7.

26. Ibid.

27. Ibid., p. 8.

28. Ibid.

29. Ibid.

30. NFC Secretariat, 'Government of Sindh's Positon on Distribution of Subvention under NFC', 2002.

31. Ibid.

32. Ibid.

33. Ibid.

34. Finance Department, 'Government of Sindh's Position on 6th National Finance Commission', 2003, p. 2, unpublished.

35. Ibid., p. 12.

36. Ibid.

37. Ibid., p. 4.

38. Ibid., p. 13.

39. Ibid., p. 4.

40. Ibid., p. 20.

41. Ibid., p. 21.

42. Ibid., pp. 2–3.

43. Ibid., p. 18.

44. Ibid., p. 22.

45. Ibid., p. 18.

46. Ibid., p. 22.

47. Ibid., p. 15.
48. Ibid., pp. 24–8.
49. Nawaz Ali Laghari, 'Impact of Distribution of 2.5% GST of Net Sales Tax under Distribution Order, 2006 in Case of Sindh', 2008, pp. 8–9, unpublished.
50. Iftikhar Ahmed, Usman Mustafa, Mahmood Khalid, 'National Finance Commission Awards in Pakistan: A Historical Perspective', *PIDE Working Paper 33*, Islamabad, Pakistan Institute of Development Economics, 2007, p. 9.
51. Ibid.
52. Ibid.
53. Ibid.
54. Pakistan Institute of Development Economics, *The 7th NFC Award: An Evaluation*, Islamabad, 2011.
55. Government of Pakistan, *Report of the National Finance Commission 2009*, 30 December 2009, <http://www.finance.gov.pk/nfc/reportofthenfc_2009.pdf>.
56. Hafiz Pasha, 'Review of 7th NFC Award', *Business Recorder*, January 2017, <http://epaper.brecorder.com/2017/01/17/20-page/840430-news.html>.
57. Ibid.
58. Pakistan Institute of Development Economics, *The 7th NFC Award: An Evaluation*, Islamabad, 2011.
59. Pakistan Institute of Legislative Development and Transparency (PILDAT), 'Taxing the Agriculture Income in Pakistan', *Briefing Paper* 42, Islamabad, 2011.
60. The statistics are reported in Agriculture Census 2010, a report published by Pakistan Bureau of Statistics.
61. Ibid.
62. Ibid.
63. Ibid., p. 9.
64. Ibid., p. 11.
65. Ibid
66. Ibid.
67. Government of Sindh, *The Sindh Land Tax and Agricultural Income Tax Ordinance 2000*, Karachi, Provincial Assembly of Sindh, 2000.
68. Ibid.
69. Lance Lochner and Enrico Moretti, 'The Effect of Education on Crime: Evidence from Prison Inmates, Arrests, and Self Reports', *The American Economic Review*, 94/1, 2004, pp. 155–89.
70. Janet Currie and Enrico Moretti, 'Mother's Education and the Intergenerational Transmission of Human Capital: Evidence from College Openings and Longitudinal Data', *The Quarterly Journal of Economics*, 118/4, 2003, pp. 1495–532.
71. R. Ahmed resident of Wahi Pandhi, 'Sindh: Water Issue', *Dawn*, 25 December 2017, <https://www.dawn.com/news/1378670>.
72. Asian Development Bank, 'Domestic Water and Sanitation Policy for Sindh', Capacity Building for Environmental Management in Sindh, Final Report, August 2006, Islamabad, Asian Development Bank, 2006, <http://www.scip.gos.pk/includes/reports/AssismentPolicyMasterPlan/Water%20&%20Sanitation%20Managment%20Policy.pdf>.
73. Pakistan Bureau of Statistics, *District-wise Census Results 2017*, Islamabad, Statistics Division, Government, 2017, <http://www.pbs.gov.pk/sites/default/files//DISTRICT_WISE_CENSUS_RESULTS_CENSUS_2017.pdf>.
74. Noman Ahmed, *Politics of Urban Water*, *Dawn*, 30 December 2016, <https://www.dawn.com/news/130525>.

Conclusion

1. Pakistan Bureau of Statistics, *Labour Force Survey 2014–2015*, Islamabad, Statistics Division, Government of Pakistan.
2. Austin Francis Louis Kilroy, Megha Mukim, Stefano Negri, *Competitive cities for jobs and growth: what, who, and how (English)*, Washington DC, World Bank Group, 2015, <http://documents.worldbank.org/curated/en/902411467990995484/Competitive-cities-for-jobs-and-growth-what-who-and-how/>, accessed 5 October 2017.
3. Roger. D. Norton, *Agricultural Development Policy: Concepts and Experiences*, West Sussex, John Wiley & Sons Ltd, 2004.
4. Ibid.
5. Sindh Board of Investment, *Sindh—The Land of Opportunities*, Online.
6. Ibid.
7. Sindh Board of Investment, 'Fisheries,' *Sindh—The Land of Opportunities*, Online.
8. Ibid.
9. Ibid.
10. Ibid.
11. Sindh Board of Investment, 'Livestock,' *Sindh—The Land of Opportunities*, Online.
12. Ibid.
13. Ibid.
14. The labour force of Sindh for the years 1998 and 2014 was 7.8 and 14.3 million respectively. The average increase in Sindh's labour force was 382,353 and the

following formula was used: Labour force/number of years = (14.3-7.8)/17 = 382,352. Source: Pakistan Bureau of Statistics, *Labour Force Survey*, Islamabad, Statistics Division, Government of Pakistan, various years.

Bibliography

Introduction

Asim, Salman, 'The Public School System in Sindh: Empirical Insights', *The Lahore Journal of Economics* 18, 2013.

Bureau of Statistics, Development Statistics of Sindh, Karachi, Planning and Development Department, Government of Sindh, various years.

Global Health Observatory (GHO) data <http://www.who.int/gho/en/>.

Government of Sindh and United Nations Development Programme, *Sindh Multiple Indicator Cluster Survey 2014*, Karachi, 2015.

Ministry of Food, Agriculture and Livestock, *50 Years of Agricultural Statistics in Pakistan (1947–2000)*, Islamabad, Government of Pakistan, 2007.

Pakistan Bureau of Statistics, *Agricultural Statistics of Pakistan (2011–2012)*, Islamabad, Statistics Division, 2013.

————, *Provisional Summary Results of 6th Population and Housing Census*, Islamabad, Statistics Division, 2017.

Pasha, Hafiz, 'Growth of the Provincial Economies', *Institute for Policy Reforms*, 2015.

Population Census Organization, 1998 Census Report of Sindh, Islamabad, Statistics Division, Government of Pakistan, 2000.

World Bank Open Data <https://data.worldbank.org/> and World Bank, *Draft Report on Sindh Growth Strategy 2015*, unpublished.

Chapter 1: Land and People

B. Pithawala, Maneck, *Historical Geography of Sind*, Jamshoro, Institute of Sindhology, University of Sindh, 1978.

Indus Ecological Programme, 'Coastal Areas', World Wildlife Fund, <http://foreverindus.org/ie_ecosystem_coastal.php>.

Pathan, Mumtaz Hussain, *Arab Kingdom of Al-Mansurah*, Hyderabad, Institute of Sindhology, University of Sindh, 1974.

Population Census Organization, *Handbook of Population Census Data Sind*, Islamabad, Statistics Division, Government of Pakistan, 1988.

————, *1998 Population Census Report of Sindh*, Islamabad, Statistics Division, Government of Pakistan, 2000.

Rehman, Mushtaqur, *A Geography of Sindh Province, Pakistan*, Karachi, Oxford University Press, 1975.

Rasul, Ghulam, *Impacts of Climate Change*, Islamabad, Pakistan Metrological Dept., Research and Development Division, n.d.

Sorley, H. T., *The Gazetteer of West Pakistan the Former Province of Sind Including Khairpur State*, Lahore, Gazetteer Cell, Board of Revenue, 1968.

Chapter 2: Administrative and Economic History

Ali, Mubarak, *The English Factory in Sindh*, Lahore, Fiction House, 2005.

Andrew, W. P., *The Indus and Its Provinces: Their Political and Commercial Importance Considered in Connexion with Improved Means of Communication*, Karachi, Indus Publications, 1986.

Cheesman, David, *Landlord Power and Rural Indebtedness in Colonial Sind (1865–1901)*, Oxford, Routledge, 1997.

Choksey, R. D., *The Story of Sind: An Economic and Social Survey (1843–1933),* Karachi, Indus Publications, 2003.

Economic Reforms Unit, *Budget Strategy Paper 2015–16 to 2017–18,* Karachi, Finance Department, Government of Sindh, n.d.

Gidumal, Dayarm, *History of Alienations in the Province of Sind Compiled from the Jagir and Other Records in the Commissioner's Office on the Authority of Bombay Government Resolution No. 12, Dated 2nd January 1878, Revenue Department,* Karachi, Commissioner's Press, 1886.

Hughes, Albert William, *A Gazetteer of the Province of Sind,* London, George Bell and Sons, 1876.

Huttenback, Robert A., *British Relations with Sind 1799–1843: An Anatomy of Imperialism,* Karachi, Oxford University Press, 2007.

Irrigation Department, 'Sukkur Barrage', Government of Sindh, n.d., <http://sindh.gov.pk/dpt/Irrigation/sukkur%20barrage.htm>, accessed 5 May 2017.

Khuhro, Hamida. *The Making of Modern Sindh: British Policy and Social Change in the Nineteenth Century,* Oxford, Oxford University Press, 1999.

Mariwalla, C. L., *Essays on British Policy Towards Sind Upto the First Afghan War 1839,* Karachi, Indus Publications, 1947, 1982.

Memon, Siddique G., *Sukkur: Then and Now,* Oxford, Oxford University Press, 2000.

Pakistan Bureau of Statistics, *Pakistan Social and Living Standards Measurement Survey 2013–14,* Islamabad, Statistics Division, Government of Pakistan, 2015.

Sorley, H. T., *The Gazetteer of West Pakistan the Former Province of Sind Including Khairpur State,* Lahore, Gazetteer Cell, Board of Revenue, 1968.

Government of Sindh, 'Sukkur Barrage', n.d., <http://sindh.gov.pk/dpt/Irrigation/sukkur%20barrage.htm>, accessed 3 August 2016.

World Bank, *Pakistan—Country Snapshot,* Washington DC, 2015.

———, *Pakistan: Country Development Landscape,* Washington DC, 2014.

Zaidi, S. Akbar, *Issues in Pakistan's Economy: A Political Economy Perspective,* Karachi, Oxford University Press, 2015.

Chapter 3: Population

Bureau of Statistics, *Development Statistics Report 2011,* Karachi, Planning and Development Department, Government of Sindh, n.d.

Census Organization, 'Population by Geographical Levels: Punjab', *Population Census of Pakistan 1972,* Islamabad, Interior Division, Government of Pakistan, 1974.

Census Organization, 'Population by Geographical Levels: Sind', *Population Census of Pakistan 1972,* Islamabad, Government of Pakistan, 1974.

Government of India, *1891 Census,* Bombay, n.d.

———, *Census of India 1931,* 8 vols., Bombay, n.d.

———, *Census of India 1941,* vol. 12, Sindh, n.d.

Home Affairs Division, *Census of Pakistan Population 1961,* Karachi, Government of Pakistan, n.d.

Manager of Publications, *Census of Pakistan, 1951,* Karachi, Government of Pakistan, n.d.

Pakistan Bureau of Statistics, *Population by Province/ Region since 1951,* Islamabad, Government of Pakistan, n.d.

———, *Provisional Summary Results of 6th Population and Housing Census,* Islamabad, Statistics Division, 2017.

———, *Population Census 2017,* Islamabad, Statistics Division, Government of Pakistan, 2017.

Pakistan Census Organization, *Census of Pakistan Population 1961,* Karachi, Government of Pakistan, n.d.

———, *1981 Population Census Report of Sindh,* Islamabad, Statistics Division, Government of Pakistan, 1984.

———, *Handbook of Population Census Data Sindh,* Islamabad, Statistics Division, Government of Pakistan, 1988.

———, *Provincial Census Report of Sindh,* Islamabad, Statistics Division, Government of Pakistan, 2000.

———, 'Statistical Report of Pakistan', *Population Census of Pakistan 1972,* Islamabad, Statistics Division, Government of Pakistan, n.d.

———, 'Statistical Report of Sind', *Population Census of Pakistan 1972,* Islamabad, Statistics Division, Government of Pakistan, n.d.

————, *Population Census of Pakistan 1972*, vol. 2: *Population by Geographical Levels Sind*, Islamabad, Statistics Division, Government of Pakistan, n.d.

World Bank, *Pakistan Urban Sector Assessment*, unpublished background paper, 2014.

'What five Sahel countries learned from Bangladesh about strengthening population policies', 2016, <http://www.worldbank.org/en/news/feature/2016/06/23/what-five-sahel-countries-learned-from-bangladesh-about-strengthening-population-policies>.

Chapter 4: Education

Aly, Javed H., *Education in Pakistan: A White Paper Revised Document to Debate and Finalize the National Education Policy*, Islamabad, Ministry of Education, Government of Pakistan, 2007.

Amjad, Ravish, *A Comparative Analysis of the Role of the Private Sector as Education Providers in Improving Issues of Access and Quality*, Lahore, Development Policy Research Center, 2012.

Aslam, Monazza, 'The Determinants of Student Achievement in Government and Private Schools in Pakistan', *The Pakistan Development Review*, 42/4, 2003.

Barnett, W. Steven, 'Long Term Effects of Early Childhood Programs on Cognitive and School Outcomes', *The Future of Children*, 5/3, 1995.

Education and Literacy Department, *Sindh Education Sector Plan 2014–18*, Karachi, Government of Sindh, 2014.

————, *Sindh Basic Education Program (SBEP)—Monitoring and Evaluation Manual*, Karachi, Government of Sindh, 2013.

Finance Department, *Finance Budget Books*, Karachi, Government of Sindh, various years.

Government of Pakistan, *National Education Policy 1998–2010*, Islamabad, 1997.

Malik, Akhtar H., 'A Comparative Study of Elite English-Medium Schools, Public Schools and Islamic Madaris in Contemporary Pakistan: The Use of Pierre Bourdieu's theory to understand "Inequalities in Educational and Occupational Opportunities"', PhD. Thesis, University of Toronto, 2012.

Ministry of Education and Scientific Research, *The New Education Policy of the Government of Pakistan*, Karachi, The Manager of Publications, March 1970.

Ministry of Education, *National Education Policy 2009*, Islamabad, Government of Pakistan, 2009.

————, *National Education Policy and Implementation Programme*, Islamabad, Government of Pakistan, 1979.

————, *The New Education Policy 1972–1980*, Islamabad, Government of Pakistan, 1972.

Ministry of Federal Education and Professional Training, *Pakistan Education Statistics 2015–16*, Islamabad, Government of Pakistan, 2017.

Ministry of Finance, *Economic Survey of Pakistan 2016–17*, Islamabad, Government of Pakistan, 2017.

Nguyen, Quynh T. and Dhushyanth Raju, 'Private school participation in Pakistan', *Lahore Journal of Economics*, 20/1, 2015.

Pakistan Bureau of Statistics, *Pakistan Social and Living Standard Measurement Report 2014–15*, Islamabad, Government of Pakistan, 2016.

Reform Support Unit, *Student Achievement Test (I to IV)*, Karachi, Government of Sindh, n.d.

Sabir, Mohammad, *Agenda for the 8th NFC: Lessons from the 7th NFC Award, Post-7th NFC Developments and Emerging Issues*, Karachi, Social Policy and Development Center, 2014.

Siddiqui, Habibullah, *Education in Sindh Past, Present and Future* (Jamshoro: Institute of Sindhology, 1987).

SEMIS, *Sindh Education Profile 2001–02*, Karachi, Education and Literacy Department, Government of Sindh, n.d.

————, *Sindh Education Profile 2005–06*, Karachi, Education and Literacy Department, Government of Sindh, n.d.

————, *Sindh Education Profile 2010–11*, Karachi, Education and Literacy Department, Government of Sindh, n.d.

————, *Sindh Education Profile 2015–16*, Karachi, Education and Literacy Department, Government of Sindh, n.d.

UNICEF, *Defining Quality in Education*, Florence, 2000.

UNESCO, *Education for All 2000–2015: Achievements and challenges*, Paris, 2015. <http://unesdoc.unesco.org/images/0023/002322/232205e.pdf>.

Chapter 5: Health

Abbasi, M. B., *Socio Economic Characteristics of Women in Sind Issues Affecting Women's Status*, Karachi, Economic Studies Centre, Sind Regional Plan Organization, Government of Pakistan, 1980.

Bureau of Statistics, *Health Profile*, Karachi, Planning and Development Department, Government of Sindh, 2010–15.

_____, *Development Statistics of Sindh* 2011, Karachi, Planning and Development Department, Government of Sindh, 2013.

_____, *Sindh Multiple Indicator Cluster Survey 2014*, Karachi, Planning and Development Department, Government of Sindh, 2015.

Dawn, 'Uplift Plans for Sindh Estimates Revised', 1979.

Department of Health, *Flood-Affected Nutrition Surveys—Sindh Pakistan*, Karachi, Government of Sindh, 2010.

Federal SAP Secretariat, *Progress of SAP based on Quarterly Report: July–December 1997*, Islamabad, Multi Donor Support Unit (MSU), Government of Pakistan, 1998.

'Five Year Plans of Pakistan', *Open Source Enclyclopedia*, n.d., <https://pediaview.com/openpedia/Five-Year_Plans_of_Pakistan>, accessed 26 May 2017.

Ghumman, Khawar, 'One in Three Pakistanis Lacks Access to Adequately Nutritious Food', *Dawn*, 22 December 2015.

Government of Punjab and UNDP, 'Bureau of Statistics Punjab, Government of Punjab', *Multiple Indicator Cluster Survey Punjab 2014*, Lahore, Bureau of Statistics, Government of Punjab, 2014.

Government of Sindh and UNDP, 'Report on the status of the Millennium Development Goals Sindh', *United Nations Development Programme Nepal*, Karachi, Government of Sindh/United Nations Development Programme, 2011.

_____, and United Nations International Children's Emergency Fund, *Multiple Cluster Indicator Survey 2004*, Karachi, Government of Sindh and United Nations International Children's Emergency Fund, 2005.

_____, *Development Initiatives and Achievements—Four Year Performance*, Karachi, Planning and Development Department, 2010.

_____, *Post-War Development Schemes (1947–1952)*, Karachi, Government of Sindh, n.d.

_____, *Sindh People and Progress*, Karachi, Directorate of Information Sindh, 1954.

HANDS, *1st Situation Analysis Survey—Tharparkar*, Karachi, HANDS Pakistan Head Office, 2014.

Holland, Sir Henry, *Frontier Doctor: An Autobiography*, London, Hodder and Stoughton, 1958.

Husain, Ishrat, *Economy of Modern Sind*, Jamshoro, Institute of Sindhology, University of Sind, 1981.

Institute of Business Management, *Economic Survey of Sindh*, Karachi, 2011.

International Food Policy Research Institute, *Global Nutrition Report 2015: Actions and Accountability to Advance Nutrition and Sustainable Development*, Washington, DC, IFPRI, 2015.

Junaidi, Ikram, 'Conditions in Teaching Hospitals Unsatisfactory, Says PMDC President', *Dawn*, 18 February 2016.

Mansoor, Hasan, '994 new cases of HIV/Aids detected in Sindh this year', *Dawn*, 28 November 2014.

Pakistan Today, '889 new HIV cases detected in Sindh this year', 24 July 2016, <https://www.pakistantoday.com.pk/2016/07/24/889-new-hiv-cases-detected-in-sindh-this-year/>, accessed 25 May 2017.

Policy and Strategic Planning Unit, *Policy and Strategic Planning* Unit, Lahore, Health Department, Government of Punjab, 2014.

Ramanna, Mridula, *Health Care in Bombay Presidency—1896–1930*, Delhi, Primus Books, 2012.

Rizvi, N. and Nishtar, S., 'Pakistan's health policy: appropriateness and relevance to women's health needs', *Health Policy*, 88/2–3, 2008.

Sathar Z. A., M. A. Wazir and M. Sadiq, *Prioritizing Family Planning for Achieving Provincial Maternal Child Health and Development Goals*, Islamabad, Population Council, 2014.

SPDC, 'Annual Reviews', various years, <http://www.spdc.org.pk/Publication.aspx?mid=15>.

Sorley, H. T., *The Gazetteer of West Pakistan the Former Province of Sind Including Khairpur State*, Lahore, Gazetteer Cell, Board of Revenue, 1968.

Standing Committee on Nutrition, *5th Report on the World Nutrition Situation: Nutrition for Improved Development Outcome*, Geneva, United Nations System, 2004.

Sheikh, Fazal M., 'Rain inundates low-lying areas', 1978.

Sindh Bureau of Statistics and United Nations International Children's Fund, *Multiple Indicator Cluster Surveys*, Karachi, Sindh Bureau of Statistics/United Nations International Children's Fund, 2005.

The News, 'Punjab to spend more on health, education than Sindh, KP', 16 June 2015, <https://www.thenews.com.pk/print/46262-punjab-to-spend-more-on-health-education-than-sindh-kp>.

UN, 'Millennium Development Goals', 2000, <http://www.unmillenniumproject.org/goals/>, accessed 29 May 2017.

———, Sustainable Development Goals', 2015, <http://www.un.org/sustainabledevelopment/sustainable-development-goals/>, accessed 29 May 2017.

UNDP, 'Human Development Reports', 1990–2015.

United Nations System Standing Committee on Nutrition, *5th Report on the World Nutrition Situation: Nutrition for Improved Development Outcome*, Geneva, WHO, 2004.

USAID, *Pakistan Emergency Situational Analysis—A Profile of Tharparkar*, Washington, DC, iMMAP, 2014.

World Bank, 'Data Portal—Pakistan', 1960–2014, <http://data.worldbank.org/indicator/SH.STA.ORCF.ZS?locations=PK>.

World Health Organization, *Constitution of the World Health Organization*, Geneva, WHO, 1948.

———, *Pakistan—Tharparkar Crisis: Overview, Response, Damages*, Islamabad, WHO, 2014.

———, 'Nutrition Landscape Information System, (NLiS)', 2017, <http://apps.who.int/nutrition/landscape/report.aspx>.

Zaidi, Shehla, Akhund, G. H., Narejo, S., and Jennifer S., 'Situation Analysis for Post Devolution', *ResearchGate* [online journal], November 2011, <https://www.researchgate.net/publication/299391057_Situation_Analysis_for_Post_Devolution_Health_Sector_Strategy_of_Sindh_Province>, accessed 27 May 2017.

Chapter 6: Labour and Employment

Agence France-Presse, AFP, 'Few lessons learned two years on from Karachi factory fire', *Dawn*, 7 January 2015.

Ahmed, Sadaf, 'Constructing a Culture of Fear: The Role of Gender Based Violence in Controlling Bonded Labour in Pakistan', eds. Ayaz Qureshi and Ali Khan, *Bonded Labour in Pakistan*, Karachi, Oxford University Press, 2016.

Amjad, Rashid, 'The Employment Challenges for Pakistan in the 1990s', ed. Anjum Rashid, *Financing Pakistan's Development in the 1990s*, Karachi, Oxford University Press, 1992.

Arif, Ghulam M., 'Bonded Labour in agriculture: a rapid assessment in Punjab and North West Frontier Province, Pakistan', Working Paper no. 25, Geneva, International Labor Organization, 2004.

Ghori, Habib Khan, 'Sindh Assembly Bans Employment of Children Under 14', *Dawn*, 26 January 2017.

Hisam, Zeenat, ed., *Status of Labour Rights 2015*, Karachi, Pakistan Institute of Labour Education and Research, (PILER), 2016.

Home Affairs Division, *Census of Pakistan, 1961,* Karachi, Government of Pakistan, n.d.

Human Rights Commission of Pakistan, HRCP), 'Rights of the Disadvantaged', *Human Rights Commission of Pakistan Annual Report 2015*, Lahore, 2016.

Hussain, Iffat, *Problems of Working Women*, Newcastle, Cambridge Scholars Publishing, 2008.

Hussein, Maliha H., et al., 'Bonded Labor in Agriculture: A Rapid Assessment in Sindh and Balochistan, Pakistan', Working Paper no. 26, Geneva, International Labor Organization, 2004.

International Labor Organization, *Key Indicators of the Labour Market*, 9th edn, Geneva, 2016.

———, 'WOMEN—Only 2 per cent trade union members in the formal and invisible in the informal economy', *ILO* [website], August 2012, <http://www.ilo.org/islamabad/info/public/pr/WCMS_187903/lang--en/index.htm?ssSourceSiteId=asia/lang--en/index.htm>, accessed 5 March 2017.

———, 'C029—Forced Labour Convention, 1930, No. 29)', *ILO* [website] <http://www.ilo.org/dyn/normlex/en/f?p=NORMLEXPUB:12100:0::NO::P12100_ILO_CODE:C029>, accessed 2 Oct. 2016.

———, Observation, (CEACR)—adopted 2013, published 103rd ILC session, 2014), 'Freedom of Association and Protection of the Right to Organise Convention, 1948 (No. 87)', *ILO* [website]. <http://www.ilo.org/dyn/normlex/en/f?p=1000:13100:0::NO:13100:P13100_COMMENT_ID:3149517>, accessed 3 October 2016.

———, R116—Reduction of Hours of Work Recommendation, 1962 (No. 116)', *ILO* [website], <http://www.ilo.org/dyn/normlex/en/f?p=1000:12100:::NO:12100:P12100_INSTRUMENT_ID:312454>, accessed 3 October 2016.

Khan, Ali and Ayaz Qureshi, eds., *Bonded Labour in Pakistan*, Karachi, Oxford University Press, 2016.

Manager of Publications, *Census of Pakistan, 1951*, Karachi, Government of Pakistan, n.d.

Ministry of Finance, 'Population, Labour Force and Employment', *Pakistan Economic Survey 2007–2008*, Islamabad, Government of Pakistan, 2008.

_____, 'Population, Labour Force and Employment', *Pakistan Economic Survey 2015–16*, Islamabad, Government of Pakistan, 2016.

Pakistan Bureau of Statistics, *Labour Force Survey 1951–52*, Karachi, Government of Pakistan, n.d.

_____, *Labour Force Survey 1960–61,* Karachi, Government of Pakistan, n.d.

_____, *Labour Force Survey 1963–64,* Karachi, Government of Pakistan, n.d.

_____, *Labour Force Survey 1971–72*, Islamabad, Statistics Division, Government of Pakistan, n.d.

_____, *Labour Force Survey 1990–91*, Islamabad, Statistics Division, Government of Pakistan, n.d.

_____, *Labour Force Survey* 1990–91, Islamabad, Statistics Division, Government of Pakistan, n.d.

_____, *Labour Force Survey 1997–98*, Islamabad, Statistics Division, Government of Pakistan, n.d.

_____, *Labour Force Survey 2001–02*, Islamabad, Statistics Division, Government of Pakistan, n.d.

_____, *Labour Force Survey 2005–06*, Islamabad, Statistics Division, Government of Pakistan, n.d.

_____, *Labour Force Survey 2010–11*, Islamabad, Statistics Division, Government of Pakistan, n.d.

_____, *Labour Force Survey 2015–16*, Islamabad, Statistics Division, Government of Pakistan, n.d.

Population Census Organization, *Population Census of Pakistan 1972*, Islamabad, Statistics Division, Government of Pakistan, n.d.

_____, *1981 Census Report of Sind Province*, Islamabad, Statistics Division, Government of Pakistan, 1984.

_____, *1998 Census Report of Sindh*, Islamabad, Statistics Division, Government of Pakistan, 2000.

PPI, 'Labour Unions Lament Risky Working Conditions', *The Express Tribune*, 23 December 2014.

Provincial Assembly of Sindh, 'Sindh Minimum Wages Act, 2015', *pas.gov.pk* [website], April 2016, <http://www.pas.gov.pk/up loads/acts/Sindh%20Act%20No.VIII%20of%202016.pdf>, accessed 30 September 2016.

Provincial Assembly of Sindh, 'The Sindh Bonded Labour Abolition Act, 2015', *Open Parliament* [website], <http://www.thepunctuationguide.com/em-dash.html>, accessed 30 September 2016.

Qazilbash, Ali, 'Beyond Setting at Liberty: A Legal Study of Bonded Labour in Pakistan', eds. Ali Khan and Ayaz Qureshi, *Bonded Labour in Pakistan*, Karachi, Oxford University Press, 2016.

Qureshi, Ayaz and Ali Khan, 'Introduction', *Bonded Labour in Pakistan*, Karachi, Oxford University Press, 2016.

Radio Pakistan, 'Sindh Governor Accords Assent to "Sindh Bonded Labour System" (Abolition) Act 2015', Radio Pakistan [website], June 2016, <http://www.radio.gov.pk/23-Jun–2016/sindh-governor-accords-assent-to-sindh-bonded-labour-system-act–2015>, accessed 3 March 2017.

Research and Development Unit, *Sindh Employment Trends*, Karachi, Sindh Technical Education and Vocational Training Authority, Government of Sindh, 2013.

Saleem, Ahmed, 'Peshgis in the Mining Sector', eds. Ali Khan and Ayaz Qureshi, *Bonded Labour in Pakistan*, Karachi, Oxford University Press, 2016.

Tahir, Nadia, *Status of Labour Rights in Pakistan 2015*, Karachi, PILER, 2016.

The News, 'Majority of Industrial Workers Unaware of Dire Health Risks', 6 October 2016.

Walk Free Foundation, 'Global Slavery Index 2016', Walk Free Foundation [website], 2017. <https://www.globalslaveryindex.org/index/>, accessed 17 January 2017.

Zhou, Mi, *Minimum Wage Setting, Implementation and Working Conditions in the Formal and Informal Sectors of the Garment Industry in Pakistan, Key Indicators of the Labour Market*, Geneva, International Labour Organization, 2016.

Chapter 7: Poverty and Inequality

Acemoglu, Daron, Simon Johnson, and James Robinson, 'Understanding Prosperity and Poverty: Geography, Institutions and the Reversal of Fortune', eds. Abhijit Vinayak Banerjee, Roland Bénabou, and Dilip Mookherjee, *Understanding Poverty*, New York, Oxford University Press, 2006.

Amjad, Rashid, 'Pakistan's Poverty Reduction Strategy: Why Employment Matters', *The Lahore Journal of Economics* 10, 2005.

Anka, Lawal Muhammad, 'Empirical Analysis of the Determinants of Rural Poverty in Sindh Province of Pakistan', PhD thesis, Sindh Development Studies Centre, University of Jamshoro, 2009.

Anwar, Talat, Qureshi, Sarfraz K., and Ali, Hammad, *Landlessness and Rural Poverty in Pakistan.*, Karachi, State Bank of Pakistan, 2002.

Asadullah, Muhammad Niaz, 'Educational Disparity between East and West Pakistan', Discussion Papers in Economic and Social History, no. 63, University of Oxford, 2006, <http://www.nuff.ox.ac.uk/economics/history/Paper63/63asadullah.pdf>.

Gazdar, Haris, 'Review of Pakistan Poverty Data', *Sustainable Development Policy Institute—Monograph Series Number 9*, Sustainable Policy Institute, 1999.

Ghauri, Irfan, 'Poverty Afflicts 75% people in rural Sindh', *The Express Tribune*, 2 July 2016, <https://tribune.com.pk/story/1135227/alarming-stats-poverty-afflicts–75-people-rural-sindh/>.

Husain, Ishrat, 'Poverty Reduction Strategy of Pakistan', <https://ishrathusain.iba.edu.pk/speeches/povertyReduction/PovertyReduction–13-Oct–05.pdf>.

Irfan, Muhammad, 'Poverty and Natural Resource Management in Pakistan', *The Pakistan Development Review*, 46/4, 2007.

Lohana, Hari Ram, '*Poverty Dynamics in Rural Sindh, Pakistan*', Working Paper No. 157, n.p., Chronic Poverty Research Centre, 2009.

Nawaz-ul-Huda, et al., 'Social and Economic Inequality in Sindh—A Factorial Analysis Approach', *International Journal of Sociology and Anthropology*, 5/6, 2013.

Naveed, Arif, and Nazim Ali, '*Clustered Deprivation: District Profile of Poverty in Pakistan*', Islamabad, Sustainable Development Policy Institute, 2012.

Pakistan Bureau of Statistics, *Household Integrated Economic Survey 2005–06*, Islamabad, Government of Pakistan, 2007.

———, *Household Integrated Economic Survey 2007–08*, Islamabad, Government of Pakistan, 2009.

———, *Household Integrated Economic Survey 2010–11*, Islamabad, Government of Pakistan, 2012.

———, *Household Integrated Economic Survey 2012–13*, Islamabad, Government of Pakistan, 2014.

———, *Household Integrated Economic Survey 2013–14*, Islamabad, Government of Pakistan, 2015.

———, *Household Integrated Economic Survey 2014–15*, Islamabad, Government of Pakistan, 2016.

Pakistan Institute for Parliamentary Services, *National MDGs Orientation for Parliamentary Task Forces*, Islamabad, Pakistan Institute for Parliamentary Services, 2014.

Sindh Bureau of Statistics and UNDP, *Multidimensional Poverty in Pakistan*, Karachi, Sindh Bureau of Statistics and UNDP, 2015.

'Poverty and Natural Resource Management in Pakistan', *The Pakistan Development Review*, 2007.

Rizvi, Ali Raza, et al., *Sindh Strategy for Sustainable Development*, Karachi, International Union for Conservation of Nature and Natural Resources, 2007.

Sen, Amartya, *On Economic Inequality*, New York, Oxford University Press, 1973.

Smith, Michael B. Todaro, and Stephen C. Smith, 'Poverty, Inequality, and Development', *Economic Development*, Boston, Pearson Addison Wesley, 2012.

SPDC, 'Social Development in Pakistan—Growth, Inequality and Poverty', *Annual Review 2001*, Karachi, Oxford University Press, 2001.

———, 'Poverty, Inequality and Social Inclusion', *The State of Social Development in Rural Pakistan*, pp. 85–115, Annual Review 2012–2013.

———, 'Counting the Poor in the Urban Context' in *The State of Social Development in Urban Pakistan*, pp. 137–57.

———, 'Financing of Urban Social Service Delivery in Pakistan', *The State of Social Development in Urban Pakistan*.

———, 'Geographical Unevenness in Urban Human Development', *The State of Social Development in Urban Pakistan*.

UNDP, *Human Development Report 2016*, New York, UNDP, 2016, accessed 5 November 2017, <http://hdr.undp.org/sites/default/files/2016_human_development_report.pdf>.

United Nations Department of Economic and Social Affairs, *World Summit for Social Development—Chapter 2*, Copenhagen, United Nations Department of Economic and Social Affairs, 1995, accessed 22 February 2017, <http://www.un.org/esa/socdev/wssd/text-version/agreements/poach2.htm>.

United Nations, Economic and Social Council, *ACC Statement of Commitment for Action to Eradicate Poverty*, accessed 22 February 2017, <https://www.unsceb.org/CEBPublicFiles/press/9818151e.pdf>.

World Bank Databank, accessed at <http://databank.worldbank.org/data/reports.aspx?Code=PAK&id=556d8fa6&report_name=Popular_countries&populartype=country&ispopular=y>.

———, *World Bank Forecasts Global Poverty to Fall Below 10% for First Time; Major Hurdles Remain in Goal to End Poverty by 2030* (4 October 2015), accessed 22 February 2017, <http://www.worldbank.org/en/news/press-release/2015/10/04/

world-bank-forecasts-global-poverty-to-fall-below–10-for-first-time-major-hurdles-remain-in-goal-to-end-poverty-by–2030>.

Zaidi, S. Akbar., *Issues in Pakistan's Economy: A Political Economy Perspective*, Karachi, Oxford University Press, 2015.

Chapter 8: Agriculture

Abbasi, M. B., *Socio Economic Characteristics of Women in Sind Issues Affecting Women's Status*, Karachi, Sind Regional Plan Organization, 1980.

Agricultural Census Organization, *Agricultural Census 2010*, Karachi, Statistics Division, Government of Pakistan, 2011.

Agriculture Marketing Information Service, *Marketing of Garlic: Problems and Prospects*, Lahore, Directorate of Agriculture, Government of Punjab, n.d.

Aazim, Mohiuddin, 'Issues in Farm Mechanization', *Dawn*, 8 December 2014.

Agriculture Department, *Investment Opportunities in Agriculture Sector*, Karachi, Government of Sindh, n.d., accessed 1 June 2017.

'History', *Agriculture Department* [website], n.d., <http://sindhagri.gov.pk/history.html>, accessed 2 June 2017.

Khan, Ahmed Fraz, 'Farms without Subsidies', *Dawn*, 4 August 2008.

Ahmed, Feroz, 'Agrarian Change and Class Formation in Sindh', *Economic and Political Weekly*, 19/39, 1984.

Ahmad, Salim, *Peasant Land Rights Movements of Pakistan*, Islamabad, Sustainable Development Policy Institute, 2008.

Bhatti, I. M. and Atta H. Soomro, 'Agriculture in Sindh', *Agricultural Inputs and Field Crop Production in Sindh*, Hyderabad, Directorate General Agricultural Research Sindh, 1994.

'Cotton', *Agricultural Inputs and Field Crop Production in Sindh*, Hyderabad, Directorate General Agricultural Research Sindh, 1994.

'Rice', *Agricultural Inputs and Field Crop Production in Sindh*, Hyderabad, Directorate General Agricultural Research Sindh, 1994.

'Sugarcane', *Agricultural Inputs and Field Crop Production in Sindh*, Hyderabad, Directorate General Agricultural Research Sindh, 1994.

'Wheat', *Agricultural Inputs and Field Crop Production in Sindh*, Hyderabad, Directorate General Agricultural Research Sindh, 1994.

Bukhari, Ashfak, 'Preventing decline of rice exports' *Dawn*, 8 August 2016.

Bullo, Momin, *Date Crop of Khairpur*, Karachi, Sindh Enterprise Development Fund, Government of Sindh, n.d.

Bureau of Statistics, *Development Statistics of Sindh 1991*, Karachi, Planning and Development Department, Government of Sindh.

———, *Development Statistics of Sindh 1997*, Karachi, Planning and Development Department, Government of Sindh, n.d.

———, *Development Statistics of Sindh 2002*, Karachi, Planning and Development Department, Government of Sindh, n.d.

———, *Development Statistics of Sindh 2007*, Karachi, Planning and Development Department, Government of Sindh, n.d.

———, *Development Statistics of Sindh 2011*, Karachi, Planning and Development Department, Government of Sindh, n.d.

———, *Development Statistics of Sindh 2014*, Karachi, Planning and Development Department, Government of Sindh, n.d.

Chaudhary, Mohammad Aslam, 'Regional Agricultural Underdevelopment in Pakistan', *The Pakistan Development Review*, 33/4, 1994, pp. 889–98.

Dawn, 'Banana cultivation in Sindh', October 2003.

———, 'Extending Poultry Farming to Rural Areas', 3 September 2007.

———, 'Factors Affecting Guava Produce', 24 October 2005.

———, 'Farmers in Sindh Get Free Sunflower Seeds', 25 March 2011.

———, 'Farmers Plan Protest across Sindh', 15 March 2012.

———, 'Hyderabad: Fertilizer Samples Found Substandard', 30 May 2002.

———, 'Hyderabad: Cut in Sindh's Fertilizer Share Slated', 29 March 2003.

————, 'Hyderabad: Riverine Forests Fast Disappearing, 18 February 2008.

————, 'Hyderabad: Samples of 10 Fertilizers Found Substandard', 16 March 2003.

————, 'Mangroves Worst Hit by Deforestation: Study', 20 June 2012.

————, 'Peasants, Rights Activists Protest against Water Shortage', 25 July 2011.

————, 'Samples of 10 Fertilizers Found Substandard', 16 April 2003.

————, 'Salinity Problems in Vegetable Crops', 4 March 2012.

————, 'Sindh Forests', 15 February 2016.

————, 'Subsidised Tractor Scheme and Farm Mechanisation', 29 March 2010.

————, 'Sukkur: Spurious Pesticides, Fertilizers Seized', 4 August 2004.

————, 'Towards Agricultural Mechanisation', 13 January 2014.

Directorate of Agriculture, *Cotton Production, Marketing and Export*, Lahore, Government of Punjab, 2006.

Government of Sindh, The Sindh Fertilizer, Control) Act, 1994', *Sindh Laws* (Website) (1994), <http://sindhlaws.gov.pk/setup/Publications_SindhCode/PUB–15–000810.pdf>, accessed 17 June 2017.

————, 'The Sindh Fertilizer (Control) Rules 1999', *Sindh Laws* (Website), 1999, <http://sindhlaws.gov.pk/setup/Publications_SindhCode/PUB–15–000555.pdf>, accessed 17 June 2017.

Hafiz, Ghufran Ali Khan, et al., 'Impact of Rising Prices of Fertilizers on Crops Production in Pakistan', *Global Journal of Management and Business Research*, 10/ 9, 2010.

Hamid, Naveed and Akmal Hussain, 'Regional Inequalities and Capitalist Development', *Pakistan Economic and Social Review*, 12 /3, 1974.

Hanif, Khan and Nauman, *Agricultural Perspective and Policy*, Islamabad, Ministry of Food, Agriculture and Livestock, Government of Pakistan, 2004.

Hasan, Arif, 'Eclipse of Feudalism', *Dawn*, 8 December 2015.

Hussain, Akmal, 'Agrarian Structure and Social Change', ed. Ayesha Jalal, *The Oxford Companion to Pakistani History*, Karachi, Oxford University Press, 2012.

Husain, Ishrat, '*Economy of Sindh: 1972/73—2012/13*', Karachi, Avari Towers, 2nd International Seminar on Sindh through the Centuries, 26 March 2014, <http://www.ishrathusain.iba.edu.pk/The_Economy_of_Sindh_Conclusing_Keynote_Address_at_the_2nd_International_Seminar_on_Sindh_through_the_Centuries.docx/>, accessed 1 June 2017.

————, '*Economy of Sindh: 1972/73—2012/13*', 2nd International Seminar on Sindh through the Centuries, Karachi, 2014, <http://www.ishrathusain.iba.edu.pk/The_Economy_of_Sindh_Conclusing_Keynote_Addres>, accessed 10 August 2017.

Islamabad Chamber of Commerce, *Report on Mangoes From Pakistan*, Islamabad, n.d.

Ilyas, Faiza, 'Drafts on Forest, Wildlife Laws Await Govt Approval for Four Years', *Dawn*, 17 January 2015.

Jamali, Dino Karim, 'Crops', *Nuclear Institute of Agriculture* [website], n.d., <http://www.nia.org.pk/crop.html>, accessed 15 June 2016.

Khan, Aamir Shafaat, 'Makers Halt Tractor Production', *Dawn*, 27 December 2011.

————, 'Poultry Rates Hit New Peak', *Dawn*, September, 2008.

————, 'Sharp Decline in Tractor Sales', *Dawn*, 6 August 2011.

————, 'Farms without Subsidies', *Dawn*, 4 August 2008.

Khan, Hafiz Ghufran Ali, et al., 'Impact of Rising Prices of Fertilizers on Crops Production in Pakistan', *Global Journal of Management and Business Research*, 10/ 9, 2010.

Khan, Mohammad Hussain, 'Sindh to Produce Less Mangoes This Season', *Dawn*, 11 April 2016.

————, 'Sindh's Big Farmers Prefer Rice Crop', *Dawn*, 9 June 2014.

————, 'Sindh's Irrational Sugarcane Pricing Policy', *Dawn*, 11 January 2016.

Hussain, Javed and Jan Khaskheli, 'Issues and Problems of Women Cotton Pickers in Sindh-Baseline Study of Matiari District', n.p., *Sindh Community Foundation*, n.d.

Junejo, Salman, 'When will the Suffering of the Sugarcane Farmers in Sindh End', *Tribune Blogs* [website], n.d., <http://blogs.tribune.com.pk/story/25974/when-will-the-suffering-of-the-sugarcane-farmers-in-sindh-end/>, accessed 17 June 2016.

Laghari, Hadi Bux, *An Overview of Banana Production Sindh*, Karachi, Sindh Enterprise Development Fund, Department of Finance, n.d.

Memon, Sarfaraz, 'In Khairpur, a Tutorial Benefits Date Growers', *Express Tribune*, 4 September 2012.

Mohil, Praveen and Usha Jain, 'Influence of Inorganic and Organic Fertilizers on Biomass Production of Amaranthus', *European Journal of Experimental Biology*, 6/4, 2016.

Ministry of Food, Agriculture and Livestock, *50 Years of Agricultural Statistics in Pakistan (1947–2000)*, Islamabad, Government of Pakistan, 2007.

Ministry of National Food Security and Research, *Agricultural Year book 2015–16*, Islamabad, Government of Pakistan, 2017.

Fruits, Vegetables and Condiments Statistics of Pakistan, Islamabad, Government of Pakistan, 2016.

Ministry of Industries and Production, *Fertilizer Policy*, Islamabad, Government of Pakistan, n.d.

Natural Resources Management and Environment Department, *Fertilizer use by crop in Pakistan*, Rome, Food and Agriculture Organization of the United Nations, 2004.

Nulty, Leslie, *The Green Revolution in West Pakistan—Implications of Technological Change*, New York, Preager Publishers, 1972.

Oxford Poverty and Human Development Initiative and United Nations Development Program, *Multidimensional Poverty in Pakistan*, Karachi, Planning Commission of Pakistan, Government of Pakistan, 2015.

Pakistan Bureau of Statistics, *Approved Crop Calendar,* Karachi, Planning and Development Department, Government of Sindh 2011.

———, *Agricultural Statistics of Pakistan (2011–2012)*, Islamabad, Statistics Division, 2013.

Qureshi, Khurshid Ali, et al., 'Contribution of Area and Yield of Total Rice Production in Pakistan: An Analysis', *Pakistan Journal of Agricultural Sciences*, 30/1, 1993.

Qureshi, Muzaffar, 'Cotton Production May Fall in Sindh', *Dawn*, 10 August 2014.

Rashid, Shehreyar and Asjad Tariq Sheikh, *Farmers' Perceptions of Agricultural Land Values in Rural Pakistan*, Islamabad, Pakistan Institute of Development Economics, n.d.

Report of the Land Reforms Commission for West Pakistan, Lahore, Superintendent Government Printing, West Pakistan, 1961.

Salma, S., S. Rehman and M.A. Shah, 'Rainfall Trends in Different Climate Zones of Pakistan', *Pakistan Journal of Meteorology*, 9/17, 2012.

Shaikh, Muhammad Ali, *Report on Agriculture in Sindh—Issues and Options,* Karachi, SZABIST Center for Information and Research, 2001.

———, *Sector Brief Dates,* Karachi, Government of Sindh, n.p.

———, *Sector Brief of Guava*, Karachi, Sindh Board of Investment, n.d.

———, *Sector Brief Poultry,* Karachi, Sindh Board of Investment, n.d.

Sorley, H. T., *The Gazetteer of West Pakistan: The Former Province of Sind Including Khairpur State*, Lahore, Gazetteer Cell, Board of Revenue, 1968.

Zaidi, S. Akbar, *Issues in Pakistan's Economy*, 3rd ed., Karachi, Oxford University Press, 2015.

Chapter 9: Irrigation

Government of Sindh, *Water Sector Improvement Project (WISP)*, Karachi, Planning and Development Department, Government of Sindh, n.d.

Khan, Ahmed Hayat, 'Water Sharing Disputes in Pakistan: Standpoint of Provinces', *Berkeley Journal of Social Sciences*, 4, 2014.

Michel, Aloys Arthur, *The Indus Rivers: A Study of the Effects of Partition*, New Haven, Connecticut, Yale University Press, 1967.

Ministry of Water and Power, *The Water Accord 1991*, Islamabad, Government of Pakistan, 1991.

Pathan, Mumtaz Hussain, *The History of Arab Period in Sindh*, unknown, 1978.

Rajput, Muhammad Idris, *Background Paper—Draft: Inter-Provincial Water Issues in Pakistan*, Islamabad, PILDAT, 2011.

———, *Kalabagh Dam and Sindh: A View Point,* Karachi, Sindh Graduates Association, 2005.

Sorley, H. T., *The Gazetteer of West Pakistan: The Former Province of Sind Including Khairpur State*, Lahore, Gazetteer Cell, Board of Revenue, 1968.

Chapter 10: Infrastructure

Bureau of Statistics, *Development Statistics of Sindh 1975,* Karachi, Planning and Development, Government of Sindh, n.d.

————, *Development Statistics of Sindh 1983,* Karachi, Planning and Development, Government of Sindh, n.d.

————, *Development Statistics of Sindh 1992,* Karachi, Planning and Development, Government of Sindh, n.d.

————, *Development Statistics of Sindh 1998,* Karachi, Planning and Development, Government of Sindh, n.d.

————, *Development Statistics of Sindh 2001,* Karachi, Planning and Development, Government of Sindh, n.d.

————, *Development Statistics of Sindh 2006,* Karachi, Planning and Development, Government of Sindh, n.d.

————, *Development Statistics of Sindh 2009,* Karachi, Planning and Development, Government of Sindh, n.d.

————, *Development Statistics of Sindh 2010,* Karachi, Planning and Development Department, Government of Sindh, n.d.

————, *Development Statistics of Sindh 2014,* Karachi, Planning and Development Department, Government of Sindh, n.d.

Finance Division, *Pakistan Economic Survey 1995–96,* Islamabad, Ministry of Finance, Government of Pakistan, n.d.

————, *Pakistan Economic Survey 1990–91,* Islamabad, Ministry of Finance, Government of Pakistan, n.d.

————, *Pakistan Economic Survey 2016–17,* Islamabad, Ministry of Finance, Government of Pakistan, n.d.

————, *Pakistan Economic Survey 2015–16,* Islamabad, Ministry of Finance, Government of Pakistan, n.d.

————, *Pakistan Economic Survey 2010–11,* Islamabad, Ministry of Finance, Government of Pakistan, n.d.

————, *Pakistan Economic Survey 2005–06,* Islamabad, Ministry of Finance, Government of Pakistan, n.d.

————, *Pakistan Economic Survey 2000–01,* Islamabad, Ministry of Finance, Government of Pakistan, n.d.

Home Affairs Division, *Census of Pakistan, 1961,* Karachi, Government of Pakistan, n.d.

Pakistan Telecommunications Authority, *Annual Report 2003–04,* Islamabad, Government of Pakistan, n.d.

————, *Annual Report 2005–06,* Islamabad, Government of Pakistan, n.d.

————, *Annual Report 2010–11,* Islamabad, Government of Pakistan, n.d.

————, *Annual Report 2015–16,* Islamabad, Government of Pakistan, n.d.

Government of Sindh, 'Highways Department', *Government of Sindh* [website], n.d. <http://www.sindh.gov.pk/dpt/worksandservices/highway.htm>, accessed 25 February 2017.

————, 'Katchi Abadis Government of Sindh- Profile of Katchi Abadis', *Government of Sindh* [website], n.d., <http://sindh.gov.pk/dpt/SKAA/status%20of%20katchi.htm>, accessed 20 April 2017.

Hasan, Arif, 'The Causes of Land Contestation in Karachi and How These Impact on Housing and Urban Development', International Institute for Environment and Development (IIED), 27/1, 2015.

————, 'The Water and Sanitation Challenge: The Conflict between Reality and Planning Paradigms', 2009, <http://arifhasan.org/seminars/the-water-and-sanitation-challenge-the-conflict-between-reality-and-planning-paradigms>, accessed 10 April 2017.

————, 'Ugly Karachi', *Dawn,* 6 November 2015.

————, 'Urban Land Reform', *Dawn,* 15 July 2015.

IUCN, *Sindh State of Environment and Development,* Karachi, IUCN Pakistan, 2004.

Manager of Publications, *Census of Pakistan, 1951,* Karachi, Statistics Division, Government of Pakistan, n.d.

————, *Census of Pakistan, 1951* [Vol. 7—Tables of Economic Characteristics West Pakistan], Karachi, Government of Pakistan, n.d.

Pakistan Bureau of Statistics, *Pakistan Social and Living Standards Measurement Survey (PSLM) 2006–7,* Islamabad, Statistics Division, Government of Pakistan, 2007.

————, *Pakistan Social and Living Standards Measurement Survey (PSLM) 2010–11,* Islamabad, Statistics Division, Government of Pakistan, 2011.

————, *Pakistan Social and Living Standards Measurement Survey (PSLM) 2014–15,* Islamabad, Statistics Division, Government of Pakistan, 2016.

Population Census Organization, *Population Census of Pakistan 1972,* Islamabad, Statistics Division, Government of Pakistan, n.d.

————, *1981 Census Report of Sind Province,* Islamabad, Statistics Division, Government of Pakistan, 1984.

————, *Handbook of Population Census Data Sind,* Islamabad, Statistics Division, Government of Pakistan, 1988.

————, *1998 Provincial Census Report of Sindh,* Islamabad, Statistics Division, Government of Pakistan, 2000.

Planning Commission, *The First Five-Year Plan 1955–60,* Karachi, Government of Pakistan, 1957.

_____, *The Third Five-Year Plan 1965–1970*, Islamabad, Ministry of Planning, Development and Reforms, Government of Pakistan, 1965.

_____, *The Fourth Five-Year Plan 1970–75*, Islamabad, Ministry of Planning, Development and Reforms, Government of Pakistan, 1970.

_____, *The Fifth Five-Year Plan 1978–83 Sectoral Programmes (Part II)*, Islamabad, Ministry of Planning, Development and Reforms, Government of Pakistan, 1978.

_____, *The Sixth Five-Year Plan 1983–88*, Islamabad, Ministry of Planning, Development and Reforms, Government of Pakistan, 1983.

_____, *The Seventh Five-Year Plan 1988–1993 Federal/Provincial Projects and Programmes*, Islamabad, Ministry of Planning, Development and Reforms, Government of Pakistan, 1989.

_____, *The Eighth Five-Year Plan 1993–98*, Islamabad, Ministry of Planning, Development and Reforms, Government of Pakistan, 1994.

_____, *The Tenth Five-Year Plan 2010–15*, Islamabad, Ministry of Planning, Development and Reforms, Government of Pakistan, 2010.

_____, *The Eleventh Five-Year Plan 2013–18*, Islamabad, Ministry of Planning, Development and Reforms, Government of Pakistan, n.d.

Sánchez-Triana, Ernesto, et al., 'Infrastructure Modernization', *Revitalizing Industrial Growth in Pakistan: Trade, Infrastructure, and Environmental Performance*, Washington DC, World Bank, 2014.

Siddiqui, Salman, 'Trade via Karachi records 15% increase', *Express Tribune*, 5 July 2016, <https://tribune.com.pk/story/1136469/imports-exports-trade-via-karachi-port-records–15-increase/>.

Chapter 11: Sindh's Industrial Structure: Past and Present

Asian Development Bank and World Bank, *Pakistan: Securing Sindh's Future—The Prospects and Challenges Ahead*, n.p., 2005.

Bureau of Statistics, *Census of Manufacturing Industries in Sindh 1970–71*, Karachi, Planning and Development Department, Government of Sindh, 1970–1.

_____, , *Census of Manufacturing Industries in Sindh 1975–76*, Karachi, Planning and Development Department, Government of Sindh, 1976.

_____, *Census of Manufacturing Industries in Sindh 1980–81*, Karachi, Planning and Development Department, Government of Sindh, 1981.

_____, *Census of Manufacturing Industries in Sindh 1985–86*, Karachi, Planning and Development Department, Government of Sindh, 1986.

_____, *Census of Manufacturing Industries in Sindh 1990–91*, Karachi, Planning and Development Department, Government of Sindh, 1991.

_____, *Census of Manufacturing Industries in Sindh 1995–96*, Karachi, Planning and Development Department, Government of Sindh, 1996.

_____, *Census of Manufacturing Industries in Sindh 2000–01*, Karachi, Planning and Development Department, Government of Sindh, 2001.

_____, *Census of Manufacturing Industries in Sindh 2005–06*, Karachi, Planning and Development Department, Government of Sindh, 2006.

_____, *Government of Sindh—Development Initiatives and Achievements—Four Years Performance 2008–09 to 2011–12*, Karachi, Planning and Development Department, Government of Sindh, 2012.

_____, *Development Statistics of Sindh 1970*, Karachi, Planning and Development Department, Government of Sindh, 1970.

_____, *Development Statistics of Sindh 1975*, Karachi, Planning and Development Department, Government of Sindh, 1975.

_____, *Development Statistics of Sindh 1980*, Karachi, Planning and Development Department, Government of Sindh, 1980.

_____, *Development Statistics of Sindh 1985*, Karachi, Planning and Development Department, Government of Sindh, 1985.

————, *Development Statistics of Sindh 1990*, Karachi, Planning and Development Department, Government of Sindh, 1990.

————, *Development Statistics of Sindh 1995*, Karachi, Planning and Development Department, Government of Sindh, 1995.

————, *Development Statistics of Sindh 2000*, Karachi, Planning and Development Department, Government of Sindh, 2000.

————, *Development Statistics of Sindh 2005*, Karachi, Planning and Development Department, Government of Sindh, 2005.

————, *Development Statistics of Sindh 2010*, Karachi, Planning and Development Department, Government of Sindh, 2010.

————, Planning and Developing, Government of Sindh <http://sindhbos.gov.pk/>, 'Rich Heritage of Handicraft', *Pakistan Economist*, 1975.

Dhakan, D. A., *Impact of the Growth of Cotton Textile Industry on the Economy of Sindh*, Karachi, Sindh Development Foundation, 2002.

Husain, Ishrat, *Economy of Modern Sindh*, Hyderabad, Institute of Sindhology, University of Sindh, 1981.

Hussain, Sahar S. and Vaqar Ahmed, 'Experiments with Industrial Policy: The Case of Pakistan', Sustainable Development Policy Institute, Karachi, 2011.

Industries and Commerce Department, Government of Sindh, <http://www.sindh.gov.pk/dpt/industriescommerce/index.htm>, accessed 14 June 2017.

IUCN Pakistan, *Sindh Strategy for Sustainable Development,* Karachi, IUCN Pakistan, Sindh Programme, 2007.

Junejo, Mumtaz Ali and Muhammad Nawaz Chand, 'Growth and Efficiency of Small Scale Industry and its Impact on Economic Development of Sindh', *Pakistan Journal of Commerce and Social Sciences*, 1, 2008.

Khan, Mushtaq, *The Political Economy of Industrial Policy in Pakistan 1947–1971*, London, Department of Economics, SOAS, 2000.

Finance Division, *Pakistan Economic Survey 2014–2015*, Islamabad, Ministry of Finance, Government of Pakistan, 2015.

National Refinery Limited. 'Production and Capacity', <ww.nrlpak.com/ProductionCapacity.aspx/>, accessed 1 August 2017.

Ravi Magazine, 'Analysis of Pakistani Fertilizer Industry—A Report', [online magazine], April 2015, <https://www.ravimagazine.com/analysis-of-pakistani-fertilizer-industry-a-report/>, accessed 18 June 2017.

————, 'Sugar Industry of Pakistan—An Academic Report', *Ravi Magazine* [online magazine], May 2015, <https://www.ravimagazine.com/sugar-industry-of-pakistan-an-academic-report/>, Accessed 20 June 2017.

Shaikh, Saleem, 'Sindh's Sagging Handicraft Business', *Dawn*, 22 March 2010.

Unlocking the Economic Potential of Sindh: An Enhanced Framework for Competitiveness, Islamabad, Competitiveness Support Fund, 2010.

Wizarat, Shahida, *The Rise and Fall of Industrial Productivity in Pakistan,* Karachi, Oxford University Press, 2002.

Yellow Pages of Pakistan, 'Industrial Zones in Sindh', <http://www.findpk.com/yp/Biz_Guide/html/industrial_zones_sindh.html>.

Chapter 12: Energy and Mineral Resources

Abrar, Mian, 'Port Qasim Coal-fired Power Project: CPEC's first project witnesses emphatic progress on ground', *Pakistan Today*, 12 May 2016.

Ali, Akhtar, *Pakistan's Energy Development: The Road Ahead,* Karachi, Royal Book Company, 2010.

Ali, Fahd, *The History of Private Power in Pakistan*, Sustainable Development Policy Institute, 2007.

Beg, Fatima and Fahd Ali. *The History of Private Power in Pakistan*, Working Paper, Islamabad, Sustainable Development Policy Institute, 2007.

Bhutta, Zafar, 'Pakistan's Oil and Gas Discoveries Touch Record', *The Express Tribune*, 29 June 2016, <https://tribune.com.pk/story/1132448/pakistans-oil-gas-discoveries-touch-record/>.

Dawn, '50 licences awarded for exploration of gas, oil', 24 January 2014, <http://www.dawn.com/news/1082218>.

Energy/Development International Price Waterhouse, *The Coal Industry in Pakistan: Requirements for Growth*, USAID, 1985.

Express Tribune, 'Norwegian firm to set up three solar power plants in Pakistan', 7 July 2015, <http://tribune.com.pk/story/916741/mou-signed-norwegian-firm-to-set-up-three-solar-power-plants-in-pakistan/>.

Hydrocarbon Institute of Pakistan, *Pakistan Energy Yearbook 1981*, Islamabad, Ministry of Petroleum and Natural Resources, Government of Pakistan, 1982.

_____, *Pakistan Energy Yearbook 1986*, Islamabad, Ministry of Petroleum and Natural Resources, Government of Pakistan, 1987.

_____, *Pakistan Energy Yearbook 1991*, Islamabad, Ministry of Petroleum and Natural Resources, Government of Pakistan, 1992.

_____, *Pakistan Energy Yearbook 1996*, Islamabad, Ministry of Petroleum and Natural Resources, Government of Pakistan, 1997.

_____, *Pakistan Energy Yearbook 2001*, Islamabad, Ministry of Petroleum and Natural Resources, Government of Pakistan, 2002.

_____, *Pakistan Energy Yearbook 2006*, Islamabad, Ministry of Petroleum and Natural Resources, Government of Pakistan, 2007.

_____, *Pakistan Energy Yearbook 2008*, Islamabad, Ministry of Petroleum and Natural Resources, Government of Pakistan, 2009.

_____, *Pakistan Energy Yearbook 2009*, Islamabad, Ministry of Petroleum and Natural Resources, Government of Pakistan, 2010.

_____, *Pakistan Energy Yearbook 2011*, Islamabad, Ministry of Petroleum and Natural Resources, Government of Pakistan, 2012.

_____, *Pakistan Energy Yearbook 2014*, Islamabad, Ministry of Petroleum and Natural Resources, Government of Pakistan, 2015.

_____, *Pakistan Energy Yearbook 2015*, Islamabad, Ministry of Petroleum and Natural Resources, Government of Pakistan, 2016.

_____, *Pakistan Statistical Yearbook 1985*, Islamabad, Statistics Division, Government of Pakistan, n.d.

_____, *Pakistan Statistical Yearbook 1995*, Islamabad, Statistics Division, Government of Pakistan, n.d.

_____, *Pakistan Statistical Yearbook 2005*, Islamabad, Statistics Division, Government of Pakistan, n.d.

_____, *Pakistan Statistical Yearbook 2011*, Islamabad, Statistics Division, Government of Pakistan, n.d.

_____, *Pakistan Statistical Yearbook 2012*, Islamabad, Statistics Division, Government of Pakistan.

_____, *Pakistan Statistical Yearbook 2013*, Islamabad, Statistics Division, Government of Pakistan.

_____, *Pakistan Statistical Yearbook 2014*, Islamabad, Statistics Division, Government of Pakistan.

_____, *Pakistan Statistical Yearbook 2015*, Islamabad, Statistics Division, Government of Pakistan.

_____, *Province-wise Details of Blocks Awarded, Bidding Details of Blocks*, Islamabad, Ministry of Petroleum and Natural Resources, Government of Pakistan, n.d.

FFC Energy, 'About Us', <https://www.ffcel.com.pk/about-us.php>.

Fraser, Julia M., *Lessons from the Independent Private Power Experience in Pakistan*, Discussion Paper no. 15, n.p., Energy and Mining Sector Board, 2005.

Finance Division, 'Energy', in *Pakistan Economic Survey 2011–12*, Islamabad, Ministry of Finance, Government of Pakistan, 2012.

International Energy Agency, 'About Hydropower', n.d., <https://www.iea.org/topics/renewables/subtopics/hydropower>.

Islamabad Chamber of Commerce and Industry, *An Overview of Electricity Sector In Pakistan*, Islamabad, 2011.

K-Electric, *Financial Data—Analyst Briefing*, Karachi, 2015.

_____, 'Our Business', 2015, <http://www.ke.com.pk/category/our-business/index.html>.

Khan, Israr, 'Govt, ADB agree on awarding contract of Jamshoro power project by Sept.', *The News*, 18 March 2017.

Khan, Nasim A. *Energy Resources and Their Utilization in Pakistan*, Karachi, Hamdard University Press, 2010.

Khan, Nasir, Ahmed Amara Konaté, and Peimin Zhu. 'Integrated Geophysical Study of the Lower Indus Platform Basin Area of Pakistan', *International Journal of Geosciences* 4, 2013.

Khan, Shakeel and Hafiz Farhan, *Analysis of Pakistan's Electric Power Sector*, Blekinge Institute of Technology, Department of Electrical Engineering, 2015.

Khyber Pakhtunkhwa Tribune, 'Swat Economy', n.d., <http://kptribune.com/index.php/en/swat/swat-economy>.

Memon, Naseer, Oil and Gas Resources and Rights of Provinces: A Case Study of Sindh, *Centre for Peace and Civil Society*, 2010.

Ministry of Petroleum and Natural Resources, *Investment Opportunities in Pakistan's Upstream Oil and Gas Sector*, Islamabad, Government of Pakistan, 2015.

National Transmission and Despatch Company, *Power Statistics 2012–13*, Lahore, WAPDA house, n.d.

Pakistan Bureau of Statistics, *Pakistan Statistical Yearbook 1976*, Islamabad, Statistics Division, Government of Pakistan.

Pakistan Meteorological Department, *An Investigation of Wind Power Potential at Gharo, Sindh*, Government of Pakistan, 2003.

Pakistan Petroleum Information Service, *Upstream Petroleum Activities, July 2016*, Islamabad, Government of Pakistan, 2016.

Rehan Energy, 'Karachi Solar Street Lights', <http://rehanenergy.com/altenativeenergies/solar/solar-street-lights/karachi-solar-lights>.

Rizvi, Jawwad, 'Demystifying Pakistan's Energy Crisis', *MIT Technology Review—Pakistan*, 2015.

Siddiqui, Usama, 'Pakistan Power Sector Reforms: Pakistan Struggles to Overcome the Power Crisis', *Express Tribune*, 25 April 2011, <http://tribune.com.pk/story/155979/power-sector-reforms-pakistan-struggles-to-overcome-the-power-crisis/>.

Siemens, 'Quarry and Raw Materials for Cement', 2016, <http://www.industry.siemens.com/verticals/global/en/cement-industry/raw-materials-cement/pages/Default.aspx>.

Sindh Board of Investment, *Sector Brief Renewable Energy*, Government of Sindh, n.d.

The News, 'Six New Oil, Gas Discoveries in Sindh, KP', 29 June 2016, <https://www.thenews.com.pk/print/131339-Six-new-oil-gas-discoveries-in-Sindh-KP>.

Ullah, Kafait, 'Electricity Infrastructure in Pakistan: An Overview', *International Journal of Energy, Information and Communications*, 4/3, 2013.

Chapter 13: Public Finance: Taxation and Resource Mobilisation in Sindh

Ahmed, Iftikhar, Usman Mustafa, Mahmood Khalid, 'National Finance Commission Awards in Pakistan: A Historical Perspective', PIDE Working Paper 33, Islamabad, Pakistan Institute of Development Economics, 2007.

Ahmed, Mahmud, '8th NFC Award: Setting Direction', *Dawn*, 4 May 2015, <https://www.dawn.com/news/1179748>.

Ahmed, Qazi, Akhtar Lodhi, 'Provincial Finance Commission: Options for Fiscal Transfers', *The Pakistan Development Review*, 47/4, 2008.

Cheema, Ali, Asim Ijaz Khwaja, and Adnan Khan, 'Decentralization in Pakistan: Context, Content and Causes', KSG Working Paper No. RWP05–034, 2005.

Currie, Janet and and Enrico Moretti, 'Mother's Education and the Intergenerational Transmission of Human Capital: Evidence from College Openings', *The Quarterly Journal of Economics*, 4/119, 2003.

Fatima, Mahnaz, and Qazi Masood Ahmed, 'Political Economy of Fiscal Reforms in the 1990s', *The Pakistan Development Review*, 40/4, 2001.

Finance Department, *Annual Budget Statements*, Karachi, Government of Sindh, various years.

———, 'Government of Sindh's Position on 6th National Finance Commission', 2003, unpublished report.

———, *Budget 2016–17*, Karachi, Government of Sindh, 2016.

———, *Sindh Tax Revenue Mobilization Plan (2014–2019)*, Karachi, Government of Sindh, 2014.

———, *Budget-in-Brief*, Islamabad, Ministry of Finance, Government of Pakistan, various years.

———, *Fiscal Operations Report*, Islamabad, Ministry of Finance, Government of Pakistan, various years.

Ghaus-Pasha, Aisha, Hafiz Pasha and Asma Zubair, 'Fiscal Equalisation among Provinces in the NFC Awards', *The Pakistan Development Review*, Pakistan Institute of Development Economics, 49/4, 2010.

Government of Sindh, *The Sindh Land Tax and Agricultural Income Tax Ordinance 2000*, Karachi, Provincial Assembly of Sindh, 2000.

Government of Pakistan and Development Partners, *Pakistan Sindh Province—Public Financial Management and Accountability Assessment*, n.p., PEFA, 2013.

Jaffery, Nighat, and Mahpara Sadaqat, 'NFC AWARDS Commentary and Agenda', *Pakistan Economic and Social Review*, 44/2, 2002.

Khan, Asim, 'Case for Agriculture Tax', *The Express Tribune*, 16 May 2016.

Khattak, Naeem Ur Rehman, Ifthikar Ahmad, and Jangraiz Khan, 'Fiscal Decentralisation in Pakistan', *The Pakistan Development Review*, 49/4, 2010.

Khuhro, Hamida, *The Making of Modern Sind*, Karachi, Indus Publications, 1978.

Laghari, Nawaz Ali, 'Impact of Distribution of 2.5% GST of Net Sales Tax under Distribution Order, 2006 in Case of Sindh', 2008, unpublished report.

Laghari, Nawaz Ali, 'Recommendation for Consideration of Provincial Committee on National Finance Commission', 2008, unpublished report.

Lochner, Lance and Enrico Moretti, 'The Effect of Education on Crime: Evidence from Prison Inmates, Arrests and Self Reports', *American Economic Review*, 94/1, 2004.

Malik, Hamza, 'Shocking Facts about Pakistani Income Taxpayer', The True Perspective (Blog), 16 March 2011, <https://www.thetrueperspective.com/2011/03/shocking-facts-about-pakistani-income.html>.

Ministry of Finance, 'Working Papers and Minutes of the National Finance Committee', 1970, unpublished report.

Mustafa, Usman, 'Fiscal Federalism in Pakistan: the 7th National Finance Commission Award and its Implications', PIDE Working Paper 73, Islamabad, Pakistan Institute of Development Economics, 2011.

National Assembly, *18th Amendment to the Constitution of Pakistan 1973*, Islamabad, Government of Pakistan, 2010.

National Finance Commission Secretariat, *Report of the National Finance Commission 2009*, Islamabad, Government of Pakistan, 2009.

National Finance Commission Secretariat, *Government of Sindh's Positon on Distribution of Subvention under NFC*, 2002, unpublished.

Pakistan Institute of Legislative Development and Transparency, 'Taxing the Agriculture Income in Pakistan', Briefing Paper 42, Islamabad, 2011.

Pasha, Hafiz, 'Growth of the Provincial Economies', Institute for Policy Reforms, 2015.

_____, 'Review of 7th NFC Award', *Business Recorder*, 17 January 2017, <http://epaper.brecorder.com/2017/01/17/20-page/840430-news.html>.

Pakistan Institute of Development Economics, *The 7th NFC Award: An Evaluation*, Islamabad, 2011.

Sabir, Muhammad, 'Dynamic Consequences of the 1997 NFC Award', *The Pakistan Development Review*, Pakistan Institute of Development Economics, 40/4, 2001.

Sabir, Muhammad, 'Financial Implications of the 7th NFC Award and the Impact on Social Services', *The Pakistan Development Review*, Pakistan Institute of Development Economics, 49/4, 2010.

Shah, Aslam, 'Local Bodies in Sindh Deprived of PFC Awards Due To Government's Non-Seriousness', *Daily Times*, 18 February 2017, <http://dailytimes.com.pk/sindh/19-Feb–17/local-bodies-in-sindh-deprived-of-pfc-awards-due-to-governments-non-seriousness>.

State Bank of Pakistan, *Special Section 2: National Finance Commissions Awards—A Review*, Karachi, 2011.

The Nation, 'Karachi Contributes 60–70Pc of Revenue', 25 July 2010.

Zaidi, S. Akbar, *Issues in Pakistan's Economy*, Karachi, Oxford University Press, 1999.

Zaidi, S. M. Abbas, 'Contribution of Sindh in Pakistan's Economy', *Pakistan Economist*, 2009, <http://www.pakistaneconomist.com/pagesearch/Search-Engine2009/S.E632.php>.

Index

A

abiana 187, 203–4, 208, 296, 326
acreage 22, 32, 164, 166, 171–2, 315
agrarian economy 184, 187, 199
agriculture 2, 4, 7, 11, 13, 16, 19–20, 25–6, 32, 40, 52–3,
    95, 110, 113, 115, 119–20, 122–30, 157–9, 163–7,
    170–80, 182–91, 193, 198–202, 204–5, 208–9, 227,
    241, 250, 253, 283–4, 294–7, 307, 312–17, 323, 325–
    6, 328, 330–2
agro 53, 122, 237, 256, 317
agro-climate 132, 153, 157, 159, 161
agro-industries 227
agro-processing 188, 330
Annual Development Programme (ADP) 321–5
arid 7, 97, 122, 161, 164, 270
automobiles 227, 235–7, 250
autonomy 86, 88, 300–1, 304

B

Badin 8, 11, 128, 139–40, 157, 169, 178, 180, 187, 191–2,
    199–201, 205, 213, 222, 253, 258, 270–1, 286
Bahawalpur 2, 8, 50, 157
Baloch 3, 9–10, 14–5, 20, 22, 26, 34, 43, 270
Balochistan 1–2, 6, 9, 49–50, 54, 69, 81, 85, 124–5, 128,
    157, 172, 179, 193–8, 201–2, 211, 252, 257–8, 260,
    263–4, 267–8, 272–3, 275–7, 279, 283–4, 294–5,
    297–305, 307–10, 316
Bangladesh 12, 45, 53, 112, 137, 175, 288–90
barrage 2–5, 18, 27–8, 30–2, 38, 40–1, 165, 167, 170, 172,
    177–8, 189–94, 197–8, 200, 202–3, 205, 277
basin 1, 167, 173, 197–8, 258–62
Benazirabad 11, 47, 72, 139–40, 179–80, 199, 238, 287
beneficiary 72, 79–80, 161, 207, 332
Bhutto, Zulfikar Ali 70, 86, 158, 166, 170, 183, 226, 245,
    255, 315
biodiversity 2, 197

biometric 64, 89
biotechnology 331
birth 18, 50, 52–3, 91–2, 95–6, 104–5
bondage 127–30
bonded labour 127–30
brick 129, 222, 249, 273, 329
bridge 34, 190–3, 206, 210–3, 215–6, 218, 224, 251, 331
buffalo 4, 11, 33, 182
bullock 23, 25, 190
bureaucracy 34, 54, 297, 328

C

camel 4, 11, 25–6, 33–4, 37, 182, 249
canal 2, 4–6, 21, 24–32, 37–8, 167–8, 173, 177, 187,
    189–94, 196–200, 202–7, 209, 224
cement 216, 226–7, 235, 239–40, 269, 293, 331
census 16, 18–9, 32–3, 41–52, 54, 107, 121, 158, 165–6,
    170, 182–3, 188, 222–3, 228–33, 235, 242–4, 246–8,
    251–2, 300–1, 305
China–Pakistan Economic Corridor (CPEC) 213–4, 216,
    255, 275, 278
citizen 39, 49, 87, 94, 139, 153, 210, 222, 295, 320–1,
    326–9, 332
city 3–6, 11, 13, 17, 37, 39, 43, 49, 52, 54, 121, 126, 141,
    187, 191, 212, 224, 229, 251–2, 274, 278, 282, 285,
    291, 295, 325, 329
civilisation 11, 13, 238
coal 3, 213, 215–16, 254, 270–6, 278–9, 291–2, 304, 328
coastal 2–3, 8, 14, 164, 168–9, 182, 196–7, 199, 201,
    214–15, 245, 258, 277–8, 329–30
commerce 11, 15, 33, 38, 76, 280, 282, 330
commercial 5, 14–5, 17, 33–6, 126, 174–5, 178–81, 213,
    217, 237, 259, 263, 269–70, 273, 275, 277, 282–5, 291
commission 11, 27–8, 74, 77, 88, 126, 129, 132–3, 135–7,
    165, 169–70, 186, 195, 198, 247, 275, 281, 299–301,
    303–5, 309–10, 320, 332

committee 11, 27, 39, 72–3, 77, 94, 165, 169, 194–5, 198, 207–8, 298

communications 9, 16, 33–8, 40, 102, 105, 115, 122–3, 192, 210, 254, 281, 326

community 9, 23, 41, 53, 65, 67, 72, 122–3, 129, 131, 139, 151, 178, 205–6, 278, 301, 329–30, 332

compensation 24, 65, 105, 109, 165, 169, 195, 254, 299, 303, 308

competition 86–7, 216–18, 226, 253, 255–6, 282

concrete 132, 192, 215

conflict 197, 204, 302

constitution 55, 67, 89, 110, 127, 299, 303, 305, 307–8, 314, 320

construction 18, 27–8, 30–1, 34, 37–8, 41, 61–2, 64, 72, 76, 114, 122–3, 165, 180–1, 189–93, 197–8, 201–2, 204–6, 208, 210–3, 215–8, 221–2, 240, 249, 274, 278, 293, 331

consumer 133, 177, 218, 226–7, 229, 235, 244, 266, 268, 278, 280–2, 285–6, 291

contraceptive 52–3, 90–1, 94, 96, 104

cotton 3, 11, 14, 25, 29, 32, 35–6, 38, 127, 157–8, 164, 172, 176–8, 180, 186, 191, 226, 238–40, 249, 306

creek 2, 4, 181, 199, 201, 258, 261

crime 54, 144, 322

crisis 95, 98, 255, 273, 282, 285

crop 3, 25, 32, 36, 95, 126, 157, 159, 163–5, 168–9, 171–2, 175, 177–9, 183–4, 186, 189, 191, 193, 209, 331–2

crude oil 260, 263–6, 273, 291–2, 300, 304–5, 307

cultivation 3, 20–1, 27, 29, 32, 36, 127, 164–5, 167, 169–70, 172, 177–81, 184, 187, 189–91, 193–4, 199

cyclones 7–8, 199–200, 322

D

Dadu 2, 5–6, 11, 14, 28, 32, 45, 128, 139–40, 157, 177–8, 189–91, 201, 203, 209, 222, 258, 270, 287, 298

dams 4, 197–8, 222, 277–8, 281, 331

decentralisation 86, 89, 124, 295, 300, 307, 309–11, 320–1, 328

delta 2–3, 5, 8, 29, 168–9, 173, 178–9, 181, 197, 205, 260–1, 270, 329–30

demographics 16, 41–3, 50, 91, 138, 310, 331

discos 279, 281–2, 287

disease 3, 39, 90, 92, 94–8, 105, 156, 179, 181, 186, 200, 206, 325, 330

diversification 254, 256, 302

domestic 52, 117, 120–1, 126, 149, 177–8, 184, 217–18, 224, 237, 244, 247, 262–4, 267, 269, 274, 277, 283–4, 291, 323, 326

drainage 11, 169, 200–7, 209, 221–2, 273, 317, 325

E

ecology 3, 158, 186

economics 69–71, 76, 107, 143, 300–1, 305

economies 92, 107, 120–1, 123, 254, 276, 294–5, 332

economy 2, 7, 10, 15, 19, 32, 37, 40, 51, 63, 87, 90, 107, 109, 111, 119–22, 133, 139, 141, 146, 150, 159, 163, 166, 178, 182–4, 187, 199, 208, 210, 213, 218, 226–7, 235, 247, 250–1, 254–5, 294–5, 302, 324, 329–32

ecosystem 173

ecotourism 329

education 21, 38, 45, 48, 50, 52, 55–68, 70–89, 92, 94, 96, 99, 101–2, 109, 112, 116–21, 126, 131, 133, 135–7, 139, 148, 153, 157, 159–62, 254–6, 296, 319, 321–4, 330, 332

Eighteenth Amendment 55, 84, 86, 88–9, 102, 161, 268–9, 295, 311, 320, 326

elections 39, 54, 76, 187, 204, 206–8

electricity 3, 61, 76, 122, 136, 210, 253, 275–86, 288–91, 330

electronics 227, 235, 243–4

embroidery 10, 248–9

employment 8, 45, 48, 50, 60, 76, 86, 107–8, 111–12, 115, 117, 119–23, 126–8, 130, 153, 158, 160–1, 178, 188, 204–5, 227, 229–31, 233–41, 248, 250–1, 253, 255, 323, 328, 330

empowerment 72, 86, 94, 96, 126, 328

encroachment 181, 209, 224

energy 7–8, 132–3, 186, 253, 255, 257, 259, 261, 263–78, 281–5, 288, 290, 300

enrolment 56–65, 67–9, 71–2, 74–8, 80–6, 88–9, 112, 137–8, 253, 308

entrepreneurship 23, 107, 126, 227, 251, 253, 323

environment 2, 6, 54, 61, 67, 73, 90, 95, 128, 131, 134, 182, 197, 199–202, 205, 223–4, 248, 255, 273, 277, 329

equality 67, 144

equity 136, 163, 167, 280, 317

ethnic 9, 54, 331–2

ethnicities 295

ethno-linguistic 331–2

expenditure 8, 23, 38, 65–6, 74, 82, 88, 90–1, 102–3, 105–6, 131, 133, 147–9, 151–3, 156, 159–62, 222, 295–7, 299, 306, 310, 318–19, 321–4, 326–7, 329, 331

exploitation 127–30, 139, 171, 182, 216, 261

exploration 82, 87, 97, 107, 120, 179, 182, 254–5, 257–8, 260–2, 269–70, 272, 329

export 10, 14, 33–8, 169, 177–9, 182, 187, 216–17, 227, 243, 248, 250, 253, 255–6, 275, 287, 298–301, 305–6, 329–31

F

fabric 87, 188, 238–40
facility 87, 92, 97–8, 100, 174, 179
factory 14–15, 181, 226, 240–1
family 51, 53, 94, 96, 104–5, 108–9, 113, 118, 122, 129, 131, 141, 149, 153, 166, 170
famine 17, 144, 191
farmers 29, 109, 115, 168–72, 174–5, 177–80, 184, 186–8, 197, 199–200, 202–4, 206–7, 209–10, 242, 277, 315, 317, 331
farming 11, 16, 129, 141, 151, 158, 164, 167, 169, 174, 177–9, 181, 183–4, 188, 209, 315, 330
Federal Board of Revenue (FBR) 296, 308, 311, 313, 331–2
federal budget 124
federal education 56–9, 63, 68, 74–5, 83, 85
federal government 10, 39, 124, 173, 183, 197, 210, 222, 255, 269, 297, 299–309, 314, 320, 322, 331–2
federalism 295, 297, 305, 311
federation 10, 126, 152, 156, 159–61, 298–9, 303–4, 307
feeder 5–6, 28, 74, 76, 178, 189–90, 192–4, 202–3, 205, 217, 286
female 18, 47, 50–3, 56–9, 70–1, 75–6, 78–82, 94, 97, 101, 108–12, 117–19, 121, 126, 129–30, 328, 332
fertiliser 172, 174, 177, 179–80, 183–4, 186–7, 216, 241–2, 254, 269
fertility 4, 50, 53, 96–8, 104, 126, 183, 241
feudalism 13, 15, 20, 126, 128, 130, 141, 158, 163, 165, 170, 184, 187–8
finance 30, 38, 54, 66, 71, 103, 106–7, 133, 145, 175–6, 188, 207, 209, 214, 217–18, 221, 245, 248, 254, 265, 275, 294, 296, 298–305, 308–15, 320–6, 332
fisheries 2–3, 5–6, 115, 122–5, 163, 181–2, 201, 209, 329–32
floods 4–5, 7–8, 24, 30, 33, 72, 95, 134, 173, 177, 191, 193, 196, 198–200, 202, 204–5, 209, 322, 331
forestry 2–3, 115, 122–5, 134, 163, 180–1, 192, 194, 197, 201, 330
fruit 3–4, 26, 32, 38, 117, 179, 186, 191, 331
fuel 136, 184, 242, 256, 263, 267, 269, 276–7, 285
funds 34, 38–9, 53, 65, 72–3, 82, 94, 99, 105, 191, 200, 211, 245, 256, 278, 300–1, 309, 318–9, 321

G

gas 3, 53, 122, 183, 242, 245–6, 255, 257–8, 260–2, 266–9, 273, 275–6, 285, 292, 296, 300, 304–8, 313, 328
GENCO 279–81
gender 18, 47, 51–2, 54, 58, 61, 71, 75, 78, 80–1, 84, 101, 105, 108–10, 119, 126, 136–7, 144, 151, 162, 249, 331

geography 3, 37, 70, 88, 97, 128, 147–9, 151, 157, 315, 331
geology 261, 270, 275
Gini Coefficient 144–5, 151, 153, 162
governance 10, 12, 38, 54, 64–5, 88–90, 94, 99, 102, 105, 121, 128, 138–9, 159, 162–3, 165, 206, 209, 218, 298, 321–2, 328–9, 331–2
governments 17, 48, 77, 105, 120, 124, 134, 144, 161, 181, 184, 187, 222, 226, 268–9, 295–7, 299–301, 304–5, 307–8, 310–11, 320–1, 324, 326, 328–9, 332
Gwadar 215–16, 261
gypsum 3, 292

H

handicraft 249–50
Haq, Ziaul 3, 86, 170, 300
hari 23, 127–9, 141, 158, 163, 165, 169–70, 174, 187–8
health 7, 38, 48, 52, 66, 90–106, 109, 112–13, 121, 126, 131, 135–9, 153, 156, 159–62, 181–2, 197, 200, 206, 251, 253, 255, 296, 319, 321–4, 330, 332
HESCO 280, 282, 285–8
Hyderabad 2, 5, 8, 11, 14–15, 17, 20, 32–3, 39, 42, 47, 49, 64, 96, 105, 109, 128–9, 137, 139–40, 157, 164, 166, 168, 178–80, 190–3, 205–6, 211–13, 217–18, 220–4, 227–30, 238, 248–50, 252–3, 270, 282, 286–7, 329
hydrocarbon 257–61, 263–73, 283–4, 288, 290
hydroelectric 276–8
hydropower 253, 276–8

I

immunisation 91–2, 95, 104–5, 136, 138, 308, 330
imports 34–7, 53, 70, 172, 180, 182–4, 186–7, 191, 216–17, 226, 244–5, 264, 269, 273–5, 281, 306
India 1–2, 9, 12–16, 26–8, 33, 37, 39, 41–5, 49–50, 90, 137, 164–5, 170, 172–3, 175, 177, 191, 195, 197–9, 210, 218, 226, 257, 273, 277, 288–90, 294, 297, 315
indicators 55, 65–6, 86, 90–3, 96–7, 102, 105, 131–2, 134–9, 144, 162–3, 306–9, 318–22, 328
industrial 2, 7, 120, 123, 125–6, 160–1, 196, 198, 200, 222, 226–9, 231, 233–41, 245, 248, 250–6, 263, 273–4, 282, 295, 328
industrialisation 52, 226–7, 245, 248, 250–1, 255
industrialists 251
industries 10, 15, 122, 126, 128, 139, 169, 181, 183–4, 186, 188, 210, 218, 220–1, 226–33, 235–7, 240, 242–56, 266–7, 269, 280, 282–4, 291–5, 323, 328–30
infrastructure 8, 16, 34, 38, 48, 53–4, 63–4, 92, 100, 121, 123, 139, 141, 162, 181–2, 188, 202–3, 205, 209–11,

213, 216, 220, 224, 240, 245, 250–1, 255–6, 269, 274–5, 279, 281, 303–4, 311–12, 320–2, 324, 326–32

institutions 9, 17, 55–6, 60, 78, 83–4, 86, 95, 101, 114, 125, 127, 163, 174–5, 181, 184, 187–8, 206–7, 209, 226, 246, 250–1, 255, 295, 328, 331

investment 8, 37, 54–5, 73, 90, 101, 117, 121, 162, 179, 181–2, 188, 213, 217–18, 221, 224, 226–7, 244, 247, 250, 253, 255–6, 275, 278, 280, 322–4, 328–9, 331–2

irrigation 2–5, 7, 11–12, 16, 18, 24–32, 38, 157, 164–5, 167–70, 172–3, 178, 183–4, 187–9, 191–4, 198, 200–9, 296, 326, 328–9, 331–2

Islamabad 7–8, 12, 41, 43–9, 51–2, 54, 56–9, 62–3, 68, 74–5, 83, 85, 100, 107–11, 114–25, 132–3, 135–7, 140, 145–57, 171, 175–6, 182, 185, 196, 214, 217–19, 223–4, 228, 230–3, 235, 242–4, 246–7, 251–2, 257, 261–73, 280, 282–4, 287–8, 290–2, 300–1, 305, 310–11

J

Jacobabad 2, 8, 11, 30, 39, 140, 157, 164, 178, 193–4, 202, 222, 248, 270, 287, 298

jagirdari 19–24, 40, 127, 158, 163, 165, 169–70, 191, 207

jobs 52, 64, 86, 95, 109, 112–13, 120, 126, 131, 141, 187, 210, 245, 250, 254–5, 296, 323, 329–31

justice 16, 137, 195

K

Kalhora 12–15, 19, 25–6, 29

Karachi 2–6, 8, 11–12, 15, 17, 19–20, 31–9, 41–50, 52, 54, 57, 60–2, 64, 66–7, 73, 75–81, 83, 91, 93–7, 99–101, 104–5, 107, 109, 112, 121–2, 137, 139–40, 142–52, 156–7, 159–62, 167, 169, 176, 181, 196, 210–24, 226–32, 234–43, 245, 250–4, 257–62, 266, 268, 270, 274–9, 282, 285, 291, 295–6, 298–9, 304, 308, 311–14, 316–17, 319, 321, 323–5, 328–30

K-Electric 274, 278–82, 285, 288

Khan, Ayub 12, 145, 158, 166, 169–70, 183, 226, 241, 245

kharif 3, 28, 32, 164, 167–8, 190, 192–6

Khyber Pakhtunkhwa (KP) 1, 48, 69, 85, 125, 130, 172, 195–7, 260, 264, 272, 303–5, 307–10

L

labour 23, 45, 48, 50, 52–3, 57, 90, 96, 100, 105, 107–30, 149, 154, 157, 178, 182, 187–8, 192, 229–30, 235, 244, 248, 251, 253–6, 295, 315, 323, 328–32

landlords 23–4, 126–30, 163–6, 169–72, 174, 187, 207, 209

land ownership 129, 141, 164–5, 169–70, 172, 174, 184, 186–8, 315

Larkana 2, 5–6, 11, 17, 32–3, 47, 49, 96, 99, 139–40, 157, 178–9, 191, 193–4, 201, 212, 222, 224, 252–3, 270, 287, 298, 329

leather 10, 14, 25, 246–9

Left Bank Outfall Drain (LBOD) 198–201

legislation 28, 127, 178, 209, 311, 319

literacy 53, 56–8, 65, 72–4, 77, 79–82, 84, 86, 90, 96, 105, 116–19, 126–7, 130–1, 137–8, 186, 253, 308, 322, 324–5

literature 9, 107, 145, 322

M

male 18, 21, 47, 51–2, 54, 56–9, 70–1, 75, 78, 97, 108–12, 117–19, 121, 126, 153

malnutrition 90–1, 95, 97–8, 104, 126, 144

mango 3, 179

mangrove 2–3, 181, 197, 201, 330

maternity 92, 95, 104

matriculation 63, 76, 84, 87, 116–17

mechanisation 113, 119, 165, 167, 183–4, 188, 213

media 70, 145, 181, 184, 188

metal 190, 232–3, 245–6, 249

microfinance 126, 174–5, 188

migration 9, 12, 17–19, 41–5, 48–50, 52, 54, 92, 95, 109, 120–3, 128, 130, 139, 141, 149, 151, 163–5, 173–4, 177, 221, 253–4, 330–1

Millennium Development Goals (MDGs) 55, 104–5, 132, 151

mineral resources 3, 232–3, 257, 291, 293, 328

mobilisation 204, 207, 211, 294, 311–12, 314, 320, 326, 331

modernisation 38, 86, 181, 188, 204–5, 213, 216, 220, 255

monsoon 2, 7–8, 197, 199–201, 303

mortality 50, 52–3, 90–3, 95–6, 104–5, 137–8

Multan 8, 13, 17, 37–8, 157, 279, 282

Musharraf, Pervez 86, 198, 201, 305

N

Napier, General Sir Charles 15, 20–1, 23–4, 27, 30, 33–4, 39, 215–16

National Finance Commission (NFC) 67, 89, 295–6, 299–311, 313–14, 320

nationalisation 55, 70–1, 86, 226, 228, 236, 245, 285

Naushahro Feroz 3, 11, 47, 139–40, 179, 238, 270, 287

Nawabshah 3, 8, 32, 99, 105, 140, 157, 164, 177, 179, 199, 213, 217, 222, 253, 286–7, 298, 329

NFC Award 67, 89, 295–6, 299–302, 304–10, 313, 320

O

OGDCL 258–60, 262, 269–70
oil 2–3, 35–6, 167, 191, 215–16, 227, 235–6, 253, 257–8, 260–6, 269–70, 273, 275–6, 285, 291–2, 300, 304–5, 307–8
organisations 53, 67, 72, 99–100, 102, 105, 122–4, 126, 198, 202–4, 206–8, 226, 248, 256
outsourcing 100, 229, 235

P

Pakistan 1, 3, 5–8, 10, 12–13, 18–19, 21–2, 33, 39, 41–59, 62–3, 67–75, 77, 83–8, 90–1, 94–7, 100–2, 105, 107–11, 113–29, 131–8, 140–62, 164, 166, 169–87, 189–90, 194–9, 202, 210–14, 216–21, 223–4, 226–33, 235–8, 241–8, 250–3, 255, 257–84, 288–95, 297–303, 305–8, 310–11, 314–15, 318–19, 323, 325–6, 328, 330
Pakistan International Airlines (PIA) 217–18, 224
Partition (1947) 12–13, 19, 24, 30, 42–3, 49, 126, 165, 170, 177–8, 181, 226, 248, 250
petroleum 3, 257–8, 261–73, 275, 283–4, 288, 290, 304, 326
pharmaceuticals 227, 243–4
plantation 3, 193, 209
population 1, 6, 8–10, 16–19, 24, 33, 40–55, 57–8, 65, 74–5, 86–8, 90–2, 96, 99–102, 104–5, 107–10, 113–14, 116–20, 123, 127, 130–2, 134, 137, 139, 141–6, 148–9, 152, 154, 156, 161–3, 165, 167, 173–7, 182, 186–8, 191, 198, 209, 214, 220–3, 251, 255, 278, 289, 294, 298–301, 303, 305–6, 308–10, 320–3, 325, 328–32
port 14, 19, 33, 37, 48, 211–12, 214–17, 224, 227, 245, 251, 274
poultry 33, 163, 175, 181–2, 331
poverty 36, 55, 63, 105, 107, 123, 131–7, 139–46, 148, 150–4, 156–9, 161–2, 187, 210, 231, 302, 306, 308–9, 320, 324–5, 329–30
property 23–4, 38–9, 130, 165, 170, 173, 221, 255, 296–7, 312–15, 325–6, 332
public 26, 28, 38–9, 45, 48, 53, 58–61, 63, 65–8, 70–5, 78, 82–90, 92–3, 96, 98–102, 105, 131, 139, 159, 161–2, 174, 178, 185, 187–8, 201, 203, 211–12, 217, 221–2, 226, 245, 248, 255–6, 277–8, 281, 290, 294–5, 318–22, 324–9, 331
public finance 38, 159, 294–5, 320, 326
public sector 58, 63, 72, 74, 84, 88–9, 92–3, 98–100, 102, 105, 211, 222, 226, 248, 277–8, 281, 322, 325, 329, 331

Q

Quetta 8, 193, 279, 282

R

rabi 3, 28, 32, 164, 167–8, 190, 195–6
rainfall 2–4, 7–8, 26, 29, 32, 172–3, 177–8, 180, 189–90, 197, 199–201, 273, 277, 303
recruitment 64, 74, 85, 89, 94, 254
refinery 227, 264
reforms 63–4, 73, 77, 79–82, 89, 94, 126, 135–7, 158, 165–6, 169–70, 187–8, 202, 204, 206–9, 227, 294–5, 317–18, 326, 331
refugees 12, 164, 170, 177, 221
regulation 86, 105, 165, 190, 209, 222
reservoir 6–7, 173, 192, 197–8, 232, 245, 277–8, 331
resource allocation 59, 64–5, 300, 308, 310
resources 3, 6–7, 25, 30, 53, 61–2, 64–5, 72–3, 82, 84, 92, 98, 102, 104–5, 113, 122, 126, 139, 143, 161–2, 170, 172, 178, 181, 187, 198, 209, 213–14, 253–4, 257, 259, 261, 263–73, 275–6, 281, 283–4, 288, 290–1, 295–7, 299–301, 303–5, 307, 310–11, 314, 320–1, 323, 326, 328–9, 332
revenue 16, 18–25, 27, 29–30, 33, 38–9, 165, 167, 169, 174–5, 187, 190, 192, 218, 295–6, 298–306, 308–20, 326, 331–2
rice 3, 5, 25, 28–9, 32, 157–8, 164, 167–8, 172–4, 176–8, 186, 189–91, 194, 203, 209
Right Bank Outfall Drain (RBOD) 5, 201–2
riparian 188, 194, 196–7
riverine 3, 181, 187, 194, 209
rivers 1–6, 9, 19, 25–7, 29–30, 33–4, 37, 107, 168–9, 173, 178, 181, 189–98, 200–2, 205, 211–12, 222, 270, 277–8, 293
Rohri 10, 14, 21, 27–8, 31, 189–91, 194, 209
rural–urban 45, 48–9, 51–2, 99, 101, 111, 120–1, 141, 149, 151, 154, 254–5, 330–1

S

salinity 20, 180, 196–9, 201, 209, 330
sanctions 28, 70, 187
sanitation 48, 54, 90–1, 97–8, 102, 105, 131, 136, 156, 160–1, 221–2, 224, 251, 321–2, 324–5, 330
seaport 52, 224, 253–4, 328
security 34, 48, 75, 95, 126–7, 141, 165, 176, 181–2, 185, 188, 253–5, 328–9
seed 23, 32, 35–6, 167–8, 172, 174, 177, 180, 184, 186–7, 191, 332

Shahdadkot 6, 11, 48, 139–40, 194, 201–2
sharecropper 5, 19, 128, 141, 165, 170
Sharif, Nawaz 195, 300
Shikarpur 2, 5, 10–11, 17, 20–1, 30, 39, 47, 139–40, 157, 178, 193–4, 220, 222, 253, 287
Sindh 1–30, 32–85, 87–8, 90–104, 107, 109–14, 116–31, 134–5, 137–44, 146–91, 193–9, 201–7, 209–15, 217, 219–24, 226–44, 246–58, 260, 262–79, 282–8, 290–321, 323–6, 328–32
socioeconomic 52, 68, 70–1, 96, 132, 163
solar 184, 276–8
students 52, 60–5, 67, 71–2, 74, 76–82, 84, 87–9, 112, 126, 332
subsidies 24, 101, 172, 181, 183–4, 287, 317, 326, 332
sugar 29, 35–6, 157, 178, 187, 200, 226, 237–8, 299–301
sugarcane 4, 32, 127, 164, 172, 176–8, 180, 189, 209, 226, 237
Sui 257–8
surplus 38, 120, 173, 177–8, 180, 187, 189, 198, 200, 296
sustainability 72, 87, 135, 204–5, 208, 277, 304
Sustainable Development Goals (SDGs) 92, 96, 105

T

taxation 15, 20–1, 24–6, 28–9, 33, 38–9, 120–1, 124, 181, 183–4, 229, 242, 253, 256, 268, 294–308, 311–20, 325–7, 331–2
teacher absenteeism 64–5, 89
teachers 55–6, 58–60, 63–5, 70, 72, 74, 76–7, 82, 84–5, 88–9, 101
technology 157, 172, 178, 210, 218, 226, 245, 247, 253–6, 273–5, 291, 318, 329
telecommunications 188, 210, 218–19, 225, 253, 255, 330
tenancy 126–9, 164–5, 169, 223
Thar 1, 3, 7, 17, 32–3, 38, 97–8, 128, 144, 203, 213, 254, 270–5, 292, 298, 325
Tharparkar 2–3, 11, 25–6, 45, 97–8, 139–40, 157, 162, 187, 222, 249, 253, 270, 283, 298
Thatta 2–3, 5–6, 9–11, 13–14, 17, 21, 32–3, 45, 47–8, 72, 128, 139–40, 157, 164, 178, 187, 191–2, 204, 222, 249, 253, 270, 277, 283, 298
topography 2, 20, 24
tourism 5, 329–30

transportation 5, 33, 54, 112, 115, 122–3, 181, 209, 211–13, 216–17, 224, 253, 255–6, 269, 329
tributaries 1, 29, 40, 181, 197
tubewells 2, 184–5, 189, 199–200, 203

U

underemployment 108–9, 113–15, 130
underutilisation 62, 109, 113–14, 213
UNDP 92, 132–3, 135
unemployment 52, 55, 108–13, 117, 130, 141, 245, 331
universities 9, 21, 59, 77, 83, 88, 92, 101, 112–13, 150, 166, 186, 253, 255, 259, 323–4
urbanisation 47–8, 53–4, 90, 112, 120–1, 123, 139, 141, 188, 229, 254, 295, 298, 304
urban–rural 89, 109, 134, 141, 149, 151, 153–4, 158, 162, 187, 332
USA 15, 260, 270

V

vaccination 92, 95, 104
vegetables 29, 32, 167, 179–80, 186, 193, 236–7, 331–2
vehicles 212, 224, 279, 312–13, 323

W

WAPDA 168, 198, 201, 270, 274, 278–81, 286
wells 2, 29, 37–8, 98, 189, 257–8, 260–1, 269–70
wildlife 5–6, 181
World Bank 48, 91, 94, 132–5, 151, 183, 195, 199, 204, 226, 266, 278–9, 289, 318, 329

Y

youth 45, 50, 56–7, 72, 85, 112–13, 117, 254–5, 331

Z

zamindari 5, 20, 23–5, 28–9, 36, 40, 129, 158, 169, 173–5, 181, 191